# CATHERINE THE GREAT

*Love, Sex and Power*

# CATHERINE THE GREAT

*Love, Sex and Power*

Virginia Rounding

HUTCHINSON
LONDON

Published by Hutchinson in 2006

1 3 5 7 9 10 8 6 4 2

Copyright © Virginia Rounding 2006

Virginia Rounding has asserted her right under the Copyright, Designs and Patents Act, 1988 to be identified as the author of this work

First published in 2006 in the United Kingdom by Hutchinson

Hutchinson
The Random House Group Limited
20 Vauxhall Bridge Road, London SW1V 2SA

Random House Australia (Pty) Limited
20 Alfred Street, Milsons Point, Sydney,
New South Wales 2061, Australia

Random House New Zealand Limited
18 Poland Road, Glenfield,
Auckland 10, New Zealand

Random House (Pty) Limited
Isle of Houghton, Corner of Boundary Road & Carse O'Gowrie,
Houghton 2198, South Africa

The Random House Group Limited Reg. No. 954009

www.randomhouse.co.uk

A CIP catalogue record for this book is available from the British Library

Papers used by Random House
are natural, recyclable products made from wood grown in
sustainable forests. The manufacturing processes conform to
the environmental regulations of the country of origin

Typeset in Bembo by Palimpsest Book Production Limited,
Polmont, Stirlingshire
Printed and bound in Great Britain by
William Clowes Ltd, Beccles, Suffolk

ISBN 0 09 179992 9
ISBN-13 978 0 09 179992 2 (From Jan 2007)

In gratitude: MR and PER
who first encouraged me to study Russian

# Contents

# List of Illustrations

Portrait of Catherine II in Profile by Virgilius Erichsen, oil on canvas, before 1762, The State Hermitage Museum, St Petersburg, Russia.

Portrait of Catherine II by Alexei Petrovich Antropov, oil on canvas, before 1766, The State Hermitage Museum, St Petersburg, Russia.

Portrait of Count Grigory Grigoryevich Orlov by Andrei Ivanovich Cherny(?), enamel on copper, late 1760s to early 1770s, The State Hermitage Museum, St Petersburg, Russia.

Portrait of Alexei Bobrinsky in a Masquerade Costume (artist unknown), oil on canvas, late 1770s, The State Hermitage Museum, St Petersburg, Russia.

Portrait of Catherine II in front of a Mirror by Virgilius Erichsen, oil on canvas, between 1762 and 1764, The State Hermitage Museum, St Petersburg, Russia.

SECTION TWO

Portrait of Stanislas II Augustus (1732–98), 1797, oil on canvas, by Marie Louise Elizabeth Vigée-Lebrun (1755–1842) Château de Versailles, France/Bridgeman Art Library.

Portrait of Prince Grigory Alexandrovich Potemkin by Johann Baptist Edler von Lampi, oil on canvas, c.1790, The State Hermitage Museum, St Petersburg, Russia/Bridgeman Art Library.

Baron Melchior Grimm (1723–1807), pencil on paper, by Carmontelle, (Louis Carrogis) (1717–1806), Musée Conde, Chantilly, France Giraudon/Bridgeman Art Library.

Giovanni Paesiello (1740–1816), oil on canvas, by Marie Louise Elizabeth Vigée-Lebrun (1755–1842) Château de Versailles, France Lauros/Giraudon/Bridgeman Art Library.

Catherine II's Uniform Dress Modelled after the Uniform of the Life-Guards Preobrazhensky Regiment, silk, metal thread, metal and galloon, gilded, 1763, The State Hermitage Museum, St Petersburg, Russia.

## List of Illustrations

Catherine II's Uniform Dress Modelled after the Uniform of the Life-Guards Cavalry Regiment, silk, metal thread, metal and galloon, gilded, 1773, The State Hermitage Museum, St Petersburg, Russia.

Portrait of Grand Duke Paul Petrovich by Alexander Roslin, oil on canvas, 1777, The State Hermitage Museum, St Petersburg, Russia.

Portrait of Grand Duchess Maria Fyodorovna by Alexander Roslin, oil on canvas, 1777, The State Hermitage Museum, St Petersburg, Russia.

Portrait of Grand Dukes Alexander Pavlovich and Constantine Pavlovich by Richard Brompton, oil on canvas, 1781, The State Hermitage Museum, St Petersburg, Russia.

Portrait of Count Semyon Zorich (unknown artist), oil on canvas, The State Hermitage Museum, St Petersburg, Russia.

Portrait of Alexander Lanskoy (unknown artist), oil on canvas, 1783/84, The State Hermitage Museum, St Petersburg, Russia.

Portrait of Alexander Dmitriyev–Mamonov by Mikhail Shibanov (copy), oil on canvas, 1800, The State Hermitage Museum, St Petersburg, Russia.

Portrait of Catherine II Wearing a Kokoshnik (Woman's Headdress) by Virgilius Erichsen (copy), oil on canvas, (original painting 1769–72), The State Hermitage Museum, St Petersburg, Russia.

Portrait of Catherine II (1729–96) by Vladimir Lukich Borovikovsky (1757–1825) Tretyakov Gallery, Moscow, Russia/Bridgeman Art Library.

Portrait of Catherine II the Great (1729–96) in a Travelling Costume, 1787 (oil on canvas) by Mikhail Shibanov (fl.1783–89) State Russian Museum, St Petersburg, Russia/Bridgeman Art Library.

Portrait of Catherine II (1729–96) (oil on canvas) by Albertrandi, Anton (c.1730–1808) © Royal Castle, Warsaw, Poland Maciej Bronarski/Bridgeman Art Library.

*Catherine the Great*

Portrait of Catherine II (1729–96) of Russia (oil on canvas) by Alexander Roslin (1718–93) Musée des Beaux-Arts, La Rochelle, France/ Bridgeman Art Library.

What is certain is that I have never undertaken anything without having been intimately persuaded that what I was doing conformed to the good of my Empire. This Empire had done everything for me: – I believed that all my individual faculties, constantly employed for the good of this Empire, for its prosperity, for its superior interest, could hardly suffice to acquit myself towards it.

Catherine II, 16 June 1791

# Foreword

Faced with the enormous task of writing about Catherine the Great – enormous both because of the length of her reign and the amount of material to be covered, and because of the eminent qualities of some of those who have written about her before – I was encouraged by two remarks of Nancy Mitford in letters to her friend, the bookshop proprietor Heywood Hill. First, discussing the project she had undertaken to write about Madame de Pompadour: 'Miss M. Trouncer [Margaret Trouncer, a Francophile biographer] has been to the library here APPALLED that I'm doing it, furiously angry, says I must be mad, there's nothing more to say on the subject.' And secondly, talking of her biography of Louis XIV: 'Actually, if there is interest in the subject at all, my book is utterly different from [Vincent] Cronin's, we hardly touch on the same things. Such an immense reign, well documented, makes that almost inevitable – each person does what interests him.' Having always admired Miss Mitford's ability to entertain her readers and to wear her learning lightly, and agreeing with her that every writer undertaking such a subject will produce something quite different from any other, I make no apology for writing about what interests me in the life of Catherine II, also called the Great, of Russia.

This does not pretend to be a definitive once-and-for-all biography, containing everything that is known about Catherine. She is someone about whom books will probably go on being written for as long as people go on writing and reading books. I deliberately do not go into lengthy detail about Russian foreign and diplomatic policy in the eighteenth century – and would refer readers to books such as Isabel de

Madariaga's *Russia in the Age of Catherine the Great* if that is what they are interested in. What I attempt to do is present Catherine the woman, the multi-faceted, very eighteenth-century woman, principally through her own words and those of her contemporaries, drawing out from the volumes of material written by them and by the Empress herself those particular observations, comments and conversations which allow her to appear most vividly before our eyes. I have chosen to tell a chronological narrative, rather than use a thematic approach, for it is in watching Catherine's life unfold day by day that one sees the sheer scope of that life, the extent of the tasks she set herself and the range of activities she managed to encompass.

In allowing Catherine to come into as clear a focus as possible at a distance of over 200 years, I do not want to tell my readers what to think of her. But I do want to put paid to the more salacious rumours which have sullied her reputation so unjustly, even in her own lifetime but particularly since her death. That this most civilised of women should be known by most people only in relation to the infamous and entirely untrue 'horse story' is one of the greatest injustices of history.

## Transliteration of Russian names

My aim throughout has been to lessen confusion for the non-Russian reader, and therefore I have wherever possible used the most familiar versions of people's names, rather than adhering strictly to a particular system of transliteration. Consequently I have chosen to use 'Alexander' rather than 'Aleksandr', 'Peter' rather than 'Pyotr' and, in the case of the Empress herself, 'Catherine' rather than 'Ekaterina'. In order to distinguish Catherine from other women with the same Christian name, I have referred to them as 'Ekaterina'. When quoting from contemporary French or English sources, I have retained the original transliterations of proper names – which can vary even within the same document. (Where the original transliteration might be particularly confusing, I have identified the character in square brackets.) The pursuit of simplicity has also led me to omit patronymics, with the exception of members of the imperial family, and unless the name is part of a direct quotation. I hope this approach will assist the reader in recognising people and places when they reappear.

*The calendar*

Dates in eighteenth-century Russia were reckoned according to the Julian Calendar, or Old Style, which at that time was 11 days behind the Gregorian Calendar or New Style, gradually coming into use throughout most of Europe. In this book dates are always given in Old Style, unless indicated by the abbreviation N.S.

*Money*

As a very rough rule of thumb, one rouble in 1780 had the purchasing power of approximately £20 sterling at today's prices.

Except where otherwise indicated in the notes, translations from French and Russian are mine.

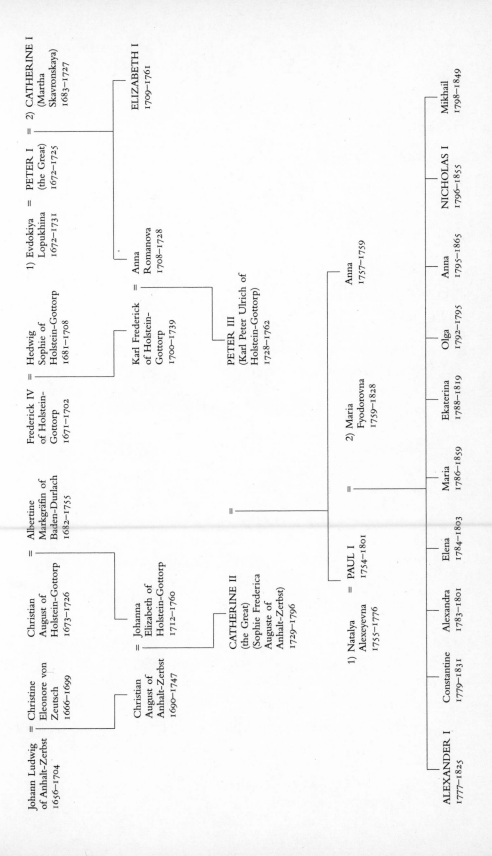

Johann Ludwig
of Anhalt-Zerbst
1656–1704

= Christine
Eleonore von
Zeutsch
1666–1699

Christian
August of
Holstein-Gottorp
1673–1726

= Albertine
Markgräfin of
Baden-Durlach
1682–1755

Frederick IV
of Holstein-
Gottorp
1671–1702

= Hedwig
Sophie of
Holstein-Gottorp
1681–1708

1) Evdokiya
Lopukhina
1672–1731

= PETER I
(the Great)
1672–1725

= 2) CATHERINE I
(Martha
Skavronskaya)
1683–1727

Christian
August of
Anhalt-Zerbst
1690–1747

= Johanna
Elizabeth of
Holstein-Gottorp
1712–1760

Karl Frederick
of Holstein-
Gottorp
1700–1739

= Anna
Romanova
1708–1728

ELIZABETH I
1709–1761

CATHERINE II
(the Great)
(Sophie Frederica
Auguste of
Anhalt-Zerbst)
1729–1796

PETER III
(Karl Peter Ulrich of
Holstein-Gottorp)
1728–1762

1) Natalya
Alexeyevna
1755–1776

= PAUL I
1754–1801

=

2) Maria
Fyodorovna
1759–1828

Anna
1757–1759

ALEXANDER I
1777–1825

Constantine
1779–1831

Alexandra
1783–1801

Elena
1784–1803

Maria
1786–1859

Ekaterina
1788–1819

Olga
1792–1795

Anna
1795–1865

NICHOLAS I
1796–1855

Mikhail
1798–1849

# Dramatis Personae

EMPRESS CATHERINE II (THE GREAT) Previously Grand Duchess Catherine Alexeyevna and originally Princess Sophie Frederica Auguste of Anhalt-Zerbst

*Catherine's family*
PRINCE CHRISTIAN AUGUST OF ANHALT-ZERBST Catherine's father
PRINCESS JOHANNA ELIZABETH OF HOLSTEIN-GOTTORP Catherine's mother
PRINCE GEORG LUDWIG OF HOLSTEIN-GOTTORP Catherine's uncle
EMPEROR PETER III Catherine's husband, previously Grand Duke Peter Fyodorovich and originally Karl Peter Ulrich, Duke of Holstein-Gottorp
THE EMPRESS ELIZABETH Aunt of Peter III and daughter of Peter I (the Great)
GRAND DUKE PAUL PETROVICH Catherine's son, later Emperor Paul I
GRAND DUCHESS NATALYA ALEXEYEVNA Paul's first wife, originally Princess Wilhelmina of Darmstadt
GRAND DUCHESS MARIA FYODOROVNA Paul's second wife, originally Princess Sophia Dorothea of Würtemberg
GRAND DUKE ALEXANDER PAVLOVICH Catherine's eldest grandson, later Emperor Alexander I
GRAND DUCHESS ELIZAVETA ALEXEYEVNA Alexander's wife, originally Princess Louise of Baden-Durlach

GRAND DUKE CONSTANTINE PAVLOVICH Catherine's second grandson

GRAND DUCHESS ANNA FYODOROVNA Constantine's wife, originally Princess Julie of Saxe-Coburg

GRAND DUCHESSES ALEXANDRA PAVLOVNA, ELENA PAVLOVNA, MARIA PAVLOVNA, EKATERINA PAVLOVNA, OLGA PAVLOVNA, ANNA PAVLOVNA Catherine's granddaughters

GRAND DUKE NIKOLAI PAVLOVICH Catherine's third grandson, later Emperor Nicholas I

*Members of other imperial or royal houses*
FREDERICK WILLIAM I King of Prussia 1713–40
FREDERICK II (THE GREAT) King of Prussia 1740–86
PRINCE HENRY Prince Royal of Prussia
FREDERICK WILLIAM II King of Prussia 1786–97
GUSTAVUS III King of Sweden 1771–92 (and Catherine's first cousin)
GUSTAVUS IV ADOLPHUS King of Sweden 1792–1809
JOSEPH II Holy Roman Emperor 1765–90

*Catherine's lovers and favourites (in chronological order)*
SERGEI SALTYKOV
STANISLAS PONIATOWSKI (subsequently King Stanislas II Augustus of Poland)
GRIGORY ORLOV
ALEXANDER VASSILCHIKOV
GRIGORY POTEMKIN (subsequently given the surname Potemkin-Tavrichesky)
PETER ZAVADOVSKY
SEMYON ZORICH
IVAN RIMSKY-KORSAKOV
ALEXANDER LANSKOY
ALEXANDER YERMOLOV
ALEXANDER DMITRIYEV-MAMONOV
PLATON ZUBOV

*Principal courtiers, officials and military men*
FYODOR BARYATINSKY Involved in Catherine's coup, subsequently a chamberlain

## Dramatis Personae

ALEXEI BESTUZHEV-RYUMIN Elizabeth's Chancellor

IVAN BETSKOY Chamberlain at Elizabeth's Court, collaborator on educational projects with Catherine

ALEXANDER BEZBORODKO Catherine's 'factotum'

ALEXANDER BIBIKOV Artillery captain and supporter of Catherine's coup, later Marshal of the Legislative Commission

PRASKOVYA BRUCE Catherine's friend and confidante, previously Praskovya Rumyantseva, married to Yakob Bruce

YAKOB BRUCE Became Governor-General of Moscow

ALEXANDER CHERKASOV Elizabeth's cabinet secretary, and President of Medical College under Catherine

ANDREI CHERNYSHEV Cousin of Zakhar and Ivan Chernyshev

IVAN CHERNYSHEV President of Naval College under Catherine

ZAKHAR CHERNYSHEV Brother of Ivan Chernyshev, gentleman of the bedchamber to Grand Duchess Catherine, subsequently President of War College

MARIA CHOGLOKOVA Principal lady-in-waiting to Grand Duchess Catherine

EKATERINA DASHKOVA Elizaveta Vorontsova's sister, a supporter of Catherine's coup, and first Director of the Russian Academy

ALEXANDER GLEBOV Appointed Procurator-General by Peter III

ALEXANDER GOLITSYN Vice-Chancellor at the time of Catherine's coup, previously Russian ambassador in London

ALEXANDER GOLITSYN (not the above) Marshal of Catherine's Court and Governor-General of St Petersburg

DMITRY GOLITSYN Russian ambassador in Paris and then in The Hague

COUNTESS GOLOVINE Niece of Ivan Shuvalov and one of the ladies at Catherine's Court

SAMUEL GREIG Scottish naval commander in Catherine's service

ALEXANDER KHRAPOVITSKY One of Catherine's secretaries

ALEXANDER NARYSHKIN Gentleman of the bedchamber at Elizabeth's Court and Chief Cup-Bearer at Catherine's Court

LEV NARYSHKIN Alexander Naryshkin's brother, gentleman of the bedchamber at the young Court of Catherine and Peter, subsequently Master of the Horse at Catherine's Court

ADAM OLSUFYEV Head of Catherine's cabinet

ALEXEI ORLOV Grigory Orlov's younger brother and naval commander, later given the surname Orlov-Chesmensky

FYODOR ORLOV Another brother of Grigory Orlov, involved in Catherine's coup

IVAN ORLOV The eldest Orlov brother

VLADIMIR ORLOV The youngest Orlov brother

IVAN OSTERMAN Vice-Chancellor under Catherine

NIKITA PANIN Governor of Grand Duke Paul, and senior member of College of Foreign Affairs

PETER PANIN Nikita's brother and army general

MARIA SAVISHNA PEREKUSIKHINA Catherine's maid and confidante

ANNA PROTASOVA Catherine's friend and lady-in-waiting

ALEXEI RAZUMOVSKY Favourite of Empress Elizabeth, and Master of the Hunt

KIRILL RAZUMOVSKY Younger brother of Alexei Razumovsky, and Hetman of Ukraine

NIKOLAI REPNIN Nikita Panin's nephew by marriage

PETER RUMYANTSEV Field Marshal who played major part in both Russo-Turkish Wars, given the surname Rumyantsev-Zadunaisky

NIKOLAI SALTYKOV Governor of Grand Dukes Alexander and Constantine

PETER SALTYKOV Governor-General of Moscow

ALEXANDER SAMOILOV Potemkin's nephew, Procurator-General in succession to Alexander Vyazemsky

STEPAN SHESHKOVSKY Senate secretary and head of Secret Branch under Catherine

VASILY SHKURIN Catherine's valet, and later chamberlain

ALEXANDER SHUVALOV Peter Shuvalov's brother, head of Secret Chancery under Elizabeth

IVAN SHUVALOV Cousin of Alexander and Peter Shuvalov, successor of Alexei Razumovsky as the Empress Elizabeth's favourite, subsequently Grand Chamberlain at Catherine's Court

PETER SHUVALOV Alexander Shuvalov's brother, Grand Master of Ordnance under Elizabeth

ALEXANDER SUVOROV Field Marshal who quashed Polish revolt, given the surname Suvorov-Rymnitsky

GRIGORY TEPLOV Deputy to Kirill Razumovsky and supporter of Catherine's coup

MIKHAIL VOLKONSKY Supporter of Catherine's coup and replacement of Peter Saltykov as Governor-General of Moscow

## Dramatis Personae

**ALEXANDER VORONTSOV** President of College of Commerce
**MIKHAIL VORONTSOV** Chancellor at the time of Catherine's coup, uncle of Ekaterina Dashkova and Elizaveta Vorontsova
**ROMAN VORONTSOV** Senator and father of Ekaterina Dashkova and Elizaveta Vorontsova
**ELIZAVETA VORONTSOVA** Peter III's mistress
**ALEXANDER VYAZEMSKY** Procurator-General under Catherine
**ZAKHAR ZOTOV** Catherine's valet

# *Prologue*

he city of St Petersburg, where Catherine spent so much of her life – that city of glittering needle spires and domes, of brightly painted façades, of long perspectives for promenading along, a European capital founded as Russia's 'window on the West' – has always been a stage set, as recognised by all the writers who have lived and worked and set their work there. St Petersburg was Catherine's city – even more perhaps than it was the city of Peter the Great – not only because she was responsible for commissioning so much of its architecture, but because it resonated so strongly with her beliefs: that nature can be improved upon by art, that human beings can become better creatures if their environment and education are improved, that order, beauty and goodness are linked and nourish one another. St Petersburg was also her stage. There was little if any privacy for a woman at the centre of an imperial Court in the eighteenth century, and Catherine was aware that she was a public figure as soon as she set foot in Russia.

Living in that constant awareness, she did what she could to control how people saw her. One of the principal ways in which she attempted to do this was by writing – or 'scribbling', as she called it – not only several versions of her memoirs but also countless letters, to her friends, lovers, family members, officials, and the philosophers she liked to think of as her mentors. Many of these letters were intended to be read far more widely than by their designated recipient. The routine interception of post that went on between the Courts of Europe was used as a form of propaganda – that is, if a monarch or ambassador or courtier sent a communication via the ordinary post rather than

I

using a private courier, it was intended to be intercepted and its contents divulged to interested parties. Even when a letter had arrived at its destination, it might not be viewed as private. Though Catherine did not wish her letters to Voltaire, for instance, to be formally published (she did not think they were well enough written for that), she knew that he would not keep the contents to himself. She relied on him to give her a good press; through presenting herself to him as an enlightened philosopher-queen, and gaining his endorsement for this persona, she knew this would be the image presented to the Courts and salons of Europe.

Just as with the media 'personalities' and celebrities of our day, there was a price to be paid in the eighteenth century by someone who was as adept at influencing public opinion and as tireless in presenting an image of herself through the media as was Catherine – and that was that others would present their own versions of the 'truth', turning the manipulator of the media into its victim. Catherine was not the only one who could write memoirs and letters for circulation, or place anonymous pieces in gazettes, and the rumours which built up around her, many of them salacious in nature, were partly just the reverse side of the coin of self-publicity.

Catherine was not concerned only with self-publicity in her writing, however. For her the very act of writing was addictive, and it was one of the chief ways in which she found relief from the stress of her daily life. In some of her correspondence, most notably that with her deepest epistolary friend, Friedrich Melchior Grimm, she was able to forget the need always to present herself in the best possible light. She called Grimm her '*souffre-douleur*' – her scapegoat or whipping boy – who could be the safe recipient of whatever she wanted to say; to him she was able to express her worries and her griefs, as well as the things that made her laugh, other people's idiosyncrasies, the delight she took in her grandsons, her dogs, and her various artistic and architectural projects. It is in the correspondence with Grimm that we find portrayed Catherine's most human face: we discover how funny she could be, what a good observer she was of other people, and we begin to understand how she could inspire such devotion from friends and servants. But as she hides little from Grimm, we also see how acquisitive she was (of people as well as objects), how demanding and difficult, how disingenuous in her relations with her son – and how like a besotted teenager she could be at the start of a relationship with a new favourite. She trusted Grimm never to misuse what she told him and to disseminate only what she asked him to. In this book I have drawn extensively on Catherine's letters to Grimm, allowing her to speak in her own voice whenever possible.

Did she and Grimm intend their correspondence to be published? They both wrote, at least some of the time, with posterity in mind and were well aware of how interesting their letters would be to historians of their lives and times. They expected a large proportion of them to be read by others eventually, but the tone of many of Catherine's letters suggests that this consciousness did not impinge on her writing, or at least not significantly enough to make her censor herself much, if at all. She gave clear instructions that the letters should not be published, or even read by anyone else, in her lifetime, and though Grimm sometimes felt that her letters were wasted on him alone and should be made available to a wider audience (on at least one occasion he made representations to her on the subject), he respected her decision not to allow this. He valued his correspondence with Catherine far too highly ever to jeopardise it by disobeying her.

Another useful and interesting source for details of life at the Courts of eighteenth-century Europe are the ambassadorial dispatches and reports of foreign ministers, though they have to be treated with caution and cannot always be taken at face value. Diplomatic dispatches were by no means immune from interception – indeed, part of Catherine's daily working life involved going through with her secretaries transcripts of intercepted dispatches and other foreign correspondence. The daily collection of these transcripts even had a name – *perelyustratsiya* (a word no longer in use and referring to the unofficial or secret copying of official documents or private letters). The knowledge of the likelihood of such interception had a number of consequences. Sometimes a dispatch was written with the intention that it should be intercepted and read by or reported to the sovereign; such correspondence might contain information the ambassador wished to reach the ear of the sovereign and was unable to communicate in any other way, particularly as all official communications would go through ministerial channels and might never normally reach the head of state. Or an ambassador might use his dispatch purely as a vehicle of flattery, ostensibly reporting to his masters at his home Court on a recent event or development at the Court where he was posted, while colouring his account in such a way as to give pleasure to the interceptors.

Of course foreign ministers did also have to attempt to communicate confidentially with their political masters and to receive confidential instructions from them. Dispatches were routinely written in cipher – and as routinely decoded, there being certain officials at every Court whose specific task was to break ciphers. Couriers were also used extensively – both ones whose sole occupation was to convey messages back and forth between countries, and merchants or other people travelling for their own purposes who also agreed to take packets with them. But even a dispatch written in cipher and sent with a courier did not carry a one hundred per cent guarantee that it would reach its destination intact and without having been read by someone other than its intended recipient. So the most potentially explosive information could not even be sent in cipher and with a courier, but would have to wait until an opportunity for face-to-face communication arose or until the ambassador was recalled.

Nevertheless, while bearing all these caveats in mind, along with the bias to be expected from men who had the interests of their own countries at heart and who were imbued with many of the usual prejudices of the time – against women, foreigners and so on – the dispatches of some of the more perspicacious of the foreign ministers at the Court of St Petersburg in the eighteenth century, such as the Prussian Count Solms and the urbane and 'clubbable' Englishman Sir James Harris, can still give a wonderfully vivid depiction of court life and provide detailed contemporary views of the Empress and how she appeared to manage her life and Empire. What may be lost in objectivity is made up for in immediacy, and the most considered of diplomats cannot altogether conceal glimpses of how life was actually lived in the place to which he was posted.

Memoirs can be more problematic than letters and dispatches because of the greater length of time that has elapsed between the experience and the recording of it, and because of the writer's desire to shape his or her recollections into a coherent narrative, which inevitably leads to rearrangements, omissions, maybe even some invention – quite apart from any deliberate colouring and interpretation of events and personalities in order to show the memoirist in the best possible light and to present his or her own point of view. Catherine's writing – and rewriting – of her own memoirs was certainly in part a propaganda exercise, though she was also a born writer and could never resist the act of writing for its own sake. Yet provided they are checked against what is known from other sources, and compared with other narratives, memoirs too can be extremely valuable in helping to produce a vibrant picture of people and places and events – and not the least of their value is the picture inadvertently painted of the writer, of his or her values, beliefs, particular ways of looking at things. As Richard Aldington wrote in his introduction to *The Private Life of the Marshal Duke of Richelieu*:

> If memoirs are not history, they may be literature: they may have all the pleasing inaccuracies of human nature. They may not relate facts with strict and impartial accuracy, but they may reveal personality . . . Memoirs will not help us to pass examinations or to qualify as examiners, but they will tell us something of interest, if it is only the tittle-tattle of generations that have long since crumbled to dust.

In an age which was so conscious of itself, of how architecture, dress, hair (or wigs), gestures, ceremonial, manners looked, and of the effect produced by all the physical aspects of life, where 'spectacle' was so important, no festivity complete without its firework display, where rank and decorations were matters of deep concern, the way in which people presented themselves in their memoirs and letters was an intrinsic part of the spirit of the age.

Everyone who passed through the story of Catherine the Great played their part on a stage, with a greater or lesser degree of awareness that that was what they were doing. Some of them – such as Catherine herself, her most famous consort Grigory Potemkin, her mother Johanna, Princess of Holstein-Gottorp, her predecessor the Empress Elizabeth, and foreign visitors such as the Prince de Ligne and the Comte de Ségur – were very conscious of themselves as actors; others seemed less aware that they were being watched, such as Catherine's husband, Peter III, who never understood his audience, or even that he had one. Some, such as her son Paul, felt they were being shunted off into the wings and resented it.

These lives, constantly under scrutiny, being played out under the gaze of courtiers, emissaries, spies and ambassadors, with what went on against each backdrop – of Petersburg, Versailles, Vienna, Berlin, London – being disseminated with varying degrees of distortion across the wider stage of Europe, with its ever-changing borders and allegiances; these lives are what are portrayed in the letters, diaries and memoirs of the various players. Through reading what they say about one another and about themselves, where they contradict or complement one another, the reader takes a seat in the auditorium, suspends judgement, accepts that not everything about a person can be known, enters into the spirit of eighteenth-century Europe, and watches as one of its most remarkable women – who in many ways embodied the principles of that century – plays out her many-faceted life.

# 1

# From Feudal Anthill
# to the Court of Russia
# *(1729–44)*

*Her demeanour was marked by such nobility and grace, that I would
have admired her even if she hadn't been to me what she is.*
Princess Johanna of Holstein-Gottorp on her daughter,
the future Catherine II

The woman who became Catherine II, the Great, Empress
of All the Russias, was born Sophie Frederica Auguste of
Anhalt-Zerbst on 21 April Old Style, 2 May New Style,
1729, in the Baltic port of Stettin in Pomerania (now Szczecin in north-
west Poland). She was the first child of her 39-year-old father Prince
Christian August of Anhalt-Zerbst and her 17-year-old mother Princess
Johanna Elizabeth of Holstein-Gottorp. Sophie and Auguste were the
names of one of the baby's great-grandmothers on her father's side,
while Frederica – which may also have been chosen as a mark of
respect to Prince Christian August's patron, King Frederick William of
Prussia – was the name of both one of her mother's elder sisters and
her mother's paternal grandmother.

Anhalt-Zerbst and Holstein-Gottorp were two of the 300 or so tiny
sovereign states, or principalities, of which the area roughly covered by
present-day Germany consisted in the eighteenth century. The pre-
revolutionary Russian historian V.O. Klyuchevsky describes these
endlessly dividing and subdividing states, with their 'princes of
Brunswick-Luneberg and Brunswick-Wolfenbüttel; of Saxe-Romburg,

Saxe-Coburg, Saxe-Gotha, and Saxe-Coburg-Gotha; of Mecklenburg-Schwerin and Mecklenburg-Strelitz; of Schleswig-Holstein, Holstein-Gottorp, and Gottorp-Eutin; of Anhalt-Dessau, Anhalt-Zerbst, and Zerbst-Dornburg', as 'an archaic feudal anthill'. Everyone in these noble families seems to have been related to everyone else, even if only through marriage and at several removes. (Many of them also seem to have had the same Christian names, in different combinations, which can be very confusing.) There were also many cross-border allegiances, the members of one princely house serving in the army or civil service of a more powerful one and being rewarded with money, position or influence. Prince Christian August's father, who had died in 1704, was Prince Johann Ludwig of Anhalt-Zerbst, himself the son of Prince Johann of Anhalt-Zerbst and Princess Sophie Auguste of Holstein-Gottorp. Sophie's mother's side of the family was rather more elevated, with closer connections to the occupants of thrones; one of Princess Johanna's great-grandfathers had been King Frederick III of Denmark. Her father was Christian August, Duke of Holstein-Gottorp, who also held the office of Bishop of Lübeck until his death in 1726 ('Bishop of Lübeck' was a hereditary title, the bishopric being in the possession of the House of Holstein-Gottorp until the secularisation of 1803). His parents were Christian Albrecht, Duke of Holstein-Gottorp, and Frederica Amalie Oldenburg, Princess of Denmark. Johanna's mother was Albertine Markgräfin of Baden-Durlach, the daughter of Friedrich VII Magnus Markgraf of Baden-Durlach and Princess Auguste Marie of Holstein-Gottorp; she had married Christian August in 1704. Albertine was the only one of Sophie's grandparents still to be alive at the time of her birth.

For any girl born into this 'feudal anthill', competition to make a good marriage and thus secure for her family a better place in the pecking order would be fierce. Sophie always felt that her parents would have preferred a boy as their firstborn, but that nevertheless her father at least was pleased by her arrival in the world. Throughout her life she retained a great respect for Prince Christian August, thinking of him as a model of integrity, honesty and erudition. One of Christian August's cousins was Prince Leopold of Anhalt-Dessau (known as the 'Alte Dessauer'), who had the reputation of being an exceedingly brave soldier and who had assisted the military martinet King Frederick William in devising the 54 movements of Prussian drill, including the ceremonial march-past with unbent leg which came to be known as the goosestep. Prince Leopold was King Frederick William's most trusted general; Christian August himself, who had also served with distinction in the Prussian army, was not far behind in the King's esteem. At the time of Sophie's birth he was the Governor of Stettin, having been sent by King Frederick William to command the garrison there just after his marriage in 1727. He was a serious and austere man and a committed Lutheran, who preferred the company of books to social gatherings.

His young wife Johanna, with her aquiline nose, arched eyebrows and curly fair hair, was of a different character altogether. She had been brought up at the Court of Brunswick by her godmother and aunt by marriage, Elizabeth Sophie Marie, the Duchess of Brunswick-Lüneberg, to whom the Duke of Holstein-Gottorp had been happy to relinquish one of his several daughters. Johanna had grown up on the same footing as the Duchess of Brunswick-Lüneberg's own daughter, and it was the Duchess who arranged her marriage at the age of 15 and provided her dowry. It would be an anachronism to draw any psychological conclusion from the fact that the young Johanna married in 1727 a man old enough to be her father and who had the same Christian names as her own father, who had died in the previous year; nevertheless, it is true to say that there was something of a father–daughter relationship between Sophie's rather ill-matched parents.

Johanna found her existence with her sober middle-aged husband in the misty grey town of Stettin at the mouth of the river Oder a far cry from the livelier atmosphere she had grown used to at the Court of Brunswick. In Stettin the Governor and his family lived in the ducal castle (now known as the Castle of the Pomeranian Princes), a sixteenth-century granite building in the main square. The city offered little scope to a young woman who hankered after an exciting social life. Neither did the advent of her first child appear to bring Johanna much joy. Her attitude towards Sophie was always ambivalent. The birth had been difficult, and Johanna appears to have felt the reward was insufficient for what she had had to endure; according to her daughter, she almost died in the process and it took her 19 weeks to recover.

The infant Sophie, who had very fair skin, blonde hair and blue eyes, was handed over to a wet-nurse and placed in the overall charge of 'the widow of a certain Herr von Hohendorf', who also acted as a companion to Johanna. Frau von Hohendorf did not retain her position for long, failing in her relations with both the child and her mother. She was given to shouting, with the result that the small girl got into the habit of ignoring any order unless it was said repeatedly and in a very loud voice. Sophie was rescued from incipient uncontrollability, however, by the advent of the Cardel sisters, part of a family of Huguenot refugees. The elder sister, Magdeleine, who had charge of her until she was about four years old, did not succeed in capturing the child's affection, but her successor, her younger sister Elizabeth, usually known as Babet, was able to win her over and secured a lasting place in her memory and in the pantheon of people she believed to have influenced her for good. Sophie saw little of her father, though she seems to have been sure of his rather distant affection ('[he] considered me to be an angel'), and even less of her mother, who, she remembers, 'did not bother much about me'. She had been supplanted in her mother's affections (if indeed she had ever been in them at all) by the much-desired son, William Christian Frederick, who had arrived 18 months after her own birth. She herself was, as she put it, 'merely tolerated' – and at times not even that. Babet Cardel made up for this lack of parental care, taking the little girl – who had become rather spoilt as well as neglected – in hand. She taught her to read, while visiting tutors provided elementary lessons in writing and dancing.

When Sophie was three years old, she had been taken by her parents to visit her grandmother Albertine in Hamburg. An even more exciting event took place when she was four: King Frederick William of Prussia came to visit the small Court at Stettin, and little Sophie was instructed to greet him formally by kissing the hem of his coat. She was, however, too short to reach it, a fact about which she claims to have complained audibly, blaming the King for not wearing a longer coat; the incident remained in Frederick William's memory so that subsequently he always asked after her. Sophie suffered the usual round of childhood accidents, including having a toy cupboard fall on her and almost sticking a pair of scissors in her eye. In early childhood she was subject to outbreaks of a skin disease which would now be called impetigo. When the rash appeared on her hands she wore gloves until the scabs fell off, and when her scalp became affected she had to have her hair shaved off and wear a bonnet.

Much of the instruction the young Sophie received consisted of rote learning, which she later came to despise as both bad for the memory and a waste of time; what was the point of learning things by heart, she wondered, when you could just as easily go and look them up in a book? She was taught both French and German, and was also instructed in religion, history and geography by a Lutheran pastor called Wagner, with whom she had several tussles over such questions as whether those who had never had a chance to hear the Gospel – 'Titus, Marcus Aurelius, and all the great men of antiquity' – could really be damned for eternity, and the nature of the chaos which preceded creation. The picture the adult woman was keen to produce in her memoirs was of an independent-minded, intellectually courageous child who would not be cowed into accepting received opinion. She also recalls asking the pastor to explain what circumcision was, a question which even the valiant Babet Cardel refused to answer.

Though her mother occasionally hit her, out of impatience and exasperation, corporal punishment was not a routine part of Sophie's childhood. Pastor Wagner, she claims, wanted her to be flogged for her impertinence in asking too many questions, but Babet Cardel was not authorised to carry out such punishments. Deprived of the rod, the pastor took to the infliction of mental torture instead, frightening the child with stories of hell and damnation until Babet noticed her charge crying by the window and persuaded him to desist. The sensible Babet used the approach of the carrot rather than the stick, rewarding Sophie for good work and behaviour by reading aloud to her.

The adult woman remembered herself as a boisterous child, who would pretend to go to sleep at bedtime but sit up as soon as she was left alone and turn her pillow into an imaginary horse, bouncing up and down on it until she was tired. (It has sometimes been assumed that what she was in fact doing was masturbating; admittedly children sometimes do, but they also pretend pillows are horses . . .) Her other night-time trick, indulged in when the family was staying at her father's country estate in Anhalt, consisted of racing up four flights of stone stairs whenever Babet left the room to go to the privy, which was along a short passage, then running back down to throw herself under the covers before the rather stout and slow-moving woman returned.

As Sophie grew older, Johanna seemed to find the company of her little girl more acceptable. In 1736 she took the child to the Court of Brunswick for the first time to meet the woman to whom she owed her own upbringing and marriage, the Duchess Elizabeth Sophie Marie of Brunswick-Lüneberg. Still aged only seven, Sophie greatly enjoyed herself, prattling away, being spoiled and petted and, as she put it herself, 'insufferably forward'. Johanna was in the habit of staying at this Court for several months of every year (escaping from the boredom of Stettin), and from now on Sophie always went with her. This was where she first experienced the routines and rituals of formal court life, a training which would prove invaluable to her. Around the time of this first visit, she became aware of the kind of future which might await her, and of the possibility of aiming high. In her memoirs she attributes this realisation to comments made by Dr Laurentius Bolhagen, a close friend and adviser of her father. Bolhagen was reading a gazette containing an account of the marriage of Princess Auguste of Saxe-Gotha-Altenburg, one of Sophie's second cousins, to the Prince of Wales (in April 1736), and he commented to Babet Cardel: 'Really, this Princess has been much less carefully brought up than ours; she is not beautiful either, but there she is, destined to become Queen of England! Who knows what future faces ours?'

In the same year, Sophie suffered her first serious illness; from the symptoms she describes – initially a violent cough and sharp chest pains – it was clearly a form of pneumonia. In the same year Johanna also suffered the death of a baby daughter, Auguste. Sophie spent three weeks in bed with a fever, the cough and chest pains continuing, only able to lie on her left side. Such medical treatment as was provided for her was experimental; as she herself recalled: 'I was given many mixtures to take, but God alone knows what they were!' When she was finally well enough to get out of bed, it was observed that she had developed a pronounced curvature of the spine. This appears rather to have frightened her parents, who were already having to cope with one disabled child, the elder of Sophie's two brothers (her second brother, Frederick August, having been born in 1734) being able to walk only with the aid of crutches. It seems more than likely that both children were affected by rickets, a condition where skeletal deformities occur as a result of vitamin D deficiency and a lack of direct sunlight. They were keen to keep the news of Sophie's apparent deformity within the family; if it were to become public, it would seriously damage her marriage prospects. Her parents' horrified reaction cannot have done much for Sophie's already fragile self-confidence. Neither can the bizarre treatment they eventually procured for her. The only local person they could find with a reputation for skill in straightening out 'dislocations' was the town's executioner. After examining Sophie in the greatest secrecy, he ordered that her back and shoulders should be rubbed every day with the saliva of a servant girl, who was under strict orders not to eat anything beforehand. It is possible that the massage may have done Sophie some good, but in addition she was made to wear, night and day, an uncomfortable corset. Curiously, the executioner also gave her a black ribbon to wear round her right arm and shoulder. After about 18 months, Sophie's spine began to grow straight again, and by the time she was 11 she was allowed to stop wearing the corset (though it would in any event have been quite normal for a girl of her age and time to wear at least a reinforced bodice to push back the shoulders and thus keep the back flat).

Clearly Sophie's parents did not believe in mollycoddling their little girl. Neither did they act with much sensitivity. Around the same time that she became ill they decided she was too old for dolls and other toys, so they were all confiscated. The grown woman claims not to have suffered much from this, as she was imaginative enough to turn anything that came to hand into a toy. Arguably, this is where she first learnt how to make the best of a not particularly good situation, how to bide her time, be watchful, retreat into her inner self and prepare for the time when she would be able to act, even though this was hardly a conscious strategy at the age of seven.

In 1737 Sophie and Johanna spent the winter at the Court of Berlin, where Sophie met the wife of Crown Prince Frederick (later Frederick the Great) and his younger brother Prince Henry, the Prince Royal. Two years later mother and daughter paid a visit to Eutin, where Johanna's elder brother and current Bishop of Lübeck, Adolf Frederick of Holstein-Gottorp, had his official residence. It was on this occasion that the 10-year-old Sophie first met her future husband, the 11-year-old Karl Peter Ulrich, Duke of Holstein-Gottorp.

Karl Peter Ulrich was the grandson of Peter the Great of Russia. His mother, Anna Petrovna Romanova, had been Peter's daughter by his second wife, Catherine. She had died of consumption at the age of 20, only two months after the birth of her son. The boy's father, who had died in June 1739 at the age of 39, was Karl Frederick, Duke of Holstein-Gottorp, a nephew of Charles XII of Sweden. Since the death of his father, Karl Peter Ulrich had been placed in the charge of his father's cousin and Sophie's uncle, Adolf Frederick. He and Sophie were second cousins.

The recently bereaved boy was at this time considered to be something of a prodigy, and was good-looking, well-mannered and courteous. He was also lonely and lost. Starved of affection, and of any female company, he took to the lively and attractive Johanna at once and seemed rather jealous of Sophie. Though Sophie herself took little notice of him, the children's relatives were already inclined to look upon them as a future couple. It was anticipated that the young Duke would one day become King of Sweden. And naturally Sophie was not averse to the idea that she might one day be a Queen. She had after all been brought up in the assumption that she would marry into some ruling family or other, and the higher her position could be, the better. But though her prospects were reasonable as far as her family connections were concerned, she had doubts about her personal attributes. She did not consider herself to be beautiful (neither Babet nor her parents were given to undue praise or flattery) and realised early on that she would have to learn to make herself attractive in other ways if she was to succeed in the art of pleasing. As yet the prospect of marriage was not a pressing concern. Back in Stettin she continued the routine of lessons with tutors and Babet, and was in no particular hurry to grow up. Various possible suitors were occasionally discussed by her family, among them Prince Henry of Prussia, but she was considered too young for this to be a serious prospect.

In 1742, when Sophie turned 13, several major family events occurred. Prince Christian August suffered a stroke which affected his left side, though he quickly made a reasonable recovery. A greater disaster was the death of Sophie's 12-year-old brother, William. Johanna was inconsolable, her grief only partially assuaged by the birth a few months later of another daughter, who was given the name Elizabeth in honour of the Empress of Russia, who stood as godmother to the child.

The Empress Elizabeth, who had seized the throne of Russia in a coup in 1741, had longstanding connections with the Holstein-Gottorps. Not only had her sister, Anna Petrovna, been married to Duke Karl Frederick, but she had herself been engaged to marry Johanna's elder brother, Prince Karl August. This marriage never took place, however, as Karl August died in Russia of smallpox in May 1727, at the age of only 20. Elizabeth, ever a sentimental woman, preserved a romantic memory of her young fiancé, and Johanna had taken care to cultivate the family connection by writing to congratulate her soon after she seized power, wishing her a long reign. The Empress reciprocated to the naming of the new baby after her by sending Johanna a small copy of her own portrait, framed in diamonds.

Prince Christian August's stroke, William's death and the birth of little Elizabeth were succeeded by a change of residence. In November 1742 Christian August became joint ruler with his elder brother of Anhalt-Zerbst, a small sovereign principality with a population of only 20,000. In order to take up his new position (his brother being joint ruler in name only), Christian August resigned from the Prussian army with the rank of Field Marshal and moved the 150 miles with his family to the medieval town of Zerbst, which, surrounded by walls, towers and a moat, provided a pleasant contrast with Stettin. Their new residence was a small baroque palace, built in the 1680s.

Another person whose life changed dramatically in November 1742 was the young Duke of Holstein-Gottorp, Karl Peter Ulrich. Summoned to Russia by his childless aunt, the Empress Elizabeth, he was named as her heir, received into the Orthodox Church, and granted the name and title of His Imperial Highness the Grand Duke Peter Fyodorovich. Such an alteration in his circumstances made him an infinitely more desirable husband for any young Princess while doing nothing to ameliorate his own sense of disorientation and loneliness. Becoming heir to the Russian throne entailed renouncing his rights to the throne of Sweden and, with the Empress Elizabeth's support, Johanna's brother Adolf Frederick was now elected Crown Prince of Sweden. Consequently, by the end of 1743, everyone connected with Sophie had risen considerably higher in the feudal anthill, and it did not pass unnoticed within the Anhalt-Zerbst ruling household that the boy whose name had almost in jest been coupled with Sophie's several years earlier was now destined for a very great future indeed. A copy of Sophie's portrait as painted by Balthasar Denner was delivered to the Empress Elizabeth by another of Johanna's brothers, Prince Frederick August, to ensure that the Empress should not forget her late fiancé's niece.

A curious interlude now took place which nearly put paid to these great ambitions. It suggests a lack of supervision, and possibly even some connivance, on Johanna's part, as well as a degree of ambivalence towards the ambitions she nursed for her daughter. Johanna, though desirous of promoting her family's interests, could never quite forgive Sophie for being able to exercise aspirations higher than her own; for having the potential to enter a world more powerful, more dazzling, more exciting than the one she had had to settle for herself. The interlude revolved around Johanna's youngest brother, Prince Georg Ludwig of Holstein-Gottorp, who was in the service of the King of Prussia and enjoyed spending time with his sister and her family. Georg Ludwig was 10 years older than Sophie. He would come to visit her in her room when her mother was out or otherwise occupied. Sophie was at first too innocent to have any idea of the nature of the attraction; Georg Ludwig was just a favourite uncle who liked spending time with her. Babet Cardel, however, was no fool. She disapproved of the visits and complained that they were interfering with Sophie's lessons. Prince Georg Ludwig left Zerbst shortly after Babet had expressed her concerns, but when he and Sophie met again in Hamburg, en route for the annual visit to Brunswick, Babet was not in the party, and the Prince was able to spend as much time as he liked in Sophie's company. In Brunswick, however, he was more circumspect, taking little notice of Sophie in public and talking to her only in the evenings, in her mother's room. Sophie – at least according to her mature recollections – persisted in regarding him only as a good friend and relative, and did not quite get the message when he bemoaned the fact that he was her uncle. When she asked him why this made him unhappy, he begged her to promise to marry him, a plea that amazed Sophie but simultaneously opened her eyes to the nature of this man's feelings for her. At first embarrassed, she gradually grew accustomed to the outpourings of passion in which he now felt free to indulge, and found herself becoming attracted to him, to the extent that she actually agreed to marry him, provided her parents gave their consent. (Such a close family relation-ship would also have required the consent of the Lutheran Church before any marriage could take place.)

Later Sophie realised what must have been obvious at the time to any percipient onlooker – that her mother knew perfectly well what was going on and had sanctioned her brother's behaviour. Once the girl had agreed in principle to Prince Georg Ludwig's proposal, he allowed himself to pursue her physically as well as emotionally, seizing on any opportunity he could find to kiss her. At other times he would sigh and moan, forget to eat and drink, and play the role of the romantic, hopeless lover, afraid that another suitor would seize his prize before he could obtain her parents' consent. But he did not appear to take any actual steps to secure that consent. Perhaps Johanna was advising him to bide his time, knowing Sophie's father would not prove tractable. When Sophie and Johanna returned to Zerbst, Prince Georg Ludwig left Brunswick too, and events soon conspired to put an end to this episode.

On New Year's Day 1744, Johanna received a letter from St Petersburg, written by Brummer, the Grand Duke Peter's Marshal, in which she and her daughter Sophie were invited by order of Elizabeth, Empress of All the Russias, to the Russian Court. Sophie had stolen a quick glance at the letter as her mother opened it, sufficient for her to realise its import. Nothing was said to her about it for three days. Her mother had been paying more attention to her of late, partly because a Swedish diplomat, Count von Gyllenburg, who had met them both in the autumn of 1743, had tried to point out to her that her daughter was more worthy of notice than she thought (he had had some cultured conversation with

Sophie, discussing ideas and books), and also because her brother Georg Ludwig's attitude towards Sophie had changed the way she saw the girl herself. In fact, she was actually beginning to consider her daughter as a future sister-in-law – someone who would be a friend and who would no longer constitute a threat to her own self-importance. The letter from Russia tore Johanna in two. On the one hand, how could she resist the excitement of a journey to what was known to be a very glamorous Court, and the honour she herself would receive as an intimate of the Empress? But on the other, how could she stomach the barely acknowledged admission that it was her daughter who was the principal object of interest to the Empress, and that the wife of the heir to the Russian throne would be of more importance than his mother-in-law? Furthermore, if, as seems very likely, she had already given a promise to her brother that she would do what she could to secure Sophie as his bride, she now found herself in a quandary. Sophie, well aware of her mother's ambivalence, and having grown up considerably over the last few months, decided to take matters into her own hands. Accordingly, she confronted her mother with her knowledge about what was in the letter, declared the whole household was talking of nothing else, and said that the invitation should not be ignored, as her whole future was at stake. Johanna, taken aback by this direct approach, floundered and protested that its political instability made Russia a dangerous place, and also for the first time mentioned Sophie's uncle as someone who had a material interest in her future. Sophie blushed at this reference, but her own mind was clearly made up, and she replied that Prince Georg Ludwig could only desire her happiness. And so Johanna took the easy option of saying 'Ask your father.'

Christian August had been specifically excluded from the invitation to Russia. (There was nothing unusual about this. When she was Empress, Sophie would follow the same procedure, inviting mothers to bring prospective brides for inspection by herself, her son and grandsons. It was important that such visits should not look too official in case the plans did not come to fruition.) Johanna would be provided with the necessary money for the journey, was instructed to preserve close secrecy about it and to travel incognito, under the name of the Countess of Rheinbeck, as far as Riga (which marked the frontier between Polish Lithuania and the Russian Empire). At Riga she was to announce herself; she and Sophie would then be provided with an escort. Once inside the Empire, they were to give as the pretext for their visit the desire to thank the Empress in person for all the favours she had granted

Johanna's family. The pretence that this was merely a friendly visit from distant relatives to their benefactress was for public consumption, both at home and abroad (not that anybody believed it).

In her memoirs Sophie claimed that it was she who persuaded Christian August to accept the invitation issued to his wife and daughter, on the dubious grounds that the journey did not actually commit them to anything, and that if on arrival in Russia they did not like it very much, they could turn round and come back home again. Christian August had considerable qualms about allowing his Lutheran daughter to go as a prospective royal bride to a country where Orthodoxy was the state religion, even though part of him must have been expecting the summons. Both parents, however, were aware that the ruler of a small German principality could not with impunity turn down an invitation – which amounted almost to an order – from the Empress of Russia.

Quelling his doubts with the help of written instructions to his daughter as to her future behaviour, Christian August allowed the journey to proceed. Pretending, for public consumption, to have been summoned to Berlin, he left Zerbst together with his wife and daughter. Babet Cardel was left behind in Zerbst. She and Sophie had not been getting on very well for the preceding few days, as Sophie had refused to tell her what was afoot. But when the moment came to say goodbye, the pair clung together weeping, both realising that they would not be seeing one another again, despite Sophie trying to keep up the pretence that they were only going to Berlin.

One of the reasons for travelling via Berlin was so that Frederick II (the Great, who had become King of Prussia in 1740) could give Johanna instructions as to how she might best serve his interests at the Russian Court. (The pay-off was an agreement that Frederick would use his influence to install Johanna's eldest sister as head of the Prussian-owned religious foundation at Quedlinburg.) Frederick was well aware of the real nature of the journey. He was a supporter of the projected marriage, hoping it might serve to increase Prussian influence in Russia. He desired, not unnaturally, to see Sophie for himself, but Johanna was implacably opposed to this idea – she seems to have felt it was too soon for her daughter to be stealing the limelight from her – and came up with all the excuses she could think of (Sophie had no court dress, Sophie was ill) to avoid having her daughter make an appearance. The King, however, insisted, and eventually Johanna had to capitulate. Sophie was given the signal honour (no doubt to Johanna's chagrin) of being seated next to Frederick at dinner while he quizzed her; she acquitted herself well and appeared to gain the King's approval.

On leaving Berlin, Christian August took the route to Stettin, while Johanna and Sophie travelled on towards Russia. This was another difficult leave-taking, as father and daughter said goodbye for what they must have suspected was the last time. For a considerable number of years to come, affection was to be in short supply for Sophie, and she would miss her dependable, upright father more than she ever admitted.

Sophie found the long journey from Berlin to St Petersburg, via Mitau and Riga, in the depths of winter very trying; her feet swelled up, and she had to be carried in and out of the carriage at each stop. The initial party was not particularly large; in addition to Sophie and Johanna, it consisted of Johanna's chamberlain, her lady-companion Fräulein von Kayn, four chambermaids, a valet, several footmen or lackeys, and a cook.

The arrangements which had to be put in hand to manage such a journey and to prepare for the travellers' arrival at various points along the way were complex. On arrival in Mitau (now Jelgava in Latvia, and then the capital of Courland), Johanna was informed that the Colonel in command of the detachment on guard duty at the castle wished to make her acquaintance. She agreed to receive him (in her memoirs Sophie volunteers the extra piece of information that Johanna put her in a separate room, out of the way) and the Colonel informed her that he had sent a courier to Riga (where the Empress's carriages had already been waiting for a week) with news of her progress and wanted to know whether she had any orders to give. On their departure from Mitau at ten o'clock the following morning, the Colonel not only provided the party with a six-man military escort, but insisted on accompanying them himself, with a couple of officers. In an inn between Mitau and Riga they found a representative of the Russian Court waiting for them – Marshal Prince Naryshkin, Grand Master of the Hunt and a court chamberlain. Naryshkin handed over letters and compliments from the Empress and took charge of the arrangements for the rest of the journey.

When they were within a mile of Riga they were met (Johanna, who kept a record of the journey for the benefit of the rest of her family and ensured throughout that she was the heroine of the story, predictably describes this as 'I was received . . .') by the Vice-Governor of the town, Prince Vladimir Dolgoruky, with all the officers of the garrison who were not currently on duty, along with various town dignitaries and representatives of the nobility. (One cannot help being put in mind of Gogol's *The Government Inspector* as everyone turns out to greet these important people, whoever they may be . . .) Prince Naryshkin introduced the assembled dignitaries to Johanna, and then she and Sophie were invited to climb aboard the coach which had been sent from Petersburg to collect them.

And so the first of the many great processions of Sophie's life set off. It consisted of a quartermaster sergeant on horseback, a sergeant with a detachment of cuirassiers from one of Grand Duke Peter's corps, Prince Naryshkin and the Colonel who had escorted the Princesses from Mitau, Prince Dolgoruky and the Commandant of Riga, another quartermaster sergeant, two officers from a Finnish regiment, the coach containing Johanna, Sophie and Fräulein von Kayn, the 'travel coaches' containing clothing and other necessities, and then the carriages carrying representatives of the nobility and of various government departments. The convoy crossed the frozen river Dvina; as the coach carrying Johanna and Sophie crossed over the great bridge just outside Riga, a cannon was fired from the ramparts. There was a large guard stationed at the gates, commanded by two officers. The Princesses entered the town of narrow streets and steep-roofed houses to trumpet fanfares and drum rolls. Here, in addition to the travellers ceasing to be the Countess of Rheinbeck and her daughter and re-assuming their real identities, the calendar moved back 11 days to the Old Style.

At the entrance to the street where they were to stay, there was another detachment of guards, and a further hundred (according to Johanna) lined up outside the house itself. Johanna and Sophie were to be accommodated in the house of a wealthy merchant and member of the nobility, rather than in the imperial mansion or castle, as neither of those could be adequately heated for their brief stay. Crowds lined the streets, and the carriages towards the back of the convoy decided to take an alternative route, rejoining the Princesses at the entrance to the house. Forty more soldiers were stationed inside the entrance, two cuirassiers were on guard at the door of the antechamber, two more at the door of the dining room. The house was clean and pleasantly furnished; Johanna reports approvingly that the furniture was English and 'of the sort one finds in Hamburg'.

Yet more introductions were made and compliments exchanged; this took place in the dining room, the only room large enough to accommodate all the people who wanted to meet Johanna. (Presumably they also wanted to meet Sophie, but one would not know this from

Johanna's account.) Naryshkin and Dolgoruky then accompanied the Princesses to the apartments prepared for them, where they were greeted by the people the Empress had sent to act as their servants. Here they were also presented with new clothing for the rest of the journey, each receiving a luxurious sable pelisse (or cloak) covered with cloth of gold, palatines (wide-shaped stoles or tippets) of the same fur, and a fur blanket covered with a rich chintz with a gold background. This blanket was to cover themselves with in the sleigh in which they would be making the next part of the journey. They then had coffee and conversation (which would have been mainly in French, the common language, though Naryshkin also knew German) with Naryshkin and Dolgoruky, and Johanna dispatched a courier to the Empress to inform her of their arrival in Riga and also to thank her for the generosity of her welcome. Supper followed, at which toasts were drunk to the Empress and to His Imperial Highness the Grand Duke.

Johanna provides a list of the people sent by the Empress to attend her and Sophie and service all their needs in Riga and for the rest of the journey. It reads like 'The Twelve Days of Christmas':

1. A detachment of cuirassiers, with a lieutenant, from the Grand Duke's Holstein regiment.
2. The chamberlain Prince Naryshkin.
3. A Master of the Horse.
4. An officer of the Izmailovsky Guards who fulfilled the functions of a manservant.
5. A steward.
6. A preserve-maker.
7. I don't know how many cooks and kitchen helps.
8. A sommelier and his assistant.
9. A man to make the coffee.
10. Eight footmen.
11. Two grenadier guards of the Izmailovsky Regiment.
12. Two quartermaster sergeants.
13. I don't know how many sleighs and stable hands.

The Princesses stayed for another full day in Riga, the Empress's Master of the Horse explaining through an interpreter that this delay could not be avoided. This meant there was time for yet more introductions and in the afternoon all the important ladies of the town came to visit them. Every time the Princesses went in for a meal a fanfare was played by trumpets, drums, flutes and oboes. Johanna disingenuously remarks: 'It never occurred to me that all this was for poor little me, for whom in some other places they hardly beat the drum and in others sound nothing at all.'

An hour or so before the Princesses' departure from Riga, all the dignitaries who had greeted them turned up again to see them off, and Johanna found her hand being kissed repeatedly. Then the party got into their sleighs. The sleigh in which Johanna and Sophie were to travel was an extraordinary contraption. Designed by Peter the Great, and normally used by the Empress herself, it was a sort of articulated bedroom and antechamber on runners, pulled by 10 horses. The outside was scarlet ornamented with silver brocade and the inside was fur-lined. It contained feather beds, silk mattresses and blankets, damask cushions and a satin cover, on top of which the travellers were to lie. There were plenty more cushions for placing under their heads and then they were covered up with the fur blanket, so that it was just like being in bed. (Sophie had to be taught the manoeuvre of getting in and out of this vehicle.) Heated stones were provided to keep the travellers' feet warm, and a wax candle lantern hung from the roof. The space between the sleeping compartment and the coachman was used both for storage and for the gentlemen of the party to occupy during the daytime and for the maids to sleep in at night. Fräulein von Kayn had a separate, less luxurious, sleeping sleigh for herself. Bringing up the rear of the great array of sleighs was one coach on wheels, in case Johanna and Sophie found they could not cope with what was for them a novel form of transport.

The convoy set off mid-morning, and again Johanna provides a full list of the order:

1. A squadron from His Imperial Highness's regiment;
2. my sleigh, in the front of which I had the chamberlain Prince Naryshkin, Her Imperial Majesty's equerry, an officer of the Izmailovsky Guards and Monsieur Lathorff; behind me were two of Her Majesty's lackeys and two Preobrazhensky Guards;
3. a detachment of the regiment that always precedes governors;
4. a sleigh containing the Vice-Governor and his Commandant;
5. 'la Kayn's' sleigh;
6. the sleighs of the chamberlain and gentlemen-in-waiting;
7. the sleighs of the magistrate, deputies, members of the nobility, and

of those officers who were not riding on horseback around my sleigh.

About a mile out of the town, the main party said goodbye to those in the seventh category of Johanna's list. The Vice-Governor and the Commandant, as well as a few officers, travelled on with the Princesses' party until suppertime, however, and then the party proper sped on through the night, stopping next day for dinner at Dorpat in Livonia (modern-day Lithuania), where they were again received with full military honours.

Late on Friday night, they arrived at Narva, a few miles inland from the Gulf of Finland (in present-day Estonia). The streets down which they were to travel had been illuminated, but they were too late and tired to see much. They set off again the following midday, travelled through the night and arrived at St Petersburg at one o'clock in the afternoon of 3 February, during the brief hours of winter daylight in this most northern of cities, to salvoes of cannon fire.

It would be a mistake to imagine St Petersburg in 1744 as quite the glorious city it later became. It was still under construction – many of the buildings were log cabins – though the Italian architect Domenico Trezzini had already contributed the Peter and Paul Cathedral, a Summer Palace, the Twelve Colleges and the Exchange. The needle spires of the Admiralty and the Peter and Paul Cathedral already existed but were not yet gilded. Much of the town was made of wood, and fires were regular occurrences, as were floods. Alongside the Neva river, to the west of the Admiralty, houses had been constructed in wood and stone for members of the Russian aristocracy and important foreigners. Elizabeth's Winter Palace was on the site occupied by the present-day one, though it was smaller (and much draughtier), but the area behind it, which would eventually become Palace Square, was a field. In fact much of St Petersburg was still wild, with wolves and bears to be found in parts of it. Nevertheless, this city on the Gulf of Finland, its population twice that of Berlin, would still have presented an impressive aspect to the Princesses of Anhalt-Zerbst.

St Petersburg was not, however, their final destination as the Court was currently residing at the old capital of Moscow. The intention was that, after a brief respite in Petersburg, the Princesses should travel on to Moscow in order to arrive by 10 February, Grand Duke Peter's sixteenth birthday. The Empress had arranged for various of her court ladies to accompany the Princesses to Moscow, and four of these now received them at the foot of the staircase of the Winter Palace, along with the Vice-Governor, Prince Repnin, and 'thousands' (as Johanna puts it) of other gentlemen of varying degrees of importance. From the description Johanna now gives, one could be forgiven for thinking that her daughter had fallen out of the sleigh somewhere en route:

> The Prince gave me his hand; I was to stay in the Grand Duke's apartments. As I got out of the sleigh, I was greeted by the firing of cannon from the Admiralty glacis. On arrival in my apartments, hundreds of people were presented to me. My tongue was dry with cold. Nevertheless I had to exchange an infinite number of compliments. I dined alone with the ladies and gentlemen provided for me by the Empress; I was served like a queen. The ladies came to see me in the evening . . . The following day, which was yesterday, I received the compliments of priests and monks. There were a lot of people there all day long. I was almost fainting by the time I returned to my inner apartments.

After dinner Naryshkin organised an entertainment for the visitors: he had a troupe of 14 elephants, given to the Empress Elizabeth by Nadir Shah of Persia, brought into the courtyard of the Winter Palace, where they performed various circus tricks.

The Princesses spent just over two days in St Petersburg, during which time a half-hearted plot was attempted by certain courtiers who did not support the proposed match to delay them and prevent them arriving in Moscow in time for the Grand Duke's birthday, which would have discredited them in the Empress's eyes. Johanna was alerted to this plot by an old acquaintance of hers, the Marquis de la Chétardie. She insisted on pressing on for Moscow as soon as possible and they duly departed on the night of 5–6 February.

The party this time consisted of between 20 and 30 sleighs; relays of horses were waiting for them at each staging post, where they were also provided with morning coffee, dinner or supper and 'all imaginable conveniences'. During this leg of the journey Johanna suffered a minor mishap, occasioned by the back of the long sleeping sleigh hitting the corner of a house as it went round a bend during the night. Her account of the incident is characteristically dramatic:

> The shock that the sleigh received caused a big iron bar, which supported the cover and was used for holding it back when you

wanted to be in the open air, to fall into the interior; this bar dragged with it a smaller one, which held up a curtain for drawing against the sun; both bars fell right on top of my head. The blow woke me up; in my struggle to get out from under my pelisse both bars fell on my chest and arm and, either from fear or pain, I couldn't get my breath. At first all I could do was tug at my daughter, who was also asleep, to wake her up. Nothing had fallen on her. While she was calling out to tell the driver to stop, I had time to sort myself out. I thought I was injured, but I wasn't, the pelisse having protected me from the full force of the blow; otherwise I would definitely have suffered a broken head, breastbone and arm. They got me out of the sleigh, rubbed me with eau de vie and I got away with a few bruises.

Her daughter's account of the accident is rather more measured: 'As we left Petersburg, the sleigh in which my mother was travelling bumped into a house at a turning and an iron hook attached to the carriage fell on her head and shoulder. She protested she had received grave injuries though nothing could be seen, not even a bruise. This accident delayed our journey for several hours.' Johanna in fact sustained fewer injuries than others of the party. One of the grenadier guards was thrown against the house, smashing his nose and chin, while 'One of the coachmen of the corps who were steering us was thrown head over heels off his seat; he fell on top of the quartermaster sergeant, the pages and the footmen who were in the front part of the sleigh and it was fortunate that he didn't crush anyone.'

Despite the accident, the convoy made good time, and by four o'clock in the afternoon of 9 February they were within 25 miles of Moscow. At this point a courier arrived to give Johanna instructions about the manner of their entry into the city; they were to proceed with haste, as Her Imperial Majesty was in a state of nervous antici-pation. The Princesses had a quick change of clothing (Sophie remem-bered that she wore a tight-fitting dress of rose and silver moiré, a heavy watered grosgrain silk) and a hurried meal, though Johanna was too nervous to swallow anything and, sending couriers before them, off they sped, this time with 16 horses to pull their sleigh, covering the distance in three hours. A couple of miles away from the city they were met by a gentleman of Her Imperial Majesty's bedchamber, who conveyed the compliments of both the Empress and the Grand Duke, neither of whom, he said, could wait to see them.

The chamberlain and gentlemen of the Court took their seats in the front of the sleigh, its cover folded back, for the arrival at the Annenhof Palace★ where the Court was in residence. Passing through the grand entrance, the sleigh ran past the windows of the Empress's apartments; the Empress came out into a small passage from where she could catch a first glimpse of her visitors without being seen herself. On getting out of the sleigh, Johanna and Sophie were greeted by Marshal Brummer, accompanied by various chamberlains, gentlemen and Guards officers. They were then escorted to their apartments, where they removed their outerwear. As Johanna was untying her headdress, Grand Duke Peter appeared and presented to her the Field Marshal Prince of Hesse-Homburg, who was the Empress's aide-de-camp. Now the moment arrived for the Princesses to meet the Empress, who summoned them to her apartments. 'And so we set off,' recounted Johanna. 'Everyone's curiosity and the way they stared at the German women from top to toe and from toe to top was inconceivable. Her Majesty came forward a few steps in what is known as her first antechamber which adjoins the bedroom and is where she sees everyone. I pulled off my gloves, and she kissed me with what I can only describe as tenderness.' Johanna then kissed the Empress's hand and made a formal speech of thanks for 'the benefits which she has showered on my family' and asking for continued protection 'for me, the rest of my family and my child whom Her Majesty has deigned to allow to accompany me to her Court'. Sophie herself was immediately impressed by the 34-year-old Elizabeth's beauty and the majesty of her bearing: 'She was a large woman who, in spite of being very stout, was not in the least disfigured by her size nor was she embarrassed in her movements; her head, too, was very beautiful.' She was wearing a very large hoop of the sort she wore for special occasions, under a dress of silver moiré ornamented with gold braid; in her hair she wore a black feather and an array of diamonds.

The Empress, after thanking Johanna for her speech, turned an attentive and appraising gaze on Sophie. She kissed her and then led them both into her bedroom (this was not as intimate as it sounds – business was frequently transacted in bedrooms) where armchairs had been placed for them but no one sat down. Johanna says that this was because the conversation was so animated that no one thought of sitting, while Sophie tersely remembers that as the Empress did not sit down, neither

★ This palace was destroyed during the Moscow plague in 1771.

could anybody else. At some point during the conversation Elizabeth left the room for a few minutes. The Princesses imagined that she had gone out to give some orders, but Johanna came to believe that the reason was sentimental: 'I have found out subsequently that, after having seen my face closely, she had found that I looked so like my late brother, that she had been unable to hold back her tears and that that was why she had gone out.'

After half an hour or so, the Empress decided that Johanna and Sophie must be tired after their journey and dismissed them. She did not eat with them that evening or on subsequent days as it was Lent and the devout Elizabeth was abstaining from the meat with which the Princesses would be served. The Grand Duke, however, was dispensed from these Lenten observances and he quite often took his meals with the Princesses, either in their apartments or in his. For this first supper Sophie sat on the Grand Duke's left, with Count Münnich, the Master of the Empress's Household, on her other side; she was struck by the fact that the Count had a habit of speaking very slowly with his eyes closed. She claimed to remember Grand Duke Peter as having a long pale face, a straight nose and a firm chin, being rather small for his age and having a great deal of nervous energy. During the meal the Empress approached the door unobserved, to see the first impressions created and received by her guests.

The next day, the Empress and the Grand Duke both sent their compliments by way of a gentleman-in-waiting. As soon as the Princesses were dressed, the gentlemen who were to attend on them were presented to them. These included two chamberlains and two gentlemen-in-waiting, four pages and 'I don't know how many others, altogether a very numerous court.' Various other gentlemen were introduced to them and then, at about 11 o'clock in the morning, the Prince of Hesse-Homburg arrived with an invitation to join the Empress in her apartments. 'That day,' wrote Johanna, 'there was a gala in honour of the Grand Duke. The antechambers were swarming with people; one could hardly move through them. I was wearing a heavy outfit, I was stiff from the fatigue of the journey, so that by the time I reached Her Majesty's apartments my legs were giving way under me.' On this occasion the Empress bestowed on both Johanna and Sophie the Order of St Catherine. After the ribbons and stars had been attached, they all departed to see the Grand Duke. The Empress, whose head, neck and bosom were bedecked with jewels and who was wearing a brown robe embroidered with silver, soon left them to go to church.

The Princesses quickly settled into the routine of the Court, living a relatively quiet life as it was Lent, dressing for dinner at midday and meeting various courtiers over coffee in the early afternoon. The rest of the afternoon would be spent in solitary occupations, and during the evenings they would visit Grand Duke Peter in his apartments, or he would come to theirs (always, in both cases, in the company of ladies- and gentlemen-in-waiting). Much of the Empress's time was taken up with her devotions, Elizabeth being a very religious, and often superstitious, woman.

Sophie now had to absorb a great deal of information very rapidly if she was to survive and prosper at the Russian Court. Principally she had to work out who was who, and whose favour it was vital to cultivate. One of the most powerful men was Elizabeth's Vice-Chancellor, Count Alexei Bestuzhev-Ryumin (he was often referred to simply as Bestuzhev). Sophie was later to describe him as 'infinitely more feared than loved . . . a great intriguer, suspicious, firm and intrepid in his principles, occasionally tyrannical, an implacable enemy, but the true friend of his friends'. He was not a supporter of Sophie as a prospective bride for Peter; he would have preferred a girl from an Austrian or English royal family. Lined up against Bestuzhev were those courtiers who supported the interests of France, Sweden and Prussia. They were led by the Marquis de la Chétardie and by Count Lestocq, Elizabeth's surgeon and a prime mover in the coup which had brought her to power. Also among those whom Sophie had to learn to cultivate was Grand Duke Peter himself. He did not appear to be a particularly happy young man. Having been brought up by a series of male tutors, he now felt lonely and bullied at Elizabeth's Court, unsure about the change of religion which had been foisted on him, with little enthusiasm for Russia or for the prospect of ruling it. To begin with, Sophie's advent must have seemed a welcome diversion, for here was a companion of near his own age, someone else rooted up from a background similar to his, someone whom – initially – he could hope to impress with his knowledge of the Russian Court. One can sense his relief at no longer being the only young person constantly in the limelight, not understanding how things worked or even what people were saying. Maybe he felt slightly protective toward Sophie; at the outset. Unfortunately, she rapidly outstripped him; her quickness of mind, her innate political sense – perhaps even the fact that she was a girl and used to absorbing a lot of information in silence and working out how to make the best use of it – as well as her ambition and determination, meant she fitted in at Court far more easily than Peter had ever done. Instead of being able to be a wise consort to his young wife-to-be, Peter found it was the other way round, and he did not, on the whole, welcome this – he had, after all, been there longer than she had, he was older (slightly) than her, and he was a boy.

Though Sophie was more adaptable than Peter, the immense change she had to go through took its toll on her physically. Quite apart from being in a foreign country whose native language was completely unknown to her, with foreign customs, she had had to emerge from the relatively relaxed and private life of an obscure German Court to one of complete visibility, where every action, word and expression counted, and would be interpreted and reported back to those in authority. Her eventual marriage to Grand Duke Peter was by no means a foregone conclusion. For those first weeks and months at the Russian Court Sophie was on trial and, if she did not want to be sent home in embarrassment and ignominy, she could not afford to put a foot wrong. She received little real guidance and could not even be sure that her mother was on her side. She was, however, provided with teachers to help her integrate as quickly as possible into Russian court life: Father Semyon Theodorsky, Abbot of the Ipatyev Monastery and later Bishop of Pskov, to prepare her to be received into the Orthodox Church (he had performed the same role for Grand Duke Peter); Vasily Adadurov to teach her Russian; and Monsieur Landé to give her dancing lessons. She was so keen to learn Russian quickly that she would get up during the night to learn her vocabulary, a practice which she believed (or at least decided the readers of her memoirs should believe) contributed to her going down with pleurisy.

Johanna, who was at first disposed to ignore her daughter's shivering, then became convinced she might have smallpox and for that reason resisted the doctors' recommendations that Sophie should be bled (bloodletting being one of the few remedies carried out for anything at that time). Johanna considered that being bled had contributed to her own brother's death from smallpox, and feared the same thing would happen to her daughter. So, while the doctors and Johanna argued and sent reports to the Empress, who was away on pilgrimage at the monastery of Holy Trinity-St Sergius, poor Sophie lay there with a high fever, groaning from the pain in her side. It was not until the fifth day of her illness that the Empress returned to find Sophie unconscious and immediately assumed control. Accompanied by Count Lestocq and another surgeon, she insisted that Sophie be bled, and the remedy (the surgeon opening a vein in her foot) appeared to bring instant relief. She was bled a total of 16 times over the next month, despite Johanna's protests; she, however, eventually had to concede that her daughter was not, after all, suffering from smallpox.

Even during the course of this severe illness, Sophie did not lose sight of the need to maintain the right image. So, for instance, while Johanna wanted a Lutheran pastor summoned to her daughter's side, Sophie asked instead for Semyon Theodorsky, who duly came and talked to her. It may have been that she had become used to the priest and valued his company and prayers, but whether or not her request was calculated, it raised her status in the eyes of the Court and of the Empress. This was, as was everything at Court, a public illness; Sophie was not left alone to languish – there were always people in her room, observing, listening, and she was already wise enough to know this. She also used her convalescence to listen and learn, pretending to be asleep while in fact eavesdropping on the conversations going on among the ladies-in-waiting. Johanna showed less wisdom, and her behaviour during the course of the illness did not endear her to anybody. It was considered that she had shown insufficient sympathy towards her daughter. Grand Duke Peter did show concern for Sophie, and, as she began to recover, got into the habit of spending the evening with her and Johanna.

On 21 April, Sophie's fifteenth birthday, she officially reappeared in public for the first time after her illness. As she recalled many years later, it was a difficult day: 'I do not think that my appearance made an edifying impression on the company. I had become as thin as a skeleton, I had grown taller, but my face and features were drawn, my hair was falling out, and I was mortally pale. I appeared to myself ugly as a scarecrow and did not feel at my ease.' The Empress sent her some rouge (made of red lead mixed with carmine or vermilion) and told her to apply it; fortunately this cadaverous appearance was only temporary.

Sophie had passed the initial tests of acceptability to the Empress and the Grand Duke, and on 3 May she wrote to her father to ask formally for his consent to her betrothal. Behind the stylised language (she assures him that her wishes will always be in conformity to his and that no one will be able to make her fail in her duty) lies her consciousness of what the real issue is as far as her father is concerned: the requirement that she convert from the Lutheran to the Orthodox (or Greek) Church. But Sophie is determined that her father's scruples – or indeed her own – should not be allowed to stand in the way of her ambitions. She repeats what she has written to him before, that she can find no difference between the Greek and Lutheran religions, and so has decided that it is right for her to convert.

She had not, however, arrived at this decision without a struggle. Her father's views and beliefs held great sway over her; she had been brought up to kneel and say her prayers morning and night, and she took her religion seriously enough for her conversion to be more than a mere formality. Semyon Theodorsky, a highly educated priest who had studied at the University of Halle, greatly eased the process for her, so that she was able to write quite early on to her father that they must have been mistaken in fearing Orthodoxy so much; the outward ceremonies might be very different, she tells him, but that is because the Church has had to take into account the 'brutality of the people' – in other words, uncivilised Russians need a lot of outward show if they are to be persuaded to take religion seriously at all. To convince oneself that there is no substantial difference between Lutheranism and Orthodoxy nevertheless requires some mental gymnastics. Apart from the theological and doctrinal differences between the Western and Eastern Churches centring on the 'filioque' clause of the Creed, there is the emphasis the Orthodox Church places on the performance of the liturgy and on outward signs of inner devotion. Sophie's sober father would have felt profoundly uneasy and out of place during an Orthodox celebration of the liturgy, with the jewel-encrusted icons, the royal doors in the centre of the iconostasis behind which only the priests can penetrate, the people constantly crossing themselves, bowing, lighting candles and kissing the icons, and bearded priests in rich vestments chanting prayers and readings in Church Slavonic, an archaic language already removed from that spoken by the people. It is interesting that even when compiling her memoirs many years later, Sophie still felt it necessary to justify – both to others and to herself – her decision to convert. Recalling her childhood and her earliest teacher in religion, Pastor Wagner, she writes: 'One day I asked this Lutheran priest, for that was what my teacher was, which of the Christian Churches was the most ancient. He told me that it was the Greek Church and that it was also the one closest to the teachings of the Apostles, he was convinced of that. From then onwards I have always had a great respect for the Greek Church and curiosity to learn about its doctrines and ceremonies.'

When Sophie wrote to her father, she was still weak from her illness, but over the next few weeks her health improved. So did the weather, and Grand Duke Peter took to outdoor pursuits – walking and shooting – with his entourage. When Sophie recalled this period of her life in her memoirs, she was at her most dismissive about her future husband, disingenuously asserting that she was only marrying him because her mother had told her to, but admitting that she was already attracted by 'the Crown of Russia'. Peter, she declared, talked only of soldiers and toys.

Having survived both serious illness and qualms of conscience, Sophie now had to contend with her mother's lack of political sense, which nearly brought their whole Russian enterprise to a disastrous conclusion. Conscious of being Frederick II's unofficial emissary, Johanna had been building up quite a circle of acquaintances at the Russian Court, including her old friend the Marquis de la Chétardie, who had previously been the French ambassador but was now at the Court as a private individual. He and Johanna had been making disparaging remarks to one another about the Empress, on his part because he was disgruntled and disappointed at having lost his former influence over her, and on Johanna's as a clumsy attempt to undermine the influence of the anti-Prussian Bestuzhev. De la Chétardie had reported some of what Johanna had said to the French Court; his correspondence had – inevitably – been intercepted by Bestuzhev himself who had, with some glee, shown it to the Empress. This was the reason for Elizabeth appearing unannounced and furious in the Princesses' apartments one day in early June and delivering a reprimand to Johanna which reduced her to tears. There were certainly some at Court who hoped this débâcle would end with both Princesses being dispatched back to Zerbst and another bride found for Peter; as for Peter himself, Sophie suspected it might be a matter of indifference. As he had to marry someone, that someone might as well be Sophie, but he would be unlikely to jeopardise his own standing with the Empress by supporting Sophie if she fell into disfavour. On this occasion, however, Johanna's tearful repentance seemed enough to satisfy the Empress, who was also by now aware of the different characters and behaviour of mother and daughter. The political consequences of the intrigue included the Marquis de la Chétardie being escorted to the frontier and ordered out of the country, and Bestuzhev being appointed Grand Chancellor. The Empress also signed a treaty with Saxony reinforcing the Austro-Russian alliance while undermining Prussian interests. So much for Johanna's championing the cause of King Frederick.

Meanwhile, Prince Christian August did as was requested of him and gave his official blessing to the Empress's plans for his daughter. All those immediately concerned seemed delighted, even Peter, and the Empress pressed ahead with the preparations, naming 28 June as the date for Sophie's admittance into the Orthodox Church, with the betrothal ceremony the day after, the Feast of Sts Peter and Paul, and consequently the Grand Duke's name-day.★

Sophie's preparation for these ceremonies was arduous, and the stamina required on the days themselves considerable. Her lessons with Semyon Theodorsky became more intensive, and on the two days before her conversion she did not appear in public. On the last day she fasted, which meant eating only fish cooked in oil. On the morning of the 28th she first of all went to confession (a pre-requisite for the Orthodox before receiving communion) and was then dressed in the Empress's apartments. Elizabeth had had made for her a scarlet and silver adrienne (a variant of the popular 'sack-dress', worn over stays with a small train and hoop), matching her own dress of rose-coloured silk with silver braid on all the seams. Sophie wore only a white ribbon in her unpowdered hair; her jewels were few and were those given to her by the Empress during her illness. Even Johanna thought her daughter who, with her long, pointed chin and thin face, was no natural beauty, looked beautiful on this occasion.

The service took place in the chapel of the Golovin Palace, also known as the Annenhof Summer Palace, on the outskirts of Moscow. (The word 'chapel' can sound misleading; the chapels of the imperial palaces were ornate churches, their only difference from other churches being that they were inside a palace rather than being separate buildings.) Johanna, a close observer as usual, provides a detailed description of the order of the procession from the Empress's apartments to the chapel:

The Court walked ahead, the Grand Master and the marshal of the Court immediately in front of Her Majesty. Her Imperial Majesty alone, flanked by the chamberlains and gentlemen of the bedchamber on duty that day; I came next, led by the Grand Duke, who was flanked by his grand marshal and his chamberlain of the day Monsieur Naryshkin, with the gentleman of the bedchamber Prince Trubetskoy next to me; my daughter followed us all on her own, accompanied

★ For Orthodox Christians, the feast day of the saint after whom they are named has always been as important as their own birthday and is celebrated in a similar manner.

by our other chamberlain and gentleman of the bedchamber; she was followed by the Princess of Homburg, the Princess Golitsyn, grand mistress of Her Majesty's household, the ladies of the portrait,* the maids of honour, the princesses and private ladies. The antechambers were packed; one could hardly move through them.

Waiting for them at the church was a semicircle of archbishops, with the Archbishop of Novgorod in the centre. A velvet cushion was placed before them for Sophie to kneel on; behind it was a carpet where the Empress was to stand. The Grand Duke and Johanna stood behind the Empress, with everyone else moving into whatever place they could find. (Everyone, apart from the old and infirm, stands throughout Orthodox services.) Sophie knelt to receive the Archbishop's blessing, then stood, bowed to the Empress, and read out loud in Russian, in a clear voice and without stumbling, the confession of faith, which ran to 50 quarto pages. At the end she recited the Creed from memory. It was, according to the sentimental Johanna, a highly emotional occasion: 'I was already so overcome in advance, that I burst into tears before she had got to the end of the first word. Her Imperial Majesty had her face covered so no one could see it. Everyone who was there was praying with us; the old men were sobbing; all the young people there had tears in their eyes.' Sophie acquitted herself superlatively: 'Her demeanour ever since she had come in and throughout the whole ceremony was marked by such nobility and grace, that I would have admired her even if she hadn't been to me what she is.'

After the confession of faith, the Abbess of the Novodevichy Convent came forward to act as witness of the anointing. She stood to Sophie's left while the Archbishop placed salt on her tongue and anointed her forehead, eyes, neck, throat, and the front and back of her hands with oil. He then recited some prayers and gave the blessing, after which Sophie kissed his hand. The imperial party, including Sophie, now left the body of the church and retired into a long gallery which adjoined it, where they remained while the liturgy of the Mass was sung, until the consecration. At that point the Empress led Sophie back into the church and, at the moment when the sacrament was distributed, brought her forward to receive communion from Father Semyon Theodorsky. She also assisted her in making all the correct gestures. More litanies

---

* Ladies of the Court who had received the honour of being allowed to wear a miniature portrait of the Empress.

and psalms were sung and then prayers were said for the Orthodox believer Ekaterina (Catherine) Alexeyevna. Sophie was now officially Catherine (and that is how she will be referred to from now on).

Afterwards, back in the Empress's apartments, Elizabeth presented Catherine with a diamond clasp for her bodice and a necklace worth 150,000 roubles. There then followed two hours during which Catherine and her mother had their hands kissed by all the ladies of the Court as well as by members of the Holy Synod, the Senate and the nobility. By now Catherine was so exhausted that she was excused dinner and went off to have a rest.

Later that day, everyone visited the Grand Duke's apartments to congratulate him on the eve of his name-day. Catherine presented him with a hunting knife and cane head, mounted in gold and ornamented with diamonds and emeralds, these gifts having been provided for her by the Empress, for as yet she had no money of her own. The Empress also provided the rings which Catherine and Peter were to exchange the following day; Johanna described these rings as 'real little monsters'. The whole party then had to change and, after supper, travel incognito (i.e. without ceremony rather than in disguise) to the Kremlin (about two and a half miles away from the Golovin Palace) where the next day's ceremony was to take place in the Cathedral of the Assumption (or Uspensky Sobor), built in the 1470s by Ivan the Great as the seat of the Russian Orthodox Church. The long cortège moved slowly through the heat and dust of the summer night. At midnight the bells of the Kremlin rang out to announce the feast day, the bells of all the other churches in Moscow clanging in response.

The day of the betrothal began with prayers said in Catherine's apartments, and then Count Lestocq arrived, bearing a portrait of the Empress framed in diamonds and another of the Grand Duke mounted in a bracelet, also decorated with diamonds, for Catherine to wear. More hand-kissing followed, this time by ambassadors and foreign ministers as well as by military men. The party then collected in the Empress's apartments and set off in procession for the cathedral, in a similar order to that of the preceding day except that this time Catherine was on Johanna's right and the Empress, who was wearing her crown and imperial mantle, had a silver canopy held over her by eight major-generals. The procession descended the flight of stairs leading from the Krasnoye Kryltso (Beautiful Porch) and crossed Cathedral Square, the Guards regiments lining the way.

The Empress was received at the door of the cathedral by the clergy.

The Archbishop, cross in hand, then led the procession into the middle of the church where there was a large dais, carpeted in velvet, on which was placed the patriarchal throne. Peter and Catherine bowed low to the Empress and then took up their places before the dais. The Empress stood near the ambo (or lectern), Johanna parallel with her, and everybody else behind. The two rings were taken by the Archbishops of Moscow and Novgorod and carried, in the company of several bishops, archimandrites and deacons, through the royal doors and placed on the altar, where they remained while a bishop read out the Empress's *ukaz* (or decree), proclaiming the forthcoming marriage of the Grand Duke to this young Princess, who from this moment would bear the titles of Grand Duchess of All the Russias and Her Imperial Highness. The Archbishop then brought back the rings, which were placed on top of the Gospel book and presented to the Empress, who blessed them in her capacity as head of the Orthodox Church. She then herself placed the rings on the fingers of the young couple, who kissed her hand. After a blessing by the Archbishop, the Empress embraced both Peter and Catherine. As Johanna explained, 'This whole ceremony took place before the Mass, in order that the Grand Duchess could be inserted in the prayers which precede it.'

In the Uspensky Cathedral there was no opportunity for the imperial party to disappear out of sight during the liturgy. Instead the Empress took her place in the high gallery belonging to the Tsars, while the Grand Duke occupied one facing it, traditionally reserved for heirs apparent. A temporary gallery had been constructed for Catherine and Johanna alongside that of the Empress. Johanna cannot have been alone in finding it all an exhausting experience: 'During the exchange of rings all the bells had been rung and the cannons fired; this was repeated during the singing of Psalm 100. Mass was followed by a sermon, given by a metropolitan. The whole ceremony took four hours, during which one could not sit down for a quarter of an hour.' The physical ordeal continued after the service: 'After coming out from [the cathedral] everyone went to their own apartments and there received the compliments of the whole empire. To say that I could not feel my back from all the bowing that I had to do in embracing this throng of ladies, and that my right hand had a real mark the size of a German florin from all the kisses I received is not at all an exaggeration; everyone here saw it.' More gifts were exchanged, the Grand Duke giving Catherine a diamond-encrusted watch and fan, while he presented to Johanna another watch decorated with rubies and diamonds, and a snuff box. Catherine gave Johanna a large string of pearls, and Johanna gave Catherine her own ruby ornaments.

Dinner was then served in the Kremlin's Faceted Palace; the seating arrangements had caused considerable diplomatic wrangling. According to Johanna, the Empress had originally intended that Johanna should join her and the young couple beneath the throne but that an enemy of hers (probably Count Bestuzhev, though she does not name him) had stirred up the foreign ambassadors to object to this preferential treatment and to declare that they too wanted to be at the dinner but that they could not possibly allow this Princess of a minor German principality to claim precedence over them. The Empress solved the problem by spreading everybody out over several halls. She, Peter and Catherine dined alone in the throne room, while Johanna was served at a separate table in an apartment above it, from where she could see and be seen by the imperial trio. The diplomatic corps was seated in another apartment. There were five toasts drunk during the meal: to the Empress, the Grand Duke, the Grand Duchess, the clergy and the loyal subjects; the first three were accompanied by cannon fire.

After the meal everyone dispersed for a couple of hours' rest, and at nine o'clock in the evening the ball commenced in the throne room. The Grand Duke and Duchess opened the ball, Peter taking the Empress as his partner and Catherine the Danish ambassador. The ball lasted for about four hours, a select group consisting of the Empress, Peter, Catherine, Johanna, the Prince and Princess of Hesse-Homburg, and the ambassadors of England, Holstein and Denmark dancing on the carpet at the foot of the throne, and the rest of the assembly on the other side of the room. It became very hot and crowded in this unusually constructed room, in which the vaulted roof was (and still is) supported by one large pillar in the centre. During the ball the Kremlin and its surroundings were illuminated and there was much firing of cannons. This exhausting day, the first in the life of Catherine, Grand Duchess of All the Russias, finally came to an end with a private supper at two o'clock in the morning.

## 2

# *Engagement and Wedding*
# *(1744–45)*

*I wanted to be Russian in order that the Russians should love me.*
Memoirs of Catherine the Great

*O*n the day following the betrothal, the Grand Duchess was serenaded both by military bands – trumpets, timpani, oboes and side drums – and by instrumentalists and church singers performing Italian music, the Empress's Italian choirmaster Francesco Araya having composed a new musical drama specially for the occasion. Manufacturers brought her gifts (perhaps, more accurately, 'samples' in the expectation of future custom) of materials and ribbons, and the Empress brought her the star and cross of St Catherine worked in diamonds and worth, according to Johanna, 70,000 roubles. The Empress also granted her an annual allowance of 30,000 roubles. One of the first things Catherine did on receipt of this new-found independence and comparative wealth (and before she had learnt that 30,000 roubles might not last very long among the extravagances of Elizabeth's Court) was to write to her father and offer to pay for the treatment of her sickly younger brother. She also gave her father a brief account of her conversion and betrothal, rather disingenuously informing him that 'Catherine' had been 'added' to her name by the Empress. She did not tell him about 'Alexeyevna' and understandably so, for by the receipt of this patronymic, her ties with Christian August were symbolically severed.

That summer there were 'balls, masquerades, fireworks, illuminations, operas and comedies' as part of the official celebrations to mark peace with Sweden (the latest war having provisionally ended in 1743). It was during these celebrations that her own Court was first established for Catherine, a number of courtiers being chosen for her by the Empress. They included three young gentlemen of the bedchamber, Count Zakhar Chernyshev, Count Peter Bestuzhev-Ryumin and Prince Alexander Golitsyn, all of whom could speak both French and German, and three maids-of-honour, two Princesses Gagarina and a Mademoiselle Koshelyova. In a supervisory role both over these courtiers and the young Grand Duchess herself was placed the lady-in-waiting Countess Maria Rumyantseva, of whom Catherine was not overly fond and towards whom Johanna bore particular animus, as Countess Rumyantseva was among those who disapproved of Johanna and her intrigues – which by now included a sexual intrigue with the 40-year-old Count Ivan Betskoy, a chamberlain at Elizabeth's Court and the illegitimate son of Field Marshal Prince Ivan Trubetskoy.* Not that Countess Rumyantseva, an old hand at the Russian Court, was a stranger to such intrigues, having herself at one time been the mistress of Peter the Great. Catherine got on very well with her daughter Praskovya, who was the same age as herself; the two girls frequently shared a bedroom where they used to 'romp about until early in the morning'.

Catherine claims in her memoirs that during this period between the betrothal and marriage Peter's Marshal, Brummer, complained to her several times about the Grand Duke's behaviour, hoping she might be able to exercise some influence over him. She refused to interfere, however, not wishing to alienate her fiancé at this early stage. On the whole the young couple found one another's company diverting, at least in comparison with that of most of the adults surrounding them. Catherine describes herself and Peter as sometimes producing an 'uproar' and being 'both brimful of childish spirits'.

At the conclusion of the peace celebrations, Catherine, Peter and Johanna set off for Kiev (a journey of some 470 miles), the Empress following a few days later. Johanna and the young people made the most of the relative freedom this journey afforded them, ensuring that they travelled with the people they liked most in their carriage (a large sleeping coach, loaded with beds) and excluding those likely to disapprove of their high spirits, such as Countess Rumyantseva, Marshal Brummer and Fräulein von Kayn. These three, along with another tutor of Peter's called Bergholz, travelled together in another carriage in

---

* Illegitimate children were often given their father's surname, minus the first syllable.

which, as Catherine describes it, they 'made sour remarks at our expense while we were enjoying ourselves'. They travelled via Serpukhov and Tula and then entered Ukraine; after passing through Hlukhiv (an important Ukrainian fortress town which Catherine denotes by its alternative spelling of Glukhov), they arrived at Kozelets and the mansion of Count Kirill Razumovsky, the younger brother of Count Alexei Razumovsky, the Empress Elizabeth's current and long-standing favourite. Here they had to wait three weeks until the Empress caught up with them.

The Empress Elizabeth, the daughter of Peter the Great by his second marriage (to his former servant and mistress, Catherine, originally Marta Skavronskaya), was a formidable woman who shared certain characteristics with her giant of a father, including his fine physique. She had initially been a reluctant monarch. Since her father's death in 1725, the succession to the Russian throne had been a turbulent affair, a situation largely of Peter's own making. On tiring of his first wife, Evdokia Lopukhina, Peter had immured her in a convent near Staraya Ladoga. His second wife, Catherine, was of peasant stock and had, before becoming Peter's mistress, been the mistress of one of his most influential courtiers, Prince Alexander Menshikov. In 1718 Peter had his own son (by his first wife) Alexei sentenced to death at the age of 28 (he died from torture before the sentence could be carried out). The crime for which he had been arrested and tortured (by, among others, his father himself) in the Trubetskoy Bastion of the Peter and Paul Fortress was to have disagreed with Peter's westernising reforms, which he had threatened to reverse had he attained the throne. In a further attempt to ensure his reforms would remain intact after his death, Peter abolished the right of primogeniture and passed a new law of succession in 1722 by which the reigning monarch should nominate his or her own successor. Unfortunately he died before fulfilling his own instruction.

Prince Menshikov, erstwhile lover of Peter's widow, had no intention of relinquishing the power he had enjoyed during Peter's reign and realised that the best way of maintaining it was to secure the throne for his former mistress, who had been elevated to the status of Empress by Peter in 1724. And so, with his help and that of the Guards regiments who supported him, the illiterate former servant became Catherine I, Empress of Russia in her own right. Functioning mainly as a figurehead, she died in 1727, after a reign of only two years. Prince Menshikov, who has to be admired at least for his persistence, now contrived to get Peter's grandson by his first marriage (the son of the murdered Alexei), a sickly 11-year-old also called Peter, on to the throne, appointing himself as Regent. Unfortunately for Menshikov, the young Peter II died of smallpox only three years later and the next person to ascend the throne was Anna Ioannovna, the niece of Peter the Great and by now widow of the Duke of Courland. The Supreme Privy Council, a small group of aristocrats of whom Prince Menshikov was a leading member and who had virtually run the Empire under Catherine I and Peter II, had offered Anna the crown in the belief that she too would be guided by them and would not try to exercise any real power of her own. She appeared to accept their conditions until she was crowned, whereupon she tore them up and assumed real instead of nominal power, ruling with the aid of her favourite, the German Ernst Biron. Anna abolished the Supreme Privy Council and exiled several of its members, including Menshikov, to Siberia; all Menshikov's goods – including his sumptuous palace on Petersburg's Vasilyevsky Island, which Peter the Great used to requisition for his larger-scale entertainments – were confiscated.

During Anna Ioannovna's reign Elizabeth lived at Court, and was described by a visiting Englishwoman as 'very fair, with light brown hair, large sprightly blue eyes, fine teeth, and a pretty mouth. She is inclinable to be fat, but is very genteel, and dances better than any one I ever saw. She speaks German, French, and Italian, is extremely gay, and talks to every body, in a very proper manner, in the circle, but hates the ceremony of a court.'

Anna Ioannovna died, childless, on 17 October 1740, after a reign of 10 years. Shortly before her death she had named as her successor Prince Ivan Antonovich, the baby son of her niece Anna Leopoldovna. In addition she had named Ernst Biron as Regent, but this proved too much for some of the Guards regiments and Biron was overthrown on 9 November, Anna Leopoldovna being proclaimed Regent for Ivan Antonovich (Ivan VI) in his stead. Amidst all this political instability, the now 31-year-old Princess Elizabeth was brought to the realisation that she would either have to exercise her claim to the throne or be in constant danger of imprisonment (at best in a convent) or even assassination; she was persuaded to stage a coup by, among others, the French ambassador the Marquis de la Chétardie (he who was later banished on account of his intrigues with Johanna). De la Chétardie, who was under instructions from the French Court to encourage a revolution which would put an end to the prevailing German influence, had provided money to help win over the influential Preobrazhensky Guards in St Petersburg. The coup, involving just 308 Guardsmen, was staged during the night of 24–25 November 1741. The child-Emperor Ivan VI was imprisoned in the island-fortress of Schlüsselburg and subsequently written out of all official documents as though he had never existed.

Elizabeth now possessed absolute legislative and executive power. The Russian sovereign (the Tsar or Tsarina and, since 1721, Emperor or Empress) could take advice from experienced statesmen, and would be wise to take note of the opinions and desires of such groups as the army and nobility, but could in theory rule as he or she wished. (The reality could be rather different, as the British ambassador Lord Hyndford pointed out: 'altho' this is the most absolute of all governments, there is none in the world so subject to factions and cabals'.) The Tsar could introduce or amend laws by means of the *imennoy ukaz*, or named decree, signed with his Christian name. Elizabeth, who was poorly educated, lazy and never betrayed any clear vision for her country, was nevertheless more liberal and civilised than previous Russian rulers. During her reign, for instance, the death penalty was officially abolished (though there were still cases of people dying after the infliction of excessive corporal punishment) and restrictions were placed on the use of torture. Other pieces of legislation included the prohibition of mixed bathing in public baths in major cities, and the banning of bears from roaming around in city centres. Elizabeth left most of the actual work of ruling, however, to her Chancellor, who was for many years Count Alexei Bestuzhev-Ryumin.

An upbringing during which coups, counter-coups and suspected plots were never far from the surface had turned Elizabeth into a very nervy person, who used her religious observances partly to help assuage her fears. She frequently went on pilgrimage, attended Matins, Mass and Vespers every day and unfailingly observed the four periods of fasting during the Orthodox liturgical year: the fast of the Nativity from 15 November to 24 December (thus slightly longer than the Western Church's Advent); the Great Lent from the Monday before what the Western Church calls Ash Wednesday until Easter; the Apostles' fast lasting from the week after Pentecost until the feast of Sts Peter and Paul on 29 June (the duration of which would depend each year on when Easter, and consequently Pentecost, fell); and the two weeks before the Feast of the Dormition of the Mother of God on 15 August. During these fasts no meat or dairy products could be eaten, and fish and vegetable oil could only be consumed on certain days such as major saints' days. Additionally, at the beginning and end of Lent nothing could be eaten at all, and even during ordinary times most Wednesdays and Fridays were fast-days.* On many of these days of devotion, such as major saints' days, no normal business could be transacted, which meant that it could take a very long time to get anything completed.

When not busy with her religious observances, Elizabeth enjoyed the outdoor sports of hunting and shooting, as well as dancing. She also had a healthy appetite for sex, her roster of lovers having included French doctors, Cossack choristers and Guards officers. Her long-term favourite, nicknamed the 'Night Emperor', was a Ukrainian half-Cossack whom she had first noticed when he was a young cantor in a church choir. Once he became her lover, she changed his name from Razum to the nobler-sounding Razumovsky and awarded both him and his younger brother Kirill the title of Count. It was rumoured that she had contracted a morganatic marriage with Alexei Razumovsky in 1742, but she never married openly or produced legitimate offspring. She was aware from the outset of her reign, however, of the desirability of bringing stability to the Empire by ensuring her succession – and preferably for more than one generation; hence her summoning of Grand Duke Peter and, subsequently, of a bride for him.

Elizabeth finally arrived to join Peter, Catherine and Johanna at Kozelets on 15 August. En route from Moscow she had made frequent stops to set up camp and go walking and shooting; she had also indulged in a few bouts of anger and had expelled several people from her entourage. On her arrival there ensued a great round of balls, concerts and card parties, at which large amounts were gambled in games of faro (a game devised in France towards the end of the previous century). At last the final stage of the journey to Kiev got under way, this time with the Empress setting off first and waiting for the remainder of the party in a camp by the Dnieper river. On 29 August the whole of the imperial party crossed the river and entered the city, the clergy coming out in a body to meet them. Everyone alighted from their carriages and made the last part of the journey to the Pechersky (or Cave) Monastery on foot, following the processional cross.

By this time Johanna was barely tolerated at Court, and she was not

* These traditions continue to be observed in the Orthodox Church, though with varying degrees of strictness.

enjoying herself very much. Catherine realised that part of the problem was that she now took precedence over her mother, which no amount of tact on informal occasions could really help, as on formal occasions the expected protocol had to be observed. 'I had made it a general rule to show her the utmost respect and deference, but that did not always solve the problem, and she continually made bitter remarks, which did her no good and did not predispose people in her favour.' Catherine herself, meanwhile, found herself by and large approved of and apparently loved by both Empress and Grand Duke. 'Everything,' she felt, 'combined to make me hope for a happy future.'

After a stay of 10 days in Kiev, the Court returned to Moscow, where social life continued through the autumn and winter with a series of theatrical performances and masquerades. Catherine expended much of her exuberant youthful energy on dancing, taking lessons with Landé in the early morning and afternoon before dancing the night away at a ball or masquerade. She was also introduced to one of the Empress Elizabeth's particular pleasures (and one shared by many European Courts of the time), the masked balls she called 'Metamorphoses': 'Every Tuesday there was a sort of masquerade at Court which was not to everyone's taste, but I, who was only fifteen, enjoyed it greatly. The Empress had ordered that only those whom she herself selected were to be invited to these masquerades and that all the men were to be dressed as women and all the women as men.' As Catherine noticed, the only person apart from herself really to enjoy these occasions was the Empress, who took pleasure in showing off her fine legs in breeches and stockings. The men of the Court detested these Tuesday evenings as they were forced to stagger clumsily around in voluminous petticoats stretched over hoops, colliding with the women, who were equally unused to having to manage their partners in such attire. At one such masquerade there was a serious entanglement as Catherine was dancing with the chamberlain Sievers, who was wearing a hooped dress lent to him by the Empress. Everyone ended up on the floor, with Catherine trapped underneath Sievers' skirt. She was helpless with laughter as various dancers struggled to right them; the chamberlain and other court worthies were less amused.

Apart from dancing mishaps, the only serious trouble Catherine ran into at this time was a common one at Court, particularly for its junior members – that of running up debt. She had found that the allowance granted her by the Empress did not cover the amount it seemed necessary to spend both on clothes for herself and presents for others. She had arrived at the Russian Court with a very limited wardrobe – and this was a Court where women were accustomed to change their dresses three times a day. As a member of the imperial family, the Grand Duchess could hardly dress less lavishly than other court ladies. She also needed to stock up on underwear, having only a dozen chemises when she arrived. Then there was bed linen to provide herself with, for until now she had been using her mother's. As to her other major item of expenditure, Catherine had rapidly reached an understanding of how the wheels turned at the Russian Court: 'I had been told that people in Russia were fond of presents and that by showing a little generosity, one acquired friends and made oneself agreeable.' In her efforts to please, she indulged not only courtiers but also her fiancé and her mother. She therefore felt her high expenditure was inevitable, though it was her mother's view that Catherine was as yet too inexperienced to manage her own finances and that she should have come to her for advice. (Johanna's indignation on this point was exacerbated by the knowledge that others at Court were equally determined that her daughter should not turn to her for advice on any subject.) Countess Rumyantseva was no help at all; as Catherine herself put it: 'the most extravagant woman in Russia . . . had been appointed to wait on me: she was always surrounded by tradesmen and advised me every day on a number of things I should purchase from them, which I often did only to offer them to her, as she seemed so eager to have them'. Yet despite her attempts to justify herself, Catherine was aware that getting into debt did not entirely fulfil her declared objectives for her new life in Russia, which she had summarised as follows:

1. To please the Grand Duke.
2. To please the Empress.
3. To please the nation.

The trouble was that these three aims could not always be fulfilled simultaneously. Buying presents to please the Grand Duke, for instance, ran the risk of displeasing the Empress through extravagance. With time it would become more and more difficult for Catherine to hold her three objectives in balance.

In November the Grand Duke contracted measles. During his illness he and his entourage were separated from the rest of the Court, and all entertainments were cancelled. On his recovery he was seen to have grown taller and stronger, but Catherine claims to have detected no other improvement: 'his mind was still very immature. He spent his time in his room playing soldiers with his valets, flunkeys, his dwarfs,* and his gentlemen-in-waiting.' Soon afterwards the Court left Moscow for St Petersburg, Johanna and Catherine sharing a sleigh for the journey, with Peter and Marshal Brummer in another. On 18 December the party stopped at Tver to celebrate the Empress's thirty-fifth birthday.

Further along the road to Petersburg, at Khotilovo, the Grand Duke suddenly fell ill again, collapsing during the evening. This time his illness betrayed clear symptoms of the dreaded smallpox. Johanna acted quickly, deciding that Catherine must leave Khotilovo at once to avoid the risk of infection. The Empress had left already and had arrived in St Petersburg; couriers were dispatched and, revealing the depth of her concern for her nephew and heir, she returned immediately to Khotilovo. The two parties travelling in opposite directions encountered one another at Novgorod, the Empress agreeing that Johanna and Catherine should travel on to Petersburg.

On their arrival in the city, mother and daughter were accommodated in a house alongside the Winter Palace, where they had four rooms each, separated by a hall at the top of the stairs, the Winter Palace itself being too small at that time to house everyone at once. The palace had originally been a private mansion and had been taken over by Anna Ioannovna when she became Empress in 1730. She had used the meadow outside as a pasture for her cows. Since then the palace had been repaired and enlarged many times, latterly by the Italian Bartolomeo Rastrelli (appointed court architect in 1738) who had added an extension to the original building which more than doubled its size. It was an extremely cold house, damp both outside and in, with cracked and smoking stoves.

The new arrangement of having an apartment each was much to Catherine's liking, while not at all to Johanna's, who felt her position and influence diminishing by the day. Johanna stayed grumpily in her own apartment with her small circle of intimate friends, while her daughter occupied herself with reading, improving her Russian and learning to play the clavichord – or, rather, dancing around the room while Francesco Araya did the actual playing.

When the rest of the Court arrived in Petersburg (minus the Empress and the Grand Duke), social life took over, a constant flow of visitors arriving at Johanna's and Catherine's apartments, and the ladies occu-

* Dwarfs were a common feature of court life in many countries.

pying themselves with playing cards and dressing (and then dressing again). Catherine joined in all the light entertainment, despite the fact that this must have been a very anxious time for her – for if the Grand Duke were to die, she as Grand Duchess would lose her *raison d'être*. Her levity incurred the mild disapproval of one of the foreign diplomats present at Court, Count von Gyllenburg. (This was the same von Gyllenburg who had been influential in Catherine's childhood, after encountering her in Hamburg and persuading her mother to take more notice of her.) He was in St Petersburg as the official bearer of the news that Johanna's brother Adolf Frederick, the Bishop of Lübeck and Crown Prince of Sweden, had married Princess Luise Ulrike of Prussia, a sister of Frederick II. One day von Gyllenburg decided to upbraid Catherine on what he perceived as her lack of seriousness. He provided her with a reading list for her self-improvement, including Plutarch's *Lives* and *Life of Cicero* and Montesquieu's *Considérations sur les causes de la grandeur des Romains et de leur décadence* ('Considerations on the causes of the greatness of the Romans and their decline'), published in Amsterdam in 1734. In a burst of enthusiasm Catherine ordered these books to be procured for her.

Grand Duke Peter pulled through, and by the end of January was sufficiently recovered to be able to return with the Empress to St Petersburg. As soon as they arrived, Catherine and Johanna went to greet them. Even in the semi-darkness of a late winter afternoon, Catherine was shocked by her fiancé's appearance:

> He had grown a great deal, but his face was unrecognisable. All his features were coarsened, his face was still all swollen, and one could see that he would without doubt remain badly scarred. As his hair had been cut off, he had an enormous wig which made him look even worse. He came up to me and asked me if I found it hard to recognise him. I stammered my congratulations on his recovery, but he had in fact become frightful to look at.

Peter's 'frightfulness' waned over the next few weeks, but he remained very self-conscious over the ravages smallpox had wrought on him. Catherine herself was not entirely recovered from her earlier bout of pleurisy. She was still very thin, and had had a recurrence of chest pains at the beginning of the year, as a result of which the doctors had advised her to drink milk and Seltzer water every morning.

On 10 February, the Grand Duke's seventeenth birthday, Catherine dined alone with the Empress, Peter not yet being prepared to reappear in public. The Empress expressed pleasure with the progress Catherine was making in her studies of the Russian language, and gave her some practice in Russian conversation. Over the next few weeks Catherine and Peter spent some time together in the evenings, but did not particularly seek out each other's company. Catherine was aware – partly because Peter, who was, she declares, 'about as discreet as a cannon ball', told her – that his favoured companions, his valets and other members of his Court, were plying him with advice on how to treat a wife, in terms unlikely to contribute to her future happiness. She decided that, at least for the time being, her best option was to listen to what he told her and appear to acquiesce with his views, so that he would feel she was a loyal friend. In fact, she adopted this as her policy towards everyone she encountered at that time, seeking to gain affection and a measure of security by pleasing. 'I tried to be as charming as possible to everyone and studied every opportunity to win the affection of those whom I suspected of being in the slightest degree ill-disposed towards me; I showed no preference for any side, never interfered in anything, always looked serene and displayed much attentiveness, affability, and politeness all round.' A serene air, with a discreet little smile, began to be her constant expression while in public.

In many ways Catherine was still a child, and these last few months before her marriage represented her last chance to enjoy a degree of childish freedom. To improve her integration into the Russian Court, the Empress had appointed eight Russian maids to attend on her, so that she had to speak Russian much of the time. These girls became her playmates; what was lacking in verbal communication was compensated for by games such as blind man's buff (which remained a favourite all her life) and constructing a slide out of the clavichord and a pile of mattresses. As far as the maids' more serious duties were concerned, Catherine made an attempt to share out the responsibilities, giving the one she liked best the key to her jewels, putting the German maid whom she had brought with her from Zerbst in charge of linen, assigning another one to her lace, another to her ribbons. One of her two dwarfs was charged with taking care of her hair-powder and combs, the other of her rouge, hairpins and *mouches* or patches (artificial beauty spots, much favoured by eighteenth-century women). But Countess Rumyantseva and the Empress reacted adversely to this small display of independence on Catherine's part, and vetoed her arrangements.

During Lent, Catherine and Peter had a disagreement over the question of their observance of Orthodox practice. Peter became irritated on learning that Catherine and her maids were in the habit of attending the chanting of Lenten prayers in her antechamber, and participating with all the correct gestures of bowing and signing themselves. Peter felt this to constitute an unnecessary show of devotion, while Catherine took the view that she was merely observing the proper rituals expected of her now that she was an Orthodox believer. Lutheranism was far more deeply ingrained in Peter than in Catherine; it was part of his identity. He had viewed his conversion to Orthodoxy as politically expedient, but his heart had not been in it and he did not intend to adhere to its practices more than was absolutely necessary. He had expected Catherine to take the same attitude, and was annoyed to discover she did not. A few days after this quarrel, a curious incident involving Johanna took place; apparently she had asked for a blood-letting, which had been clumsily carried out and caused her to faint. Catherine could not understand why she had asked this to be done, as she had always been afraid of the procedure. It is possible that this fainting episode was connected to the fact that Johanna was now preg-nant by Count Ivan Betskoy; she may in fact have had a miscarriage, or even tried to induce one. Also in Lent poor Johanna suffered another painful blow: the news arrived from Zerbst that Catherine's little sister, the three-year-old Elizabeth, had died. This was sudden and unexpected; Johanna grieved deeply for the little girl whom she had not seen for more than a year, and Catherine too was 'very stricken'.

In March the Empress announced that Peter and Catherine's wedding would take place in four months' time. Elizabeth was determined to vie with Versailles and Dresden in splendour, and the preparations were so elaborate that the wedding had to be postponed twice. It was finally scheduled for 21 August.

In May the Empress and the Grand Duke moved into the Summer Palace (constructed of timber and surrounded by wonderful gardens, parterres and fountains), while Catherine and Johanna were accom-modated in a stone building alongside the Fontanka river and next to Peter I's original little Summer Palace (completed by Domenico Trezzini in 1712). According to Catherine, the short distance which now separ-ated her from Grand Duke Peter's apartments made it too much of an effort for him to bother visiting her very often. This lack of affection upset her and she shed a few tears in private, while putting on a brave face in public; she had, after all, had plenty of practice in her child-hood at living without demonstrations of affection. Neither did her mother have much time for her during these weeks, absorbed as she was in her own dramas and crises. At what must have been a perplexing and anxious time for a young girl, Catherine had very little, if any, support and sympathy: 'On the whole, I found life very irksome but took care not to speak of it ... I persisted more and more in my desire to win the affection of the unimportant as well as of the great, neglecting no one and making it a rule to believe that I needed everybody. Accordingly I behaved in such a way as to win general approval – and in this I succeeded.' She was too immature to be able to have much understanding for her fiancé, who must also have been nervous and may have been avoiding her because he did not know how to behave with someone he was soon to marry.

A few weeks later the entire Court moved to the imperial palace at Peterhof, 18 miles away from St Petersburg on the south coast of the Gulf of Finland. The site is a split-level one, the Great ('Upper') Palace built on high ground by Johann Friedrich Braunstein, with huge additions by Rastrelli, while the little ('Lower') Palace of Monplaisir is situated by the sea. Both palaces were begun in 1714, and from the outset Peterhof was designed as a single composition of palaces and pavilions, gardens, cascades and fountains, all facing towards the coast. The Empress, Grand Duke, Johanna and Catherine all lived in the original part of the Upper Palace, the Empress and Grand Duke on the top floor, Johanna and Catherine beneath the Grand Duke's apartments. They dined every day with Peter in the open air, under a tent, or on the terrace adjoining his apartments, and he came to their apartments for supper. The Empress was away frequently, visiting various country estates, while Catherine and Peter spent their time walking, riding (Catherine had recently begun to take riding lessons) or driving in a carriage around the extensive grounds. Peter was also spending an increasing amount of time on his military games and exercises, including teaching his fiancée how to handle a rifle: 'He made me stand at arms with my musket, on duty at the door of the room between his and mine.' Catherine did her best to keep up her spirits by remembering the imperial position of the person she would soon be marrying, rather than his personal attributes. Meanwhile Johanna also went off on visits to neighbouring country houses, returning to scold Catherine for having taken too many liberties in her absence, such as going out for midnight walks with her ladies-in-waiting and valets. She also unjustly accused her daughter of having ventured into the Grand Duke's apartments at inappropriate times; it seems she was suffering from an uneasy conscience over not supervising the young people properly during the Empress's absence. Johanna's disagreeableness at least served the purpose of forging a link between Catherine and Peter, who sympathised with her over the matter of her mother. Johanna was also still carrying on her inept political intriguing, continuing a clandestine correspondence with King Frederick of Prussia, unaware that the Russian authorities were reading the letters.

Towards the end of June, the whole Court returned to St Petersburg. Anticipation of her marriage was by now preoccupying Catherine, who one night arranged for all her ladies-in-waiting and maids to sleep in her room so that they could have a prolonged discussion about 'the differences between the sexes'. It appeared that none of the girls, including Catherine, was at all well informed; she promised them that she would question her mother about it the next day, but Johanna, preoccupied with her own sexual and emotional problems, did not wish to discuss the matter. Catherine was not the only one experiencing anxieties about the sexual aspect of the forthcoming marriage; the court doctors had tried to suggest to the Empress that the Grand Duke was not yet physically developed enough to marry and should wait a few years. But to no avail. The Empress was of the opinion that there was no time to lose.

As the wedding day approached, Catherine became subject to bouts of nervous hysteria, bursting into tears for no apparent reason. Her female entourage did what they could to divert her. In addition to discussing the mysteries of sex with them, Catherine used her ladies-in-waiting to experiment with fashion, persuading them to join her in adopting the latest French hairstyle, which involved cutting the hair short at the front and curling it.

Once the day was finally fixed for the wedding, public announcements were made on three consecutive days by heralds dressed in coats of mail, preceded by drum-rolls and escorted by a detachment of the Horse Guards and dragoons. On the day before the wedding, the Court moved from the Summer to the Winter Palace and finally, that evening, Princess Johanna came to talk to Catherine and explained something of what married life would entail. This mother–daughter *tête-à-tête* took place against a background of cannon fire and the ringing of all the church bells, which lasted from nine o'clock till eleven.

On the morning of 21 August, everyone in the Winter Palace and adjoining houses rose early (they can have had no difficulty waking, as at five o'clock cannons were again fired from the Peter and Paul Fortress and the Admiralty, as well as from a warship and a number of other vessels lying at anchor in the Neva). Princess Johanna and Countess Rumyantseva went with the ladies-in-waiting to Catherine's apartments, where they dressed her initially in a simple *déshabillé* of white and gold, worn over a small hoop. At eight o'clock she was summoned by Her Imperial Majesty's duty chamberlain to the Empress's state bedroom, where the Empress was also in her *déshabillé* though her hair had been dressed. Before the dressing of the bride got under way, both Catherine and Johanna made short formal speeches of thanks to the Empress, who responded graciously.

First Catherine's hair needed to be prepared, and a tussle ensued between Empress and hairdresser over the new-fangled curls. The Empress wanted Catherine's hair to lie flat so that the jewels she was to wear could be fixed securely; but the hairdresser was not prepared to relinquish the cherished curls without a fight. Countess Rumyantseva was employed as a go-between, Catherine kept diplomatically quiet, and the Empress, irritated with all the toing and froing, finally told the hairdresser he could do what he liked. Once Catherine's hair was ready (Johanna describes it as black, glossy and unpowdered), the Empress reappeared to place the grand ducal crown on her head and to tell her she was free to wear as many jewels as she wished. Then the ladies-in-waiting helped her into her very heavy formal dress of cloth of silver, embroidered with silver on all the seams and hems, and designed to emphasise her narrow waist. Over it she wore a cloak of silver lace, and on her face she wore a little rouge. Johanna thought she looked splendid. The Grand Duke, who was being dressed in the adjoining room, wore clothes which matched Catherine's, and was resplendent with sword and glittering diamonds.

The Guards regiments, including mounted Horse Guards, took up their posts around the palace, along the route, and outside the church, and the carriages began to arrive at the palace to collect those designated to travel in each one. The great procession to the church of Our Lady of Kazan moved off at 10 o'clock. First came a detachment of cuirassiers followed by a deputy master of ceremonies in an open chaise. Then came the carriages of the Grand Duke's and Grand Duchess's gentlemen of the bedchamber, beginning with the youngest and each preceded by four lackeys. The carriages of the grand ducal chamberlains and of the Empress's gentlemen of the bedchamber were each preceded by eight lackeys and escorted by a heyduck (a liveried personal servant). The number of lackeys, running footmen and heyducks increased in proportion to the seniority of the occupants of each carriage, major generals being preceded by two running footmen and ten lackeys, generals-in-chief, ministers, senators and 'blue ribbons' (knights clad in the insignia of their order) meriting two pages on the running board, a heyduck, several Moors and hussars, four running footmen, twelve lackeys and a mounted equerry. Behind the Empress's Grand Master of the Court and the Field Marshals came a detachment of Horse Guards, led by their drummers. Twenty-four coaches were occupied by the maids-of-honour, ladies of the bedchamber and ladies-in-waiting.

Johanna's brother, the Bishop of Lübeck, was present for the ceremony. He travelled in a magnificent coach preceded by four running footmen, fourteen lackeys, two gentlemen of the bedchamber and two pages, with four heyducks by the door and a liveried footman walking at the head of the horses, which were also accompanied by four grooms. When the Grand Master of Ceremonies came to inform Princess Johanna that it was her turn to take her place, she followed him out into the courtyard with the Princess of Hesse-Homburg and with her train supported by Monsieur Latorff. She and the Princess of Hesse-Homburg travelled together, their cortège being in the same formation as that of the Bishop of Lübeck.

The cortège of the Empress was the most splendid of all:

Her Imperial Majesty's cortège was opened by the Court trumpets and drums. The Grand Master of Ceremonies in an open chaise, his wand in his hands. The Marshal and the Grand Marshal of Her Imperial Majesty's Court also in open chaises, carrying their marshal's batons. The 14 sergeants who always accompany the Sovereign in this country, when [she] goes out in public. 4 Quartermaster Sergeants of the Bedchamber, 6 ordinary Quartermaster Sergeants of the Court. The governor of the pages on horseback. 36 pages on horseback . . . Her Majesty's chamberlains two by two, each of them with two running footmen at the head of their horses. Two ordinary equerries. The principal equerry. 24 mounted grooms. 12 lackeys of the Bedchamber. 40 lackeys.

Johanna describes the Empress's coach, in which the Grand Duke and Duchess travelled with the Empress, as resembling 'a real little castle'. It was pulled by eight horses, each horse being led by grooms. Two pages rode standing on the running board, six Moors and twelve heyducks walked and two adjutants-general and the Master of the Horse rode alongside. The Empress's robe was similar to Catherine's, except that it was made of chestnut-coloured silk. She also wore her imperial crown and mantle.

As each part of the procession arrived at the square in front of the church, people made their way to their allotted places. Princess Johanna, her brother and the Princess of Hesse-Homburg waited for Her Imperial Majesty at the foot of a high bridge-like structure covered with a red cloth, where the clergy as a group – that is, the Bishops (or in some cases Archbishops) of Moscow, Novgorod, Pskov, St Petersburg, Pereslavl, Krutitsy and Jerusalem, many archimandrites, priests, and deacons holding censers – as well as the choir were to receive the Empress. When Elizabeth arrived, the Archbishop of Novgorod presented the Gospel to her to be kissed and then went into the church, followed by the other clergy two by two. Behind the clergy walked the Master of Ceremonies, the Marshal and Grand Marshal, and then the Empress, her train being carried by her Grand Master and four chamberlains. Peter's Grand Marshal and Grand Chamberlain preceded him and Catherine, who was on Peter's right, her train being held by two chamberlains.

The service was conducted by the Archbishop of Novgorod. The celebration of the Mass took place first, followed by a short prayer; at its conclusion the Archbishop approached the Empress, bowed low, and requested her orders to begin the ceremony of marriage. Having received them, he went back through the royal doors. The Master of Ceremonies, wand in hand, and the Marshal and Grand Marshal of the Empress's Court went to stand on either side of a small raised platform in the centre of the church opposite the royal doors. Her Imperial Majesty descended from her throne while the bride and groom emerged from the gallery where they had heard the Mass, and Princess Johanna and the Princess of Hesse-Homburg from another. The Empress took the bride and groom by the hand and led them to their places, the Grand Duke on the right and the Grand Duchess on the left. Then the Archbishop returned from the sanctuary, accompanied by two other bishops, each carrying a golden crown. The first crown, which was for the Grand Duke, was handed to the Bishop of Lübeck; the second, for Catherine, to the Master of the Hunt (and the Empress's lover), Count Razumovsky. As is the custom at Orthodox weddings, the crowns were held over the heads of the bride and groom throughout the ceremony, Johanna remarking on how tiring this must have been for her brother and Count Razumovsky. When the couple made the customary circling of the ambo, Catherine's train was carried by two of the chamberlains who had carried that of the Empress during the entry into the church. After the Gospel had been sung, the Archbishop took, exchanged and blessed the rings (of plain gold) and presented them to the Empress for her to bless them too; then he handed them to the bridal couple for placing on the same finger as their engagement rings. At the end of the ceremony both bride and groom prostrated themselves before the Empress, who raised them up and heartily embraced them. She also kissed Johanna. Then Father Semyon Theodorsky preached the sermon, in which he spoke of the miracles of Providence in uniting these two offspring of the houses of Anhalt and Holstein, destined to reign over the Russian people. The sermon was followed by the Te Deum, which was accompanied by triple firing of cannon and the clanging of all the bells of all the churches.

The Master of Ceremonies then discreetly marshalled everyone to leave in the order in which they had arrived and the cortèges returned the way they had come: along the Great Perspective Road (the name originally given to what became the Nevsky Prospekt) towards the Admiralty, passing under a triumphal arch along the way. When the Empress's cortège came into view, a signal came from the Admiralty to fire all the guns again, the noise swelled by the cries of the troops and the acclamations of the people lining the route.

Back at the Winter Palace, the ambassadors and all the foreign ministers were waiting to greet the Empress in her apartments. She did not stop with them for long but quickly returned for dinner, which was served in the grand gallery. The Empress sat under a specially erected canopy, along with the Grand Duke and Duchess, who sat at either end of the long top table. This time Johanna had nothing to complain about in the seating arrangements, as she was placed on one of the tables at right angles, only one step down, next to Peter and opposite the Bishop of Lübeck, who was next to Catherine. All the grandees, nobility and clergy were served at other tables, of which there were several hundred. After the second course the health of each person in the Empress's party was drunk, beginning with the bride and groom, one goblet of wine circulating for each toast while cannons were fired, the signal for the guns being given by an officer stationed on a high platform outside from where he could see what was happening. There then followed a 'magnificent' dessert, and the meal ended at 11 o'clock in the evening.

After this late dinner the Empress retired while the gallery was prepared for the ball which was to follow. By now Catherine was suffering from the weight of her clothes and particularly of the crown, but special permission had to be sought from – and reluctantly bestowed by – the Empress before she could remove it, which she did while the preparations were carried out. It was then replaced on her head. The ball, during which only polonaises (a processional dance for couples arranged in line by rank) were danced, lasted for no more than an hour and a half. Then came the ceremonial procession to the apartments of the newly-weds and their ritual preparation for the marriage bed, all described by Johanna:

> Her Imperial Majesty, preceded by the Masters of Ceremonies, the Grand Master of her Court, the Grand Marshal and Marshal and the Grand Chamberlain of the Grand Duke's Court and followed only by the young spouses hand in hand, me, my brother, the Princess of Hesse, the Grand Mistress, the ladies-in-waiting, the Ladies of the Bedchamber and the maids-of-honour, set off for the nuptial apartment, from which the men came out as soon as all the women had entered and the doors were closed, while the young spouses went into the apartment where they were to change their clothes. First the bride was undressed. Her Imperial Majesty removed her crown; I ceded to the Princess of Hesse the honour of putting on her chemise, the Grand Mistress handed her the dressing gown and the rest of the ladies put the finishing touches to the most magnificent *déshabillé* in the world . . .
>
> Once the Grand Duchess was dressed [sic], Her Imperial Majesty went to see the Grand Duke, whom the Master of the Hunt Count Razumovsky and my brother had helped to undress. The Empress brought him out to us; all his attire was identical to that of his spouse, but he was not nearly so handsome in it.
>
> Her Imperial Majesty then gave them her blessing which they received with one knee on the ground. She embraced them tenderly and left to us, the Princess of Hesse, Countess Rumyantseva and myself, the task of putting them to bed.

Catherine was installed in the double bed in the luxuriously decorated bedroom (the walls lined with red velvet and embellished with pilasters and silver bosses) and left alone for the first time in days. Peter now disappeared. In later years Catherine could see the comic side of her wedding night:

Everybody left me and I remained alone for more than two hours, not knowing what was expected of me. Should I get up? Should I remain in bed? I truly did not know. At last Mme Krause, my new maid, came in and told me very cheerfully that the Grand Duke was waiting for his supper which would be served shortly. His Imperial Highness came to bed after supper and began to say how amused the servant would be to find us in bed together.

If Peter had any idea at all of what he was supposed to do, he showed no inclination to do it. When Catherine finally realised that, despite what her mother had led her to expect of a husband, nothing was going to happen, she ended her wedding day by turning over and going to sleep.

The wedding celebrations lasted for 10 days. On 22 August, Catherine and Peter received official congratulations from ambassadors, foreign ministers, lords, senators, ministers, officers and clergy before travelling for the first time alone together in a carriage (though 'alone' is a relative term, as they were preceded by a cortège as splendid as that of the day before) to the Summer Palace to dine with the Empress. Elizabeth presented Catherine with more jewels (emeralds and sapphires) and provided her with a complete wardrobe of linen, lace and dresses. Catherine and Peter returned to the Winter Palace at about four o'clock in the afternoon, to prepare for the evening's ball. The Empress arrived at the Winter Palace towards eight o'clock and was received at the foot of the staircase. The Grand Duke and Duchess opened the ball, Catherine taking as her partner her uncle the Bishop of Lübeck, and Peter taking first Johanna and then the Princess of Hesse-Homburg. The ball lasted until midnight and was followed by supper at a table decorated with specially constructed fountains. Everyone apart from Catherine and Peter, who sat in the centre, received their places by lot. Only Her Imperial Majesty's health was drunk on this occasion, again to the sound of cannon fire.

The following day, 23 August, was a rest-day, during which Catherine and Peter paid Johanna a visit, and vice versa. Countess Rumyantseva sent word to say the Empress had decided she should no longer be employed in supervising Catherine now that she was married; Catherine felt no regret over this. Meanwhile, Madame Krause, appointed by the Empress, was already exerting her authority over Catherine's other maids, discouraging them from speaking to her in private or romping about with her as they had previously done.

On 24 August there was a dinner at the Winter Palace, the imperial party dining in state before an audience. It had also been arranged for the general populace of Petersburg to join in the marriage festivities, a free feast, or cockaigne, consisting of fountains from which wine would flow, mountains of bread, and six whole roasted oxen, each stuffed with poultry and other roast meats, having been prepared outside the palace. The feast was due to commence after the dinner inside the palace had finished and once the ambassadors had arrived at Court; the crowds of people were being held back by a fence and an inadequate guard. The officer whose job it was to provide the signals for the cannon fire to accompany the toasts was also supposed to give the signal for the feast to begin. Unsurprisingly, the excited and hungry crowd, which had been gathering since the previous night, did not have the patience to wait for their signal, 'but as soon as they noticed the one for giving the first toast, bursting through the fence they knocked over the guards and threw themselves on their prey'. The Empress was informed of her subjects' riotous behaviour; at first she only laughed, but then decided to punish them by not turning on the wine fountains. The foreign ministers arrived at about five o'clock and there was then a concert of Italian music given in the grand gallery. Afterwards members of the Court went for a drive around the city to see the illuminations.

On the next day an opera was performed at the Summer Palace, and on 26 August there was a domino ball at the Winter Palace. The domino was originally an all-embracing black silk gown, which had spread throughout Europe from Venice as an ideal garment for the masquerade, enhancing the disguise by completely enveloping the wearer. Dominoes could also, as in this case, be brightly coloured. This ball involved four sets of 16 couples, dancing quadrilles and dressed in dominoes of matching colour schemes. The first set, led by the Grand Duke, was in rose and silver; the second, led by Catherine, in white and gold; the third, led by Johanna, in blue and silver; and the fourth, led by the Bishop of Lübeck, in yellow and silver. Each set was instructed to dance in its own corner of the room, and not mingle with the others. Catherine was in a sufficiently overwrought state by now to be almost reduced to tears at this restriction, as the men in her set were elderly and could not dance at all well. There was another ball the following day, featuring the same quadrilles, and on 29 August there was a public masquerade, which included the staging of Molière's play *La Princesse d'Elide*. The masquerade, which took place in various apartments of the

Winter Palace, lasted well into the night, the play finally finishing at three o'clock in the morning.

The final day of festivities was 30 August, the feast day of St Alexander Nevsky. At nine o'clock in the morning all the knights of the order of St Alexander Nevsky assembled in the Empress's apartments, where she joined them wearing the uniform of the order (a white dress decorated with silver braid, with a flame-coloured lining, jacket and cuffs) and her crown. The knights kissed her hand and then got into the carriages which were awaiting them outside the palace. The Empress followed, accompanied by the Grand Duke. Princess Johanna and Catherine came behind, along with the Grand Mistress, the ladies-in-waiting and the maids-of-honour, all two by two, and the convoy set off for the monastery dedicated to the warrior-saint, at the other end of the Great Perspective Road from the Admiralty.

When the convoy arrived outside the monastic complex, the archimandrite, at the head of his clergy, stepped forward to receive the Empress who then walked to the boundary, the knights marching two by two ahead of her and the ladies following. A triple discharge of cannon announced her arrival. First of all the party entered the church, where the liturgy was celebrated, followed by the Te Deum, again to a triple discharge of cannons fired by the squadron which had escorted Peter the Great's little boat (*botik*), which was brought to the monastery every year. The Empress then sat down to dinner with the knights.

The *botik* was (and still is) one of the most revered symbols of Peter the Great and of the transformation he wrought on his country, in particular his creation of its naval fleet and the beginnings of its career as a maritime power. Various legends accrued around this boat, the so-called 'grandfather of the Russian Navy', which Peter had discovered in 1688 in an outhouse when he was 16 years old and which inspired his first dreams of building a fleet. One of the legends was that the boat was originally the gift of Elizabeth I of England to Ivan the Terrible; it is now believed to have been constructed in the 1640s either in England or by Dutch craftsmen in Russia following an 'English-type' design. Having first learnt to sail in this little boat, Peter stored it for safekeeping in the Kremlin in 1701; it was later removed to the Peter and Paul Fortress, where it was kept on a plinth inscribed: 'From the amusement of the child came the triumph of the man.'★

---

★ A replica of the *botik* can still be seen in the Boat House at the Fortress; the original is preserved in the Central Naval Museum on Vasilyevsky Island.

The *botik* was too old and fragile to be placed directly in the water, so it was carried inside a larger boat which was itself pulled by two longboats. After dinner the Empress was rowed out to board the *botik*, where she kissed the image of her father which was kept in it. She then returned to her own longboat, which flew the imperial standard and was preceded by four galleys from which drums and trumpets sounded. The rest of the party followed in other longboats and galleys, to be met by more boats, including a type of gondola, at the entrance to the Great Neva. From here the regatta sailed up towards the Admiralty, from which the Empress took the salute, as well as from the Fortress. Her galleys returned the salute, and the court trumpeters and drummers responded from the balconies of the palace to the musicians in the galleys. The Empress then accompanied the *botik* back to its resting-place in the Fortress.

Back at the palace, yet another ball began. It was followed by a firework display, which in turn was followed by a meal in the gallery where Her Imperial Majesty supped again with all the knights of the order of St Alexander Nevsky. And so, records Johanna, 'thus finished the most lavish of festivities ever perhaps to have taken place in Europe'.

The days which followed can only have been an anticlimax. Apart from the novelty of sharing a bed, nothing in Peter's way of life appeared to have changed. According to Catherine, he still preferred playing soldiers with his valets – 'performing military exercises and changing their uniforms twenty times a day' – to spending time with his new wife. In later life, she summed up her disillusionment thus: 'I would have been ready to like my new husband had he been capable of affection or willing to show any. But in the very first days of our marriage I came to a sad conclusion about him. I said to myself: "If you allow yourself to love that man, you will be the unhappiest creature on this earth."' She occupied herself with reading novels and spending time with her mother, the preparations for whose departure were now underway.

In early September, Catherine, Peter and Johanna were sent to the imperial palace of Tsarskoye Selo (about two hours' drive away from St Petersburg) while the Empress went to Count Razumovsky's country estate at Gostilitsy. This interlude, at the palace (built for Catherine I) and park which would one day become Catherine II's favourite place, was not a success, spoilt by bickering between old and young.

Princess Johanna left St Petersburg and subsequently the Russian Empire on 28 September. The Empress had given her the considerable sum of 60,000 roubles to pay her debts, but it turned out that she owed more than the same amount again, and this was a burden which rested heavily on her daughter, who took over responsibility for the outstanding debts, for years to come. A few days before her departure, Johanna had had a long talk with the Empress, and she left the Russian Court under a considerable cloud, the scandal over her affair with Ivan Betskoy and her continued meddling having pleased no one. Catherine and Peter went as far as Krasnoye Selo (another summer residence to the south of St Petersburg) with Johanna to see her off. Catherine was very upset and 'cried abundantly'; Johanna was idiosyncratic to the last: 'my mother, in order not to swell my grief, left without saying goodbye'.

# 3

# Early Married Life
# (1745–52)

*After the dogs I was the most miserable creature in the world.*
Memoirs of Catherine the Great

Soon after the departure of Princess Johanna, an incident occurred at the young Court (as the Court of the Grand Duke and Duchess was known) which was to set a pattern: Catherine's favourite among her maids-of-honour was suddenly dismissed, for no apparent reason – other than that she was Catherine's favourite. A few weeks later it was the gentleman of the bedchamber, Count Zakhar Chernyshev, who was removed; in this case Catherine believed his removal had been requested by his mother, out of fear that he might fall for the young Grand Duchess (as indeed, several years later, he did).

During the autumn and winter of 1745–6 Catherine and Peter were installed in the Winter Palace in adjoining apartments, separated by a large staircase. In winter it was cold and draughty to cross from one set of apartments to the other; there was nevertheless much coming and going on a daily basis. During this first winter Catherine frequently used to play billiards in the evenings with Peter's tutor Bergholz in the Grand Duke's antechamber, while Peter himself 'romped with his gentlemen-in-waiting in the other room'. Despite the separate apartments for use during the day, the couple generally shared a bedroom at night.

Court life proceeded in its usual manner, which included two masquerades a week (outside the penitential fast seasons), one at Court and the other at one of the principal houses in the town, members of the nobility taking it in turn to host these events. Catherine did not remember these masquerades with enthusiasm: 'One pretended to be entertained by them but in fact one was bored to extinction at these balls which, in spite of the masks, were ceremonious and attended by so few people that the Court rooms were empty; and the town houses were too small to accommodate even the few people who went there.' She nevertheless admits that her life was fairly pleasant at that stage, and that she and Peter were getting on reasonably well. Peter was already, however, preferring other, less challenging, women to his wife; indeed, he had told her that he was in love with one of the Empress's ladies-in-waiting even before they were married.

As Catherine's memoirs focus on her married life, they become increasingly biased and have to be taken with ever larger pinches of salt. She is concerned to demonstrate that she was in no way to blame for the failure of her marriage, that Peter was an impossible husband and would have been, had she allowed him to continue, an impossible Tsar. Whatever she says, the marriage was not viewed – by the participants or anybody else – as hopeless from the start, despite the lack of success in bed. Peter's behaviour at this time was undoubtedly adolescent, but he was not uncultivated; desirous of emulating his hero Frederick the Great, he combined a predilection for military drill with an interest in the arts, particularly music. What he seems principally to have lacked is empathy, the ability to understand the effect his words and actions had on others – a legacy of his solitary upbringing, the early loss of his mother and his lack of siblings or other childhood companions.

On 7 March 1746 Princess Anna Leopoldovna, the mother and erstwhile Regent of the little Ivan VI, died in childbirth in the northern town of Kholmogory, not far from Arkhangelsk. She and her children (apart from Ivan, imprisoned in the Schlüsselburg fortress) had been exiled by Elizabeth, their intended destination being the remote Solovetsky Monastery on an island in the White Sea, but bad weather and bad roads had prevented them ever getting that far. Now her body was returned to St Petersburg, where it lay in state in the Alexander Nevsky Monastery until the funeral a fortnight later. Anna Leopoldovna had given birth to two more children while in Kholmogory, each child of hers having a potential claim to the Russian throne. Her death and burial brought this threat to the surface of Elizabeth's mind and increased her sense of urgency that Catherine should produce a child. Merely being married to the Grand Duke was no guarantee of safety. Elizabeth could still disinherit Peter if she chose, and there were precedents for the disposal of imperial spouses; if Peter the Great could send his first wife to a convent, it could have occurred to Elizabeth to solve the problem of an unsatisfactory niece-in-law in the same way. And whenever Peter was ill – as he was in this same month, suffering from a violent fever from which it took him a long time to recover – the precariousness of Catherine's position inevitably increased. The British ambassador, Lord Hyndford, certainly expected everything to change if Peter were to die: 'The great duke still continues in a very weakly condition, and if any accident should happen to him, your lordship [i.e. the Earl of Harrington, to whom Hyndford was making his report] would soon hear of Ivan being recalled.' Nevertheless, Catherine records that at this time the Empress was kind to her, was pleased by her grief and anxiety over Peter's illness, and promised that she would not abandon her under any circumstances.

After Easter, by which time Peter was almost restored to full health, he set up a puppet theatre in one of his rooms and invited ladies and gentlemen of the Court to attend performances. Catherine claims to have been unimpressed, describing the puppet show as 'insipid' (one of her favourite words for describing Peter and his doings). She also describes how Peter's impetuosity got him into trouble with the Empress. One day, while working alone on his puppet theatre, he realised he could hear sounds coming from the other side of the blocked-up door connecting his apartments with those of the Empress. He couldn't resist using the tools he had with him to drill holes in the door to see what was going on in the next room, which was one the Empress used for private dinner parties, and where there was a mechanical table which could be hauled up and down between this floor and the one below to collect and remove dishes, thus dispensing with the need for servants in the room.★ Peering through the holes he had drilled, Peter espied the Empress's favourite, Count Razumovsky, in a brocade dressing gown, dining with the Empress, along with a handful of her closest friends. (A 'dressing gown' was a rather more

---

★ This was a popular court installation, there having also been one at King Frederick William's schloss in Berlin and later at Frederick the Great's palace of Sanssouci, as well as in the small, moated, two-storey building Peter the Great had called his hermitage at Peterhof; they were designed to ensure the privacy of the guests and their conversation rather than out of any desire to give the servants time off. Elizabeth had another such device in her own hermitage, built in the 1740s, at Tsarskoye Selo.

substantial garment in the eighteenth century than it is now and was worn over other clothes. What Peter saw was the Empress's party dressed informally, rather than ready for bed.) Unable to keep his discovery to himself, he invited his entourage to peer through the holes – which they did – and then extended his invitation to Catherine and her ladies. He even went so far as to place benches and stools around his peep-holes. When Catherine realised what was going on, she refused to take part, apparently more able than was Peter to picture the Empress's fury if she were to discover she was being spied on. Catherine's reaction cooled the ardour of the others for this singular entertainment, even Peter becoming slightly apprehensive and returning to the work on his puppet theatre.

The Empress, inevitably, did find out, and arrived in Catherine's apartments after church on the following Sunday to upbraid her nephew. Peter who, unlike Catherine, had not been to church, wandered in wearing a dressing gown with his nightcap in his hand. After the customary kisses in greeting, Elizabeth accused him of gross ingratitude towards her and of behaving like a child. He made the mistake of starting to protest, which further infuriated the Empress, who began to heap imprecations on him. Even Catherine became upset, though Elizabeth told her she was not included in the reprimand. When her torrent of abuse had exhausted itself, she said goodbye and left. Peter and Catherine were both sufficiently subdued at having witnessed the Empress in a rage – 'like a Fury', as the Grand Duke put it – to need to discuss it between themselves and not to want any company at dinner, dining together in Catherine's apartments.

The repercussions did not end there, as the incident was used as a pretext for closer supervision of the Grand Duke and Duchess. In May the Court moved to the Summer Palace and at the end of the month the Empress appointed a new principal lady-in-waiting for Catherine, Maria Choglokova. Five years older than Catherine, she was Elizabeth's own cousin, and, in Catherine's words, 'uneducated, malicious, and full of self-interest'. Her husband Nikolai, who was temporarily absent on a minor diplomatic mission, was one of the Empress's chamberlains. Madame Choglokova was also close to the Chancellor, Count Bestuzhev, towards whom Catherine still felt much mistrust and who was now ordered by the Empress to draw up instructions – 'for the persons attached to the service of the Grand Duke and the Grand Duchess' – as to how the Choglokovs were to fulfil their supervisory role. From the instructions concerning Peter, it is clear that he was having some trouble learning what was acceptable behaviour at Court (he might have been perfectly at home at the Court of his grandfather, Peter the Great, who liked nothing more than playing jokes on his courtiers and foreign visitors):

> The person selected to keep the Grand Duke company will endeavour to reprimand certain unseemly habits of his Imperial Highness. He must not, for instance, when at table pour the contents of his glass over the servants' heads, nor must he address coarse expressions or improper jokes to those who have the honour to come near him, including foreigners of distinction received at Court; or publicly make grimaces and continually jerk his limbs.

The areas of concern over Catherine's behaviour were different and suggest that she may not have been behaving quite so perfectly as her memoirs record. She was told to adhere zealously to Russian Orthodoxy, not to interfere in matters of state, and not to offend her husband or treat him coldly. It was made very clear to her, if it was not so already, that her purpose was to produce an heir. The main reason for the Empress having appointed Maria Choglokova to this supervisory post was that she was disturbed that, after nearly a year of marriage, Catherine showed no signs of pregnancy. Choglokova's brief was both to find out the reason for this disappointing state of affairs and to inspire her charge with uxorious devotion. As Catherine recalled: 'She had the reputation of being very virtuous, because she adored her husband; hers had been a love marriage, and such a good example thrust in front of my eyes was obviously meant to inspire me with the desire to emulate it.' On the day after appointing Choglokova, Elizabeth lashed out verbally at Catherine, accusing her of either being in love with another man or deliberately refusing to get pregnant as a result of being in league with the King of Prussia, like her mother. Catherine, who feared the Empress might be about to hit her, burst into tears but managed not to make Peter's mistake of trying to contradict Elizabeth and waited for the storm to abate. On this occasion Peter did not come in for any of the abuse, Elizabeth having apparently decided that the situation was entirely of Catherine's making. Catherine claims to have been so upset after this outburst (her first ever entirely private 'conversation' with the Empress) that she thought of suicide, one of her maids coming upon her in the act of trying to force a rather blunt knife through her stays.

The suspicion that Catherine might be in love with someone else had arisen from her friendship with Andrei Chernyshev, the cousin of Zakhar and his brother Ivan, all three of whom had been among the members of Peter's entourage (until Zakhar had been removed). The Grand Duke was particularly fond of Andrei and regularly employed him to convey messages to Catherine. Andrei provided Catherine with information about goings-on at Court (in such a Court everyone needed their spies and confidants) and it is possible that, starved of other male affection, she became rather too fond of him and made her feelings obvious enough to place herself in danger. Her own valets certainly thought so and were concerned to protect her from her indiscretion. Apprised of the danger they were in, Andrei decided to follow the common practice of Russian courtiers when faced with potential trouble – to stay in bed. He feigned illness for several weeks, and later, at the same time as Maria Choglokova received her appointment, all three Chernyshevs were sent away from St Petersburg to serve as lieutenants in regiments based near Orenburg on the Yaik river (later named the Ural).

The increased supervision did nothing, however, to remedy the fact that the marriage was still unconsummated, and the longer the situation continued, the harder it became for the young couple to overcome their embarrassment – both in relation to one another and over the sense that everyone was watching them. Catherine was also convinced that, while the Empress was attempting to force them into marital relations, others at Court were equally determined to force them further apart: 'I have every reason to believe that there was a great desire at that time to create trouble between me and the Grand Duke. For very soon afterwards Count Devier, without rhyme or reason, told me of the Grand Duke's infatuation for Mlle Karr, lady-in-waiting to the Empress, and later on confided that he had noticed my husband showing the same feelings towards Mlle Tatishchev.'

The apartments in the Summer Palace where all this was going on were not designed for anyone's convenience. Catherine's remarks about them also provide an insight into toilet arrangements in the palace:

They formed a suite of rooms with two entrances, one by the stairs through which everyone who came to see us had to pass, and the other leading into the Empress's State apartments, so that to do their work in our rooms our servants had to pass in and out through one or other of these doors. One day it happened that as one of the

Foreign Ministers arrived for an audience with us, the first thing he saw was a commode being taken away for emptying.

Moving from palace to palace through the year also involved taking a lot of furniture with them, as there were not enough mirrors, beds, chairs, tables and chests to furnish all of the palaces in use at different times. Gradually Catherine began to acquire her own furniture to overcome this deficiency.

At the beginning of July 1746, Peter and Catherine accompanied the Empress on a tour of inspection to Reval (now Tallinn, and capital of Estonia). It was not an easy journey, as at every stop accommodation at the post-houses was taken up by the Empress and her entourage; the young Court had to make do with tents or servants' quarters. Catherine retained a clear memory of the inconveniences, and of the difficulties caused by the Empress's whims and lack of routine: 'I remember dressing one day on that journey in front of a stove where bread had just been baked and another time there was water above my ankles when I walked into the tent where my bed had been put up. To make matters worse, the Empress never had any fixed hours either for departures or arrivals, for meals or for rest; thus, we were all excessively harassed, both masters and domestics.' The arrival at the town of Catherinenthal was a good example of Elizabeth's lack of planning; she had wanted to arrive with much pomp and ceremony during daylight hours, but instead they turned up at half past one in the morning amidst pouring rain: 'We were all very elaborately dressed, but as far as I know no one saw us, for the wind had blown out all the torches.'

Back in St Petersburg, Catherine found herself prey to depression, chest pains and frequent crying fits brought on by boredom and constant criticism from Maria Choglokova (who had now been rejoined by her husband). Having made no progress so far in discovering what was amiss with the grand ducal marriage, the Empress now decided to draw her clergy into the investigative process. She ordered the Grand Duke and Duchess to prepare themselves to take communion on the Feast of the Dormition on 15 August; the required preparations included fasting and confession. On this occasion their usual confessor, Bishop Semyon Theodorsky, questioned both Peter and Catherine closely about their respective relationships with the Chernyshevs. He soon realised that there was no truth in the innuendoes that so worried the Empress, both the Grand Duke and Duchess still being disconcertingly innocent. Catherine concluded: 'I suppose that our confessor communicated our confession to the Empress's priest and that the latter repeated it to Her Imperial Majesty, which certainly could do us no harm.'

The Empress spent early August at Peterhof and in the second half of the month moved to Tsarskoye Selo, while the young Court was dispatched to the imperial estate of Oranienbaum on the southern shore of the Gulf of Finland. Oranienbaum had originally belonged to Prince Menshikov and had passed into imperial possession when he was sent into exile; Elizabeth had presented it to Grand Duke Peter in 1743. The large palace, built during the reign of Peter the Great and later modified by Rastrelli, consisted of a domed central structure connecting by means of long galleries to pavilions on either side. It sits on a high cliff with terraces descending to a large formal garden, and commands a fine view of the sea. There was (and is) extensive parkland at Oranienbaum, trees overhanging the alleys so thickly that in places they block out the sun. Here Peter was able to indulge his love of military exercises: '[he] immediately placed his whole retinue under arms: the Chamberlain, the gentlemen-in-waiting, the courtiers . . . the servants of the Court, the gamekeepers, the gardeners, all were armed with muskets. He exercised them every day and made them mount guard.' In the evenings rather bad-tempered balls took place, the company not being large enough for people to enjoy themselves properly. Those courtiers who did not like being put through their military paces all day felt tired and disgruntled. It was during this 'irksome life' at Oranienbaum, 'where the five or six women lived in isolation, dependent on each other's society from morning till night', that Catherine first really began to engage with literature; it was to become a major solace and inspiration for the rest of her life. She had been reading novels, of which she had become rather tired, but now she discovered the letters of Madame de Sévigné and then the works of Voltaire.

After a summer and autumn of shuttling back and forth between Oranienbaum, Peterhof and the Summer Palace in St Petersburg (the short stays at each place making it very difficult for business to be conducted, to the frustration of ambassadors and foreign ministers), the Court returned to the Winter Palace, and this time Peter and Catherine were lodged in the apartments in which Peter had lived before their marriage. They greatly preferred these rooms, but their improved living arrangements did not lead to any change in marital relations. Catherine was now suffering almost continuous headaches and insomnia. She thought the reason for the headaches had been diagnosed correctly by the court physician, Dr Boerhave, who felt her skull and said it was still like that of a child and that the bones had not yet fused. Sustained tension and an unconsummated marriage would seem to offer a more likely explanation.

Catherine is at pains in her memoirs to stress the philistinism of Elizabeth's Court, making such comments as 'Science and art were never touched on, as everybody was ignorant of those subjects; one could lay a wager that half the Court could hardly read and I would be surprised if more than a third could write.' The reality was rather different; among the arts, music was a particularly important feature of Elizabeth's Court, the court choir which she had founded being of very high quality. Having always taken great pleasure in the music of the Russian Orthodox Church, Elizabeth was committed to preserving its ancient traditions and even sang in the choir herself in the small private chapel near her apartments. Secular music was also encouraged, Francesco Araya composing a new opera at least once a year, to be performed on the Empress's birthday or on the anniversary of her coronation. The first Russian theatre was also founded at Elizabeth's Court by a group of students from the elite Cadet Corps school, under the direction of the poet, historian and playwright Alexander Sumarokov. They performed works by Racine, Molière and Shakespeare. Grand Duke Peter himself often organised concerts in the evenings at which he played the violin. (New violin concertos were being published in St Petersburg at this time, composed by the court concert master and violinist Luigi Madonis, a pupil of Vivaldi, as well as symphonies by the Paduan violinist and composer Domenico Dall'Oglio.) Catherine, who was not musical, found these concerts tiresome and did not always attend. On other evenings all the young Court assembled in the grand ducal apartments to play parlour games, and twice a week they could attend a performance in the theatre located opposite the church of Our Lady of Kazan.

Despite the insomnia and headaches, and her boredom with music, Catherine remembers enjoying the winter of 1746–7: 'In short that winter was the gayest and best devised in all my life. We spent practically all our days laughing and dancing.' Early in 1747, after taking part in a pilgrimage to view the famous wonder-working icon of the Mother of God at Tikhvin near Novgorod, the Grand Duke and Duchess were informed they would have to move out of the apartments they liked and return to the ones they had occupied the previous year. Catherine was convinced that this was done in order to cast a blight on their enjoyment, which she felt was resented by both the

Choglokovs and Count Bestuzhev. Peter was now suffering, as Catherine had previously, from the experience of those closest to him in his entourage being sent away. On attaining his majority (for German princes, this was the age of 18), he had been forced through political considerations to dismiss all the men he had with him from Holstein, including Brummer and Bergholz. In addition, a valet to whom he was close was sent to the Peter and Paul Fortress, and a *maître d'hôtel* whose dishes he particularly enjoyed was dismissed. So Peter was forced in his loneliness and despair to turn more to Catherine, to whom he could still talk openly. But the couple did not draw any closer physically or emotionally. Catherine felt sorry for him, but he also irritated her:

> I realised his position and was sorry for him, and therefore tried to offer all the consolation that was in my power. Often I would be annoyed by these visits which lasted several hours, even exhausted by them, because he never sat down and one had to walk up and down the room with him all the time. He walked fast and took large steps, so that it was difficult to follow him and at the same time continue a conversation about very specialized military details, of which he spoke with relish and, it sometimes seemed, interminably.

Catherine admits that Peter enjoyed reading as much as she did, but asserts that his favoured reading material was 'stories of highwaymen or novels' – or Lutheran prayerbooks. This is unlikely to have been a full or fair picture of the Grand Duke's intellectual life. Nor was her description of Peter's skill as a violinist as accurate as it is amusing: 'He did not know a single note, but had a good ear and showed his appreciation of the music by the strength and violence with which he drew sounds from his instrument.'

On 5 March Catherine's father died in Zerbst. Catherine received the news of her bereavement shortly after returning from a trip with the Grand Duke and the Empress to Gostilitsy to celebrate Count Razumovsky's name-day. She was deeply upset. She had probably never expected to see her father again, but he represented stability and fidelity, and she liked to think of him as someone who loved her – perhaps even as someone she could return to should it ever become necessary. Elizabeth considered Catherine's grief to be excessive. For her it implied an attachment to her past and a discontent with her present situation which did not bode well for the early production of offspring – for should not a young wife love her husband more than her father? Catherine was left alone to mourn for a week, after which she was told firmly to dry her tears; Maria Choglokova reported that the Empress's orders were that she should stop crying as her father 'had not been a king'. Catherine retorted that though this was indeed true, he had still been her father. But the instruction was reiterated for her to rejoin court life on the following Sunday; nevertheless she was permitted to wear mourning for six weeks.

With all the spies and watchdogs at the young Court, it is not surprising that sometimes those who were supposed to be in charge fell out with one another. The German woman in charge of the maids, Madame Krause, disliked the Choglokovs and set out to undermine their authority. One result of this feuding was the rather strange scene, as depicted by Catherine, of the marital bed becoming a playground:

> She procured for the Grand Duke toys, dolls and other childish play-things which he adored. During the day they were hidden inside and underneath my bed; the Grand Duke would be the first to go to bed after supper, and as soon as we were both in bed, Mme Krause would lock the door, and then the Grand Duke would play until one or two o'clock in the morning. I was obliged willy-nilly to join in with this delightful entertainment, as was Mme Krause.

One night towards midnight, Maria Choglokova knocked at the door and the miscreants had to hide all the toys hurriedly under the blankets. She grumbled that they were awake so late but could find nothing else to complain of; and as soon as she had gone out again, Peter retrieved the toys and carried on playing until he fell asleep.

In the autumn of 1747 conditions at the young Court became even more strict, with the intention of forcing Peter and Catherine together. No one was allowed to enter the Grand Duke and Duchess's apartments without the permission of one of the Choglokovs. Even the ladies- and gentlemen-in-waiting were to penetrate no further than the antechamber. Neither were they, or the servants, permitted to have any private conversations with the Grand Duke or Duchess; all conversation was to be conducted in loud tones. Peter and Catherine were united in protest at such conditions, which they both felt were un-deserved – and which did not have the desired effect of getting them to perform together in bed.

That winter Catherine paid much attention to her appearance. She was now 18, and aware that she was becoming more attractive physically. Whenever possible she had her hair dressed twice a day by a young Kalmuk man who was a particularly skilled hairdresser. She described her appearance at this time as follows: 'I was tall and had a magnificent figure, but I could have allowed myself a little more weight, as I was rather thin. I did not like using powder, and my hair was a soft brown, very thick and well planted on the forehead. The fashion for leaving one's hair unpowdered was, however, beginning to wane, and that winter I used it now and then.'

On 6 January 1748 she woke up feeling ill, with a sore throat, headache and pains all over her body. Nevertheless she got up as usual and prepared to attend the liturgy, which would be followed by a procession outside to the Neva for the blessing of the waters, which took place every year on this day, the Feast of the Epiphany. But this year the Empress had decided not to attend the blessing of the waters, and excused Peter and Catherine as well. Catherine returned to bed, became feverish during the night, and woke the next morning with her hands and chest covered in small red spots. There was the usual fear that it might be smallpox, but her physician diagnosed measles. During her illness her bed was moved to a warmer room, for the alcove where she and Peter usually slept was very draughty, separated only by thin boards from a vestibule (where Peter liked to keep hounds); Catherine believed she contracted colds every winter from sleeping in a draught. During her convalescence Peter decided to organise masquerades in her bedroom, dressing up the servants and making them dance while he played the violin. Catherine does not appear to have been impressed by these attempts to cheer her up: 'Pretending a headache or weariness, I would lie on the sofa, though also wearing a mask, and was bored to death by the dullness of these balls which amused him so prodigiously.' But Peter was making an effort to extract some enjoyment from a very restricted existence, in the knowledge that any mark of favour he showed could result in that person disappearing: 'When Lent came another four men were removed from his entourage, among them the three pages whom he liked best. These frequent dismissals upset him deeply, but he either did nothing to stop them or protested so clumsily that it only made matters worse.'

Catherine continued to have trouble with her finances. Her expenditure consistently exceeded her income, and provoked periodic outbursts of anger from the Empress. On one occasion Elizabeth let it be known via a chamberlain that she had declared at dinner that every-thing Catherine did was 'fraught with stupidity', that she had an inflated sense of her own worth while being a 'nobody', and that it was far more important to keep an eye on her than on the Grand Duke. Catherine naturally was upset to hear this, but was becoming used to the Empress's moods. She knew that the only response to make was one of apparent submission and, via the same chamberlain, she conveyed sentiments of respect, obedience and deference to Elizabeth. She was not alone in her debt problems; in November 1747 Chancellor Bestuzhev found himself in such difficulties after having spent more than 100,000 roubles on his new stone mansion on the Admiralty side of the Neva that he was reduced to taking out a mortgage on the property with the British consul, James Wolff, for 50,000 roubles.

At the beginning of May 1748 the Empress invited Peter and Catherine to join her at Tsarskoye Selo. The usual repressive measures were lifted during this 11-day break, Peter and Catherine being allowed to eat with the Empress's courtiers when she herself was otherwise engaged. Unfortunately the experience was marred by Peter's lack of self-control. According to Catherine:

> the Grand Duke spoilt everything through his uncontrolled gaiety: for lack of better company he had become accustomed among his valets to vulgar, common behaviour and language, which in the present company was considered offensive, even when used as a joke . . .
>
> This is the effect that can be produced by an indiscreet word, uttered imprudently – it is never forgotten. Really these words were no more than a silly outburst from a young man beside himself with laughter, who was only forced to frequent bad company because of the way in which his dear aunt and her minions kept him impris-oned. This young man, frankly speaking, deserved pity rather than censure.

After this stay at Tsarskoye Selo, the Court returned to St Petersburg, then travelled to Gostilitsy for the Feast of the Ascension. During this visit there was an alarm early one morning as the house where the young Court was staying began to fall down. Nikolai Choglokov woke Catherine and told her to get up and leave with him immediately as the foundations were crumbling. She asked him to leave the room while she got out of bed and hastily pulled on stockings, petticoat, skirt and a short fur jacket before going to wake Madame Krause. As they left the latter's room, the house began to move under them. 'Mme Krause screamed:"It's an earthquake!"' The stairs collapsed, and Catherine had to be passed down through a series of Guards officers, then carried out of the house and into a field. Here she found the Grand Duke in his dressing gown. One of Catherine's ladies-in-waiting had been badly injured by bricks which had fallen on to her head from a collapsing stove (one of the large tiled stoves used for heating). Sixteen workmen who had been sleeping in the basement were killed. The house had been built in haste during the autumn, and the bailiff had ignored some of the architect's instructions; the thaw had then precipitated the collapse. Count Razumovsky was in despair over the accident, though everyone tried to play down what had happened when the Empress (who was staying in another house) was informed; consequently she was cross with Catherine for suffering from shock.

Peter and Catherine again spent some time that summer at Oranienbaum, where Catherine took up duck-shooting, getting up at three o'clock in the morning and dressing in men's clothes to accompany an old huntsman. They would cross the garden on foot, shouldering their guns, climb into a fisherman's skiff which was waiting for them, and set off along the Oranienbaum Canal, which stretched out about a mile into the sea. At times this seems to have been fairly dangerous: 'We often rounded the canal and so sometimes found ourselves in stormy weather out at sea in the skiff.' Peter would sometimes join them an hour or two later. At about 10 o'clock Catherine would return to her apartments and dress for the midday dinner. Afterwards everyone rested (Catherine was reading Hardouin de Péréfixe's seventeenth-century history of Henri IV of France as well as the works of the sixteenth-century Abbé de Brantôme, which included lives of famous and captivating ladies – '*dames illustres*' and '*dames galantes*'), and in the evenings there were musical parties (organised by Peter) or they went riding. (The long northern summer days made it possible to be out both early and late.)

Back in Petersburg, Madames Krause and Choglokova had one of their periodic fallings-out. Choglokova won a decisive battle this time, and persuaded the Empress to dismiss Madame Krause, who retired to live with her son-in-law. She was replaced by a Madame Vladislavova. During the autumn Catherine began to correspond secretly with her old friend, Andrei Chernyshev (he had initiated the correspondence), sending him money and small gifts. They used a wardrobe girl called

Katerina Petrovna, who had a fiancé among the court servants, as a conduit for getting the letters in and out. Catherine's description of handling Andrei's first letter gives an indication of how closely she was watched: 'During the day I carried the letter in my pocket. When I undressed I pushed it under my garter into my stocking and before getting into bed pulled it out and hid it in my sleeve; I dared not leave it in my pockets for fear of their being searched. The girl could only speak freely to me when I was on my commode.' Nevertheless, the atmosphere among Catherine's ladies and maids was slightly more relaxed, as Madame Vladislavova was a less strict supervisor than Madame Krause. Katerina Petrovna also brightened things up, as she 'was naturally inclined to all sorts of pranks and gave a remarkably good imitation of the way Madame Choglokov walked when she was pregnant. For this she pushed a large pillow under her skirt and made us all laugh as she promenaded about the room.'

In the middle of December, the Court set out for Moscow. Preparations had been underway for weeks, the Senate and Colleges (or government departments) having been given official notification of the move in October. Many people sent provisions ahead, before the major frosts began, fearing both that they would not be able to get what they wanted in Moscow and also that the wine might be spoilt if it had to travel through the freezing conditions of a Russian winter. Some, including Chancellor Bestuzhev, even took supplies of Neva water with them since, though it tended to give foreigners 'Neva tummy', it was still considered less noxious than the water in Moscow. The foreign ministers, who had not received notification to prepare for the journey until some time after the rest of the Court, had to wait several weeks before setting out, as there were no horses to be had. About 100,000 people were involved in this migration, and they had to wait for the horses who had made the first trip (and as horses were changed at every staging post, the numbers involved were enormous) to return to Petersburg. Catherine and Peter had departed slightly ahead of the Empress, travelling at night in a large sleigh, with the gentlemen-in-waiting in the front. During the day Peter moved into a closed sleigh which he shared with Choglokov, while Catherine remained in the large one which she kept open, talking to the various courtiers sitting opposite her. The Empress caught up with the grand ducal party in Tver, which caused them some inconvenience: 'as the houses and provisions prepared for us were taken by her retinue, we remained there for twenty-four hours without horses or food. We were very hungry but towards the evening Choglokov managed to get a roast sturgeon for us and it seemed delicious.'

During the journey Catherine learnt from a gentleman of the bedchamber, Prince Alexander Trubetskoy, the details of the disgrace which had befallen Elizabeth's physician, Count Armand Lestocq, in mid-November. Accused of being in secret correspondence with and in the pay of the Courts of France, Sweden and Prussia and of having spoken disrespectfully of the Empress, he had been imprisoned in the Fortress, tortured (specifically, 'hung up by the arms backwards for a considerable time') and sentenced to exile in Siberia. All his goods had been confiscated, and his house given by the Empress to General Stepan Apraksin (who had headed the commission which examined him). Having previously been warmly disposed towards Catherine, Lestocq had warned her to avoid him just before his arrest, when he knew he was under suspicion.

In Moscow, Peter and Catherine were allocated the apartments in which Catherine had lived with her mother on their arrival in Russia. 'Nothing could have been more uncomfortable than the way we were lodged, the pair of us. Our apartment formed a double wing; as one entered, my rooms were on the right, the Grand Duke's on the left; neither could move without disturbing the other.' Catherine recollected her dislike of Peter's proximity with vehemence:

> At that time the Grand Duke had only two occupations. One was to scrape the violin, the other to train spaniels for hunting. So, from seven o'clock in the morning until late into the night, either the discordant sounds which he drew very forcefully from his violin or the horrible barking and howling of the five or six dogs which he thrashed throughout the rest of the day, continually grated on my ears. I admit that I was driven half-mad and suffered terribly as both these musical performances tore at my ear-drums from early morning till late at night. After the dogs I was the most miserable creature in the world.

Almost immediately, Catherine was afflicted by spots on her face. Dr Boerhave first prescribed sedatives, which had no effect, then gave her oil of talcum to dilute in water and wash her face with once a week. This cleared them up quickly. Less easy to cure was the perennial problem of being deprived of congenial company. Soon after the Court's arrival in the old capital, instructions were received that the merry

Katerina Petrovna was to be married as soon as possible. Yet again, the only reason for this appeared to be that Catherine favoured the girl and that she made everyone laugh. 'She got married, and no more was said about her.' But the correspondence between Catherine and Andrei Chernyshev, who was now near Moscow en route to his regiment, continued, this time through the agency of Catherine's valet, Timofei Yevreinov. In time he too was dismissed, the pretext being a quarrel he had with a servant whose job was to bring in the coffee.

Late January 1749 saw the first of the many health scares which would afflict the rest of the Empress's life, sending the Court into parox-ysms of fear about what might ensue if and when she died. This first scare happened in the middle of the carnival, when the Empress suffered what Catherine describes as 'an attack of constipation which threat-ened to become very serious'. In the event of the Empress's death it would not just be a simple matter of Peter's taking over as Tsar – and both Catherine and Peter were well aware of their vulnerability. A palace coup, orchestrated by someone like Count Bestuzhev, could result in their banishment, imprisonment or even assassination. They were well aware that during this crisis Count Bestuzhev, General Apraksin and others were holding secret meetings. The Choglokovs told them nothing but were quite clearly involved and, as Catherine expressed it, were 'noticeably looking down their noses' at the Grand Duke and Duchess. A dispatch from Lord Hyndford confirms, with tantalising vagueness, that dangerous plots were afoot, although the Grand Duke's opponents seem to have been as frightened of him as he was of them: Hyndford writes that the two Counts Razumovsky, Chancellor Bestuzhev and General Apraksin had 'taken proper measures, for their security, in case of an accident, for they are by no means in favour with the great duke (I dare say no more upon this subject, altho' in cypher)'.

Peter (according to Catherine) was beside himself with apprehen-sion. Catherine did what she could to calm him, promising to try and get information from her servants about the state of the Empress's health and reassuring him that, if the worst came to the worst, she would help him to escape from their apartments, which at the time they dared not leave without permission. If necessary, she told him, they could even jump out of their ground-floor windows. She also let him know that she was in contact with several Guards officers, as well as with Count Zakhar Chernyshev (Andrei's cousin), on whom she could rely. It is interesting to note that even at this early stage Catherine, far more

aware than Peter of the strategies needed for survival, had been carefully building up a network of support; she had clearly not just been
sitting quietly listening to the music during court entertainments. She
had also continued her policy of trying to please people, which had
paid off in improved relations with both Choglokova and Vladislavova.
('My cheerful disposition was also much appreciated and all these Arguses
and Cerberuses were often amused in spite of themselves by the conversations I held with them.') Thus reassured, Peter 'returned to his corner
with his dogs and his violin'. Madame Vladislavova turned out to be a
very valuable source of information, as some of her relatives and friends
were in close attendance on the Empress and she was also on intimate
terms with some of the court priests and cantors, who followed up the
liturgy she assiduously attended with gossip. The constipation crisis
passed (the ending of the 'blockage' coinciding with the arrival of the
Empress's menstrual period) and the intrigues, for the time being, faded
away.

During the summer the Empress undertook a lengthy pilgrimage to
the Holy Trinity–St Sergius Monastery. She had decided to walk the
whole 30 miles there from Moscow, which she did at the rate of about
two and a half miles a day, with a few days' rest in between each day
of walking. Catherine and Peter meanwhile were sent to stay in a house
called Rayovo, between Moscow and the monastery, which belonged
to Maria Choglokova. Catherine spent all her time hunting and riding:
'I rode like mad all day; no one stopped me and I could break my
neck if I wished – no one interfered with me or cared.' Likewise Peter
was out shooting all the time, the couple only coming together for
meals or in bed – and even then Peter arrived after Catherine had
gone to sleep and left before she woke up. The monotony was inter-
rupted on some days by visits from Count Kirill Razumovsky, the
favourite's brother; years later he told Catherine that the reason behind
these visits was that he was in love with her, which she had not
suspected at the time. When the Grand Duke and Duchess rejoined
the Empress, Elizabeth was shocked by Catherine's sunburnt complexion
and told her to apply a liquid made of lemon, egg white and eau-de-
vie to her face. This remedy (which Catherine also recommends for
cold sores) had the desired effect.

For the next few months Catherine was afflicted with chronic
toothache, which intensified during the journey back to St Petersburg
at the end of the year, during which she and Peter travelled day and
night in an open sleigh. On arrival, she summoned Dr Boerhave and

beseeched him to extract the troublesome tooth. After failing to dissuade her from this course of action, he summoned her surgeon Gyon to assist him. Catherine sat on the floor, Boerhave and Choglokov on either side to hold her still, while Gyon yanked out the tooth. It wasn't easy, and Gyon pulled out some of her jawbone at the same time. The pain was so violent that, as Catherine put it, 'tears streamed from my eyes and nose as though water had been poured from a teapot'. She was put to bed, and continued to suffer for about four weeks (even after this gruesome operation, one of the roots of the tooth remained in her jaw). She was so bruised that she was unable to appear in public until the middle of January.

During Lent of 1750 the Empress initiated another attempt to find out why no child had been produced; she conveyed her intention via Maria Choglokova to discover 'whose fault it was' and sent a midwife to examine Catherine and a doctor to examine Peter. But after she had vented her feelings, her anger died down again. The lack of grand ducal offspring was becoming an accepted fact of life in various quarters; more than a year previously Lord Hyndford had reported to the Duke of Newcastle that it was probable that the Grand Duke would never have any children. In mid-March Elizabeth went to Gostilitsy to celebrate Alexei Razumovsky's birthday, while Peter and Catherine visited Tsarskoye Selo. With them went their own Court and the Empress's ladies-in-waiting, chief of whom was the Princess of Courland. Peter was very partial to this Princess, partly because she spoke German and in spite of Catherine's contemptuous dismissal of her as 'small and hunchbacked'. Catherine reckoned that all the men of the house of Holstein were attracted to deformed women, saying of her uncle, the Bishop of Lübeck and soon to become King of Sweden, that he 'never had a mistress who was not hunchbacked, lame, or one-eyed'. She stated, however, that she was not overly worried about Peter, convinced that his desire for the Princess would 'never go much further than languorous ogling'. The Grand Duke and Duchess and their entourage entertained themselves with strolling about, hunting, or playing on the swing during the day, and with the usual card games in the evening. The Grand Duke's chamberlain, a certain Sergei Saltykov, fell in love with one of the Empress's ladies-in-waiting, Matryona Balk, while she was on the swing, going so far as to propose marriage. She accepted, and they were married soon afterwards.

One night in Tsarskoye Selo Catherine had gone to bed early with a headache. Madame Vladislavova presumed her real ailment was jealousy provoked by the attentions the Grand Duke was paying the Princess of Courland, and she expressed how sorry she felt for the Grand Duchess – which the proud Catherine hated to hear. When the Grand Duke came to bed – somewhat the worse for drink – he began telling her how much he admired the Princess and became irritated when she, feigning sleep, failed to respond. According to Catherine, he then gave her 'two or three rather violent punches on the side'. Who can say if this really happened? Certainly Peter was known to get drunk, and Catherine's description of what happened next sounds realistic enough: 'I cried a lot that night because of all this and because of his having hurt me, also because of my whole position, which was as unpleasant in every way as it was tiresome. Next day he seemed to be ashamed of what he had done. He did not mention it and I pretended nothing had happened.'

Catherine continued to spend much time on horseback. The Empress feared that riding astride would lessen the Grand Duchess's chances of becoming pregnant, so she had to go side-saddle, at least when Elizabeth was watching. She had, however, a special saddle made for her to her own design, which could be adjusted, along with the stirrups, to enable her to ride astride when it was safe to do so. The coat of her riding habit was made of an azure silk camlet (a closely woven worsted, which shrank in the rain and faded in the sun so that it constantly had to be replaced) with silver braid and crystal buttons; with it she wore a three-cornered black hat decorated with a string of diamonds. The skirt was split so that it could fall on both sides of the horse (and thus make it hard to see whether she was riding side-saddle or not). Catherine was conscious of how good she looked on horseback, and was pleased to be able to show off in front of the Empress. That summer, when the young Court moved to Oranienbaum, they went hunting every day. In this way Catherine worked out a lot of her frustrations, both physical and mental, and also found it helped reduce her premenstrual tension: 'I passionately loved riding; the more violent the exercise the more I enjoyed it, so that if a horse ever broke away I galloped after it and brought it back.' She was also fond of dogs, and the Grand Duke gave her a small English poodle; she and her women enjoyed dressing him up and letting him eat with them at table, a napkin tied round his neck.

Back in St Petersburg, a full round of court entertainments was planned for the autumn and winter: the French comedy two days a week, masquerades on another two days, a concert in the Grand Duke's apartments on one evening, and a ball on Sunday. One of the weekly masquerades was restricted to members of the Court or specially invited guests of the Empress (numbering between 150 and 200 people), while the other was open to all the titled people in town, down to the rank of colonel, as well as to Guards officers, and involved up to 800.

Rank (*chin*) played a vitally important part in the life of the Russian nobility. The Table of Ranks, instituted by Peter the Great in 1722, was based on military hierarchy, and applied not only to the armed forces but also to the civil service and the Court. There were 14 ranks (14 being the lowest), most military ranks having a naval and civil equivalent with several having a court equivalent as well.★ Sometimes military titles were used to denote civilians of equal rank – hence there was a number of men called 'General' who had little connection with the army. On reaching the eighth rank (major, third captain, or collegiate assessor), a commoner would be granted noble status, along with all his descendants. Wives shared the rank of their husbands. Children, even of nobles, had to work their way up the ranks from the bottom; in consequence, many sons were enrolled in regiments at extremely young ages so that they could attain a higher rank by the time they actually came to serve. Guards officers stood two ranks higher than ordinary officers in any official appointment, so competition to enlist in the elite Guards regiments was fierce and required an influential patron. Rank dictated every aspect of life: one's style of dress, how many horses could be harnessed to one's carriage, the number of servants in attendance, the livery they wore, the way one was addressed, the place one could occupy in church and the order of precedence on all official occasions.

At the masquerades Catherine showed herself to be as energetic a dancer as she was a rider, often changing her dress three times during the course of a ball. At the public balls she would never wear the same outfit twice, liking to surprise and impress the onlookers; she dressed more simply for the private court balls, aware that this would please the Empress (who herself had an enormous wardrobe). Some of the masquerades continued to be transvestite and for these she wore what she describes as 'superb clothes, all embroidered or of an elaborate style'.

★ For example, the military class 2 rank was General-in-Chief, the naval class 2 Admiral, the civil class 2 Vice Chancellor or Real Privy Counsellor, while at Court the Chief Chamberlain, Chief Marshal, Chief Steward, Chief Equerry, Chief Master of the Hunt and Chief Cup Bearer were all ranked as class 2. Lower down the scale, a gentleman-of-the-bedchamber held a court rank equivalent to the military rank of Brigadier.

For once such competition did not displease the Empress; she was gratified that Catherine should enter so whole-heartedly into the spirit of
her cross-dressing entertainments. Despite the problems Catherine had
encountered in her relationship with the Empress, despite the latter's
capriciousness and tendency to make life difficult for the people around
her, Catherine continued to admire Elizabeth, particularly for her physical attributes. Recollecting her at these masquerades engendered some
of the most fulsome praise she ever accorded another woman:

> The only woman who looked really good and perfectly right as a
> man was the Empress herself. As she was very tall and rather power-
> fully built, male costume suited her wonderfully. She had the most
> handsome legs I have ever seen on a man, and her feet were
> admirably proportioned. She danced to perfection and had a special
> grace in everything she did, whether dressed as a man or as a
> woman. One always wanted to keep one's eyes trained on her,
> turning them away with regret, because there was nothing that
> could replace her.

These two attractive and forceful characters, each with a strong sense of
her own physical presence, responded to one another, recognising kindred
spirits (even though Catherine would come to censure and reject many
aspects of the way Elizabeth conducted herself as sovereign):

> One day at one of these balls I watched her dancing a minuet. When
> she had finished, she came up to me. I took the liberty of telling
> her that it was very fortunate for women that she was not a man,
> for a portrait of her looking like that would be enough to turn the
> head of more than one woman. She took what I said in very good
> part and replied to me in the same tone, in the most gracious manner
> possible, that if she were a man it would be to me that she would
> present the apple.

Apart from the Empress, Catherine enjoyed upstaging all the other
women at Court, and being at the forefront of fashion. One day she
appeared at a masquerade dressed all in white, with her long hair tied
back with a white ribbon, a white gauze ruff around her neck, a rose
in her hair and another in her corsage. Such daring simplicity, which
could only be carried off by a young and very slim woman, drew all
eyes to her.

As Catherine had matured she had begun to get on much better with Maria Choglokova, whose marriage had long since ceased to be exemplary. In fact, her husband Nikolai had made advances to the Grand Duchess, which she had repulsed, thus earning Maria's gratitude. The latter liked Catherine to spend the afternoons with her; otherwise she read, or walked up and down with the Grand Duke when he wished to talk to her. In her memoirs she was utterly dismissive of this time spent with her husband: 'Resolved though I was to treat him with patience and good nature, I admit frankly that I was often worn out by his visits, walks, and conversation, which was of an insipidity beyond parallel. When he left me, to read the most tedious book seemed a delightful pastime.'

That winter Catherine was also the recipient of attentions from Count Zakhar Chernyshev. He began sending her posies, and before she knew where she was, the two were in regular 'sentimental correspondence', notes being passed back and forth by one of the ladies-in-waiting. Catherine's pent-up emotions came bursting out as she wrote to him that she loved him as no other woman had loved him (he was 29 years old to her 22), and that she could not imagine Paradise without him. Nevertheless, the relationship never became anything more than epistolary, and at the beginning of Lent 1752 Count Chernyshev left St Petersburg to return to his regiment.

# 4

# *Catherine Grows Up*
# *(1752–55)*

*I drew myself up and, with head erect, stood as one bearing great responsibilities rather than a humiliated and oppressed person.*

Memoirs of Catherine the Great

By 1752 Peter and Catherine were far from being the children they had been when they married. They had each established a life for themselves at the Russian Court and both were becoming sexually attracted, and attractive, to other people. Catherine had been on the verge of entering into a sexual relationship at least once. Yet they had made absolutely no progress in fulfilling their marital duty towards one another, even though they knew perfectly well that this was also perceived as their duty towards the Russian Empire. Peter and Catherine's refusal, or inability, to have, or even to try to have, sex – despite being forced together, practically imprisoned in their bed night after night – suggests an extraordinary degree of either stubbornness or helplessness on the part of one or both of them. Their refusal to produce the required heir could be viewed as an act of rebellion against the Empress and her Court, the only means the Grand Duke and Duchess had of exercising any power or taking any independent action – or, in this case, inaction. But the fact that this course of inaction was also injurious to themselves, laying them open to being dismissed as useless, would suggest that they were unable to help themselves.

After Easter, when the Court moved to the Summer Palace, Catherine began to notice that the chamberlain Sergei Saltykov – he who had proposed to his wife-to-be after seeing her on the swing at Tsarskoye Selo – was more and more often in attendance. He seemed to be trying to win the favour of the Choglokovs, which she found curious, as none of the young courtiers usually had a good word to say for the pair or showed any desire to spend time with them. Catherine began to wonder if he had some ulterior motive, and during a concert Saltykov made it clear that he had set his sights on seducing her. Catherine, who imagined initially that she was in control of the situation, asked him what he expected to gain from pursuing such a relationship. He replied in ecstatic terms, whereupon she reminded him that he had married someone he had shown every sign of being in love with only two years previously. He declared that this had been a mistake and he no longer loved his wife. Catherine tried to resist his attentions, but 'unfortunately I could not help listening to him; he was handsome as the dawn; there was no one to compete with him in that, not at the Imperial Court, and still less at ours. Nor was he lacking in intelligence or the accomplishments, manners, and graces which are a prerogative of the *grand monde*, but especially at the Court.'

Catherine was easy prey. Sergei Saltykov was 26 years old, thus three years older than Catherine, and sexually experienced. He came from a noble family and, as Catherine put it, 'knew how to conceal his faults'. She managed to resist his blandishments for several weeks, and then Nikolai Choglokov presented him with an opportunity to pursue her more determinedly, by arranging a hunt on his island during which Saltykov managed to get Catherine to himself in order to 'start upon his favourite subject'. At first Catherine was silent while Sergei made his protestations of love, but finally she had to admit that he was 'agreeable' to her. That evening there was a storm, and the hunting party was stranded at the Choglokovs' house on the island until the early hours of the morning. As Sergei continued to make passionate verbal love to Catherine, she realised that this was a situation she might not be able to control. She was, in fact, falling in love: 'I had believed it possible to govern and influence both his heart and mine but now realized that this was going to be a difficult if not an impossible task.'

Saltykov's assiduous attendance at the young Court, and particularly the attention he paid the Choglokovs, soon became the subject of gossip which, inevitably, reached the ears of the Empress. Catherine believed that it was actually because of her suspected involvement with Saltykov that the Empress had expressed annoyance with her over an arrangement for all the members of the young Court to wear matching outfits at Oranienbaum that summer – 'grey below, blue on top, with a black velvet collar, and no other ornament'. Elizabeth, who was visiting Oranienbaum for a day (she herself was staying at Peterhof), also told Maria Choglokova that she was still convinced that Catherine's habit of riding astride was preventing her getting pregnant and that she shouldn't walk around in masculine riding habit all day. For once Choglokova seems to have refused to beat about the bush, even with the Empress: '[she] replied that there was no question about my having children; these, after all, could not appear without something being done about it and that though their Imperial Highnesses had been married since 1745 – nothing *had* been done about it yet'. Poor Madame Choglokova then came in for her share of abuse from the Empress – who must surely have suspected the truth even if no one had had the courage to say it to her face before, but who was now blaming Choglokova and her husband for not having somehow forced Peter and Catherine into having sex. After this conversation was reported to them, both Sergei Saltykov and gentleman of the bedchamber Lev Naryshkin, whose name was also being linked with Catherine's, decided it would be politic to retire from the scene for a few weeks, on the pretext of family illness.

Nikolai Choglokov also now retired to one of his country seats for a month, and while he was gone, his wife set to work seriously in an attempt to fulfil the Empress's wishes for the grand ducal consummation. Together with one of the Grand Duke's valets, she selected the pretty young widow of the German artist Georg Christoph Grooth, who had been Elizabeth's court painter and curator of her art collection, to undertake the Grand Duke's belated sex education. According to Catherine, 'It took several days to persuade her, promising her I do not know what, and then to instruct her in what was expected of me and what she had to agree to do.' Madame Grooth duly initiated Peter into what was expected of a husband; it is possible to interpret the following passage from Catherine's memoirs as suggesting that the marriage was now finally consummated: 'At last, after many efforts, Mme Choglokov obtained what she wanted and when she was certain of her facts, she informed the Empress that everything was going on according to her wishes. She had dreamt of great rewards for her efforts, but was mistaken; she got nothing, though she kept repeating that the Empire was in her debt.'

Catherine's sexual initiation thus seems to have involved two men, husband and lover. Opportunities for physical intimacy with Sergei

Saltykov must have been few and far between at this stage. And on his return to Court in the autumn, he only increased Catherine's desire for him by appearing to lose interest in her. That winter the Court again removed to Moscow. Catherine was now in the early stages of pregnancy, and at the last post-station before Moscow she miscarried 'with violent haemorrhages'. The accommodation assigned to the Grand Duke and Duchess in Moscow was far from satisfactory:

> We were living in a wooden wing, newly built that autumn, so that water flowed down the panelling and the rooms were singularly damp. This wing had two rows with five or six rooms on each side; those on the street were for me, and those on the other side the Grand Duke's. In the room which was to be my dressing-room they put all my women and maids with their servants, so that there were seventeen women all in one room which, though it had three very large windows, had no other exit but my bedroom through which they had to pass for all their necessities, which was not comfortable either for them or for me.

Catherine, who was not feeling at all well, tried to improve conditions by creating partitions in her bedroom with large screens.

Sergei Saltykov arrived in Moscow several weeks later and contrived to be absent from Court for much of the time. Catherine was upset but Sergei, clearly an experienced philanderer, persuaded her that there were good reasons for his behaviour. Around this time, partly in the hope that it would ease Sergei's position at Court as an acknowledged friend of the Grand Duke and Duchess, Catherine took steps to reduce the antagonism between the young Court and Chancellor Bestuzhev. The latter was feeling threatened by the increasing ascendancy of the Shuvalov family (the 22-year-old Ivan Shuvalov had recently replaced Alexei Razumovsky as the Empress's official favourite) and their friend Mikhail Vorontsov, the Vice-Chancellor. In this atmosphere of shifting allegiances, the Chancellor responded positively to the Grand Duchess's overtures and the two began to establish a cautious friendship. (In addition to having a career as a politician and statesman, Bestuzhev had dabbled in chemistry as a young man and had invented and patented a sedative, which came to be known as 'Bestuzhev's drops'. They were made from a solution of ferric chloride, ether and alcohol, and were sufficiently well known to receive a mention a century later in Victor Hugo's *Les Misérables*. In later life Catherine swore by them as a remedy for 'spasms'.)

It was now clear to Madame Choglokova that, despite her best efforts, Catherine and Peter were not having sex often enough or effectively enough to guarantee a successful pregnancy and that it would be wise to take further steps to ensure the birth of an heir. In a rather roundabout manner she set out a plan to Catherine: 'She started in her usual way with a long dissertation on her affection for her husband, on her wisdom, on what had or had not to be done to secure love and facilitate conjugal relations, and then suddenly declared that there were certain situations of major importance which formed exceptions to the rule.' Her idea was that Catherine should become pregnant by either Sergei Saltykov or Lev Naryshkin, whichever of the two she preferred. Whether Choglokova was acting on her own initiative or at the Empress's instigation is impossible to know. Certainly the Empress's impatience may have prompted Choglokova's desperate search for a solution, fearful as she was for her own position. It is also possible that Saltykov might have proposed the idea himself during their long chats as he sought to ingratiate himself with Catherine's minders. His access to the Grand Duchess was eased as soon as Choglokova had decided it was in her interests to promote their union. Nevertheless, his desire for Catherine seems to have diminished significantly once he had seduced her, and the fact that he was now being actively encouraged to go to bed with her may have dampened his ardour still further.

In May 1753 Catherine was pregnant again. She and the Grand Duke spent several weeks at a country estate which the Empress had given to Peter some six or seven miles from Moscow. The houses in which they were to live were built around them while they slept in tents. They returned to Moscow towards the end of June, Catherine feeling very tired and sleeping much of the time. On 29 June, the Feast of Sts Peter and Paul, she fulfilled all the usual obligations of attendance at the liturgy followed by dinner, a ball and supper. The next day she had severe backache and miscarried again during the night. On this occasion Madame Choglokova had realised what was happening and had summoned a midwife to attend her. She had been about two or three months pregnant, and was convalescent for six weeks during which she was very bored and unhappy, forced to stay in her room, in the heat of a Moscow summer and with hardly any company. Meanwhile the Grand Duke, according to his wife, spent his time getting drunk in his room along with his servants, who showed him little respect, 'for in their state of inebriation they did not know what they were doing and forgot that they were with their master and that their master was the

Grand Duke'. Catherine also relates that one day Peter decided to make an example of a rat who had eaten two of the toy sentinels on guard in a cardboard fortress; the rat was hanged and 'exposed to the public for three days'. When Catherine laughed in derision, Peter was greatly put out, and she had to apologise for her 'womanly ignorance of military law'. In addition to the eccentric Grand Duke, there were several genuine cases of mental illness at Court that summer, including a monk who had cut off his private parts with a razor, and a major of the Semyonovsky regiment who professed the belief that the late Nadir Shah of Persia was God; Elizabeth had them all lodged near Dr Boerhave's apartments, 'so that a small lunatic asylum gradually collected at Court'.

On the afternoon of 1 November 1753, the wooden palace in which the Court was housed was burnt to the ground. Catherine paints a vivid description of the fire:

> I set off straightaway for my room and, passing through an antechamber on my way, I saw that the balustrade in a corner of the great hall was on fire. That was twenty feet away from our wing. I entered my rooms and found them already full of soldiers and servants carrying out as much of the furniture as they could. Madame Choglokova had followed hard on my heels, and as there was nothing else for us to do in the building than wait for it to catch fire, Madame Choglokova and I left, and finding at the door the carriage belonging to the choirmaster Araya, who had come for a concert at the Grand Duke's (whom I had warned myself that the house was on fire), she and I got into this carriage, the street being covered in mud, because of the continuous rain that had been falling for several days, and from there we watched the fire as well as the furniture being brought out from all parts of the building. Then I saw an amazing thing – an astonishing number of mice and rats coming down the staircase in single file, without even bothering to hurry.

Catherine and Madame Choglokova had left the building at three o'clock; by six there was no sign of it left. The heat of the fire became so intense that the onlookers had to move into the fields a hundred yards away. Most of Catherine's clothes and other belongings, including her books (she was at that time reading Pierre Bayle's *Dictionnaire Historique et Critique*, at the rate of a volume every six months – there were five volumes in total) were salvaged from the fire. The Empress, however, lost all 4,000 dresses she had brought to Moscow. (The clothes restored to Catherine included some belonging to the Countess Shuvalova, the underskirts of which were lined with leather at the back because the Countess had been incontinent since the birth of her first child.) The Empress departed for her estate of Pokrovskoye while the Grand Duke and Duchess were temporarily lodged at a house belonging to Choglokov. They found this house to be horrible – rotting, draughty and 'filled with vermin'.

In February 1754 Catherine realised she was pregnant again. During this third pregnancy she was watched over very carefully and her physical activities were curtailed. She remained at home, for instance, during Easter week, when a party of gentlemen-in-waiting, including Sergei Saltykov, went out riding with the Grand Duke. On 21 April, Catherine's twenty-fifth birthday, Nikolai Choglokov, who had been ill for some time, was declared to be beyond hope of recovery. Catherine was upset, as she had learnt how to manage him and had also succeeded in turning his wife into a loyal friend. Elizabeth's main concern was that he should be taken home to die, away from the Court, 'as she was afraid of the dead'. As soon as he had died, the Empress appointed the feared Count Alexander Shuvalov, a cousin of Ivan and head of the Secret Chancery, to assume Choglokov's functions in the grand ducal household. Shuvalov, it appears, suffered from a facial twitch, 'a sort of convulsion that affected the entire right side of his face, from the eye to the chin, whenever he was overcome with joy, anger, fear, or anxiety'.

In May the Court returned to St Petersburg. Catherine was greatly relieved to find that Sergei Saltykov and Lev Naryshkin were both to be travelling in the same party as herself and Peter, but it turned out that she could not see Saltykov at all during the long and tedious journey (it was deliberately taken very slowly, on account of Catherine's pregnancy) because she was sharing a carriage with Alexander Shuvalov and his wife, along with Madame Vladislavova and the midwife who had been appointed to be in constant attendance.

After nearly a month of travelling they arrived back at the Summer Palace, where the Grand Duke resumed the staging of concerts. The supervisor of his education, Jakob Stählin (a member of the Petersburg Academy of Sciences, who also acted as imperial pyrotechnician), records that Peter was sufficiently accomplished as a violinist, having been taught by various Italian musicians, to join in the performance of symphonies and ritornellos in Italian arias. Stählin also explains why it was difficult for Peter to assess his own abilities, for even when he played a wrong note or fudged a tricky passage, his teachers would exclaim, 'Bravo, your Highness!' That he did have a great love for music is undeniable; he also built up a very valuable collection of violins made by Amati, Jacob Stainer and other masters.

Catherine was suffering from melancholy. Saltykov was showing signs of withdrawing from her, and she feared that he might be sent away. She felt no better when the Court removed to Peterhof, where she went for long walks, 'but all my troubles followed me relentlessly'. On their return to the Summer Palace, Catherine was shocked to discover that the apartments being prepared for her confinement were along-side those of the Empress; 'they were dismal like all the rooms in the Summer Palace. They had only one entrance, were badly furnished in red damask, contained little furniture and no comfort.' And she would find it very difficult to receive her chosen visitors there.

On 20 September 1754 Catherine gave birth to a son. As soon as she had gone into labour during the previous night, both the Grand Duke and Alexander Shuvalov had been woken, and the Empress herself had arrived at about two o'clock in the morning. Catherine had what she described as 'a very hard time' on the birthing couch, and the baby arrived at noon. The mother was given no time to experience any maternal satisfaction or to hold her son: 'As soon as he was swaddled the Empress called for her confessor who conferred on the child the name of Paul, after which the Empress ordered the midwife to take the child and follow her.' The birth was announced by 201 salvoes of cannon fire from the Fortress, and members of the nobility began arriving at the palace to congratulate the Empress.

Whether Paul Petrovich was indeed the son of Grand Duke Peter, or that of Sergei Saltykov, is a question which will never be satisfac-torily answered unless and until DNA tests are carried out on the remains of Peter III and Paul I. In at least one version of her memoirs Catherine seems to want the reader to infer that Saltykov was the father. It is of course quite possible that Catherine herself was unsure as to the child's paternity. But the evidence in support of the argument that Paul was in fact Peter's son is strong and lies both in his unpre-possessing appearance as an adult (Sergei Saltykov was considered to have been exceptionally handsome) and in aspects of his character in which he closely resembled Peter. Similar characteristics were also evident in Paul's second son, Constantine. Whatever the truth of the matter, the boy was accepted as legitimate by the Empress Elizabeth and treated from the moment of his birth as a future Tsar.

After Paul had been removed and taken to the Empress's apartments,

Catherine was left alone. No one thought to attend to the young mother, but left her lying on the bed on which she had given birth. She asked Madame Vladislavova to change her soiled linen and help her back to her own bed, but Vladislavova said she couldn't do that without specific instructions. She wouldn't even give Catherine a drink of water. After three hours Countess Shuvalova arrived and was horrified to see the Grand Duchess's condition. 'It was enough to kill me,' she said – which was very reassuring for me. I had been in tears ever since the birth had taken place, particularly because I had been so cruelly abandoned, lying in discomfort after a long and painful labour, between doors and windows which did not close properly, with nobody daring to carry me back to my bed although it was close by and I was too weak to drag myself there.' Countess Shuvalova went to fetch the midwife, who arrived about half an hour later; up to that point the Empress had demanded her complete attention for the baby. Catherine was finally carried back to her bed, then left on her own again for the rest of the day. Neither the Grand Duke nor the Empress bothered to come and find out how she was; it could not have been made clearer to her that, having fulfilled her task of producing a child, she was herself of no account. Meanwhile there was much rejoicing over the birth.

The following day, Catherine was in considerable pain all down her left side, and was unable to sleep. Again no one bothered about her, although the Grand Duke did look in briefly – long enough to say he had no time to stay. Madame Vladislavova sat with her for a while, but could do nothing to help, and Catherine, though unable to stifle her tears and moans, hated betraying her misery.

Six days after his birth, Paul was baptised. Catherine believed he had almost died, after suffering from ulceration in his mouth. But such news as she received she could only gather furtively, as to ask too many questions would have implied distrust of the Empress's care of her son. Catherine had in fact no confidence in Elizabeth's methods of child-rearing. In her memoirs, she ascribed many of Paul's later ills to the way he was treated as a baby:

He was kept in an excessively hot room, swaddled in flannel, laid in a cot lined with silver fox, covered with a satin, wadded quilt over which was another counterpane of pink velvet lined with silver fox. Later on, I often saw him lying like that, bathed in sweat from head to toe so that when he grew up the slightest whiff of air brought on colds and sickness. In addition, he was surrounded by a great number of old matrons who with their half-baked remedies, resulting from ignorance, inflicted upon him much more physical and moral harm than good.

On the day of the baptism (which Catherine did not attend; even had she been well enough to do so, religious custom dictated that she remain in close confinement for 40 days after the birth), the Empress came to see her in her rooms, bringing her some jewels (described by Catherine as 'a miserable little necklace with earrings and two dingy rings which I would have been ashamed to give to my maids') and an order that she was to be granted a gift of 100,000 roubles. Unfortunately she soon had to lend the money back to the Empress, not receiving it finally until January – the reason being that Grand Duke Peter had reacted most indignantly on learning that Catherine had been given a present, demanding the same amount for himself. Cashflow difficulties meant that the Empress's cabinet secretary, Baron Cherkasov, had to borrow back the money from the Grand Duchess in order that the Empress might give it to the Grand Duke.

Balls, illuminations and fireworks were organised to celebrate Paul Petrovich's baptism, while his mother languished on her bed, unwell and unhappy. The Grand Duke had begun to visit her in the evenings, but principally in order to see her maids-of-honour, in particular Elizaveta Vorontsova, niece of the Vice-Chancellor, who now became the chief focus of Peter's affections (and who was generally referred to by the courtiers as '*das Fräulein*', or simply by her patronymic, Romanovna). All the women Peter had fallen for had been considerably below his own social standing and level of education, and *das Fräulein* was no exception. She was also considered to be rather coarse. But she came to love Peter, and he loved her. It seemed that with Elizaveta Vorontsova he could relax and be himself with no fear of censure, whereas with his wife he constantly felt he was being judged and found wanting. Even though she had long considered their marriage a failure and had been unfaithful herself, Catherine was unhappy to see her husband (whom she had previously imagined incapable of forming any viable relationship) being attracted to someone else – particularly when she saw that someone else as an inferior. It was a blow to her pride. To add to her misery, two and a half weeks after Paul's birth, Catherine was informed that Sergei Saltykov had been sent away, the pretext for his removal from Petersburg being his appointment as the official messenger of the news of the birth to the Court of Sweden. 'I buried myself even deeper in my bed, where I could sorrow in peace. To remain in it I pretended the increased pains in my leg prevented me from getting up, but the real truth was that I could not and would not see anybody in my grief.'

The thirtieth of October marked the end of the 40 days of confinement, and a 'churching ceremony' was held in Catherine's rooms, attended by the Empress. For the first time since the birth, Catherine was allowed to see her son: 'I found him beautiful and the sight of him made my heart rejoice, but the moment the prayers were over the Empress had him carried away.' Two days later Catherine received official congratulations. The room next to her bedroom was richly furnished for the occasion, and she sat on a bed covered with pink velvet embroidered with silver as people lined up to kiss her hand.

The Court then returned to the Winter Palace, where Catherine resolved not to leave her room until she had overcome her depression. She devoted the rest of 1754 to reading and thinking. Her reading material included works by Voltaire, Montesquieu's *L'Esprit de Lois* ('The Spirit of Laws', which became a great influence on her legislative activity as Empress) and the *Annals* of the Roman historian Tacitus, as well as all the Russian books she could lay her hands on, which included 'two immense volumes of Baronius translated into Russian'. (Caesar Baronius was an Italian prelate and ecclesiastical historian who died in 1607.) Catherine managed to summon sufficient energy to attend the liturgy at Christmas, but it took all her strength: 'in church I was overcome with ague and pains in the whole body, so that back in my room I undressed and lay down on my bed, which was in fact no more than a couch which I had had placed against a blocked-up door because it seemed to me that no draught could come through it'. She had set up her bed in this small room because her usual bedroom, with windows looking out to the east and north, was so cold. But she also had the desire of someone suffering from depression to confine herself in as small a space as possible, and she spent the whole winter secluded in this narrow little room, screening herself from the draughts as best she could.

Between Christmas and Lent there were many balls given at Court and in the town, to celebrate the recent birth. 'Everyone surpassed everyone else in their desire to give dinners, suppers, balls, masquerades, firework displays and illuminations, each more splendid than the last.' Catherine attended none of them, pleading illness as her excuse. Towards the end of this carnival period, Sergei Saltykov finally returned from Sweden. During his absence Catherine had been able to receive news of him and to exchange messages via Chancellor Bestuzhev and Madame Vladislavova (whose son-in-law was the Chancellor's first clerk). She had learnt through the same channel that the intention for the immediate future was to employ Saltykov as Russian minister to Hamburg. This intelligence did nothing to improve her spirits, but even worse was the lack of urgency which Saltykov displayed on his return to fulfil a rendezvous with his erstwhile mistress. Madame Vladislavova had arranged their first meeting, but Sergei did not turn up: 'I waited for him till three o'clock in the morning, but he did not come; I underwent agonies wondering what could have prevented him.' Saltykov claimed next day that he had been waylaid by Count Roman Vorontsov (a senator and the father of Elizaveta Vorontsova) and taken to a meeting of freemasons, but Catherine, through questioning Lev Naryshkin, soon realised that he could have made the tryst, had he really wanted to. She was deeply hurt, but when he finally did come to see her, she forgave him readily enough. And it was Sergei who managed to persuade her to reappear in public, which she did on 10 February 1755, Grand Duke Peter's twenty-seventh birthday. She emerged a changed person. She had realised during the long weeks and months after little Paul's birth that no one would fight for her if she did not fight for herself. She would have to create her own destiny in Russia.

# 5

# Sir Charles Hanbury-Williams and Stanislas Poniatowski (1755–58)

*I do not know what I am saying, or what I am doing. I can truly say that it is the first time in my life that I feel like this.*
Grand Duchess Catherine to Sir Charles Hanbury-Williams

After Easter of 1755 the Grand Duke and Duchess went to Oranienbaum. Before they set off, the Empress allowed Catherine to see her baby once more: 'I had to cross all Her Majesty's apartments before reaching his room where the heat was suffocating.' The Grand Duke displayed a spectacular lack of political awareness by virtually turning Oranienbaum into an enclave of Holstein, summoning a whole detachment of Holstinian troops to take up residence there. To add insult to injury, he took to wearing his own Holstein uniform every day except official court days, despite his being Lieutenant-Colonel of the Preobrazhensky Guards, and spent his time exercising his Holstinian troops in a camp he had set up for them. Though she deplored his action, Catherine said nothing and spent her time going for long walks with the married gentlemen-in-waiting and their wives, taking care to go in the opposite direction from the army camp. Peter, Catherine claimed, had begun to exude a constant odour of alcohol and tobacco. She, on the other hand, was acquiring a reputation for intelligence and for being a willing and thoughtful listener. Even Peter referred to her as 'Madame Resourceful' and would come to her for advice, though 'once he had got it, would rush away again as fast as he had come'.

On 29 June a supper to which all the ambassadors and foreign ministers were invited took place at Oranienbaum, in celebration of the Grand Duke's name-day. Catherine was seated next to the British ambassador, Sir Charles Hanbury-Williams, whom she had first met some months earlier. She recalls the supper at Oranienbaum with fondness:'I remember that Sir Hanbury-Williams [*sic*], the British Ambassador, was my neighbour at table, and we had a pleasant and gay conversation. He was witty, well-informed, and knew the whole of Europe, so that it was not difficult to converse with him. I learnt later that he had come away from that evening as well entertained as I had been and that he had talked of me with great admiration.' On this occasion Sir Charles was accompanied for the first time by his young Polish secretary, Stanislas Poniatowski, who immediately attracted Catherine's attention as she and Sir Charles watched him dance.

Sir Charles himself was a wealthy gentleman originally from Monmouthshire. Born in 1708, he had made an advantageous marriage (to Lady Frances Coningsby, by whom he had two daughters but from whom he separated amicably after 10 years), had been a Whig Member of Parliament and was knighted in 1744. A friend of Horace Walpole, he was also well known in England as a wit and as the author of satirical and occasionally rather bawdy verse.* He was a member of the Hellfire Club, a coterie of aristocratic and establishment gentlemen reputed to indulge in wild orgies; in fact they did what such men have always done – drank, visited prostitutes and actresses, and pulled strings for one another. Sir Charles, whose principal commission as ambassador was to conclude an Anglo-Russian treaty (which he succeeded in doing, with Chancellor Bestuzhev's help, in September 1755), had brought with him to St Petersburg some goldfish, the gift of Lord Chesterfield. Despite this somewhat eccentric persona, he was a cultivated man, with a particular penchant for bringing out talented young people. He and the Grand Duchess were bound to find much of interest in one another.

Stanislas, Sir Charles's companion at the Oranienbaum supper, was the son of Count Poniatowski, who had fought alongside King Charles XII of Sweden in the war with Peter the Great (the Great Northern War, which ended in 1721). Subsequently he had become one of the

---

* See, for instance, 'A Lamentable Case submitted to the Bath Physicians', in *The Works of the Right Honourable Sir Chas. Hanbury Williams*, with notes by Horace Walpole, Earl of Orford, Edward Jeffery & Son, London, 1822, Vol.1, pp.237-8.

most loyal partisans of King Stanislas Leczinski of Poland. Stanislas's mother was Princess Constance Czartoryska, a member of one of Poland's most powerful families. Stanislas himself had toured Europe, and had first encountered Hanbury-Williams in Berlin in July 1750, when the latter was British minister there. He had also made an impression in Paris, where he had struck up a particularly close relationship with the literary and artistic hostess Madame Geoffrin, whose weekly literary salon he frequented and who liked him to call her 'Mama'. (He seems to have had something of a talent for acquiring surrogate parents.) Soon after his arrival in St Petersburg, Sir Charles had written to Stanislas, inviting him to join him as his secretary in the ambassadorial mansion near the Winter Palace. Stanislas had wasted no time, arriving in Petersburg in June.

Poniatowski's arrival within her orbit coincided with Catherine hearing unfavourable reports about Sergei Saltykov. She learnt that he had been indiscreet about their relationship at the Courts of Sweden and Dresden, and that he had also been flirting with other women on his travels. She had been half aware of Saltykov's imperfections for some time, and the presence of this attractive young Pole, with his aura of European sophistication, finally allowed her to admit that her relationship with Sergei was not worth pursuing. He had in any event now been sent to Hamburg. The gentleman of the bedchamber, Lev Naryshkin, who seemed to enjoy his role of arranging the young Court's amours, soon noticed Catherine's interest in Stanislas and took it upon himself to cultivate it. He became friendly with Poniatowski, and kept trying to persuade him to take advantage of the Grand Duchess's inclination. For some time Poniatowski refused to listen, wary of court intrigues and of the potential danger in undertaking such a dalliance. He was aware that Catherine had already had a lover, but believed that she was more interested in pursuing her own ambitions and that they would not really have anything in common. Consequently it took him about three months to be persuaded to respond to Naryshkin's hints. Catherine also claimed that it was other people who were determined to bring them together, writing in 1774: 'We took no notice of him, but good people, with their empty suspicions, forced me to notice that he existed, that his eyes were of unparalleled beauty and that he directed them (though so near-sighted he doesn't see past his nose) more often in one direction than another.'

Eventually Naryshkin wore Poniatowski down, particularly after Catherine exchanged a few words with him at Court. Soon afterwards he sent her a note, to which Naryshkin brought him a reply on the following day. Then, as Stanislas put it in his memoirs (for he was another 'scribbler'), 'I forgot that Siberia existed.' One evening, a few days later, Naryshkin brought Stanislas to Catherine's apartments, without having given her much warning; as Peter was expected in about a quarter of an hour, she had no alternative but to take Stanislas into her private rooms. He describes what she was like at this time:

> She was 25 years old [actually she was 26]. She had only just recovered from giving birth for the first time. She was at that peak of beauty which most beautiful women experience. She was of a vivid colouring, with dark hair and a dazzlingly white complexion, large, slightly prominent and very expressive blue eyes, very long dark eyelashes, a Grecian nose, a mouth which seemed to invite kisses, perfect hands and arms, and a narrow waist. On the tall side, she moved with extreme agility yet at the same time with great nobility. She had a pleasant voice and a laugh as merry as her disposition.

Poniatowski also commented on her ability to switch with rapidity and ease between different occupations, able one moment to be indulging in a childish game and the next to be all concentration over some arithmetical problem. She was fearless, affectionate, and had a talent for identifying a person's weak spot. At this first rendezvous she was wearing a dress of white satin, with some fine lace intertwined with pink ribbon around her neck.

Stanislas also wrote a description of himself, at Catherine's request, in which he said he would prefer to be a little taller than he was, to have nicer legs, a less aquiline nose, a smaller mouth, and better eyesight and teeth. He thought he nevertheless had a noble and expressive face, and that he bore himself with distinction. He was aware that he had benefited from an excellent education, knew how to conduct himself in conversation, was enamoured of the arts and loved reading. He was perceptive, quick to recognise other people's hypocrisy and sometimes too hasty to point out their shortcomings. He considered himself to be sensitive, with a tendency to melancholy, as well as ambitious and desirous of serving his country. Twenty-two years old and still a virgin, he was ready to throw himself into a love affair with passion, as was Catherine.

In the autumn, the Grand Duke and Duchess had returned to the

Summer Palace, and the Holstein troops had been sent back home. With the onset of winter the whole Court moved to a temporary Winter Palace, constructed by Rastrelli out of timber in the space of a few months, while at the same time he started work on the building of the new permanent Winter Palace on the site of the old one. Elizabeth had decided she could stand the discomfort of the draughty and much modified old building no longer, and Rastrelli's plans for the new palace had been approved and the foundation stone laid in 1754. Rastrelli was to start again, building an almost entirely new and grander palace; although it was rebuilt after the great fire of 1837, in appearance this is essentially the Winter Palace we see today. It took a year to clear the buildings which were already on the site. The temporary wooden palace, into which the Court now moved and where it was to be accommodated for the next six years, was located on a previously empty site which ran from the Malaya Morskaya to the Bolshaya Morskaya streets, on a corner of the Great Perspective Road. On part of this site Elizabeth had a theatre constructed, which was the first to be devoted to Russian comedy and tragedy.

Catherine's apartments in the temporary palace were admirably suited for a clandestine affair. She had plenty of space and did not have to suffer the proximity of the Grand Duke. They had each been allotted four large antechambers and two inner rooms with an alcove – and now that a child had been produced, they were no longer obliged to sleep together every night. Peter used his greater degree of freedom to indulge in a favourite pastime, combining his love of all things military with his earlier interest in puppet theatres:

> In those days, and long afterwards, the Grand Duke's principal play-thing in town was an enormous number of model soldiers, made of wood, lead, starch, and wax, which he lined up on narrow tables occupying the whole room – one could barely make one's way between them. He nailed narrow strips of wire across the tables with string attached to them. When the strings were pulled, the strips of wire made a noise which, according to him, was just like the rolling fire of guns. He celebrated all the Court holidays with great regularity, making these troops produce a rolling fire: besides that, every day there was the Changing of the Guard – that is, the dolls which were supposed to be on duty replaced others which were removed from the tables. He himself attended this ceremony

in uniform – top boots and spurs, gorget and sash – and those of his servants who were admitted to these wondrous exercises were obliged to dress in the same way.

Around this time Catherine thought she might again be pregnant, and she had a blood-letting. All she gave birth to, however, were four wisdom teeth.

Every week throughout that winter the Grand Duke organised a concert on Tuesday and a ball on Thursday, attended by the ladies- and gentlemen-in-waiting of the young Court with their respective spouses. The concerts would start at four o'clock in the afternoon and go on until nine. The performers included Italian, Russian and German instrumentalists and singers who were in the personal service and pay of the Grand Duke – such as two German sopranos, one of whom, Eleonora, was a particular favourite of Peter's and regularly used to have supper with him in his apartments – as well as members of the imperial court choir. The Grand Duke himself always played first violin throughout the performance, and he also persuaded a number of court officials and Guards officers to play various instruments. The total number of performers at each concert averaged between 40 and 50.

Lev Naryshkin, who got on well with both Grand Duke and Duchess, was a regular attender at the entertainments of the young Court as well as being in the habit of paying more personal visits. When he arrived at Catherine's rooms he would often stand outside the door and miaow, until she responded in kind, and then he would enter. He continued to facilitate encounters between Catherine and Stanislas Poniatowski, the most daring of these involving night-time excursions when Catherine would dress as a man and, at the appointed signal, leave the palace with Naryshkin to go and spend a few hours with a small circle of friends, including Poniatowski, at the house where Lev lived with his brother and sister-in-law. Given that Catherine was not supposed to go out at all without the Empress's permission, embarking on this kind of adventure posed a considerable risk. The first such excursion took place on 17 December 1755 and was followed a few days later by a reciprocal visit, the nocturnal visitors smuggling themselves into the palace and then into Catherine's apartments. The secret meetings among this group of friends became frequent, signs often being exchanged at the theatre to let one another know where to gather that night. On two occasions the carriage arrangements failed and Catherine had to walk home, but somehow she managed never to be discovered.

During that winter the Empress's health deteriorated. At first people thought her trouble might be merely menopausal, but no one was sure. The Shuvalovs began to court the Grand Duke in case his aunt was near to death. As Catherine portrayed it, 'There was a lot of whispering among courtiers about Her Imperial Majesty's illness, which was considered to be more serious than had at first appeared; some called it hysteria, others spoke of fainting fits, convulsions, or nervous disorder.' It was probably epilepsy, which left her tired and weak for several days after the fits.

At the head of the Shuvalov clan was Ivan's cousin, Peter Shuvalov, who dispensed advice and favours from his grand Petersburg residence. He also held the monopoly for salt, tobacco and tunny-fish, while his brother Alexander, the head of the Secret Chancery, held that for champagne. The brothers, who already enjoyed commercial links with France, wished to conclude a Russo-French alliance, to aid them in marketing Russian tobacco in France.

In 1756 Antonio Rinaldi was appointed architect to the Grand Duke's Court and commissioned to build at Oranienbaum. He made a sort of miniature fortress for Peter, with five bastions and twelve cannon, to the south-east of the Great Palace. Inside the bastion he constructed a small stone palace for Peter himself, which was known as the Peterstadt, and a barracks for the Holstein troops whom Peter brought back for the summer. Catherine took up horse-riding again, having lessons every morning except Sunday in a space she had had cleared in her private garden as a manège. Peter continued to organise concerts. In 1750 a small stage had been constructed in the great hall of the Oranienbaum palace, alongside the library and picture gallery, where for the most part Italian *intermedi* (musical entertainments written to be inserted between the acts of plays) were performed. In 1756 this stage was transformed into a large opera theatre, built by Rinaldi in the latest Italian style. From now on a new opera was staged here every summer, composed by the Grand Duke's *maestro di capella* Vincenzo Manfredini.

By the summer of 1756 Catherine was deeply involved with Stanislas Poniatowski, both physically and emotionally. Theirs was a sentimental relationship, in keeping both with their youth and with the sensibility of the age in which they lived. In later life Catherine found Poniatowski's breed of sentimentality rather cloying, but for now she abandoned herself to this romantic attachment. This was the first time in her life she had found a man fully responsive to both her sexual and emotional needs, and she was prepared to take many risks in order to spend as much time with him as she could. Though only a small circle of friends knew about the affair, there was always the danger that it could become more public knowledge – a small dog belonging to Catherine threatened to give the game away, for instance, when it greeted Stanislas ecstatically in the presence of a third party – and Poniatowski's position as Sir Charles Hanbury-Williams' secretary offered him no diplomatic protection. It was in the hope of securing an official diplomatic position that would afford him such protection and guarantee a long stay in Russia that Stanislas went to Poland that summer – for what he, Catherine and Sir Charles all hoped would be a short absence.

On his departure, the Empress made him a gift of a snuff-box worth 4,000 roubles, which she sent after him by courier to Riga. She had also written to Augustus III, the King of Poland, commending Stanislas's conduct in St Petersburg. But despite Elizabeth's ignorance of his relationship with the Grand Duchess, Stanislas was already the subject of gossip at Court. A story went the rounds that he had been panic-stricken on being pursued by the Empress's courier, imagining he was about to be arrested either for his relationship with Catherine or for his meddling in foreign affairs at this tense time for the powers of Europe (what became known as the Seven Years' War was about to begin). But Stanislas denied having experienced any such fear.

His desire to persuade Augustus III to appoint him as a diplomatic envoy and to return swiftly to Russia was frustrated by international events. The Prussian invasion of Saxony took place in August 1756, and by the autumn of that year Augustus III (who was also the Elector of Saxony) was cut off from Poland, and the Sejm (the Polish parliament) could not sit. Stanislas was stranded in Warsaw. Austria, followed by France, went to Saxony's aid while Russia, who had a 10-year-old defensive treaty with Austria but was not bound by it to join in, initially did nothing.

To console herself during Poniatowski's absence, and to do whatever she could to get him back, Catherine entered into an almost daily correspondence (conducted in French) with Sir Charles Hanbury-Williams. He had been aware of, and had indeed encouraged, the relationship between Catherine and Stanislas from the start (perhaps seeing it as one means to foster good relations between England and the young Court). Catherine wanted to be able to unburden her heart to someone who sympathised with the affair and who esteemed Stanislas as highly as she did herself. She also felt in need of the advice of an older man and wise counsellor, particularly at a time when she was seriously contemplating her future role in the governance of Russia. Through this correspondence Sir Charles played an important part in Catherine's political education. He was also the recipient of her first attempt at autobiography, as she wrote for him a 40-page memoir detailing her difficult life in Russia and her unhappy marriage.

Always conscious of the possibility of interception, even when they used trusted intermediaries to convey their letters back and forth, Catherine and Sir Charles used disguised names for the people they wrote about and for one another. Sir Charles addressed Catherine as 'Monsieur', they referred to Poniatowski as 'our absent friend' and to the Empress as 'a certain person'. Likewise, in the letters which passed between Sir Charles and Poniatowski, Catherine was referred to as 'the Countess of Essex' (actually the title of one of Sir Charles's daughters) or as 'Collette'. Poniatowski himself was designated by the name of the card game 'L'Ombre' or by 'Le Cordon Bleu'. Ivan Shuvalov was known as 'Accajou' ('Mahogany'), the Empress as 'La Prudence', Chancellor Bestuzhev as 'Le Patron' ('the Boss') and Sir Charles as 'La Sagesse' ('Wisdom'). Poniatowski in particular seems to have enjoyed writing in this sort of code; he suggested they might also rename Petersburg Paris, Peterhof Versailles and Oranienbaum Choisi, and he referred to money as 'tea'.

The health of 'a certain person' is a constant subject of speculation in the correspondence between Sir Charles and Catherine. The latter described Elizabeth's problem as 'water in the lower part of her belly', asserting that she had even tried witchcraft to cure it. It did not surprise Catherine as much as it did Sir Charles that the Empress could believe simultaneously in the Orthodox faith and in witchcraft. After 12 years at the Russian Court she had become used to such apparent contra-dictions, remarking that 'to disordered minds the same thing can appear as black and white at the same time'. Such derogatory comments about the Empress in a letter to a British diplomat would have been enough to land the Grand Duchess in serious trouble if discovered, to say nothing of the speculation about the Empress's death and whether one day soon Catherine would 'wear the crown'. (Some anticipated, if vague, form of power-sharing between Catherine and Peter is an underlying assumption running through the correspondence.) Sir Charles seems to have viewed the Empress's illness almost with relish, writing in reply: 'There is short shrift for those who have water in the belly; and I know at first hand that the cough is returned, with great shortness of breath' and continuing: 'I implore you to tell me everything you hear about the health of a certain person. There is nothing in the world which interests me so much.' The shortness of breath meant that the Empress could not manage to walk as far as the chapel in the Winter Palace from her apartments. A few days later Sir Charles is quite clearly longing for the Empress to die or, more accurately, for Catherine (and presumably Peter) to succeed her: 'My fondest hopes are founded upon the great event which will soon occur, notwithstanding the Devil, the witches and the witchcrafts.'

In Catherine's letter to Sir Charles of 9 August, she hints that Elizabeth may have been considering cutting Grand Duke Peter out of the succession and naming instead the little Paul Petrovich as her heir. Sir Charles's letter of 18 August confirms that Elizabeth was dissatisfied with Peter, though he opines that this is more to do with the influence of other people than with her own feelings: 'I am told that the Empress has always a soft spot for the Grand-Duke; but if she never sees him, if she is never told his Imperial Highness's real words and real actions, if his enemies alone have the ear of Her Majesty and always speak against him and you, the same story told and re-told time after time will have its effect, and will stifle the tenderest feelings.' Catherine was expecting Elizabeth to die at any moment, and she seemed ready to act to ensure that she and Peter took the throne together, with her supporters, including the all-important Guards officers, in place: 'Afterwards [i.e. after Elizabeth's death], within two or three hours, every dirty trick will certainly be played; yet whether they wish to exclude us or tie our hands, they will not be able to do it alone. There are but few officers who are not in the secret; and, provided that my arrangements for being informed in time do not fail, and that even only one among eight people gives me warning, it will be my fault if they gain the upper hand.'

It is clear from such comments that Catherine was running a comprehensive system of spies at and around the Court. She was playing for high stakes and knew it: 'I shall either perish or reign.' Sir Charles had recognised an innate power in her and was determined to nourish it. 'You are born to command and reign,' he wrote, 'and old age alone will kill you.' His support was not only in words; he had also made arrangements for Catherine to receive funding from the Court of St James: 'the forty thousand roubles are at your disposal and await your orders'. This money had been made available on the direct authority of King George II, who had conveyed to Sir Charles 'how pleased he is with the many marks of friendship which he receives from her Imperial Highness; and you are to assure her, in the name of the King, that he is ready, and will always be ready, to give her marks of his complete confidence and affection'. Catherine conveyed her thanks gracefully, but she wanted it to be quite clear that she was acting in the interests of Russia rather than for her own personal gain. It was very important to all concerned that no one outside the very small circle of conspirators should know that this money had been procured for Catherine by Sir Charles. Consequently certain procedures had to be followed, as Sir Charles instructed Catherine: 'First, I shall get the money from Wolff [the British consul]. I shall settle his account, and after that I shall send word to you how much remains in my hands; and you will draw that sum by [Naryshkin] as you require it, from time to time, for my own security demands that no one should ever be able to prove that I procured you money.' Catherine was also nervous about the subvention being discovered: 'I must tell you that I felt worried at writing the bond for the money, on account of the risk of it falling into strange hands: try to keep it in your possession.'

Sir Charles gave Catherine much useful advice – for instance, 'to weigh things well and carefully before coming to any important decision. But once you have made it, never change.' He promised always to tell her the truth and not succumb to flattery: 'I shall never be troublesome to you, I shall faithfully guard your secrets, I shall oppose everything which you propose that I consider contrary to your interests. I shall give you the best advice I can. I shall tell you nothing but the truth. I shall help you in all that in my power lies, and never shall I flatter you.' Sir Charles was the first man Catherine had encountered since parting with her father in 1744 whom she could trust to tell her the unbiased truth as he saw it, and this made him immeasurably valuable to her, both as an ally and an educator. Nevertheless, from the outset of the correspondence, he reveals a sentimental attachment to the Grand Duchess: 'There must always be comfort for me in your letters, for I feel a delight at opening them even before I read them.'

Sir Charles also passed messages between Catherine and Stanislas, both forwarding letters and conveying their feelings toward one another in his own letters: 'For six years I have been, so to speak, guardian and instructor to our friend, and he is certainly under some obligations to me, but none which can compare to the service which I shall now render him, when I tell him the truth of truths, that you love him.'

On 18 August, when the Empress's health seemed to have taken another turn for the worse, Catherine spells out in detail to Sir Charles what her plans are. She writes that, on being informed of the Empress's death, she will go straight to collect her son and, if possible, leave him with the Grand Master of the Hunt (Count Alexei Razumovsky) and the men under his command. If she cannot find Razumovsky, she will take the child to her own room. Then she will send a trusted messenger to warn five Guards officers she has lined up ready, who each have 50 soldiers they will mobilise in her support, to act as a reserve 'in the case of any difficulty'. (At this point she confirms that she is acting in concert with the Grand Duke, though clearly not expecting him to be able to take the initiative; she appears to consider that the best course of action is for Peter to stay with the infant Paul.) She will then order Chancellor Bestuzhev and Generals Apraksin and Lieven to attend on her; meanwhile she will enter the room where Elizabeth is lying and instruct the captain of the guard to take the oath of allegiance to her. If any trouble ensues, she intends to have the Shuvalovs arrested. She will also dispense bribes liberally wherever necessary (it was partly for this purpose that she needed money from England).

In presenting her plan to Sir Charles, she betrays a sneaking suspicion that it may all sound too good to be true. She is evidently very excited:

> The extreme hatred for the [Shuvalovs], which all those who do not belong to them feel, the justice of my cause, as well as the easy sequence of everything which runs its natural course, makes me hope for a happy issue. You must tell me, and that clearly; it is for that reason also why I place it before you. The novelty of the whole thing, and the haste with which I communicate it to you, have necessitated a very great effort of imagination on my part.

Nevertheless Sir Charles approved her plan in principle, though he also expressed concern that she should guard against difficulties that might occur before Elizabeth's death rather than worry solely about what might happen after it. He urged Catherine to make more effort to improve relations with the Shuvalovs, or at least to prevent them exercising so much influence over Bestuzhev and Apraksin. 'While your friends remain under the rod of your enemies, I venture to say that they are useless to you, to say the very least.'

Meanwhile Chancellor Bestuzhev was also angling for money from England. In his letter of 23 August, Sir Charles told Catherine that

Bestuzhev had requested him some time ago to see if a 'large pension' could be arranged for him, as he could not afford to live according to his rank on the salary he was paid in St Petersburg (only 7,000 roubles a year, according to him). The quid pro quo would be that he would support English interests at the Russian Court. In this letter, Sir Charles portrays himself as something akin to the knight in a chivalric romance paying homage to his idealised lady: 'My heart, my life, and my soul are all yours. I look upon you in everything as a being superior to me. I adore you, and this adoration goes so far that I feel certain that I can never be worthy of your esteem.' He has a fantasy that one day when Catherine is Empress he will return to Russia as English minister, to 'live a great deal with you as a faithful servant and a humble friend'. He confesses: 'I should like the right to come and go and to profit by your leisure hours: for I shall always love Catherine better than the Empress.' That Catherine had a powerful ability to charm cannot be denied. She also had a strong sense of her own destiny: 'I would like to feel fear, but I cannot; the invisible hand which has led me for thirteen years along a very rough road will never allow me to give way, of that I am very firmly and perhaps foolishly convinced.'

On 31 August Catherine took the step of writing to Chancellor Bestuzhev to tell him that she wanted Poniatowski back in Petersburg. Sir Charles had primed the Chancellor and persuaded him to promise his assistance, having realised that only he could bring about Poniatowski's return, by asking the first minister of Poland and Saxony, Count Heinrich von Brühl, to arrange it for him as a personal favour. Sir Charles had also informed Bestuzhev of the nature of the relationship between Poniatowski and Catherine, the latter believing that the Chancellor would be prepared to help her and could be entrusted with the secret. (It was Poniatowski's opinion that Bestuzhev was half in love with Catherine himself, and also that he had tried to supply her with at least one lover of his own choosing.) On the same day Catherine complained to Sir Charles that the Grand Duke was in her apartments rather more often than usual, disturbing her privacy, on account of his 'new penchant for a Greek girl, who is in my service'. She laments the curtailment of her freedom this causes her, but the days of jealousy are now past.

On 4 September Catherine reported to Sir Charles that the Empress – who was still very much alive – was angry with the Grand Duke. She had complained that his views 'conflicted with all that was being done here and . . . were anti-Russian, and . . . she said that it was those cursed Holsteiners who inspired him with these sentiments. She said all this to the Chancellor herself on Sunday, and never went out at all, although fully dressed, as she was so cross.' Catherine also commented that, thanks partly to the advice he was himself receiving from Sir Charles, the Grand Duke was making every effort to change his anti-Russian opinions, and that he had become 'very reasonable about many things'. Two days later she reported with amusement, if somewhat unkindly, on the Empress's latest fanciful idea:

> Here is something to raise a laugh. The person, on whose cough you were counting yesterday, does nothing but talk in the privacy of her chamber of going to command the army in person. One of her women said to her the other day, 'How can you? You are a woman.' She replied, 'My father went; do you believe that I am stupider than he?' The other answered, 'He was a man, and you are not.' She began to get angry, and persisted in saying that she wished to go to the war herself. They add that the good lady, far from being able to perform such a feat, cannot climb her own stairs without losing her breath.

Bestuzhev had now definitively fallen prey to Catherine's charms, and was jealous of both Sir Charles and Poniatowski because they shared her favour. There was more to this than simple jealousy, however: what power Bestuzhev was able to exercise over the Shuvalovs was a result of the influence he was believed to have over Catherine, the probable future Empress. It was therefore important to him that he, rather than Sir Charles or Poniatowski, continue to be seen as the person most closely allied to her. Bestuzhev's complaints on this score had the effect of making Catherine even more determined to press him to bring about Poniatowski's return. She was in considerable distress by now, longing for Stanislas to the point of becoming ill, and not at all sure of success. Sir Charles was also putting pressure on Bestuzhev, making it clear he would receive no further financial assistance from him and would not get his pension from the English Court if he failed to deliver on this matter. He urged Catherine to keep up the pressure too: 'He can do what you ask, if he pleases.' As the situation became ever muddier and more fraught with danger, however – because of suspicions being raised in the Empress's mind about Poniatowski's trustworthiness – Sir Charles warned Catherine: 'you will make me speak and act in everything that you wish; but when I see troubles for you and the fact that passion no longer listens to reason, I shall oppose your desires with a firmness equal to the eagerness which I shall always feel in obeying you in all that can be of use, or even of pleasure, to you'.

But Catherine was desperate. As she wrote to Sir Charles on 11 September, 'I do not know what I am saying, or what I am doing. I can truly say that it is the first time in my life that I feel like this.' Sir Charles replied in a far from ambassadorial manner:

> One word from you is my most sacred law. When I think of you, my duty to my Master [i.e. King George] grows less. I am ready to carry out all the orders you can give me, provided they are not dangerous to you; for in that case I shall disobey with a firmness equal to the obedience with which I would carry out all others . . .
>
> I am yours, yours only, and all yours. I esteem you, I honour you, I adore you. I shall die convinced that there was never a sweetness, a soundness, a face, a heart, a head, to equal yours.

Friday 20 September was Paul Petrovich's second birthday, and a supper was given at Court in the evening, which both the Grand Duchess and Sir Charles attended. On the 22nd Sir Charles was unwell with a severe headache which prevented him attending Court as would have been usual on a Sunday evening; the indisposition lasted for several days. His position as British ambassador was becoming increasingly difficult, as relations between Russia and England deteriorated. As Sir Charles explained in a letter he dictated to Catherine:

> As soon as it is known in London that Russia has acceded to the Treaty of Versailles [by which her allies agreed to give financial and military assistance to Austria in the war against Prussia], my country will look upon the Empress as worse than an enemy, as a treacherous friend, who has betrayed us by prevarications, false assurances and delays, and who, after ratifying a treaty [i.e. the Anglo-Russian treaty, agreed during the previous year] guaranteed by her own signature and under the Great Seal of her Empire, has construed it in a manner that nullifies all the promised defence.

Catherine was nevertheless buoyed up by now as two days earlier she had been able to send Sir Charles a copy of a letter written by Bestuzhev to Count von Brühl, in which he recommended Poniatowski as an ideal envoy extraordinary for Poland.

On 15 October the Empress was ill again, suffering a fit during which 'the fingers of her hands were bent back, her feet and arms were cold as ice, her eyes sightless'. She recovered after being bled. The next day she suffered three attacks of giddiness, and was terrified of going blind. Catherine received all the latest reports from her well-placed spies: 'My surgeon, a man of great experience and good sense, expects an apoplectic seizure, which would certainly carry her off.' It was Sir Charles's opinion that if the Empress were to die now, the Grand Duke and Duchess would be safe: 'Everyone will bow down, everyone will prostrate themselves before you, and you will ascend the throne with the same ease as I sit down to a meal.'

At the end of October, Stanislas Poniatowski was nominated envoy extraordinary to the Court of St Petersburg by Augustus III and shortly afterwards invested as a knight of the White Eagle. But Poniatowski's mother, a devout Roman Catholic, whom Stanislas revered, was deeply worried about her son returning to St Petersburg and to an adulterous – and dangerous – relationship. Stanislas described the scene to Catherine with characteristic melodrama: 'she wrung my hand and went away, leaving me in the most horrible predicament that I have ever had to face in my life. I dashed my head against the walls, shrieking rather than weeping. I never closed my eyes all night. I looked like a corpse the next day.'

The Empress continued to frustrate Sir Charles's and Catherine's plans by staying alive. She 'went to shoot blackcocks the day before yesterday, but was taken so ill that they despaired of bringing her round. She came back, and is better.' Sir Charles himself was ill again on 10 November, having to dictate his letter to Catherine because of a fever and severe headache. He warned her against trusting Bestuzhev, whom he suspected might try to get rid of both Poniatowski and himself in the near future. Meanwhile Bestuzhev was congratulating himself on being firmly in the Grand Duchess's good graces for having managed to deliver Poniatowski, who was to be accommodated in a house opposite the church of Our Lady of Kazan.

News of the Empress's state of health had travelled all round the Courts of Europe, and Sir Charles had been requested by the British minister at the Court of Frederick the Great in Berlin to let him know the Grand Duke's and Duchess's attitudes towards Prussia. Catherine provided him with a reply in which she played down the likely extent of her own future influence but which also committed her to nothing vis-à-vis Prussia and articulated her guiding principle in foreign affairs: 'The Grand-Duke, from his military inclinations, is Prussian to the death; and this goes so far that it has become a prejudice and is engrained in his disposition. It is almost useless to speak of the Grand-Duchess, since it is not settled that she will then have much authority; but we will satisfy your curiosity. She will never advise anything which she does not believe will contribute to the greatness and interests of Russia.' Sir Charles himself – still in very poor health, and not managing to keep down any solids – was now preparing to ask for his recall, aware that there was nothing further he could do to restore good relations between Russia and England (at least until the Empress died). Despite what she had written to him, Catherine suffered from no real doubt as to her future influence, writing on 23 November: 'I promise you that I shall firmly rebuild all that they are now pulling down, if the decease ever gives me the opportunity.' Two days later she tried to cheer Sir Charles by giving details of how ill Elizabeth really was:

> The Empress – for it is very right that I should speak to you of her in a manner which will comfort you a little, is in a pitiable state. She went out yesterday evening just as dinner was served. She came to the Grand-Duke and me, and said, 'I am feeling well, and have no more cough nor shortness of breath, but I cannot put on a tight dress on account of great pains in my stomach.' As she had previously spoken of oysters, I said, 'Madame, that pain may come from having eaten too many.' 'No,' she said, 'I have had it for a year and a half, and it never leaves me.' I beg you to realize that she could not speak three consecutive words without coughing and without being out of breath, and that, unless she thought us both deaf and blind, she could not tell us that she was free from those complaints. As this made me smile, I tell it to you. It is comfort for those who have no other comfort.

On 26 November Sir Charles expressed the hope that one day Catherine would make Stanislas Poniatowski King of Poland. He also informed her that the Shuvalovs entertained a very low opinion of Grand Duke Peter; they claimed that he was drunk every day and predicted that he would die an early death. Sir Charles, however, seems to have respected the Grand Duke, despite his appreciation of Catherine's greater talents: 'The kindness which his Imperial Highness has always shown me since my arrival at this court, calls for infinite gratitude from me, and I shall never fail to prove it to him when the opportunity arises.' (He appears not to have counted facilitating the Grand Duke's wife's affair with another man as ingratitude.) He was also worried about what might befall Poniatowski on his journey to Russia (as both Prussia and France were keen to prevent this posting, which they feared would militate against their own interests). He advised Catherine on how she should behave once Stanislas was safely back:

> I am too much afraid of the tricks and treachery of nearly everyone here not to beg of you on my knees to be extremely careful when Poniatowski arrives, for I cannot divest myself of the idea that the Chancellor is resolved to keep you entirely in his own hands, and he will allow no one to share your favour with him . . .
>
> Be very circumspect, therefore, Monsieur, in your interviews with Poniatowski, and above all see him at his own house or at that of a third person, but *never at your own*. If you go out at night and are recognized, it will only make the world talk and create suspicion. But, if he were caught entering your house, the game is up, and his fate is sealed beyond repair.

Poniatowski had finally set out to return to St Petersburg on 2 December. There was indeed an attempt to ambush him en route, but, having been warned in time, he managed to avoid his would-be captors. On 21 December Catherine wrote impatiently, 'He certainly keeps us waiting for him; he is said to be at Riga', but by the 24th he had arrived. By 28 December she had seen him again and was able to report that he was 'marvellously well'.

Poniatowski's primary mission in St Petersburg was to negotiate Russian military assistance for Augustus III against Prussia. This put him politically at odds with his friend Sir Charles, as England had been an informal ally of Prussia since signing the Convention of Westminster in January 1756. Consequently he had to appear to be keeping his distance from the ambassador, though the two men communicated via Catherine and sometimes in person. On the last day of 1756 Poniatowski had an audience with the Empress at which he made an eloquent speech about the Prussian 'Hydra'. But other diplomats persisted in regarding him as a double agent in the service of the English.

Russia officially joined in the war in January 1757 by acceding to the Franco-Austro-Saxon alliance against Prussia. This made Sir Charles's position even more impossible, and he left St Petersburg to seek some respite in the country. On 22 March Catherine wrote to warn him that a secret order had been issued to open all the letters of foreign ministers, and that the order was aimed particularly at him. She also said that she was studying English for three hours every day (she never in fact learnt to speak English, or even to understand or read it very well). Sir Charles confirmed that he would be on his guard, though in fact he believed his mail had been opened routinely for at least the past year. He also wondered if Catherine was pregnant: 'The wish is very near my heart, Monsieur, that your son should have a brother.' Her reply was sent the next day: 'I am marvellously well, and have good hopes! I send you this news, because you wish me well.'

At the beginning of spring, the Grand Duke and Duchess went as usual to Oranienbaum. In April (the 21st was her twenty-eighth birthday), Catherine wrote to ask Sir Charles to praise her qualities to the Grand Duke, 'advising him, as his true and faithful friend, to follow the beneficial advice of that excellent head [i.e. her own]'. She spent her time at Oranienbaum that year planning and planting in her garden, walking, riding, driving in a dogcart, and reading, while the Grand Duke occupied himself with his Holstein troops and in giving parties and masquerades. In May Catherine asked Sir Charles to arrange a further secret loan for her. She used some of this money to stage a masked feast and entertainment in her garden on 17 July (by which time she was about five months pregnant), with the aim of improving the Grand Duke's bad temper. It was a highly elaborate affair, as Catherine describes:

> On a site some way away from the wood, I . . . had a great chariot built by Antonio Rinaldi, the Italian architect who worked for me at the time: an orchestra of sixty men could be placed on it, musicians as well as singers. The Court Italian poet composed the verses and the choirmaster Araja the music. In the garden, a wide alley was decorated with lamps and curtained off from where the table was laid for supper.

The weather was perfect. After the first course the curtain concealing the alley was raised to reveal the orchestra arriving on Rinaldi's chariot, pulled by about 20 garlanded oxen and accompanied by dancers. Everyone stood to watch the spectacle and listen to the music, and then resumed their seats for the second course. This was followed by a kind of tombola, free lottery tickets being distributed for prizes of

china, flowers, ribbons, fans, combs, purses, gloves, sashes and 'other frippery'. After dessert there was dancing until six o'clock in the morning.
The whole event was judged a great success; 'there was not a breath
of intrigue or malice to interfere with my fête and His Highness and
everybody else were ecstatic about it and kept complimenting the
Grand Duchess on her feast'. The event cost Catherine the equivalent
of almost half her annual income.

On 19 August there was a victory for the Russian forces at Gross-
Jägersdorf. On the day of the Te Deum to celebrate the victory, Catherine
gave another feast in her garden for the Grand Duke and all the
members of the Court at Oranienbaum, and also had an ox roasted
for the labourers and masons. Peter enjoyed the party, during what was
a difficult time for him, as his natural sympathies lay with Frederick
the Great and the Prussians.

The situation now began to get very complicated for Catherine and
her friends. The first signs of trouble were connected to Marshal (previously General) Apraksin's decision not to capitalise on his victory at
Gross-Jägersdorf by pursuing the Prussians. In her memoirs Catherine
supports the theory that the Marshal, in anticipation of the Empress's
death and a subsequent change of policy, had used the pretext of shortness of supplies to justify a retreat. At the time, however, she herself
was suspected by the Empress's supporters of plotting, together with
Bestuzhev, to undermine the Russian victory. Poniatowski was also
under suspicion of having subverted both Catherine and Bestuzhev,
out of secret loyalty to the English. Catherine admits that she was
indeed in correspondence with Apraksin, but claims that she only wrote
to him at Bestuzhev's behest to warn him of the rumours circulating
about him in Petersburg and to urge him to advance: 'I explained that
his friends found it difficult to justify the speed of his withdrawal and
begged him to resume his advance and execute the Government's
orders. Chancellor Bestujev sent this letter on to him. Marshal Apraxine
did not reply to me.'

On 8 September the Empress suffered an epileptic fit at Tsarskoye
Selo, outside the parish church where she had gone to attend the liturgy
for the Feast of the Nativity of the Virgin. A crowd of people surrounded
her while she lay unconscious, which meant that her illness could no
longer be kept hidden behind court doors. She was bled where she
was, then borne away on a sofa. Shortly afterwards she regained
consciousness, but was not able to speak properly (having bitten her
tongue during the fit) or recognise where she was.

By the end of September the Grand Duke was finding Catherine's very obvious pregnancy a source of irritation. One day he declared in the presence of Lev Naryshkin and several others: 'Heaven alone knows how it is that my wife becomes pregnant. I have no idea whether this child is mine and whether I ought to recognize it as such.' Naryshkin came rushing to Catherine to report this remark. Alarmed, but quick-thinking as always, she decided to call the Grand Duke's bluff, assuming he would not wish his performance in the marital bed to be a matter for public discussion. She instructed Naryshkin to ask Peter to swear on his honour that he had not slept with her, and tell him that, if he were prepared to swear such an oath, Naryshkin would at once inform Alexander Shuvalov in his official capacity as head of the Secret Chancery. Naryshkin did as he was told and Peter, whose remark had been uttered out of bad temper and resentment rather than a desire to cause Catherine harm, replied: 'Go to hell. Do not talk to me any more about it.' (Both Peter's remark and Catherine's response suggest that they were still sleeping together occasionally, despite the fact that they were also both having affairs with other people; Catherine may indeed have contrived to sleep with Peter on realising she was pregnant. There is thus a remote possibility that Catherine was carrying Peter's child, though it has generally been assumed that the child was Poniatowski's, even though he gives no indication of this in his memoirs.)

Sir Charles Hanbury-Williams left Russia in October.* In the same month Poniatowski received notification that he was to leave Petersburg. This, if anything, increased the frequency of his trysts with Catherine, as they both felt they had to make the most of whatever time they had left.

On 8 November the Empress asked Poniatowski in public why he had been recalled. He replied that his Court was acting under pressure from the French. Only a few days later, French prestige collapsed with the news of the defeat of their armies by Frederick the Great at Rossbach. The pressure for Poniatowski to leave ceased for the time being. Catherine persuaded Bestuzhev to protest about the recall to von Brühl, who then instructed Poniatowski to delay asking for his farewell audience.

Catherine's daughter Anna Petrovna was born on 29 November 1757 between 10 and 11 o'clock in the evening. The Empress decided she

---

* A little over two years later he was to take his own life. The symptoms which had begun to plague him during those last months in Russia turned out to be an early indication of mental derangement.

should be named after her deceased elder sister, Peter's mother. Whatever doubts he had expressed about the child's paternity, Peter seemed pleased: 'he arranged great celebrations in his rooms and ordered that festivities should also be arranged in Holstein and accepted all the congratulations with every sign of satisfaction'. The same procedure was followed as after Paul Petrovich's birth: the child was removed to be cared for by the Empress and her servants; she was baptised on the sixth day after her birth; the Empress made presents of money (60,000 roubles apiece) to both Grand Duke and Duchess, and there were celebrations at Court and in the town after the baptism. The treatment meted out to Catherine was also the same as before, but this time she was prepared. She decided to turn her confinement to her own and her friends' advantage by arranging her bedroom in such a way as to screen off a private alcove containing a sofa, mirrors, small tables and chairs. The alcove could be accessed through a private door leading from an antechamber which served as a storeroom. If other people came in, all they would be able to see was the large screen. If they asked what was behind it, Catherine would reply, 'the commode'. Poniatowski would sneak in disguised as a court musician, in cloak and blond wig. Leaving his carriage or sleigh some distance away, he would enter the palace via a private staircase, the guard (presumably having been warned of his arrival beforehand) not challenging him. After her confinement had ended, the Grand Duchess herself would sometimes leave by the same staircase at a pre-arranged time, dressed as a man, and Poniatowski would take her in his carriage to his own house.

One day when he was waiting for her, an officer of the guard chanced upon his sleigh and began to question him. Poniatowski pretended to be asleep, as though he were a lackey waiting for his master. He broke out into a sweat despite the freezing temperature, but fortunately the soldier left before the Grand Duchess arrived. That same night the sleigh hit a stone with such force that Catherine was thrown out. She was briefly unconscious, and Stanislas was terrified that she might be dead. Then, on her return (having actually sustained only bruises), she discovered that her wardrobe girl had locked the door of her room – which she normally re-entered from the private staircase – but fortunately after a short wait someone else opened it.

This chapter of accidents was of minor significance compared to the arrest, on 14 February 1758, of Chancellor Bestuzhev. As Catherine described it, 'He was relieved of all his decorations and rank, without a soul having been able to reveal for what crimes or transgressions the first gentleman of the Empire was so despoiled, and sent back to his house a prisoner.' Although the arrest took place in the same palace in which the Grand Duke and Duchess were living, and not far from their own apartments, they knew nothing about it at the time. Catherine only heard the news the following morning, from a note written by Poniatowski smuggled in by Lev Naryshkin. Poniatowski also informed her of several other arrests: of her friends Ivan Yelagin (who was also a friend of Poniatowski) and Adadurov (Catherine's former Russian teacher) and, most worryingly for her, of Bernardi, an Italian jeweller, who had long acted as her confidant and courier, particularly in her correspondence with Sir Charles Hanbury-Williams. It was clear to Catherine that she too was under suspicion. She dressed and attended the liturgy as though nothing had happened, but 'with the iron in my soul'. No one said a word about Bestuzhev or any of the others.

The following day Bestuzhev succeeded in getting a message to Catherine, to let her know that he had managed to burn everything incriminating before his arrest. Catherine relates in her memoirs that Bestuzhev had drawn up a plan 'according to which, at the death of the Empress, the Grand Duke would be declared Emperor by law and at the same time I would be declared as participating with the Grand Duke in the rule of the country. All the offices were to continue and he, Bestujev, would be made lieutenant-colonel of four Guards regiments and the president of three Imperial Colleges – those of Foreign Affairs, War, and the Admiralty.' Catherine had not endorsed the plan, apparently viewing it as too difficult to execute, but she had a draft of it in her possession while a copy of it and some of her letters were with Bestuzhev. Fortunately for her, these were documents he had been able to destroy. He also managed to set up various channels of communication, employing musicians, valets and guards as messengers. At least one of these channels was intercepted, however, causing further alarm and distress.

No specific crime could be pinned on the former Chancellor. Instead, it was alleged that he had attempted to sow discord between the Empress and Their Imperial Highnesses, and that sometimes he had acted against the orders and wishes of the Empress (as she had very rarely issued him with any orders at all, this was impossible either to prove or disprove). Those intent on bringing about his ruin included the Shuvalovs and the Vice-Chancellor Mikhail Vorontsov, as well as the Austrian and French ambassadors. Vorontsov and the Shuvalovs had succeeded in convincing the Empress that Bestuzhev, because of his standing in Europe, had been usurping the glory which should have been hers. The case dragged on, but no verdict was reached. Bestuzhev was nevertheless stripped of all his honours and exiled to his country estate. Yelagin and Adadurov were also sent into exile, and Bernardi was imprisoned in Kazan. (Poniatowski gave the latter's wife money so she and her children could return to Venice, and also provided her with a pension for the rest of her life.)

As Poniatowski was shown to have corresponded with Bestuzhev, his recall was now demanded formally by the Russian government. Catherine burnt all her potentially incriminating papers (including the evidence of money she had received from England). She was now completely isolated: 'The Grand Duke hardly dared speak to me and avoided coming into my rooms, where I was all alone, not seeing a soul. I refrained from asking anyone to come and visit me, for fear of exposing them to some unpleasantness or disaster; at Court, afraid of being shunned, I avoided approaching all those whom I suspected would do so.'

But Catherine was not prepared to sit and wait for something to happen, and she decided to seize the initiative by requesting an interview with the Empress. She wrote a careful appeal in Russian, begging that, since she had had the misfortune to arouse Elizabeth's displeasure, she might be sent home to her relatives. She was prepared to call the Empress's bluff, just as she had done earlier with Peter over the question of her daughter's paternity. She suspected the Shuvalovs in particular of favouring her banishment, but believed Elizabeth would be very unlikely to approve such a drastic step, for fear that any change to her succession plans would arouse the supporters of the deposed Ivan VI. Elizabeth granted the interview, though appeared to be in no hurry to appoint a day and time; this was both because she disliked giving fixed times to anything and because a thorough investigation was now being conducted into Catherine's behaviour. The Grand Duke had been informed of the impending interview and was doing all he could to ensure that he would be present.

'Waiting for this interview to take place,' Catherine wrote, 'I remained quietly in my apartments. I was convinced in my heart of hearts that if there was any idea of banishing me or intimidating me with such a project, the steps I had taken would upset the Shuvalovs' plans, which certainly would not be approved of by the Empress, for she was not at all inclined to such spectacular measures.' Catherine was also convinced that the only negative point that could actually be proved against her was her unsatisfactory marriage – 'that I did not consider her august nephew the most amiable of men, just as I did not appear to him the most amiable of women'.

As the weeks went by with no sign from the Empress, Catherine tried another tactic to break the impasse herself. One of her ladies-in-waiting was the niece of the Empress's confessor – who at the time was also Catherine's confessor – and she suggested Catherine summon him and ask him to intercede on her behalf. The priest turned out to be sympathetic to Catherine and helped secure an interview on 13 April 1758.

Catherine dressed and prepared herself at 10 o'clock in the evening, then lay down on the sofa and fell asleep. Count Alexander Shuvalov finally came to fetch her at half past one in the morning. On her way through the antechambers she saw the Grand Duke also making his way to the Empress's apartments. The room in which the Empress received Catherine was long, with three windows; there were two dressing tables, on which Elizabeth's golden toilet set was spread out, a sofa and some high screens. Ostensibly only four people were present – Elizabeth, Peter, Alexander Shuvalov and Catherine herself – but Catherine suspected, rightly as it turned out, that Ivan Shuvalov was hiding behind one of the screens. As soon as Catherine entered, she fell to her knees and, sobbing, begged the Empress to send her back to her relatives. The Empress seemed more sad than angry, and asked how she could want to go when she had children, to which Catherine replied (with justification) that her children were in the Empress's hands and could not be in better ones. Elizabeth told Catherine to rise.

The interview lasted for an hour and a half, during which the Empress walked up and down the room, addressing Catherine and Peter in turn, as well as Alexander Shuvalov – who was also discussing the situation with Peter. Elizabeth 'listened with particular attention and a kind of unwilling approval to my steady and balanced replies to my distinguished consort's exaggerated statements which showed as clear as day that all he wanted was to sweep me aside and put in my place, if possible, his mistress of the moment'. Peter blustered about like a bull in a china shop, while his wife's every word and gesture was calculated to attaining her end.

[Peter's] behaviour became so objectionable that the Empress came up to me and whispered: 'I have many more things to say to you, but I find it difficult at the moment, as I do not want to make things worse between you than they are already,' and with a movement of the eyes and head she showed that it was because of the presence of the two others. Seeing this intimate and friendly demonstration to me at so critical a moment, I opened my heart to her and whispered back: 'I, too, find it difficult to speak now, in spite of the great desire I have to tell you all there is in my heart.'

It was not until almost three o'clock in the morning that the Empress terminated the interview. Peter left first, followed by Catherine: 'The Grand Duke always took large strides when he walked; this time I was in no hurry to follow him; he went back to his rooms and I to mine.' While Catherine was starting to undress, Alexander Shuvalov arrived and asked her to dismiss her maids. He gave her a message from the Empress: Catherine was not to have too heavy a heart and she would have another conversation with her before long. Shuvalov warned her not to mention this second projected conversation to the Grand Duke.

Catherine remained closeted in her apartments, pleading ill health. She spent her time reading, including looking through the early volumes of Diderot and d'Alembert's *Encyclopédie*. She saw and heard nothing of the Grand Duke, whom she believed to be waiting impatiently for her to be sent away so that he could marry Elizaveta Vorontsova. Meanwhile Poniatowski received permission from the Court of Saxony to leave his posting whenever he wished.

The second conversation was eventually granted in May, after a visit Catherine had been permitted to make to her children. This time the two women were completely alone:

I began by thanking her for allowing me to come, adding that the gracious promise alone of that visit had brought me back to life. She said to me after that: 'I insist that you tell me the truth about everything I am going to ask you.'

I assured her that she would hear nothing but the exact truth from my mouth and that all I wanted was to open my heart to her entirely, without any restriction. She asked me then if I had really written only three letters to Apraxine. I swore to her that it was so, which was indeed the truth. Then she asked me for details about the life of the Grand Duke . . .

Here Catherine's memoirs break off. She never did reveal precisely what passed between her and the Empress, but subsequently she felt sufficiently restored to favour to emerge from her retirement and for Stanislas once again to delay his departure. That summer he came to see her frequently at Oranienbaum, his nocturnal visits made more convenient by the fact that he was staying at Peterhof on account of the presence there of Prince Charles of Saxony, the son of Augustus III. Stanislas was in danger of becoming rather blasé about these visits, until one night in late June:

> The good fortune which I had enjoyed up to then with my disguises and everything relating to this course of action had made me so oblivious to the risks, that on [25 June] I took the chance of making a visit without having arranged it beforehand with the Grand Duchess which I had always done before; as usual I travelled in a small covered carriage driven by a Russian *izvozchik* [coachman] who did not know me. On the back of the carriage sat the same footman in disguise who had always accompanied me in the past. That night (which wasn't really night in Russia) we were unfortunate enough to meet the Grand Duke with his entire suite, all of them half-drunk. They asked the *izvozchik* who his passenger was. He replied that he didn't know; my footman answered that it was a tailor. They let us pass. But Isabelle [*sic*] Vorontsova, maid-of-honour to the Grand Duchess and mistress of the Grand Duke and who was with him, sniggered suggestively about this so-called tailor, and this put the Grand Duke into such a bad mood that, after I had spent several hours with the Grand Duchess in the remote pavilion she was then occupying under the pretext of taking baths, on leaving I found myself suddenly assaulted a few paces away by three men on horseback and armed with sabres. They seized me by the collar and took me like that to the Grand Duke who, on recognising me, simply ordered my captors to follow him. They led me for some time down a path which led to the sea. I thought my end was near, but on the shore they took a right turn to another pavilion, where the Grand Duke began by asking me in forthright terms whether I had . . . [*sic*] his wife.

Although Peter assured him that things would be easier for him if he told the truth, Stanislas insisted, 'I cannot tell you I have done something I have not done.' Peter then decided he would let Stanislas sweat it out for a while, and left him under guard. After about two hours Alexander Shuvalov arrived, which convinced Stanislas that the Empress had been informed of his arrest. Shuvalov, with his usual frightening facial twitch but feeling somewhat nervous himself, demanded an explanation. Stanislas had had time to work out how to handle the situation, and decided to brave it out: 'I am sure you will agree, Sir,' he said, 'that it is important to the honour both of your Court and of myself, that all this should end with as little fuss as possible, and that you should promptly get me out of here.' Shuvalov returned an hour later to say that a carriage was waiting to take Poniatowski back to Peterhof. But Stanislas' trials were not over yet:

It was a wretched little carriage, and seemed to be constructed of mirrors, or rather windows, on all sides like a lantern. It was in this supposed incognito that I sadly made my way, in broad daylight at six o'clock in the morning, pulled by two horses through deep sand which made the journey feel as though it was lasting forever. At some distance from Peterhof I stopped the carriage and sent it back, and then walked the rest of the way wrapped in my cloak and with my grey hat pulled down over my ears. I must have looked like a brigand, but I thought my appearance would still attract less attention from curious onlookers than that delightful carriage would have done. Having got back to the building where I was staying with several of the gentlemen of Prince Charles' suite, in small low rooms on the ground floor, all with their windows open, I decided not to go in by the door for fear of meeting someone. I thought I was doing very well by climbing through the window to my room – but I had got the wrong window, and jumped into the room of my neighbour, General Ronslad, who was shaving and thought he was seeing a ghost. We were both struck dumb for several moments and then burst out laughing. I said to him: 'Don't ask me where I've been, or why I came in through the window, but give me your word of honour as a good compatriot never to speak of it.' He promised, and I went off to try to get some sleep, but in vain.

Stanislas spent an anxious couple of days. It was clear from people's expressions that his adventure was widely known, though no one referred to it. Catherine, meanwhile, was busy trying to smooth things over and, with her usual political instinct, had realised that the best way to achieve this was to win over the Grand Duke's mistress. She succeeded in doing this and sent a note to Stanislas to tell him so. Stanislas had his own opportunity to speak to Elizaveta Vorontsova on 29 June (three years to the day since he had first seen Catherine), when the Grand Duke and Duchess came to Peterhof for a ball to celebrate the Grand Duke's name-day. Poniatowski danced a minuet with Vorontsova, during the course of which he said to her: 'You have it in your power to make several people happy.' Vorontsova replied that it was almost done, and instructed him to come at one o'clock in the morning to the Lower Palace of Monplaisir where the Grand Duke and Duchess were staying. Not knowing what to expect, Stanislas duly turned up at the appointed hour. Vorontsova came out to meet him and told him to wait, as the Grand Duke was smoking a pipe with a few friends and wanted them to leave before receiving Poniatowski. Eventually she told Poniatowski to come in.

Vorontsova had succeeded so well in her peace-making mission that the Grand Duke now seemed more than happy to accept the situation, his only reproach to Poniatowski being that he had not told him the truth: '"How foolish not to have been frank with me," he said. "None of this mess would have happened then."' Stanislas proceeded to ingratiate himself with Peter by congratulating him on the smooth execution of his arrest.

> He was so flattered by this, and made so happy that, after a quarter of an hour, he said: 'Now that we are such good friends, I find there is someone missing here.' He crossed over to his wife's room, dragged her out of bed, leaving her time only to put on her stockings and no shoes, and slip on a Batavia dress without an underskirt, and then brought her in, saying, as he pointed to me: 'Here he is! I hope I shall have satisfied everybody!'

Catherine, in Poniatowski's words, caught the ball immediately and replied: 'All that's missing is a note from you to Vice-Chancellor Vorontsov asking him to make arrangements in Warsaw for the prompt return back here of our friend.' Peter immediately wrote the note, which he got Elizaveta Vorontsova to countersign. Then they all behaved as though they had not a care in the world, and stayed up laughing and talking until four o'clock in the morning.

Peter enjoyed these sessions *à quatre* so much that he insisted on Stanislas repeating his visit four times: 'I arrived in the evening, walked up a secret staircase to the Grand Duchess's room, where I found the Grand Duke and his mistress. We had supper together, after which he took his mistress away, saying to us: "Well, my children, I do not think you need me any more," and I remained as long as I liked.' Catherine did not feel entirely easy, aware that the knowledge her husband – and others – had obtained could one day be used against her.

Despite these improved relations, Poniatowski soon realised it would still be safer for him to leave St Petersburg. In August he departed for Poland. He and Catherine both imagined he would be returning soon.

# 6

# Empress of All the Russias
# (1759–62)

*So many favourable circumstances cannot be brought together without the hand of God.*

Memoirs of Catherine the Great

Although Poniatowski and Catherine wrote frequently to one another over the next year, their letters being conveyed by both British and French diplomats, the period after her Polish lover's departure was a time of retrenchment for Catherine. Despite her reconciliation with the Empress, she was still dangerously isolated at the Russian Court. The arrest of Bestuzhev and its fall-out – his sentence of exile was publicly announced on 8 April 1759, Vice-Chancellor Mikhail Vorontsov being promoted to Chancellor in his stead – had made her aware of how close to disaster she had been. And the affair with Poniatowski had, by the time he left, become worryingly public. Catherine missed him greatly, particularly in the first weeks and months of their separation. For some time she would feel animosity towards those who had made his departure inevitable, but a part of her, that cool part which planned and plotted and was determined that she would play a vital role in the governance of Russia, was relieved that her demanding and melodramatic young lover had left the scene.

Catherine could not easily avail herself of the solace which the company of her young children might have afforded her, as the visits she was permitted to make to them were still rationed by the Empress, the absolute maximum being once a week during the summer. The four-year-old Paul was a nervous child. One day, when one of the

Empress's ladies slammed the door, he was so scared that he rushed to hide under the table. Grand Duke Peter took no interest in him, or indeed in his mother. He was by now committed emotionally to Elizaveta Vorontsova. And then, on 9 March 1759, Catherine's 15-month-old daughter Anna died. Her funeral and burial took place at the Alexander Nevsky Monastery six days later. Catherine attended the funeral and never mentioned the baby again.

The Empress Elizabeth continued to suffer from bouts of ill health, including frequent nosebleeds. Her dropsy, or oedema (which Catherine had earlier referred to as 'water in the lower part of her belly'), became progressively worse. Speculation on the succession did not diminish either. Rumours were circulating constantly that the Empress intended to disinherit her nephew Peter in favour of his son Paul. But, as Catherine explained in some notes she wrote years later under the title 'Last Thoughts of Her Imperial Majesty Elizabeth Petrovna':

> It is impossible to say what Her Imperial Majesty Elizabeth Petrovna's last thoughts were about the succession, for she had no clear ideas on the subject. There is no doubt that she did not like P.III [i.e. Peter] and considered him incapable of ruling; she knew he did not love the Russians, she thought of death with fear and horror, as well as of what would come after; but as she was slow in taking any decision, particularly in her last years, one can guess that she also hesitated on the question of the succession.

As Catherine began to accept that the political situation precluded Poniatowski's return, she sought out and found exactly the right man for the next phase of her life.

Lieutenant Grigory Orlov of the Izmailovsky Guards was one of five brothers, and the most handsome. Their surname, deriving from *oryol*, the Russian for 'eagle', was apposite. Sons of a provincial governor, the Orlov brothers had received little formal education and Grigory had enrolled in the Izmailovsky Guards at the age of 18. Now in his mid-twenties, he was a man of gigantic physique. He had already acquired a reputation for bravery, having fought on at the battle of Zorndorf – a particularly bloody engagement of the Seven Years' War which had taken place in August 1758 – despite having been wounded three times. All five Orlov brothers enjoyed bear-hunting and cock-fighting as well as organising and participating in boxing matches, with two teams of 50 boxers in a long line.

Grigory Orlov had returned from the war to St Petersburg in March 1759, accompanying Count Schwerin, one of Frederick the Great's adjutants who had been captured at Zorndorf. On his return to the capital, Grigory was appointed adjutant to Count Peter Shuvalov, at that time Grand Master of Ordnance. He then proceeded to have an affair with the Count's mistress, Princess Elena Kurakina, a renowned beauty and the daughter of the late Marshal Apraksin (who had died of a stroke in August 1758). This served the vain and pompous Shuvalov right, as he had deliberately chosen the handsome Orlov for his adjutant in order to complement his beautiful mistress. Inevitably, Catherine heard of the exploits of this young officer who was rapidly becoming the talk of the town. The legend is that she first caught sight of him from a window in the timber Winter Palace. But their first meeting is most likely to have occurred during an official engagement at Court. It was not until some time in 1761 that the two became lovers, Orlov having extricated himself from his entanglement with Shuvalov's mistress. This time Catherine kept her affair a carefully guarded secret. Only a very few close friends, such as Countess Praskovya Bruce (who as Praskovya Rumyantseva had been Catherine's friend since adolescence), were in the know. The contrast between Orlov and Catherine's previous lover could not have been greater. Where Poniatowski was all high-flown European sensibility, Orlov was pure Russian physicality. He and his brothers also provided a link between Catherine and the Guards regiments, vital components of any forthcoming power struggle.

On 19 May 1760 Catherine's mother had died in Paris, where she had gone to live after leaving Prussian-occupied Zerbst in 1758. She was only 47 years old. Catherine wrote to the Empress asking for money to buy some of Johanna's belongings, which she had had to pawn before her death. She writes that if she cannot buy them back now, they will be sold at public auction in March 1761 and that it would be best to avoid the shame of this, particularly as most of the items in question had been gifts from the Empress herself. Elizabeth complied with the request. Catherine was also relieved to learn that Johanna had taken care to destroy the letters her daughter had been sending her, by clandestine means, over the course of several years.

From handwritten notes Catherine compiled in 1761 it is clear that, as Elizabeth drew nearer to the end of her life and Peter continued to be seen in many quarters as an unsatisfactory figure to be a future Emperor, she herself was studying, thinking and planning how best to exercise power once it came her way. She was increasingly conscious that she had many supporters, people willing to help her seize control when the time was right, and her new connection with the Orlov brothers made what may have previously appeared theoretical become a very practical possibility. The ideas and maxims she collected and wrote down for herself were not original – they came from her reading of Montesquieu, the cameralist★ writer and jurist Baron Jakob Friedrich von Bielfeld, and others – but her notes do demonstrate her powers of assimilation and organisation, and her attempt to apply general concepts to the particular situation and country in which she found herself. Some of the precepts she lists are written as little homilies to herself, summarising the qualities required in a perfect ruler. The didactic, slightly hectoring tone is typical of her; Catherine always evinced a great desire to teach – both herself and anybody else who would listen. Her notes also demonstrate her fundamental belief, characteristic of the Enlightenment philosophers she spent much time reading, that, through the application of reason, solutions to most human problems can and must be found.

Her notes begin with a question about how a school for young ladies, modelled on that of St Cyr, the famous establishment founded in France by Madame de Maintenon (the second, morganatic wife of Louis XIV), might be instituted in Russia. She expressed the hope and belief that, though it would be necessary to accept the assistance of French teachers to begin with, after several years 'we would have managed to form sufficient subjects of our own nation to teach in the house'. She goes on to examine a variety of questions, ranging from the very practical – how to stop officials delaying payments to beneficiaries in the hope of getting a bribe, how to ensure the arts of war are not lost during a prolonged period of peace – to high-flown sentiments addressed primarily to herself: 'Power without the trust of the nation is nothing for the one who wishes to be loved and to have glory; it is easy to win it: take the good of the nation and justice, which is never separated from it, for the rule of your actions, of your statutes. You have and should have no other interest. If your soul is noble, there is its aim.' She addressed – briefly – the thorny issue of serfdom, declaring: 'It is against the Christian religion and justice to make slaves of men (who are all born free)' but going on realistically to note that emancipating

---

★ Cameralism was the science of government worked out in the small German courts in the 17th and 18th centuries; its central tenet was that the state could achieve its aims by minutely regulating all forms of activity in government and society.

the serfs 'would not be the way to make oneself loved by stubborn, prejudiced landowners'. Her suggested solution is for gradual emancipation, to take place every time a piece of land changes hands. Her optimistic projection is that this will produce 'a free people' in the space of a hundred years. (Coincidentally, her great-grandson Alexander II did indeed emancipate the serfs precisely one hundred years later.) Another problem which concerns her is the very high mortality rate among the children of Russian peasants. She envisages some practical solution – 'able doctors who are more philosophers than the average run of them' must be able to come up with 'some general rule' – which can then be implemented for the good of the country: 'for I am persuaded that the little care taken of very small children is the principal cause of this evil; they run round naked, in just a chemise in snow and ice. The one who survives is very robust, but nineteen die, and what a loss for the State.' Catherine also had criticisms to make of Moscow, a dislike of the old capital and an urge to reform it being one of her constant preoccupations. Again she is determined to find a practical solution:

> The majority of our manufactories are in Moscow, perhaps the least favourable place of Russia; there are innumerable people, the workers there become licentious, the production of silk goods cannot be of high quality, the water there is muddy – especially in the spring, the best season for the dyeing of silk. This water affects the colours, they are either tarnished or coarse. On the other hand a hundred small towns are falling into ruins; why not move a manufactory into each one, chosen according to the produce of the province and the quality of the water. The workers would apply themselves harder there and the towns would flourish more.

Next she gives herself some sound advice about the introduction of new laws (which her husband would have done well to follow). The only way to find out whether a law is going to work, she says, is to stimulate discussion beforehand and find out exactly what people are saying. Springing something unexpected on the people, she suggests, may not bring about the desired results.

Catherine also sets out some guidelines on how a ruler ought to behave towards his or her courtiers. She intends, she writes, to use flattery to ensure that they are not afraid to tell her the truth. She will talk to each official about the particular task entrusted to him, and will only dispense favours if she is directly asked for them or if she has already made up her mind to do so without the encouragement of any third party, for 'it is important that the obligation be owed to you, not to your favourites etc.'. She believes that one of her most important tasks will be to select the right people to work for her: 'he who does not seek merit, he who does not discover it, is unworthy and incapable of reigning'. Catherine ends her notes with a quotation from Bielfeld on the importance of respecting religion but of not allowing it to influence matters of state. There is also a remark about her growing favour, which she is aware is the corollary of the disfavour Grand Duke Peter had aroused in various quarters. Her words convey the impression of someone moving cautiously, but steadily, towards her goal.

One of Catherine's chief supporters was the little Grand Duke Paul's governor, Nikita Panin. The son of one of Peter the Great's generals and senators, Panin had long been a friend of the Empress Elizabeth and had also, through the patronage of Bestuzhev, served as Russian ambassador to Sweden from 1748 to 1760. He was a cultivated, well-educated man and, like Catherine, interested in European political theory and in particular the works of Montesquieu. He had hopes for a constitutional monarchy for Russia, and imagined that allying himself with Catherine might represent a way towards achieving it. He was known for his consciously outdated appearance. According to another of Catherine's supporters, the Princess Ekaterina Dashkova, he 'wore a wig with three ties hanging down his back, was studied in his dress, always the perfect courtier – a somewhat old-fashioned one, truth to tell, like a picture-book idea of those at the court of Louis XIV'. His brother Peter was an army officer who had recently been promoted to general after his exploits against the Prussians.

The young Princess Dashkova had a decidedly inflated view of her own importance in Catherine's circle of supporters and conspirators. Her usefulness to Catherine lay in her connections. Born Ekaterina Vorontsova, she was a niece of Chancellor Mikhail Vorontsov and the younger sister of Grand Duke Peter's mistress, Elizaveta Vorontsova, and thus a most valuable source of information. She herself imagined that her primary worth to Catherine was as a close friend and fellow intellectual. She was certainly a great deal better educated than most women at the Court of St Petersburg. Nevertheless, it was what she overheard when in the company of the Chancellor or the Grand Duke and what she could pick up from her sister, rather than her views on literature, that made her valuable to Catherine.

The Empress Elizabeth died on 25 December 1761 at three o'clock in the afternoon, after having suffered a violent nosebleed. Catherine records: 'At the moment of H.I.M.'s death, Princess Dashkov sent word to me: "You have only to give the order and we will enthrone you." I sent back my reply: "For God's sake do not start this chaos; what God wills will happen in any case, but your idea is both premature and immature!"' What Dashkova did not know was one of the reasons why a coup in favour of Catherine would have been premature. Catherine was at least five months pregnant, a condition she had managed to conceal even while watching by the Empress's bed for the last two nights of Elizabeth's life.

Catherine's relationship with the Grand Duke had by now deteriorated to such an extent that there could be no possibility of convincing him or anyone else that the child might be his. Concealment of the pregnancy was her only option. What happened next was quite different from anything imagined during the Grand Duchess's correspondence with Sir Charles Hanbury-Williams. Peter departed for the Senate, telling Catherine to stay by Elizabeth's body until she received further instructions. The Empress's body was washed, disembowelled and embalmed (presumably not in Catherine's presence), before being dressed in a silver robe with lace sleeves. According to Catherine, Peter did not intend to spend much time mourning: 'The body had hardly been laid out and placed on a bed with a baldaquin when the Court Marshal sent me word to say that there would be a supper that evening in the gallery (three rooms away from the body) at which we were ordered to wear light-coloured dresses.' Catherine was then summoned to the palace chapel, where Peter took the oath as Emperor Peter III (no mention being made of his wife or son), a Te Deum was sung in thanksgiving, and the Archbishop of Novgorod, Metropolitan Dmitry Sechenov, delivered a speech to the delighted Emperor.

Three days after Elizabeth's death Catherine went to visit Paul (it is noticeable that she did not rush to see him, even though now there was no one to prevent her from doing so). She also visited Count Alexei Razumovsky, Elizabeth's former favourite, who was prostrated with grief. Initially Elizabeth's body lay in her state bedroom, while priests recited the Gospel and soldiers stood at guard. After three weeks the body was carried in an open coffin to one of the large state rooms. Here it was installed on a dais, beneath a canopy crowned with a double-headed eagle. A golden crown was placed on Elizabeth's head, inscribed with her name and dates, and the words 'Most Pious Autocrat'.

The walls of the room were draped in black and many candles burned around the catafalque. For the next 10 days the people of Petersburg were able to file past twice a day to pay their respects.

Catherine, clothed in black, spent most of these weeks of mourning praying beside the bier. Her dignity, her visible grief and her observance of the Orthodox rites won her great respect among the faithful, as she knew they would. Peter did not mourn any more than was strictly necessary. Thus, while appearing to do nothing, Catherine managed to underline the contrast between herself and her husband. The voluminous mourning robes also had the advantage of helping to disguise her advanced state of pregnancy. When Peter made haste to move himself and his mistress into the barely completed new Winter Palace, Catherine stayed on in the temporary palace – which was where Elizabeth had died and was lying in state – pleading ill health (while in fact preparing for the birth of her child).

Elizabeth's funeral took place on 25 January 1762. Her body was 'taken with great pomp from the Palace across the river to the Peter and Paul Cathedral in the Fortress'. Catherine asserts that Peter's behaviour on this occasion was particularly scandalous:

> The Emperor was very gay that day and during the sad ceremony invented a game for himself; he loitered behind the hearse, on purpose, allowing it to proceed at a distance of thirty feet, then he would run to catch up with it as fast as he could. The elder courtiers, who were carrying his black train, found themselves unable to keep up with him and let the train go. The wind blew it out and all this amused Peter III so much that he repeated the joke several times, so that I and everybody else remained far behind and had to send word to stop the ceremony until everybody had caught up with the hearse. Criticism of the Emperor's outrageous behaviour spread rapidly and his unsuitable deportment was the subject of much talk.

Peter found the Requiem Mass celebrated for the late Empress at the Roman Catholic church of the Franciscans more to his taste than the Orthodox devotions. His *maestro di capella* Manfredini had composed a new setting of the Mass which was performed by the court singers – including the castrati and a renowned German bass – as well as by a full orchestra (whereas music in the Orthodox Church is always entirely vocal). This lasted for two hours, and Jakob Stählin reported that 'The

Emperor himself listened attentively from the beginning to the end and was invited after divine service to breakfast in the refectory.'

Peter's passion for music was such that he lifted the prohibition on performances at Court, which was a traditional element of the prolonged period of mourning for a sovereign. He allowed music to be performed at assemblies, during dinners and on other occasions as soon as the Empress Elizabeth had been buried. He also continued to play himself, as leader of the orchestra, and encouraged the amateur instrumentalists who used to play with him in private to join him in these concerts. He was very keen to increase the numbers of foreign virtuosi at the Russian Court, expressing an ambition to gather around himself in as short a time as possible the most famous musicians of Europe. He had in his sights both the great violinist and composer Giuseppe Tartini, and the composer, harpsichordist and *maestro di capella* of San Marco in Venice Baldassare Galuppi; Tartini could not be enticed away from Padua, while Galuppi did eventually make it to Petersburg in 1765.

But Peter's musical activities were of small significance compared with his far-reaching political initiatives. On 18 February 1762, barely eight weeks since he had taken power, a manifesto was published freeing nobles from compulsory service to the State during peace-time. Though this was welcomed in many quarters, it nevertheless provoked some disquiet. There was a fear that the nobility might lose their traditional role in society, and find that role – and its accompanying influence – usurped by bureaucrats and imperial favourites. It also upset the balance of society. The service given to the State by the nobles was considered to be the other side of the equation from the service demanded by the nobles of their serfs. As Catherine expressed it, 'The nobles were all agog about their new freedom and had forgotten that it was owing to the Army service that their ancestors had acquired the ranks and property which they themselves had now inherited.' Rumours spread about the countryside that it would next be the turn of the serfs to be liberated from service to their masters, and this unfounded idea earned the name of Peter III much popularity among the peasants. But he had failed to prepare the ground for his reform or to think through the possible consequences. Catherine had addressed the question of noble service in her 1761 notes, acknowledging that the current system of compulsory and lengthy service had its drawbacks, particularly when it meant that members of the nobility were unable to attend to the proper management of their estates. But she would never have introduced such a major change without extensive preparation, including both theoretical study and consultation of interested parties. An equally ill-thought-out reform was the secularisation of monastic property (including serfs); Peter's obvious lack of sympathy for the Orthodox Church exacerbated the anger provoked by this measure, which did not even allow for any compensation to the monasteries. Peter is also alleged to have told the Archbishop of Novgorod that all icons other than those portraying Jesus should be removed from churches, and that the clergy should shave off their beards and dress like Western priests. He ordered the closing of private chapels in the mansions of wealthy nobles and merchants, which also alienated many priests in the major cities, and he upset the members of the ordinary clergy by lifting the exemption from conscription in the armed forces formerly granted to the sons of priests and deacons.

On 21 February the Emperor published a less controversial decree, abolishing the Secret Chancery. Several prominent people were also brought back from exile. On 9 March he ordered that humiliating punishments involving the use of whips and sticks should no longer be inflicted on soldiers, sailors and other subalterns. In future only swords and canes were to be used. Unfortunately for Peter, these moves towards liberalism went almost unnoticed – and the abolition of what was effectively the imperial secret police probably also prevented him from discovering the seriousness of the plot to dethrone him.

Now Peter made the even more disastrous mistake of alienating the armed forces. The Russian forces were on the point of crushing those of Frederick the Great, having taken the fortress of Kolberg and occupied East Prussia, when Peter called an immediate halt to the war. He concluded peace with Prussia in May 1762. Frederick had known that only a miracle could save him, and the death of Elizabeth and accession of Peter III became known as 'the miracle of the House of Brandenburg'. Peter refused to accept any territorial gains from Prussia, even though Frederick was prepared to cede East Prussia to him. This sudden change of policy came as a painful shock not only to those engaged in the conflict, but to all those who had lost sons, fathers, brothers or husbands during the war which had been going on for the last five years. The Emperor appeared to be making a mockery of the great victories the Russian army had won. He also injured its pride by seeking to remould it after the Prussian model. He ordered new uniforms in the Prussian style, and awarded his Holsteiners an ever higher status. He was known to dislike the elite Guards regiments, and some feared that he might be planning to abolish them altogether. Peter further inflamed Russian sentiments by making preparations for a war with Denmark in order to recover Schleswig (this had been part of an ongoing dispute between Denmark and Holstein since the Treaty of Roskilde of 1658, and had been a major factor in the Great Northern War). This was to involve active cooperation with the Prussians. Peter assembled troops in Livonia, while those who had been serving in Westphalia languished unpaid. This projected war was a clear demonstration that Peter's interests continued to lie with Holstein, and not with the Empire of which he was now the sovereign. It was no help either to his public image that he spoke Russian poorly and rarely; he also took no steps to hold a coronation, failing to grasp the significance the Russians attached to this religious ceremony. An Orthodox coronation, held in the ancient capital of Moscow, could have done much to make the faithful accept him as their rightful, divinely appointed Tsar.

On 10 April, 11 days before her thirty-third birthday, Catherine gave birth to her son by Orlov, attended only by her maids and a midwife. He was given the Christian name Alexei, and his father was acknowledged by his patronymic, Grigoryevich. He acquired the surname Bobrinsky on account of his being wrapped in beaver fur, a beaver being *bobyor* in Russian. The child was dispatched immediately to the care of foster-parents, Catherine's trusted valet Vasily Shkurin and his wife. And as soon as she had recovered (as this was all secret, there was no question of her observing the customary confinement period or churching ceremony), Catherine moved into her apartments in the new Winter Palace.

As had also been the case with the Empress Elizabeth, part of Catherine's determination to seize power was fear of the alternative. She had already expressed to Sir Charles Hanbury-Williams her intention to 'perish or reign', and Peter had made it quite clear that there would never be any question of her sharing his power. Princess Dashkova was convinced that Peter was intending to rid himself of Catherine, by whatever means, in order to marry her sister Elizaveta Vorontsova. She recalled that Peter always referred to his wife as 'she' and that he advised her, Dashkova, to cultivate her sister's good opinion, for her own future benefit. It was the French attaché Bérenger's opinion that a coup in favour of Catherine had become inevitable and was bound to be supported by the nation:

The abandonment, the state of humiliation to which the Empress had been reduced, the daily outrages she endured with incredible patience, her inviolable respect for religion and its ministers, her air of goodwill towards everyone, the talents and the knowledge she was known to possess, her dignity and decorum put alongside the bizarre and ferocious character of the Tsar, in short the virtues of this admirable Princess had sustained the wishes and prayers of the nation for a long time in her favour.

Things came to a head at a gala dinner on 9 June, held to celebrate the confirmation of the peace treaty with Prussia. Princess Dashkova described the scene:

> The Empress [i.e. Catherine] began by the toast to the Imperial family. When she had drunk it, Peter III sent his General A.D.C. Gudovich, who was standing behind his chair, to ask her why she had not risen from her seat when drinking to the health of the Imperial family. The Empress replied that as the Imperial family consisted only of His Majesty, her son and herself, she did not conceive it possible that the Emperor should require her to do so. When Gudovich came back with this reply, the Emperor ordered him to tell her that she was a fool (*dura* – a much stronger word in Russian) and ought to have known that the Imperial family included also his two uncles, the princes of Holstein.★ Fearing, apparently, that Gudovich would not use the same expression, he repeated it loudly enough to be heard by the whole table.

According to Princess Dashkova, Catherine burst into tears, but then attempted to divert attention from this public insult by asking Count Stroganov, who was in attendance behind her chair, to recount some amusing stories. His support of her was noted and, after the dinner, he was ordered to retire to his house near Kamenny Ostrov and stay there until further notice. Peter was on the verge of issuing a warrant for Catherine's arrest, and was only dissuaded by the representations of her uncle Prince Georg Ludwig – who had sighed after her when she was a young girl. Peter had invited him to St Petersburg soon after his accession and had even bought for him the palace and gardens formerly belonging to Count Peter Shuvalov, who had died in January. He had

---

★ The fact that the Princes of Holstein-Gottorp were actually Catherine's rather than Peter's uncles makes this strange scene even stranger, and suggests that the Emperor was casting around for any excuse to humiliate his wife.

also named him general-in-chief of all his Holstein armies and administrator of his estates in Holstein.

News of the incident at the gala dinner circulated quickly around town and Court, and increased sympathy for Catherine. The time for taking decisive action was approaching.

In a despatch to his Court written shortly after the coup, the French attaché Bérenger identified the principal conspirators as: Count Kirill Razumovsky, hetman (or chief) of the Ukraine, brother of Elizabeth's former favourite and a long-time friend and admirer of Catherine's – he was also president of the Academy of Sciences and well liked by the Izmailovsky Guards, of whom he was the colonel; Princess Dashkova (whose Guards officer husband was also willing to support Catherine); Catherine's private secretary Odart, a Piedmontese by origin, who helped to arrange a loan of 100,000 roubles for Catherine from an English merchant called Felton; Grigory Teplov, one of the best-educated men in Russia and deputy to Kirill Razumovsky; Nikita Panin; three of the Orlov brothers; the Archbishop of Novgorod, Dmitry Sechenov, who, even if he refrained from actively conspiring, was sympathetically inclined; Prince Volkonsky (whom Bérenger described as having joined the conspiracy in the last few days before its execution); Bibikov, an artillery captain; and Lieutenant Passek of the Preobrazhensky Guards. Other people Bérenger believed to have been involved included Count (now General) Ivan Betskoy, recently arrived from Paris, and Procurator-General Glebov (who had been appointed by Peter). Bérenger also reported that each conspirator was to be trailed by someone, who would report immediately to the others if one of the group were arrested or defected. Catherine herself, with the assistance of the Orlov brothers, acted as coordinator, divulging only such information to the others as she deemed necessary, and financed by secret loans in particular from the anti-Prussian governments of Denmark and Austria. She described the organisation of the conspiracy in a letter to Stanislas Poniatowski a month after the coup had taken place:

> The Guards were all prepared and at the end there were thirty or forty officers in the secret and about ten thousand subalterns. There was not one traitor during the three weeks, because the plotters were divided into four separate sections and only the leaders met for the execution of the plan, while the real secret remained in the hands of these three [Orlov] brothers. Panin wanted the

declaration to be made in favour of my son, but all the others were against it.

Rumours reached Peter that a coup was being planned, but he took no notice and continued to amuse himself much as he had in the days when he was Grand Duke. At an informal supper he gave at the Summer Palace as a further celebration over peace with Prussia, he had to be carried from the table at four o'clock in the morning. That evening, before becoming incapacitated, he had conferred the Order of St Catherine on Elizaveta Vorontsova.

On 25 June Peter made a determined effort to stamp his authority on the Russian Orthodox Church by issuing a decree to the Synod affirming the equality of all Christian creeds, and directing that the fasts of the Orthodox church year should no longer be obligatory. The decree stipulated that the Synod should obey the Emperor's will without question. All serfs belonging to monasteries were to be taken over by the State, and adultery was no longer to be condemned as criminal. This particular reform led to some wild rumours. It was suggested that the Emperor intended to divorce all the court ladies from their husbands and force them to marry other men of his choosing. At around the same time the Lutheran church which Peter had had built at Oranienbaum, primarily for the use of his Holstinian troops, was consecrated. The Emperor took part in this ceremony with devotion, even, according to some reports, receiving communion.

On the evening of 26 June, Peter and Catherine were both present at a dinner at Count Alexei Razumovsky's estate of Gostilitsy. Afterwards Catherine returned to the palace of Monplaisir at Peterhof and Peter to Oranienbaum. He had instructed his wife to ensure that a good dinner was prepared for his forthcoming name-day celebration. On the following day, one of Catherine's chief conspirators, Lieutenant Passek, was arrested, following some unguarded remarks made by one of the soldiers he had recruited. The other conspirators realised that, instead of waiting until Peter returned to St Petersburg later that summer as had been intended, they needed to act immediately, before details of the plot could be tortured out of Passek.

In the early hours of Friday 28 June 1762, Grigory Orlov's younger brother Alexei (similar to Grigory in build and appearance but with a prominent scar on his face, acquired in battle) entered Catherine's bedroom at Monplaisir. She described the moment in a letter to Poniatowski: 'Alexei Orlov came in very calmly and said: "All is ready for the proclamation, you must get up." I asked for the details, he said: "Passek has been arrested." I hesitated no longer, dressed promptly, without further ado, and got into the carriage in which Orlov had arrived.'

Catherine and Alexei left Monplaisir in such haste, by a back door and with no servants, that there was no time to attend to her hair and she was still wearing her lace nightcap. During the journey they were fortunate enough to meet her French hairdresser travelling in the opposite direction. He climbed into her carriage and arranged her hair en route, though there was no time to powder it. (Catherine had by now begun to powder her hair regularly, so that in pictures she appears to have fair hair rather than her natural dark brown.) A little further on they encountered a carriage carrying Grigory Orlov and Prince Fyodor Baryatinsky, and Catherine was transferred into this carriage as the horses pulling the one in which Alexei Orlov had travelled were by now exhausted. She arrived at the barracks of the Izmailovsky regiment just outside St Petersburg at eight o'clock in the morning. There the officers and men, led by their colonel, Count Kirill Razumovsky, took the oath of allegiance to Catherine, Empress of All the Russias, in the presence of a priest holding a cross. Catherine then resumed her seat in the carriage and, with the priest walking in front with the cross and accompanied by the Izmailovsky Guards, proceeded to the Semyonovsky regiment, where the troops again took the oath without hesitation in, as Catherine described it, 'a frenzy of joy'. Towards nine o'clock the growing cavalcade, which now included the Semyonovsky Guards, arrived at the church of Our Lady of Kazan (where Catherine had been married to Peter). Here the ranks were swelled by the soldiers of the Preobrazhensky regiment, though the officers initially remained loyal to Peter. The Archbishop of Novgorod and other members of the clergy were waiting at the church. The Te Deum was sung and Catherine took the oath of sole sovereign of All the Russias, naming her son the Grand Duke Paul as successor (using a proclamation which she had written herself in the early days of the conspiracy). Meanwhile the British ambassador, Robert Keith, was just being alerted to events – as he reported a few days later: 'Last Friday morning about nine o'clock (as I was preparing to go to Peterhoff to meet the Emperor) one of my servants came running into my room with a frightened countenance, and told me that there was a great uproar at the other end of the town, that the guards, having mutinied, were assembled and talked of nothing less than dethroning the Emperor.'

From the Kazan church the Empress Catherine made her way in a two-seater carriage, with Grigory Orlov on the running board, through an immense crowd to whom she waved and smiled, to the new Winter Palace, where the Senate awaited her. Regiments of troops stood guard outside the palace, where they swore the oath of allegiance read out by Metropolitan Venyamin, Archbishop of St Petersburg. Nikita Panin had ordered the seven-year-old Grand Duke Paul Petrovich to be woken at dawn, dressed hurriedly, and conveyed under armed escort from the Summer Palace. He appeared alongside his mother on a balcony of the Winter Palace, to tumultuous acclamation. Inside the palace the oath was administered to many court, military and ecclesiastical officials, this process lasting until about two o'clock in the afternoon. Robert Keith noted how quiet and normal the atmosphere in the city seemed to be, with few signs on the English Embankment of anything out of the ordinary; all he had noticed were some pickets placed on the bridges and some horse guards patrolling the streets.

Troops were now assigned to guard every approach to Petersburg, to stop anyone leaving and to detain anyone arriving from Oranienbaum or Peterhof. There was little resistance. The soldiers of the Life Cuirassiers regiment, which had been one of Peter's favourites, were hesitant to support the coup at first and only agreed to swear the oath after the arrest of the regiment's German officers. Catherine's uncle, Prince Georg Ludwig of Holstein-Gottorp, was also arrested and temporarily confined to his house.

Now that Catherine was firmly in control of the capital, the next step was to deal with Peter. Even as the oath of allegiance was being sworn to Catherine at the Winter Palace, Peter and his companions, including Elizaveta Vorontsova, were on their way in six carriages from Oranienbaum to Peterhof, expecting to celebrate the eve of the Emperor's name-day. They were intercepted by a servant sent by the Grand Marshal of the Court with information about what was going on in St Petersburg. But Peter seemed not to understand the significance of what he was told and pressed on for Peterhof where, on arrival at Monplaisir, he was surprised not to find Catherine. He searched for her in all the rooms, even looking under the beds and in the wardrobes – as though he thought his wife might be playing hide-and-seek. As Robert Keith put it, 'From that moment the unhappy Emperor seems to have lost himself, and there was nothing but despair and confusion amongst the small number of his attendants.'

Before setting off for Peterhof, Catherine gathered her ministers together in the old Winter Palace, with Grigory Teplov acting as secretary, to draft the manifestos and orders which needed to be published immediately. The first manifesto, composed in advance by Razumovsky and Teplov, printed, and then concealed by Catherine's private secretary Odart, had already been proclaimed that morning. It announced Catherine's assumption of the throne, justifying her accession by claims that Peter had endangered Orthodoxy, sullied Russia's military glory and undermined the Empire's institutions. A note was now sent to Admiral Ivan Talyzin, who had that day been appointed Commandant of the Kronstadt Island Fortress where he had made the entire garrison swear allegiance to the Empress, authorising him to do whatever he thought fit. Rear-Admiral Miloslavsky was ordered to administer the oath to naval units in the Gulf of Finland and to guard against any attacks coming from that direction. An order was issued for Peter Panin to take command of the Russian troops from General Rumyantsev. Catherine also lost no time in sending for ex-Chancellor Bestuzhev. Lastly she issued a decree to the Senate in which she informed the senators that she was now leaving with the troops to consolidate the coup, entrusting them in her absence with 'the fatherland, the people and my son'. A few men from every regiment were ordered to remain behind in Petersburg as guards for Paul.

It must have felt to Catherine that she had lived all her life in preparation for this day as she rode at the head of between 14,000 and 20,000 men (accounts vary as to the numbers), creating an enduring image of herself as the powerful and charismatic leader of the Russian nation. She was deliberately creating symbols on this day, conscious of every nuance of appearance. Instituting herself as Colonel of the Preobrazhensky Guards (the rank enjoyed by Peter the Great), she donned the Guards' green and red uniform (borrowing one for the occasion from an officer) and mounted her grey thoroughbred stallion Brilliant, sabre in hand and with oak leaves adorning her tricorn hat. A young and striking-looking guardsman noticed that she had forgotten to attach a sword-knot to her sabre and, galloping across to her, handed her his own. This was the first encounter between Catherine and Grigory Potemkin, who in years to come would be the most important man in her life. (She mentioned him a month later in a letter to Poniatowski: 'a petty officer called Potemkin displayed discernment, courage and action'.) Princess Dashkova, also in a borrowed Preobrazhensky uniform, rode with her, as did Count Buturlin, Count Razumovsky, Prince Volkonsky and Quartermaster-General Villebois. Several hours earlier,

Alexei Orlov had left at the head of an advance guard of cavalry and mounted hussars, followed by artillery units. The soldiers had already cast off the new Prussian uniforms which Peter had made them wear and put on their old Russian ones.

As Catherine and her troops were leaving the city, Chancellor Vorontsov arrived and tried to remonstrate with her. Unable to prevent what was happening, he nevertheless refused to take the oath of allegiance (or not at once) and retired to his own house. Prince Trubetskoy and Count Alexander Shuvalov made ineffective efforts to rally some troops to oppose Catherine, but they quickly desisted and were taken off to swear the oath of allegiance. Catherine's army, the third of the three detachments taking the road along the Gulf of Finland, did not make fast progress – both through tiredness and a lack of urgency as no great resistance was anticipated. At two o'clock in the morning of 29 June they stopped for a rest at Krasny Kabachek, three miles outside Petersburg.

Peter had spent most of the rest of 28 June, after failing to find Catherine, sending couriers off to try to get information. But they either found the roads blocked or never returned. He had dinner served at the end of one of the alleys overlooking the sea, and drank his usual quantity of alcohol. There were about 600 Holstinian troops at his disposal at Oranienbaum but, even had they been sufficient to take on Catherine's overwhelming forces, he gave no indication of knowing how to deploy them. All those years of playing at soldiers proved to be of no use when confronted with the real thing. Eventually, prompted by General Münnich, he decided that his only hope was to go by sea to Kronstadt and perhaps escape from there on a Russian man-of-war to Holstein, where he could raise an army. Accordingly, at four o'clock in the afternoon, General Count Devier was sent to Kronstadt to tell the 3,000-man garrison to prepare for the Emperor's arrival.

Peter ordered the embarkation to Kronstadt to take place at midnight, when the 47 officials and courtiers (women as well as men) who were with him climbed on to a galley and a yacht and set off. Approaching the harbour at Kronstadt, they found their access blocked by a floating barrier. The Emperor's galley dropped anchor and sent a boat to request the removal of the barrier, but the sentry refused to comply. At first Peter assumed the man was merely obeying the orders he had himself given to General Devier, so he shouted out that he was the Emperor and demanded entry. The sentry shouted back that the garrison no longer recognised Peter III, only Catherine II. The alarm sounded, and

Peter and his flotilla were told to leave or they would be fired on. An armed vessel was blocking the approach to the open sea, so Peter's party had no option but to turn around, the galley (with Peter aboard) going to Oranienbaum and the yacht sailing back to Peterhof. Peter retired to his cabin and collapsed.

At five o'clock in the morning of Saturday 29 June, Peter's name-day and the eighteenth anniversary of his betrothal to Catherine, her army resumed its march on Peterhof. Along the road they arrested several hussars from Peter's Holstein regiment who had been sent to reconnoitre, as well as encountering former supporters of the Emperor who had already deserted him. At one point they were met by the Vice-Chancellor, Alexander Golitsyn, bearing a letter from Peter to Catherine in which he acknowledged that he had been unjust to her, promised to change and asked for a reconciliation (for all the world as though this were merely a marital tiff). No reply was vouchsafed to this request. News was brought that Alexei Orlov and his troops were already occupying both Oranienbaum and Peterhof and that they had encountered no resistance. A second pencil-written letter arrived from Peter in which he implored forgiveness, renounced the throne, and requested to be allowed to return to Holstein, taking with him Elizaveta Vorontsova and General Gudovich, his aide-de-camp. In answer to this, the act of abdication was dispatched to him for signature.

On arrival at Peterhof the troops were lined up and Catherine made her entry, still on her grey stallion which she handled with ease, to the acclamations of the soldiers. It was here that she received the signed act of abdication. She verified Peter's handwriting, and handed the document to an adviser for safe-keeping. She then retreated inside the Upper Palace, in order to avoid witnessing the humiliation of her husband, who arrived an hour later, in an old carriage, having been brought from Oranienbaum to Peterhof. Vorontsova and Gudovich were led away under arrest. As Peter emerged from the carriage, 300 trusted troops were deployed to protect him, to prevent his being set upon by any of the soldiers. Accompanied by Alexei Orlov, he was taken to a room in which he had often stayed when at Peterhof and made to divest himself of his Preobrazhensky uniform and to hand over his sword and the ribbon of St Andrew. Overcome with misery and shock, he fainted. About two decades later, Peter's hero Frederick the Great commented to the Comte de Ségur that Peter had allowed himself to be dethroned like a child being sent to bed.

Later that afternoon Peter was transferred to Ropsha, an estate about

20 miles inland which had been granted to him by the Empress Elizabeth. He was transported there in a large coach pulled by more than six horses, with drawn curtains and armed guards on the running boards, in the charge of Alexei Orlov, Fyodor Baryatinsky and a Lieutenant Baskakov. The intention was that he would stay at Ropsha until permanent accommodation was ready at the island fortress of Schlüsselburg. Catherine told Poniatowski that 'respectable and comfortable rooms were being prepared' for him.

The Russian historian V.O. Klyuchevsky sums up Peter III's reign succinctly: 'A chance guest of the Russian throne, Peter flashed across the Russian political horizon like a shooting star, leaving everyone bewildered as to why he had appeared there.' Robert Keith owned to a lack of surprise about the dramatic course of events, while also admitting that he had not expected things to happen quite so soon:

> Several other little circumstances greatly exaggerated, artfully represented and improved, contributed to the fall of this unhappy Prince, who had many excellent qualities, and who never did a violent or cruel action in the course of his short reign; but who from an abhorrence to business, owing to a bad education, and the unhappy choice of favourites who encouraged him in it, let every thing run into confusion, and by a mistaken notion he had conceived of having secured the affections of the nation by the great favours he had so nobly bestowed upon them, after his first mounting the throne, fell into indolence and security that proved fatal to him. To conclude not only I, but several persons of sense and discernment, thought they could perceive, latterly, in this Prince, a considerable change from what he was for some months after his accession, and that the perpetual hurry in which he lived, and the flattery he met with from the vile people about him, had in some measure affected his understanding.

After Peter's abdication and departure, Catherine also left Peterhof, this time in a carriage preceded by a detachment of horse guards. She stayed overnight at a house belonging to Prince Kurakin where she had a short sleep while still fully clothed, an officer pulling off her boots for her.

On the morning of Sunday 30 June 1762 Catherine re-entered St Petersburg in triumph, riding into the capital at the head of the Preobrazhensky Guards, along with other Guards regiments and artillery.

She arrived at noon at the Summer Palace to be greeted by little Paul and many government and church officials, and went immediately to the palace's chapel for the singing of the Te Deum. Afterwards she was exhausted, having hardly eaten or slept for three days. Before going to bed she issued an order to General Suvorov that Peter's violin and pug-dog should be sent to him from Oranienbaum, along with his doctor Lüders, his negro Narcissus and his head valet Timmler.

The common people celebrated Catherine's accession in time-honoured fashion by getting drunk. On that Sunday all the drinking establishments were opened to the troops, who went wild, consuming as much vodka, beer, mead and champagne as they could. (Claims were later submitted by tavern-keepers and spirits merchants for a total of about 105,000 roubles' worth of drink lost during Catherine's accession; the claims were still being processed in the Senate three years later.) Dashkova relates that some 30 soldiers broke into a cellar, where they found gallons of Hungarian wine which they were happily drinking out of their hats. During the course of the evening the drinking and looting increased and, amidst all the shouting and singing, a rumour spread that the Prussians were coming to kidnap Catherine. There was danger of a riot, which not even Grigory Orlov and his brother Fyodor were able to quell. Eventually Lieutenant Passek (who in the end had been imprisoned for only 12 hours and had not given anything away) was sent to awake the exhausted Empress after midnight and take her out in a carriage to visit the Izmailovsky Guards. Only after the soldiers had seen her did they calm down.

In her letter to Poniatowski, describing the main events of these momentous days, Catherine paid honour to her supporters: 'The Orlovs shone by their art of leadership, their prudent daring, by the care introduced in small details, by their presence of mind and authority. They have much common sense and generous courage. Enthusiastically patriotic and honest, passionately attached to me and friends among each other, as brothers rarely are, there are five of them in all, but only three were here.' She is also quite blunt in her estimation of Ekaterina Dashkova, whose reputation nevertheless as the heroine of the hour resounded throughout Europe:

Princess Dashkov, younger sister of Elizabeth Worontsov, (though she wants all the honour of the execution of the plot attributed to her, simply because she knew some of the leaders) was in bad odour on account of her sister, nor did the fact that she was only nineteen

years old impress anyone. Though she pretended to be the intermediary through whom everything reached me, everybody had been
in touch with me for six months before she even knew their names.
It is true that she is intelligent but she behaves ostentatiously and is
an intriguer and disliked by our officers; only the heedless and the
rash told her what they knew, which was not much more than a
few details. I[van]. Shuvalov, the lowest and meanest of men, has, I
am told, written to Voltaire that a girl of nineteen has changed the
face of the Empire. Please undeceive this great writer.

Catherine's sense that she was fulfilling her destiny was validated
completely by these three extraordinary days. As she also wrote to
Poniatowski: 'At last, God brought everything to the end He wished
and all this is more a miracle than an organized and planned event, for
so many favourable circumstances cannot be brought together without
the hand of God.'

# 7

# Murder, Coronation
# and Conspiracy
# (1762–63)

*The Empress will need all her strengths and talents to avert the storms that I see forming at her Court.*

Report of the French attaché, Bérenger

*T*he problems which faced Catherine on her accession were considerable, as she recalled some years later when she wrote of an unpaid army and a state in financial disarray. No one in the Treasury had any idea of what was in the coffers, and everywhere people were bringing 'complaints of extortion, bribes, oppression and miscarriages of justice'. Prisons were bursting at the seams and there were reports of peasants indentured to factories rebelling against their owners. Nothing, according to Catherine, was working properly. The attitude amongst officialdom was 'but we've always done it this way' – and there were plenty who had been happily lining their pockets in the process. There was much here for Catherine the administrator and lover of order to tackle. She took over the bureaucratic machinery of government virtually intact, so far as its personnel was concerned; unlike any previous occupant of the Russian throne, she did not prosecute or exile any of the high-ranking officials who had served under her predecessor. Her attitude seemed to be that they had had no choice in the matter and, provided they gave her their undivided loyalty from now on, she would not reproach them with their past. Very few of Peter's officials were dismissed, and some who initially were moved to posts outside the capital were soon returned to high office. Eventually even Ivan Shuvalov, the late Empress's favourite, rose to a position of eminence and trust at Catherine's Court. Chancellor Vorontsov, despite his protestations on the day of the coup, remained in post, though his power was inevitably diminished by the fact that Catherine, unlike Elizabeth, did not intend to sit back and let her officials get on with their work in the way they saw fit. It was something of a culture shock for the Russian senators (of whom there were about 20, the Senate being the highest government institution, which was supposed to coordinate the work of all the Colleges and of the provincial governors) to experience a ruler who actually joined in their sessions and expected a degree of accountability from them. It was also something of a shock to the Empress to discover the levels of disorganisation and ignorance pervading some of her organs of government. On first attending the sessions of the Senate, for instance, she was horrified to find that not only were the senators unable to answer her questions about how many towns there were in the country, but they did not even possess a map of Russia. She immediately sent someone out to obtain one from the Academy of Sciences.

Catherine did not intend to repeat Peter's mistake of neglecting to arrange a coronation. One of the very first appointments she made was of Prince Nikita Trubetskoy, whom she put in charge of planning the event, with an initial budget of 50,000 roubles. Vasily Shkurin, who was to be in charge of Catherine's wardrobe, was allotted 20,000 roubles and the Empress also ordered 120 oak barrels of silver coins for distribution to the populace. The event was to take place as soon as reasonably possible, and in Moscow, the old capital and traditional place of coronation. The German-born Catherine intended that this should emphasise her Russian-ness, her sense of tradition and the divine imprimatur for her rule.

On 2 July the foreign ministers were summoned to attend Court at 11 o'clock in the morning, where they were presented to the Empress by the Chancellor. On the same day Catherine wrote to Stanislas Poniatowski who, on receiving news of the coup, seems to have imagined that he should now rush back to St Petersburg where he would be welcomed by his former lover, now Her Imperial Majesty, with open arms. She was anxious to disabuse him of that idea:

> I beg you most urgently not to hasten to come here, as your arrival in the present circumstances would be dangerous for you and do

me much harm. The revolution which has just taken place in my favour is miraculous. Its unanimity is unbelievable. I am deeply engaged in work and would be unable to devote myself to you. All my life I will serve and revere your family but at the moment it is important not to arouse criticism. I have not slept for three nights and have eaten twice in four days.

While the new Empress was beginning to take stock of the work that lay ahead of her, the ex-Emperor was trying unsuccessfully to accommodate himself to being held in close confinement at Ropsha, where he was lodged under guard in one room and was not even allowed to go out on to the terrace. He wrote pathetically to Catherine, requesting more space and privacy:

I beg Your Majesty to have confidence in me and to have the sentries removed from the second room, as the one I occupy is so small that I can hardly move in it. As Your Majesty knows I always stride about the room and my legs will swell if I cannot do so. Also I beg you to order that no officers should remain in the same room with me, as I have needs that I cannot possibly indulge in front of them. I beg Your Majesty not to treat me as a criminal as I have never offended Your Majesty. I recommend myself to Your Majesty's magnanimity and beg to be reunited with the indicated persons in Germany as soon as possible. God will repay Your Majesty.

Your very humble servant,

Peter

PS. Your Majesty may be sure that I will not undertake anything against her person or her reign.

He also wrote a brief note to ask Catherine to restore Elizaveta Vorontsova to him, and a further request to be allowed to leave for Germany with the people he had asked to accompany him.

Peter was still in the charge of, among others, Alexei Orlov and Fyodor Baryatinsky. Orlov appears to have treated him reasonably well, helping him pass the time by playing cards. The men all ate together, the meals accompanied by the quantities of wine to which they were accustomed. It was a volatile situation. On 2 July Alexei wrote a cryptic note to Catherine which should have alerted her to the potential danger Peter was in: 'We and the whole detachment are all well, only our

Monster [i.e. Peter] is gravely ill, with an unexpected colic. I fear that he might die tonight, but even more I fear that he might live. The first fear is caused by the fact that he talks nonsense the whole time which amuses us, and the second that he is really a danger to us all and behaves as though nothing had happened.' Peter had been taken ill with acute diarrhoea – an affliction he must have found deeply embarrassing, as he hated having to relieve himself in the presence of guards. On the evening of Wednesday 3 July he was attended by his physician Dr Lüders, who gave him some medicine. The next day Dr Lüders called in Staff Surgeon Paulsen for a second opinion; both doctors concluded by the evening that Peter had recovered. On 5 July the French attaché Bérenger wrote optimistically to the Comte de Choiseul: '[Peter] proposes to live as a philosopher; I think that all he will be lacking is freedom.' But by that evening Peter had fallen ill again, and then on the following evening Catherine received an anguished and confused note from Alexei Orlov:

Your Majesty, our little mother!* How can I tell you, how can I describe what has happened; you will not believe your slave, but I will tell you the truth as before the Lord. Your Majesty, our little mother! I swear that I cannot understand how this has happened. We are finished if you do not pardon us, our little mother, he is no more! No one wanted it to come to that, how would we dare to raise our hand against our sovereign! Nevertheless, Your Majesty, the misfortune has happened. At table he got into an argument with Prince Fyodor [Baryatinsky], and before we could have time to separate them, he was no more. We cannot ourselves remember what we were doing; but we are all guilty, we deserve death. Forgive me, if only because of my brother. I have admitted everything to you, it would be useless to have an investigation. Pardon me or sentence me to death at once. Life disgusts me: we have aroused your anger and lost our soul.

Orlov's letter was locked in a cabinet in Catherine's study, where it lay hidden throughout her reign.

No one knows the degree of Catherine's complicity in the murder of Peter. Many people at home and abroad assumed her to be guilty,

---

* '*Matushka*', a traditional way of addressing the tsarina, and the feminine equivalent of '*batyushka*' ('little father', used for both tsars and priests).

even if they did not say so openly. Few bought the official version – that Peter had died of a 'haemorrhoidal colic' – though this verdict was never questioned overtly, at least not in Russia. The general feeling seems to have been that Peter's death was an inevitable consequence of his dethronement. It was hard to imagine him being locked up indefinitely, with his violin and his Lutheran Bible but also with his periodic fits of drunken instability. And it was harder still to think of him being allowed to return to Holstein as he desired. Years later, Frederick the Great laid the blame on the Orlovs but not on Catherine:

> Catherine, crowned and free, believed, as a young woman with no experience, that everything was done; such a cowardly enemy did not appear dangerous to her. But the Orlovs, more audacious and far-seeing, not wanting anyone to use this prince as a standard to raise against them, murdered him.
>
> The Empress did not know about this heinous crime, and learnt of it with a despair that was not feigned; she had a just presentiment of the judgment which everyone would today bring against her; for the guilt of this judgment is and must be ineffaceable, since, in her position, she had harvested the fruits of this assassination, and saw herself obliged, in order to have support, not only to spare, but even to keep alongside her the authors of the crime, since they alone could save her.

In referring to Catherine as 'a young woman with no experience', Frederick was underestimating her well-developed political and strategic sense. It seems most likely that Catherine had given at least tacit consent to Peter's assassination. With the three Orlov brothers and Fyodor Baryatinsky, she had reached the conclusion that Peter must be disposed of, and the arrangement was that, while Catherine must never be seen to have been involved, she would protect her husband's assassins and ensure they were never brought to trial. But the inevitable questions surrounding her own involvement presented her with an additional hurdle to overcome in establishing herself in the eyes of Russia and the world as a legitimate monarch. She would always now have to contend with the reputation encapsulated by Bérenger in his colourful report to the Comte de Choiseul: 'What a picture, Monseigneur, for the nation once it has returned to its right mind and can judge in cold blood! On one side, the grandson of Peter I dethroned and put to death; on the other, the grandson of Tsar Ivan languishing in irons, while a Princess of Anhalt-Zerbst usurps the crown, beginning her reign with a regicide.'

Catherine had learnt of Peter's death a few hours after it occurred, but no public announcement was made until the following day. The foreign ministers were informed of the event in a document issued by the College of Foreign Affairs, which said that 'the late Emperor, after having suffered greatly from haemorrhoids and from a violent stomach-ache with which he was often afflicted, died yesterday'. A manifesto was also read out in the churches, announcing the death of the former Emperor from a severe colic and inviting prayers for the repose of his soul.

Catherine arranged for an autopsy to be performed on Peter's body which confirmed death by natural causes. His body was then exposed for two days at the Alexander Nevsky Monastery, where people were free to come and pay their respects – though the names were taken of any significant people who did so. No foreign ministers went to see the body, but Bérenger sent a friend who reported back to him that Peter's 'face was extraordinarily black, that he was oozing through the skin an extravasated blood which could be seen even on the gloves which covered his hands'. 'Finally,' wrote Bérenger, 'people claim to have noticed on the corpse all the symptoms which may indicate poisoning.' Peter was clothed in his beloved light blue Holstinian uniform; the signs of strangulation were obscured by an ample cravat covering his throat and a large hat concealing much of his face.

The burial took place on 10 July. As Robert Keith described it, 'The late Emperor was buried at Newsky on Wednesday morning, without ceremony, only those of the first five classes were ordered to attend the funeral.' Catherine did not attend. The coffin was placed on top of that of Anna Leopoldovna. Peter's burial in the Nevsky Monastery, away from the rest of the Romanov dynasty in the Peter and Paul Cathedral, was designed to underline both his political insignificance and his unwor-thiness to be considered a true descendant of Peter the Great. The fact that he had never actually been crowned as Tsar was also now used as a reason for relegating him to this relatively lowly place of burial.

Two days after Peter's funeral, the former Chancellor Bestuzhev arrived back in Petersburg. He was met by Grigory Orlov 20 miles outside the city and driven the rest of the way in the imperial coach. Catherine was waiting to greet her old ally at the Summer Palace. She immediately restored all his ranks and titles and presented him with his own carriage and a splendid house, with all the needs of his table provided at court expense. (His former house on the embankment alongside St Isaac's Square, on which he had taken out a mortgage from the English consul, became the headquarters of the Senate in 1763.) A manifesto was proclaimed confirming Bestuzhev's innocence of the charges laid against him by the Empress Elizabeth. The other courtiers exiled over the affair were also recalled (one of them, Ivan Yelagin, quickly became one of Catherine's most trusted officials) and were treated with great honour. Within a few weeks of the coup, Catherine's uncle, Prince Georg Ludwig, was awarded 100,000 roubles for the losses he had sustained when soldiers had looted his house, and allowed to return to Holstein with 62 other natives of that principality.★ As for Peter's former mistress, Elizaveta Vorontsova, Catherine gave permission for her to live in her father's house in Moscow, until such time as she had a house of her own. She was told to live quietly and not give people any reason for talking about her. Catherine subsequently instructed Elizaveta's father, Roman Vorontsov, to ensure she was adequately provided for by making over to her what would have been hers had she married. The Empress herself also made arrangements for a house to be bought for her in Moscow.

On 2 August Catherine wrote again to Stanislas Poniatowski, providing him with full details of the events of the coup: 'All minds here are still in a state of ferment,' she said. 'I beg you not to come here now, for fear of increasing it.' She also gave him a version of what had happened to Peter:

> Fright had given him a colic that lasted three days and passed on the fourth. On that day he drank excessively – for he had everything he wanted, except liberty. The illness affected his brain, it was followed by a great weakness and in spite of all the assistance of physicians, he gave up the ghost, after asking for a Lutheran priest. I had him opened up – but his stomach showed no traces of ill-health. The cause of death was established as inflammation of the bowels and apoplexy. He had an inordinately small heart, quite withered.

---

★ Prince Georg Ludwig died on 27 August 1763, at the age of 44. Catherine arranged for the Prince's sons, 11-year-old William and 9-year-old Peter Frederick Ludwig, to be brought to Petersburg; they were looked after and educated at Court.

Should Stanislas still be entertaining any lingering hopes that their former relationship could now be revived, the Empress Catherine put paid to them: 'I received your letter. A regular correspondence would be subject to a thousand inconveniences, I have twenty thousand precautions to take and have no time for harmful little love-letters.' Catherine was very aware that she now had to do everything within her power to be accepted as a legitimate Russian ruler, and that to draw attention to her own foreignness by maintaining a close relationship with another foreigner – and, worse, a Roman Catholic – could be fatal. She tried to indicate this to Poniatowski, explaining that during the coup 'everything was carried out on the principle of hatred of the foreigner; Peter III himself counted as such'. She did not tell her former lover in so many words that he had been replaced in her affections by another man, but she did hint at it: 'I feel very embarrassed . . . I cannot tell you what it is about, but it is true.' At the end of the letter she almost sounds a note of apology: 'Good-bye, the world is full of strange situations.'

A week later St Petersburg's official gazette announced awards to all the principal leaders of the coup. Kirill Razumovsky, Nikita Panin and Mikhail Volkonsky all received pensions of 5,000 roubles a year, while 17 others, including Grigory and Alexei Orlov, Lieutenant Passek and Princess Dashkova, each received 800 serfs (gifts of serfs always came with the land they occupied and worked for the benefit of their owner) or 24,000 roubles.

Preparations for the coronation were proceeding apace. Elements of the Petersburg administrative departments had begun leaving for Moscow in late July. Catherine herself, preceded by Grigory Orlov, set off on 1 September, her suite consisting of 23 persons with 63 carriages and carts, pulled by 395 horses. Her son Paul had left several days earlier, in the company of his governor Nikita Panin, in a convoy of 27 carriages with 257 horses. Although Catherine's convoy travelled slowly, it caught up with Paul's party, which had halted its journey at a posting station when the child had become feverish. He seemed to be feeling better by the time his mother reached him, however, so she pressed on. On 10 September Catherine wrote to Panin from Petrovskoye, Count Kirill Razumovsky's estate outside Moscow, expressing concern about Paul's attack of fever, but ascribing it to overexcitement.

The health of the nearly eight-year-old Grand Duke Paul had long been a subject of some anxiety, and during the preceding month, the court doctor, Kruz, appointed by the Empress to be Paul's general physician, had compiled a summary of his illnesses to date and the measures which had been taken to combat them. The picture he paints is of a little boy chronically affected by digestive problems, including diarrhoea and vomiting. The principal cause of his ailments, according to Dr Kruz, was 'the acidity which dominates in his stomach and digestive tract', a problem which the doctor believed to have been exacerbated by remedies – 'oils', 'syrups' and 'dilutants' – prescribed in Paul's infancy, which had 'engendered a slowness in the body's juices, by further weakening the solid parts'. Dr Kruz nevertheless commends Mr Panin (whose supervision of the Grand Duke extended to the most minute particulars) for his 'extraordinary wisdom and prudence' in ensuring that Paul followed 'a highly scrupulous diet and way of life'. He recommended that Paul should now have a diet consisting of meat and alkaline substances to 'correct the juices', take salts, 'soapy remedies' and Seltzer water to 'unblock the glands', be administered a variety of drugs (he lists the ingredients of two powders to be made up for him, one of which is a laxative) and take some physical exercise to strengthen 'the solid parts'. His lower abdomen was also to be massaged daily, and other recommended remedies included spa water with goats' or asses' milk, and Peruvian bark. His suppurating glands were to be dressed every day 'according to the rules of surgery in order to form a perfect scar, which does not disfigure the face'.

Despite Paul's indisposition, he and Panin managed to catch up with Catherine in time to join her for the triumphal entry into Moscow on 13 September, a fact which enhanced the glory of the occasion. The presence of her son, the undoubted (at least as far as the crowds knew) descendant of Peter the Great, conferred on Catherine a kind of legitimacy – even though she never for one moment considered herself merely a regent ruling in her son's name. There were others who imagined, however, that this had been the assumption behind her coup. It is certainly possible that Catherine allowed Nikita Panin to entertain such a belief as the price of his support, while knowing that he would be over-ruled by the majority of her supporters, who wanted her to be Empress in her own right. In all her planning as Grand Duchess, as well as in the proclamations drawn up weeks before her accession, there was never any suggestion that Catherine saw herself as only occupying the throne in trust for her son, but the rumour plagued her throughout her reign that the original plan had indeed been that she should rule as regent but that in the excitement of the moment she had been proclaimed Empress almost by accident. Catherine never gave any clear indication of the role she expected her son to fulfil during her lifetime, either as child or man (other than that it would be negligible), but she capitalised on his popularity with the people and recognised his importance for her image. She also knew that if anything untoward were to happen to him, it would be disastrous. His position as heir to the throne acted as a guarantee of stability to her own reign, so she was keen to have him by her when on display, and he was well looked after. But there is little indication that she particularly liked him, and she rarely chose to spend time with him (not that there was anything unusual about the maintenance of such a distance between mother and child in an eighteenth-century aristocratic family). As for the sickly boy, the weeks since he had been roused from bed in the early morning to greet the crowds alongside his mother from the balcony of the Winter Palace must have passed in a confused blur, despite Panin's best efforts to ensure he led an ordered life. He had hardly known his father, but he was well aware that he had been the Emperor, that now he was dead and that his mother was all-powerful instead. How much his recurrent illnesses were psychosomatic can only be guessed at, but it is hard to avoid the conclusion that at least some of his symptoms may have been caused by stress and unhappiness.

Catherine's coronation took place on Sunday 22 September 1762, two days after Paul's eighth birthday. The child was unable to attend the ceremony as he was ill again, this time with a high fever and a swollen leg. Twenty-one cannon fired a salute at five o'clock in the morning, and at eight o'clock soldiers took up their positions inside the Kremlin as all the church bells of Moscow began to clash. At ten o'clock Catherine emerged from her private apartments to the accompaniment of trumpets and drums. In the audience chamber she was greeted by the senior gentlemen of the Court and high-ranking church dignitaries. Then, preceded by her confessor who sprinkled the path before her with holy water, she descended from the Krasnoye Kryltso and proceeded to the Cathedral of the Assumption, where she had been betrothed to Peter in 1744.

Catherine wore a magnificent gown of silver silk embroidered with eagles and trimmed with ermine. Her long train was carried by six chamberlains. The imperial purple velvet mantle, which had been made in Paris for the coronation of Catherine I in 1724, was encrusted with hundreds of double-headed golden eagles. The dazzling crown, which she placed on her head herself, had been specially commissioned. It was based on an ancient Byzantine design of two half-spheres connected by a garland of oak leaves and acorns, and contained a total of 4,936 diamonds set in silver, the whole topped by an enormous dark ruby. In shape it was not dissimilar to the mitre of an Orthodox bishop, the ruby taking the place of the cross, and this similarity would not be lost on Catherine, who as Empress was also head of the Russian Orthodox Church. Cannons were fired in salute as she stood before the diamond- and ruby-studded throne, with the sceptre in her right hand and the orb in her left. She was anointed by the Archbishop of Novgorod, received communion, and then went to venerate the icons in the Cathedrals of the Archangel and the Annunciation.

Her confessor once asked her, fairly late in life, whether she believed in God, and she was amazed to have been asked such a question, as she recounted to her secretary, Alexander Khrapovitsky:

> I was asked a strange question at confession, which I have never been asked before: do you believe in God? I at once recited the whole Creed and, if they want proof, then I will give them such proofs as they have never thought of. I believe everything affirmed at the seven Ecumenical Councils, because the Holy Fathers of those times were closer to the Apostles and could understand everything better than us.

Catherine was thus an Orthodox believer in that, as a member of the Orthodox community of faith, she identified herself as Christian and accepted the teachings of the Church. She did not view faith as a matter of individual belief in the way we view it today, which is why she found the question posed by her confessor so surprising. As an Orthodox believer she fulfilled the requirements of Orthodoxy – which means 'right worship' – through the observances of fasting, attending the liturgy, going to confession and receiving communion at the prescribed times, and making the correct signs of crossing oneself, bowing, reverencing icons, kissing the priest's sleeve and so on. She would not have thought it necessary to do any more than that – there are many feast days in the Orthodox calendar on which one had to attend the liturgy, and Orthodox liturgy is never short – or to question her faith. The Enlightenment philosophers she favoured did not require her not to believe – merely that belief should be consistent with reason, which she interpreted as meaning it should not be extreme or fanatical, and that religion should not interfere in statecraft or politics (which suited her very well). Catherine also took her position as head of the Orthodox Church in Russia very seriously. The Church, managed in the right way, lent stability to the State. The guiding principle for Catherine was order, and the Orthodox Church, with its orders of bishops, archimandrites, priests and deacons, and the people as obedient worshippers, contributed to the rightful ordering of a peaceful, well-regulated State, where everyone knew his place and contributed appropriately to the whole. In the ordering of Catherine's personal life, however, religion seems to have played a very small part, and the response she made to her confessor when asked if she believed would suggest that she was not given to minute examination of conscience in these encounters.

After the coronation the Empress returned to the Faceted Palace to receive the homage of the courtiers and to award decorations, ranks and gem-studded swords. Grigory Orlov was named adjutant-general, and all five Orlov brothers were elevated to the title of Count, as was Nikita Panin. That evening all the buildings of the Kremlin were illuminated, and at midnight Catherine emerged on to the Krasnoye Kryltso where she was greeted by loud acclamations. According to the French ambassador the Baron de Breteuil, some of these acclamations were stage-managed (Communist leaders of the twentieth century were not the first occupants of the Kremlin skilled at orchestrating popular enthusiasm) and at one point they nearly went disastrously wrong:

> At one of these moments it happened that, instead of crying, 'Long live the Empress Catherine II', the soldiers and people began to shout . . . 'Long live our Emperor Paul Petrovich' by which they meant the Grand Duke. The Court, informed of the error of this acclamation, immediately sent some officers who made them be silent, saying with kindness to the soldiers that the Empress was persuaded of their joy and begged them to moderate it for today. This little circumstance caused some alarm in the interior of the Court, but there were no repercussions.

There then followed a week of festivities and celebrations, culminating in a firework display on 29 September. The festivities were made all the more glorious by the fact that, for the first six months of Catherine's reign – which coincided with the second six months of the period of mourning for the late Empress Elizabeth – public performances of music were banned both at Court and throughout the country (in deliberate contrast to Peter's neglect of this pious observance). An exception was made for the coronation and subsequent celebrations, mourning being cancelled for those days, so that the sense of rejoicing and splendour must have been particularly memorable. Jakob Stählin had been sent from Petersburg to Moscow to put on theatrical performances, and Vincenzo Manfredini had composed a new opera – *Olimpiade*, with a libretto by the Italian poet Pietro Metastasio (who provided the libretti for many eighteenth-century operas) – which was performed several times on the imperial stage. After the coronation festivities, music was again silenced until the end of the year.

For Catherine two things marred the coronation celebrations and the days immediately following them. The first was Grand Duke Paul's continued ill health; he suffered a serious relapse at the end of the festivities and spent the first two weeks of October in bed. His mother was so worried that she made a vow to endow a public hospital in Moscow in her son's name. (The astute Catherine, no matter how genuine her anxiety, was never one to let such a public relations opportunity pass her by.) The second cause for concern was brought to Catherine's attention on 3 October, when Vasily Shkurin reported a conspiracy among the Izmailovsky Guards, led by one Peter Khrushchev. Catherine immediately ordered Colonel Kirill Razumovsky to conduct a secret investigation within the regiment, and 15 people were arrested within the space of 48 hours. It emerged that a Captain Ivan Guryev had mentioned a conspiracy of various nobles to install the captive Ivan VI as Emperor. Guryev's brother Semyon was involved; he had invented a story about Ivan being brought from Schlüsselburg and had been motivated largely by jealousy at seeing other people receiving rewards while he had received none, despite having stood watch at Peterhof during Catherine's coup.

On Catherine's orders, Peter Khrushchev and Semyon Guryev were beaten with sticks (*batogi* – a form of punishment in which two men sat on either end of the prostrate victim, both beating his naked back with two sticks) to see if they would confess anything more, but neither did. The investigators concluded that the whole 'conspiracy' amounted to no more than drunken posturing and recommended that 11 men be transferred to other regiments or distant garrisons. Catherine demanded harsher sentences, however, to act as a deterrent, to which the investigators responded dutifully by proposing death sentences for five of the men. The Empress then passed these recommendations to the Senate which, as expected, softened them somewhat, condemning only Peter Khrushchev and Semyon Guryev to death by decapitation.

In the event Catherine commuted the sentences still further; Khrushchev and Guryev were to be deprived of rank, noble status and surnames, to have their swords broken over their heads and to be sent to eternal imprisonment in Kamchatka. Three other so-called conspirators were stripped of rank and condemned to exile. The sentences were carried out on 28 October, and the convicts sent off to Siberia.

Catherine had been involved in too many conspiracies herself not to take them seriously. She was quick to re-establish the imperial secret police, albeit under another name: while confirming the abolition of the Secret Chancery and forbidding anonymous denunciations, she simultaneously ordered that any matters concerning potential rebellion or treason be referred to the Senate, from which there soon emerged a Secret Branch. This organisation effectively took over the role of the Secret Chancery and lasted throughout Catherine's reign.

The Earl of Buckingham, who had recently replaced Robert Keith as British ambassador, reported on 14 October on Catherine's visible strain: 'The Empress seems to have a settled melancholy upon Her countenance. She mentioned to me, last night, in conversation, that She had lately found Herself absent in company, and that the habit of it imperceptibly grew upon Her, She knew not why.' The Earl had his first official private audience with the Empress that day and presented his credentials; he returned to Court in the evening where, he reported, 'I had the honour of playing at picket with Her Majesty. She asked me a great many questions about England and upon the whole Her behaviour to me both there and at my audience was extremely gracious.' (This was indeed quite an honour, as 'picket' or piquet, pronounced 'peeket', was a card game for only two people.) A month later, after Buckingham had had time to observe the characteristics of the various officials in Catherine's government, he wrote up some of his conclusions in a dispatch to the Earl of Halifax:

The Chancellor [Mikhail Vorontsov] has the air and address of a man of condition, but if ever he had any abilities, they are greatly impaired, and his mind and body are too greatly relaxed for him to be capable of that intense application to business, which his situation requires . . . The Vice-Chancellor [Alexander Golitsyn] has been so long in England,★ that it is unnecessary to say any thing

★ Golitsyn had been Russian ambassador in London before returning to Petersburg to take up the post of Vice-Chancellor in the last months of Elizabeth's reign.

of his character, abilities, or connections. Mr Bestucheff is old, and has the appearance of being still older; if he is now capable of business, it cannot last long: it is said, he is greatly consulted; and his behaviour to me at least implies that he would have thought it so. Mr Panin, who seems better qualified than most of the Russian Ministers to hold the first place, probably shares the Empress' confidence with him; but the Empress Herself, from all the observations I can make, and all the lights I can obtain, is, in talents, information, and application, greatly superior to every body in this country.

The Empress's lover, Grigory Orlov, was having to adjust to the life of an imperial favourite, a far cry from being the secret lover of a Grand Duchess. Their relationship was now openly acknowledged – though the Empress was very rarely demonstrative in public, and no one seemed to be aware that Grigory had been Catherine's lover *before* the coup. His presence near Catherine since early 1761, if it was noticed at all, had been explained as a result of unrequited affection, as is clear from the Baron de Breteuil's comments to the Comte de Choiseul (the Baron had been privy to the relationship between Catherine and Poniatowski, being one of those who had facilitated their correspondence):

> I do not know, Monseigneur, what will come of the correspondence which the Tsarina is carrying on with Monsieur Poniatowski, but there no longer seems to be any doubt that She has given him a successor in the person of Monsieur Orlov, whom she made a Count on the day of her coronation . . . He has been in love with the Tsarina for several years and I remember that one day She pointed him out to me as a ridiculous character, and told me the extravagance of his sentiments, but since then he has deserved that She should take them more seriously; apart from that, it is said, he is a great fool. As he only speaks Russian, it will not be easy for me to judge of that very soon – this attribute of stupidity is hardly rare among those who surround the Tsarina these days.

In November the Baron remarked that Grigory had landed himself in trouble with the Empress for having been imprudent enough to spend 24 hours away from the palace indulging in gambling and drunkenness. Grigory's relationship quickly aroused the suspicion and jealousy of other courtiers – not so much sexual and emotional jealousy, as envy of the honours he and his brothers were awarded combined with a fear of their influence and access to the Empress. Only Catherine and the Orlovs themselves were fully aware of the extent of the role they had played in the coup. Consequently, the immediate favours they reaped seemed disproportionate to onlookers who imagined that Catherine was motivated only by her sudden – as it appeared – infatuation with the handsome Grigory, who seemed to have come out of nowhere to a highly prominent position. Bérenger had reported on the hostility as early as 5 July: 'I have no time, Monseigneur, to go into details about the intrigues and cabals which are already appearing at the new Court. They conspire against Orlov and secretly prepare his downfall. The Empress will need all her strengths and talents to avert the storms that I see forming at her Court.' A few months later the Prussian envoy, Count Solms, summarised for Frederick the Great what he thought he knew about the Empress's favourite. Given the inflated and inaccurate role accorded to her here, some of his information may have come from Princess Dashkova:

This man who plays today the principal role at the Russian Court was a lieutenant captain in the artillery in the time of the late Emperor Peter III. Unable to gain access to great houses because of his passion for gambling and his small amount of wealth, he was obliged to consort with his comrades and people considerably lower than them. Today one could perhaps find artisans and lackeys who used to sit with him around the same table. His frequenting of gambling dens and taverns made it easy for him to learn the sentiments of the soldiers and the people, and so he was used to prepare their minds for the revolution which was being planned. It was Princess Dashkova who introduced him to the Empress and who told her he was a trustworthy man. He did in fact show himself to be very zealous in the preparations and more assiduous than others after the coup had been struck. His eagerness was noticed and the gratitude which the Empress believed she owed him, supported on his side by a handsome figure and a kind and prepossessing physiognomy, soon drew him out of his original obscurity. He was overwhelmed with wealth and honour and is now count, chamberlain, lieutenant-general, aide-de-camp of Her Majesty, and knight of the Order of St Alexander. He lives at Court, where all his expenses are paid. His three [*sic*] brothers have profited from

his good fortune and enjoy the benefits of Her Majesty's particular protection.

Meanwhile Catherine continued to make changes in her administ
ration. She dealt with her courtiers and officials in much the same way
she had dealt with her supporters before the coup – very few of them
were ever allowed to see the full picture, each of them imagining that
they were more completely in the Empress's confidence than they actually were. For the time being Russia was at peace. The new Empress
had immediately cancelled both the incipient war with Denmark and
the alliance Peter had formed with Prussia, while assuring the Prussians
that she had no intention of fighting them. Her policy of peace was
conducted with the aim both of calming tensions at home and of easing
the financial burden imposed by armed conflict. As a first step to sorting
out the embittered relations between Church and State, Catherine had
abolished the College of Economy, the state agency responsible for the
administration of ecclesiastical properties, and appointed a commission
(always useful for the buying of time) to examine the thorny issue of
the secularisation of church and monastic property. Then on 27
November she reinstated the College under a different name as part
of a general reform to specify the budgets and staffing of all ecclesiastical institutions. Many clerics grumbled about what was seen as another
move towards secularisation, but there was little active protest. In
December Catherine issued secret orders that torture was to be used
only very sparingly in order not to let the innocent suffer, and in the
same month she dispatched Quartermaster-General Prince Alexander
Vyazemsky to Kazan with a manifesto exhorting submission from the
rebellious peasants assigned to factory work in the Urals. Vyazemsky
was also authorised to investigate the workers' complaints – but only
after their submission had been obtained.

Throughout this period Nikita Panin had been working on a plan
– with, as he believed, the Empress's approval – to establish a council
of ministers to work alongside Catherine. She would have the power
to appoint the members of this council but not to dismiss any of them,
and all her decrees would have to be countersigned by them. Catherine
now quietly allowed further consideration of this plan to be dropped.
The Orlovs had insinuated to her that Panin's real aim was to introduce an aristocratic constitution that would curb her own power and
pave the way for Paul's succession – but that she would ever have seriously considered a plan that attempted to limit any of her powers, with

or without the Orlovs' interference, is highly improbable. As had been the case before her accession, she was prepared to allow Panin to elaborate his own theories while she carried on arranging the pieces on her imperial chess board. Eventually Panin would find she was gently yet firmly controlling him, rather than the other way about. From a comment the Earl of Buckingham made in one of his dispatches, it can be inferred that Chancellor Vorontsov and Vice-Chancellor Golitsyn preferred the good old days when the sovereign did not interfere: 'The Chancellor, and Vice-Chancellor mentioned, that Her Imperial Majesty applied Herself so much to business, as might be prejudicial to Her health; that She would see and form her own opinion upon every thing.'

There was at least one entrenched custom at the Russian Court which was not amenable to being changed overnight, as a dispatch from the Earl of Buckingham makes clear: 'If the Treaty of Commerce is concluded upon terms agreeable to His Majesty [i.e. George III], I should rather think it advisable, that presents should be made to [Orlov], to Bestucheff, Panin, and the Vice-Chancellor . . . I must add, that possibly an expence [*sic*] of this kind is not absolutely necessary, though they have been but too much used to presents here.' During the same month the Earl attended an 'entertainment' at Court, on which he reported with enthusiasm (fully expecting his dispatch to be intercepted and his fulsome praise relayed to the Empress):

> It was a Russian tragedy, which was performed at the Palace before the Empress, in a most magnificent hall fitted up for the occasion, with a stage, scenes and all proper decorations. The subject of the drama was a Russian story, and as far as any judgement may be formed upon reading an incorrect French translation, the sentiments and the dialogue would do honour to any author, in any country. The Countess Bruce acted the principal part, with a spirit, ease, and propriety, which is seldom met with even amongst those, who are bred to the stage. Two other characters were admirably represented by Count Orloff, and a son of the late Marshal Schuwaloff's [this was Andrei Shuvalov]. Count Orloff's figure is very striking, and bears some resemblance to that of the Earl of Errol. After the play there was an entertainment of dancing performed by the Maids of Honour, and several of the first nobility. I believe so many fine women were never seen upon any stage, and must add, that few countries could produce them. The Countess

Catherine's father, Christian August of Anhalt-Zerbst, as portrayed by Antoine Pesne in 1725.

Catherine's mother, Johanna Elizabeth of Holstein-Gottorp, probably also painted by Antoine Pesne in about 1746.

A portrait of the Empress Elizabeth by Louis Tocque, painted two years before her death. Catherine said of her: 'She was a large woman who, in spite of being very stout, was not in the least disfigured by her size nor was she embarrassed in her movements; her head, too, was very beautiful.'

Grand Duke Peter and Grand Duchess Catherine, painted by Georg Christoph Grooth around the time of their marriage. The artist died in 1749, and it was his widow who was called upon to initiate Peter into the mysteries of sex, after Catherine had failed to do so.

Grand Duke Peter, painted
by Fyodor Stepanovich Rokotov
in 1758. By this time, Catherine's
relationship with her husband
was beyond repair.

Grand Duke Paul, Catherine's –
and probably Peter's – son, painted
in his classroom by Virgilius
Erichsen. Paul's education included
languages, history, geography,
mathematics, drawing, dancing,
fencing and music.

A portrait of Grand Duchess Catherine by Virgilius Erichsen. Painted before her coup of 1762, this shows the mature woman, poised to take control of her destiny.

The Empress Catherine in her coronation robes, with crown, sceptre and orb,
as painted by Alexei Petrovich Antropov.

A portrait of Alexei Bobrinsky, Catherine's son by Grigory Orlov, in masquerade costume, by an unknown artist. Bobrinsky inherited his mother's pointed chin.

A miniature of Grigory Orlov, Catherine's lover from about 1761 to 1772 and a close friend until his death, probably painted by Andrei Ivanovich Cherny.

Catherine II in the early years of her reign, painted in front of a mirror by Virgilius Erichsen.

Strogonoff, daughter to the Great Chancellor, the Countess Narishkin and a young Lady, sister to Colonel Sievers, who was in England, and daughter of the Great Marshal of the Court distinguished themselves particularly. The orchestra was composed of gentlemen. The elegance and magnificence of the whole was such, that what may appear a laboured description, is but barely doing justice to it.

The good Earl cannot resist expressing his surprise that such an entertainment could have been performed so well in this country believed by the rest of 'civilised' Europe to be 'backward': 'When we consider how few years have elapsed since the politer arts were first introduced into this country, and how considerable a part of that time they have been but little cultivated, it will appear very extraordinary, that a performance of this kind can have been planned and executed in a few weeks.' The late Peter III would have found little that was extraordinary about it, and would indeed have delighted in it. In his report on the same event to the Duc de Praslin, the Baron de Breteuil focused on Catherine's ever greater infatuation (as he saw it) with her favourite:

The Empress's passion for Count Orlov seems to increase and everything suggests that he will gain a very considerable ascendancy over Her. A few days ago, Monseigneur, a Russian tragedy was performed at Court, in which this favourite played very gauchely the principal role. This Princess [i.e. the Empress] was nevertheless so enchanted by the charms of the actor, that She called me over several times to tell me about them and ask me what I thought. She went even further with the Comte de Mercy [the Viennese ambassador], who was sitting next to Her. She exclaimed ten times a scene, praising Orlov's nobility and beauty, adding a thousand little comments of that nature, and elaborating beyond all measure to the Ambassador on her lover's qualities of heart and mind; then no doubt supposing that the Ambassador of Vienna was insufficiently persuaded of these last, she informed him that Count Orlov deliberately set out to make himself appear a ninny, but that those of her courtiers who let themselves be taken in by this were highly gullible.

During carnival time, a giant masquerade was staged in the streets of Moscow, entitled 'Minerva Triumphant'. This three-day spectacle involved a mile-long procession of 4,000 actors and musicians. At the head of the masquerade scenes of drunkenness, ignorance, deceit, bribery, hardship and pride were depicted; these were succeeded by portrayals of a golden age of peace and virtue which, it was to be inferred, had now dawned with the advent of Minerva herself, the Empress Catherine II.

In the spring of 1763 the stand-off between Church and State over the issue of secularisation came to a head, with Metropolitan Arseny of Rostov, a 65-year-old member of the Holy Synod, who had long been opposed to any interference of the State in church affairs, sending a denunciation to the Synod in early March. It was heard by other members of the Synod a week later and they, fearful of compromising their relations with Catherine, decided that it contained insults to the Empress. A Guards officer was dispatched to Rostov the Great to bring the Metropolitan to Moscow to be tried; he arrived under arrest on 17 March. The examination of Metropolitan Arseny was conducted by the Synod at night in order to keep it secret. They refused to accept the Metropolitan's protestations that he had meant no offence to the Empress, but treated him as though he were engaged in a conspiracy against her, and tried to extract from him the names of accomplices and followers. On 7 April he was stripped of his office and rank, and sentenced to incarceration in a northern monastery where he was to be denied access to pen and ink. The Empress capitalised on the whole affair by re-establishing the College of Economy as a prior measure to the secularisation of church lands, which she now declared to be illegally gained and improperly held. The Synod could hardly protest without appearing to be on the side of the disgraced Metropolitan Arseny.

In a 'most secret' dispatch of 15 March, the Earl of Buckingham had commented on the increasingly obvious favour being shown to Grigory Orlov: 'Her Imperial Majesty shows Orloff every day fresh marks of distinction; Her partiality is indeed so far decided, as to offend those who think themselves, from their rank, situation, and ability better entitled to her favour.' He also complained that the foreign ministers could not, as yet, work out who was in charge of foreign affairs: 'The foreign Ministers seem all equally ignorant where to find the real Minister. M. Panin has the first sight, after the Empress, of all foreign correspondence, which from him is carried to M. Bestucheff: They thwart each other, and every body else; they have each of them weight enough to keep Her Imperial Majesty undecided, but neither of them sufficient to bring Her to a determination.' By the middle of May he considered the situation at Court to be worsening: 'People of all ranks are displeased with the great favour shown to the Orloff family, and express their dissatisfaction much more freely than has been usual in this country.'

There was a fear that the Empress, widowed and still of childbearing age, might be persuaded by the Orlovs to marry Grigory. If she did, not only would Paul's position as heir apparent be in jeopardy, but Catherine – a mere woman, as the men around her reckoned – would inevitably end up devolving power to her husband, if not relinquishing it to him entirely. Catherine's other supporters had not, they felt, removed an unsatisfactory Tsar from the throne only to find themselves ruled by an upstart, uneducated Guardsman and his hard-drinking, hard-fighting brothers. Whether Catherine herself ever seriously considered marrying Grigory is open to doubt. She had been fiercely determined to gain power for herself and had planned her use of it so carefully that it is hard to imagine that she would have placed herself voluntarily in a position where she might have to give any of it up. But she was also a woman who needed a man, and at this stage in her life she depended absolutely on Grigory for emotional support, as well as needing his company to help her relax and put the cares of state to one side at the end of each working day. She also felt that she owed Grigory and his brothers a great deal. She was still in the process of learning how to manage her private life (which could never again be truly private) alongside the demands of the throne. The vehemence of some of the opposition to any suggestion of her marrying Grigory Orlov startled her and made her realise – if she had ever really doubted it – that her private life was part of her political life. To remain unmarried was by far the more sensible option for a female autocrat who wished to maintain her absolute power. She also learnt that rumours of marriage might actually prove dangerous to her lover.

On 26 May Grigory himself compiled some notes for Catherine concerning a conspiracy whose central character was one Fyodor Khitrovo, or Khitrov, who had originally been a supporter of Catherine at the time of the coup against Peter. According to Grigory, Khitrovo had been talking to a few fellow officers and others, including Princess Dashkova, about what should be done if the Empress were determined to marry Orlov. Grigory himself they considered to be 'stupid' and of little real consequence, but his brother Alexei was 'a great rogue and the reason behind the whole business'. Khitrovo proposed nothing less than murdering all five brothers. He also claimed that Catherine had promised Panin before her accession that she would rule only as regent – a claim which, when she heard of it, she vehemently denied. Khitrovo was arrested and eventually banished to his estate.

On 7 June the Prussian envoy, Count Solms, one of the most percipient of contemporary diplomats, wrote to Frederick the Great to acquaint him with the discontent rife at the Russian Court, and identified Princess Dashkova as a principal focus of intrigue and opposition:

> [Princess Dashkova] has lost the confidence and friendship of the Sovereign, she has been made to leave the Imperial palace, where she was living, in order to live in the town and she has not re-appeared since at Court except rarely and on grand occasions. This woman of romantic spirit, who wants only to make a name for herself in history and to see statues put up to her during her lifetime, has not been able to bear the affront directed at her. She considers the behaviour of the Empress towards her to be ungrateful and, surrounded in her house by handsome wits and flatterers, she receives all those who have reasons to be discontented with the Court. She is the kind of woman to attempt a new revolution every week, just for the pleasure of it.

Solms reports the rumour that Ekaterina Dashkova was actually the daughter of Nikita Panin – the evidence for this, it seems, being that the two spent a lot of time together and that Panin acted in a fatherly way towards the hot-headed young Princess, attempting to restrain her wilder flights of fancy. Panin certainly enjoyed the company of attractive young women – it was a particular weakness of his – and Dashkova got on well with anyone who made her the centre of their attention. According to Solms, Panin and the Empress had both grown somewhat disenchanted with one another after the first few optimistic months:

> In those early days [Panin] was the spirit of counsel and the Empress, knowing his zeal for the public good and his disinterestedness, could not have confided in a better person, as he shared all the views of that Princess on reform, of which he recognised the necessity . . . He tried to undertake so many things at once, of which up till now not a single one has been achieved, new rules being mixed up with old mistakes, that affairs are come into such confusion that those who want to profit from them do so with the same success as in the past. The effect having not at all equalled what he promised, the

Empress has naturally had to lose the high idea she had conceived of him and now consults other people, such as Bestuzhev, who has grown old in malice and chicanery, Suvorov – a brutal and coarse man, Shakhovskoy and Nepluyev, both of them senators, intelligent men but with no knowledge, their only merit being that they are disinterested and incorruptible.

What Solms had in fact identified, without quite recognising it, was that Catherine, nearly a year into her reign, was still working out how best to harvest the talents of the people around her. She was determined not to rush such important decisions and was still in the process of testing and trying out different combinations before making her final selections. Ex-Chancellor Bestuzhev, as Solms realised, had aged too much during the time of his exile to be capable of taking up a responsible post:

I have noticed myself in trivial conversations I have had with him at Court that he is unable to concentrate on a speech all the way through without repeating himself and forgetting by the end what he said at the beginning. If one considers that in addition every day he drowns in wine and strong liquors the little good sense which he has left, it is impossible to understand how this old man can have gained so much credit.

At the end of Catherine's first year as Empress, Count Solms summed up the situation thus:

Returning to the source of the discontent against the present government, one will find it in the three reasons which I have indicated: in the precipitous hurry of a general reform, in the bad choice of people in credit, and one can add to that: in the passionate enthusiasm for the favourite. This last has made the Empress lose the advantageous idea which the public had conceived at the beginning of her reign of her superiority of spirit over other people. One sees in her only the woman, who likes pleasure and sensual delight, who will sooner or later surrender herself into a lover's hands and abandon to him the reins of empire. The effect of the second is that no one truly attaches himself to Her Majesty and that she cannot count on having friends among the persons of standing, for she has shown no recognition for the services rendered to her, except to the Orlov family alone which is without credit and support in the empire, and has not given her trust except to a few people and moreover to those who enjoy no esteem with the public, the greatest number and the first lords of the country are not at all interested in having anything to do with her. The wisest among them and the most moderate search for pretexts to stay away from Court and try, if they can, to obtain permission to leave the country altogether, in order to find cover from the storm which they fear. Finally the first reason gives rise to recollections which are advantageous to the memory of the late Emperor. One thinks of the innovations in the military, in imitation of Your Majesty's troops as regards the change of the officers' uniforms with the addition of reveres and shoulder straps, one thinks of the projected confiscation of ecclesiastical lands and several other new regulations which are the same ideas as those the deceased person had; those very things which were imputed to him as crimes his successor, after having seized the sceptre from him, is using to glorify herself. These ideas which are beginning to germinate among the people may be that much more dangerous to the Empress as she has in the person of her son, the Grand Duke Paul, a rival in whom everyone recognises a more justly founded right than hers to occupy the throne of Russia. All it requires is a hothead and one could see in Russia a tragic scene like that of last year. The actors who took part in that one could perhaps be persuaded to take an equal part in this, all the more so as the intention of several of them, and indeed of Count Panin himself, or so it is said, had been to give only the regency to the Empress now and to confer the supreme authority on the Grand Duke Paul, but she cleverly managed to profit from the initial enthusiasm and took possession of the first place, whereas only the second had been destined for her. Such is the present situation, Sire, of this Court.

Count Solms then ventured a prediction: 'if an opinion can acquire some authority by unanimous consent, then it is certain that the reign of the Empress Catherine II, like that of the Emperor her husband, will make only a brief appearance in the history of the world'.

# 8

# Catherine Sets to Work
# (1763–67)

*My single aim is the greatest well-being and glory of the fatherland.*
Catherine II to Procurator-General Vyazemsky

*O*n 28 June 1763, the first anniversary of her accession and after nearly 10 months based in Moscow, Catherine made her public re-entry into St Petersburg, accompanied in the imperial coach by Grand Duke Paul. Ahead of the coach rode 26 men on horseback followed by the carriages of the principal courtiers, each dressed in the habit of the order to which he belonged. Count Grigory Orlov, in his uniform as Grand Master of Ordnance (an appointment he had received this year), rode immediately behind the imperial coach at the head of a detachment of horse guards, and then came the principal ladies of the Court in their carriages. Another detachment of guards brought up the rear. An immense crowd lined the streets to welcome their Empress back to her capital. Having stopped at various points along the route to be greeted by the members of the government Colleges, Catherine finally arrived at the Summer Palace at seven o'clock in the evening where the foreign ministers were waiting on the steps to congratulate her on her safe return. She proceeded first to the chapel for prayers and then to the throne room for the ceremony of hand-kissing, before retiring to her apartments. She reappeared towards half past eleven and was accompanied by the foreign ministers and courtiers to the end of the garden in order to watch a firework display over the Neva. The following day, the Feast of Sts Peter and Paul and hence the Grand Duke's name-day (as it had been his father's), Catherine and Paul attended the liturgy at the Peter and Paul Cathedral. In the evening there was a ball and supper at Court, and the day was also marked by the distribution of various awards and gifts to people who had supported the Empress during the first year of her reign.

Throughout the rest of 1763 Catherine concentrated on getting her administration into full working order, making appointments, issuing instructions and, occasionally, rebukes. She gave her favourite his first administrative role, as president of the new Chancery of Guardianship for Foreigners whose responsibility was to oversee the immigration of people, mainly German, to settle the Empire's southern territories. This appointment was designed to test Grigory's capabilities – he proved an able and enthusiastic administrator – to keep him occupied, and to minimise the envy of existing officials. As this was a completely new post, nobody could complain that Grigory had taken their place. Catherine also instructed Grigory's brother Fyodor to observe the Senate's sessions and everyday affairs, as preparation for a possible administrative appointment. Another protégé of hers, Grigory Potemkin, who had a particular interest in religious and theological matters, was assigned to a similar role in the Holy Synod. These two, while learning the ropes, also acted as useful informants, reporting the proceedings to the Empress. Bestuzhev was too old and failing to be given any official post, but Catherine kept the old man on at Court, in semi-retirement, out of consideration and in recognition of past services. He died on 9 April 1766.

In September 1763 Catherine issued an instruction as to when she would see each of the ministers of her personal cabinet. Grigory Teplov (who, along with Ivan Yelagin, assisted the Empress in composing decrees) was to have an audience every Monday and Wednesday at eight o'clock in the morning. Tuesdays and Thursdays were reserved for Adam Olsufyev (who headed the cabinet, received petitions and disbursed monies), and Fridays and Saturdays for Yelagin (who also acted as her personal secretary). These three were soon joined by three other state secretaries: Sergei Kuzmin, Grigory Kozitsky and Stepan Strekalov. Catherine herself had soon established a pattern for her working day to which, with minor variations, she adhered throughout her reign. She described it in a letter to the Parisian hostess, and old friend of Stanislas Poniatowski, Madame Geoffrin:

I get up regularly at 6 o'clock in the morning, I read and write all alone until eight, then someone arrives to read business to me, everyone who needs to speak to me enters, one by one, one after the other, that lasts until at least eleven o'clock, then I dress. On Sundays and feast-days I go to Mass, on other days I go out into my antechamber where a lot of people are usually waiting for me, after half or three quarters of an hour of conversation, I sit down to dinner, after that *the naughty General* [Mme Geoffrin had referred thus to Ivan Betskoy, who had spent much time in Paris and was a friend of hers] arrives to indoctrinate me, he takes up a book and I take up my knots.★ When our reading is not interrupted by packets of letters and other hindrances, it lasts until half-past five, when I either go to a spectacle, or I play, or else I chatter with whoever is the first to arrive until supper, which is over before eleven o'clock when I go to bed, in order to do the same thing the next day – and this is all ruled like manuscript paper.

Catherine frequently had to chivvy her officials to work as hard as she did herself. On 3 August she had written to the Senate to complain that the senators had been failing to carry out both her oral and written edicts. She attached a list of 148 of her personal instructions which had not been fulfilled, and ordered the senators that they were to work not only from 8.30 a.m. to 12.30 p.m., but also three times a week in the afternoons until the backlog was cleared up. And some time in 1764 she wrote to Yelagin, addressing him by his patronymic: 'Listen Perfilyevich, if by the end of this week you haven't brought me the instructions or statutes of the gubernatorial duties, the manifesto against the leather-flayers and the Beketov business with it all completed, I will declare you to be the laziest person in the world and that there is nobody who drags out so many things entrusted to him, as you do.' Indolence was not one of General Betskoy's faults, but he both amused and irritated Catherine by dumping things on her furniture, as she explained to Madame Geoffrin when thanking her for the gift of a small table:

I will avoid this pretty little table suffering the fate of all the ones which are in my room and which are on the verge of collapse

---

★ 'I take up my knots' refers to the popular ladies' pastime of knotting, in which linen or silk thread was knotted with a small shuttle into a braid, which would then be used as ornamentation for dresses or small textile objects. It is typical of Catherine that she would not sit with her hands empty.

under the weight of what is on them, from time to time I tell them to bring me another one, this time, I say, I will keep it clear, *but it is a vain effort and I am sure* that after a few days it will be covered, all the world contributes to it and the General at the head of them, he begins by putting his book and his magnifying glass on it, then a map, a few scrolls, some envelopes, his letters, finally both carved and uncarved stones often things he's found in the street and under his feet, and he ends by saying: 'Oh Madame! there is never a corner in your room where one can put anything.'

Count Nikita Panin was formally appointed the senior member of the College of Foreign Affairs in October 1763, and took charge of Russian foreign policy. This meant he was effectively playing the role of chancellor – but Catherine took care never to give him, or indeed anyone else in her administration, this title, thus making it quite clear to her courtiers and officials that ultimate power in every sphere resided with herself. The existing Chancellor Mikhail Vorontsov's role gradually diminished until it virtually disappeared, and he was never officially replaced. Despite Panin's considerable responsibilities in the realm of foreign affairs, he also kept his post as Paul's governor or, to give this role its formal title, Grand Master of the Grand Duke's Court. This provided him with a secure base at Court and living quarters in the various imperial palaces. His dual role could also, however, lead to a frustrating slowness in the conduct of foreign affairs, as Buckingham explained to the Earl of Sandwich:

Great as the delay of all business is at this Court, it will appear less extraordinary, when it is considered, that Mr Panin has the whole direction of Foreign Affairs, for (as to the Vice-Chancellor, he rather embroils than assists him, even with regard to those trifles, in which he is permitted to interfere) he also has the care of the Grand Duke, superintends his Education; attends him almost every where, dines with him, and lodges in the same room; add to this, though a sensible and a worthy man, long used to business, he is indolent in the taking it under consideration, and tedious in the agitation of it; his constitution is weak, and he has a taste for pleasure, and dissipation: when your Lordship considers these circumstances . . . you will think dilatoriness, in some sort, excusable.

Many years later, after Panin's death, Catherine told Friedrich Melchior Grimm an anecdote about him: 'Count Panin, talking through his nose and going hem hem at each pose, used to say: *Kings, kings are a necessary evil which one cannot do without,* and when I used to complain that this or that was not going as it should, then he would say to me: *What are you complaining about? If everyone was perfect or was capable of being perfect, we would not need you kings.'* Catherine and Panin established a working relationship in which both continued to entertain doubts about the other while acknowledging one another's gifts. And each tried constantly to get the upper hand. The Empress realised he was a man she needed to have on her side in the early years, for otherwise he could have been a very powerful focus of opposition.

On 12 November Catherine issued a decree establishing a Medical College, whose brief was to expand medical care for the population as a whole, to increase the number of Russian doctors and other medical personnel and to supervise the working of apothecary shops. The first president of the College was Baron Alexander Cherkasov. In December the Senate secretary Stepan Sheshkovsky began working in the Secret Branch, the precise nature of his duties being carefully concealed from the public. At the end of the year Catherine decided on one of her most significant and successful appointments, replacing Alexander Glebov as Procurator-General of the Senate with Prince Alexander Vyazemsky (whom she had already used to quell the peasant disturbances in the Urals). Vyazemsky remained in this post, working closely with Catherine, for most of her reign. At the beginning of 1764 she provided Vyazemsky with detailed — and top-secret — instructions about his new role. This document (written in Russian, as was all the official work of the State and most of what Catherine wrote to her ministers) provides a fascinating glimpse into the workings of the Russian government and demonstrates how closely Catherine had been observing her officials and their characteristics — and, in many cases, their shortcomings — during the first 18 months of her reign. Alexander Glebov had fallen short of Catherine's expectations for her Procurator-General through his self-interest and lack of openness and sincerity towards her. Furthermore he had, she believed, been corrupted by his youthful association with the late Count Peter Shuvalov. Catherine explained to Vyazemsky what he could expect in his dealings with her:

If I see that you are loyal, hard-working, open and sincere, then you can be assured of my unbounded confidence. Above all I love the truth, and you must feel free to say it, without fear; you can argue with me without danger, provided that the end result is good. I hear that everyone considers you to be an honest man, and I hope to be able to demonstrate to you that people with such qualities thrive at this Court. Furthermore I will add that I do not require flattery from you, but only sincerity and a firm attitude towards business.

Catherine told him that he would find two 'parties' in the Senate, but that it was important not to accord too much consideration to either of them, so that neither would become strong. Eventually they would wither away. 'I have been watching them,' wrote Catherine, 'with an unwinking eye, and I have deployed people according to their capabilities.' She warned Vyazemsky:

In one you will find people of honest morals, but not of very far-sighted intellect; in the other, I think they see further, but it is not clear that they can put their views to good use . . . You must favour neither one nor the other, but treat them both courteously and impartially, listen to everyone and, guided solely by the dictates of justice and the good of the fatherland, proceed firmly and by the shortest route to the truth. Ask me about anything you are unsure of, and rely completely on God and on me; seeing such satisfactory behaviour towards me, I will not betray you.

Catherine diagnosed the Senate's current problems as having been partly caused by 'the lack of application to work of several of my predecessors', the result being that the senators had become used to interfering in matters which should not concern them, such as the distribution of honours, and to abusing their authority. She also warned Vyazemsky that the people most likely to try to deceive him were the 'small fry', the clerks who worked for the Senate. The easiest way to deal with them, she suggested, was simply to sack them.

On 14 September 1763 the vow Catherine had taken the previous year had been realised with the opening of Paul's Hospital on the outskirts of Moscow, in a wooden house formerly owned by Alexander Glebov. At the beginning it had 25 beds and three members of staff. Financed entirely by Catherine, it offered free treatment to the curable poor of both sexes. Then on 21 April 1764, Catherine's thirty-fifth birthday, the Moscow Foundling Home and lying-in hospital for unmarried and destitute mothers was opened. Intended to discourage infanticide (and inspired by British and European models such as the Thomas Coram Foundling Hospital in London and the Ospedale della Pietà in Venice), the five-storey Foundling Home (which also included within its complex a church and a dairy farm with 80 cows) received babies without any questions asked. A mother could ring the doorbell and a basket would be let down into which she could place her baby, with a note of its name and whether it had been baptised. Then the basket would be drawn back up and the woman would go on her way. By the end of 1764 the home had received 523 babies, and there were 14 births at the hospital during the course of the year. The mortality rate of the home, however, was disturbingly high, causing it, and its later Petersburg counterpart, to be known as 'angel factories'. The children who did survive received a good education and appeared happy. Closely involved with Catherine in the founding and administration of the Foundling Home and lying-in hospital was Ivan Betskoy, the official and friend (and erstwhile lover of her mother) who used to read to her in the afternoons. The other major project on which they worked together was the Smolny Institute, a girls' boarding school founded in the Smolny Convent (built by Rastrelli for the Empress Elizabeth on the south-west bank of the Neva) and which took as its inspiration Madame de Maintenon's establishment at St Cyr which Catherine had long desired to emulate.

Catherine's activities as an art collector also began in 1764, with the purchase of 225 Old Master paintings from the Berlin dealer Johann Gotzkowski. They were mainly by Flemish and Dutch masters, and included Franz Hals's *Portrait of a Young Man Holding a Glove* and Rembrandt's *A Polish Nobleman* and *Joseph accused by Potiphar's Wife.* The paintings had originally been accumulated on instructions from Frederick the Great, but at the end of the Seven Years' War the economic situation in Prussia was such that he was in no position to buy them. Catherine's aim in purchasing them was as much political as artistic, intended to demonstrate Russia's superiority to the whole of Europe. Peter the Great and Elizabeth had both collected some artworks, but it was with Catherine that systematic collection began, and it was with this first major purchase from Gotzkowski that the great collection which came to be synonymous with the word 'Hermitage' was born. Construction began that year of the Academy of Arts on Vasilyevsky Island, designed by the French architect Jean-Baptiste Vallin de la Mothe, and one of the first Classical revival buildings in Russia. Catherine was so impressed that she commissioned him to design the first extension to the Winter Palace – the Small Hermitage, which was to be connected by a covered bridge to the main palace and was intended as a private place where the Empress could entertain her friends without ceremony and hang her burgeoning collection of pictures.

The relationship between Catherine and Grigory Orlov was now an established feature of court life, provoking continual covert grumbling but no major disturbances. There was no further serious talk of their marrying. On Catherine's return to the Winter Palace in the autumn of 1763 she had taken over the rooms originally occupied by Peter III and Elizaveta Vorontsova in the south-east corner of the first floor and made them into her private apartments. Grigory was given apartments above her own, so that the lovers could visit one another by means of a private staircase. On 19 September the Earl of Buckingham encountered the Empress when he was visiting Orlov: 'She came in at a private door, and He retired for the greater part of the time She stayed, which was about half an hour.' Catherine's first lover, Sergei Saltykov, was now serving as a plenipotentiary envoy; he wrote to her from Paris in April 1764, thanking her for money (20,000 roubles) which had been sent to him to pay off his debts, and asking for his salary and expenses for the previous year to be paid now. Nikita Panin confirmed to Catherine that this money had been sent, and asked whether Saltykov should now be posted to the Court of Saxony. Catherine's opinion of him was not high; she replied to Panin: 'Hasn't he already got into enough mischief? but if you can vouch for him, then send him, only wherever he is, he will always be a fifth wheel on the carriage.'

Plans were also afoot to deploy Stanislas Poniatowski to Russia's – and ostensibly his own – advantage. King Augustus III of Poland had died on 25 September 1763, provoking some excitement among the European rulers who wished to continue or extend their influence in that country. Catherine wrote to Panin: 'Don't mock me because I leapt up from my chair when I heard the news about the death of the King of Poland: the King of Prussia jumped off the table when he heard.' Panin's nephew by marriage, Prince Nikolai Repnin, was immediately dispatched to Warsaw with an endorsement of Stanislas Poniatowski as the Russian choice for the next King. Repnin, along with the Russian ambassador in Warsaw, Count Keyserling, was instructed to threaten force, and even annexation of Polish territory, if there were any opposition to Poniatowski's candidacy. Russia had exercised an informal protectorate over Poland for decades, ever since Peter the Great had guaranteed its constitution in 1716. Catherine herself had a contemptuous attitude towards the country and its chaotic system of government (particularly on account of the *liberum veto*, which made it possible for any member of the Sejm to prevent the passage of legislation), an attitude which included disdain for militant Roman Catholicism. She also believed her former lover to be of a fundamentally weak character and that he would in consequence be dependent on her. Poniatowski was elected King of Poland unanimously, taking the name Stanislas II Augustus, on 26 August 1764 (with the presence of both Russian and Polish troops to ensure the vote went the right way). Catherine wrote to Nikita Panin in triumph at their joint achievement (and to complain of a backache):

> Dear Nikita Ivanovich
>
> I congratulate you on the king that we have made. This event greatly increases my confidence in you, as I can see how there were no mistakes in all the measures you took; I wanted you to know how pleased I am about this. I have such dreadful backache that I am in no state to hold a pen for long, so would you please, instead of me on this occasion, write to Count Keyserling and Prince Repnin to express my pleasure at their work and zeal, by which they have obtained no small glory for themselves and for us; and order a letter to the new King to be prepared for my signature, in reply to his. Either I have rheumatism in my back or I am dying: I fear it might be a stone; except that after a bath for the first time it felt easier, so perhaps it's only a chill.

Poniatowski was crowned in Warsaw on 14 November.

It was during a conversation about Poland at the Grand Duke's dinner table, to which Panin was accustomed to invite senators, generals and senior officials including foreign ministers, that little Paul made a remark which demonstrated that he fully expected to be Emperor when he attained his majority. The Earl of Buckingham reported the incident, which must have taken place shortly before the death of Augustus III, to the Earl of Sandwich:

> When I am speaking of Poland, I am tempted to mention something which fell from the Grand Duke; he was at dinner with some company, and in the course of conversation, asked a Foreign Minister, who was at table, the age of the King of Poland; he answered him

sixty seven; then, replied the Grand Duke, he may live ten years longer, and if he should, I will make You King of Poland. Your Lordship will easily imagine that this saillie made no small impression upon the company: Mr Panin was particularly struck with it, and did not look up for some time.

Mr Panin might well not look up, as he must have been responsible for the Grand Duke's belief about his future – a belief definitely not sanctioned by the Empress, and which would most certainly displease her if she heard about it.

The Grand Duke's education, which included languages, history, geography, mathematics, drawing, dancing, fencing and music, was carefully supervised. He was taught physics and astronomy by the distinguished mathematician and scientist Franz Aepinus, who also taught at the Corps of Cadets, and science and mathematics by a graduate of that institution, Semyon Poroshin. Religious instruction was provided by Archimandrite, later Metropolitan, Platon, one of Russia's most enlightened and well-known churchmen. The catechism he prepared for Paul was translated and published throughout Europe, and he inculcated in the Grand Duke a strong sense that he was called by God to rule Russia. Catherine had tried unsuccessfully to persuade the French philosopher Jean le Rond d'Alembert to come to Russia as Paul's tutor, but he had declined politely and firmly (while quipping to his friends that he suffered from piles – which could prove fatal in Russia). Training in war and military matters did not play a part in Paul's education, except in so far as they impinged on diplomacy and finance. He showed early signs, however, of having inherited Peter III's fascination with everything to do with soldiers, weaponry, uniforms and parades (this predilection, which went well beyond normal boyish enthusiasm and was not encouraged by the very non-militaristic Count Panin, is perhaps one of the strongest indications that Paul was indeed Peter's son). Paul was instructed in dancing by the ballet master Franz Gilferding, and his participation in 1764 in a ballet based on the legend of Acis and Galatea, in which he danced the part of the god Hymen, brought the house down. He danced 'so charmingly, with such confidence and skill, that he aroused genuine applause which went on and on and over which the orchestra, which was largely composed of noble amateurs, could hardly be heard'.

The little boy was not always quite so charming, as is clear from the entries in Semyon Poroshin's diary. On Thursday 7 October 1764,

His Highness woke up at six o'clock. On completion of his toilet, he got on with his studies . . . He played battledore and shuttlecock during his break . . . At six o'clock in the evening he wanted to attend a theatrical presentation. They were performing a French play, *L'Ecole des femmes* . . . His Highness applauded several times . . . Twice, the public began to clap without waiting for him, and he got cross about it. Back home, he was still grumbling . . .: 'In future, I will ask permission to send away those who applaud in my presence when I am not doing so. It is not as it should be.'

This was an early indication of the character of the future Paul I. On 15 November he was disagreeable to Poroshin, who recorded: 'Today I had a sore finger; and besides, I have never liked carving at table. To amuse himself, His Highness deliberately sent all the dishes to me, so that I could cut them up and serve them. Then he said, jumping up and down on his chair as he does when he's in a good mood, "Poor Poroshin, look how hard he's working!"'

In early May 1764 one Lieutenant Vasily Mirovich, stationed at the Schlüsselburg fortress, began to make plans with a fellow officer, Apollon Ushakov, to free Ivan VI from captivity and proclaim him Emperor in Petersburg while Catherine was away on a tour of the Baltic provinces, planned for late June. The Earl of Buckingham had already identified the former baby-Emperor, about whom he admitted that reports were very contradictory, as a possible focus of dissent: 'It is asserted by many, that he is absolutely an idiot; others on the contrary, declare, that he appears deficient no otherwise, than from want of education and that, conscious of his own situation, he politically conceals his abilities.' Quite how these 'many' people could possibly have gained an informed opinion about this young man who had been incarcerated for almost his entire life in virtual solitary confinement in Schlüsselburg is not explained; it was a case, as usual, of rumours masquerading as reports.

Lieutenant Mirovich had been born in Siberia, the son of an exiled Ukrainian nobleman and the grandson of a Cossack officer who had been involved in rebellions against Peter the Great. A Ukrainian patriot, Mirovich longed to regain his family's fortune and position. He entered the army and was stationed in St Petersburg at the time of Catherine's coup. He made continued efforts to reclaim the Ukrainian land confiscated from his family, although Kirill Razumovsky, the hetman of Ukraine, had assured him his case was hopeless. When his regiment was moved to Schlüsselburg he began to take an interest in 'Nameless

Prisoner No. 1' – the deposed Ivan VI, known familiarly to the soldiers as 'Ivanushka'.

Nikita Panin had been entrusted with the arrangements for Ivan's security. Catherine hoped to be able to persuade the young man to become a monk, which would have put him out of the running to be a candidate for the throne, and the officers who were charged with guarding him were supposed to be attempting to push him in this direction. The other convenient alternative would be for him to die of natural causes, and he was expressly denied medical attention in the hope of assisting nature. But Panin also reinforced the orders given by the Empress Elizabeth and confirmed by Peter III: in the event of any attempt to escape, the prisoner was to be killed. That this instruction had been reconfirmed by Catherine's minister was never made public, however.

According to Mirovich's plan, Apollon Ushakov would arrive at Schlüsselburg by boat during a night on which Mirovich would be on sentry duty. Ushakov would pretend to be a courier from the Empress, bearing a decree ordering Ivan's immediate release, which Mirovich would then announce to the troops. Together they would arrest the commandant of the fortress and release the prisoner. The conspirators would then transport Ivan and his supporters down the Neva to Petersburg, where the oath of allegiance would be made to him by the troops and people.

The ambitious plan began to go wrong when Ushakov had to leave Petersburg, as he was ordered unexpectedly to join a party taking army funds to Smolensk. He either became ill or pretended to be ill en route, and turned back for Petersburg. But on his way back he drowned – by accident or possibly suicide – in a river. After receiving the news, Mirovich tried to persuade a few lackeys and soldiers to join his crazy enterprise, but eventually decided he would have to act alone.

Catherine embarked on her tour of Estonia and Livonia, to consolidate her authority throughout the Empire, on 20 June. Count Solms reported to Frederick the Great: 'On the part of the nation there is a lot of discontent and fermentation, and much courage and firmness at least in appearance on the Empress's side. She left here with the most serene air and the most assured countenance.'

On 4 July, having drafted a manifesto announcing Ivan VI's accession and the oath of allegiance to him, Vasily Mirovich exhorted the troops in his command to support his plan. Some agreed, on condition that everyone else would join in too. The night of 4–5 July was very foggy. At about two o'clock in the morning Mirovich called his men to arms and they seized control of the main gates. When the commandant was alerted and came out to see what was happening, Mirovich knocked him out with his musket butt, and then marched his men to the cell where Nameless Prisoner No. 1 was confined. Fire was exchanged between the attackers and Ivan's guards. Mirovich read out his manifesto to inspire his men, but it was already too late. The guards ceased firing, and showed Mirovich the body of 'his Emperor', lying in a pool of blood. They had carried out their secret instructions, killing him as soon as they realised an attempt was being made to free him. Reverently Mirovich kissed the body and gave himself up.

Catherine received the news of the assassination of Ivan VI in Riga, from where she wrote to Nikita Panin:

> I have read with great amazement your reports and all the marvels which have taken place at Schlüsselburg: the Divine guidance is wonderful and inexhaustible! I have nothing to add to your extremely good instructions, except that now an investigation of the guilty parties must be carried out without publicity or concealment (since of itself the matter cannot remain secret, more than two hundred people having taken part in it).

She ordered that 'the nameless prisoner' be buried quietly at Schlüsselburg, and instructed the investigation into the whole affair to be undertaken by a General Weimarn who, she said, 'is a clever man, and will not go further than he is ordered'. She wrote again to Panin two days later, after she had read the transcript of Mirovich's first interrogation. She could not quite believe that Mirovich had had no accomplices, and recommended that the drowned Ushakov's brother be questioned in case he knew anything. Catherine also decided she would travel back to Petersburg sooner than originally planned in order to help cut short any speculation about the seriousness of the plot. She hoped there would soon be 'a speedy end to this whole mad business'.

It was also while she was in Riga that another great eighteenth-century character, Giovanni Giacomo Casanova, first set eyes on the Empress. He watched her presiding over a game of faro in such a way as to ensure that the subjects whom she was entertaining would win. Casanova described Catherine as 'not precisely handsome' but nevertheless of pleasing appearance. He subsequently visited St Petersburg, where he enjoyed one or two pleasant conversations with the Empress.

He does not seem, however, to have made a lasting impression on her.

Catherine spent 13 July in Mitau, the only occasion on which she ever travelled outside the bounds of her Empire. Five days later she wrote to Ivan Nepluyev and Prince Vyazemsky to thank them for their part in investigating the Schlüsselburg affair, but advising against arresting Mirovich's relatives unless there was any proof of their involvement in his plot. She did not want, she stressed, the innocent to suffer. On 17 August a manifesto was published, giving the official version of Ivan's death. It included the statement that Ivan had been insane, and announced that Mirovich would be tried by a special court of 48 dignitaries drawn from the Senate, the Synod, the heads of all the Colleges, and members of the top three ranks of the nobility. This court was empowered to review Weimarn's findings and to determine sentences, which would then be subject to confirmation by the Empress. No mention was ever made of the secret instruction to assassinate Ivan (though this was widely known, as is clear from the Earl of Buckingham's account of the event in a 'most secret' report to the Earl of Sandwich). The two guards who had carried out the act were rewarded with promotion and 7,000 roubles apiece, both for their action and for their silence. The 16 soldiers who had served under them were likewise sworn to eternal secrecy and rewarded (with smaller amounts). Catherine's correspondent in Paris, Madame Geoffrin, was clearly unimpressed by the manifesto when it reached France, as Catherine defended it to her indignantly:

> You like the truth, you want people to say it to you as you say it yourself, and so I am tempted to tell you that you are reasoning about this Manifesto like someone who is colour-blind. This document was not written for the foreign powers but in order to inform the Russian Empire that Ivan was dead, and so it had to be said how he died, there were more than a hundred witnesses of his death and of the attack by the traitor, and therefore it had to be a very precise account. Not to have done so would have been to give credence to the wicked rumours that the Ministers of Courts who envy me and do not like me were spreading around, it was a delicate business, I believed that to tell the truth was the only path to take. The Senate Printer had this Manifesto translated into several languages, a step which prevented less exact translations.

It may have taken rather longer to disseminate information – and misinformation – in the eighteenth century than it does in the twenty-first,
but Catherine's was just as much an age of 'spin' as is our own, and
she was as adept at manipulating versions of the facts as any modern
spin doctor. To conclude her self-defence to Madame Geoffrin she
cheerfully claimed that the end justifies the means: 'Well, the goal was
reached and my Manifesto did not fail to achieve its object, *ergo* it was
good. You think I'm stubborn, don't you?'

On 9 September 1764 the special court sitting in judgement on the
Mirovich affair signed its sentence. Mirovich was condemned to death
by beheading, and a number of soldiers judged to have conspired with
him were sentenced to run the gauntlet (the six most unfortunate
would have to run between 1,000 men 10 or 12 times); they would
then (if they survived this fearsome punishment) be sent into exile. Six
days later Mirovich was executed in St Petersburg. When his head was
held up to the crowd, it had a terrifying impact, the death penalty not
actually having been exercised in Russia for 22 years. Mirovich himself
faced his execution calmly, convincing some of the bystanders that he
was expecting to be pardoned at the last minute. His remains were left
on public display until the evening, when they were burnt along with
the gallows.

And so the first two years of the reign of Catherine II, who set so
much store by reason and enlightened principles, had included two
assassinations and an execution. But Catherine was also a realist and
not given to wasting time or energy indulging in useless regrets. She
felt more secure on her throne with both Peter III and Ivan VI dead;
and she had much work before her to complete the task Peter the
Great had begun of transforming Russia into a powerful, and European,
Empire. On the second anniversary of her coronation, and two days
after Paul's tenth birthday, the Empress and Grand Duke dined together
in state, with Nikita Panin standing behind the Grand Duke's chair to
serve him. For the anniversary celebrations Manfredini had composed
a new opera, *Carlo Magno* ('Charlemagne'), in which the Venetian singer
Colonna made her debut as prima donna on the imperial stage. This
opera, however, did not find favour with the Court, despite Colonna
herself being a success; it seems to have been considered too clever and
not entertaining enough. A similar judgement had been passed on
Manfredini's two preceding offerings, and this prompted the Court
Marshal General Sievers to search for another *maestro di capella*, the
result of which was the arrival in St Petersburg the following summer

of Baldassare Galuppi (whom Peter III had had on his want-list in 1762). Manfredini was henceforth relegated to composing ballets, and to teaching music to Grand Duke Paul.

Despite all the difficulties she had so far encountered, Catherine was enjoying herself as Empress. 'If I were not afraid of boring you by talking so much about myself,' she wrote to Madame Geoffrin,

> I would tell you that the dreadful occupation I have undertaken is imperceptibly becoming routine, that on those days when I am less harassed, I feel as though I'm missing something, and the next day I am more eager than ever for work, I have made it a rule to begin always with the most difficult most awkward and most tedious matters, with that out of the way the rest seems easy and agreeable, and I call that rationing pleasure . . . On what you say about truth and friendship fleeing from sovereigns, I certainly want you to know that I weary myself with shouting it on every conceivable occasion, and I accustom those who approach me to tell me the unvarnished truth, even if it is against myself, and I have found this very profitable.

Her courtiers may have been encouraged to tell her the truth, but most of them still found it difficult to be natural in her presence, as Catherine complained in another letter to Madame Geoffrin: 'when I enter a room, anyone would think I was the medusa's head, everyone is petrified, and each person has a strained look, I often shriek like an eagle against these ways, I admit that isn't the way to change them, for the more I shriek the less people are at their ease'.

In November Count Kirill Razumovsky was induced to retire as hetman of Ukraine, the Empress having developed doubts, reinforced by Grigory Teplov, about the efficiency of his administration. She wrote to Nikita Panin about the conversation she had had with Razumovsky: 'The hetman was with me, and I had an explanation with him, in which he said the same thing as he had said to you, and in the end he asked me to take away from him such an onerous and life-threatening office. To that I replied that I had no doubt at all of his loyalty and would talk with him further in the future. Now please tell him in my name that today or tomorrow he should put down in writing what he said to me.' When everything was settled, Razumovsky was awarded an annual pension of 60,000 roubles as well as substantial amounts of Ukrainian land in compensation, and retained his prominence as a senator and wealthy host and patron. The Empress appointed no further hetmen and instead established a College to administer Ukraine under the supervision of Governor-General Peter Rumyantsev.

Towards the end of 1764 the Baron de Breteuil drew up a waspish résumé for the next French ambassador, describing the characteristics of certain principal players at the Russian Court, including Catherine herself:

> One must certainly consider that she places herself well above all the prejudices men respect the most, and believe that the only driving force of her conduct is and always will be her ambition and the satisfaction of her desires. These two motives are often enough the bases for the behaviour of most men. But there are nevertheless considerations which hold them back, and one can feel certain that there are no such considerations capable of stopping Catherine II in matters of her taste, her pride or her interest. Despite her intelligence, the excess of these first passions will blind her to the latter and will surely drag her more than once beyond the limits imposed by judgment and reason.

Panin, suggests Breteuil, can be managed with careful handling:

> He is honest and disinterested, generally wants the good and the glory of his country, but is vain and gets bad-tempered when his ideas are not adopted without reservation. One can pull him out of his anger in large part by applauding his projects, praising their greatness, the disinterestedness of his views, and being quick to condemn the blind insults which have been made about his knowledge and opinions. Mr Panin is also very sensitive to friendship. He responds to little signs which indicate the interest one takes in his position. He likes to hear it said that this particular sentiment towards him is independent of business and of the representative character of the one who evinces it towards him. There are hardly any confidences which cannot be extracted from him by these methods of flattery. He is also very fond of gaiety and, although he puts on a show of being very serious, he very much likes the company in private of people who know how to stop being serious. For the rest, he is very distrustful and fairly subtle, and it would be dangerous to try to gain his confidence too quickly by any of these methods.

Chancellor Vorontsov was by now of little consequence (and retired, at Catherine's behest, at the beginning of 1765): 'His sentiments for us are sincere and well-known, as is his extreme weakness which renders him null in every case of any importance.' There were few people, in Breteuil's opinion, at the Russian Court who could not be bribed; even Catherine's private secretary and friend, Ivan Yelagin, was susceptible: 'This is a very subtle young man, very circumspect, he likes the table and pleasure. He wants to be flattered. His poverty which is great makes him want to be paid, but one must not make this proposition to him until some time has elapsed and after having established friendship and society with him.'

The health of the Grand Duke seemed to be improving as he grew older, though he was still subject to many minor ailments, including headaches, of which, according to Semyon Poroshin, he was something of a connoisseur:

> His Highness woke up at six o'clock, complained of a headache and stayed in bed until ten . . . We talked later about the classification which the Grand Duke has drawn up of his migraines; he distinguishes four of them: the circular, the flat, the ordinary and the crushing. 'Circular' is the name he gives to the pain at the back of his neck; 'flat' is that which gives him a pain in the forehead; the 'ordinary' migraine is a light pain; and the 'crushing' is when his whole head hurts him greatly.

Part of Paul's problem – and certainly one of the contributory factors to his digestive difficulties – was that he was always in too much of a hurry: 'His Highness has the bad habit of rushing things; he rushes to get up, to eat, to go to bed. At dinner-time . . . how many ruses he will think of to gain a few minutes and sit down to eat sooner! It's the same with supper . . . When he goes to bed in the evening he is already thinking about getting up earlier the following morning. This happens nearly every day, although we are trying to make him give up the habit.' The inability to sit still had also been a characteristic of Peter III.

On 25 December the Empress and her son opened a ball together with a minuet. There followed quadrilles, which the Grand Duke did not know how to perform, and Panin gave him permission to dance as he wished. The child, whom the ladies watching dubbed 'dear little Punyushka', was delighted as he 'pranced about in his own way, jumping and running around the room'. Poroshin commented about his charge: 'His Highness has a fault common to all those who are used to seeing their desires satisfied more often than frustrated. They are impatient, they want to be obeyed immediately.' This was another characteristic which Paul retained throughout his life.

In early 1765 the Earl of Buckingham was replaced as British ambassador by Sir George Macartney, who arrived in Petersburg equipped with the usual array of prejudices against his new host country:'notwithstanding the general ferocity of the inhabitants, the women here seem to have as much sway, as amongst the most civilised nations'. He also anticipated trouble when Paul Petrovich came of age: 'according to every appearance, the Empress seems at present, to be firmly fixed on the Throne, and I am persuaded that Her Government will remain, at least for some years, without alteration, but it is not impossible to foresee what will happen when the Grand Duke approaches to maturity'. He ended his first report with a sentiment that will resonate with anyone familiar with Russia at any stage in its history: 'there are many paradoxes here that would demand uncommon ingenuity to reconcile'.

Now that Catherine had finalised her official appointments and felt that she was making progress on getting her government to work effectively, she decided it was time to turn her attention to her first major project of internal reform; the subject was one which she had known from the start needed to be tackled. On 28 March 1765 she reported to Madame Geoffrin that for the past two months she had been working for three hours every morning on the laws of the Russian Empire. This was, as she said, 'an enormous undertaking'. She declared that her aim was to 'put everything into a more natural state, acknowledged by humanity and founded on public and individual utility'. The last codification of laws had taken place in 1649, since which thousands of new ones had been promulgated, often without any clear reference to previous laws on the same subject. It happened frequently that even the courts did not know what the law actually was, a situation which led to constant lawsuits followed by lengthy appeals. The anonymous compiler of the *Authentic Memoirs of the Life and Reign of Catherine II* provides a vivid summary of the work that needed to be done:

the laws of this vast empire were voluminous to a degree of the greatest absurdity, perplexed, insufficient, in many cases contradictory, and so loaded with precedents, reports, cases, and opinions, that they afforded an eternal scene of altercation, and were scarcely to be reconciled or understood by the very professors of them. The particular laws of the different provinces were also continually interfering and clashing, and caused such confusion, that the whole presented an endless chaos, and effaced almost every trace of original system or design.

There was no tradition of legal training in Russia; hence none of the government officials surrounding Catherine were experts, and Catherine herself only knew what she had picked up from her reading. The books she drew on in compiling the document which was to become known as her 'Great Instruction' included Montesquieu's *L'Esprit de Lois*, the recently published *On Crimes and Punishments* by the Italian legal theorist Cesare Beccaria, and Bielfeld's *Institutions Politiques*. Catherine was assisted in her work by one of her secretaries, Grigory Kozitsky, whose job it was to translate into Russian the material she selected from her reading. In June she began to show portions of her work to selected confidants.

One effect of Catherine's commitment to work was that her life as Empress was in danger of becoming very sedentary. The days when she spent most daylight hours on horseback were long past — she hardly seems to have ridden at all since the time of her coup — and Grigory Orlov, among others, used to nag her to be more physically active and get out of her 'eternal armchair', particularly during the winter months. In the summer she managed to get out and about more, June 1765 being a particularly busy month, in which she sailed with her fleet on the Baltic, visited all her country houses (including the building site of her Chinese Palace at Oranienbaum, which was then under construction to Rinaldi's design) and attended, with Paul, the army's summer camp manoeuvres at Krasnoye Selo (Paul was so excited about this that he made himself ill). Catherine protested to Madame Geoffrin: 'There is enough to make the Ladies of Paris faint in the Turbulent Life I am leading.'

On 5 August the Grand Duke was again indisposed, which Poroshin put down to his bad eating habits: 'His Highness complained of having a headache and feeling sick. He went to his room and got undressed. The doctor was sent for. Count Nikita arrived at that moment. The Grand Duke brought up nearly all his dinner. His Highness . . . is often subject to what is called indigestion: he eats too fast, doesn't chew properly, and so charges his stomach with an impossible task.' Paul now seemed to be developing a precocious interest in women — specifically in his mother's maids-of-honour – which Panin, a ladies' man himself, did nothing to discourage. For some months Paul was infatuated with Vera Choglokova, the orphaned daughter of the same Choglokovs who had had the task of supervising Catherine and Peter in the early years of their married life. After the death of her parents, Vera had been brought up at Court. On 9 October Paul was allowed to visit the observatory on the top of Catherine's apartments, which treat was followed by another even more exciting one for him. 'After the meal,' related Poroshin,

> Grigory Orlov came to see His Highness on behalf of Her Majesty to invite him to the observatory which had been built above the Empress's apartments. On his arrival, His Highness found Her Majesty there. One could see the whole town. When it was time to go back, Count Grigory asked His Highness if he would like to go and say hello to the maids-of-honour who lived not far from there. The Grand Duke was burning to do so, but did not know how he should reply in the presence of Her Majesty. The Empress settled it by telling His Highness that he could go. Never was an order carried out with such alacrity. Count Nikita and Count Grigory were of the party. They went round all the maids of honour. Once he was back, the Tsarevich talked about his expedition with rapture. 'Guess where I went today,' he said to everyone who came to see him. Overcome by retelling the story, he threw himself on to the couch in a voluptuous languor. He called me [i.e. Poroshin] to him and told me that he had seen his lady-friend and that she enchanted him more and more.

Catherine had 20 maids-of-honour, several of whom were only children. They were distinguished by being allowed to wear the initial letter of her name, set in diamonds. That year she was in search of a governess or supervisor for them, commissioning an old friend of her mother's in Hamburg, Madame Bielke (who subsequently became a frequent and trusted correspondent) to find one for her. The ideal woman to fulfil this post, Catherine stipulated, would be 'not young and not of the Catholic religion'. She should be of good morals, but not prone to nit-picking; should know how to insist, but at the same time be gentle; should have 'wit, prudence, accomplishments' and should like reading; if suitable, she could also be a companion for Catherine herself, but should never presume on this. 'When you have found this marvel,' wrote Catherine, 'please let me know, so that we can get ourselves ready. I will not be at all difficult about the conditions – lodged, heated, lit, fed, carriaged and dressed goes without saying: that is so at all Courts.' Perhaps to no one's great surprise, Madame Bielke never did succeed in finding such a marvel.

Baldassare Galuppi had arrived in St Petersburg, for the start of a three-year contract, in July 1765 and had quickly won the Court's – and Catherine's – approval. His standard of performance – his own and that which he expected from others – was evidently higher than that of his predecessors. On Wednesday afternoons concerts of chamber music took place in the Empress's antechamber, at which Galuppi impressed everyone by the accuracy of his playing on the clavichord. To help the elderly virtuoso cope with his first Petersburg winter, Catherine made him a present of a red velvet kaftan embroidered with gold and lined with sable, as well as a sable hat and a muff of another fur. For the Empress's name-day (24 November) Galuppi was commissioned to write an opera, *Didone abbandonata* ('Dido abandoned') to a libretto by Pietro Metastasio. At the first rehearsals he was dissatisfied with the orchestra, and therefore he arranged more frequent rehearsals, at which he shouted and scolded the musicians in Venetian dialect for the slightest mistake. There was a marked and rapid improvement in the orchestra's playing, but because of the number of costumes and the amount of scenery that had to be prepared, the opera was not ready for performance by Catherine's name-day and had to be postponed till carnival time. It was put on twice in the week before Lent – that is, in the last days of February 1766 – with great success. A few days after the second performance, the Empress sent Galuppi a gold diamond-encrusted snuff box and 1,000 ducats. Signora Colonna received, for playing the role of Dido, a diamond ring valued at 1,000 roubles. The opera was performed again at Easter, and received its final performance on Catherine's name-day that year.

In 1766 Catherine learnt from her ambassador in Paris, Prince Dmitry Golitsyn, that the French writer and compiler of the *Encyclopédie*, Denis Diderot, was in dire straits financially, and so was offering his personal library for sale at 15,000 livres. Catherine had long taken an interest in Diderot, having first written to him shortly after her accession offering to continue publication of the *Encyclopédie* in Russia, as the publication of any further volumes had just been banned in France. On this occasion Diderot had declined her assistance, preferring to publish in Switzerland. This time she made him an offer he could not refuse – namely,

16,000 livres on condition that the books remain in Diderot's home during his lifetime. She further appointed him librarian of his own library, with a salary of 1,000 livres a year, to be paid for 50 years in advance. Not surprisingly, Diderot was overcome with gratitude and in return he became Catherine's artistic adviser in Paris, searching out great paintings for sale and securing them on her behalf. Prince Golitsyn, a cultured man and at home in the intellectual circles of Paris, also acted in this capacity, buying works for Catherine by contemporary painters such as Greuze and Chardin. Catherine's purchase of Diderot's library provoked an adulatory letter from Voltaire, with whom she had been in correspondence since 1763:

> Madame! It is now towards the northern star that all eyes must turn. Your Imperial Majesty has found a path towards glory unknown to all other sovereigns before her. No one has thought of lavishing their beneficent acts seven or eight hundred leagues away from their own states. You have truly become the benefactress of Europe; and you have acquired more subjects through the greatness of your soul, than others could conquer by force of arms.

In Catherine's reply she declared with due modesty, if disingenuously, that 'the light of the northern star is only an aurora borealis', and returned compliment for compliment: 'You have fought the united enemies of men, superstition, fanaticism, ignorance, chicanery, corrupt judges . . . It requires many virtues and qualities to overcome these obstacles. You have shown that you possess them: you have conquered.'

The conduct of foreign affairs, always a slow business at the Russian Court, threatened to become slower still in 1766 because of Panin's somewhat scandalous involvement with the young and beautiful Countess Stroganova, the married daughter of the ex-chancellor Vorontsov. According to Sir George Macartney, Panin had conceived a 'violent passion' for Countess Stroganova, who was a 'Lady of uncommon beauty, and of a lively wit, improved and embellished by every advantage of education, and travel'. She had been separated from her husband for about a year,★ both parties to the marriage being keen to regain their freedom (Count Stroganov wanted to marry Princess Trubetskaya

---

★ Vorontsov had written to Catherine about his daughter some time previously, asking her approval for a divorce; Catherine had replied that this was not a matter for her — she was personally indifferent to it — but for the ecclesiastical authorities to deal with.

instead). Sir George predicted dire consequences for Panin over this passion of his, which both the lady herself and her friends were doing all they could to keep alive:

> The ill effects arising to Mr Panin, from this unfortunate connection are, that, by his negligence and dissipation, all business is either at a stand or moves with more than Russian slowness; that he begins to lose the respect of the public, which can scarce pardon an undisguised boyish passion, in a man of his years, station and experience; that his enemies have not failed to lay hold of this opportunity, to represent the indecency, and ill example of such weakness in the Minister of Her Majesty and in the Governor of the Heir of her empire.

On 6 April, a couple of weeks before her thirty-seventh birthday, Catherine reported to Madame Geoffrin that her great work on laws and her tapestry were advancing at the same rate, the work on the laws being done for two hours during the morning and the tapestry while being read to in the afternoon. She also told her correspondent that she had read out to Grigory Orlov a section of a letter in which Madame Geoffrin had commented on how hard-working she was; Grigory's reaction to this had pleased Catherine, and confirms that he was not given to easy flattery of his imperial mistress: 'He, who makes a profession out of laziness, despite being very clever and talented by nature, exclaimed "That's true", and that was the first time I had ever heard any praise from his mouth and it is to you Madame that I owe it.'

In a chatty letter which Catherine wrote to her friend Madame Bielke from Tsarskoye Selo that summer, she explained how she liked to play blind man's buff in the evenings – with or without Paul; how she had little time for doctors, particularly if they took themselves too seriously (one of her court surgeons used to say that after hearing her speak on the subject, 'no one would give a glass of water to a doctor'); how there had been a rumour recently circulating around the Courts of Europe that she had been poisoned, whereas actually she was in very good health and had been since she became Empress; and how she had never found it easy to spend time with women, blaming this on the fact that she was not allowed to talk freely with members of her own sex when she was a Grand Duchess: 'I will admit to you that there are no more than two women in the world to whom I can talk for half-an-hour at a time. From 15 to 33 years old I had no women to talk to and only dared have chambermaids with me; if I wanted to talk I had to go into another apartment where there were only men, thus be it habit or taste I can only make conversation well with them.' Catherine also confirmed to Madame Bielke that she would be going to Moscow in the winter and staying there for a year.

In a letter to Madame Geoffrin of 21 October 1766, Catherine reported her 'acquisition' of the sculptor Etienne Maurice Falconet, who had been recommended by Diderot to create a statue of Peter the Great. Falconet had contributed the article on sculpture to the *Encyclopédie* and had been working for the previous nine years at the Sèvres porcelain factory, modelling small classical figures that could be reproduced in porcelain. He was enthusiastic about the idea of working on a monumental scale and, at 25,000 livres a year for an estimated eight years, put in a lower bid for the Peter the Great statue than the other sculptors who had been approached by Catherine's ambassador in Paris, Prince Golitsyn. On his arrival in Petersburg, Falconet was provided with a workshop and studio on the site of the Empress Elizabeth's throne room and kitchen in the old timber Winter Palace which Catherine had had demolished. Next door, on the same site, what had been Elizabeth's theatre was remodelled as an apartment for him.

In early December Sir George Macartney reported on Catherine's work on the laws in such glowing terms that his dispatch was clearly designed to be intercepted and relayed to the Empress:

> At present the Czarina's attention is principally engaged by a favourite project, the success of which will do Her more real honour, and be of greater advantage to Her, than the winnings of a battle or the acquisition of a Kingdom. She, whose penetrating genius is equally happy in discovering defects and in finding resources to remedy them, has long beheld with regret the confusion, tediousness, ambiguity, and injustice of the laws of Her Empire: to correct them has been long the object of Her ambition . . . A most noble undertaking, and worthy the ambition of a great Prince, who prefers the title of legislator to the fame of conquest, and founds his glory upon providing for the happiness, and not the destruction of mankind.

The Empress now issued a call for the selection of deputies to form a Legislative Commission. Major institutions such as the Senate and the various Colleges, and certain segments of the population – the nobility, townsmen, Cossacks (irregular cavalry formations, living on the margins of settled society) and free peasants (but not serfs, who comprised approximately one half of the rural population) – were invited to draw up 'instructions' about their legal concerns and send deputies to the Commission. The clergy were supposed to be represented through the Holy Synod, which was invited to send a deputy as though it were any other government department, and officers and soldiers were represented through the Military College. Grigory Potemkin was appointed to be one of three 'Guardians of Exotic Peoples', the other two being Vyazemsky and Olsufyev. This was intended to be the kind of large-scale consultation advocated by Diderot in one of his articles in the *Encyclopédie*. Such a consultation had not been held in Russia for more than 100 years.

In a letter to Madame Bielke, Catherine made a rare allusion to her married life, making a claim which she would repeat in her memoirs: 'I pity the poor Queen of Denmark for being so little celebrated, there is nothing worse than having a child-husband.* I know it by experience, and I am one of those women who believe that it is always the fault of the husband if he is not loved, for in truth I would have loved mine very much, if it had been possible to do so, and if he had had the kindness to want it.' She went on to tell Madame Bielke her projected timetable for her forthcoming journey: 'I will be leaving, Madame, towards 10th February our style for Moscow . . . I will be there after four days of travelling . . . After that in May I will go to walk around Kazan, as if I were going to one of my country houses, and at the end of June I will be on my way back to Moscow, in order to start work on a new law code of which you have already heard, and before a year is out I will be on my way back here, God willing.'

---

* Caroline Mathilde, the daughter of Frederick, Prince of Wales, married King Christian VII of Denmark in 1766; the mentally unstable Christian declared he could not love Caroline Mathilde, as it was 'unfashionable to love one's wife'. The marriage was dissolved in 1772.

# 9
# Laws, Smallpox and War
## (1767–69)

*My device is a bee which, flying from plant to plant, collects honey to carry to its hive, and its inscription is utility.*

Catherine II to Voltaire

atherine left for Moscow on 7 February 1767, Panin and the Grand Duke having set off a few days earlier. She had instructed Panin to ensure that the palaces where she was to stay en route were aired before her arrival, as she feared that otherwise she would get headaches. Before leaving she drew up an instruction for Senator Ivan Glebov, who was to be left in charge of law and order in St Petersburg: he was to pay special attention to preventing the activities of thieves and robbers in the town and on the approaching roads, to remind householders to lock their gates at night and to make use of night-watchmen and dogs, and to ensure that the night patrols did their patrolling properly rather than passing the night in taverns or other inappropriate places.

As ever, Catherine was quick to compare Moscow and St Petersburg and knew which she preferred. She found Moscow, an ancient town which had grown haphazardly and whose long history was reflected in a mix of architectural styles, intractable compared with her beloved Petersburg which she could shape at will and where everything was ordered and planned, at least in appearance. She particularly disliked the density of Moscow's population and what she called its 'false air of Ispahan', by which she meant the Asiatic influences resulting from the invasion of the Mongol hordes in the thirteenth century.

199

Catherine left Moscow towards the end of April and embarked on a journey down the Volga, travelling initially by road to Tver, accompanied by a suite of nearly 2,000 people, including members of the diplomatic corps. At Tver the travellers exchanged their coaches and carriages for boats, a flotilla of 11 galleys starting downstream on 2 May. The Empress's galley, which she likened to a 'whole house', accommodated not only herself and her personal attendants, but also Grigory Orlov and his brother Vladimir, Zakhar and Ivan Chernyshev (friends of Catherine's youth, who now held influential posts in her government), and several other courtiers and officials. The enormous galleys made stately progress down the Volga, with plenty of stops along the route. People would turn out to greet the Empress from the river-banks, serenading her with French horns, trumpets, kettle drums and choirs of villagers, in a mixture of spontaneity and previously orchestrated arrangements. At times the journey was hampered by the weather, Catherine reporting to Panin on 8 May that they had spent the whole of the previous day at anchor because of a very strong and cold contrary wind. She quickly became frustrated whenever she was deprived of news from Moscow and St Petersburg on account of couriers being delayed or miscalculating where to find her on a particular day.

By 10 May she had reached the historic town of Yaroslavl, from where she wrote to Panin: 'I arrived here yesterday, at nine o'clock in the evening and I am well, thank God, as is my whole suite, and in the space of twenty-four hours I received three couriers from you. Say thank you to the Grand Duke for his second letter, to which I will reply at leisure, but now I am getting ready to visit several manufactories, and I will not be leaving here before Sunday.' Uncharitably the Empress remarked in a letter to Mikhail Vorontsov that the women of Yaroslavl had pretty faces, but that in their girth and clothing they resembled the *mappa mundi*. A few days later she was in Kostroma, lodged in the famous Ipatyevsky Monastery from where, as she reminded Panin, the first of the Romanov dynasty had been summoned to Moscow in 1613 to be crowned Tsar. A reception was held in Kostroma at which several members of the imperial suite, including Ivan Chernyshev who 'wept throughout dinner', were overcome at the warmth of the welcome they received from the local nobility. The members of the diplomatic corps were now to take their leave of the Empress and return to Moscow where they would, trusted Catherine, fulfil her publicity purposes; 'They will tell you,' she wrote to Panin, 'how I was received here.'

On 26 May Catherine finally made her entry into Kazan, where the welcome was even more overwhelming than it had been in Kostroma. For the local peasantry the Empress was the closest thing they had ever seen to God. Some of them attempted to offer candles to be carried before Catherine, as though she were an icon – until they were unceremoniously chased away. For all that she wanted her subjects to adore and be grateful to her, Catherine did not like such 'excess' and reported to Panin that otherwise 'everything is going extremely decorously'. The Governor of Kazan laid on a magnificent entertainment at his house; Catherine indicated her pleasure by staying up beyond her usual bedtime and not leaving until after midnight. As is usual with royal or state visits, everyone worked hard to present a glowing picture to the Empress and she was duly impressed: 'Here the people all along the Volga are wealthy and very satisfied and, although the prices are high everywhere, everyone has bread to eat and no one complains or suffers need.' At Simbirsk, the party disembarked from the galleys and prepared to return to Moscow (where Panin, in the Empress's absence, had been spending much of his time with Countess Stroganova). Though Catherine had shown no inclination to seek out her less fortunate subjects, this journey did open her eyes to the diversity of her people and she commented to Voltaire on the difficulty of making laws to apply equally – 'and what a difference of climate, people, customs, even ideas!'

Back in Moscow Catherine immersed herself in the final preparations for the opening of the Legislative Commission. On Sunday 30 July the Empress left the Golovin Palace for the Kremlin at ten o'clock in the morning in a coach drawn by eight horses, preceded by 16 carriages bearing her courtiers and followed by Grigory Orlov with a detachment of horse guards. Grand Duke Paul also followed in his own ceremonial coach. At the Kremlin the deputies marched across the square two by two in a specified order behind Procurator-General Vyazemsky to join the Empress at the Cathedral of the Assumption. During the religious ceremony the representatives of the non-Christian minorities remained outside. Catherine had great hopes for the way her Commission would cross religious divides, describing in a letter to Voltaire how 'the Orthodox sitting between the heretic and the Muslim . . . They have so completely forgotten the custom of roasting one another that if anyone were unwise enough to propose that a deputy should boil his neighbour to please the supreme being, I answer for everyone in saying that every single person would reply: he is a man as I am.'

After the service the deputies signed their oath of office, while Catherine proceeded to the Faceted Palace, where she received them in the reception hall. Wearing the imperial mantle and a small crown, Catherine stood before the throne. Copies of her Great Instruction and the Commission's rules of procedure were displayed on a table draped in red velvet on her right, while to her left stood Grand Duke Paul (now nearly 13 years old), along with court and government officials and the foreign ambassadors. The most important ladies of the Court were also present. The Metropolitan of Novgorod, Dmitry Sechenov, who was the deputy chosen by the Synod to represent the Church, made a speech in praise of Catherine, and then Vice-Chancellor Golitsyn read a motivational greeting from the Empress.

The first working session of the Commission was held next day in the Faceted Palace. The first item on the agenda was for the deputies to listen to a reading of Catherine's Great Instruction; this was not completed until the fifth session on 9 August. The Great Instruction or, to give it its official title, 'The Instructions to the Commissioners for composing a new Code of Laws', consisted of more than 500 maxims, setting out Catherine's fundamental beliefs about the law and how it should operate in Russia. It was a compendium of general principles on which good government and an orderly society should be based. Much of it was a reworking and expanding of the maxims and observations she had compiled for herself in 1761. She ended her Great Instruction optimistically: 'Nothing now remains for the Commission to do, but to compare every Part of the Laws with the Rules of these Instructions.' The deputies were also given rules as to their behaviour during sessions: they were not to interrupt one another, swords were not to be worn in the assembly, and brawling would be punishable by fines or even exclusion. On completion of the reading, the deputies were supposed to get to work, a number of committees having been formed to consider different areas of the law. But first they made a formal response to the Great Instruction by requesting that the Empress accept the title of 'The Great, most Wise, and Mother of the Fatherland'. Catherine drafted a reply to be relayed to the deputies: 'About the titles which you wish me to accept from you, I reply as follows: 1) the Great – I leave it to time and to those who come after me to judge dispassionately what I have done. 2) Most Wise – I cannot call myself this, since God alone is most wise. 3) Mother of the Fatherland – to love the subjects entrusted to me by God I consider to be the duty of my calling; to be loved by them is my desire.' Catherine demonstrated her wisdom by refusing these titles, but the very offer of them by the deputies (which may have been engineered behind the scenes with Catherine's concurrence) strengthened her position on the throne, and dismissed any question of viewing her merely as regent for her son. Despite the official refusal, the Senate accepted for safekeeping a document detailing the request that Catherine should accept these titles, and promised that it would be published in gazettes and newspapers in Russian, French and German. With such affirmation from her subjects, and with someone of the stature of Voltaire telling her that he considered her Great Instruction to be 'the most beautiful monument of the century', Catherine received no more assistance in assessing the true measure of her intellectual and literary abilities than did her late husband in understanding the limits of his musical talent. This is part of the loneliness of absolute power – particularly for someone who realises that people do not generally tell the unvarnished truth – and is one reason why Catherine so valued the presence and affection of a man like Grigory Orlov, who did not flatter her.

Throughout her time in Moscow Catherine was in correspondence with Etienne Falconet, who was busy working on the clay version of his equestrian statue of Peter the Great, using two imperial horses – Brilliant and Caprice – as models. He had them both ridden in sequence up a specially constructed ramp, while he sketched them over and over again. Falconet was a demanding correspondent and showed himself needy for his imperial patron's approval from the start of his time in Petersburg. Catherine managed to find time to write to him during the days when her Great Instruction was being read to the deputies, pointing out that she was not in a position to give an informed opinion on his work (Catherine never pretended to know more about art and music than she did, content to rely on her specialist advisers) as well as warning him against believing gossip about her intentions or plans:

Monsieur Falconet, I have kept putting off replying to you from one day to the next, I moved around so many times this spring that it was not until this morning that I unearthed your last letter from among my papers; but first of all be assured and have no further doubt that I will return to Petersburg around Christmas. There has never in fact been any real doubt about this return; but there are story-tellers here as there are in Paris who see, or it wouldn't take much for them to see, the moon at mid-day, and who reason according to what they think they see . . . I believe that you have done your best; but how can you refer it to me for approval? I cannot even draw; this will perhaps be the first good statue which I will have seen in my life: how can you content yourself with such a slender judgment? the least schoolboy knows more about your art than I do . . . Goodbye, Monsieur Falconet; I am so busy these days now that I have placed such a heavy burden on my shoulders that I have hardly time to write these words to you.

Before leaving Moscow at the end of the year, Catherine halted the sessions of the Legislative Commission. They would reopen two months later in St Petersburg. On 23 January 1768 she was back at Tsarskoye Selo and three days later she returned to the town, telling Panin that 'Petersburg seems like paradise compared to Ispahan'.

There was now a surprising development in Nikita Panin's life, as reported by Count Solms to Frederick the Great:

I cannot resist informing Your Majesty about an unexpected future event, news of which has just seeped out here, before the interested parties wanted to make it known – that is, the marriage of Count Panin with the eldest daughter of the Grand Chamberlain Count Sheremetev. It is the most significant match that could be made in Russia, as much in terms of family as of wealth; through wealth inherited from her mother, the young Countess already enjoys during her father's life-time an income of more than 40 thousand roubles, as well as an establishment complete with houses, china, jewels and other things, so that, for these reasons alone, one can only congratulate Count Panin on his good fortune. Nevertheless one cannot help but be surprised by his decision. His bodily infirmities had made one believe that, if he were to decide to marry, he would not be looking for a young person. Moreover, as his position at Court and the place he holds in relation to the Grand Duke do not permit him to live outside the palace, he will not be able to enjoy the pleasures of society and of a life of ease in his house, and it is not credible that he should want to leave his post of Grand Master, which gives him such great credit in the nation. As he has nevertheless taken this decision as suddenly as it is unexpected, I am tempted to believe that he is looking towards the future and that he desires by establishing himself thus to secure a sure retreat, independent of favour, for his later years.

The English diplomat Henry Shirley also reported on this surprise engagement: '[Panin] is very soon to be married to the countess Anna Petrowna Scheremetew, a lady of almost unlimited ambition. His connections with countess [Stroganova] which have done him so much harm are now at an end, and we may hope to see him become the same excellent man that he was five years ago.'

But poor Panin's happiness was short-lived. Within three months of the engagement Anna Sheremeteva had fallen ill with smallpox. This was the disease of which Catherine had been in constant fear since childhood and she had, on at least one occasion, rebuked Panin for having allowed Grand Duke Paul to be in a public place where he might come into contact with infected people. All Europe had been horrified by the ravages smallpox had wrought on the Habsburg Court in May 1767, when both the Empress Maria Theresa and her daughter-in-law Maria Josepha had come down with the disease. Maria Theresa had survived with some scarring, but Maria Josepha died within the space of a week. On 4 May 1768 Catherine wrote a consolatory letter to Panin from Tsarskoye Selo:

> I am extremely sorry about the illness of your fiancée, but I do not despair: God is merciful, and her youth can easily overcome illness. I see from your letter that you are grieving sooner than you need and, if God makes her better, then I fear that you will fall ill. Please take care of your health and be assured of the sympathy which I bear towards you in all circumstances . . . Give my son my blessing; I commission him to try to comfort you.

A secret letter which she wrote the next day to Ivan Yelagin reveals both the depth of her anxiety over Paul's proximity to the deadly disease and her genuine concern for her minister. The letter begins: 'Ivan Perfilyevich, I am in enormous embarrassment on account of A[nna] P[etrovna].'s smallpox; if I followed my inclination, I would immediately bring the Grand Duke here, and Nikita Ivanovich would follow him in a couple of days, but I think that this would seem distressing to Nikita Ivanovich. You know that he does not like moving, above all having to part from his fiancée.' Catherine admits that bringing the Grand Duke to Tsarskoye Selo will not be without inconvenience to herself as it will mean rearranging other plans, but 'provided the Grand Duke is safe, then I would not worry about that'. Her concern for Paul was not solely a matter of maternal feeling – though that was part of it – but also an awareness that carelessly allowing him to become infected with smallpox would 'not be without reproach from the public'. Feeling unable to broach the matter with Panin herself, she asked Yelagin to raise it in conversation with him, to work out what to do, and tell her. 'I am very anxious and cannot decide what is best; for everything in this critical situation is bad.' Whatever Yelagin said to Panin resolved the matter, and Catherine's next letter to Yelagin mentions the preparations which were being made to receive the Grand Duke at Tsarskoye Selo. On 15 May Catherine wrote to Panin to reassure him about her own health (she had had a sudden fainting fit the day before): 'Seeing from your letter to I[van] P[erfilyevich] Yelagin, that my paroxysm of yesterday, which didn't mean anything, has added to your worries, I take up my pen myself to tell you that this morning I slept until ten o'clock and got up feeling almost better, just a little weak; please don't worry, for there is no need. Doctor Ens assures me that your fiancée will come through these difficult days.'

But Dr Ens's optimism was misplaced. Henry Shirley reported to Lord Viscount Weymouth two days later: 'I must not neglect to let you know that the countess Anna Petrowna Scheremetew, Mr Panin's bride, a young lady of uncommon merit, beautiful, and immensely rich died this morning at five o'clock of the small pox. I have not yet any news of the Count Panin, but by the anxiety he was in during all the time of her illness, he must be inconsolable. He loved her so much, that we are not without apprehension for him.' Nevertheless, within three days Panin was preparing to rejoin the Grand Duke at Tsarskoye Selo; he seems to have decided that the only way to cope with his bereavement was to get back to normal existence as soon as possible, and forget the hopes he had entertained of a different kind of life. Panin's name was never again associated with romance or marriage.

Countess Sheremeteva's illness and death made Catherine all the more determined to proceed with a course of action which she had been quietly investigating and planning for some time. A form of inoculation against smallpox, in which a tiny amount of material from a pox pustule was inserted in the nostril or at the hair-line, had long been practised as a part of folk medicine in Europe and Asia; a mild form of the disease appeared in the patient, which was not particularly dangerous and which conferred lifelong immunity. In recent years some trained medical men had attempted to make this procedure appear more 'professional' by adding purges and bleeding to cleanse the system, and inserting the infective material into a large incision, usually in the arm. As often as not this procedure led to a severe dose of the disease with the complication of the wound becoming infected – so that the patient might have done a lot better just to catch the disease in the normal way. Some untrained practitioners, however, among the best known of whom were the Sutton family, father and son, were doing rather better by using the basic folk method. Thomas Dimsdale, a fellow of the Royal College of Physicians in London who had long been interested in smallpox inoculation, combined the best of both worlds by being a qualified medical practitioner but also developing a method similar to that used by the Suttons. More importantly, his method seemed to be successful. He published a treatise on the subject in 1767 which attained a wide circulation, and it was through this that Baron Alexander Cherkasov, the president of the Russian Medical College, came to hear of his work. Knowing that Catherine was intent on introducing inoculation to Russia, provided it could be demonstrated to work, Cherkasov suggested to the Russian ambassador in London that Dr Dimsdale be approached. The project which was proposed to him involved nothing less than coming to Russia to inoculate the Empress and her son. He rose to the challenge, and in July 1768 the 56-year-old Dr Dimsdale and his 22-year-old son Nathaniel (a medical student at Edinburgh) set out for St Petersburg.

A new British ambassador to Russia in the person of Lord Cathcart arrived shortly ahead of the Dimsdales. His children's tutor, William Richardson, described the experience of first seeing the city as the travellers approached by boat: 'The palaces of Oranibaum [*sic*] and Peterhoff have a magnificent appearance to the sea; and the face of the country is agreeably diversified with woods and little hills. The country around St Petersburgh is very woody: so that in approaching it, the steeples and spires, which are covered with tin and brass, and some of them gilt, seemed as if they arose from the midst of a forest.' The first public event which Lord Cathcart and his family attended was the laying of the foundation stone of the new St Isaac's Cathedral, designed by Rinaldi, on 8 August. (The earlier, wooden, church in St Isaac's Square had been demolished to clear the space where Falconet's equestrian statue of Peter I would eventually stand; Rinaldi's church was to be built further back in the square.) Both Lord Cathcart and Mr Richardson described the event in some detail: 'All the space to be occupied by the church had been previously railed in; and into this place, only persons of high rank, and those who had a particular permission were admitted. An immense multitude of people were assembled without.' Lord Cathcart's party was shown into a tent, where they were introduced to most of the ladies of the Court. An arch 'supported upon eight pillars of the Corinthian order, and adorned with garlands' had been erected over the place where the altar was to be, and underneath the arch there was a table 'covered with crimson velvet, fringed with gold' and a small marble chest had been placed on the table. Smaller side-tables bore the items to be deposited in the foundation stone, which included medals and coins, a gold box for them to be placed in and 'two pieces of marble in the form of bricks'.

The first procession to arrive was that of the Grand Duke and his retinue. 'This young Prince,' wrote Richardson, 'the heir apparent of the Russian empire, is of a pale complexion, with dark eyes, more remarkable for their good colour, than expression; and of a shape more delicate than genteel. He seems of a cheerful disposition, of affable and easy manners. He was dressed in the uniform of the navy, and wore a blue ribbon of the order of St Alexander Nevsky.' Then cannon fire from the Admiralty and the beating of drums announced the arrival of the Empress, who was preceded by a procession of deacons swinging censers and bearing banners of St Isaac, priests carrying crosses, candles and a large icon, followed by choristers and bishops. Richardson provides a detailed description of the now 39-year-old Empress Catherine:

The Empress of Russia is taller than the middle size, very comely, gracefully formed, but inclined to grow corpulent; and of a fair complexion, which, like every other female in this country, she endeavours to improve by the addition of rouge. She has a fine mouth and teeth; and blue eyes, expressive of scrutiny, something not so good as observation, and not so bad as suspicion. Her features are in general regular and pleasing. Indeed, with regard to her appearance altogether, it would be doing her injustice to say it was masculine, yet it would not be doing her justice to say, it was entirely feminine . . . She wore a silver stuff negligee, the ground pea-green, with purple flowers and silver trimming. Her hair was dressed according to the present fashion. She also wore a rich diamond necklace, bracelets, and ear-rings, with a blue ribbon of the highest order of Knighthood; and the weather being very warm, she carried in her hand a small green umbrella. Her demeanour to all around her seemed very smiling and courteous.

Lord Cathcart gave a brief description of Grigory Orlov which would suggest that the imperial favourite had taken pains to educate himself in the ways of courtiers since Catherine's accession: 'Count Orloff is of a stature much above the common size, and is graceful in his person and the character of his countenance is modest and mild. He speaks very good French.'

Divine service was performed, with much praying, singing, sprinkling with holy water and censing. Then the medals were blessed and placed in the marble chest, and the Empress was the first to use a golden trowel to embed some coins in a stone. The Grand Duke added some mortar, as did Lord Cathcart and various state dignitaries. When everything had been placed in the marble chest, the table was removed through a trap door and the Empress operated the pulley whereby the chest was lowered down through the platform and into place. Archimandrite Platon then delivered a sermon, and the service concluded with mutual hand-kissing between priests and Empress, the priests – according to Richardson – kissing the Empress's hand with 'good-will and a loud noise'.

Later that same month Lord Cathcart went to view the proceedings of the Legislative Commission from a gallery alongside the one the Empress used, when she wished to see what was going on and hear what was being said without being seen herself, in the hall in the Winter Palace where the plenary sessions were held. The ambassador arrived during a break:

The room seemed so full, and the different groups so busy in conversation that it was impossible to look down upon the assembly without thinking of a beehive. The Empress's throne fills one end of the room, the other end and both sides have benches as in the house of Commons; on the left side of the throne is a table of State. At the upper end there was a chair for the Marshal of the commission, and on one side two other chairs, one for the director who minutes the proceedings, and the other for the procureur-général who is there as commissioner from the Empress and who has a right to interpose in her name, in case the standing orders should be attached.

The members are classed according to the governments to which they belong, every district furnishing a noble, a merchant or artizan, and a free peasant, and the seats being numbered they place themselves accordingly. The clergy have but one commissioner who is an archbishop and sits alone on the right of the throne. When the house was resumed, they all took their places and observed the most perfect silence and attention till one o'clock when they adjourned.

Lord Cathcart's final fact-finding trip around this time was to the Smolny Institute:

[Betskoy] was so obliging on Tuesday evening as to show us the convent so called, where the Empress educates at her own expense two hundred and fifty young ladies of distinction and 350 daughters of burghers and free peasants. They are received at four years of age, and remain till nineteen.

They are divided into five classes and remain three years in each class during which time they are instructed in every thing necessary for their respective situations. I saw their dormitories and was present at their supper; nothing can exceed the care or success of Mr de Betskoy and the ladies employed in this seminary which is but in its infancy, there being no more than two hundred and twenty as yet received, and the house which was really intended for a convent by the late Empress and is very magnificent not being near finished.

The 'young ladies of distinction' studied religion, Russian, foreign languages, arithmetic, geography, history, heraldry, drawing, music, knitting and sewing, dancing and how to behave in society, while the daughters of burghers and free peasants took many of the same subjects but with foreign languages being replaced by more domestic skills. The pupils lived at the Institute during the whole 15 years of their education. Their parents were able to view them and admire their progress on days when they performed for visitors, but there was no going home for holidays, Catherine and Betskoy believing that if the next generation was to be an improvement on the present one, separation from family during the period of education was essential.

On the morning of 28 August Dr Dimsdale and his son, having arrived in Petersburg and been accommodated temporarily in an apartment on Millionnaya Street, were privately received by Catherine. The only other people present at this first meeting were Nikita Panin and Alexander Cherkasov, the latter, who could speak English, acting as an interpreter as Dr Dimsdale's French was not up to holding a conversation unaided. The doctor was impressed by how well informed the Empress was on the subject of smallpox inoculation as she questioned him with 'extraordinary penetration and soundness'. The Dimsdales were invited to join the Empress at dinner, where she presided at the head of a long table of about a dozen people. 'Dinner consisted of several excellent dishes, prepared in the French manner, and afterwards with dessert of the best fruits and preserves.' Dimsdale's attention was particularly taken by a Russian pineapple, which 'although small was very tasty'. The Empress, relates Dimsdale, was courteous and attentive to each of her guests, who all seemed relaxed in her company.

The reason for the Dimsdales' presence in St Petersburg was, as Lord Cathcart put it, 'a secret which everybody knows'. The Empress was prepared to be inoculated immediately, but Dimsdale wanted to carry out the procedure on 40 or 50 other people first, as it was believed that different climates could affect the outcome. He had assured Lord Cathcart (who was understandably nervous, as was King George III, about a British subject carrying out such an operation on the Russian sovereign) that both the Empress and the Grand Duke were in a state of perfect health for the procedure to be a success, and, reported the ambassador, he was 'charmed with their gracious and engaging behaviour towards him'. During their preparatory work, for which they used a number of young people of poor families both for procuring infective material and for testing out the inoculation, the Dimsdales were struck by the prevalence of the belief among lower-class Russians that fresh air was dangerous, particularly for the ill and convalescent. One family had to be bribed to open a window in the room of their sick child – but even then they agreed to open it only when the Dimsdales were there and closed it a short time after they were gone.

Anticipation of being inoculated was not Catherine's main concern during the summer and autumn of 1768. The international situation had been tense for some time. There had been rebellions in Poland by anti-Russian and anti-Poniatowski Polish patriots, in response to which Catherine had moved larger forces into the country. This was perceived as Russian arrogance, particularly by the French, who made use of the opportunity to bribe Turkey into challenging Russia. Things were brought to a head by the incursion into Turkish territory of a group of Russian Cossacks in pursuit of some Polish rebels. Once there the Cossacks had set to massacring Jews and Tatars. In response, on 25 September the Turks declared war in their traditional manner – that is, by imprisoning the Russian envoy, Alexei Obreskov, in the Castle of the Seven Towers.

One of the first victims of the Russo-Turkish War was the Legislative Commission, whose plenary sessions were now abandoned, as many of the deputies needed to depart for military service. Nothing had yet received final approval in the Commission, though the debates, discussions and lists of grievances it had generated provided Catherine with a wealth of information from which she was able to draw in the future. The 19 sub-committees which had been formed also carried on with their work, preparing draft legislation to be considered by the Empress at a later date.

Three recruiting levies were ordered on the outbreak of war, and between October and December approximately 50,000 men were conscripted into the armed forces. The levies always caused bitterness and anguish in the villages, as the unfortunate recruits left in columns, sometimes chained together, for what was at that time lifelong service, their families and neighbours bidding them goodbye as though they were already dead. Catherine now set up a small Council of State, composed of her closest advisers and officials, to coordinate the military effort, to define the Russian war aims and lay down the general lines of Russian foreign policy. The Council, being a purely ad hoc body which only discussed the matters Catherine put before it, was not concerned with the general administration of the country. The Empress herself usually, though not always, attended the meetings.

The outbreak of war did not disrupt the inoculation plans. Dr Dimsdale described the secrecy surrounding the event:

Through the agency of Baron Cherkasov everything was stipulated and arranged according to the wishes of the Empress, and at nine o'clock in the evening, by prior agreement, a messenger appeared at Wolff's house [i.e. the house of the British consul] with the order to come immediately, bringing with us the sick person from whom the material for the smallpox inoculation was to be taken. No one apart from my son and myself knew the real reason for this order being given, and we looked as amazed as everyone else. Nevertheless we immediately did as requested.

The child I had chosen as the most suitable for this, and who was by now displaying symptoms of smallpox, had already fallen asleep. My son picked him up, wrapped him in his own overcoat and carried him to the carriage. We were the only people in it; we were driven to the great entrance of the palace, the one by Millionnaya Street, where we were given an apartment when I arrived in the town.

We entered the palace by a secret door, where Baron Cherkasov met us and led us to the Empress.

Lord Cathcart reported that the only people in attendance at the inoculation were Nikita Panin, Caspar von Saldern (a Holstinian minister at that time close to Panin and the Grand Duke) and Baron Cherkasov; Grigory Orlov was away on a hunting expedition and had not been informed.

On the day after her inoculation Catherine went to Tsarskoye Selo for a period of isolation in the country air. Here she followed the 'cool regimen' prescribed by Dimsdale, which included spending two or three hours a day outside. On 21 October Lord Cathcart was able to report to Lord Weymouth that the operation had been a success:

It is with great pleasure I have the honour to acquaint Your Lordship that the Empress who has only had the slightest indisposition, and has never been confined to her apartments since the operation, had yesterday a very favourable eruption of small pox, very few in number, and of a quality entirely to Dr Dymsdale's satisfaction. This I have just heard from Mr Panin to whom Her Majesty wrote every day (except one that she had a head ache) with her own hand. He at the same time told me it was a very great secret, and not to be owned here till the Grand Duke's inoculation is over. I assured him the news will give the King the greatest satisfaction, as His Majesty expected from Dr Dymsdale's going abroad that the resolution was taken, and would, I knew, be under anxiety until all was happily over.

A few days later Count Solms provided more graphic details – which he also claimed to have received from Panin – for Frederick the Great: 'The eruption took place without causing a very violent fever, Her Majesty felt it for two days, for which she was obliged to stay in bed. She had a few pustules on her face, a hundred over all of her body of which the majority were on both arms; they are already beginning to peel, so as far as one can humanly predict, she has no further danger to fear.' Catherine was delighted with both herself and Dr Dimsdale, as is evident from a cheerful letter to Madame Bielke (from which it is also clear that Dr Dimsdale had become an object of gossip throughout Europe):

Madame! Whatever anyone may have told you against Monsieur Dimsdale who is neither a charlatan nor a quaker, he inoculated me on 12th October and in less than three weeks here I am recovered thanks be to God, and delivered for ever from all fear of this horrible disease. A number of people have followed my example, among others the Grand Master of Ordnance Count Orlov and Marshal Count Razumovsky. All Petersburg wants to be inoculated, and all those who have been are well. My doctor is a prudent, wise and disinterested man and is extremely upright; his parents were quakers and so was he, but he has left them, retaining only the excellence of their morals. I will be eternally grateful to this man; those who would decry a man of such merit can only be charlatans with an interest in doing so.

Catherine reported to Voltaire that, on the day after his inoculation, the intrepid Grigory Orlov went hunting in a snowstorm.

Next to be inoculated was the 14-year-old Grand Duke whom, despite his recurrent childhood illnesses – which the doctor, like Catherine, attributed to the manner of his early nurture by 'certain old ladies' to whom the Empress Elizabeth had entrusted him – Dr Dimsdale described as 'of fine physique, hale and hearty, strong and without any congenital disease'. Paul received his inoculation on 2 November, with no complications; on the same day a Te Deum was sung to celebrate Catherine's recovery. Her reply to the Senate's congratulations demonstrates that she attached great importance to her inoculation – which had not been without personal risk: 'My object was by my own example to save from death countless of my loyal subjects, who, not knowing the benefit of this method, and fearing it, were remaining in danger. By this I have fulfilled part of the duty of my calling, for, according to the Gospel, the good shepherd lays down his life for his sheep.'

William Richardson wrote a detailed description of the service held in the chapel of the Winter Palace on 22 November to celebrate the recovery of both Catherine and Paul. His account is written very much from the point of view of a somewhat bewildered Western observer and he clearly had no appreciation of icons; it is nevertheless a very accurate, if uncomprehending, description of Orthodox liturgy and worth reproducing:

On each side of the chapel, which is a very lofty and spacious room in the winter palace, is a row of gilt Ionic pillars. The walls are covered with glaring and ill-executed pictures of Russian saints. On the roof over the altar (or rather, the place corresponding to the altar in English churches), the Supreme Being is represented as an old man in white apparel. On the inside of a rail which extended across the room, and close by the pillar which was next the altar, on the south side, stood the Empress and her son: and also on the inside of the rail, and on each side of the altar, was a choir of musicians. All the rest who witnessed, or took part in the solemnity, excepting the priests, stood on the outside of the rail.

The ceremony began with solemn music; and then were pronounced the prayers and ejaculations which constituted the first part of the service. This having lasted some time, two folding-doors close by the altar were opened from within, and displayed a magnificent view of the interior and most holy part of the chapel. Opposite to us was a large picture of the taking down from the cross: on each side, a row of gilt Ionic pillars; in the middle, a table covered with cloth of gold; and upon the table were placed, a crucifix, a candlestick with burning tapers, and chalices with holy water. A number of venerable priests, with grey hair, flowing beards, mitres, and costly robes, stood in solemn array on each side of this magnificent sanctuary . . .

From this place advanced a priest, with 'slow and solemn pace,' carrying a lighted taper: he was followed in like manner by another, reciting prayers, and carrying a censer smoking with incense. Advancing towards her Majesty, he three times waved the censer before her; she all the while bowing, and very gracefully crossing her breast. He was succeeded by another priest, who carried the Gospel; out of which having read some part, he presented it to the Empress, who kissed it.

The priests then retired; the folding-doors were closed; the choristers sung an anthem: they were answered by musical voices from within: the music was deep-toned, and sublime. The folding-doors were again set open: the ceremonies of the taper and incense repeated: two priests then advanced, and carried the bread and wine of the Eucharist, veiled with cloth of gold. Having administered these, they retired. The doors were closed, and the solemn music resumed.

The doors were set open a third time, with the same ceremonies as before; and a priest ascending the pulpit fixed to the pillar opposite to the Empress, delivered a discourse . . . After this, some priests came from the inside of the chapel, and concluded the service with prayers and ejaculations.

On St Catherine's Day, 24 November, the Empress made Dr Dimsdale a Baron of Russia, a title which was to be hereditary. She also gave him a present amounting to £10,000 and a pension of £500 a year. In addition he was awarded the rank of counsellor of state, which made him equivalent to a major general. The young boy from whom the infective material had been taken, Alexander Markov, was ennobled with the honorary surname of Ospenny (*ospa* being Russian for smallpox, this surname could perhaps be translated as Smallpoksky – a rather dubious honour, one might think).

Dr, now Baron, Dimsdale continued to practise in Russia for several months. A vaccination house was established in what had once been a wool factory where the citizens of Petersburg could walk in and receive the treatment free of charge. Dimsdale commented in the notes he wrote during his stay that both the Empress and the Grand Duke had allowed material to be taken from them to inoculate many other people, which helped to dispel the belief that it was dangerous to donate material in this way. Catherine's power to charm had operated in its highest degree on Baron Dimsdale. He described her as being of more than medium height and having much natural grace and majesty. He found her courteous, affable and good-humoured as well as highly intelligent – 'one cannot help but be amazed by her'. He was impressed with her command of Russian, French and German, as well as her ability to read Italian and to understand some English. He reported that she observed the rites of the Orthodox Church 'in an exemplary manner', that she was very abstemious in her consumption of wine, of which she drank only one or two glasses mixed with water at meal-times, and that she worked tirelessly on affairs of state: 'the encouragement and flourishing of the liberal arts, the good of her subjects – these are the matters to which, in times of peace, her great gifts are constantly devoted on a daily basis'. The Baron was hardly less impressed by Grand Duke Paul, whom he described as being of medium height, with pleasant facial features and a fine physique. He found him cheerful and friendly, and witty in conversation, and was impressed both by the quality of his instructors and by the attention he gave to his studies: 'He spends the morning mostly with [his teachers]; towards mid-day he goes to pay his respects to the Empress; after that he spends some time with the courtiers who have the honour to dine at his table. Having finished dinner, after coffee he goes to his inner apartments where he studies until the evening.'

Even as she was immersed in legislation, war and medical advances,

Catherine did not neglect her art collection, which expanded considerably during these years. In 1768 Prince Dmitry Golitsyn was transferred as ambassador from Paris to The Hague, where he managed to secure for the Empress two small but significant collections of Dutch and Flemish paintings – those of the Prince de Ligne and Count Cobenzl. The Cobenzl collection also contained about 4,000 Old Master drawings. Then in 1769 Catherine acquired the collection of the late Count Heinrich von Brühl, the Saxon minister who had been instrumental in getting Stanislas Poniatowski appointed as envoy extraordinary in 1756. Her ambassador in Saxony had alerted her to the sale by Brühl's descendants and she had pronounced herself ready to buy the paintings, provided they were really by the artists to whom they were attributed. The haul, of both Old Masters and contemporary works, consisted of over 600 paintings, including works by Rembrandt, Rubens, Jacob van Ruisdael and Watteau, and 1,000 drawings, including a large group of Poussins, many Rembrandts, works by Paolo Veronese and Titian, and a large number of engravings. Catherine paid 180,000 guilders for the collection, which arrived by boat from Hamburg, the drawings mounted in 14 leather-bound volumes. The collection nevertheless suffered some sea-water damage.

The way in which Catherine relied on her artistic advisers in the acquiring of works for her collection is demonstrated in a note she wrote to Falconet in July 1769: 'You tell me that the 33 pictures of which Monsieur Collin has sent you the catalogue are by an able man, but you don't tell me whether they are good; if you find that they are, Monsieur, then you will oblige me by asking your friend for the price.' She did not, however, agree to buy anything and everything merely on the say-so of her advisers; in August 1769 she turned down the offer of a work by the painter Carle Vanloo because, as she explained to Falconet, 'I don't understand it enough to see what you see.' The Small Hermitage, which incorporated a hanging garden (in which songbirds were kept) built over the stables with apartments at either end, was ready for use this year. Catherine asked for picture galleries to be added down each side of the garden. Some statues were introduced into the hanging garden, which did not make for the happiest combination with the songbirds, as Falconet was at pains to explain to the Empress: 'the marble figure of Love is covered and spoilt by bird droppings, and these droppings leave indelible marks on the marble'.

Early in 1769, the first issue of a short weekly satirical periodical entitled *Vsyakaya vsyachina* ('All sorts of things') and modelled on the

English *Tatler* and *Spectator* was published. Its policy was to aim gentle satire at such defects in Russian society as 'ignorance, superstition, corruption, inhuman treatment of peasants, worship of all things French'. Catherine herself, never one to pass up an opportunity to engage in didactic writing, contributed anonymous pieces to this enterprise – which suggests that she was also instrumental in setting it up. A number of other satirical periodicals began to appear around the same time, including *Truten* ('The Drone'), edited by Nikolai Novikov, *Adskaya Pochta* ('Hell's Post'), edited by the novelist Fyodor Emin, and *Smes'* ('Miscellany'). None of these periodicals, not even *Vsyakaya vsyachina*, lasted for more than about a year, as the reading public in Russia was not yet large enough to maintain them all. William Richardson commented on how difficult it could be to find out what was really going on politically in Russia, in the absence of the kind of newspapers to which he was accustomed in England and with the distances from one end of the country to the other to contend with: 'The half of Russia may be destroyed, and the other half know nothing about the matter.' Richardson was also finding the Russian winter something of a challenge:

> Cold! desperately cold! We have had winter without the least abatement of its rigour since the first of November, and it may continue, we are told, without the least mitigation, till the beginning or the middle of April. The frost has been all this while uninterrupted. The wind has blown almost constantly from the north-east. It comes howling and cold from the heights of Siberia, and has brought with it immense quantities of snow. In the beginning of winter the snow fell, without intermission, for several days. In the country, nothing appears but a boundless white desert; and the rivers are almost one chrystalline mass.

That winter Catherine had a 'feverish cold' which, unusually, kept her in bed for six days – 'something I found very inconvenient for someone who loves to move about and who mortally hates being in bed'. Dr Dimsdale, who was still in Petersburg, supervised her care and forbade her to do any work for 10 days. It was a mark of her particular respect for this member of a profession she generally laughed at that she obeyed him – in her own fashion – by spending the time as soon as she could get up in letter-writing.

On 6 March Lord Cathcart provided the Earl of Rochford with his judgement (marked 'most secret and confidential') of the principal members of the Russian Court. He began with an indictment of Russians in general, who, he wrote, 'are men of no education or principles of knowledge of any sort, though not without quickness of parts'. He declared that some of them had 'great pretensions' but that their only policy was 'cunning, which may deceive a stranger and embarrass rivals, but never will be able to conduct affairs or gain the confidence of discerning friends'. Of Catherine herself – not of course a Russian – he had the highest opinion: 'The Empress has a quickness of thought and discernment, an attention to business and a desire to fill her throne with dignity and with utility even to the lowest of her subjects, and to the rising and future as well as present generation, which without seeing her it is difficult to imagine.' Lord Cathcart also held Grigory Orlov in high esteem, absolving him from the faults he perceived in most Russians:

> Count Orloff is a man gentle, humane and accessible, and his demeanour towards his sovereign most respectful.
>
> He is a man of very little education, but of extremely good natural parts, and the most distant possible from any sort of pretensions, which in this country is a commendation cannot be bestowed with truth on many people, he has taken a great deal of pains and with good success to instruct himself of late years, and having had an opportunity of talking with him one evening when he was heated with dancing and had drunk a glass more than common, I can venture to offer it as my opinion that he is a man of honour and truth, and detests and despises the least deviation from either in others.

Catherine had built around her, according to Lord Cathcart, two distinct circles, one comprising the officials in the various departments whom she had chosen for their particular capabilities, and another purely for entertainment and relaxation after the fatigues of the day – a circle which tended to consist of younger, less serious people. All the officials, opines Cathcart, hankered after being part of this second, informal circle – apart from Nikita Panin who, perhaps after his hopes of a glittering marriage were so sadly dashed, 'is of a different turn, and of different manners, and does not conceal that he finds it too much for him, and that he aims at no ground but utility and integrity which does honour to his sovereign and gives stability to her government'. Catherine's old admirer Count Zakhar Chernyshev, on the other hand, was planted firmly in both circles and 'though very little younger than Mr Panin is at the head of all the festivities of private parties'. The ambassador had little to say about Grand Duke Paul, other than that he was 'a very promising Prince, entirely under the conduct of Mr Panin, who lies in the room with him and never allows him to stir out without him'. No wonder that he also said of Panin: 'he has too much to do'.

The twenty-first of April 1769 was Catherine's fortieth birthday. Tommaso Traëtta, previously court composer in Parma, who had replaced Galuppi when the latter's three-year contract had expired in the summer of 1768, composed an opera – *Olimpiade* – for the occasion. Catherine wrote cheerfully to Madame Bielke: 'Courage, keep on moving forward, words which have seen me through good and bad years alike, and now I have forty of them under my belt and what is the present evil compared with the past? But since you are so interested in my successes, let me tell you, Madame, that on 30th April new style, which was our Easter, we won a battle fought under the walls of Khotin against an army of fifty thousand Turks.'

## 10

# The Heroic Orlov
# (1769–72)

*Thanks to the indefatigable care and zeal of Count Orlov, the diseases
of Moscow have considerably diminished.*
                    Catherine II to her friend Madame Bielke

*O*n 4 August 1769 Catherine told Voltaire that 'my soldiers go
to war against the Turks as if they were going to a wedding'.
The import of the war and of the rise of Russia as a naval
power had not as yet aroused any concern in the mind of the British
ambassador, particularly as the Russian navy was heavily dependent on
British expertise: 'I think it is my duty to observe that there is nothing
at present so near the Empress's heart, or indeed more a national wish
here, than to put the Russian naval forces upon a respectable footing;
that may be done with the assistance and cooperation of England, and
by no other means whatever, but it is impossible that she should ever
be a rival capable to give us jealousy, either as a commercial, or as a
warlike maritime power.'

Throughout that summer Etienne Falconet had been struggling with
the public reaction to his equestrian statue. A particular point of
contention was the serpent which the sculptor had introduced into the
ensemble. Several people had told Falconet that it was inappropriate
and ought to be removed, not realising that without the serpent on
which Peter's horse is trampling, as Falconet explained to Catherine,
'the support of the statue would be most uncertain. They have not
made as I have the calculation of the forces which I need. They do
not know that if their advice was unfortunately followed, the work

would not survive at all.' Catherine had no intention of getting involved in the controversy, replying to Falconet: 'There is an old song which says *what will be, will be,* that is my response to the serpent, your reasons are good.' Catherine wrote again on the subject to him the following April: 'I hear only praise of the statue, I have heard from only one person a comment which was that she wished the clothing was more pleated, so that stupid people would not think it was a chemise; but you can't please everybody!' A granite boulder which had been split by lightning and so was known as a 'thunder stone' had been located at Lakhta in Karelia and was judged ideal to form the plinth of the equestrian statue. After Catherine had been to see the stone herself, she decided to advertise a prize to be awarded to the person or persons who could come up with the best suggestion for transporting it to Petersburg. The winning solution involved rolling the stone along a specially constructed road from Lakhta to the northern coast of the Gulf of Finland, an enterprise which took five months. From there it was towed in a large barge along the Neva to its final destination. Towards the end of May 1770 Catherine was still having to reassure a prickly Falconet, who this time was worrying about the lack of re-action to his work, the clay version having recently been unveiled: 'I know that you have removed the tarpaulin, and that in general everyone is very happy; if people don't say anything to you, it is out of delicacy; some feel they aren't qualified enough, others are perhaps afraid of displeasing you by telling you their opinion, still more can't see a thing. Don't . . . take everything the wrong way.'

During 1770 Catherine realised she needed a larger purpose-built space to house her expanding art collection, and Yuri Felten, an archi-tect born in Petersburg but of German extraction, was commissioned to build a Neo-classical extension to the Small Hermitage; this larger building became known as the Old Hermitage. It was to contain not only galleries, but also a library, a medal cabinet and a billiard room (billiards having always been one of Catherine's favourite pastimes). Around this time Catherine was also becoming increasingly interested in gardens and gardening. In May she issued orders for an 'English park' – a term which had come to designate a picturesque or landscape garden in which artifice was employed to create a 'natural' effect – to be laid out at Tsarskoye Selo. Two years later Catherine elaborated on what she meant by the term 'English garden' when she wrote to Voltaire: 'Right now I adore English gardens, curves, gentle slopes, ponds in the form of lakes, archipelagos on dry land, and I have a profound scorn for straight lines, symmetric avenues. I hate fountains that torture water in order to make it take a course contrary to its nature; statues are relegated to galleries, vestibules etc.; in a word, anglomania is the master of my plantomania.'

From 24 to 26 June 1770, the Russians engaged with the Turks at Chesme Bay in the Aegean, winning a resounding victory in which most of the Turkish fleet was destroyed. Catherine related what she had been told of the battle in a letter to Voltaire (and hence to the rest of Europe):

> My fleet, under the command not of my admirals but of Count Alexei Orlov, first beat the enemy fleet and then burnt it completely in the port of Chesme ... Nearly a hundred vessels of all sorts have been reduced to ashes. I dare not say how many muslims perished: it is said to be nearly twenty thousand ...
>
> War is a wretched business, sir! Count Orlov told me that the day after the burning of the fleet, he saw with horror that the water of the port of Chesme, which is not very large, was the colour of blood, so many Turks had perished there.

Ten days later the battle of Larga took place. This also resulted in a victory for the Russians. One of the officers to be decorated for his part in this battle was Grigory Potemkin, by this time a Major-General of the Cavalry. He was awarded the Order of St George third class (the Empress having founded this order on 26 November 1769). On 20 July the Empress attended the singing of a Te Deum at the church of Our Lady of Kazan in celebration of the victory at Larga. The battle of Kagul took place the following day and the Empress was present for the singing of another Te Deum on 2 August.

In addition to casualties incurred in the ordinary course of military engagements, the Russo-Turkish War opened up the Russian Empire to the threat of bubonic plague, for it was rife in Turkey and its immediate surroundings. The authorities had been aware of this danger from the start, and towards the end of May the Empire's foremost authority on the subject, Dr Johann Lerche, had been sent to the Second Army, commanded by General Peter Panin (Nikita Panin's brother), which was then on its way to besiege the Turkish fortress of Bender. On 27 August Catherine secretly ordered quarantine precautions to be taken in Kiev, which served as a major supply depot and was thus a place from which plague might enter the rest of the Empire. Unfortunately the plague had already reached

Kiev, though its first manifestations went undetected. The presence of the disease was finally announced by the Governor-General of the city on 9 September. Ten days later the Empress ordered cordons to be established all around Ukraine. The Governor-General of Moscow, Field Marshal Peter Saltykov, was also ordered to place a checkpoint at the river crossing in Serpukhov. By 3 October the authorities in Kiev were talking of 'fever with spots', which was generally thought to be less dangerous than the 'pestilential distemper' or plague. Nevertheless, on 10 October Dr Lerche arrived in the city to supervise the anti-plague measures, and on 1 November the Empress dispatched a special emissary to oversee all containment in Ukraine.

Meanwhile Catherine had to put her anxieties to one side, at least to outward view, in order to entertain Prince Henry of Prussia, King Frederick's younger brother (who had first met Catherine when she was barely out of childhood and when he had been discussed as a possible suitor). He arrived in Petersburg towards the end of October. The political object of his visit was to promote a partition of Poland which would be to the benefit of both Prussia and Russia, though to the casual observer he seemed to be there primarily to renew his acquaintance with Catherine and see the sights of Russia. At the end of October the Empress and the Grand Duke, who had recently turned 16, accompanied Prince Henry to Tsarskoye Selo for a few days. Catherine told her friend Madame Bielke that the Prince was very attentive and friendly towards her, though she feared that he might be rather bored. From William Richardson's description of him, it is clear that the Prussian afforded the Russian courtiers some amusement:

He is under the middle size; very thin; he walks firmly enough, or rather struts, as if he wanted to walk firmly; and has little dignity in his air or gesture. He is dark-complexioned; and he wears his hair, which is remarkably thick, clubbed, and dressed with a high toupee. His forehead is high; his eyes large, with a little squint; and when he smiles, his upper lip is drawn up a little in the middle. His look expresses sagacity and observation; but nothing very amiable: and his manner is grave and stiff rather than affable. He was dressed, when I first saw him, in a light-blue frock [i.e. a frock coat], with silver frogs; and wore a red waistcoat and blue breeches. He is not very popular among the Russians; and accordingly their wits are disposed to amuse themselves with his appearance, and particularly with his toupée.

On Sunday 28 November a masquerade was given at Court in Prince Henry's honour. It was attended by 3,600 people, and filled 21 apartments of the Winter Palace. William Richardson described some of the costumes:

A great part of the company wore dominos, or capuchin dresses. Though, besides these, some fanciful appearances afforded a good deal of amusement . . . The Empress herself, at the time I saw her Majesty, wore a Grecian habit; though I was afterwards told, that she varied her dress two or three times during the masquerade. Prince Henry of Prussia wore a white domino. Several persons appeared in the dresses of different nations, Chinese, Turks, Persians, and Arminians. The most humorous and fantastical figure was a Frenchman who, with wonderful nimbleness and dexterity, represented an overgrown, but very beautiful parrot.

The Frenchman dressed as a parrot decided to amuse himself at the solemn Prussian's expense:

He chattered with a good deal of spirit; and his shoulders, covered with green feathers, performed admirably the part of wings. He drew the attention of the Empress; a ring was formed; he was quite happy; fluttered his plumage; made fine speeches in Russ, French, and tolerable English; the ladies were exceedingly diverted; every body laughed but Prince Henry, who stood beside the Empress, and was so grave and so solemn, that he would have performed his part admirably in the shape of an owl. The parrot observed him; was determined to have revenge; and having said as many good things as he could to her Majesty, he was hopping away; but just as he was going out of the circle, seeming to recollect himself, he stopped, looked over his shoulder at the formal Prince, and quite in the parrot tone and French accent, he addressed him most emphatically with *Henri! Henri! Henri!* and then diving into the crowd, disappeared. His Royal Highness was disconcerted; he was forced to smile in his own defence, and the company were not a little amused.

Trumpets announced the arrival of Apollo with the seasons and months of the year, played by children from the Cadet Corps and the Smolny Institute. Apollo made a speech to the Empress and then invited her, along with 119 guests, into supper which was served at 12 tables laid for 10 people each. Every table was in its own niche representing one of the months. The large oval room was 'lit by more than two thousand candles; above the niches there was a large gallery, where there were four orchestras and a great number of masked revellers'. Supper was accompanied by vocal and instrumental music and the children performed a ballet. The scene was so enchanting that even Richardson forgot his habitual air of English superiority: 'at different intervals persons in various habits entered the hall, and exhibited Cossack, Chinese, Polish, Swedish, and Tatar dances. The whole was so gorgeous, and at the same time so fantastic, that I could not help thinking myself present at some of the magnificent festivals described in the old-fashioned romances.' Afterwards the company retired into an adjoining room where a stage had been constructed and the children provided further entertainment. It was after midnight when the formal programme ended, and dancing carried on until five o'clock in the morning. 'Thus ended this masquerade,' wrote Catherine to Madame Bielke, 'with which everyone seemed very pleased.'

At the beginning of December Prince Henry left Petersburg for Moscow, where he stayed for most of the month. He travelled incognito, so that he could avoid the protocol which would have had to attend the brother of Frederick the Great travelling in an official capacity. And he remained quite oblivious to the threat of plague which was now hanging over the old capital. Moscow harboured immense numbers of rats, drawn both by the vast amounts of grain stored in and shipped from the town, and by the quantity of water – a particular attraction for the Norway rat, which habitually infested sewers and drains. Thousands of house rats would also have found a home in the predominantly wooden constructions of the city. No one in 1770, however, understood the connection between bubonic plague and flea-bearing rats. Most people, including Catherine, believed the plague somehow originated from subterranean sources in the form of invisible vapours, through direct personal contact, or through contaminated articles such as textiles, money and paper – hence the nature of many of the precautions which were put in place. Prince Henry arrived back in Petersburg three days after the Moscow authorities learnt that plague had indeed broken out in their city.

This particular epidemic turned out to be a small one, limited to two outlying wooden barracks at the annexe of the Moscow General Infantry Hospital. There was some disagreement among the local medical practitioners as to whether this really was plague; those who took the view that it was believed that it had reached Moscow from Constantinople by way of the Danubian principalities, Poland and Ukraine. The Moscow police and Governor-General Marshal Saltykov took the usual precautions of isolation and fumigation.

By the New Year, Catherine had got over her fears that Prince Henry might be bored in Russia and told Madame Bielke that she thought he had been enjoying himself:

> I have never in my life met anyone in whom I have found a greater conformity of ideas with my own than I find in him: often we both open our mouths, and it is the same thing that we want to say; perhaps that is why he likes being with me. I admit to you that no visit from a prince could be more agreeable to me than his is . . . in truth he is very estimable: his disposition is cheerful, and his character honest and humane, his mind elevated and polished; in a word, he is a hero who shows me a great deal of friendship. Goodbye, madame, forgive the confusion of this letter; I have been interrupted three times while writing it.

William Richardson was less inclined to believe that Prince Henry had been having a good time: 'This city, since the beginning of winter, has exhibited a continued scene of festivity and amusement: feasts, balls, concerts, plays, operas, fireworks, and masquerades in constant succession; and all in honour of, and to divert his Royal Highness Prince Henry of Prussia, the famous brother of the present King. Yet his Royal Highness does not seem much diverted.' The German-born Empress was perhaps better able to read the taciturn Prussian than was the English tutor.

Prince Henry left for home on 19 January, the same day on which a contract was signed for the employment of one John Bush to work on the imperial gardens. Mr Bush, originally Johann Busch, was born in Hanover but had settled in London in the mid-1740s where he established a flourishing nursery garden in Hackney. From here his reputation spread throughout Europe. Catherine had sent one of her architects, Vasily Neyelov, who was one of the first to be involved in the design of the English garden at Tsarskoye Selo, to England, accompanied by his son Peter, both to study English garden design and to persuade Bush to come and work for her. Selling his business, Bush moved with his large family to Russia and was initially employed at

Oranienbaum, receiving a salary of 1, 500 roubles a year. Catherine's concept of her garden at Tsarskoye Selo was by no means limited to trees, plants and ponds, or even to rustic follies for their own sake. She used the open spaces here to create her Empire in microcosm and to commemorate her conquests in monumental and symbolic form. This process began in earnest in 1771 with Rinaldi creating designs for the Triumphal Gates and the Rostral Column (also known as the Chesme Column) in the centre of the Great Pond to commemorate the victory of the Russian fleet commanded by Alexei Orlov and Captain Samuel Greig, a native of Scotland who had entered the Russian service to fight against the Turks, and who rose to become one of the most important Russian admirals. 'If this war continues,' Catherine commented to Voltaire on 14 August, 'my garden at Tsarskoye Selo will soon look like a game of skittles, for at each brilliant feat I have some monument erected.'

Early in 1771 Catherine began to intensify a search she had initially instigated as early as 1768 – for a suitable fiancée for Grand Duke Paul. This, she deemed, was not only a necessary step to ensure an uninterrupted succession to the throne in the form of grandchildren; it would also be a way of taking the young Paul's mind off any idea he might be entertaining, now he was nearly grown up, of sharing power with her during her lifetime, or even – heaven forbid – of ousting her from the throne. She had far too much work to do to allow her son to jeopardise her position. She was now even more sure of the necessity of retaining power and of the inestimable benefits her reign was bringing and would continue to bring to the Russians. Catherine was determined not to make the same mistakes with her son that the Empress Elizabeth had made with her nephew Peter, and so steps had been taken when Paul was barely 14 years old to initiate him into the mysteries of sex. Again a young widow was employed to provide the instruction, and she proved to be far more than a one-night stand. Her name was Sophia Chartoryzhkaya and she was the daughter of a former governor of Novgorod. The adolescent Paul – who had already proved himself to like women – was captivated by Sophia, and the relationship lasted for some years, Sophia bearing him a son in 1772. (For some reason the son was named Semyon Veliky, or Semyon the Great; he died in the West Indies in 1794.) Paul was, however, made to understand that this liaison could only be temporary and that no emotional entanglement would be allowed to stand in the way of his making an appropriate marriage. The man Catherine chose to aid her in her quest was Baron

Assebourg, who had been the Danish minister to her Court and who seemed to have access to all the necessary sources of information. The Baron and the Empress proceeded to discuss – not to say dissect – the young princesses of Europe in merciless fashion.

The first girl to emerge at the top of Catherine's list of possibles was Princess Louise of Saxe-Gotha, whose paternal grandmother was of the house of Anhalt-Zerbst and Catherine's father's first cousin. Furthermore, Princess Louise's uncle had married one of Catherine's aunts on her mother's side, and Catherine suggested to Baron Assebourg that this double relationship might provide sufficient pretext for the Princess's mother to visit her with her two daughters in tow, in the expectation that Catherine would make some provision for her young relatives even if neither of them proved suitable brides for Paul. Catherine's tactics in this whole process were almost identical to those of the Empress Elizabeth when she and her mother were summoned from Zerbst all those years ago. She even made the comparison explicit: 'If you need an example to persuade the Princess to agree to this journey, you could cite mine: my mother came here under the pretext of thanking the late Empress in the name of her family for the various benefits which She had given them.' 'The worst that could happen,' Catherine continued, 'would be that bad luck interfered and that neither of the two suited us; so then what could she lose? She will gain thereby a dowry for her daughters, with which she can establish them elsewhere. For the rest, the expenses of the journey would hardly ruin her, as those expenses will be reimbursed to her here, and she can keep her incognito until she arrives in Russia, where her expenses will be paid.' Catherine asked the Baron to ensure, if possible, that Princess Louise, who had been brought up a Lutheran as she had been herself, should not yet be confirmed in that faith before setting off for Russia – 'because Protestants become obstinate from that moment, and until then they have the choice of their belief'. Catherine's real favourite for a future daughter-in-law was the Princess Sophia Dorothea of Würtemberg. But at only 11 years old, she was too young to be considered seriously. The Empress wanted to keep the matter confidential at this stage (probably an impossible objective as far as the various Courts of Europe were concerned): 'I think that the fewer confidants there are in this business, the easier it will be to ensure that, whichever direction chance takes, it finishes to our reciprocal satisfaction.' Paul's opinion during these preliminary negotiations was not sought at all, though his governor, Count Panin, was involved.

During a brief thaw in early March, the authorities in Moscow discovered an unusually high number of deaths had been taking place in the heart of the city, at a huge textile manufactory known as the Big Woollen Court. In addition a number of people living or working there were found to be ill, exhibiting the alarming symptoms of dark spots and swollen glands. The manufactory was immediately isolated. Two days later physicians investigating the cases at the Big Woollen Court concluded that the disease closely resembled plague, and during the night of 13–14 March (in order to keep the operation as secret as possible) the police evacuated the remaining inhabitants – some 640 of them – to suburban quarantines and pesthouses. Towards the end of the month Catherine endorsed an emergency programme of precautions in Moscow and appointed the senator Lieutenant-General Peter Yeropkin to administer them. She also placed Count Yakob Bruce, the husband of her closest confidante, in charge of quarantine measures in Petersburg and its surroundings. By early April the plague threat appeared to have declined substantially in Moscow, which led Catherine and many others to conclude that the disease afflicting the city had not been plague at all. Nevertheless Catherine ordered a halt to the foundation work on a new Kremlin palace for fear of releasing 'subterranean vapours'.

Catherine's preoccupations at this time were manifold, including but not limited to war, plague, a partition of Poland and finding a wife for Paul. In May her Council of State agreed that Russia might take Polish Livonia and compensate Poland with Moldavia and Wallachia. In the same month there were further developments in the bride-hunt. Count Panin wrote to Baron Assebourg (on Catherine's authority) with some clarifications about the kind of girl who would be acceptable. First, she had to be Protestant (and, it was understood, willing to convert to Orthodoxy). Roman Catholics were absolutely out of the question. Secondly, while she could if necessary be a Countess from an illustrious family rather than a Princess of a ruling house, there were certain families whose progeny could not be considered since they were known to possess hereditary defects. Thirdly, she must not be older than the Grand Duke, but she must have reached puberty. Further investigations into Princess Louise of Saxe-Gotha had revealed her to be unsuitable after all; she had put on too much weight (Catherine, not mincing her words, referred to her 'excessive corpulence') and her mother was vehemently opposed to any change of religion. Next to be considered was Princess Wilhelmina of Darmstadt, Catherine giving qualified assent to her as a possibility:

[She] has been described to me, particularly as regards her kind-heartedness, as a masterpiece of nature; but apart from the fact that I know there is no such thing in the world, you tell me that she has a quick mind and is inclined to dissension; that, added to the character of her father and to the considerable number of her sisters and brothers either established or yet to be established, gives me some doubt about her; nevertheless, do please take the trouble to investigate her again.

The 42-year-old Catherine was beginning to feel her age, at least some of the time. She told Madame Bielke that she liked to escape from the city and head for Tsarskoye Selo every year around the time of her birthday – for 'what pleasure is there in celebrating a day that makes one a year older?' She was also concerned to inform her friend, and thus to disseminate around Europe, that rumours of plague in Moscow were untrue: 'Tell whoever said to you that the plague is in Moscow that he is lying: there have only been putrid fevers and purple fevers; but in order to calm panic and prattle, I have taken all the precautions that are taken in case of plague.' Plague (or not-the-plague) in Moscow was followed by fire in Petersburg, a series of conflagrations sweeping the city on 23 and 24 May. Short of going there herself to put out the flames, Catherine sent the next best thing, Grigory Orlov. 'Since yesterday I have been like Job,' she wrote to Panin.

> Every hour brings worse news, and I cannot imagine that a fire such as yesterday's on Vasilyevsky Island can have occurred without a dereliction of duty on somebody's part. I sent Count Orlov to the town with the instruction that he was not to return while a single spark remains. He was there by nightfall on my orders for, catching sight of three places burning in the town, I was on the point of galloping off there myself. He returned at five o'clock and at eleven he galloped off again, for I think the Chief of Police's head was spinning at the sight of so much trouble, and it is indeed easy for such a thing to strain a man to breaking point.

The following day Catherine informed Panin that her suspicions of arson had been unfounded, and that all the fires had resulted from householders' carelessness.

At the end of the month Falconet reported to Catherine that Diderot and other acquaintances of his in Paris believed him to be the author of a work called *The Antidote,* which was itself a riposte to another work by a Frenchman, the Abbé Jean Chappe de l'Autoroche, his book being called *Voyage en Sibérie.* Falconet requested that Catherine obtain a copy of *The Antidote* for him, so that he could read what was being attributed to him. She replied to him the next day: 'I do not have the book you ask for: I told you this before and I haven't found any for sale here; I have ordered some to be sent from Holland.' What Catherine did not tell Falconet – or anybody else – was that she herself, having been roused to fury by what she perceived as the calumnies perpetrated by the Abbé Chappe, was the author of *The Antidote.*

*Voyage en Sibérie* had been published in 1768, its author being a French ecclesiastic and astronomer who had visited the Siberian town of Tobolsk in June 1761 in order to observe the passage of Venus over the sun. His book was a compilation of his observations about Russia and the Russians, made during his journey from St Petersburg to Tobolsk. It contains a considerable amount of hearsay (about which Catherine was most scathing, remarking to Voltaire that the Abbé, travelling 'posthaste in a firmly closed sleigh', had seen 'everything in Russia') interspersed with geographical and botanical details as well as first-hand accounts of his own experiences in the 'backward' country. The *Voyage,* which was already out of date and dealing with a previous reign by the time of its publication, did not enjoy a great deal of success even in France. But Catherine was feeling particularly sensitive to criticism both of herself and of her adopted country as a result of the appearance of an account by another Frenchman, a diplomat and secretary of the Baron de Breteuil, Claude Carloman de Rulhière. His narrative, which he read aloud to salon audiences (it was published later), concerned the coup of 1762 and was entitled 'Anecdotes on the Russian Revolution'. It portrayed Catherine as a cynical usurper and probably complicit in murder. The Abbé Chappe following hard on the heels of de Rulhière provoked Catherine into writing, in French, a point-by-point refutation of his criticisms of Russia, its inhabitants and customs, which she published anonymously in 1770 as *The Antidote.* This reached an even smaller readership than the offending *Voyage* but it did arouse some speculation about its authorship (as witnessed by Diderot and friends wondering if Falconet was responsible) and provided a healthy outlet for Catherine's indignation. She was concerned constantly with improving the image of Russia and the Russians, commenting to Voltaire: 'When this nation is better known in Europe, many errors and prejudices about Russia will be overcome.'

The summer brought yet more anxiety for the Empress: Grand Duke Paul was sick again. This illness, which may have been influenza or even typhus, continued for weeks, with several false recoveries followed by relapses. Catherine was sufficiently worried to spend much time by her son's bed. Paul's state of health combined with the cold, grey weather led to the decision that the Grand Duke should not celebrate his name-day at Peterhof that year, as Count Solms reported to Frederick the Great:

> The Grand Duke's illness has become more serious than it was thought to be at first, and it has even persuaded the Empress to come to town to see him. At the moment one is completely free of anxiety about him, although as His Imperial Highness is still very weak and has slight recurrences of fever every day, he has not gone to Peterhof. This incident has prevented me from seeing Count Panin for the whole of the last week, as he is very assiduous in his attentions to his august pupil and is kept busy by his illness.

Paul's condition fluctuated almost daily:

> The signs of the Grand Duke's convalescence have not been sustained, as had been believed. I learnt yesterday at Court that the night before last he had violent diarrhoea, which was regarded as a favourable crisis, as at the time it did not increase his weakness, but after having a new attack of fever yesterday evening, he is weaker than before so that, while one could not say that he is worse than he was, as the fever had never entirely left him, neither can one assert that he is entirely out of danger. Today is the twelfth day of his illness; one must wait until tomorrow to see if his strength will return; for it is this great weakness which is the worst thing about his condition.

It continued to be very difficult throughout July for the foreign ministers to conduct any business with Count Panin, 'who is occupied solely with looking after his august pupil, receives no one, and one can only see and speak to him very superficially every Sunday at Court, when he passes from the apartments of the Grand Duke into those of the Empress'. Paul's illness also caused a slight delay in the process of searching for a wife, Catherine writing to Baron Assebourg on 27 July: 'I received your letter of 9th (20th) June a few days before the dreadful illness which attacked my son and from which, thank God, he is now recovering. You can easily imagine that the anxious state I was in made it hardly the right time to reply to you.' Princess Wilhelmina of Darmstadt was still under investigation, Catherine and Assebourg having received contradictory assessments. On 30 July Catherine told Madame Bielke that Paul's illness was definitely over: 'we were anxious about my son's illness: it was a catarrhal fever that lasted for almost five weeks. Thank God, he is now better, apart from being a little weak; some say that he had to have the fever to make his beard grow; I have never liked beards anyway, but if that is the case, then from now on I will detest them heartily.' By the end of August the Grand Duke was appearing again in public, having grown a great deal (and having indeed sprouted facial hair).

In June Lieutenant-General Yeropkin had reported a new outbreak of disease in the Moscow suburbs, but he did not believe it to be plague. Nevertheless, in response to this news the Petersburg authorities reinstituted most of their anti-plague precautions and Catherine instructed Dr Lerche to leave Kiev for Moscow. Then at the beginning of August the shocking news arrived from Yeropkin that the plague – he had finally admitted that that was what it was – was more widespread than ever. What happened next revealed how unprepared the Moscow authorities were for any major crisis, despite the months they had had to prepare. Those who could depart – principally the nobility who possessed country estates – did so, leaving the city and its less fortunate inhabitants to their fate. Factories and workshops ceased business, and the population of workers and peasants found themselves gradually left without money or food or any means of escape from a disease which seemed to attack their class in particular. In the absence of any competent government, and feeling that no human authority cared whether they lived or died, many people turned to all they had left – a religion of wonder-working icons.

On 5 September the Empress chaired a council session which received confirmation of an impending disaster. Up to 400 people were dying in Moscow every day. Abandoned corpses lay in the streets, and there was worsening hunger among the people. There were also suspicious outbreaks of disease in the Pskov and Novgorod districts. A week later a desperate plea arrived from Governor-General Saltykov, requesting that he be allowed to leave Moscow until the winter set in. On the 14th, not waiting for permission (which he would not have received from the Empress), Saltykov fled the city, as he believed the situation to be out of human control, with deaths in excess of 800 a day.

The situation was desperate (quite how desperate the authorities in Petersburg did not yet know), and once more Grigory Orlov came forward as the man to tackle it. He had proved himself capable of taking control and restoring public order at the time of the Petersburg fires; he was a man of action, an experienced officer with an impressive physique whose very presence had the power to quell potential rioters, and he carried the Empress's full authority. For Catherine, sending Orlov was the next best thing to going herself, and her Council would never have agreed to their Empress setting off for plague-ridden Moscow. So when Grigory volunteered, Catherine accepted his offer gratefully, although fearing for his safety. (Some of his rivals at Court were probably not too averse to the idea of his succumbing to the plague.) On 20 September, Grand Duke Paul's seventeenth birthday, Lord Cathcart reported to the Earl of Suffolk on Grigory's decision, which he had from the horse's mouth:

> This morning Count Orloff told me he was convinced the greatest misfortune at Moscow was the panic which had seized the highest as well as the lowest, and the bad order, and want of regulations arising from that cause, and that he intended to set out to morrow morning to endeavour to be of what use he could . . .
>
> He said plague or no plague he would go to morrow morning: that he had long languished for an opportunity to do some signal service to the Empress and his country, that such an opportunity seldom fell to the share of private men, and never without risk, that he hoped he had found one, and that no danger should deter him from endeavouring to avail himself of it.

Grigory duly set out on the evening of 21 September, with an entourage of administrators, doctors and military men. The following day, the ninth anniversary of her coronation, Catherine appeared at Court as usual, despite having not been very well. Lord Cathcart commented on her distress: 'She is said to be infinitely hurt by the misfortunes of her subjects at Moscow, and the dastardly behaviour of the nobility, and people in power, who have left the city, and abandoned it to every sort of calamity. To these circumstances, the danger to which Count Orloff exposes himself, is thought to make no small addition.' Two days after Grigory had left for Moscow, Catherine received the horrifying news about what had actually been going on there.

In early September people had begun assembling at the Varvarskiye Gates in the wall at the eastern edge of Kitai-gorod (a walled commercial quarter alongside the Kremlin). Above the gates there hung an icon of the Most Holy Mother of God which became the subject of miraculous tales. People began to stop to pray there and a lamp was brought to hang before the icon by a soldier of the Semyonovsky Guards regiment, Savely Byakov, and a worker at a gold-braid manufactory, Ilya Afanasyev. Five priests, probably from the ranks of Moscow's innumerable priests without a parish, known familiarly as crossroads clerics, arrived to lead prayers. Byakov, Afanasyev and a third man, a peasant called Peter Ivanov, began collecting alms to buy a silver cover for the icon. Crowds began to flock to pay homage to it, and within the space of two days more than 200 roubles had been collected towards the silver cover. The Archbishop of Moscow, Father Amvrosy, a man appointed by Catherine and whom she admired for his vigorous efforts to reform the city's lax ecclesiastical establishment, became concerned at this outpouring of popular piety – both because such a large gathering contravened anti-plague regulations and because he suspected corruption, possibly involving some of the clergy, in amassing such quantities of money supposedly for the icon cover. Accordingly, on the evening of 15 September he sent some of his officials to seal the chest in which the people's offerings had been collected. But some of the assembled crowd, who had run out of patience with officialdom and many of whom sincerely believed that the wonder-working icon could save them, began to cry out (as Catherine reported it later to Madame Bielke): 'The Archbishop wants to steal the blessed Virgin's treasure, he must be killed!' People began to fight among themselves, but the more incensed among them ran to the Kremlin. There, again in Catherine's words, 'they broke down the doors of the monastery where the Archbishop lived,* then looted this monastery, got drunk in its cellars and, having failed to find the one they were searching for, one group set off for the Donskoy Monastery, from where they dragged out the old man and cruelly murdered him'.

With the help of a small band of soldiers and two cannon, order was restored in some measure by Lieutenant-General Yeropkin. According to his initial reports, at least 100 people died in the Kremlin and 249 were arrested, many of them wounded. A few days later he

---

* This was the Monastery of Miracles, which was on the site now occupied by the Presidium building in the Kremlin.

provided Catherine with amended figures: 78, it was affirmed, had been killed, and 279 arrested. Nineteen members of Yeropkin's forces had been wounded, one of whom subsequently died. On 27 September Catherine authorised the publication of the official account of the Moscow plague riots, as they became known, in the hope of fore-stalling wild rumours. On the same day Lord Cathcart reported on the 'melancholy' event to the Earl of Suffolk, adding of the Empress: 'She is much affected with these calamities, and cannot, though she endeavours, conceal it.'

On his arrival in the stricken city on 26 September (bad roads had prevented his getting there any sooner), Grigory Orlov implemented a series of measures aimed at restoring public order and confidence in the authorities. These included promising freedom to serfs who volun-teered to work in the hospitals, the opening of orphanages, the distri-bution of food, clothing and money, and the reopening of the public baths. The closure of the baths had been undertaken originally as a quarantine precaution, but the unpopularity of this decision had helped spark the riots. More than 3,000 old houses were burnt, and 6,000 were disinfected. Precautions were also taken to prevent plague spreading out from Moscow, particularly towards St Petersburg. At the end of September the Senate forbade all governmental offices in Petersburg, apart from the Colleges of Foreign Affairs, War and the Admiralty, to receive couriers directly from Moscow. All messengers were to stop at Torzhok to be met by couriers from Petersburg who would take the dispatches the rest of the way. Mail from infected localities was to be handled with tongs, and the letters were to be fumigated. All house-holders and residents in Petersburg were also to observe various precau-tions, regarding how they received visitors, the fumigation of baggage, and the reporting of any cases of sudden death or fever. Old clothes sold by pedlars were especially suspect. On 17 October Catherine inter-rupted a meeting of her Council to announce the introduction of addi-tional anti-plague measures; it was agreed to institute a cordon around Petersburg, whereby everyone arriving was to undergo further quar-antine. William Richardson commented: 'There is no appearance of any pestilential distemper in this city. Every precaution, however, is used against it: the communication with Moscow, and all suspected places, is interrupted; vinegar is burnt in great quantities in every house; and the utmost attention is paid to the health of the lower ranks. Yet it is not very pleasant to be within two or three days journey of so dreadful a neighbour.' In late October Catherine also instituted special anti-plague protection for Tsarskoye Selo. Checkpoints and barriers were put in place on the approach roads and nobody was allowed to pass them after sundown or without documentation from the cordon guards. The palace and gardens were to be kept locked.

On 3 October Orlov informed Catherine of his decision to postpone military recruitment in Moscow and the surrounding province, as recruiting levies always provoked tension and no one desired crowds of recruits coming into the city at this juncture. He also issued an order for convicts to be sent from provincial jails to act as gravediggers in Moscow. The following day he staged a splendid funeral for Archbishop Amvrosy at the Donskoy Monastery, using the occasion as an opportunity to publicise appeals for individual precautions to be taken and for cooperation with the authorities, both ecclesiastical and state.

The Moscow plague riots, and in particular the murder of the Archbishop, constituted a serious shock to Catherine the educator, who believed that she was leading her people towards the light of reason. Such blind fanaticism and barbarity could hardly be squared with her pride in a people who were being encouraged to embrace inoculation and whom she had endeavoured to instruct to undertake with her a major reform of the legislation. Admittedly the 'rabble' who had been involved in the riots were hardly those from whom the deputies of the Legislative Commission had been chosen, but she had nevertheless hoped that civilised values of tolerance and a lack of 'excess' might have begun to filter down to the broad mass of her subjects. That had clearly not happened yet, and Catherine wrote gloomily to Voltaire, lamenting: 'In truth, what a lot this famous eighteenth century has to boast about! how very wise we have become!' It was also a vital part of her self-image as Empress to imagine her subjects as happy and reaping all the advantages of her beneficent rule. Murder, mayhem and disease severely compromised such a positive picture. The fact that the riots had taken place in Moscow, however, helped Catherine to recover her optimism. It underlined what she had always felt about the old capital, with its lack of order, its teeming masses and its 'false air of Ispahan'. The ability of her favourite Grigory Orlov to impose order, even if ending the plague proved beyond his powers, further cheered her. The defection of the Moscow nobility, and particularly of Governor-General Saltykov, was what angered her most. She spoke more harshly about Saltykov than she generally did of any of her officials, telling Alexander Bibikov, who had served as Marshal of the Legislative Commission: 'The weakness of Field Marshal Saltykov passed all understanding, for he was not ashamed to ask for leave at a time when he was particularly needed there in person, and, without waiting for permission, he went away – if you can credit it – to amuse himself with his dogs.' She added as a postscript: 'I forgot to say in my letter that that old sod of a Field Marshal has been dismissed.'

On 12 October the Commission for the Prevention and Treatment of the Pestilential Infectious Distemper sat in Moscow for the first time. Subsequently meeting every day at 11 o'clock in the Kremlin, its members assumed jurisdiction over all medical practitioners, apothecary shops, quarantines and pesthouses. By 18 October Orlov, while outwardly confident, was privately in despair as he confessed to Catherine his failure so far to check the pestilence. The daily death toll was still running at about 600. Fortunately the arrival of cold weather began to accomplish what Orlov could not, the first snow falling in Moscow during the night of 21–22 October. Hard frosts set in on the 30th, and the following day Catherine was able to inform her council that the epidemic in Moscow had declined significantly. On 6 November the Empress dispatched Prince Mikhail Volkonsky to replace Saltykov as Governor-General and to recall Orlov. A week later Catherine reported on the situation to Madame Bielke, lavishing fulsome praise on her favourite:

Thanks to the indefatigable care and zeal of Count Orlov, the diseases of Moscow have considerably diminished, and as the frosts have arrived, it is to be supposed that in a few days it will suddenly end; that, they say, is the course of this disease. Count Orlov will leave Moscow in ten days' time; Prince Volkonsky will take his place. I have thanked Marshal Saltykov for the care he took of this capital by removing the government of it from him; the poor man had outlived his glory. I would willingly have taken care of his old age, but it was incompatible with the public good for him to stay there.

Although Count Orlov was very exposed, he and his suite are well, and in general this disease is only among the common people: the people of quality are exempt, either because the precautions they take preserve them, or because that is the nature of the disease. Every imaginable precaution is being taken for the spring, lest this detestable disease comes back. The fanaticism, of which the poor Bishop of Moscow was the victim, has ceased; Count Orlov has those people under his thumb; he has not only forbidden the dead to be buried in the town, but he does not even allow the people to hear Mass except by standing outside the church during divine service. Our churches are small and everybody stands, so normally people get very squashed; moreover they can hear perfectly well outside, as the Mass is always said out loud and in full chant. Through these exhortations the people have become so sensible that they do not even pick up the coins they find under their feet.

Grigory Orlov left Moscow on 22 November and Catherine, missing him badly by now, wrote to tell him she considered there to be no danger in his coming to Court without observing the full 30-day quarantine (particularly as no one in his suite was ill and they had not brought anything with them from Moscow). Grigory was welcomed back by the Empress on 4 December. His heroism was celebrated with a gold medal and marble medallion, and the commissioning of a set of triumphal gates at Tsarskoye Selo. The total number of deaths in Moscow from the plague epidemic was estimated at about 55,000 (that is, about one fifth of the city's population), and in the Empire as a whole at about 120,000.

With the danger to her population from the plague having now diminished, Catherine turned her attention to ending the war – on favourable terms to Russia – and by the end of 1771 she had decided to open peace talks with the Turks the following summer. Early in 1772 Russia renewed its alliance with Prussia, the two countries agreeing a convention which specified the shares of Polish territory they were to award themselves. A treaty leading to the first partition of Poland was signed on 17 February. In March Austria joined in the agreement over the partition. (During the same month Catherine could not write for several days, having cut herself when trimming her nails.) Catherine also brought off a considerable artistic coup around this time, with the purchase of the most important private collection in France to have been built up during the early part of the century, that of the banker Pierre Crozat. Though Crozat had died in 1740, his collection had not come on the market until 30 years later, following the death of his nephew Baron Thiers. A catalogue was prepared for Catherine at Diderot's instigation by François Tronchin, a banker, dramatist and art lover from Geneva, and, advised by Tronchin, Catherine acquired 500 paintings from the collection – including eight Rembrandts, six Van Dycks, three paintings and some oil sketches by Rubens, a Raphael *Holy Family*, Giorgione's *Judith* and Veronese's *Lamentation over the Dead*

*Christ* – for the sum of 460,000 livres. There was a great outcry in France over this sale to Russia.

On 28 April, a week after Catherine's forty-third birthday, she reported to Madame Bielke that Grigory Orlov and Alexei Obreskov had set out that week to conduct peace talks with the Turks. She also told her about her enthusiasm for gardens and garden design:

> I regret very much the fate of your peach and apricot trees, and I share your distress on this subject. I entirely sympathise, for I have myself been attacked by plantomania: I could not live in a place where I could neither plant nor build; every beautiful place in the world would then become insipid for me. I am just like that here; I often infuriate my gardeners, and more than one German gardener has said to me in my life: 'Oh my God! Whatever are you thinking of now?'* I have found that most of them are no more than stick-in-the-mud pedants; they are frequently scandalised by the changes from routine which I suggest to them, and when I see that routine is going to win, I employ the first obedient boy-gardener I come across, and the master of the art is left out of it – disagreeable for him, I admit, but my garden belongs to me and I know what I like. There is no one whom my plantomania amuses more than Count Orlov: he spies on me, he imitates me, he mocks me, he criticises me; but before leaving he left his garden in my charge for the summer, and this year I will be able to commit indiscretions there in my own way. His grounds [at his estate of Gatchina] are very near here, and I am very proud that he has recognised my merit as a gardener.

There was no sign in all this of any cloud on the horizon between Catherine and Grigory, and every indication that she would be welcoming him back, at the conclusion of the peace talks, with open arms.

---

* '*Aber, mein Gott! War wird denn das werden?*'

# 11

# Confusion and Unrest
## (1772–73)

*This affair is an impenetrable chaos, and there is in the conduct of the Empress a contradiction in which no one can understand anything.*
Prussian envoy Count Solms to Frederick the Great

y 1772 Catherine and Grigory Orlov had, to all appearances, settled into what was almost a version of married life, even though their relationship was never formalised. They had been lovers for 11 years and, despite all the dire warnings issued by diplomats and others over the course of those years, Catherine's choice of this favourite seemed to have contributed to her own stability and to the success of her reign. Grigory had not abused his position; he was well spoken of by most impartial observers and he provided Catherine with times of much-needed relaxation and with a relationship that was devoid of sycophancy. He was someone – possibly the only person – which whom she could completely let down her guard. And lately he had taken on an important troubleshooting role, distinguishing himself in the quelling of the plague riots. He was now set to add further laurels to his brow in the negotiations with the Turks. Perhaps his eagerness to set off for Moscow and now for Fokshany in Wallachia indicates that he was tiring of his gilded life at Court and did not wish to remain as a 'kept man' for ever. But he and Catherine had shown themselves able to adapt their relationship to changing circumstances before, and there was no reason to think his desire for action could not be accommodated within the bounds of his position as imperial favourite. That Catherine still found him attractive (he was

38 to her 43) is clear from the way she wrote of him, particularly to Madame Bielke.

But Orlov's influence with the Empress had never ceased to be a source of disquiet in certain circles at Court, most notably in that surrounding Count Panin. Although the two men went through phases of apparent amicability and there was rarely overt hostility, the cold war between the Panin and Orlov factions was viewed by many as an inescapable aspect of life at Court. One of Panin's complaints, which he voiced to Count Solms (who duly reported it to Frederick the Great), was that Grigory's presence at council meetings could delay the making of sensible decisions, 'for as [Orlov] believes that he is allowed to say whatever he wants, he often makes rash arguments, which the others are obliged to refute with much circumspection'. (For the notoriously slow Panin to blame Orlov for holding up business seems unreasonable; in a list Catherine once drew up for her own amusement as to how each of her courtiers was likely to meet his end, she predicted that Count Panin would die 'if he ever hurries'.) Panin had always viewed Grigory and his brothers as potential threats to the position of his protégé, the Grand Duke Paul, who was himself no friend of his mother's favourite. Grigory's prolonged absence from Court (the peace talks were expected to last for several months) gave Panin an opportunity to undermine the former's standing with the Empress, an opportunity he did not intend to forgo.

For the next 18 months the Court had all the appearance of a chess board. Intricate moves were played, 'check' was called several times by different parties, and it was never quite clear who was actually moving the pieces.

The spring of 1772 was very cold in Petersburg and its environs, preventing Catherine from indulging in her latest obsession of gardening. During that spring construction began at Tsarskoye Selo of Vasily Neyelov's Neo-gothic buildings, the Admiralty pavilion on the far shore of the Great Pond, and the Hermitage Kitchen near the old Hermitage pavilion. On 12 May Catherine reported to Madame Bielke that Grigory Orlov and Alexei Obreskov, her 'angels of peace', had passed through Moscow and would shortly be arriving in Kiev. On the 18th she was joined at Tsarskoye Selo by Grand Duke Paul and Count Panin (who was returning to town once a week to attend a meeting of the Council). Eight weeks later she told Madame Bielke that she thought her 'angels of peace' would by now be face to face with the Turks. She mentioned Grigory in the tones of a fond lover, describing him as 'without exaggeration, the most handsome man of his time'. That day Catherine had left Tsarskoye Selo in order to go to 'the detestable, hateful Peterhof, which I cannot bear, to celebrate my accession to the throne and the feast of St Paul there'. She was writing from a hunting lodge en route where she would be spending the night. She had particularly enjoyed her few weeks at Tsarskoye Selo, her 'favourite domicile', despite the cold weather in May, and had been taking a new pleasure in the company of her son:

> We have never enjoyed ourselves more at Tsarskoye Selo than during these nine weeks which I have spent there with my son, who is becoming a handsome boy. In the morning we breakfasted in a delightful salon situated next to a lake; then we retired after much laughter. Afterwards everyone attended to their own affairs, and we dined; at six o'clock there was a walk or a spectacle, and in the evening we made a great din to the delight of all the rowdy people who surround me, of whom there are a good number.

What Catherine did not mention to Madame Bielke was that during the spring and early summer she had also uncovered a particularly disturbing – if not very well thought out – plot by a number of junior officers of the Preobrazhensky Guards. As Count Solms described it to Frederick the Great, 'Several young and debauched gentlemen . . . bored with their condition and imagining that the shortest route to reach the summit was that of making a revolution, had conceived the ridiculous plan of putting the Grand Duke on the throne.' They had managed to gain the support of about 30 soldiers, and their audacious scheme was to go to Tsarskoye Selo to capture Paul and bear him off to Petersburg there to proclaim him Emperor. Meanwhile they would also seize Catherine and turn her over to Paul, to deal with as he thought fit. They had determined the fate of all the major courtiers, deciding whom they would keep, whom banish – and chief among their targets to dispose of were the Orlovs and all their connections. The officers' imaginations seem to have run away with them as, writes Count Solms, 'the most extravagant plan of all was that, if the Grand Duke refused to lend himself to their designs, then one of these junior officers, the author of the plot, would take upon himself the government of the Empire'. This same officer then derailed his own plot by confiding it to Prince Fyodor Baryatinsky, one of the principal conspirators in the coup which had placed Catherine on the throne. At this time he was one of her chamberlains. The young officer appears to have imagined that because Baryatinsky had been involved in one coup, he would be predisposed to back another. But he had reckoned without the chamberlain's loyalty to the Empress (who, for one thing, had protected him from the consequences of his participation in the murder of Peter III). Baryatinsky went immediately to the major of the Preobrazhensky Guards to inform him of the plot. The conspirators were arrested and confessed all. Corporal punishments were administered, ranging from the knout for the officers (the application of the knout, when skilfully performed by the executioner, could remove all the skin, in long strips, from a person's back) to being beaten and having ears and nostrils torn for the common soldiers. Then all the miscreants were dispatched to Siberia. Despite the ludicrous nature of this plot, Catherine was unnerved by it. 'No precautions . . . are neglected,' commented the new British ambassador, Robert Gunning, 'to guard against sudden attempts, there is not a corner of the gardens and environs of Peterhoff (the place she is most exposed at) in which sentinels are not placed when she resides there.' Gunning also mentions what he had heard about Grigory Orlov, from someone clearly not in the Orlov camp: 'He has, I am told, some amiable qualities, but no great ones, is imprudent and dissipated to a remarkable degree, frequently absenting himself from the Empress on hunting parties, and others less compatible with his connection with her.'

On 1 August Catherine appointed as a gentleman of the bedchamber one Alexander Vassilchikov, a 28-year-old lieutenant in the Horse Guards. This was the first official sign of something many courtiers had been suspecting for several weeks – that this young man was well on the way to replacing Grigory Orlov as imperial favourite.

What surprised contemporary observers – and continues to be baffling – is not that Catherine chose this period of Grigory's absence to take another lover, but that her choice should have fallen on someone so unremarkable. Inoffensive, courteous, obedient (all those qualities perhaps constituting a relief from the exigent Grigory), Vassilchikov displayed no particular talents or even physical attributes to recommend him to the usually discriminating Empress. Count Solms reported: 'this is not a man of distinguished countenance, nor has he ever sought to make himself noticed, and he is little known in society'. On 4 September he provided Frederick the Great with a few more details:

I have now seen this Vassilchikov and realised that I had seen him often enough before at Court, where he was just part of the crowd. He is a man of average height, about 28 years old – dark and with a nice enough face. He has always been very polite towards everybody and had a very gentle, but very timid, bearing, which he still has. It appears that he is embarrassed by the role he is playing and does not yet know how to cope with his good fortune.

Catherine's later rationalisation of what had happened is contained in a 'sincere confession' which she wrote for Grigory Potemkin in February 1774. In this document, which details all the lovers she had had up to that date, she asserts that on the very day Grigory Orlov left Tsarskoye Selo for the peace congress, she was informed that he had been having affairs with other women. So it was out of desperation and unhappiness that she cast around for a replacement. This explanation does not tally with Catherine's other correspondence. A few days after Grigory had left Tsarskoye Selo at the end of April, she was telling Madame Bielke how much she was looking forward to working on his garden at Gatchina. And as late as 25 June, at the end of the weeks she had so much enjoyed at Tsarskoye Selo and during which she had first begun to take an interest in Alexander Vassilchikov, she had written of Grigory as 'the most handsome man of his time'. What seems most likely is that someone – and the someone was very probably Count Panin – was pulling strings behind the scenes, pushing Vassilchikov forward as a potential replacement and ensuring that Catherine had noticed him before informing her of Grigory's alleged infidelities. As Count Solms summed it up: 'Luck presenting a new object of affection, the affair came about of itself, without anyone being able to say that someone had prepared it deliberately.'

Vassilchikov had first come to Catherine's notice at Tsarskoye Selo, where he happened to be in command of the small detachment assigned to guard duty while the Court was in residence. When the Empress left to go to Peterhof she sent him a gold box to thank him for having 'maintained such good order among his men'. Both the change of mood Catherine admitted to on her departure from Tsarskoye Selo to Peterhof (she wrote to Madame Bielke of shutting herself up in her room to hide her bad temper) and the fact that it was at Peterhof that Vassilchikov began to take care 'to be seen everywhere the Empress of Russia passed' would suggest that it was at this point that information began to be fed to her about Grigory. Solms evinced little doubt as to who was behind these machinations, commenting: 'The person who will gain the most will be Count Panin; his credit, although always preponderant, will have no further competition to fear, and he will have a far freer hand, as much for external affairs, as for those which concern internal government,' and later remarking: '[Vassilchikov] is attached to Count Panin, who protects and directs him.'

In mid-August Catherine returned to Tsarskoye Selo, having stayed at Peterhof much longer than she had intended. The cold spring had been succeeded by an extremely hot summer and Peterhof, being both on the edge of the sea and on higher ground than Tsarskoye Selo, was considerably cooler. Ten days later Grigory Orlov, having been informed via members of his family of what was taking place at Court, suddenly abandoned the peace conference and set off for St Petersburg. If Catherine had previously been deeply hurt by what she had learnt of Grigory's behaviour, she now had reason to be very angry at a dereliction of duty which could only have negative consequences for the peace talks, which were not proceeding well. In fact they had already ground to a halt, and Grigory had made a ministerial report in which he had asked for permission to remain with the army until the negotiations resumed. But the news he had received from Petersburg, and his falling out with the army's general-in-chief Marshal Count Rumyantsev, resulted in an abrupt change of plan. As soon as Catherine heard the news, she took steps both to ensure he could not suddenly burst in upon her and to remind him of his position as her subject.

Meanwhile Grand Duke Paul, having recovered from his illness, seemed to be flourishing under the unexpected attention he was receiving from his mother. Catherine confided to Madame Bielke that he wanted to be near her all the time and would even change his place at table so that he could sit next to her. She also allowed him at this time to go through various reports with her twice a week, a move from which he may have hoped for more than eventually resulted. For Catherine's part, this experiment seems to have convinced her that Paul was not yet suitable to be given any responsibility. But for the time being all was sunny between mother and son, with courtiers and diplomats alike attributing these improved relations to the absence of Grigory Orlov. Count Solms evinced some scepticism about the genuineness of what he described as the 'air of bourgeois cordiality and reciprocal trust' between 'these two August persons', suspecting that more might be going on than met the eye:

> I cannot be sure that a little dissimulation is not involved, at least of affectation on the Empress's part, for all her speeches to us foreigners in particular take as their topic the Grand Duke; but whatever the aim may be, it is certain that this extraordinary change of conduct towards her son must do damage to Count Orlov because, not having been such during the time of his favour, one must suppose that it was he who prevented it.

Alexander Vassilchikov proceeded to consolidate his position (or have it consolidated for him). On 30 August he was appointed adjutant-general to the Empress and moved into an apartment in the Winter Palace. Three days later he was also made a chamberlain and, as always happened with Catherine's favourites, his family benefited too, his brother Vasily being made a gentleman of the bedchamber on the same day. Not everyone at Court was pleased about this change of favourite. Many of the Empress's servants, valets and ladies, reported Count Solms, appeared 'dejected, pensive and discontented', for they were used to Grigory; he had been almost as much a part of their lives as of Catherine's for a decade, and some of them felt they owed their positions to him. The anticipated reaction of the Orlov brothers was also a subject of speculation. As Robert Gunning expressed it, 'the violence and impetuosity of Alexis [i.e. Alexei Orlov], (who not only thinks, but has even been heard to say, that it was he who placed the Empress upon the throne) may be the just occasion of some alarm'. Most people at Court could not yet decide quite how to react, as Count Solms explained: 'One fears the resentment of the former favourite, if one plumps too soon for the side of the new one, who will perhaps not have the good fortune of maintaining the position, and one is apprehensive of displeasing the new one, if one waits too long to show him deference; fortunately, he is still without any pretensions and he is therefore leaving everyone time to take their sides.' Catherine was demonstrating a blithe lack of concern over the perplexity of her courtiers and servants, being herself in 'the best mood in the world, always happy and content and involved in nothing but festivals and pleasure'. One other person was also energised by these developments: 'There is no doubt that Count Panin is profiting from all these circumstances to ensure the loss of his rival, and that he is working to hold his sovereign to the estrangement of her former favourite, in order to gain all her confidence for himself alone.'

As Grigory Orlov galloped towards St Petersburg, he was intercepted by a courier bearing an order from the Empress, instructing him to go directly to his estate at Gatchina. The pretext for the order was that he needed to spend time in quarantine, after having been in the plague-infested regions of the south. Grigory did as he was told. But what puzzled courtiers was that, although he was barred from coming to St Petersburg, Orlov was not treated like someone in disgrace. On the contrary, he was 'sent provisions from the Court and is served [at Gatchina] by the officers and liveried servants of the Court, just as in the past'. Negotiations now began between the Empress and her former lover (both of whom had by now been unfaithful to one another), the principal go-between being Grigory's elder brother, Count Ivan Orlov. The empress showed no desire to humiliate Grigory, proposing that he should keep his rank and all his honours; the points to be agreed concerned his future position at Court and his participation in civil or military service – and, by implication, the nature of his future relationship with Catherine. The Empress's initial position seems to have been that she wanted Grigory to resign from all his official posts, in return for a generous pension and other emoluments. But Grigory refused. Messages went back and forth, Count Solms observing that Orlov was being negotiated with 'not as a private individual, but as an equal'. Meanwhile Grigory remained at Gatchina, where 'It is said that he eats and drinks of the best and is enjoying himself very much. General Bauer, who came back with him from the army, and others of his former creatures are keeping him company, and from time to time a few people visit him from the town.'

The twentieth of September 1772 was Grand Duke Paul's eighteenth birthday. In the midst of all the intrigues surrounding Orlov and Vassilchikov, it seems to have passed virtually unnoticed. 'It was expected by several,' remarked Robert Gunning,

> and I believe his Imperial Highness was not himself without hopes, that some small degree of independence would have been allowed him, and an establishment formed, upon his majority; but instead of this, the contrary has been affected and his governor exercises the same degree of power he did before. No promotions were made that day, that no one may be indebted to him even in the most remote degree for their advancement.

Eighteen was, nevertheless, the age of majority for German princes, and Catherine now made over to Paul the administration of his hereditary estates in Holstein. She marked the occasion by delivering him a speech about the duties of sovereigns, and the necessity of governing with both justice and gentleness. The only people present at this ceremony, apart from Catherine and Paul, were Count Panin and Caspar von Saldern. Any satisfaction Paul may have gained from this event was short-lived, however, as in the autumn of 1773 Catherine managed to complete the transfer of the duchy of Holstein-Gottorp to Denmark (something which would have been anathema to her late husband), in exchange for the duchies of Oldenburg and Delmenhorst, which went to a minor branch of the Holstein family. Paul was thereby denuded of any possible power base outside Russia. Catherine had agreed the treaty over this exchange in 1767, but had had to wait for Paul's majority before it could be ratified. He clearly had no choice in the matter.

The day after Paul's birthday Count Solms reported to Frederick the Great that 'Count Orlov persists in his refusal to agree on the degrees of his disgrace, and the Empress still cannot bring herself to tell him what he must do.' The fear was beginning to surface at Court, among the anti-Orlov faction, that if Catherine were to see her former lover again, she might be persuaded to take him back – but, opined Solms, 'Count Panin, who would risk too much through such a return, has no doubt taken the necessary measures to ensure that such a thing, which could have disastrous consequences, will not happen.' One consequence of the whole affair was that business was proceeding even more slowly than usual. Count Panin was absorbed in trying to consolidate his own position, and even Catherine was showing less inclination for work than usual. The sticking point was Grigory's refusal to decide for himself which of his employments he should keep and which resign. He seems to have been unwilling to resign voluntarily from any of his official posts and wanted Catherine to make the decision, knowing that she would not be able to bring herself to sack him.

Catherine's new choice of favourite was doing nothing for her international reputation, Robert Gunning reporting to the Court of St James:

The successor that has been given [Orlov] is perhaps the strongest instance of weakness and the greatest blot in the character of her Imperial Majesty, and will lessen the high opinion that was generally and in a great measure deservedly entertained of her. When I first came to the knowledge of this resolution, which was very soon after it was formed, I could scarcely give credit to it; neither the person of the man nor his abilities giving the least appearance of probability to the report.

Gunning was quick to perceive the hand being played by Count Panin, even if the situation was too complicated to be fully understood:

> The intention at that time was not to have brought [Vassilchikov] forward; but the opportunity it afforded of overturning the Orloffs was too favourable not to be made use of. Mr Panin seized it, entered into the little broils of the antichamber, and into a series of intrigues unworthy of a man, much more so of a minister of so great an Empire: and the imprudence of Count Orloff in breaking up the congress in order to prevent if possible by his return here the dangers that threatened him, gave Count Panin and the Empress a fair pretext for excluding him from her presence. It is said that she has already shown some degree of remorse and that her affection for him has returned; which added to the fear of placing too unlimited a power in the hands of Mr Panin, gives her an uneasiness that is apparent. Count Zachar Chernicheff though no friend to the Orloffs considers the removal as disadvantageous to his own interest on account of the additional influence it gives to Mr Panin.

Further machinations involved Nikita Panin's brother Peter, whom Nikita wanted to be the vice-president of the College of War – but Zakhar Chernyshev was so opposed to this idea that he was even prepared to help restore the Orlovs to favour. As Gunning commented – and perhaps this was the most accurate of all his statements – 'The intrigues which all this gives rise to, throws [*sic*] a veil over the measures pursuing here which it is impossible for the keenest sagacity to pierce.'

By the end of September the negotiations between Grigory and Catherine at last reached some kind of conclusion. The terms were agreed in the form of a letter, drafted by Catherine, to Ivan Orlov. There were no recriminations, no attempts to affix blame or to take revenge. Catherine showed herself generous to a fault in accepting that people and relationships do change with changing circumstances. Her main desire was to salvage what still existed of friendship and mutual respect. She was very aware of how much she owed to Grigory and his brothers, and did not wish to antagonise them. In her letter Catherine offered to consign all that had passed 'to complete oblivion', including the collapse of the peace talks which she was prepared to ascribe only to the actions of the Turks. Count Zakhar Chernyshev had informed her, and it had been confirmed by Ivan Orlov, that 'it is both the desire and request of Count Grigory Grigoryevich Orlov to avoid any explanation'. She agreed with this, and so there were to be no post-mortems or embarrassing face-to-face meetings. Furthermore, she felt it would be difficult for them to encounter one another during the first year of what really amounted to a divorce, so she proposed that Grigory should take special leave for a year, under the pretext of ill health, and go either to Moscow, to his estate, or somewhere else of his own choosing. The amount of 150,000 roubles, which he had been given every year by Catherine, would continue in the form of an offi-cial annual pension. In addition he would receive a one-off payment of 100,000 roubles for the furnishing and setting up of the new house which was being built for him by Rinaldi on the Neva embankment (this was to become known as the Marble Palace, on account of the facings of different-coloured Russian stone used by the architect), which house was to be his in perpetuity. Until the Marble Palace was ready, he was to be allowed to live in any of the imperial palaces near Moscow or anywhere else, provided it was away from the Court. He could keep Catherine's servants and carriages for as long as he needed them, and she also awarded him 6,000 serfs, in addition to the 4,000 already awarded to his brother Alexei for his victory over the Turks at Chesme Bay. The brothers could choose their 10,000 serfs (which was a contem-porary shorthand for 'land with 10,000 male serfs tied to it and paying their dues, in labour and/or money, to the landowner') from whichever area of the country suited them best. In addition Grigory was to be given a silver dinner service which had been made to order in France and had never yet been used, 'as well as the one which was bought for everyday use from the Danish ambassador'. During the course of his year of leave, Catherine proposed that Grigory should work out for himself how he wished to serve her and the country in future. She concluded her document with the words: 'I seek nothing other than mutual peace, which I wholeheartedly intend to preserve.' Count Solms remarked: 'The affair has been handled in the end so mysteri-ously between this sovereign and her former favourite, through the mediation of the latter's brother, that one does not know exactly what conditions were made between them. It still seems that Her Imperial Majesty used great circumspection and that she fears to push the Count to a certain degree of despair.' Once the terms had been agreed, the aspects of the agreement deemed to be for public consumption were announced in a decree to the Senate and thence to all the government Colleges.

There were more surprises to come. Nearly 10 years previously, Grigory had received from the Court of Vienna, at Catherine's request, a diploma naming him a Prince of the Holy Roman Empire. It had become customary in the eighteenth century for Russian rulers to request this honour from the Holy Roman Emperor when they wished to name someone 'Prince', as the title existed in Russia only among the descendants of ancient royal houses. At the time Grigory had received this diploma, however, he was not permitted to make use of the title, Catherine having been persuaded that it was contrary to the glory of Russia for her favourite to sport a foreign title. Now Grigory requested that he be allowed to use it, and permission was granted. Count Solms characterised this gesture of Orlov's as 'a sort of bravado' and as of no great significance. 'Prince' Orlov was now expected to be leaving for Moscow as soon as the cold weather set in and the sleighs began to run.

By mid-autumn Grigory had still shown no sign of going anywhere, and there was inevitable speculation that Catherine was beginning to regret her haste in switching favourites. On 23 October Count Solms reported that 'she is sometimes affected by it to the extent of tears' and she still could not bring herself to order Grigory to set off on his travels. It seems that Panin was being excluded from whatever correspondence was passing between the Empress and her former favourite; she may well have come to the conclusion that she had been misled. Attempting to manipulate Catherine could only bring very short-term benefits, as Panin was to spend the rest of his life finding out. Nevertheless Vassilchikov remained in his new position and, as far as anyone could see, he was giving the Empress no cause for complaint. They were inseparable. And the good relations between the Empress and her son also seemed set to continue. Count Solms spoke for many observers when he lamented: 'In short, this affair is an impenetrable chaos, and there is in the conduct of the Empress a contradiction in which no one can understand anything.'

A different sort of chaos was stirring in the Ural region. In November 1772 a 30-year-old Cossack and army deserter called Emelyan Pugachev turned up in the Cossack capital of Yaitsk on the Yaik (later Ural) river and told his Old Believer★ hosts that he was Peter III, saved miraculously from death and returned from travelling in Egypt, Constantinople and Poland. Pugachev was not the first person since Peter's death to have claimed his identity. There had in fact been nine such cases since 1764, and most recently a runaway serf called Bogomolov had been impersonating Peter in the Volga region. (He was arrested and sent into exile in December, but died on his way to Siberia.) The vast expanse of Russia, where millions of illiterate peasants lived in almost complete ignorance of how or by whom their country was governed, had always been fertile ground for the emergence of pretenders. And a young tsar who had died in mysterious circumstances after only a few months of rule made an ideal candidate for impersonation. It hardly mattered to his audience of disaffected Cossacks, assorted soldiers and peasants that the stocky and dark-haired Pugachev, his hair cut in a Cossack-style 'pudding basin', bore no resemblance whatsoever to the deceased Emperor. No one in Yaitsk had ever seen Peter anyway, dead or alive. His short reign and the nature of the reforms he had attempted to introduce had also given rise to legends of a tsar who loved his people and was working to improve their lot, before being struck down by the evil German woman who now ruled over them with a rod of iron, forcing them to enlist in the army to fight her war against the Turks.

Pugachev had himself served in both the Seven Years' War and the Russo-Turkish War from 1768 to 1771, during which he earned promotion to the lowest Cossack officer rank. He had deserted in 1771, and began wandering around from relatives (he came from a Don Cossack family) to various Old Believer settlements. In August 1772 he had taken advantage of an amnesty to get himself a passport, claiming to be a native of Poland. He then continued his wanderings, sometimes passing himself off as a wealthy merchant. The situation among the Cossacks was already tense when Pugachev arrived in Yaitsk, a mutiny having been put down with brutal reprisals by tsarist forces during the summer. The Cossacks had always been an unstable element of the Empire's population, their communities or 'Hosts' comprising a mixture of escaped criminals and serfs, dissidents, army deserters and freemen, making a living by raising horses or less legal activities, including

---

★ The Old Believers, or *raskolniki*, were – and are – schismatics who did not accept various reforms to texts and practices inaugurated by Patriarch Nikon in 1666 to bring the Russian Orthodox Church more into line with the Greek Church.

robbery and pillage. They also formed irregular forces, loosely under state control, to act as border guards and light cavalry.

As yet Catherine knew nothing about the emergence of this new pretender, and the Court continued to be immersed in the intricacies of the Orlov affair. On 6 November Count Solms reported that Grigory was now making a 'repeated and pressing request' to be allowed to come to Petersburg for 48 hours. So far his request had been neither granted nor refused. The anti-Orlov faction and those who had by now decided to back Vassilchikov as the man of the moment (*vremenshchik*, the Russian word for 'favourite', means precisely that) still feared that, if the Empress were to accede to this request and receive Grigory in person, she might fall for him all over again and upset the new allegiances. Two days later, Orlov's younger brother Fyodor, also recently returned from the army, did come to town and was received at Court by the Empress as though nothing had changed. (Indeed there is no evidence to suggest that the break with Grigory ever did change Catherine's attitude or behaviour towards his brothers.) On the same day Count Solms provided Frederick the Great with a perceptive assessment:

[Orlov] has gained too strong an ascendancy over her mind; she reproaches herself for having mistreated him and, to tell the truth, She is so used to him that she finds it hard to do without him. She experiences an emptiness at not having someone to whom she can open her heart on everything, and the new favourite is not at all suitable to fill it. He is a very honest man, but absolutely new to everything, so that all one can hope for is that this Princess may hold firm in her resolution for the year, but I doubt there will be any way to hold her back beyond that.

By the end of November Catherine had agreed that Grigory might come to Petersburg to say farewell to her in person. Having received permission, he now seemed in no hurry to avail himself of it. Catherine's behaviour was hard to read. On the one hand she seemed absorbed in a passionate affair with her new favourite – 'abandoning herself to it with all the vivacity of a young person', according to Count Solms, and taking more care over her appearance than previously – while on the other supervising personally the preparation of linen destined for the body and house of her former favourite, with whom she seemed to be in close correspondence.

Grigory Orlov finally appeared at Court on 24 December; Count Solms reported on the event the following day:

Very unexpectedly Count Orlov arrived in town the day before yesterday in the evening, and went to stay at his brother's. Yesterday he had his first audience with Her Imperial Majesty, who received him in the presence of two people in her confidence: Mr Yelagin, and Mr Betskoy. He went from there to the Grand Duke's and spent some time alone with Count Panin in his study. He returned to dine at his brother's, and in the afternoon attended Vespers of Christmas Eve at Court, and it was there that the public really got to know of his arrival. From there he went to make visits in town and came back in the evening to attend the Empress's card-party. I saw him this morning at Court, where he received me with the same air of frankness and friendship which he has always shown towards me. He mingled with the other courtiers and it felt as though he had never been absent.

It is clear from a further letter from Solms that Grigory's 'two days' had been extended:

Count Orlov is still here, and has not seen the Empress alone. I am even better informed than I was last time and know that neither has he had a private interview with Count Panin; but he lives here on the same footing as any noble of the country on a visit to the capital. He attends Court morning and evening at the normal hours at which the Empress is accustomed to make her appearance. She speaks to him in a manner which betrays neither predilection nor embarrassment. I was a witness yesterday evening to their conversation which turned upon pictures. For his part, he has a far more respectful air towards the Empress than he had before; apart from that, he is just as he always was. He acts the comedian as he always did, talks to the new favourite and his friends as if nothing had happened, and pays visits all round the town. I have paid him mine; the other foreign ministers have done the same, and he repaid them to us the same day, so that one can neither foresee nor predict what will come of all this.

At the beginning of 1773 Count Solms was wondering whether this might not all be some elaborate play:

Unless the Empress and her former favourite have an understanding and are playing roles studied in advance, in order to fool everyone, it does not appear that the latter's return will produce the slightest effect of any consequence. He is staying with his brother, using a hired carriage, and visits Court only a little. He is the first to joke about his situation, in a way designed to embarrass those to whom he speaks. To see and judge from his outward manner, one would say that he is a man who feels relieved of a burden, who wants to enjoy his freedom, and that he only wanted to return to Court in order to triumph over those who wanted him to be kept away, to enjoy their embarrassment and to show himself to the public who might have suspected him of being guilty. For her part the Sovereign has maintained in society all the gaiety which she showed during the summer. Last Friday there was a masquerade at Court, and Her Imperial Majesty promenaded openly with the chamberlain Vassilchikov, and as she was not feeling very well that day and retired early, Count Orlov only came to the ball afterwards and stayed very late.

Grigory finally took his departure during the first week of January, with Count Solms continuing to view the whole affair as an impenetrable drama:

Count Orlov's first act has been played and he left last Saturday for Reval. Till the end he kept up the role he had begun. After the first few days of his arrival, he avoided the Court and the Empress's presence, in a marked manner. He spent time only with his intimate friends and flirted very publicly with all the pretty women of the town, even at the theatre and in the sight of the Empress and everybody. For her part Her Imperial Majesty showed no eagerness to have him approach her person and there is no doubt that she did not entertain him in private and showed him no attentions that anyone could have complained about. He was for example rarely invited to dine at Her table. She did not give him the Court carriages, although he had always had them in the country, nor the guard of honour of the Grand Master of Ordnance which he could have claimed, as he has not relinquished this post, nor any other that he held, but has only dispensed with exercising them for a year. On saying goodbye, Her Imperial Majesty did not say a word to him about his return. She received him very graciously and wished him a good journey and every sort of prosperity. Despite these appearances, it is nevertheless thought that there is dissimulation in the conduct of them both, but one cannot penetrate into what it consists of, nor in what it will end. The Empress's strong passion for her new favourite is more and more obvious; nevertheless, the departure of the former one made her sad and cross, and for 3 days she sent back all business. It is certain that She still feels a lot of friendship for him, and it is possible that She is carrying on a secret correspondence with him, and everyone is convinced that he has only to express a desire for something that would give him pleasure to be certain of obtaining it.

On the international front, Catherine had become war-weary by late January, wanting the peace with the Turks to be concluded. At times a very different voice sounds from that of the conquering Empress. She told Madame Bielke, for instance, that she thought war was 'a stupid thing: for every victory we won, we sang a Te Deum, that is in the nature of things, and I don't dispute it at all; but I could never help thinking that it was like the crow of a cock who, when he has beaten another, goes crying everywhere "cock-a-doodle-doo"'. But in March the truce expired; Turkey refused any further concessions, and warfare resumed a few months later.

At home the Court was thrown into a further flummox when Grigory Orlov came back from Reval at the beginning of March, having been away for all of two months. The Empress made a point in the public circle at Court of conversing equally with both her former and present favourites. Count Solms observed:

Count Orlov's most recent stay still offers nothing remarkable; it is, if one may say so, a comedy which it pleases Her Imperial Majesty to play in order to fool everybody, and which She could finish if She wanted to. It is certain that She wants to make him return, at the end of the year's leave which was granted him, into all his employments, but She observes circumspections of which one does not know the motive; he, while waiting, affects indifference and shows an extraordinary freedom of spirit. He seeks only to amuse himself and frequents all the entertainments in town . . . He says he intends to go and inspect his estates in Russia, but that he is not sure whether this will happen, that he remits the decision about his fate into the Empress's hands; that he will do everything She orders, but that without her express orders he will not resume any of his charges before the year has elapsed.

Around this time Emelyan Pugachev first came to Catherine's notice, when she confirmed a sentence for him to be knouted and exiled to Siberia for attempting to foment unrest among the Yaik Cossacks. Two months later, however, he managed to escape and went on the run.

On 10 April Catherine set off for her spring visit to Tsarskoye Selo, being joined there two days later by the Grand Duke and Count Panin. Grigory Orlov, meanwhile, had gone to Gatchina; the courtiers were now getting used to his presence again, and were relieved that he showed no sign of wanting to exact vengeance on those who had not taken his side. 'It even seems that he has no desire to return to Court with the same degree of favour as he used to enjoy,' reported Count Solms, 'and that on the contrary he is very happy to be entirely his own master, to be highly regarded everywhere he goes and to have 200 thousand roubles to spend. At least boasting of his wealth is his favourite topic at the moment.' But Catherine decided his leave had lasted long enough. On 20 May, barely nine months since he had abandoned the peace congress at Fokshany, Orlov resumed all his former offices. On 3 June he attended a meeting of the Empress's Council. His brother Alexei continued to command the naval forces in the war against Turkey, occupying several eastern Mediterranean seaports and aiding Arab rebels against the Turkish Sultan. Everything was more or less back to normal.

Catherine was now free to turn her attention to arranging the marriage of her son. Baron Assebourg's investigations into the character of Princess Wilhelmina of Hesse-Darmstadt had proved encouraging. It was time for a personal inspection, and on 15 June 1773 the Landgravine* of Hesse-Darmstadt and her three daughters – Amélie aged 18, Wilhelmina aged 17 and Louise aged 15 – arrived at Tsarskoye Selo. Catherine sent a flotilla to Lübeck to transport the Landgravine and her daughters – and their suite of 40 people, including three ladies, two gentlemen, eight chambermaids, two valets, a secretary and various other servants – to Reval. There the travellers were to be accommodated in the palace of Catherinenthal (built by Niccolo Michetti under

---

* The feminine form of Landgrave or Landgraf, the ruler of a landgraviate; a landgraviate was a territory over which a nobleman held jurisdiction.

Peter I and named in honour of Catherine I); it was only partly furnished, and Catherine instructed Baron Cherkasov to check that everything necessary was provided. Cooks and servants had been sent to the palace, and Baron Cherkasov was also to supervise them. His instructions were to greet the visitors as soon as the ships docked, and conduct them straight to Catherinenthal, where he was to convey a message to them from the Empress, saying how pleased she was that they had arrived in her dominions and that she was awaiting them with impatience at her Court. (Here she was copying the formula Elizabeth had used when she and Johanna had first arrived in the Russian Empire.) In brief, Baron Cherkasov was to 'anticipate their desires and study what would give them pleasure'. Catherine had also given some thought as to how she should herself meet her visitors for the first time. She explained with some glee to Madame Bielke:

In order to avoid any awkwardness of a first meeting, Prince Orlov sent ahead of the Landgravine to invite her to dine at his estate of Gatchina which, although it is off the main road, nevertheless shortened the Landgravine's journey by several versts.* She arrived there just after two o'clock. The Prince, receiving her at the gate and leading her up the staircase, told her that she would find several ladies already here. How astonished the Landgravine was when, on entering the room, she saw me accompanied only by Countess Bruce. She leapt backwards and exclaimed out loud. I accosted her, saying: 'I have given you a surprise, Madame; I do not know whether it is a pleasant one, but I thought it necessary in order to diminish all the awkwardness of a first interview.' At that we kissed each other, and the princesses arrived, rather astonished and a little nervous. Prince Orlov curtailed this scene: he came to request me to go into another room, while the princesses went to freshen up. We were served, and there we were at table as though we had been dining together all our lives. On getting up from table, I proposed that the Landgravine should accompany me in a very comfortable carriage for six people which I had brought on purpose; she agreed, and we set off, she, her three daughters, Countess Bruce and I.

Paul took to Wilhelmina right from the start. Catherine gave him three days to see whether he would change his mind and, as she also found

* A verst measured approximately 0.66 of a mile.

Wilhelmina superior to her two sisters, on the fourth day the Empress made the proposal to the Landgravine that her middle daughter should marry the Grand Duke. Neither mother nor daughter raised any objection, and Russian lessons and instruction in the Orthodox faith were immediately arranged. Catherine told Madame Bielke of her satisfaction with the whole family, from the mother to the young bride-to-be:

> We are now waiting for the consent of the Landgrave. His wife is a pleasure to know: she is noble in heart and mind; she is an estimable woman and of much merit in every way; her conversation is entertaining, and it appears that neither she nor her daughters are at all bored with us. The eldest is very pleasant; the youngest seems very intelligent; the middle one is everything we could ask for: she has a charming face, regular features, she is affectionate, and intelligent; I am very pleased and my son is smitten.

Despite Paul's pleasure over the young woman his mother had found for him, relations between the Empress and her son had deteriorated badly by the end of July. Paul's animosity was caused by a number of factors – disappointment that attaining adulthood had brought no change in his circumstances (apart from his impending marriage), the loss of Holstein-Gottorp, the return of Grigory Orlov to a central role at Court, and a strong suspicion that his mother's recent show of affection had been prompted by ulterior motives. There was also something of the rejected and jealous lover about Paul in his relations with his mother from now on, a sense that his affection for her had been spurned, that he had been deemed unworthy of her love, which she preferred to dispense on other young men. The twice-weekly meetings to look over reports had led to nothing, and as he approached his nineteenth birthday and his 'Russian majority', any hopes he may have entertained of sharing in government by the time he was an adult had been shown to be completely unfounded.

Outwardly, however, all was joyful at Court as on 15 August Princess Wilhelmina converted to Orthodoxy, reading the declaration of faith in Russian, as Catherine herself had done nearly 30 years previously, and being given the name Natalya Alexeyevna. On the following day the official betrothal took place, and Natalya received the titles of Grand Duchess and Her Imperial Highness. Catherine awarded her an annual allowance of 50,000 roubles, remarking to Madame Bielke that 'I only had thirty [thousand] when I was Grand Duchess, but I admit that I never found it enough.'

Mindful both of the difficulties she had herself experienced as Grand Duchess and of her youthful attempts to interfere in political matters (behaviour which she was determined no wife of Paul should emulate), Catherine had drawn up a set of instructions for Natalya Alexeyevna, which she entitled 'Brief maxims for a princess who will have the happiness to become the daughter-in-law of Her Imperial Majesty the Empress of Russia and the wife of His Imperial Highness the Grand Duke'. From these 'maxims' (a form of writing which Catherine never could resist) it is clear that she intended the young Grand Duchess to be as strictly supervised and circumscribed as she had herself been by the late Empress Elizabeth. The main difference was that Catherine was more overt and methodical about this tyranny than was the less businesslike Elizabeth.

The Grand Duchess, writes Catherine, is (like any young bride of her time and class) to 'conform herself to the tastes and habits' of the man she is to marry and to learn to fit in with the way of life to which he has been accustomed. She must have complete trust in her husband and in his mother, for whom she must also have 'the most tender attachment'. She is never to forget the importance of unity within the imperial family, and must never even listen to those who would seek to destroy that unity. More than that, she must inform on them, for she 'is under an obligation to disclose to the Empress and the Grand Duke, her husband, those who through indiscretion or dishonesty would have the audacity to wish to give her sentiments contrary to that of the attachment she must have for the Empress and for the Grand Duke, her husband'. It follows that 'she must give her trust and esteem only to those who will be chosen for her by the Empress, and who have a recognised attachment for their Sovereign and for the Grand Duke'. It is of course anticipated that the Grand Duchess is to enjoy herself, in the way of young people, at balls or other entertainments, but she should 'never forget the rank she occupies' and 'remember that familiarities can have consequences, such as the lack of regard, even of the respect which is owed to her, which can often result in scorn'.

In so much of this Catherine could have been addressing her youthful self; she certainly knew from first-hand experience the potential pitfalls for an Empress in having a bright and attractive young woman at the centre of a separate establishment at the Court, capable of acting as a focus of dissent for all the disaffected courtiers and a conduit for the schemes of foreign diplomats. Consequently she had no intention of allowing Paul and Natalya to set up their own 'young Court', and she emphasised that the Grand Duchess must 'avoid all the insinuations which can be given by the ministers of foreign Courts'. Catherine stressed that Natalya was to learn Russian and 'conform herself to the customs of the nation'; she must also learn to manage her expenditure wisely, which would require a careful balancing act in order to be neither profligate nor penny-pinching. To this end, and given her inexperience, 'she cannot do better than ask the Empress and the Grand Duke to nominate a person to assist her in this matter'. Above all, the Grand Duchess must never be idle, for 'idleness breeds boredom, which often gives rise to bad temper and capriciousness'. Catherine states reading to be the best way of filling leisure hours, but also recommends music and 'all sorts of handiwork'. The young wife is to take pleasure in society, particularly in the opportunity it affords for conversation with learned and enlightened people, but she must also cultivate her inner resources so that she is not dependent on the company of others. As a result of following these maxims, declares Catherine, 'the Princess can be sure of a most happy future'.

In the same month as Paul and Natalya's betrothal ceremony, Emelyan Pugachev reappeared among the Yaik Cossacks. This time he backed up his claim to be Peter III by displaying what he said were 'the tsar's marks', stigmata on his body 'proving' his divinely appointed kingship. (These were in fact scrofula scars on his chest, which he proudly showed while he was in the bath.) From this point his claims began to gain momentum, and he and a small group of followers started to plot how they could persuade the Yaik Cossack Host as a whole to accept him as their tsar. Those people closest to him knew perfectly well who he really was. But while some were merely using the ploy of proclaiming their leader a tsar as a means of gathering supporters to a rebel cause, others allowed themselves to be carried away with the fantasy of a saviour-tsar who could both protect and liberate his people. Pugachev's followers dressed him in an 'imperial' outfit of red kaftan and velvet cap and provided him with a secretary, as he was himself illiterate. In mid-September he and his band of rebels proclaimed a revolt. The pretender rapidly gained support by making the kinds of declarations and promises his audience of Cossacks and Kazakh nomads most wanted to hear, telling them that he would free them from the repressive regime of

Catherine, to whom he referred as 'the German' and 'the Devil's daughter'. Specifically he promised them land, food, money, weapons, freedom of religion (important to Old Believers), and exemption from taxes and recruiting levies. The day after the declaration of his initial proclamation, Pugachev's supporters already numbered 300. The rebels failed to capture Yaitsk, but they did take a few small outposts (so-called forts which were really slightly fortified villages, peopled by Cossacks, peasants and small garrisons of soldiers) and by early October they had set up their 'imperial' headquarters near the town of Orenburg.

Back in Petersburg, where the extent of the rebellion was as yet unknown, Paul and Natalya Alexeyevna were married on 29 September. Nine days earlier, Paul's long-awaited Russian majority, which had been anticipated with so much speculation over the years, was celebrated with a ball in the evening, but otherwise passed unremarked. The wedding was followed by the usual array of festivities, including a feast for the common people in front of the Winter Palace.

The occasion of the wedding was also marked by the beginning of one of the most important and long-lasting relationships of Catherine's life. Largely epistolary, and with no romantic element, it developed into a sustained and sustaining friendship. The man in question was Friedrich Melchior Grimm, who arrived in Petersburg as a member of the suite escorting Natalya Alexeyevna's elder brother, Ludwig, who had come to attend the wedding. Grimm was a German courtier of noble birth (born in Regensburg in 1723, he was six years older than Catherine) who had moved to Paris where he had been in the service of the Prince of Saxe-Gotha and the Duc d'Orléans. There he also became a close friend of Diderot and the other *philosophes*. Since 1754 he had been producing an exclusive fortnightly newsletter, *Correspondances littéraires*, founded by the Abbé Raynal (a writer and priest dismissed for unexplained reasons from the parish of Saint Sulpice in Paris), which was intended to keep the crowned heads of Europe au fait with the latest thinking on books, poetry, theatre, paintings and sculpture. The 15 or so subscribers received copies through their embassies in Paris. This was just the kind of publication to appeal to Catherine, and she had long been a subscriber.

Almost as soon as he had arrived in Petersburg, after having been presented to the Empress and the Grand Duke, Grimm received a completely unexpected request from Catherine that he should remain in Russia and enter her service. Throughout the marriage ceremonies

Grimm agonised over how to reply. It was the Landgravine's firm opinion that he should accept, and Grimm opined that the Empress did not expect a refusal. Many years later he recollected that she talked graciously to him over cards in the evenings, but that a chill began to descend as the days went by and still he gave no answer. There was no hint of coldness, however, in the way Catherine wrote of Grimm to Voltaire: 'I find his conversation a delight: but we still have so many things to say to each other, that so far our discussions have had more heat than order and coherence. We have talked a lot about you. I told him, what you have perhaps forgotten, that your works taught me to think.' Desirous of an answer, Catherine sent Count Vladimir Orlov, the youngest and most intellectual of the Orlov brothers, to see him towards the end of the wedding festivities to ask him to explain what the problem was. Grimm replied that if he could have a five-minute audience with Catherine in private, without courtiers to overhear, he would open his heart to her. The interview was granted for the following evening; Grimm described it himself:

When I entered, she had that imposing dignified look which came so naturally to her; there was nothing severe about it, but it disconcerted me. 'Well, sir,' She said, 'you wished to speak to me, what have you to say?' I replied: 'Madame, if Your Majesty continues to look like that, I shall have to leave, as I feel that I will not be able to express myself freely and will fail to make good use of these moments which you have kindly accorded me, which would be pure loss for me.' At these words she reassumed her usual smile and said: 'Sit down, and let us discuss our business.'

Reassured, Grimm explained that, though he could not help but be flattered by Catherine's proposal, he felt too old at 50 to make such a radical change as coming to live in Russia. He did not think he would be able to learn Russian and could not see how he could be useful in a country when he did not know the language. The Empress replied somewhat tartly that it would be up to her to decide how he could be of use. According to his later recollections, Grimm felt very drawn to accept Catherine's invitation. His real fear was that such good fortune could not possibly last, that if he threw everything up to follow his inclination and come to serve her in Russia, it would all go wrong, and he would find himself displaced and with nothing to show for such an upheaval. The interview lasted not for five minutes but for an hour and a half. At the end of it, Grimm was as undecided as at the beginning.

Following that first interview, Catherine frequently summoned Grimm for a private conversation after the evening's card-playing. She would sit at her table with some embroidery or other handiwork, make him sit down opposite her, and keep him until half past ten or eleven o'clock. (Talk with an interesting and intelligent man seems to have been of more interest to the Empress before bedtime than any pleasures Vassilchikov might have had to offer.) Before long these sessions became a daily occurrence, and further conversations took place at other times. Sometimes there was one before and another after dinner, and a third before bed. Grimm found himself spending almost all his time in the imperial presence, either in public or private, going back to his own lodgings only between four and six in the afternoon. He found, to his surprise, that he felt completely free in his conversations with Catherine and that she had an extraordinarily quick understanding, even when he felt he had not expressed himself well.

Meanwhile another great conversationalist, Grimm's friend Denis Diderot, had arrived in Petersburg for a long-awaited visit to his benefactress. He had been delayed on his journey by illness and arrived, still unwell, on the day before the grand ducal wedding. His initial enthusiasm knew no bounds as Diderot's other friend currently in Petersburg, Etienne Falconet, reported to Catherine a few days later:

> At last, Madame, he has come and he has seen you, this Diderot who does not cease to express his delight. *Yes, I have seen her, I have heard her*, he says, *and I swear to you, my friend, that she does not know all the good she has done me. What a sovereign! what an astonishing woman* . . . he says all sorts of other things and what is most singular, is that he says it to me as though he were teaching me, and not as if I had been telling him the same thing for the last seven years.

Another move on the court chess board now took place as Paul's marriage gave Catherine the opportunity to diminish Nikita Panin's influence. Now that Paul was officially adult, he had no further need, reasoned Catherine, of a governor, and so the man who had acted in many ways as his substitute father must now relinquish his position in the Grand Ducal household and, consequently, give up his accommodation rights in the imperial palaces. Panin's golden handshake included an estate yielding an income of 30,000 roubles a year, a pension of the same sum, and any house of his choosing in Petersburg, along with the means to furnish it and acquire all he needed in the way of dinner services, carriages and a wine cellar. The Count – and the Grand Duke, to whom this also came as an unpleasant surprise – had no choice but to submit to the Empress's will. He could hardly negotiate in the way Grigory Orlov had done a year previously. Catherine had effectively turned the tables on him, and there was little doubt who was the current winner in the Orlov/Panin rivalry. None of these undercurrents was voiced aloud, of course, Panin outwardly being accorded great esteem, as reflected in Sir Robert Gunning's report of 27 September:

> A very gracious and flattering letter from the Empress to Mr Panin has reconciled him to the immediate quitting the apartments he has in the palace. She tells him in it, that the good of the Empire requires, that both she and he should dedicate the remainder of their days to its service; that their time should now be wholly employed in procuring to it a peace, and begged he would devote all his to that purpose; she would therefore dispense with his attendance any longer on the Great Duke: who on his part has been prevailed upon to agree to this separation, on a promise of Mr Panin's having free access to him, whenever he pleases.

A week later news of Pugachev's revolt reached Catherine. By now he had amassed an 'army' of 3,000 men and over 20 cannon, and was sowing terror through the countryside around Orenburg. His followers had massacred noblemen and officers, often mutilating their victims before hanging them upside down, and had raped or taken for the 'Emperor's' harem any women they did not kill. Catherine and her advisers, however, still did not appreciate the seriousness of what was happening and seemed to think it was no more than a minor repetition of the previous year's Cossack mutiny. Consequently an inadequate force was sent out under General Karr to try to deal with the disturbances. The British diplomat Richard Oakes commented on the worsening situation on 5 November:

> Every thing relative to the insurrection in the province of Orenburg is kept as secret as possible, but it is known that the accounts from thence are more and more unfavourable. Three couriers are arrived from Cazan within these few days. It is said the number of the cossacks the pretender's followers is already increased to upwards of

twenty five thousand men who lay waste the country, and plunder the inhabitants; and that they have hanged the governor of the Russian fortress. It is even apprehended that they will attempt Orenburg. Two regiments have been ordered in addition to the force already sent to quell them, and artillery has been conveyed thither by post horses. This is certainly an affair of a very alarming nature at present.

The rebellion which became known as the Pugachevshchina (the most serious event of its kind to occur during Catherine's reign) was one of the elements that put an end to this strange interlude in the Empress's life, at the beginning of which she had seemed to be losing her grip both on herself (in the sudden infatuation with Vassilchikov) and on her courtiers (who were prepared to manipulate her weakness to further their own ends). By the end of 1773 she was firmly back in control of her Court, but the emotional and psychological gap left by the retirement of Grigory Orlov as official favourite was yet to be filled. Alexander Vassilchikov (whose part during this whole drama was as a puppet and otherwise purely decorative) had proved inadequate to fulfil Catherine's emotional needs. And he was incapable of providing any support or assistance during the rapidly developing crisis of internal unrest combined with continuing external warfare. With the same instinct which had first drawn her to Orlov in her last months as Grand Duchess, Catherine now began to focus her attention on a man who had, throughout the Vassilchikov period, been waiting in the wings. In November 1770 Grigory Potemkin had been chosen by Field Marshal Rumyantsev to deliver the news to St Petersburg of the Russians' successes against the Turks. During the several months that he stayed in the capital he had dined with the Empress on frequent occasions, and had both then and subsequently made his admiration of and devotion to his sovereign abundantly clear. He was now serving again with the army on the Danube front, participating in the siege of Silistria. On 4 December 1773 Catherine sent Potemkin a note which its recipient chose to interpret as a direct invitation:

Lieutenant-General and chevalier, I expect you have your eyes too trained on Silistria to have any time for reading letters; and although I do not yet know whether your bombardment has been successful, I am nevertheless convinced that everything undertaken by you has as its sole motive your ardent zeal towards me personally as well as to the dear fatherland, whose service you love. But as far as I am concerned I particularly want to preserve eager, brave, clever and talented people, and so I request that you should not needlessly expose yourself to danger. On reading this letter, you may ask: why was it written? To this I answer: so that you should have confirmation of how I think about you; for towards you I am always well-disposed.

# 12

# Passion and Pretenders
## (1774–76)

*The trouble is that my heart is loath to remain even one hour without love.*
Catherine II to Grigory Potemkin

A s a young man Grigory Potemkin had studied theology at
Moscow University, where he had been presented to the
late Empress Elizabeth as one of the glowing hopes of the
faculty. But soon after that encounter he gave up his formal theological studies, while remaining passionately interested in matters of Church
and religion. When, several weeks after his return to St Petersburg at
the beginning of 1774, the Empress Catherine had still made no definite move to dismiss Alexander Vassilchikov as favourite and instal
Potemkin in his place, the latter decided to put his famed devotion to
religion to good purpose and call the Empress's bluff. Accordingly he
let it be known that he had decided to take holy orders, and moved
into the Alexander Nevsky Monastery, where he ostentatiously adopted
the life of a monk, even beginning to grow a beard. By this ploy he
succeeded in spurring Catherine into action. She dispatched her close
friend and confidante Countess Bruce to bring him back to Court.
The incorrigible Potemkin, in a mixture of comedy and piety, kept the
Countess waiting while he completed his devotions. After deigning to
hear her message, however, he at once shaved, washed and changed
into uniform before riding to Tsarskoye Selo. He arrived on 4 February
at six o'clock in the evening, and was presented to the Empress. The
two immediately retired into her private apartments, where they
remained for an hour.

Potemkin's passion for religion was typical of his approach to everything in life; he had a consuming interest in many subjects and a capacity for absorption – in the sense both of being absorbed in what he was doing and being able rapidly to absorb information and ideas – which more than matched Catherine's own and which was one of the things that drew her to him. Life with Potemkin would never be boring – as life with Vassilchikov had quickly proved to be. He was the kind of man one would either love or hate. Like Grigory Orlov, Grigory Potemkin was of impressive physique, but he was far more cultured, educated and intellectually able than Orlov. His facial appearance was somewhat marred by loss of sight in his left eye (the result of an accident and not, as rumour-mongers liked to assert, because Grigory Orlov had punched him in the face); this eye was half-closed and Potemkin was very self-conscious about it, always insisting that portraitists paint him on his 'good' side. His self-consciousness cannot have been helped by the nickname awarded him by the Orlovs and others of 'Cyclops'. He had a pale face and long brown, almost auburn, hair, over which he sometimes wore a grey wig. His fine healthy teeth constituted one of his best assets. At 34 he was 10 years younger than Catherine.

The Empress herself was still in her prime, her attractiveness enhanced by the sense of majesty which showed itself in her bearing and made her appear taller than she was. She had good skin, bright eyes, a smile almost permanently on her shapely lips, and despite increasing plumpness, she retained her pointed chin. She generally wore a full dress with broad sleeves, both for comfort and ease of work and to disguise her tendency towards corpulence. She wore her dark hair powdered, and applied a bright spot of rouge to each cheek, as was the custom among Russian women at the time.

From the start Catherine was astounded by the strength of her feelings for Potemkin. She liked to think of herself as 'one of the best heads of Europe', but could not stop herself dashing off several infatuated little love-letters every day, mainly in Russian but sometimes interspersed with passages in French, to her darling, sweetheart, precious dear, brother, *toton* (French for a child's top, suggestive of how Potemkin was always whirling with energy), her little Grisha, Grishenka, or even Grishifishenka. (Potemkin kept most of these letters and notes, whereas she burnt most of the ones he sent her, so that a largely one-sided correspondence has been preserved, though it is easy to see how this one side constitutes part of a continuous dialogue.) The couple were always competitive as to which of them loved the most, Catherine generally convinced that she loved Potemkin more than he loved her, while he constantly seemed to need reassurance that she would continue to love him, and only him. Touchy and quick to take offence, he was a demanding and jealous lover, jealous even of those who had preceded him in Catherine's affections. Very early on in their relationship he seems to have upbraided her for the number of her previous lovers, accusing her of having had as many as 15. This prompted her 'Sincere Confession' of 21 February 1774, from which it is clear that she had indeed intended to summon Potemkin with her letter of the preceding December, in order to test the assertion made by Countess Bruce (whom she refers to familiarly as 'Bryusha') that he was in love with his Empress, as she desired him to be. She refers to him as a Hero or Knight (*bogatyr* in Russian, the mythical hero of medieval Russian epic songs, defending ancient Russia against all her enemies), implying perhaps that she thought of both herself and her Empire as damsels in distress, needing to be rescued by a knight in shining armour. She denies the number 15, and recounts the list of her five lovers – Sergei Saltykov ('unwillingly'), Stanislas Poniatowski, Grigory Orlov, Alexander Vassilchikov ('in despair') and now Potemkin himself. She also denies any imputations of wantonness or debauchery, for which she declares herself to have no inclination, still believing that had she been fortunate enough to have had a husband whom she could have loved, she would have remained faithful to him. She then freely admits the crux of the matter, her constant need to have someone to love and to be loved by: 'The trouble is that my heart is loath to remain even one hour without love.' And the way for a lover to keep her, she advises Potemkin, is to show her as much friendship as affection, to continue to love her and to tell her the truth.

It took several weeks for Potemkin's arrival in the position of favourite to be fully registered at Court and for Vassilchikov to be declared redundant. On 9 February Potemkin attended a formal dinner at the Catherine Palace at Tsarskoye Selo. On the same day Catherine updated her friend Madame Bielke on the situation regarding Pugachev and his rebels. In a letter of the previous month she had denied that a revolt was in progress, admitting merely that there were gangs of highwaymen operating in the Orenburg province and that one of their leaders sometimes declared himself to be Peter III and at other times his representative. These gangs of robbers, she said, had hanged more than 500 people of both sexes and all ages over the past three months. Major-General Karr had been sent against them, but had only made the situation worse. She had sent General

Bibikov to take his place. It was Catherine's opinion that the Bashkirs, who inhabited the district of Orenburg, had been 'extremely restless people, engaged in pillage since the creation of the world', but she declared herself optimistic that matters would soon be under control: 'It is very probable that all this will soon come to an end. General Bibikov has everything necessary. And, furthermore, something which lacks either sense or order cannot survive once it encounters order and reason.'

One of the many difficulties in dealing with the disturbances was that they had resulted in communications between Petersburg and the affected region being delayed, if not cut off entirely. Accounts of what was happening had to come by way of Kazan, so that the information received was immediately and even more than ordinarily out of date. Pugachev's army was numbering by now about 10,000. In the rebel camp he established his own 'court', based on the actual one, his 'courtiers' even using the same names as Catherine's. Thus the man who acted as treasurer of the copper coins (Pugachev keeping the silver himself), one Shigayev, called himself Count Vorontsov, one of Pugachev's military leaders called himself Count Panin, another called himself Count Orlov, another Field Marshal Count Chernyshev. Pugachev (or his secretaries, bearing in mind his inability to write) issued decrees (*ukazy*), some of which were even printed. Seals – including the seal of a distillery – were used to add a further degree of spurious authenticity. Pugachev had recently abandoned his legal wife and children in the Don region, and taken for his second wife the daughter of a Yaik Cossack, Yustina Kuznetsova. She received all the honours of an empress at his 'court', Cossack women being appointed as her maids-of-honour. This bigamous marriage did nothing to strengthen Pugachev's position as Peter III, however, as it was well known among his supporters that the Tsar was married to the usurping Catherine. The latter assured Madame Bielke that General Bibikov was gradually restoring control around Orenburg, and that four or five of the miscreants had been hanged. Determined to portray Russian justice as superior to that practised in other European countries, she commented: 'these very rare hangings are a thousand times more effective here than in those places where people are hanged every day'.

General Bibikov had been given authority by the Empress to establish the Kazan Secret Commission, a temporary local department of the Secret Branch, and in March she wrote to him to advise caution in the treatment of suspected rebels:

Please tell the secret commission to be careful in the investigation and punishment of people. In my judgement, the soldiers Aytugan and Sangulov were unjustly beaten; and why is there any need to beat people under interrogation? During the twelve years of my supervision the secret branch has not beaten any man during questioning, and yet each matter was investigated thoroughly and we always found out more than we needed to know.

The Empress could not, however, personally supervise the proceedings in Kazan, and there is some evidence to suggest that Bibikov dealt with her merciful inclinations by not keeping her fully informed about the methods actually used during the interrogation of suspects.

On 14 February the Court returned from Tsarskoye Selo to the Winter Palace and on the following day there was a dinner which included both Vassilchikov and Potemkin among the 20 guests. On the 18th the Empress attended the Russian comedy and afterwards stayed up with Potemkin, talking or making love, until the unusually late hour for her of one o'clock in the morning. It was a constant feature of this relationship that the lovers' timetables did not mesh. Catherine routinely went to bed several hours before Potemkin and was hard at work in the morning well before he was awake. Consequently they rarely spent the night together, and each partner frequently found the other was not available when required. Catherine, despite being the Empress and in theory free to do whatever she liked, frequently behaved like an illicit lover during her affair with Potemkin, feeling that she had to hide her assignations with him. She was also afraid that he would not respond as she desired. On 26 February she wrote: 'As soon as I had gone to bed and the servants had withdrawn, I got up again, dressed and went to the doors in the library to wait for you, and there I stood for two hours in a draught; and not until it was nearly midnight did I return out of sadness to lie down in bed where, thanks to you, I spent the fifth sleepless night.' She did not even have the consolation of conversations with Grimm, as he had fallen ill with a fever.

Perhaps Potemkin was playing hard to get until his position was consolidated. Thirty-six hours after the Empress had spent this miserable night, Potemkin wrote to ask to be made a general and her personal aide-de-camp. He could not bear to think that he might be considered 'less worthy' than others and begged that 'my doubt be resolved by rewarding me with the title of adjutant-general to Your Imperial

Majesty'. Catherine was pleased that Potemkin felt he could make such a very direct request of her, and she ordered the necessary edict to be drawn up straightaway. That day she and Potemkin met in the baths – the Russian *banya* installed in the basement of the Winter Palace which became a regular venue for their trysts. Food had been prepared for them and Catherine warned Potemkin not to take any of it away, so no one would know their secret.

In her 'Sincere Confession' Catherine had been happy to disparage Vassilchikov, telling Potemkin that every caress from the young man had made her cry. Apparently, he also sulked for months at a time. But she would not permit the jealous Potemkin to speak ill of Grigory Orlov, for whom she retained affection and respect. Orlov himself had always spoken well of Potemkin, she declared, and she remained firm in her loyalty to all the brothers: 'He loves you, and they are my friends, and I will not part with them. Now there's an admonition for you. If you know what's good for you, you'll heed it.' Yet despite the depth of her long relationship with Grigory Orlov and her earlier romantic attachment to Stanislas Poniatowski, Catherine was in love with Grigory Potemkin in a way which was new to her:

> In order for me to make sense, when you are with me, I have to close my eyes or else I might really say what I have always found laughable: 'that my gaze is captivated by you.' An expression which I used to think was stupid, improbable and unnatural, but which I now see might be possible. My stupid eyes will become fixed in looking at you; not a penn'orth of reason can penetrate my mind and God knows how foolish I'm becoming. I need not to see you for about three days, if that is possible, to give my mind time to calm down and for me to come to my senses, or you will soon grow bored with me, and how could it be otherwise? I am very, very angry with myself today and scolded myself and tried in every way to be more sensible.

Potemkin was confirmed in his appointment as adjutant-general to the Empress on Saturday 1 March. Catherine made arrangements for him to accompany her into the Diamond Hall, a room in her apartments in the Winter Palace where the imperial jewels were kept, so that he could thank her in private. On the same day she told him in a letter that Alexei Orlov (war being a seasonal activity, he was back at Court during the winter) had asked her in an amused and friendly manner

'Yes or no?' on the subject of love. He had then told her that he knew they met in the baths, because he had noticed a light shining in them later than normal for the past four days. In the same letter Catherine complained about the 'boring and suffocating' Vassilchikov who, though now surplus to requirements – and pensioned off with a generous yearly sum, estates and a mansion in Petersburg along with the requisite china, table linen and silver dinner service – was proving reluctant to leave the Empress's side. Keen not to create a scene, Catherine suggested that Potemkin should instruct Panin to find a third party who would persuade Vassilchikov to go away to take the waters. He seems eventually to have taken the hint.

Potemkin entered immediately into political and state matters, advising on the war and the Pugachev rebellion. He was a naturally political animal, as was she, and their endless conversations slipped easily from sex-talk to questions of state, via laughter, through literature and philosophy, and back again to sex. One of Potemkin's great gifts to Catherine was that he made her laugh and could keep her entertained for hours. And he longed for 'glory' as much as she did – for the Empire, its Empress, and himself. Once Potemkin had been created adjutant-general, Sir Robert Gunning was quick to perceive the significance of his emergence, reporting to the Earl of Suffolk on 4 March:

> A new scene has just opened here, which, in my opinion, is likely to merit more attention than any that has presented itself since the beginning of this reign.
>
> Mr Wasiltchikoff the favorite whose understanding was too limited to admit of his having any influence in affairs, or sharing his mistress's confidence, is now succeeded by a man who bids fair for possessing them both, in the most supreme degree. When I acquaint your Lordship that the Empress's choice is equally disapproved of by the Great Duke's party and the Orloffs, who both appeared satisfied with the state in which things had for some time been, you will not wonder, that it should occasion, as it has done, a very general surprise, and even consternation.

Sir Robert's initial assessment of Potemkin was equivocal, based at least as much on a low opinion of Catherine's other courtiers and officials as on a high estimation of Potemkin's own abilities:

His figure is gigantic and disproportioned, and his countenance very far from engaging. From the character I have had of him he appears to have a great knowledge of mankind, and more of the discriminating faculty than his countrymen in general possess, and as much address for intrigue and suppleness in his station as any of them; and though the profligacy of his manner is notorious, he is the only one who has formed connections with the clergy. With these qualifications, and from the known inactivity of those with whom he may have to contend he may naturally flatter himself with the hopes of rising to that height which his boundless ambition aspires to.

One of Potemkin's initial tactics in negotiating the tangled web of allegiances and interests at Catherine's Court was to attempt to ingratiate himself with Nikita Panin, in the hope of also making inroads with the Grand Duke, who much preferred his mother's favourites to be of the insignificant variety. To begin with, Panin was a cautious supporter of Potemkin, if only because he was delighted to see any diminution in the influence of the Orlovs. Potemkin's obvious talent in both the political and military arenas was an immediate cause of concern to existing post-holders. Well might Panin, the Grand Duke, the Orlovs and the Chernyshevs (Zakhar was the president of the College of War) be alarmed. Potemkin's rise to a position of considerable power proceeded with unprecedented speed. On 15 March he was appointed Lieutenant-General of the Preobrazhensky Guards, an honour formerly enjoyed by Alexei Orlov, Catherine herself being the Colonel of the regiment. And at the end of the month he was appointed Governor-General of New Russia, the vast territory in the south bordered by the Tatar Khanate of the Crimea and the Ottoman Empire. After a fortnight in the early spring spent at Tsarskoye Selo, the Court returned on 9 April to the Winter Palace, where Potemkin was installed in his own apartment. In order to distinguish himself from his predecessor, he had refused to move into Vassilchikov's old apartment (which was converted into a council chamber) and had a new one decorated for himself, directly below that of the Empress and connected by a private green-carpeted spiral staircase. Both apartments looked out on to Palace Square and an internal courtyard. Rooms were also prepared for Potemkin at the other imperial residences. On the day after their return to the Winter Palace, Catherine told Potemkin that it was not easy for her to come and see him in the mornings. She also expressed in this letter how dependent she had already become on his love:

> Fear not that one can free oneself from your webs, but from hour to hour one becomes more entangled. But should you yourself somehow lessen my passion, you would make me unhappy. And even then I would probably not stop loving you. But I pray God that I might die at that hour when it seems to me that you are not the same towards me as you have deigned to be these seven weeks. Only whatever happens, I need to think that you love me and the slightest doubt about this troubles me cruelly and makes me unspeakably sad.

In April Friedrich Melchior Grimm left St Petersburg, travelling initially to Italy. He had been ill for much of 1774, the Empress thus being deprived of the conversations she had so much enjoyed and of which she had written with such enthusiasm to Voltaire at the end of 1773, including Diderot in her praises: 'I see them very often,' she had written on 27 December, 'and our conversations never end.' She described Diderot as having 'an inexhaustible imagination' and as being one of the most extraordinary men who had ever existed. It did not take Catherine long, however, to discount Diderot's ideas as having no practical application in the ruling of her vast and trouble-some Empire, commenting to Voltaire (and not omitting to flatter him by alluding to *Candide*) in January 1774: 'It is a most extraordin-ary mind he has; the calibre of his heart should be that of every man; but in the end, as everything is for the best in this best of all possible worlds, and things cannot be altered, one must let them go their way, and not clutter up one's brain with useless pretensions.' Years later Catherine described her conversations with Diderot to the Comte de Ségur:

> 'I had long and frequent conversations with Diderot,' Catherine said to me, 'but with more curiosity than profit. If I had followed his advice, everything would have been turned upside down in my Empire; legislation, administration, politics, finance – I would have upset everything in order to substitute impractical theories for them.
> 'Nevertheless, as I listened to him more than I spoke, anyone witnessing us both would have taken him for a severe pedagogue and me for his humble pupil. He probably thought this himself; for after some time, seeing that none of the great innovations he had

recommended to me had been implemented in my government [innovations such as the abolition of serfdom], he expressed his surprise to me with a sort of displeased haughtiness.

'And so, speaking to him frankly, I said: *Monsieur Diderot, I have listened with the greatest pleasure to everything which your brilliant mind has inspired you to say; but with all your grand principles, which I understand perfectly well, one could produce good books and bad governance. You forget in all your plans of reform the difference between our two positions: you work only on paper, which permits everything; it is uniform, supple, and presents no obstacles either to your imagination or to your pen; whereas in my case, poor Empress that I am, I work on human parchment, which is on the contrary irritable and sensitive.*

'I am convinced that after that he took pity on me, regarding me as a narrow and vulgar person. From then on he talked to me only about literature, and politics disappeared from our conversations.'

However docile Catherine may have been in listening to the tempestuous Diderot (who was even reputed to have slapped her thighs with enthusiasm when he got too carried away) – and however disillusioned the Frenchman may have been at finding that at least some of the enlightened ideas of his benefactress operated more on the level of theory than of practice – Catherine had no doubts that she could hold her own in conversation with the most advanced philosophers of her age. She could not, however, quite reconcile this image of herself as an intellectual with the mad and girlish lover she seemed to have become: 'How awful it is for someone with a mind to lose it!' she wrote to Potemkin. 'I want you to love me. I want to appear lovable to you. But I only show you madness and extreme weakness. Oh, how awful it is to love extraordinarily. You know, it's an illness. I am ill, only I don't send for an apothecary and neither do I write long letters. If you like, I'll summarise this page for you in three words and will cross out all the rest: here it is – I love you.' She was also uncomfortably aware that if such delirium continued indefinitely, it would damage her ability to manage the affairs of her Empire, as it made her feel like 'a headless chicken'. 'I think that the fever and the agitation of my blood come from the fact that for several evenings, I don't quite know why, I've been going to bed very late for me. It's always one o'clock. I'm used to going to bed at ten. Do me a favour and leave earlier in future. Really, it's bad. Write to tell me how you are, darling, I hope you slept well. I love you, but don't have time to write, or anything to say.'

Before Grimm left St Petersburg, General Bauer was sent to ask him whether he had changed his mind about entering the Empress's service in Russia. He managed to refuse (helped by the fact that the doctors advised a change of climate for him), while promising that he would return for a second visit after he had been to Italy. Diderot, who was not pressed to extend his visit though who continued to benefit from Catherine's patronage and to correspond with her, had left a month earlier.

Relations between the Empress and her son were in a state of cautious neutrality. Paul was very much occupied with the joys of married life, and initially Catherine too was very happy with her daughter-in-law, describing her to Madame Bielke as a 'golden girl'. Paul had gained some credit with his mother early in the year by confessing to an intrigue he had foolishly allowed himself to be drawn into by Caspar von Saldern, who was currently engaged in diplomatic business in Copenhagen. Saldern's idea seems to have been that Paul should be enabled to assume an equal share in the government of Russia, taking as his pattern the joint rule over the Austrian lands enjoyed by Holy Roman Emperor Joseph II with his mother the Empress-Queen Maria Theresa. Paul had gone so far as to sign a document authorising Saldern to act as his representative and political agent in this matter. In some alarm afterwards at what he had done, Paul had gone to Panin for advice. Horrified at the way the Grand Duke had exposed himself to danger and charges of treachery, Panin repudiated the proposal and destroyed the incriminating document, but forbore to tell the Empress what had been going on. Knowing nothing of Saldern's plotting, Catherine continued to hold him in high regard. But as the time for his return from Copenhagen drew near, Paul decided that the safest and most honourable course was to inform his mother of Saldern's duplicity and express his own repentance. The information threw the Empress into a fury. She instructed Panin to forbid Saldern to use any of the titles or ranks he had gained during his Russian and Holstinian service, and to threaten him with arrest if he ever dared set foot on Russian soil again. Paul himself did not come in for any censure.

The early part of 1774 was a very difficult time for the Grand Duchess Natalya, who had to cope both with (false) rumours that she was pregnant and with bereavement; the news in March of the death of her grandmother was swiftly followed by the deeply upsetting news of the death of her mother. Catherine too was distressed by this, for she had come to like the Landgravine during the weeks she had spent in Russia.

On the day the Court had returned to the Winter Palace from Tsarskoye Selo, Catherine had written to Madame Bielke to assure her that the Pugachev rebellion was being brought under control. The siege of Orenburg was broken and the besiegers scattered (though Pugachev himself had managed to escape):

The day before yesterday I received two couriers from General Bibikov, who informs me that Major-General Prince Peter Golitsyn, after having had a very lively combat with those wretches at forty versts from Orenburg, routed them totally and has delivered the town from the blockade in which those wretches had been holding it for several months. I have letters from the governor which say that an abundance of foodstuffs has succeeded the scarcity during which he was only able to give half-portions to his people for three months. M. Bibikov has despatched troops from all directions to mop up the little bands of robbers overrunning the roads, and I hope that tranquillity will succeed this sudden disturbance, which it has pleased people in foreign countries to exaggerate in an unheard-of manner.

What Catherine could not tell Madame Bielke, as she did not yet know it herself, was that on that very day General Bibikov had suddenly died of fever. Shocked and saddened though she was when she eventually received the news, she considered that by and large the General had fulfilled the task he had been sent to do. Thousands of the rebels were captured at Orenburg, and a new Orenburg Secret Commission was established to examine all aspects of the revolt and to determine Pugachev's personal role in it. A particular concern of the Empress was to find out whether the rebellion had been provoked by some foreign power, in an attempt to destabilise the Russian Empire.

On 21 April 1774, Catherine's forty-fifth birthday, Potemkin received the Order of St Alexander Nevsky and, from the King of Poland, the Order of the White Eagle. Catherine herself placed the ribbons on him after attending the liturgy. He also received a gift of 50,000 roubles – a sum for which Grand Duke Paul would have been grateful in order to pay off his wife's debts, Grand Duchess Natalya finding it no easier to stay within her budget than had Grand Duchess Catherine. He was the recipient of no such largesse, however, having to make do with a new watch. Catherine wrote to Madame Bielke about her birthday: 'getting old is a very disagreeable thing'. She wrote in similar vein to Grimm, who by this time was in Courland: 'I hate this day like the plague; a lovely present it gives me! Every time it gives me a gift of one more year, a thing I could well do without. Wouldn't an Empress who remained fifteen years old all her life be a delightful thing?'

The day after her birthday Catherine sent Potemkin a mild reprimand, which suggests that he had been audacious enough to criticise her in front of others: 'We ask that in future you don't humiliate us, but that you cover our vices and mistakes with a stole★ and don't parade them in front of people, for that cannot be pleasant for us. And anyway it's inappropriate to treat a friend, let alone your w[ife], like that. Now there's a reprimand for you, though a most affectionate one.' The fact that she refers to herself here as Potemkin's 'wife' seems to me to be a small piece of evidence against the theory that the couple were married secretly on 8 June, or later. Either they were married before that date or, as seems more likely, they thought of one another as husband and wife, because of the intensity of their passion and as a way of assuring one another that their relationship was of far more significance than any either of them had had before. Potemkin was already making swaggering declarations that he would kill any successor to himself as Catherine's favourite. For this she reproached him, as she did not believe in love as something that could be forced or made constant through fear. In any event, she thought he would sooner tire of her than she of him. As though to prove this, on 8 May, when they were back at Tsarskoye Selo, Catherine wrote to reproach Potemkin for using the excuse of being sleepy to leave her, adding that when she had come looking for him, not only was he not asleep, he wasn't even in his apartments. She complained that he only visited her 'on forays' and appeared to be bored with her, always having more important business to rush off to. There is a suggestion in what she writes that this was how Grigory Orlov had behaved too. It did not suit either of these formidable men to appear to be tied to the apron strings of a woman, not even when that woman was Empress of All the Russias.

On 5 May Potemkin became a member of Catherine's Council, and his inexorable rise continued later in the month when he was made vice-president of the College of War, and awarded the rank of general-in-chief. Not only did this latest promotion severely threaten the position and power of Count Zakhar Chernyshev, it also provoked the ire of the usually pacific Prince Grigory Orlov, who stormed in to see

---

★ A Russian Orthodox priest covers the head of a penitent with his stole when pronouncing absolution.

Catherine on 2 June. Sir Robert Gunning reported what he had heard of this meeting: 'Something more than an explanation, a very warm altercation passed between her and the prince, on this subject, which is said to have moved her more than she was ever known to have been; and to have determined him to travel, which he means to do, as soon as he returns from Moscow, where he is now gone.' Orlov's protest and decision to leave the Court upset Catherine but had no effect on her treatment of Potemkin, whose cousin Pavel was appointed during the same month to take charge of the Secret Commission in Kazan. Also in June there was progress in the Russo-Turkish conflict. Field Marshal Rumyantsev's forces recrossed the Danube in strength, and subsequent gains under Generals Suvorov and Kamensky forced the Turks to sue for peace.

On 8 June, back at the Summer Palace in Petersburg, Catherine and Potemkin attended a dinner in honour of the Izmailovsky Guards. After the dinner Catherine went for a walk along the bank of the Fontanka river, and towards midnight (when it would still have been light) she set off on a mysterious expedition by boat, accompanied by her loyal maid and confidante Maria Savishna Perekusikhina. Potemkin had slipped away earlier to another boat that was waiting for him. The legend is that, docking at a jetty on the Little Nevka on the unfashionable Vyborg side, Catherine proceeded in a coach with drawn curtains to the church of St Sampson, where she found Potemkin waiting for her. Both were still wearing the regimental dress of the Izmailovsky Guards, Catherine's being in the form of a lady's riding habit, trimmed in gold lace. The story continues that here, in the presence of Catherine's maid, an unnamed priest and two men to hold the crowns – the chamberlain Yevgraf Chertkov and Potemkin's nephew Alexander Samoilov – Potemkin and Catherine were married. Other versions alter the location to a church near Moscow or assign the event to a different year. No proof has as yet been found, though it has been asserted that certificates were written and given to the witnesses. That a ceremony of some sort took place, intended by Catherine and Potemkin to express their commitment to one another, in the presence of a few of their closest friends and with the blessing of a priest, seems to be entirely possible; Potemkin, a devout man, may well have wished for this most important relationship in his life to receive the Church's blessing. That this was in any sense a formal, legal marriage is far more doubtful.

Two days later the Court repaired to Peterhof, where they remained for several weeks on account of the heat. Catherine continued to write loving little notes to Potemkin whenever she had a spare moment, often several times a day. They were in the nature of modern-day e-mails or text messages, and did now frequently use the imagery of husband and wife, as well as more equivocal nicknames such as Giaour (a pejorative Turkish term for a non-Muslim), Muscovite, Cossack – even Pugachev – when Potemkin was being difficult: 'My dear soul, priceless and measureless, I cannot find the words to tell you how much I love you. Don't worry about having diarrhoea. It will clean the stomach. But you must take care of yourself, dear h[usband], little sir.' Or 'Giaour, Muscovite, Cossack, do you want to make peace? Stretch out your hand, if the madness has passed and a spark of love remains in you.' This was an exhausting love, full of arguments and jealousies: 'My little dove, I will write a reply tomorrow, but today my head hurts. I am not angry and I beg you also not to be cross or sad. Moreover I will remain a f[aithful] w[ife] to you to the grave, if you will allow it; if you won't, then you are a G[iaour], a M[uscovite], a C[ossack].'

Catherine was also by now in regular correspondence with Grimm, commiserating with him on 19 June over his ill health and advising him to steer clear of doctors: 'I really don't like the sound of your frequent consultations with doctors: these charlatans always do more harm than good, witness Louis XV, who was surrounded by ten of them and who now *mortus est* [is dead]; in fact I think that that was nine more than necessary to die at their hands. I also think it is shameful for an 18th-century king of France to die of smallpox.' Throughout their correspondence Catherine frequently gave Grimm news about her dogs, particularly Sir Tom Anderson or Mr Tom, her Italian greyhound which had been presented to her, along with a bitch, by Baron Dimsdale, and of whom Grimm seemed nearly as fond as she was herself:

Mr Thomas, who should be very touched by the honour of your remembering him, has for some time lived more in the bosom of his family than with me; he is madly in love with his wife and with his five children who resemble him like peas in a pod. That makes a whole pack of them, who run with me over all the gardens and then modestly return to their kennel where papa follows, for them sacrificing kings' palaces, sofas, gold-upholstered armchairs and philoso-comical conversations.

Catherine referred in this letter to Potemkin, who two days later was made commander-in-chief of all irregular forces (that is, of the Cossacks) and of the cavalry, as someone 'who makes me laugh fit to burst'. She was always quite open with Grimm about her relationships with her favourites, while never going into any sexual details. A few weeks later she referred to Vassilchikov as 'a certain excellent, but very boring citizen' and described his replacement as 'one of the greatest, funniest and most entertaining originals of this iron century'.

On 10 July Field Marshal Rumyantsev and the Turkish representatives agreed peace terms at the obscure Bulgarian village of Kuchuk-Kainardji. The treaty, which was signed on 21 July, and which took its name from this village, recognised Russia's protectorate over Turkey's Christian subjects and prepared the ground for the annexation by Russia of the Crimea, the Kuban river, and the northern shore of the Black Sea, which was opened up to Russian navigation. While returning to Turkish sovereignty the Danubian principalities as well as several strongholds in the Caucasus and all the Greek islands seized during the war, Russia received the fortress-ports of Kerch and Enikale at the entrance to the sea of Azov, as well as Kinburn, which gave access to the estuary of the Dnieper and Bug rivers and thence to the Black Sea. When Rumyantsev's son arrived at Peterhof with news of the signed peace treaty, Catherine immediately left the chamber concert she was attending to offer prayers of thanksgiving.

The news of the satisfactory conclusion of the Russo-Turkish War did not come a moment too soon, as only two days previously the Empress had been informed of the latest disastrous turn the Pugachev revolt had taken. The rebels had managed to storm and sack the town of Kazan on 12 July. Nikita Panin wrote to his brother Peter to describe the council meeting which took place on receipt of the news; his account provides a vivid first-hand description of what an imperial council meeting could be like when the Empress was under stress and her councillors were all jockeying for position, as well as of Panin's own wheeler-dealing behind the scenes. Grigory Orlov had not, as yet, left the Court, and his resentment at the position attained by Potemkin is apparent:

> This morning we received the news about the destruction of the town of Kazan and that the governor and all his detachments have been locked up in the fortress there. Here in the meeting of our council we saw the Sovereign extremely affected, and she expressed

her intention of leaving this capital and going herself to save Moscow and the interior of the Empire, demanding and insisting very heatedly that each of us give her his opinion about this. We were all very silent ... Then Her Majesty, with perceptible annoyance, argued how useful her presence everywhere would be and she was particularly supported, against me, by our new favourite. The old one listened to everything with scornful indifference, said nothing, and excused himself on the grounds that he wasn't feeling very well, had slept badly, and therefore had no ideas. Those confirmed fools Razumovsky and Golitsyn distinguished themselves by a determined silence ... Meanwhile I decided on the following plan of action. After dinner I took the new favourite aside, and remonstrating with him over his audacious suggestions, which neither his age nor experience justified, and repeating what I had already said about the possibility of destruction threatening the Empire, I explained to him that because of my repugnance at this idea I had decided that either I myself must go to fight Pugachev or that I would answer for you, my dear friend, that you in all your decrepitude would take it upon yourself to save the fatherland, even if it were necessary to carry you there on a stretcher − provided the Sovereign wished it, or unless she could find someone better than you, and I said that he should go and tell Her Majesty this. I went to her myself soon afterwards, and repeated the same thing to her.

Though Catherine refused to invest General Peter Panin with all the powers his devoted brother demanded for him (she noted in a letter to Potemkin a week later, 'You will see, my dear, from the items attached herewith, that Sir Count Panin deigns to make his brother a potentate with unlimited power in the best part of the empire'), no one better than he could be found to deal definitively with Pugachev and his cohorts. General Panin duly set off to head the forces already engaged in putting down the revolt. Meanwhile, on 6 August, Pugachev sacked Saratov, where the priests who had gone over to his side administered the oath of allegiance both to him and to his so-called wife. He did not, however, manage to hold on to either Kazan or Saratov for more than a few days, and on 25 August he suffered his final defeat south of Tsaritsyn. Three weeks later his former supporters among the Cossacks handed him over to the tsarist forces at Yaitsk.

In October Catherine provided Voltaire (and thus the rest of Europe) with an account of the capture and initial questioning of

Pugachev who, having acknowledged final defeat, had dropped all pretence and now seemed inclined to throw himself on the Empress's mercy. Catherine allowed herself a grudging admiration for this disturber of her peace:

I will willingly, sir, satisfy your curiosity about Pugachev: this will be all the easier for me as a month ago he was captured or, to put it more accurately, he was bound and gagged by his own people, in the inhabited plain between the Volga and the Yaik, where he had been driven by the troops sent against him from every direction. His companions, deprived of food and of the means to take in fresh supplies as well as worn out by the cruel acts he was committing, and hoping to obtain their pardon, delivered him to the commandant of the fortress of Yaik, who in turn sent him to General Count Panin in Simbirsk. He is now on his way to Moscow. Brought before Count Panin, he naively admitted in his first interrogation that he was a Don Cossack, named his birthplace, said that he was married to the daughter of a Don Cossack, and that he had three children; that during these troubles he had married another woman, that his brothers and nephews were serving in the first army, that he himself had served in the first two campaigns against the Porte, etc.

As General Panin has many Don Cossacks with him, and the troops of this nation have never risen to the bait of this brigand, all this was soon verified by Pugachev's compatriots. He does not know how to read or write, but he is an extremely brave and determined man. So far there is not the slightest indication that he was the instrument of a foreign power, or that he was inspired by anyone else. It is to be supposed that Monsieur Pugachev is a master brigand, and no valet of any soul who lives.

I think that there has hardly been anyone so destructive of the human race since Tamerlain. In the first place he hanged, without mercy or any form of trial, all the members of the nobility, men, women and children, all the officers, all the soldiers that he could catch; no place he visited was spared: he pillaged and ransacked the very people who, in order to avoid his cruelties, sought to curry his favour by welcoming him: no one was safe in his presence from pillage, violence and murder.

But what demonstrates the extent of the man's delusion is that he dares to have hope. He imagines that I might accord him grace on account of his courage, and that he can assign his past crimes to oblivion through his service in the future. If it were me alone that he had offended, he might be right and I could pardon him; but this is a matter which concerns the Empire, and it has laws.

Pugachev arrived in Moscow on 4 November, transported in a specially constructed iron cage, like a dangerous wild animal. The final report on the rebellion was compiled a month later, those charged with leading the investigation having reached the conclusion that there were no external forces at work and that the causes of the revolt were principally to be found in the natural rebelliousness of the Yaik Cossacks. Wishing to dissociate herself from any act which could be interpreted as revenge, and desirous of demonstrating that Russia had surmounted her trials through the forces of law and order, the Empress empowered the Senate to pass sentence on Pugachev, dispatching Procurator-General Vyazemsky to Moscow to supervise the trial, which was held secretly in the Kremlin on 30 and 31 December. Pugachev confessed everything on his knees. Catherine had also provided Vyazemsky with secret instructions that any executions, which were to be few in number, were not to include torture. She was supported in this humane resolve by Grigory Potemkin. Both were concerned to diminish any stain on the image of an enlightened Russia which they felt the whole rebellion already represented. Officially, Pugachev was sentenced to be quartered before he was beheaded (Catherine reported to Voltaire that the criminal was so petrified that he was having to be carefully prepared for his sentence to prevent him dying prematurely of fright). But on the day of his execution in front of a huge crowd on Bolotnaya Square near the centre of Moscow, the executioner appeared to make a mistake by cutting off Pugachev's head before severing his limbs. That this 'mistake' was made on Catherine's orders was not known at the time, though Catherine herself implied as much in a letter to Madame Bielke.

Steps were then taken to try to erase the memory of Pugachev altogether, the Yaik Cossacks being renamed the Ural Cossacks, and the Yaik river and the town of Yaitsk being renamed respectively the Ural and Uralsk. Pugachev's native village on the Don was ordered to be razed, rebuilt on the other side of the river and renamed Potemkinskaya, and Pugachev's brother Dementy, who had taken no part in the revolt, was forbidden to continue using the family name. Pugachev's two wives and three children were incarcerated in the fort of Kexholm in Russian Finland, where they were given freedom of movement within the walls. A few of the leading rebels were executed alongside Pugachev, but

Catherine's main concern now was pacification, and on 19 March a manifesto was promulgated which proclaimed an amnesty for all offences committed during the revolt.

The stress of these months took their toll on Catherine, and she suffered her usual symptoms of headaches, digestive problems and other minor ailments. As Potemkin was also prone to bouts of minor illness – and hypochondria – some of the notes which passed between them were more like medical bulletins than love-letters. At some point during the year Catherine had a bout of sleep-walking, during which she wandered round the palace and entered various rooms, before waking herself up by going outside. For a few nights afterwards her doors were locked at night, to prevent her from wandering off and meeting with some accident. Her main regret about this was that Potemkin would not be able to get in if he tried to come and visit her.

The Grand Duchess Natalya was also feeling unwell. But this, according to her mother-in-law, was her own fault. The honeymoon period was clearly over between the Empress and her erstwhile 'golden girl'. 'Everything is done to excess with that lady,' Catherine told Grimm on 21 December:

If she goes for a walk, it's for twenty versts; if she dances, it's twenty quadrilles and as many minuets, without counting the allemands; in order to avoid the apartments being overheated, she has no fire lit in them at all; if other people rub ice over their faces, she turns her whole body into a face: in short the middle way is unknown here. Fearful of wicked people, she distrusts the entire world and listens to neither good nor bad advice; in a word, so far there is neither grace, nor prudence, nor wisdom in any of this, and God knows what will become of her, for she listens to no one and has a very stubborn head on her shoulders. Just think that after more than a year and a half she still doesn't speak a word of the language; she says she wants to be taught it, but doesn't apply herself to it for a moment during the day; everything is in a constant spin; she cannot bear this or that; she is indebted to the tune of more than twice the amount she has, and she already has more than practically anybody else in Europe.

During the summer of 1774 Paul had drafted a memorandum on current politics which he hoped would serve as a contribution to the formation of policy. Although his work showed thought and intelligent reading, the fact that it was critical of certain of Catherine's existing policies merely demonstrated his own political ineptitude in presenting it in the first place. The request he made to join her Council (which continued in existence despite the ending of the war) met with a severe rebuff in which his mother accused him of sulking. A sentence which the Empress seems to have left out of the fair copy of the letter she sent him expresses her attitude succinctly: 'I do not judge it appropriate to have you enter the Council. You must be patient until I decide otherwise.'

Towards the end of the year preparations were put underway for the Court to repair to Moscow, where it had been decided that the celebrations over the ending of the war with Turkey would be held in the summer of 1775. Catherine was very aware of the propaganda value of showing herself to her people in the ancient capital at this juncture, to demonstrate the solidity of her rule, after the disturbances associated with both Pugachev and the Moscow plague riots of a few years previously. She also relied on Madame Bielke (and the interceptors of mail) to disseminate information about improved conditions in the country, as she described to her friend aspects of her journey of 56 hours (not counting stops in Novgorod and Tver). The dwellers along the route had clearly been well prepared for the passage of their Empress:

On the way I saw one town newly built and two others with their foundations laid, and I was astonished to see how, despite the war, the plague and a number of fires, this road and its inhabitants have prospered in the eight years since I last travelled this way. Before one used to see little barefoot children in chemises running in the snow in these villages; now there isn't a single one who doesn't have a suit of clothes, a pelisse and boots. The dwellings, although still made of wood, are larger, and most of the houses now have two storeys. In several places I was pleased to see schools, and there are two seminaries where a thousand sons of the clergy are being taught, in addition to the language of the country, Greek, Latin, German and French. I am in truth pleased with all this; another ten years like the last ten and I give you warning that all this will be visible to anyone who has not sworn to be blind.

Catherine made her public entry into Moscow on 25 January 1775, accompanied by the Grand Duke and Duchess and preceded by the officials and ladies of the Court. The procession passed under two triumphal arches decorated with emblematical representations of the major victories of the war, and Catherine went first to make her devotions in the Kremlin's Cathedral of the Assumption and thence to the newly constructed Prechistensky Palace, where she received the first three classes of the nobility and the foreign ministers. This new palace had in fact been constructed out of several existing houses and was from the start an inconvenient building in which to live, as Catherine described in a letter to Grimm:

> It is like drinking the sea to orient oneself in this labyrinth; I was here for two hours before I could work out the way from my study without mistaking the door; it is a triumph of exits. I have never seen so many doors in my life; I have already condemned half a dozen of them, and I still have twice as many as I need; but, to be fair, you should know that in the construction of a great hall, two immense galleries and half a dozen state rooms, I have managed to join together three very large stone houses. I am living in one which the brother of the Vice Chancellor has lent me; my son is in another which I have bought, and a third, which I have also purchased, is destined for those who absolutely need to live at Court. The rest of my people are camped in ten or twelve houses which I have rented; so, all that makes a labyrinth, of which I despair of giving you a true idea.

Much of Catherine's time in 1775 was taken up with what she referred to as a new attack of 'legislomania'. The resulting statute, which would eventually be issued in November and was known as the Guberniya Reform, went through at least six drafts. Catherine's personal input, which was considerable, focused particularly on the explanatory preface and the sections dealing with the duties of local officials, the functions of the bureaus of public welfare to be established for the first time, and the reorganisation of the judicial system.

Grigory Orlov had now left on his travels, going by way of Vienna to Italy and expecting to be away for two years, as Catherine reported to Madame Bielke on Easter Day, 12 April. Despite all that had passed between them, Catherine was still able to expound her former favourite's attractions: 'If you ever see him, you will see without doubt the most handsome man you have seen in your life; nature has done everything for him as regards body, heart and spirit, and all that he is he owes to this nature, for his education was completely neglected; he is the spoilt child of nature and having received everything as a gift, he has become lazy, but despite this flaw he knows a prodigious amount.' Catherine also indicates how strenuous Orthodox Easter observances can be, concluding her letter: 'Farewell, madame, that is enough for Easter Day, when we stand up for four and a half hours; that is, from two o'clock in the morning until six. It is now just after mid-day; but I am not in the least bit tired.'

During the spring and summer of 1775 another potential pretender to the Russian throne emerged. In early May the Earl of Suffolk wrote from London to Sir Robert Gunning to warn him of the imminent arrival in Russia of a strange young woman:

In the month of January last Sir William Hamilton gave an account of the arrival of a lady at Naples from Ragusa, whose story had so much the air of romance that I did not think it necessary to take any notice of it in my letters to you, but as she appears to have become an object of the attention of the court of Russia, and as she is probably, by this time, arrived in the Empress's dominions, I would not omit to give you the following particulars; and I am persuaded you will learn what may be her real history. On her arrival at Naples she had nine persons in her suite, some of whom wore the Polish dress, and she soon afterwards called at Sir William Hamilton's door, to desire he would procure her a pass, from the minister, to go to Rome, stiling herself Countess of Bamberg.

At first Sir William declined to assist the self-styled Countess, but she became so insistent and distressed that he did eventually concede to her request and obtained a pass for her, whereupon she wrote to him to thank him, this time calling herself 'Princess Elizabeth' and claiming to be the daughter of the late Empress Elizabeth and Count Razumovsky. Subsequently she sent Sir William a longer letter which he obligingly passed on to Count Alexei Orlov, who was then with part of the Russian fleet at Pisa. Alexei in turn sent the letter to Nikita Panin, to whom 'Elizabeth' had written independently as well. He also suggested that he might inveigle the pretender on board a Russian ship and dispatch her to Petersburg. After securing Catherine's agreement, Alexei invited 'Elizabeth' to inspect the fleet in Livorno. Once she and her companions were safely on board Admiral Greig's ship, Orlov disappeared, 'Elizabeth' was placed under arrest and after two days, during which all her belongings were seized and placed on board, the ship set sail for Kronstadt. Catherine instructed Field Marshal Prince Alexander Golitsyn, the Governor-General of Petersburg, to take charge of the investigation when she arrived and to conduct her to the Peter and Paul Fortress. Together with her suite of two Poles, five menservants and one female servant, 'Elizabeth' was duly delivered to the Fortress on 26 May at two o'clock in the morning.

In Prince Golitsyn's first report to the Empress, he described the captive as being of medium height, rather thin and stately, with black hair and brown eyes with a slight squint, and a longish hooked nose which made her look rather Italian. She could speak French and German fluently, knew English and Italian and some Arabic, but spoke no Russian at all. She was not well, sometimes coughing blood. She was most indignant and astonished at finding herself in prison. Golitsyn had stressed the importance to her of telling the truth about herself, but admitted that the version she had given him of her life thus far resembled a fairy story.

In her deposition, 'Elizabeth' claimed she was 23 years old, that she had been born in Kiel in Holstein (Peter III's birthplace), but that she did not know who her parents were. She lived in Holstein until she was nine years old but was then sent with her nurse, Katerina, to Russia, ostensibly to find her parents in Moscow. Instead she was taken to the border with Persia, where 'they left her with her nurse in a house, but in which province and town, she does not know'. Here she stayed for 15 months, a neighbouring old woman telling her that she was being held there by the decree of the Emperor Peter III. Her resourceful nurse learnt the local language and persuaded some peasants to help them escape, and they eventually ended up in Baghdad. Here they were kept initially by a rich Persian called Gamet at whose house they met an even richer man called Prince Gali, who took them to Ispahan. It was Gali who kept telling her that she was the daughter of 'the late Sovereign Empress Elizabeth Petrovna, that this was confirmed not only by those living in his house, but by people coming to see him, who reasoned about her father differently: some called him Razumovsky, but others said that he was somebody else – only they could not remember the name of this latter'.

'Elizabeth' stayed with Prince Gali in Ispahan until 1769. Then the Prince was forced to flee, and proposed that she should accompany him to Europe, to which she agreed provided he did not take her to Russia, where she feared further imprisonment. Gali assured her she would be safe if she travelled through Russia with him dressed in men's clothes, which they did. And so the story went on and on and on, involving stops in Petersburg, Riga, Königsberg, Berlin and even London, until the girl fetched up back in Schleswig-Holstein, where she claimed the Count of Limburg had asked her to marry him. Apparently this proposal gave her a renewed urge to discover her true parentage, so off she set again, this time to Venice, where she encountered the Polish dissident Prince Radziwill, who convinced her she ought to travel to Constantinople, but she never made it further than Ragusa (present-day Dubrovnik). While in Ragusa she claimed to have received anonymous packets by courier, in which she was encouraged to go to Turkey, as it lay in her hands to end the Russo-Turkish War. Perhaps fortunately for everybody it ended in the meantime without her intervention. It was around this time that she enlisted Sir William Hamilton's help and ended up being tricked by Count Alexei Orlov and delivered into captivity.

Though most of this story clearly represented the delusions of a disordered yet intelligent mind, the allusions to Holstein, Poland and Turkey could not but alert Catherine, in the wake of both internal and external strife, to the possibility at the very least of hostile elements using this young woman to further their own ends. So she was determined that the investigation should be thorough. In addition to her official deposition, 'Elizabeth' wrote letters – in idiosyncratic, poorly spelt and ungrammatical French – both to Prince Golitsyn and to Catherine herself, advising the Empress that she was in a position to procure 'great advantages for your Empire'. These letters roused Catherine's ire to an extreme degree, particularly as the young woman had had the temerity to sign herself merely 'Elizabeth' – and the only person who could legitimately sign letters with Christian name only was the Empress Catherine herself. The latter wrote in anger to Prince Golitsyn:

> Send to say to the woman in question that if she wants to lighten her fate, then she should stop playing the comedy which she is carrying on in her last letters to you, even extending her impertinence so far as to sign herself Elizabeth; order to be added to this that no one has the slightest doubt that she is an adventuress, and that therefore you advise her to stop it and frankly confess who put her up to this role, and where she was born, and whether this trickery was devised a long time ago. Go to see her and tell

her very seriously that she must come to her senses. What an inveterate scoundrel she is! The impertinence of her letter to Me surpasses all expectation, and leads me to think that she is not in her right mind.

Later that month information came via British diplomatic channels that the young woman was actually an innkeeper's daughter from Prague. When this was put to her she denied it vehemently, saying that 'she had never during her whole life been in Prague; and if she knew who had abused her by suggesting this parentage, she would scratch his eyes out'.

On 10 July lavish peace celebrations began in Moscow. Catherine went in procession to the Cathedral of the Assumption for the opening ceremony, a solemn liturgy and Te Deum, flanked by Field Marshal Rumyantsev and Potemkin, and accompanied by the Grand Duke and Duchess and all the officers and ladies of the Court. The Empress wore a small crown and the imperial mantle, a purple canopy being held over her head by 12 generals. Her train was carried by guardsmen in red and gold uniforms with silver helmets and ostrich plumes. After divine service the procession returned to the Faceted Palace where Procurator-General Vyazemsky delivered a speech in praise of the Empress, the reply on behalf of the sovereign being read by the Vice-Chancellor. Then the keeper of the privy purse read out the list of honours and awards with which the Empress was pleased to mark the occasion. These included land, money, a silver service for 40 people, a collection of pictures, a jewel-encrusted hat, a diamond star and shoulder knot for Field Marshal Rumyantsev, along with the honorific addition of 'Zadunaisky' ('beyond the Danube') to his surname. Alexei Orlov received the similar addition of 'Chesmensky' in recognition of his victory at Chesme, as well as 60,000 roubles and a diamond-studded sword. Potemkin became a Count and received a miniature portrait of the Empress encrusted with diamonds to wear, an honour which Grigory Orlov had previously been the only man to hold. There were numerous other awards for military prowess, including the promotion of Rear-Admiral Greig to the rank of Vice-Admiral and the post of Commandant of Kronstadt. The 21-year-old Alexandra Engelhardt, one of Potemkin's nieces who was to become a close friend of Catherine's, was appointed maid of honour to the Empress, and Catherine also appointed Colonel Peter Zavadovsky, a handsome and well-educated 37-year-old Ukrainian who had been recommended to her by Field Marshal Rumyantsev, to her personal cabinet as a secretary to receive petitions, and Alexander Bezborodko, also recommended by Rumyantsev, as her secretary for literary activity.

After this glorious opening the remainder of the peace celebrations had to be postponed for 10 days, as Catherine fell ill on 11 July with stomach ache, followed by a fever and acute diarrhoea from which she only recovered after being bled. A story circulated at the time, particularly around the Courts of Europe, that this bout of sickness was actually a pregnancy, the result of which was a daughter by Potemkin, but there is no evidence to support this theory. Catherine herself explained later to Grimm that she thought that what had made her ill was that in a distracted mood she had eaten 20 peaches one hot afternoon, and that she had not taken any notice of the warning signs of insomnia and pain when she went to bed.

The resumed peace celebrations included a cockaigne, or feast for the common people, at which they were provided with roast oxen and fountains flowing with wine, set out in the Khodynskoye Field on the north-west edge of the city, which had been transformed into a magical landscape representing the scenes of the recent Russian victories and territorial acquisitions. One road represented the Don and another the Dnieper, the sea of Azov became a banqueting hall, Kinburn a theatre, Kerch and Enikale ballrooms. The 'river banks' were adorned with country scenes, windmills, trees and illuminated houses, and the magnificent firework display, featuring hundreds of Catherine wheels, stars, suns and fountains of fire, was set off 'beyond the Danube'. This whole idea was conceived by Catherine and Potemkin themselves and entrusted to Vasily Bazhenov for implementation, Catherine vastly preferring it to 'all those damn temples of divinities' which had been in her architects' original plans.

On 26 August, the Grand Duchess's name-day was celebrated with a performance of the French comic opera *Annette et Lubin* in the woods at the newly acquired imperial estate of Tsaritsyno, near Kolomenskoye, south of Moscow – 'to the great astonishment of the peasants of the surrounding area,' wrote Catherine to Grimm, 'who had thus far lived in complete ignorance that there was such a thing as comic opera in the world'. In the same letter Catherine told Grimm that the Grand Duchess was three months pregnant, and that she seemed well.

In late October Governor-General Golitsyn informed the Empress that the woman prisoner in the Fortress, who persisted in refusing to change her story, was now in the advanced stages of consumption and was not expected to live much longer. She died on 24 December; her body was buried hastily in the grounds of the Fortress and her guards sworn to perpetual secrecy. The strange name of Princess Tarakanova (literally, Princess of the Cockroaches) was awarded to her after her death, in one of the many tales that circulated about her for decades afterwards.

The Guberniya Reform, representing the first attempt to penetrate the Russian state to the local level, was issued on 7 November 1775. In addition to reorganising provincial Russia, in terms of how the Empire was divided up into provinces and managed by governors-general all personally appointed by the Empress, the reform included an attempt to modernise the Russian penal system by establishing prisons where people were to be held while awaiting trial or deportation, as well as houses of correction for the detention of those who had committed minor crimes, and workhouses for the poor. Education was also an important plank of the reform, the statute charging boards of public welfare in each province to establish schools in the towns, to be financed out of the interest on a grant of 150,000 roubles which was awarded to each board. The reform, many aspects of which arose out of the concerns raised by deputies to the Legislative Commission, was to a large extent Catherine's own work; she had been assisted particularly by her new secretary Peter Zavadovsky (who was duly rewarded with the cross of St George, fourth class, on 26 November) and by Potemkin. The implementation of the reforms was to be introduced gradually, with the first trial of the reorganisation being undertaken in Tver, where Governor-General Sievers was authorised to oversee the foundation of the Tver *guberniya* in January 1776.

The Court returned from Moscow to St Petersburg on 26 December. Since the end of July Peter Zavadovsky had been dining at Catherine's table, and accompanying her as a member of her suite on short trips she made out of Moscow into the surrounding countryside. Once back in Petersburg he frequently made a third with Catherine and Potemkin, working alongside them and dining with them – either as a threesome or in a small group. On 1 January Potemkin was entrusted with the command of the Petersburg troop division, and his mother was made a lady-in-waiting. The following day Zavadovsky was made adjutant-general to the Empress.

# 13

# New Lovers and a New Daughter-in-Law (1776–77)

*All will pass, except my passion for you.*
Catherine II to Peter Zavadovsky

The introduction of Peter Zavadovsky into the relationship between Catherine and Potemkin was an attempt to resolve the conflicts and stresses inherent in that relationship without destroying it altogether. Zavadovsky acted as an extra ingredient, having a diluting effect on their passionate intensity, enabling a little space to be created between them in which it might be possible to work out a new *modus operandi* acceptable to both parties. The presence of this affable and intelligent Ukrainian also provided Catherine with some relief from Potemkin's unpredictable mood swings and demands. Perhaps unconsciously at first, Catherine was looking for a way out from the all-consuming nature of her love – so inconvenient for the efficient running of her Empire – while continuing to benefit from the positive, sustaining effects of her relationship with Potemkin. Meanwhile Potemkin was also desperate to find some solution which would guarantee his position as the most important man in the Empress's life – and in her Empire – while according sufficient autonomy for him not to feel that he was merely the male equivalent of a *maîtresse en titre*, liable to lose his power when no longer required in the imperial bed.

They both needed to find a way of preserving all that was valuable in their relationship, without grinding it and one another down with continual wrangling and arguments followed by tearful reconciliations. If Catherine constantly needed a man to love and be loved by, she needed even more a relationship with a degree of predictability that gave her a sense of balance and stability, and that did not interfere with her work. She wanted a sunny rather than a tempestuous love, and she wanted to be able to make her lover happy. Reading her letters as responses to comments made by Potemkin, it seems that when he was feeling angry and insecure he would accuse her of hypocrisy and declare that her tears (of which she shed many during this period) were manipulative and of no account. He also had a tendency to blame her for the shortcomings of her other friends and the people she employed, and was in the habit of stomping off angrily and slamming doors behind him. He was given to sulking, a characteristic which Catherine, herself very ready to seek reconciliation in her personal relationships, always found hard to tolerate. They were also both making themselves ill.

If Catherine and Potemkin really were husband and wife, albeit secretly, then Potemkin's overwhelming sense of insecurity is hard to understand. Certainly Catherine found it so, and made her clearest reference to their married state in a letter of this period, in which she writes about their being attached to one another by the 'bonds of Holy Matrimony'. That she eventually managed to accommodate Potemkin, giving him almost enough power to satisfy him while never compromising her own position as Empress, and working through to a personal relationship that sustained them both for the rest of Potemkin's life, represents one of Catherine's most extraordinary achievements.

On 21 March Potemkin was granted permission to use the title of Prince of the Holy Roman Empire, an honour which had been requested for him by the Empress via her ambassador in Vienna. She also presented him with a gift of 16,000 peasants, and Denmark sent him the Order of the White Elephant. This latter award seems to have made the third member of the *ménage à trois* (for by now Catherine was emotionally and sexually involved with Zavadovsky, while still trying to work out her relationship with Potemkin) jealous, or at least cross that he had not been told about it, for Catherine remarked in an undated letter to him: 'My darling, you order me to justify myself. About the elephant and about dinner I learned no earlier than ten o'clock, and wanted to tell you about it at the meeting with you.' The other Prince of the Holy Roman Empire, Grigory Orlov (though from now on Potemkin was often referred to as 'the Prince', as though there could only be one), had been back in St Petersburg since early February. The Empress received him very graciously, according to the British chargé d'affaires Richard Oakes, but it was thought that he would soon ask for retirement from all his posts, which looked likely to be given to Potemkin. Alexei Orlov, who had already resigned from service – to Catherine's distress – arrived in the capital a few weeks after his brother, by which time the latter had been taken ill with, as Richard Oakes put it, 'a stroke of the palsy' or partial temporary paralysis; he was also overweight. A rumour circulated that Potemkin had poisoned him, the rumour gaining currency partly because Catherine went to visit Orlov twice during his illness, which gave rise to 'a very warm altercation' between her and Potemkin. What is more likely than poisoning, however, is that Prince Orlov was suffering symptoms of the tertiary stage of syphilis, a result of his fabled sexual adventuring.

On Saturday 2 April Prince Henry of Prussia arrived in Petersburg, on what turned out to be a most fortuitous visit. The following day he invested Prince Potemkin with the order of the Black Eagle, had an interview with the Empress in her private apartments after she had attended the liturgy, and then dined with her.

A week after Prince Henry's arrival, in the early hours of 10 April, Grand Duchess Natalya went into labour. Catherine wrote to Potemkin later in the day to tell him that she had been with her daughter-in-law at four o'clock in the morning, and that when the pains had abated a little she had gone to drink some coffee. By the time she returned Natalya was again in torment, but then fell into a deep sleep, snoring. Catherine left again at about 10 o'clock to attend to her toilet, believing that the baby was now on its way, and ordering that she should be summoned if matters took a turn for the worse. She also told Potemkin that she had backache herself, attributing it to anxiety. She returned to the Grand Duchess's room at noon.

Catherine provided a more detailed description of Natalya's labour in a letter to Grimm:

On 10th April at four o'clock in the morning my son came to get me, because his wife was feeling labour pains. I leapt out of bed and ran there; I found her in great pain, but without there being anything extraordinary about it; time and patience should pull her through. A woman and an able surgeon were helping her. This state continued until night-time; there were intervals of tranquillity, even of sleep; her strength did not diminish at all. Monday passed in waiting and in a similar and very worrying state; besides her doctor, who stayed in the antechamber, the Grand Duke's doctor and another obstetrician, the most able doctors we had were also summoned to give advice. They produced no new expedients or relief; on Tuesday they asked for my doctor and a former able obstetrician in order to renew their consultation. The latter having arrived, they decided that they needed to save the mother, as the child was probably dead; instruments★ were used; a combination of unfortunate circumstances, occasioned by the structure and by various accidents, rendered all human science useless throughout Wednesday; on Thursday the Grand Duchess received the sacraments. Prince Henry suggested his doctor be consulted; he was admitted, but he agreed with his colleagues; on Friday the princess gave up the ghost at five o'clock in the evening.

For the last two days of Natalya's life, Paul was 'in inexpressible distraction', Prince Henry, at Catherine's suggestion, staying with him for most of that time. None of the physicians and surgeons consulted seems to have thought of attempting a Caesarean section, though the procedure was hardly unknown in the eighteenth century. Although it frequently resulted in the death of the mother, the child was sometimes saved. But in this case they waited too long, and the child died before any real medical intervention was attempted – and even then they did not manage to extract the child. By the fourth day infection, followed by gangrene, had set in, as was inevitable, the dead baby infecting the mother, and Natalya knew she was dying. Catherine told Grimm:

> You cannot imagine what she had to suffer, and we with her; my soul was torn apart by it; I did not have a moment's rest for the whole five days, and I did not leave the princess either day or night until her eyes were closed. She said to me: 'You make an excellent nurse.' Imagine my situation: needing to console one, to strengthen the other, while having no more strength of body or soul myself, and being obliged to encourage, take decisions and think of everything which needed to be remembered. I admit that never in my life have I been in a more difficult, horrible and distressing situation: I forgot to drink, eat or sleep, and I don't know how my

---

★ Obstetrical forceps and probably crotchets, sharpened hooks used to dismember and remove a dead child.

strength kept up. I began to think that if this adventure does not upset my nervous system, then nothing will.

Immediately after the Grand Duchess's death, the whole Court, including Prince Henry who was continuing his task of saving the Grand Duke from despair, set out for Tsarskoye Selo. On that same day Catherine drew up a plan of action:

1. First thing tomorrow I will ask Prince Henry to send a courier and write to the Princess of Würtemberg to persuade her to come to Berlin with the two princesses her daughters as soon as possible . . .

2. In a few days from now His Imperial Highness [i.e. Grand Duke Paul] will say out loud that he would like to go to Riga or Reval for rest and recuperation; a few days after that he will say he has permission to go to Riga and that he would like to see the works on the Dvina, and he will say no more than that. This journey will dovetail with the time the Princess of Würtemberg arrives in Berlin.

3. His Imperial Highness and His Royal Highness [i.e. Prince Henry] will leave here together; they will go to Riga, and from there straight to Berlin to see the princesses.

4. His Imperial Highness will write to let me know his choice, a definite yes or no, and then he will return. In the case of a yes, I will appoint Prince Henry the bearer of my word and, the consent obtained, I will be written to so that I can send the Field Marshal's wife [i.e. Countess Rumyantseva] and all her entourage to Memel [now Klaipėda in Lithuania] where the princesses will come and place the bride-to-be into the hands of the people nominated to receive her.

5. The future duchess will embrace the Greek religion in Petersburg, where the betrothal and marriage will also take place.

6. The Princesses her mother and sister will return from Memel to Berlin.

7. Silence until all this is underway.

On the day following her death, an autopsy was performed on the late Grand Duchess in the presence of 13 physicians and surgeons. From this it appeared that the young woman could never have given birth to a living child by the conventional route, a deformation of her skeleton making it impossible for her to provide a wide enough birth canal. In addition, a curvature of the spine had possibly been worsened in childhood by a 'charlatan', as Catherine wrote to Madame Bielke, having been employed to straighten her up 'with blows of his fists and knees'. This also explained why the Grand Duchess had been unable to bow (Catherine had earlier put this down to pride). She concluded her account to Madame Bielke: 'I was very upset by the loss of this princess, and did everything possible that she should be saved; I did not leave her for five days and five nights, but in the end, as it was demonstrated that she could never have a child or rather that she could never bring one into the world, it is better not to think about it any more.'

Catherine's determination 'not to think about it any more' and to get to work on the very day of Natalya Alexeyevna's death with arranging her replacement inevitably appears callous – certainly from the perspective of our more sentimental age, with its belief in 'closure' and 'coming to terms' with tragic events – but it is also indicative of Catherine's whole approach to dealing with grief, both her own and that of those close to her. In her own case, her usual prescription for getting over an old love was to acquire a new one as fast as possible – she rarely gave herself much time for solitary reflection or post-mortems – and she seems to have assumed that her son would react in the same way. Her sense of urgency was increased by the awareness that her original first choice for Paul's consort – Princess Sophia Dorothea of Würtemberg – was now old enough for him and still available, but that she would not be for very much longer. She was in fact already promised to, of all people, the deceased Grand Duchess's elder brother Ludwig, the Hereditary Prince of Hesse-Darmstadt, who had attended Paul and Natalya's wedding. But Catherine was confident that, with pressure applied by Prince Henry and his brother the King of Prussia, this little difficulty could be overcome. There was also the purely practical consideration of providing heirs to the Russian throne; Paul needed a healthy wife suitable for child-bearing, and the sooner he had one the better. From what she wrote to Grimm, it is clear that Catherine did feel genuine pain at the suffering Natalya had had to endure, but that she also never forgot her own sense of responsibility to make the best of the situation and to prevent the total collapse of her son:

There were moments when it seemed to me that I could feel the tearing of the womb as I watched all the suffering, and that with each scream I felt the pains myself. On the Friday I turned into stone, and I still can't feel anything now; there are some hours when I feel weak and others when I am strong; I have a sort of intermittent fever, but it is more mental than physical. No one knows anything about that, at least they haven't seen or felt it. Just think that I, who am a weeper by profession, saw her die without shedding a tear; I said to myself: 'If you cry, the others will sob; if you sob, the others will faint, and then everyone will lose both their head and their bearings.'

All that was now required was for Paul to fall in with her plans. He was assisted in getting over Natalya by being informed – by his mother – of an alleged intrigue she had been carrying on with his friend and favourite chamberlain Count Andrei Razumovsky (who was duly banished from Court). Several weeks later Catherine offered an explanation to Grimm (in which she severely mixes her metaphors) as to why she had acted so swiftly to replace one Grand Duchess with another and how she had gone about kindling her son's interest in a new bride:

Having seen the ship capsize on one side, I lost no time: I threw him over the other side, and straightaway put my irons in the fire to repair the loss, and through that I succeeded in dissipating the profound grief which was overcoming us. I began by suggesting journeys, comings and goings, and then I said: the dead being dead, we must think of the living; having believed oneself happy and then having lost that belief, is it necessary to think one will never be so again? Let's see, let's look for another, but who? Oh, I've got one up my sleeve. – What, already? – Yes, yes, and she's a jewel. So now did he not become curious? – Who is she? What is she like? – brunette, blonde, small, tall? – Gentle, pretty, charming, a jewel, a real jewel, the sort to make one rejoice: that made him smile; one thing leads to another, a third is summoned, a certain nimble traveller whom those he leaves behind miss to the point of cursing; recently arrived precisely to console and distract; here he is established as the go-between, the negotiator; a courier despatched, a courier returned, a journey arranged, an interview organised; all with unprecedented speed, and now heavy hearts begin to be gladdened; though still sad, they are necessarily occupied with preparations for a journey which is indispensable for health and distraction.

Catherine related that Paul had then asked for a portrait of the girl. One arrived forthwith by courier, but he dared not look at it in case it was disappointing. It stayed face down on a table near Catherine's writing desk for a week until Paul, receiving an assurance from his mother that she thought the girl looked pretty, stole a look at it and, immediately pocketing it, began to speed up his preparations for departure.

Potemkin does not seem to have provided much support, judging from a note Catherine sent him around this time: 'If my peace is dear to you, do me a favour and stop grumbling.' Prince Henry, on the other hand, had done all that was asked of him. He was constantly on hand to comfort Paul and wrote as requested to Sophia Dorothea's mother, who was his niece and who could be expected both to rejoice at this splendid opportunity for her daughter and to do what her uncles required of her. Henry assured the Princess that Sophia Dorothea 'could not marry a more amiable and honest man than the Grand Duke and that she could not find a more tender mother-in-law, or one more worthy of respect, than the Empress'. Even at this very early stage – the day after his wife's death – Grand Duke Paul knew what was being planned and raised no objections.

The funeral of Grand Duchess Natalya took place on 26 April 1776, five days after Catherine's forty-seventh birthday, at the Alexander Nevsky Monastery. There she had lain in state, clothed in white satin, and was buried along with her dead child. Paul did not attend, though Catherine did. An official mourning period of three months was announced.

At the end of the month Prince Henry wrote to his brother Ferdinand to enlist his aid in bringing about the wedding of Princess Sophia Dorothea and Grand Duke Paul:

I ask you, my dear Ferdinand, to do everything possible to get the Prince and Princess of Würtemberg to ask the Prince of Darmstadt to desist. If he has the slightest shred of honesty, he will not at all want to disturb the happiness of two states whose union could be so useful to the peace of the whole of Europe and, if he has any soul, he will not want to stand in the way of the happiness of a family which, through the generous sentiments of the Empress and the Grand Duke, will find itself in a flourishing condition compared with that in which it currently is.

The Hereditary Prince Ludwig of Hesse-Darmstadt (who was at that time in Potsdam at the Court of Frederick the Great) had little choice but to release Sophia Dorothea from her betrothal to him. He decided to cut his losses and asked to marry one of her younger sisters instead. The Princess of Würtemberg was thus able to reply to Prince Henry within three weeks, confirming that she and her daughter would shortly be setting off for Berlin. She foresaw no problem with her daughter converting to Orthodoxy, particularly as she had not yet been confirmed as a Lutheran. In any event Prince Henry was of the opinion that all conversion really amounted to was a change of name. Catherine herself was convinced that divine providence had somehow arranged for the girl she had originally preferred to be available at just the right time, as though poor Natalya had been nothing more than a divinely appointed stopgap. She wrote in this vein to Grimm:

> I don't know, since 1767 I always felt particularly inclined towards this young lady; reason which, as you know, misleads instinct, led me to prefer the other, because the first was too young at the time to allow this arrangement; and was it not now, at the moment when I would have lost her for ever, that the most unfortunate event gave me my predominant inclination? So what is all that about? You will reason in your own way; you will attribute it to chance; not at all: that is not enough for me, being a believer: I need something greater than myself.

Despite all attempts at secrecy, by late May James Harris, who was then British ambassador in Berlin, was fully apprised of the Grand Duke's marriage plans, as he reported to Lord Suffolk:

> Several couriers have been received in the course of this last fort-night from Prince Henry, and it was told me in the greatest confidence that the last who arrived at Potzdam, and met the King on the road, brought the Empress's entire consent and approbation of marrying the Grand Duke to the Princess of Würtemberg, at present promised to the Hereditary Prince of Hesse d'Armstadt, and that it is settled, that his Imperial Highness, under pretence of dissipating his grief, is either to return with or immediately to follow Prince Henry to Berlin. That the Princess will meet him there, and that the affair is then to be finally determined; this event is to take place towards the months of July or August, and orders are already given for the Opera singers to hold themselves in readiness for the occasion.

Catherine and Potemkin were still struggling to resolve the tensions in their relationship while, as usual, the courtiers and diplomats looked on, unable to fathom the situation. By early May it was expected that 'the Prince' would soon be asking leave to go and take up his duties as Governor-General of New Russia, and that his request would be granted. The frustration Potemkin's behaviour was causing Catherine is clear from a letter she wrote to him during this month:

I believe that you love me, although very often there is no trace of love in what you say. I believe it because I am scrupulous and fair, I do not judge people by their words when I see that they are at odds with common sense. You write in the past tense, you say 'was, were'. Yet throughout all these days my actions have been aiming for harmony in the present. Who desires your peace and tranquillity if not I? Now I hear that you were happy with how things were in the past, but at the time it didn't seem to be enough for you. But God forgives and I do not reproach you, I do you justice and will say to you what you still haven't heard: that is, that although you have greatly insulted me and endlessly annoyed me, I can never in any way hate you, and I think that since beginning this letter and seeing you in your right mind, everything is more or less back to how it was. If only you would remain in this frame of mind, and if you do, you really won't regret it, dear friend, my soul. You know the sensitivity of my heart.

Potemkin continued intermittently to be very angry with Catherine, while she remained convinced that if only he would calm down, all could be resolved. One thing Potemkin found very hard to accept was that Catherine never forgot that she was the Empress and Potemkin her subject. When she found it necessary, she would exert her imperial authority, as she had clearly done in an incident which provoked his anger and this reply from her:

You scolded me all day yesterday for no reason. Thank God you found one today. I wrote a letter that upset you, but if you could think about the issue for a moment, without getting worked up about it, you would see that this is a letter from an Empress to a subject who has offended her by thoughtlessness, extravagance, and lack of judgment, and that this Empress has punished the subject who has offended her, as she should; but that at the same time she has not forgotten that this subject has often risked his life, as is his duty in her service.

In Catherine's view, it was Potemkin who constantly created discord between them, and she who poured oil on troubled waters. At some point during May or June, Potemkin asked her to dismiss Zavadovsky. But she refused, replying that her glory would greatly suffer if she acceded to such a request, and that the discord between herself and Potemkin would thus become firmly established. She added that it would in any event be unjust to treat Zavadovsky in this way. Catherine was also very annoyed to realise that Potemkin had been discussing their difficulties with other people – something she had not, she said, ever done herself. She concluded by emphasising that she had not banished him from her room, or from anywhere else (despite, the implication runs, having taken Zavadovsky as a lover). Potemkin's sensitivity at this time was such that if Catherine was preoccupied with some matter which caused her not to give him her full attention when he entered the room, he assumed that he was not welcome, or that she was embarrassed by his arrival.

Meanwhile Catherine's dogs continued to provide her with moments of relaxation; she described to Grimm the antics of a five-month-old puppy, one of the numerous family of Sir Tom Anderson: 'She already tears up everything she finds, throws herself on and bites the legs of those who enter my room, chases birds, flies, stags or any other animal four times as big as herself, and makes more noise on her own than her brothers, sisters, aunt, father, mother, grandfather and great-grandfather put together.' In the same letter she told Grimm that she was in excellent health and felt that her habit of bathing in cold water was particularly beneficial: 'you know that with this universal remedy, as long as you're bathing you can't be dead'.

On the evening of 13 June the Grand Duke departed for Riga, en route to Berlin, accompanied by his friend Prince Alexander Kurakin and Field Marshal Rumyantsev-Zadunaisky. Prince Henry set off a day later, so that he could be welcomed to Riga by the Grand Duke; he then left Riga before Paul, in order to be able to greet the latter at Königsberg. Once these diplomatic niceties had been observed, the Duke and the Prince travelled on together.

On 22 June Catherine gave Potemkin the Anichkov Palace, along with a grant of up to 100,000 roubles to have it redecorated to his taste. This palace, located on the Nevsky Prospekt overlooking the

Fontanka river, had originally been commissioned by the Empress Elizabeth from the architect Mikhail Zemtsov in 1741 as a gift for her favourite Count Alexei Razumovsky, from whom Catherine had now bought it for her own favourite (or ex-favourite). After Zemtsov's death it had been completed by Rastrelli. At around the same time Potemkin left the Court to go and inspect the Novgorod province; he was away until late July. Though Catherine told him that on his return she expected him to continue living in his apartments in the imperial palace, this period does mark an official change in the positions of both Potemkin and Zavadovsky. The latter's position as favourite was formally recognised by his promotion on 28 June to the rank of major-general; he also received gifts of 20,000 roubles and 1,000 serfs.

The classically educated, handsome and hard-working Peter Zavadovsky was the same age as Potemkin. There the similarities ended. By contrast with Potemkin, Catherine's new companion was modest and reserved, almost to the point of shyness. He must, at least initially, have provided a relaxing counterbalance to the ebullient and demanding Prince. Though Catherine wrote less flamboyantly to Zavadovsky than to Potemkin, using a smaller collection of loving epithets (she addressed him by the affectionate diminutives of 'Petrusa' and 'Petrusinka', or as 'darling' and 'sweetheart'), her notes to him nevertheless demonstrate a passionate attachment on her part, even if it did not last for very long. And unlike Potemkin, who nearly always addressed Catherine respectfully as 'little Mother' or 'Sovereign Lady' (however disrespectful he might be to her face), Zavadovsky reciprocated by calling her 'Katya' or 'Katyusha'. As was usual with her, at the start of their sexual and emotional relationship Catherine had high hopes for its permanence, writing in one note: 'Petrusa dear, all will pass, except my passion for you.' While Zavadovsky received no significant political responsibilities of his own (there was no need for this from the Empress's point of view, as she still had Potemkin as her principal adviser and collaborator), he continued to work in the Empress's cabinet, fulfilling what would be a common enough role for a modern woman – that of the secretary and personal assistant turned mistress. In addition to carrying on the daily routine of work, he had to switch personas from secretary to lover when required. Catherine, being the Empress, set the timetable – and she was very strict about apportioning her time, so that her work should not suffer – though 'darling Petrusa' was not always available when she wanted him, which distressed her. He also had to endure his private life being under constant scrutiny, and had to get used to being the recipient of a flood of requests to intercede on behalf of others with the Empress. It would take a remarkable man to sustain such a role. Zavadovsky, who already felt unsure of himself when faced with Catherine's erstwhile favourites and other experienced courtiers, soon began to buckle under the pressure, despite Catherine's many assurances that she loved him. He was not a natural courtier, but a born administrator. His French was not strong enough for him to enjoy social conversations conducted in that language, and court life in general held little to interest him. He was very attached to Catherine emotionally, but she had no more sympathy for his attacks of insecurity and jealousy, and attendant sulks, than she had had with any of her previous lovers. He also had to cope with Potemkin's continued presence.

On 1 July Richard Oakes reported on the changes apparent in Potemkin's position, although all was by no means clear:

> Notwithstanding the high degree of favour, in which the Orloffs at present stand with their Sovereign, and the resentment which Count Orloff is supposed to entertain against Prince Potemkin, appearances are still preserved towards the latter, which are looked upon as extraordinary. In his trip to Novgorod he is served in every article from court, and it is affected to be said, that he will return hither in a few weeks; but I cannot help believing his favour to be absolutely at an end, and am assured that he has already removed some furniture, belonging to him, from the apartments which he occupied in the winter palace.

Oakes also predicted that Potemkin might well end his days in a monastery, as the 'best refuge from the despair of an impotent ambition'.

In Berlin there was now much excitement as the time drew near for the arrival of Prince Henry and Grand Duke Paul. 'The commotion this unexpected visit makes in this place,' reported James Harris,

> is beyond all description; the King himself having set an example of magnificence not heard of in this country since Frederick the First's time. His loyal subjects are vying with each other who shall be finest. Those whose finances do not allow them to bear a share in this competition, and whose credit is exhausted, pretext urgent business in the country, or occasional sickness; but every possessor of a few hundred crowns employs them in lace and embroidery.

The Grand Duke made his public entry into Berlin on 10 July, in a procession led by uniformed members of trading companies, and travelling with Prince Henry in a silver-topped carriage drawn by eight horses and preceded by a troop of body guards. Frederick the Great used the opportunity of this visit to the full, showering the Grand Duke and his suite with all possible distinctions and gifts. As James Harris wryly commented: 'not one of them will return to Petersburg without being infatuated with his affability and goodness'. Paul himself, very conscious of his own dignity and importance, seemed less aware of the propaganda value to be attained through generosity and affability. As reported by Harris:

> The Grand Duke's conduct here has by no means reconciled to him the good will either of the people or nobility. He received all the acts of homage they did him as if they were his due, and, at his levee, took not the smallest pains to be affable. His donations, too, are exceedingly below par; a disappointment the more felt as the ideas were raised very high here of Russian magnificence, and valuable presents as much expected as wanted. Marshal Romanzow [Rumyantsev] spoke very freely to the Grand Duke on this subject; but whether His Imperial Majesty is naturally economical, or whether he was limited by the Czarina, it produced no effect, except a great coolness between the Prince and his adviser.

Nevertheless, such behaviour had no adverse effect on the principal object of the journey to Berlin, and on 26 July Richard Oakes wrote: 'On Sunday last the Empress received the news, by a courier from the Great Duke, of his Imperial Highness being betrothed to the Princess of Wirtemberg, on which joyful occasion there was a ball at court. And yesterday morning early, Count Goërtz arrived with compliments of congratulation from the King of Prussia to her Imperial Majesty on the same happy event.'

Oakes also mentioned another arrival: 'Prince Potemkin arrived here on Saturday evening, and appeared at court the next day. His returning to the apartments he before occupied in the palace made many people apprehensive of the possibility of his regaining the favour he had lost.' Potemkin eventually settled neither in the Anichkov Palace nor in his old apartments, though he remained in the Winter Palace, moving into a small building facing on to Millionnaya Ulitsa, known as the Shepilov house. This building was attached to the main palace by a covered walkway and gave him continued private access into Catherine's rooms, and she into his. He used the Anichkov Palace for entertaining and for housing his library.

On 18 August Catherine updated Grimm on her acquisition of a new bride for Paul:

> You ask me about my travellers, and I have the honour to inform you that half of them returned last Sunday, that is, the Grand Duke and his suite; the Princess is still to come, and we will not have her for another ten days. Once we do have her, we will proceed to her conversion. Well, to convince her, we'll need a fortnight, I think; I don't know how long it will take to teach her to read her profession of faith in intelligible and correct Russian; but the sooner that can be sorted, the better. In order to speed it all along, Monsieur Pastukhov has gone to Memel so that he can teach her the alphabet and the profession en route; conviction can come afterwards. You will see from this that we are looking ahead and planning in advance and that this conversion and profession of faith is going post-haste. I am arranging the wedding for a week after that act. If you want to come and dance at it, all you have to do is hurry.

Apartments were being prepared for the future Grand Duchess, Catherine herself writing instructions about how they were to be decorated and furnished. The bedroom for ordinary use was to have blue glass columns, white damask wall coverings with a pink dado and a bed to match, while the walls of the state bedroom were to be decorated in gold brocade with a dado of blue velvet embroidered with gold. The dining room was to be decorated in stucco with gilded ornamentation.

Princess Sophia Dorothea, accompanied by Countess Rumyantseva, crossed the Russian border at Riga on 24 August. James Harris had described her with moderate enthusiasm: 'Her person, though rather inclined to be fat, is far from unpleasing, and great pains have been taken with her education. Nothing can equal the joy, both of her and all the House of Wirtemberg on this occasion.' A week later Paul and Sophia Dorothea were received together at Tsarskoye Selo. Catherine wrote enthusiastically to Madame Bielke about the 16-year-old Princess (who, like herself, had been born in Stettin):

I admit to you that I am infatuated, but literally infatuated, with this charming princess: she is precisely what one wanted her to be: the figure of a nymph, peaches and cream complexion, the most beautiful skin in the world, tall and well-formed, yet light of foot; her face expresses sweetness, goodness of heart and candour; everyone is enchanted by her, and whoever did not love her would be very wrong, for she is born and made just for that . . . In a word, my princess is everything I wished, and that's me content.

Catherine was clearly looking forward to seeing Grimm again, writing to him: 'I will be staying here at Tsarskoye Selo until 6th September, when I return to town with my Princess. If you arrive, and I am here, come and find me as soon as seems good to you, and we will chatter like one-eyed magpies; forgive the comparison.' Grimm duly fulfilled his promise to return after his travels in Italy, arriving in time for the wedding. As on his first visit (apart from the time he was ill), he saw the Empress daily, having a private conversation with her at least once a day, and sometimes as many as three times. Their conversations normally lasted for two to three hours, though on one occasion they talked for as long as seven, and Grimm was so stimulated by them that he often found it difficult to get to sleep at night. One thing Grimm admired about Catherine was her ability always to be the Empress while at the same time behaving like a dear friend. A sense of dignity seemed to come naturally to her – a close friend could be familiar with her, but never overfamiliar.

On the afternoon of Tuesday 6 September, Catherine and the grand ducal pair left Tsarskoye Selo for St Petersburg in a magnificent parade coach. Sophia Dorothea's conversion took place on 14 September, when she was given the name of Maria Fyodorovna, followed on the next day by the betrothal, both events taking place in the chapel of the Winter Palace. During the meal which followed the betrothal, a concert of Italian vocal and instrumental music was performed, and in the evening there was a ball.

This time it was Paul, rather than his mother, who provided written instructions for the behaviour of his future wife (though Catherine knew about and approved what he had written). The widower intended to dominate this marriage in a way he had not managed in his first. He urged his betrothed to take her religious duties seriously, to observe all the required rituals, and to depend entirely on himself and on the Empress for advice in all matters. She should avoid using intermediaries and never complain about the Empress; instead she should seek to speak to her directly if there was anything she did not understand. Her only goals should be to serve the Empress and the Grand Duke, her husband. He admitted that he was a difficult person to live with, being volatile and impatient, and that his wife would have to accommodate herself to him. Moreover, he would have the right to criticise and instruct her in any way he thought appropriate, and she was not to take offence – even if he should be wrong, as he admitted he was quite likely to be. Maria Fyodorovna, being a practical and pragmatic young woman, seemed unsurprised at these instructions and was prepared to do whatever was necessary to make the marriage work.

The wedding took place on 26 September, six days after Paul's twenty-second birthday. The crown was held over the Grand Duke's head by Grigory Orlov. Nikita Panin was conspicuously absent from the ceremony – he had been ill, but was also irritated not to have been consulted over the marriage arrangements. The festivities, which included the usual public feast in the square in front of the Winter Palace, lasted for nearly three weeks and concluded with a firework display on 15 October.

Grigory Orlov had plans to be married himself, in a match which his brothers viewed as unsuitable but which the Empress, when asked by them to intervene, had refused to prevent. Grigory's proposed bride, Ekaterina Zinovyeva, was only 15 years old and had been appointed a maid of honour to the Empress the previous year. The problem presented by Grigory's having fallen for this girl, however, was less to do with her youth than with the fact that she was his own first cousin, and he was having to seek special permission from the Church for the marriage to be allowed to proceed.

While Grimm was in St Petersburg, Catherine made one last attempt to get him to stay permanently, offering him the job of running the imperial schools. By now she and Grimm knew and trusted one another sufficiently for there to be no need for circumlocution or prevarication: 'I want you to say to me quite clearly: "I will or I will not, I stay or I go"; I will be very pleased if you give me the answer I want, but I will not think any less of you if you reply in the negative.' He did in fact refuse her offer, again citing the fact that he spoke no Russian.

By the spring of 1777 Peter Zavadovsky was in a state of near mental and physical collapse. Catherine began to worry that his consistently gloomy mood might be a sign of impending madness, though she continued to try to calm him with soothing notes: 'My advice is –

1) stay with me; 2) believe it when I say something; 3) do not quarrel hourly about trifles; 4) reject hypochondriac thoughts and replace them with amusing ones; 5) Conclusion; all this feeds love, which without amusement is dead, like faith without kind deeds.' She felt that a period of respite was needed for them both, and told Zavadovsky that she would talk to Potemkin about it (which proposal can hardly have cheered Zavadovsky).

The experiment with Zavadovsky, while unsatisfactory for him, had proved to Potemkin that a *ménage à trois* did provide a way forward for his own relationship with the Empress, freeing him from constant personal attendance while maintaining his influence and central position in her life and Empire – always provided that he chose the right man to be the third party. So now he moved quickly. The man he settled upon was Semyon Zorich, a 31-year-old major of hussars and the son of a Serbian officer in the Russian army. Zorich had acquired a degree of celebrity in the army by the audacious way in which he had survived capture by the Turks. Having learnt that they were executing ordinary soldiers but offering nobles for ransom, he had immediately declared himself to be a Count. On his return from captivity he had written to Potemkin and been accepted into his entourage. By early May Potemkin had presented Zorich to Catherine, who wrote to say, 'What a funny creature you have acquainted me with.' The handsome, swarthy and curly-haired Zorich soon came to be known as 'Adonis' by some of the court ladies, while in other circles he was called '*le vrai sauvage*'. By 22 May Catherine was referring to him as 'Senyusha' or 'Sima' and sending him little notes, care of Potemkin – while also telling the latter how much she missed him. On the 27th she also sent Potemkin a watch to give Zorich, as he didn't have one of his own. On that day Potemkin had hosted a dinner for the Empress at his new estate of Ozerki, outside Petersburg; the 35 guests had included the Prince's nieces and cousins and, for the first time at an official reception, Zorich.

With Catherine's permission, Count Kirill Razumovsky was chosen by Zavadovsky to act as an intermediary. Although wanting to cease being the Empress's favourite, Zavadovsky was upset to the point of tears and asked that he still be allowed to come and see her, to which she consented. Clearly he remained very fond of her, or at least emotionally dependent; in addition he wished to ensure that he would be well provided for. Ivan Yelagin also assisted with the negotiations, which resulted in Zavadovsky receiving 4,000 serfs in Byelorussia (or White

Russia, now Belarus), generous financial settlements and the usual silver dinner service (though for only 16 people, in his case). He was advised to go and relax in his native Ukraine for a while, with the question of his return to service left open.

On 5 June, Grigory Orlov attained his objective and married Ekaterina Zinovyeva. The wedding was celebrated in a field outside Petersburg, and the 43-year-old bridegroom danced for joy. Catherine promoted the new Princess Orlova to the rank of lady-in-waiting, and subsequently went to dine with the couple at their Gatchina estate.

On the same day as Grigory's wedding, the King of Sweden, Gustavus III, arrived in Petersburg by sea and was received by Catherine at Tsarskoye Selo that afternoon. Gustavus was Catherine's first cousin, the son of her mother's brother Adolf Frederick, and was 16 years her junior. He was travelling under the name of the Count of Gotland, having requested not to be treated with the full honours of a king during his visit, so that he could move around in relative freedom. The cousins dined together on that first day and met several more times during the month-long stay of 'brother Gu', as Catherine referred to him subsequently in her correspondence with Grimm. The Empress arranged for him to be shown all the sights of Petersburg, and they exchanged costly gifts, Catherine awarding him the Order of St Alexander Nevsky and giving him a cane whose knob was made of a single diamond worth 60,000 roubles, as well as a blue fox-fur pelisse. (Gustavus also laid the foundation stone of Chesme church, built to commemorate the naval battle.) Gifts were also constantly being exchanged between Catherine and Potemkin to give to Zorich, whom they treated rather like an amusing plaything.

Grimm finally left St Petersburg in August; despite his refusal to stay in Russia, he was now officially on Catherine's payroll, with an annual salary of 2,000 roubles. His responsibilities were to include acting as her confidential agent in Paris and purchasing works of art for her. The correspondence between the two immediately resumed, Catherine reporting on the progress being made in her garden at Tsarskoye Selo and on two recent arrivals – the 36-year-old Italian composer Giovanni Païsiello and an infamous Englishwoman, the Duchess of Kingston:

> Païsiello's opera will not be performed until September; while waiting he goes for walks here and it is said that he is mad about my garden which becomes more beautiful every day: a path is being created on

the Grand Caprice,★ which seems superb to me; but *so far only in the imagination*, for trees have not yet been planted there, and there are only two banks of grass . . .

Talking of madness: the Duchess of Kingston has arrived here in her own yacht flying a French flag; that's an astute thing to do; she certainly isn't lacking in intelligence: she likes me very much, but as she is rather deaf and I cannot shout, she won't profit much by it.

The Duchess of Kingston, also Countess of Bristol, had been born Elizabeth Chudleigh in 1720 and had led a scandalous life in London, attaining notoriety by her appearance in the nude at a ball given by the Venetian ambassador. Her marriage to the extremely wealthy Duke of Kingston in 1769 was bigamous, Elizabeth secretly having married Augustus Hervey, later third Earl of Bristol, in 1744. The Duke of Kingston died in 1773, and in 1776 the Duchess was tried for bigamy before the High Court of Parliament. She was found guilty, but was punished only by a fine. She then embarked on her travels around the continent of Europe to escape personal involvement in a lawsuit launched by her late husband's nephew with the aim of retrieving the Kingston fortune (the Duchess's lawyers eventually won the case in her favour).

On 10 September there was a catastrophic flood in Petersburg. Catherine, who had returned to town from Tsarskoye Selo the day before, wrote immediately with an eye-witness account to Grimm:

At ten o'clock in the evening the wind announced itself by blowing open a window in my room with a crash: it was raining a little, but from then on it started raining all sorts of things: tiles, iron sheets, windowpanes, water, hail and snow. I was sleeping very deeply but was woken at five o'clock by a gust of wind; I rang and they came to tell me that the water was at my door and trying to get in; I said: in that case, bring in the guards on sentry duty in the small court-yards so that they don't perish trying to prevent the water's entry. No sooner said than done. I wanted to get a closer view of things so went into the Hermitage; it and the Neva looked like the destruc-tion of Jerusalem: the quay, which is not finished, was covered with three-masted merchant vessels; I said: 'Good God! the exchange has moved; Count Munich will have to establish the customs house

★ An archway through a man-made hill, created by Vasily Neyelov between 1770 and 1774.

where the Hermitage Theatre used to be.' So many broken windows and overturned flowerpots! And as though to keep the flowerpots company, I found porcelain ones from the chimneypieces spread out on the floors and sofas . . .

I am dining at home; the water has gone down and, as you can see, I have not been drowned; but few people have so far come out of their lairs. I saw one of my gentlemen arriving in an English carriage; the water was covering the back axle of the carriage and his footman, who was standing behind, had his feet in the water. But that's enough talk of water; it will have to be mixed with wine, all my cellars have been flooded and God knows what will come of that.

One of the casualties of the flood was the Summer Garden; most of the marble statues which Peter the Great had introduced into it were swept away, as were the aviary, hot-houses, orangeries, gazebo and the Garden's centrepiece, the elaborate system of fountains which was fed from the Fontanka river and powered by a steam engine designed by Peter himself. 'Just imagine, the recent flood spoilt more than two hundred toises* of quay,' Catherine reported to Grimm. 'Since that day I've been cross with the town of St Peter; in several houses they've eaten fish caught in the courtyards. Count Panin went fishing in his manège; nearly all the windows in my Hermitage have been smashed. A hundred and forty boats perished on the Neva and beneath my windows.'

In November Catherine suffered an attack of colic. Always happy to discuss her digestive system, she described her symptoms to Grimm in some detail:

Today I woke up between five and six o'clock in the morning with violent pains in my body; I tried to sit up and the pains moved up to my chest, leaving me breathless. I rang; someone came; I didn't know what was the matter with me; I couldn't find any way of getting comfortable in my bed; what could it be? Monsieur Kelchen declared it to be a windy colic. This hurricane in my insides lasted non-stop for five hours, and then went the same way it had come, with no why or wherefore. May the good Lord preserve you from anything like it: both Imperial patience and medical science were at their wits' end.

---

* 200 toises = 390 metres.

Towards the end of that month Etienne Falconet updated the Empress on the progress of his long-awaited equestrian statue, explaining that a second casting had succeeded in rectifying some of the problems he had encountered. He begged the Empress to visit his studio to see 'the product of my eleven to twelve years of labour', and he also reminded her that he had not yet been paid for the marble busts of the Grand Duke and the late Grand Duchess Natalya. It appears that Catherine did not respond to Falconet's plea to visit his studio, as in a letter to her in 1778 the sculptor refers to the statue as 'an object which [Your Imperial Majesty] has not yet seen'.

Unlike Falconet, the Grand Duchess Maria Fyodorovna had speedily fulfilled the prime purpose of her summons to St Petersburg. On 12 December 1777 a new phase began in Catherine's life, with the birth of her first grandson, Alexander.

# 14

# Grandsons and Other Acquisitions (1777–79)

*I am fashioning out of him a funny little person who does everything I want.*
Catherine II on her grandson, Alexander

wo days after Alexander Pavlovich's birth, Catherine wrote in delight to Grimm:

Do you know Monsieur Alexandre? . . . I bet you don't know Monsieur Alexandre at all, at least not the one I'm going to tell you about. He is not Alexander the Great, but Alexander the very little who has just been born, on the 12th of this month at a quarter to eleven in the morning. In other words the Grand Duchess has just given birth to a son who, in honour of St Alexander Nevsky, has been given the pompous name of Alexander, and whom I call Monsieur Alexandre.

All Catherine's thwarted maternal instincts – thwarted by the Empress Elizabeth's commandeering of her first two children at birth and by the necessity of concealment in the case of her son by Orlov – were channelled into her love for this grandchild. But this was not only love; Catherine had a strong sense that here at last was a little human being whom she could mould entirely after her own ideas and theories, with no one able to interfere. She had always felt that Paul had been damaged both physically and mentally by his early upbringing at the hands of Elizabeth and her attendants, with their old-fashioned

ideas about swaddling and overheated rooms, and Catherine was determined that no such damage should be inflicted on Alexander whom
she intended, from the start, to make into a worthy successor to herself.
By the time of his birth she had developed very definite ideas on how
children should be raised (many of them were gleaned from Jean-
Jacques Rousseau's *Emile*, published in 1762), and they were diametri-
cally opposed to the practices which had been employed in rearing her
own son; she had of course written them down:

> Children should not be dressed or covered too warmly either in
> winter or summer.
> It is better that children should also sleep at night without a
> bonnet.
> As often as possible children should be washed in cold water.
> They should wear slight shoes, without heels.
> For the first year they should have bare head and feet.
> It would be good to teach a child to swim, as soon as he is old
> enough.
> Make them go out often in the fresh air.
> Let them stay near the fire as little as possible even in winter.
> Let them play in the wind, in the sun and in the rain without a
> hat.
> Children's clothes should never be tight, especially around the
> chest.

In some respects Catherine behaved with her grandson very much as
Elizabeth had behaved with Paul, taking over all responsibility for his
care from the moment of his birth. There was no question of Alexander
being regarded merely as Paul and Maria Fyodorovna's son; he was also
heir, after his father, to a vast Empire, and his upbringing was therefore of an importance which did not allow personal considerations such
as paternal and maternal feelings – especially on the part of young,
inexperienced parents - to interfere. At least so Catherine thought, and
Alexander's parents had no choice but to fall in with her plans. (They
were rewarded for having produced the child by being given the large
estate which came to be known as Pavlovsk, to the south of Tsarskoye
Selo and including 15,000 acres of virgin forest.) Her commandeering
of the baby was not as drastic as Elizabeth's had been, however. Paul
and Maria Fyodorovna always had more access to their children than
Catherine had ever been allowed to hers, but they were given no part

in any decision-making regarding their sons. For the first week of Alexander's life, until his baptism on 20 December (one of his godfathers being, in absentia, King Frederick the Great), he was allowed to stay in his mother's apartments, though Catherine had immediately picked him up after his birth, taken him to be washed and supervised his being wrapped up – very lightly, and definitely not swaddled. He was then placed in a basket which in turn was placed on a divan behind a screen; Catherine was adamant that he should not be put in any kind of cradle which could be rocked. From day one, Monsieur Alexandre was not to be mollycoddled. The wife of a young gardener at Tsarskoye Selo was appointed as his wet-nurse, while the wife of General Benkendorff was placed in overall charge of the nursery – reporting, of course, to Catherine.

After his baptism Alexander was conveyed into his own room, where he slept on an iron bedstead, on a mattress covered with animal hide, with a pillow and light eiderdown. The emphasis was on fresh air; the temperature was never allowed to go above 14–15°,* no more than a couple of candles were allowed to be lit at once, and the baby's bed was railed off by an elbow-high balustrade to prevent people crowding round him. Every morning (even though this was the middle of winter) the windows were opened to air the room, while Alexander was carried elsewhere and brought back once the room had been reheated. He was washed every day in a tub of water, the one concession to his newborn status being that for the first few weeks the water was allowed to be lukewarm. (Later it would be cold, drawn the previous evening and left in his room overnight.)

Another novelty in Catherine's life at this time was a breakthrough in her appreciation of music. The composer Païsiello clearly had studied his patron and her tastes and had determined not to create anything too demanding on the ear. The musical comedies he composed at this time, combining gentle social satire with lively, easily remembered tunes, were just the sort to appeal to the Empress, whose sense of humour was not a great deal more refined than was her ear for music (she could be rather obtuse, sometimes completely missing the point of a subtle joke). Before Païsiello had arrived, the only composer whose music Catherine had enjoyed had been Galuppi – who had also been gifted in what might be termed 'baroque easy

---

* Probably this is on the Réaumur scale; 14–15° Réaumur would be about 18°C or 65°F.

listening' – and Catherine wrote to Grimm in some bewilderment at Païsiello's ability to entertain her:

> Do you know that Païsiello's opera is a charming piece? I forgot to tell you about it before; I was all ears for this opera, despite my eardrums' natural lack of sensitivity towards music; I place Païsiello alongside Galuppi. This recently arrived buffoon is very funny; even the music he sings makes me laugh: God knows how that is done. Listen, you developed man, develop me the following question: how is it that this buffoon's music makes me laugh, whereas the music of French comic operas inspires me – who neither loves nor knows anything at all about music – with scorn and indignation?

At the beginning of 1778 Grimm sent Catherine a collection of New Year presents, including asparagus from Tours, barley sugar made by the nuns of Moret-sur-Loing (which rather ungratefully Catherine fed to her dog, Lady) and a pair of stockings made of rabbit fur – which, according to Catherine, Grigory Orlov had wanted to claim for himself. The new year brought a new British ambassador to St Petersburg in the shape of James Harris, who had been in Berlin at the time of the Grand Duke's visit and who brought with him his sister and his 16-year-old wife. 'Prepared even as I was for the magnificence and parade of this Court,' reported Harris soon after his arrival,

> yet it exceeds in everything my ideas: to this is joined the most perfect order and decorum. The Empress herself unites, in the most wonderful manner, the talents of putting those she honours with her conversation at their ease, and of keeping up her own dignity. Her character extends throughout her whole administration; and although she is rigidly obeyed, yet she has introduced a lenity in the mode of government to which, till her reign, this country was a stranger.

As was the case with all the foreign ministers, if he was to make any progress Harris knew that he would have to learn to get on with Nikita Panin, through whom all foreign business was transacted. He described him as a man of 'great good nature, great vanity, and excessive indolence'. He considered him to be honourable, however, and beyond the reach of corruption. Harris was also quick to make an assessment of the state of play regarding Catherine's current favourite, reporting to the Earl of Suffolk:

> The present favourite, Zoritz, seems on the decline. He has received and dissipated an immense fortune; but what does credit to one raised to so high a rank, he has employed his influence in doing good, and rendering services to those he thought neglected. It is probable Potemkin will be commissioned to look out for a fresh *minion*, and I have heard named (although I can by no means assert it), that he has already pitched on one Acharoff, *Lieutenant* of the *Police* at Moscow.

Zorich was reported to be expecting his dismissal imminently but also determined to 'cut off the ears' of any successor. Harris also reported that Grigory Orlov was inseparable from his new wife, who was 'capricious, headstrong, and very young' (though he could hardly talk, given the age of his own wife). After a month in St Petersburg, the British ambassador had formed the opinion that the Empress's worst enemies were the flattery of others and her own passions – by which he meant her predilection for young men.

Whatever Semyon Zorich's pretensions about his position as favourite, Potemkin remained at the heart of Catherine's life, as regards both affairs of state and the more ephemeral business of the Court. As part of the celebrations to mark Alexander Pavlovich's birth, Potemkin and Catherine worked together to stage, in her apartments, an elaborate entertainment. Potemkin acted as the host, disguising himself as an African gentleman by the name of Francisque Azor. The specially invited guests (all high-ranking Russians) attended the opera at Court and were then conducted from the auditorium up a spiral staircase into a room where three velvet-covered tables were set up ready for games of macao (a card game similar to baccarat; its aim was to hold a hand of cards totalling nine points). Each table also contained a little box of diamonds and a golden spoon; the diamonds, which James Harris (who, along with other foreign dignitaries, was allowed to see the stage-set of this entertainment, after the event) reported to have been worth 50 roubles each, were awarded to players who scored nines. The game lasted for an hour and a half, after which the remaining diamonds were shared out among the guests. They then went back down the staircase to find the room through which they had passed earlier transformed. It was lined with mirrors, not only on the walls but also on the ceiling,

and on either side of the crossing opposite the staircase was suspended a large 'A' (in honour of Alexander), made out of diamonds and over two feet high. Twenty pages, dressed in cloth of gold with blue satin sashes, were standing ready to serve the guests at supper; the tables, richly adorned with jewelled centrepieces, were placed along the walls so that the guests faced the mirrors. Catherine ordered an engraving to be made of the scene, in order to impress as many people as possible.

Not all the company was quite as glittering as the setting; in the description of the event which Catherine wrote for Grimm she referred to some of those present as 'pea soups' – evidently a designation they had used earlier together in conversation – and the ingredients of which she later defined as 'essence of prattle and long speeches about nothing worth recording, topped with a seasoning of conjectures, of which most of the time not a single one is just or true, and that is how the world is run and the fate of nations often decided'.

In a letter to Grimm which Catherine began writing on 2 March and finished two days later, she expressed how much she enjoyed their correspondence, that with him she 'chatted' rather than 'wrote'. She continued: 'So go on! Bombard me, bombard me with letters: it is a good thing to do, for it entertains me, I read and re-read your packages, and I say: "How he understands me! oh, heaven! almost no one understands me as well as he does."' She reported that the healthy little Alexander had not given rise to a moment's anxiety since he was born, and she expressed amusement at having been told that Voltaire was in the habit of referring to her as 'Cateau'. She also mentioned the famous 'cameo' porcelain dinner and dessert service for 60 people which she had ordered from Sèvres, at phenomenal expense: 'The Sèvres service I have ordered is for the first nail-biter of the universe, my dear and well-beloved Prince Potemkin and, in order to ensure that it's beautiful, I have said that it's for me.' Permission had been gained from Louis XVI for copies to be made of some of the antique cameos in his collection to be used in the manufacture of this service, which was of a beautiful turquoise colour. Designs for one of the plates went back and forth between Sèvres and Petersburg eight times before agreement was finally reached, and the technical difficulties of making such a vast service were such that 3,000 pieces were fired to achieve 800 of sufficient quality. The centrepiece of the service featured an image of Catherine herself as the goddess Minerva. (As an expression of thanks for this gift, Potemkin presented the Empress with an Angolan tomcat.)

With the advent of warmer weather, baby Alexander had his first taste of life in the open air, being carried outside (bonnet-less) to sit on the grass or sand or even to sleep for a few hours on a cushion, in the shade of a tree. When he was four months old Catherine, wanting to lessen the amount of time he was carried around, presented him with a three-metre-square rug for him to lie on in his room and start to learn to crawl. The Empress reported proudly on his progress to her cousin the King of Sweden, clearly wishing her ideas on child-rearing to be admired and disseminated; she even sent Gustavus a little doll to illustrate how the baby had been wrapped after birth:

> It is a pleasure to see him sprawl [on his rug]: he gets on all fours; he goes backwards when he can't go forwards. His favourite clothing is his very short chemise and a very loose-fitting little knitted jacket; when he goes out, a light little gown made of linen or taffeta is put on over that. He knows nothing about getting cold, he is big, tall, well and very happy, having no teeth and hardly ever crying.

That spring Catherine was having changes made to the Catherine Palace at Tsarskoye Selo, which included the great staircase at one end of the palace being knocked down and rebuilt in 'the small aisle which adjoins the entrance door on the Gatchina side'. Her intention was to have 10 new rooms constructed, using as her source for the decor she envisaged a library of books on architecture which had been given her by the Abbé Galiani from Naples, a friend of Grimm and the *encyclopédistes*. She also wanted to ensure that the design of the palace would enable her to enjoy an unimpeded view over her gardens.

By May James Harris was feeling frustrated over the lack of progress he was making in attempting to negotiate an offensive and defensive alliance by which Russia would provide naval reinforcements to aid the British in the war with the American colonies. The French Court had recently taken the decision to acknowledge American Independence, and Harris felt that both Count Panin and the Empress were stonewalling him: 'The Empress is gracious to me beyond measure, and I cannot help thinking she means by this extraordinary affability to mislead me . . . Whenever I attempt to lead her to converse on our concerns, she is instantly silent or changes the subject.' Harris also reported that Grigory Orlov, who had always been warmly disposed towards England, had told him that he no longer had any influence at Court, and that 'the opposite party had prevailed, and

that he owed too much to Her Imperial Majesty to attempt the over-
setting it by means which necessarily would give her great pain and
uneasiness'. The Empress herself was not feeling very well, as she
complained to Grimm; she was perhaps experiencing the after-effects,
she thought, of a period of intense work:

> My head feels completely unhinged; I've noticed that these attacks
> are quick to follow legislomanic moods; I was attacked by the latter
> in the month of December; they've lasted until now with strength
> and energy: all was fire and genius, enough to send me into raptures;
> alas, I don't eat, or drink, or sleep; Monsieur Kelchen has difficulty
> finding my pulse; I have a tight chest. My friends scold me; they go
> on at me and insist that this is no good; I'm well aware of that; they
> consult the doctors, they believe me to be ill; they want cures; I
> consent: provided they leave the choice to me, it won't be difficult
> to swallow. Well then, what do you think of all that? Doesn't it prove
> I'm unhinged?

In addition to having a tight chest, Catherine reported an uncharac-
teristic repugnance for pen and paper, an inability to concentrate and
a lack of interest in talking about anything. James Harris had also
claimed to notice that she did not have 'that ardour for business she
was used to be famous for'. Though this could well have been, in
part, a reaction to overwork, it was also connected to the continued
instability in the Empress's personal life. Harris's earlier speculations
about Zorich's imminent dismissal and replacement may have been
premature and inaccurate (Catherine did not take up with the man
Harris had identified as 'Acharoff', or with a 'Persian candidate' whom
he had also mentioned), but Zorich had not proved to be the submis-
sive plaything Potemkin had envisaged when he initially selected him.
Indeed, he had been trying to take on Potemkin himself and to
diminish his influence, something which neither the Prince nor the
Empress could countenance. Zorich would have to go, sooner rather
than later.

The situation had become highly volatile after a particularly aggres-
sive confrontation between Zorich and Potemkin in early May. The
well-informed Harris was soon made aware of what had happened:

> A few days ago Prince Potemkin, displeased with Zoritz, presented
> to the Empress, as she was going to the play, a tall hussar officer,

one of his adjutants. She distinguished him a good deal. Zoritz was present. As soon as Her Imperial Majesty was gone, he fell upon Potemkin in a very violent manner, made use of the strongest expressions of abuse, and insisted on his fighting him. Potemkin declined this offer, and behaved on the occasion as a person not undeserving the invectives bestowed upon him. The play being ended, Zoritz followed the Empress into her apartment, flung himself at her feet, and confessed what he had done; saying, that, notwithstanding the honours and riches she had heaped upon him, he was indifferent to everything but her favour and good graces. This behaviour had its effect. When Potemkin appeared, he was ill received, and Zoritz seemed in high favour for a day or two.

Potemkin left Czarsco-Zelo, and came to Petersburg. Zoritz however has since been sent here [i.e. Petersburg], and the Empress ordered him to invite Potemkin to supper, *de raccommoder l'affaire, puisqu'elle n'aimait pas les tracasseries* [to sort out the matter, as she did not like fuss and bother]. This supper took place a few days ago: they are apparently good friends; but Potemkin, who is an artful man, will in the end get the better of Zoritz's bluntness and singularity. Potemkin is determined to have him dismissed, and Zoritz is determined to cut the throat of his successor. Judge of the tenour of the whole Court from this anecdote.

The man Potemkin had presented to Catherine was one Ivan Rimsky-Korsakov, whom he had appointed as an adjutant to himself on 8 May. Despite the apparent patching up of relations with Zorich, the latter's last recorded day at Court was 13 May. On the 22nd Harris was able to report that Zorich had finally been dismissed and that his successor was waiting in the wings – though he would not be officially acknowledged until the impetuous Zorich was at a safe distance. The semi-public way in which Catherine's private life was conducted did no good to her reputation at home or abroad, as is clear from Harris's account:

Your Lordship [i.e. Lord Suffolk] was not unacquainted with the altercation that passed at Czarsco-Zelo between Prince Potemkin and General Zoritz. The spirited behaviour of the latter had only a transitory effect; the complaisant and useful part Prince Potemkin acts got the better of every other consideration, and Mons. Zoritz, a few days ago, received his final dismission. It was conveyed to him by the Empress herself in very gentle terms, but received by him in a very different manner: forgetting to whom he was speaking, he was very bitter in his reproaches; painted this mutable conduct in the strongest colours, and foretold the most fatal consequences from it. I am assured this language was felt, but it made no alterations in the plan laid down. Zoritz, with an increase of pension, an immense sum of ready money, and addition of seven thousand peasants to his estates, is going to travel. His successor, by name Korsac, will not be declared till this journey has taken place; the impetuosity of Zoritz's character making it not safe for any man to take publicly this office upon him while he remains in the country. Both court and town are occupied with this event alone, and I am sorry to say it gives rise to many unpleasant reflections, and sinks in the eyes of foreigners the reputation of the Empress, and the consideration of the empire.

Catherine expressed great gratitude to Potemkin for having introduced her to (perhaps 'procured for her' would be more accurate) the 24-year-old Rimsky-Korsakov, whom she described as an angel and likened to a Greek statue (she often referred to him as 'Pyrrhus, King of Epirus'). She had for a while considered recalling Zavadovsky, particularly after Grigory Orlov had remonstrated with her over the damage this rapid progression of favourites was doing to her reputation, but Rimsky-Korsakov's dark good looks had proved too captivating to resist.

By 26 May the Empress had returned from Tsarskoye Selo to Petersburg, still not completely recovered from her indisposition and wondering if, as she entered her fiftieth year, such health problems were the pattern of things to come. The Grand Duke, according to James Harris, was embarrassed by his mother's behaviour and was keeping himself to himself. Rimsky-Korsakov was appointed adjutant-general to the Empress, the rank habitually held by the official favourite, on 1 June 1778. Zavadovsky, in lieu of being reinstated as favourite, was brought back into service in an administrative capacity, the area in which his true talents lay. Thus Catherine had managed to retain the loyalty and friendship of three of her former lovers: Zavadovsky, who worked faithfully for her for many years; Grigory Orlov who, despite outbursts of anger and reproach, remained a constant supporter of the woman he had helped place on the throne; and Grigory Potemkin, who was her firmest friend and confidant – and maybe still occasional lover, possibly husband. To retain the affection of these men, all remarkable in their way and often in competition with one another, was no mean achievement.

The Court returned to Tsarskoye Selo on the evening of 8 June. The turbulence of her personal life was still having an adverse effect on Catherine's health, and on Sunday 10th her headache was so bad that, after attending the liturgy, she slept for three hours instead of having dinner. She then dressed, attended a review of a regiment of grenadiers, and went for a walk around the Great Pond, though still plagued by her headache. The next day it was better, though she felt rather dull-witted.

On 21 June Catherine lamented to Grimm over the death of Voltaire:

Alas! I can only describe to you the regrets I felt on reading your letter No. 19.* Until then I had hoped that the news of Voltaire's death was false, but you assured me of its truth, and all at once I had a reaction of universal discouragement and felt a very great contempt for all the things of this world. The month of May has been very fatal for me: I have lost two men whom I have never seen, but who loved me and whom I esteemed – Voltaire and Lord Chatham;† there will be no one to replace them, and particularly the former, for a very, very long time, perhaps never, and for me they are irreparably lost; I feel like crying.

Horrified at the Roman Catholic Church's refusal to allow Voltaire to be buried in consecrated ground in Paris, Catherine upbraided Grimm – only partly in jest – for not having had the presence of mind to make off with the great man's body himself and bring it to Russia for burial. She now asked Grimm to set in train negotiations for her to purchase Voltaire's library – which consisted of approximately 7,000 volumes bound in red morocco and annotated by their owner – as well as whatever existed of his papers, including her own letters to him.

By the end of June, Ivan Rimsky-Korsakov was firmly established as favourite and Semyon Zorich had departed. Catherine felt completely

---

* Catherine and Grimm kept a careful catalogue of their letters, ostensibly in order to avoid confusion as their replies went back and forth; they were also aware, however, of the value their letters would have for posterity.
† William Pitt the Elder, who had died on 11 May [N.S.]

restored to health and good spirits, writing to Potemkin: 'thanks to you and to the King of Epirus I am as merry as a lark and I want you to be equally merry and well'. If Zorich had been treated as a plaything by Catherine and Potemkin, the younger Rimsky-Korsakov was treated almost as though he were their child; Catherine even refers to him as 'the child' and tells Potemkin, at some point during the summer, that 'the child' has asked that she kiss Potemkin on the lips should he arrive during his own absence. It is hardly surprising that Catherine's real child, Grand Duke Paul, should have found this quasi-incestuous relationship difficult to accept. Not that he found her relationship with Potemkin much easier to bear, particularly as the latter, after an initial attempt to court Paul's favour, had abandoned the effort as a waste of time and took little notice of him. As James Harris expressed it: 'The Grand Duke and Duchess are treated by Potemkin and his set as persons of no consequence; he feels this slight, and is weak enough to resent it in his conversation, though he does not dare do more.'

From her own point of view, now that her personal life was sorted out, Catherine could return wholeheartedly to business, and on 11 August she wrote angrily to Grimm about a recent action by an American privateer against some of her merchant vessels:

> Do you know what wrong those American ship owners have done me? They have seized some merchant ships which were setting off from Arkhangelsk; they carried out this delightful business in the months of July and August, but I sincerely promise you that the first to meddle in the commerce of Arkhangelsk during this coming year will pay me dearly for it, for I am not Brother G. [i.e. King George III]: one doesn't push me around with impunity; they can do what they like to Brother G., but not to me, without getting their fingers burnt; I am angry, very angry indeed.

A week later, still exercised about the American action, Catherine wrote to Grimm about the consignment of statuary and other things she was expecting from Rome:

> I have not yet received a single case or package sent by Monsieur Reiffenstein, containing marbles etc., acquired by order of Monsieur Shuvalov, NB, who is here at the moment [this was Ivan Shuvalov, the Empress Elizabeth's former favourite], because the frigates which sailed from Livorno have not yet arrived, consequently neither have

all the other beautiful things which are sailing out at sea, and may God save the Raphael loggias from tempests and from the hands of American ship owners, with whom I am very angry, because they are ruining my trade from Arkhangelsk.

This first reference in Catherine's letters to Grimm of the Raphael loggias refers to drawings of the famous gallery created in the sixteenth century in the Vatican Palace by the architect Donato Bramante, the walls and vaults of which had been painted by Raphael's pupils after his sketches and under his supervision. When Catherine received these drawings on 1 September she immediately went into an acquisitive ecstasy over them and determined that she must have replicas of the loggias for herself. She wrote at once to Grimm so that he could pass on her instructions to Johann Friedrich Reiffenstein, his artistic contact in Rome:

I'll die, I'm sure I'll die: there's a strong wind blowing from the sea, the worst kind for the imagination; this morning I went to the baths, which made my blood rise to my head, and this afternoon the ceilings of the Raphael loggias fell into my hands. I am sustained by absolutely nothing but hope; I beg you to save me: write at once to Reiffenstein, I beg you, to tell him to get these vaults copied life-size, as well as the walls, and I make a vow to Saint Raphael that I will have loggias built whatever the cost and will place the copies in them, for I absolutely must see them as they are. I have such veneration for these loggias, these ceilings, that I am prepared to bear the expense of this building for their sake, and I will have neither peace nor repose until this project is under way. And if someone could make me a little model of the building, the dimensions taken with accuracy in Rome, the city of models, I would get nearer to my aim. Well, the divine Reiffenstein could have this lovely commission as well, if Monsieur the Baron Grimm so desires; I admit that I would rather charge you with this than Monsieur Shuvalov, because the latter is always raising doubts about everything, and doubts are what make people like me suffer more than anything else in the world.

Reiffenstein subsequently commissioned a group of artists to copy the murals on to canvas, under the supervision of the Austrian painter Christopher Unterberger. This project to reconstruct a part of the

Vatican Palace in St Petersburg was the most extreme example of Catherine's desire to bring the aesthetic wonders of the world to herself. The advantages gained, to her way of thinking, by such a course of action were twofold: she did not have to leave her Empire and thus expose herself to political instability and the fear of a coup in her absence, and the works of art became hers – and the Russian Empire's – in perpetuity.

On the evening of 20 September, Grand Duke Paul's twenty-fourth birthday, James Harris played cards at the Empress's table, in the company of both Potemkin and Alexei Orlov, who had arrived unexpectedly at Court a few days previously. Harris claimed to detect tensions between the two men as well as a general flummox among all the men close to Catherine or in positions of power at the sudden reappearance of Count Orlov, all such feelings, he said, 'concealed by the most masterly hypocrisy'. Catherine's new favourite, already promoted to the rank of major-general, was proving ambitious. Potemkin had suggested Rimsky-Korsakov be made a gentleman of the bedchamber, but the young man had not felt this was enough and had requested he be made chamberlain straightaway. In acceding to his request, Catherine had appointed Potemkin's cousin Pavel to be one as well, in order to assuage the Prince. Catherine's intimacy with Potemkin was rarely threatened by her relationships with her other favourites, her *vremenshchiki*. To use the terms coined by two equally unusual lovers from the twentieth century, Simone de Beauvoir and Jean-Paul Sartre, the relationship between Catherine and Potemkin was essential, while the other loves they both engaged in were contingent. Potemkin would always be the man to whom Catherine turned when she felt in particular need of advice or support; for instance, a note she sent him during these years reads: 'Many thanks for coming. Could you not come to me for an hour, even if only on the small staircase? Je voudrais Vous parler. [I want to talk to you.]' Nevertheless, Catherine did not expect her other loves to be temporary, always imagining that this time she had found the right young man to fulfil her sexual and emotional needs, while slotting into the role designed for him by herself and Potemkin, for years to come.

By now Catherine and Grimm were involved in the minutiae of negotiating the purchase of Voltaire's library with his niece – and erstwhile mistress – Madame Denis, who had lived with him in his chateau at Ferney. The price arrived at was 30,000 roubles, plus diamonds and furs. Catherine was intending to buy not only the library, but also the librarian, Wagnière – though whether he came to Petersburg with the library, or remained in France with a pension, was to be left up to him. (He eventually settled for the first option.) The Empress was also occupied in collating and having copies made of all the letters she had herself received from Voltaire; the intention was to send them to Grimm for him to catalogue and add to the library. Catherine complained that she thought Falconet (who, on completion of his work, had left Petersburg without taking his leave of her) might have gone off with some of the letters she had lent him. Grimm was expressly forbidden to make copies of her own letters to Voltaire or to allow any of them to be printed; 'I don't write well enough for that,' Catherine remarked. She now had two busts of the great man on display in her Hermitage, one by Houdon and one by Collot; she preferred Houdon's, as here the philosopher was portrayed without a wig, and 'you know my aversion for wigs,' she told Grimm, 'and particularly for busts with wigs on: I always think that wigs are specially designed to make one laugh'.

In mid-October Catherine ordered Grimm to obtain for her 100 copies of the new edition of Voltaire's works, so that she could place them where she thought fit, as part of her continuing campaign to educate and enlighten her people (or at least the upper echelons of her people): 'I want them to serve as an example; I want them to be studied, learnt by heart, for minds to be nourished by them: this will help in the formation of citizens, geniuses, heroes and authors; it will develop a hundred thousand talents, which would otherwise be lost in the night of shadows and ignorance etc.' She was even thinking of having a replica of the philosopher's house at Ferney built at Tsarskoye Selo, but this plan did not materialise.

Catherine was also in raptures over Ivan Rimsky-Korsakov, whom she described to Grimm in hyperbolic terms, contrasting his natural perfections with ephemeral works of art which arouse only infatuation:

Infatuation, infatuation! do you realise this term is not at all suitable in talking of Pyrrhus, King of Epirus, the painters' pitfall, the sculptors' despair? Nature's chefs-d'oeuvre inspire admiration, Monsieur, and enthusiasm; beautiful objects fall and break, like idols before the ark of the Lord, before the characters of the great. When Pyrrhus takes up a violin, even the dogs attend; when he sings, the birds flock to listen, as they did to Orpheus. Never does Pyrrhus make an ignoble gesture or ungraceful movement; he shines like the sun, he spreads brilliance all around him; and yet there is nothing effeminate in him, he is all male and just as you would wish a man to be; in short, he is Pyrrhus, King of Epirus: everything is harmonious in him; there is no piece detached from the whole; this is the effect of the precious gifts harvested from nature in all her beauty, art is of no consequence here, the artificial is ten thousand leagues away.

James Harris, who was not blinded by love, made a rather different assessment of the imperial favourite, describing him as 'very good-natured, but silly to a degree, and entirely subservient to the orders of Prince Potemkin, and the Countess Bruce'. Unfortunately Catherine was not the only woman to be smitten by Ivan's physical charms; Countess Bruce had herself conceived what Harris described as a 'violent passion' for the young man. When Catherine had first been made aware of this, she had warned off the Countess – who was also her oldest friend and confidante – and appeared to think that that would be the end of the matter. Ivan's musical talent (which would be inherited by his most famous descendant, the composer Nikolai Rimsky-Korsakov) made Catherine particularly regret her own very limited appreciation of music: 'It all depends on how one is made, doesn't it? I am made incorrectly; I'd give my life to be able to hear and love music, but there's nothing I can do, it's just noise to me. I would like to send a prize to your new society of medicine to be given to any person who can invent an effective cure for insensitivity to harmonious sounds.' If Catherine found it difficult to enjoy music, she had no such problems with her dogs, whom she could recognise individually by their barks; on 30 November one of her small greyhounds was trying to impede her letter-writing to Grimm:

You will excuse me if the whole of the last page was very poorly written: I'm very hampered at the moment by a certain young and beautiful Zemira, who of all the Thomassins [i.e. offspring and descendants of Sir Tom Anderson] is the one who places herself closest to me and pushes her claims so far as to put her paws on my paper; in addition to that, she chatters to me constantly and yelps for all her needs, caprices and desires; in her I see my prophecy that the Thomases will talk one day near its fulfilment; this hope stops me disciplining her, for fear of harming or delaying the development of speech in the race.

Towards the end of the year Catherine was irritated to find that her negotiations with Madame Denis, and even her request for the plans of the chateau at Ferney, were being reported in the French gazettes. She ended her letter to Grimm of 25 December rather tetchily: 'But farewell, it must not be said in my biography that I spent my whole life writing to you.'

A few weeks later Catherine was telling Grimm that Ivan Shuvalov had become a religious zealot and that he was therefore of limited use in helping her to purchase new works of art. He did not like to suggest she acquire a Venus by Titian, for instance, for that would be sinful. He was also becoming crippled, which Catherine attributed to his having spent entire nights on his knees in prayer. She also urged Grimm to use reading glasses, which she had been using herself for the past five to six years.

On 3 February Païsiello's *Le philosophe ridicule ou Le faux savant* (called in Italian either *Gli astrologi immaginari* or *I filosofi immaginari*) was performed in the theatre of the Winter Palace. (It would have been performed in Italian, with a French translation provided for the audience.) Catherine continued to be enthusiastic about the composer, as he alone seemed capable of breaking down her resistance to music. The libretto of this two-act light drama by Giovanni Bertati told the story of a conceited elderly father, his two daughters and the suitor of one of them, a man called Giuliano, who passes himself off as 'the famous philosopher Argafontida'. The aria Catherine liked the most could have been specially composed – and probably was – to appeal to someone who generally found music to be 'just noise': it was a song in which Païsiello had set a coughing fit to music. The Empress thought it was wonderful, enough to make one 'die laughing'. Païsiello received a snuffbox for his pains, and his wife a sprig of diamonds.

Catherine and Grimm now had to discuss the practical arrangements for the transportation of Voltaire's library to Petersburg: 'I think that in this wretched time of troubles and dissensions,'\* she wrote on 5 February, 'it would be better to send the cases containing the library over land as far as Lübeck, than to send them from Amsterdam to Petersburg by sea, where more than one disastrous accident might happen to them; in Lübeck I will have them taken by one of our ships.' The publicity surrounding Catherine's acquisition of the library had resulted in a spate of thinly disguised begging letters arriving

---

\* The War of the Bavarian Succession was going on between Austria and Prussia.

from Paris; the writers were keen to praise her generosity – 'but so far I've refrained from proving it to them', she wrote. The Empress had also recently entered into negotiations with the third Earl of Orford over the purchase of paintings belonging to his late grandfather, Sir Robert Walpole, acquired for his gallery at Houghton Hall in Norfolk; Catherine eventually purchased 204 of these paintings for the bargain price of £40,000. (A frigate was sent from Petersburg to collect them in August 1779.)

In the spring of 1779 Grand Duchess Maria Fyodorovna was expecting her second child. Alexander was continuing to delight his grandmother, who described him to Grimm as 'always cheerful' and reported that he was beginning to walk and talk. The only discipline which seemed to be necessary was to confiscate his doll if he mistreated it. The second child took his time in arriving, Catherine complaining to Grimm from Tsarskoye Selo on 12 April: 'The Grand Duchess has still not given birth; if she goes beyond the 14th, I will declare that the entire faculty [of medicine] doesn't know what it's talking about when it insists that women are pregnant for nine months, and that in future they must always add: *apart from Mother Nature's variations.*' A few days later Catherine instructed Grimm to ask Reiffenstein to undertake another commission for her in Rome; this time it was architects she wanted:

Ma si il signor marchese del Grimmo volio me faré un plaisir, he will have the goodness to write to the divine Reiffenstein to ask him to find two good architects for me, Italian by nationality and able by profession, whom he will engage in the service of Her Imperial Majesty of all the Russias by contract for so many years and whom he will expedite from Rome to Petersburg like a package of tools. He will not give them millions, but an honest and reasonable salary, and he will choose honest and reasonable people, not somebody difficult like Falconet, with their feet on the ground, not in the air; he will address them to me or to Baron Friedrichs, or to Count Bruce, or to Monsieur d'Eck, or to Monsieur Bezborodko, or to the devil and his grandmother, provided they come, because all mine have become either too old, or too blind, or too slow, or too lazy, or too young, or too idle, or too grand, or too rich, or too solid, or too stale . . . in a word, anything you like except what I need.

Paul and Maria Fyodorovna's second son, Constantine, was finally born on 27 April, six days after Catherine's fiftieth birthday. 'The little rascal had kept us waiting since mid-March,' Catherine told Grimm, 'and then once he set out, he descended on us like hail, arriving in an hour and a half . . . And so here is Constantine, as big as a fist, and here am I with Alexander on my right and Constantine on my left.' When not surrounded by babies, she was surrounded by dogs: 'One of the Thomases is lying partly on a cushion which is behind me and partly on my shoulder. NB. he is preventing me from writing.'

From the start poor little Constantine could never hope to compare in the eyes of his grandmother with his paragon of a brother who, now that he was nearly 18 months old, had become of consuming interest to Catherine, as she reported to Grimm at the end of May:

> But do you realise that in talking to me of Monsieur Alexandre, you are taking advantage of my weakness? I have told you before that this was a Prince who was doing very well, but now he is something else altogether: he is beginning to show a singular intelligence for a child of his age; I am besotted with him, and the infant would spend his whole life with me if he were allowed to. His mood is always equable, because he is well, and this mood consists in being always happy, welcoming, considerate, fearing nothing and being as beautiful as a cupid. This child delights everyone, and especially me; I can make of him what I want; he can walk unaided; when he is teething, even pain doesn't change his mood; he shows where it's hurting while continuing to laugh and frolic; he understands everything that is said to him, and has formed his own very intelligible language using signs and sounds.

Alexander had also succeeded in captivating Païsiello who would get the court orchestra to play the child's favourite tunes, after which Alexander would thank the players 'in his own way'. Constantine, on the other hand, held as yet no charm for his grandmother. She was extremely dismissive of the baby, who so far displayed none of the robust good health which had been Alexander's from birth: 'I am not putting great expectations yet on this Monsieur Constantin . . . it is a very feeble existence, crying, sullen, not looking anywhere, avoiding the light and hiding his nose in his blankets to avoid the air; if he stays alive, I'll be very amazed.'

On 5 July Catherine gave Grimm a further report on Alexander's progress and on the educational play she enjoyed with him (it is clear from this account that the child's parents were not deprived of his company, although they certainly had no control over his upbringing):

> I legislate in the morning; then the day's reports arrive; then at half past ten Monsieur Alexandre; it is said that while I dress I am also fashioning out of him a funny little person who does everything I want, and who is as happy and friendly as his age allows; he was spoilt for four days when I didn't see him, but all is now repaired to the very marked contentment of Mamma and Papa (oh, that is no small thing), who cannot get over it. I have told you before, and I repeat, that I am besotted with this infant. Every day we learn new things – that is to say, out of every toy we make ten or twelve, and you never know which of the two of us will develop our genius the most; it is extraordinary how industrious we are becoming . . . After dinner my infant comes back as often as he likes, and spends three to four hours every day in my room, often without my attending to him; if he gets bored, he goes away, but that hardly ever happens.

In the same letter Catherine asked Grimm to send her the recent book by the French naturalist the Comte de Buffon, 'which says that the world has lasted for 74,000 years and will last for another 95,000: I want to know the why of that'.★ Wagnière, Voltaire's library and the model of the Raphael loggias were all now on their way from Lübeck, and the nearly 70-year-old Rinaldi (one of Catherine's architects who were becoming 'too old') was recovering from a bad fall he had sustained while working on a building.

On 12 July Païsiello's *Le philosophe ridicule* was staged for the second time. (During the previous month the composer's wife had jumped into a pond at Tsarskoye Selo for fear that a swan was about to attack her.) Païsiello had achieved the remarkable feat of composing tunes that would stay in Catherine's head, and she asked to hear the work again two days later, when she told Grimm:

> The more I see it the more astonished I am by the singular use he knows how to make of tones and sounds: even the cough, for

---

★ Catherine is referring to Buffon's work *Epoques de la Nature* ('Epochs of Nature'), published in 1779; Buffon estimated the age of the Earth to be 75,000 years, from experiments on the cooling of rocks.

example, becomes harmonious, and it is all full of sublime follies, and you do not know what this musician does to gain the attention of organs which are the least sensitive to music, and those organs are mine. I come out of his music, my head filled with music; I can recognise and almost sing his composition: oh, what a singular head is Païsiello's!

She was now starting to teach Alexander to read, even though he was not yet able to talk. He could already recognise the letter A. Next they were going to do the other vowels, and then whole syllables.

A masquerade was staged in honour of the Grand Duchess's name-day, at which Catherine actually sang one of Païsiello's tunes back to him. On this occasion Sir (as he had recently become) James Harris obtained, through the good offices of his newly acquired friend Prince Potemkin (he had abandoned the idea of making any progress through Count Panin), the unusual opportunity of having a face-to-face conversation with the Empress on foreign affairs. He described the event to Lord Viscount Weymouth:

On Monday, 22nd July, at the masquerade given in honour of the Grand-Duchess's birthday [sic], some time after Her Imperial Majesty's card-party, at which I had assisted, was finished, Mons. Korsakoff came up to me, and, desiring me to follow him, conducted me a back way into the Empress's private dressing room, and, on introducing me, immediately retired. The Empress, after making me sit down, began of her own accord, by saying, that, after her own affairs, ours were those she had the most at heart; that they lately had occupied very seriously her attention; that she was ready to hear what I had to say concerning them; and should be happy if I could obviate the obstacles which ever presented themselves to her mind in every plan she had formed to be useful to us . . . She assured me, that if she had not been well-disposed to hear all I had to say, and that if she had not also a particular regard for me, she never could have been brought to see me in so unusual a manner; she therefore desired I would speak without reserve, that she would hear both my sentiments and counsels, if I had any to give. Thus encouraged, I endeavoured, to the best of my abilities, to set before her eyes the present state of Europe in general, and in particular that of England . . .

Our conversation having now lasted upwards of an hour, she

dismissed me, and it being quite dark, it was with some difficulty I found my way through the intricate passages back to the ballroom.

On 23 August Catherine told Grimm that there was no tune from Païsiello's opera she did not know by heart, and that she thought Païsiello must be a sorcerer as he was able to conjure up any sentiment he pleased. She also told Grimm about the arrival of her new architect, Charles Cameron: 'At present I have got hold of Mr Cameron, Scottish by nationality, Jacobite by calling, a great draughtsman nourished on antiquities, known by a book on the ancient baths; we are fashioning with him a terraced garden with baths underneath, gallery above.' Cameron claimed to be a direct descendant of Cameron of Lochiel, whose coat of arms he used, but he was in fact the son of a speculative builder in London who, when Charles left for Russia, was in debtors' prison. As Catherine mentioned, Charles had published a book in 1772 on the ancient Roman baths, which is what had convinced the Empress and her ambassador in London that it would be worth inviting him to Russia to work for her.

The partnership between the Empress and her Scottish architect proved extremely fruitful. The plans Catherine mentioned in her letter to Grimm took shape eventually at Tsarskoye Selo as the Agate Pavilion and Colonnade, which became known as the Cameron Gallery. First of all, however, Cameron (who initially was given a workroom in the flat above the orangery at Tsarskoye Selo occupied by the gardener John Bush and his family) was set to work to fulfil Catherine's plans for the conversion of rooms within the Catherine Palace. He worked first on a suite of eight rooms at the north end of the palace, known as the First Apartment; these were to be for the use of the Grand Duke and Duchess and they consisted of the Blue Drawing Room, the Chinese Cabinet, an anteroom, the Green Dining Room, a bedchamber, a music room, a studio for painting and ivory carving, and a serving room.* Catherine loved the work Cameron did here – which was completed in 1782 – much preferring his Neo-classical style with its muted colours and sense of space and symmetry to the baroque indulgences of Rastrelli.

* This apartment, which later came to be known as the suite of Empress Elizaveta Alexeyevna, the wife of Alexander I, was completely destroyed by German bombs during the Second World War but has since been restored to its original glories by Soviet architects and artists working directly from Cameron's plans.

Cameron later worked on the south end of the palace on two further suites, the Fourth and Fifth Apartments, comprising the Empress's public and private rooms.

Catherine was also pleased that Reiffenstein had succeeded in finding another architect for her, the Italian Giacomo Quarenghi, who would soon be arriving with his wife. The Empress hoped that the latter would be a welcome companion for Païsiello's wife. Her letter of 23 August ended in characteristic praise of her elder grandson, who was continuing to be all she could desire:

> But here comes Monsieur Alexandre; I am making a delightful infant out of him; it is astonishing that, though he can't yet talk, this child has knowledge at 20 months above the ability of any other child of three years. Grandmamma is making of him what she wants: damn it, he will be lovable; I will not be wrong about that: as he is cheerful and willing, he seeks to please right from the start. Goodbye. I must go and play with him.

While Catherine was playing with Alexander, Ivan Rimsky-Korsakov was off playing somewhere else. It seems that almost everyone at Court apart from Catherine knew that the Countess Bruce's 'violent passion' for the handsome young man had not been dampened for long and that Ivan had been sufficiently flattered to respond. Countess Bruce being the same age as Catherine – and her oldest friend – Rimsky-Korsakov did not even have the excuse that he fancied a younger woman. All Catherine seems to have noticed is that she often did not know where her favourite was. In early July she had told Grimm that 'Pyrrhus' had been unwell for a while, but was now looking prouder and more mischievous than ever (as well he might).

A detailed description of the formal side of life at the Russian Court at this time is provided by an Englishman, Archdeacon William Coxe, who visited Russia as the companion and tutor of the teenage nephew of the Duke of Marlborough, who was undertaking a five-year 'Grand Tour' of Europe. Coxe and his charge were presented to the Empress by Sir James Harris on 20 September 1779, Grand Duke Paul's twenty-fifth birthday, and he wrote a full account of the event:

> At the entrance into the drawing room stood two centinels [*sic*] of the foot-guards: their uniform was a green coat, with a red cuff and cape, and white waistcoat and breeches; they had silver helmets

fastened under the chin with silver clasps, and ornamented with an ample plume of red, yellow, black, and white feathers. Within the drawing room, at the doors of the passage leading to her majesty's apartments, were two soldiers of the knights body-guard; a corps perhaps more sumptuously accoutred than any in Europe. They wore casques, like those of the antients, with a rich plumage of black feathers, and their whole dress was in the same style: chains and broad plates of solid silver were braided over their uniforms, so as to bear the appearance of a splendid coat of mail; and their boots were richly ornamented with the same metal.

In the drawing room we found a numerous assembly of foreign ministers, Russian nobility, and officers in their different uniforms, waiting the arrival of the empress, who was attending divine service in the chapel of the palace, whither we also repaired. Amid a prodigious concourse of nobles, I observed the empress standing by herself behind a railing; the only distinction by which her place was marked. Immediately next to her stood the great-duke and duchess; and behind an indiscriminate throng of courtiers. The empress bowed repeatedly, and frequently crossed herself, according to the forms used in the Greek church, with great expressions of devotion. Before the conclusion of the service we returned to the drawing room; and took our station near the door, in order to be presented at her majesty's entrance. At length, a little before twelve, the chief officers of the household, the mistress of the robes, the maids of honour, and other ladies of the bed-chamber, advancing two by two in a long train, announced the approach of their sovereign. Her majesty came forward with a slow and solemn pace; walking with great pomp; holding her head very high; and perpetually bowing to the right and to the left as she passed along. She stopped a little way within the entrance of the great drawing room, and spoke with great affability to the foreign ministers while they kissed her hand. She then advanced a few steps, and we were singly presented by the vice-chancellor Count Osterman, and had the honour of kissing her majesty's hand. The empress wore, according to her usual custom, a Russian dress; it was a robe with a short train, and a vest with sleeves reaching to the wrist, like a Polonaise; the vest was of gold brocade, and the robe was of light green silk; her hair was dressed low, and lightly sprinkled with powder; her cap ornamented with a profusion of diamonds; and she wore a great deal of rouge. Her person, though rather below the middle size, is majestic; and her countenance, particularly when she speaks, expresses both dignity and sweetness. She walked slowly through the drawing room to her apartment, and entered alone. The great-duke and duchess followed the empress to the door, and then retired to their own drawing room, where they had a levee; but, as we had not yet been presented to them at a private audience, we could not, according to the etiquette of the Russian court, follow them. The great-duchess leaned upon the arm of his imperial highness; and they both inclined their heads on either side to the company, as they passed along the line which was formed for them.

In the evening, beginning at about six o'clock, there was a ball at the Winter Palace, which was again described by Archdeacon Coxe:

The great-duke opened the ball by walking a minuet with his consort; at the end of which his imperial highness handed out a lady, and the great-duchess a gentleman, with whom they each performed a second minuet at the same time. They afterwards successively conferred this honour in the same manner upon many of the principal nobility, while several other couples were dancing minuets in different parts of the circle: the minuets were succeeded by Polish dances; and these were followed by English country-dances. In the midst of the latter the empress entered the room: she was more richly apparelled than in the morning, and bore upon her head a small crown of diamonds.

Upon her majesty's appearance the ball was instantly suspended; while the great-duke and duchess, and the most considerable persons who were present, hastened to pay their respects to their sovereign: Catharine [*sic*], having addressed a few words to some of the principal nobility, ascended a kind of elevated seat, when, the dancing being again resumed, she, after a short time, withdrew into an inner apartment.

Here the Empress sat down to a game of macao with the Duchess of Courland, Countess Bruce, Sir James Harris, Potemkin, Count Razumovsky, Count Panin, Prince Repnin and Ivan Chernyshev. Coxe further observed:

In the course of the evening the great-duke and duchess presented themselves before the empress, and stood by the table for about a quarter of an hour, during which time her majesty occasionally entered into conversation with them. The empress seemed to pay very little attention to the cards; conversed familiarly and frequently with great vivacity, as well with the party at play, as with the persons of rank standing near her. About ten her majesty retired; and soon after the ball concluded.

As Archdeacon Coxe explained, the same pattern of events was followed on every 'court day' – that is, on Sundays and other festivals:

There is a drawing room at court every Sunday morning, about twelve o'clock, and on other particular festivals, at which the embassadors [sic] are usually present, and which all foreign gentlemen, who have been once presented, are permitted to attend. The ceremony of kissing the empress's hand is repeated every court day by foreigners in the presence chamber; and by the Russians in another apartment; the latter bend their knee on this occasion; an expression of homage not expected from the former. No ladies, excepting those of the empress's household, make their appearance at the morning levees.

On every court day the great duke and duchess have also their separate levees at their own apartments in the palace. Upon particular occasions, such as her own and the empress's birth-day, etc. foreigners have the honour of kissing her imperial highness's hand; but upon common days that ceremony is omitted.

In the evening of a court day, there is always a ball at the palace, which begins between six and seven. At that time the foreign ladies kiss the empress's hand, who salutes them in return on the cheek. Her majesty, unless she is indisposed, generally makes her appearance about seven; and, if the assembly is not very numerous, plays at Macao in the ball-room; the great-duke and duchess, after they have danced, sit down to whist. Their highnesses, after a short interval, rise; approach the empress's table; pay their respects; and then return to their game. When the ball happens to be crouded [sic]; the empress forms her party, as I have before-mentioned, in an adjoining room, which is open to all persons who have once been presented.

Coxe was very struck by the splendour and richness of the Russian Court, which he declared to retain 'many traces of its antient Asiatic pomp, blended with European refinement'. He also provided details of court dress, for both male and female courtiers:

The court-dress of the men is in the French fashion [i.e. breeches, long waistcoat and jacket, made of cloths of gold and silver stuff, decorated with embroidery and precious or semi-precious stones]: that of the ladies is a gown and petticoat, with a small hoop; the gown has long hanging-sleeves and a short train, and is of a different colour from the petticoat. The ladies wore, according to the fashion of the winter of 1777 at Paris and London, very lofty head-dresses, and were not sparing in the use of rouge. Amid the several articles of sumptuousness which distinguish the Russian notability; there is none perhaps more calculated to strike a foreigner than the profusion of diamonds and other precious stones, which sparkle in every part of their dress. In most other European countries these costly ornaments are (excepting among a few of the richest and principal nobles) almost entirely appropriated to the ladies; but in this the men vie with the fair sex in the use of them. Many of the nobility were almost covered with diamonds; their buttons, buckles, hilts of swords, and epaulets, were composed of this valuable material; their hats were frequently embroidered, if I may use the expression, with several rows of them; and a diamond-star upon the coat was scarcely a distinction.

The dénouement of the affair between Ivan Rimsky-Korsakov and Countess Bruce occurred in October. At the beginning of the month the Empress was still blissfully unaware of any problem in her personal life. On the 3rd she wrote in her usual good spirits to Grimm, yet again expressing delight in her elder grandson and pride at the nature of her relationship with him:

This child loves me instinctively; simply the sight of me puts him at his ease; he holds strictly to what I say to him; if he is crying and I come in, he stops; if he is happy, his happiness increases. I talk reason to him within his understanding; he yields and gives in to such reason. The other day Prince Orlov, seeing all this, was astonished and said: 'But here is a child who is not yet two, who can't talk but who listens to reason.' Well, this child is not so docile for everybody. As for the other one, he isn't anything yet.

A week later Rimsky-Korsakov was formally dismissed, by the Empress herself. Potemkin, having decided the situation could not be allowed to continue and realising that subtle measures would be ineffective, had arranged for Catherine to come upon her best friend and her favourite in a compromising position, if not actually *in flagrante delicto*. After that everything came out, and the Empress realised that the couple had been deceiving her for months. Supported by Potemkin, she sustained what must have been a severe blow with remarkable fortitude. She was ill for a few days, but responded to the situation with characteristic magnanimity towards an ex-favourite, resolving, as usual, not to waste time and emotional energy crying over spilt milk. Via Ivan Betskoy she had conveyed to Rimsky-Korsakov her intention to provide well for his future, requesting that he should go away, travel, and eventually marry someone suitable. But the arrogant, immature Rimsky-Korsakov was still too full of himself and cocksure about his ability to charm women to respond appropriately. He continued to wreak havoc, not only by refusing to leave Petersburg, and gossiping about his sexual adventures with the Empress, but by betraying Countess Bruce into the bargain, embarking on an affair with the beautiful Countess Ekaterina Stroganova, who was so bowled over that she left her husband and child for him. (Poor Count Stroganov was not very fortunate with his wives; his first wife, Anna, had been the woman involved in a love affair with Nikita Panin and whom he had been on the point of divorcing when she died.) Even Catherine was now roused to ire, and the dangerous young man was sent away to Moscow. Countess Bruce had completely lost her head over him; having also lost her position at Court, she followed Rimsky-Korsakov to Moscow. But he no longer wanted her, and she was forced to return to her long-suffering husband, Count Yakob Bruce. Her friendship with Catherine was beyond repair. (Countess Bruce died in Moscow on 7 April 1785, Catherine commenting on this at the time in a letter to Grimm with typical generosity and understatement: 'it is impossible not to mourn her when one has known her well, for she was very lovable; six or seven years ago this would have pained me even more, for since that time we became a little more distant and separated than before'.)

Before making his move to bring about Rimsky-Korsakov's disgrace, Potemkin had lined up yet another young man to replace him in the Empress's favour and affections. On this occasion, however, Catherine seems to have followed her own inclination and selected a 22-year-old officer of the Horse Guards called Alexander Lanskoy. Despite the inauspicious circumstances in which this hurried choice was effected, it turned out to be one of the most successful Catherine ever made.

## 15

# The Empress and the Emperor
# (1779–81)

*If I were to begin singing his praises, I would never finish.*
Catherine II on the subject of Joseph II

With her increasing years, and her status as a grandmother, there came a change in the way Catherine reacted to her favourites. Though she was still a fervent admirer of male beauty, and needed to have a young man as a loving and beloved companion, the emphasis turned away from sex (which may never have played as important a part in her relationships as both contemporary and later commentators have liked to imagine) and towards pedagogy and a desire to share her artistic and architectural enthusiasms. The need to instruct and educate both herself and others had always been a crucial component of Catherine's make-up, but it was as though the advent of her grandsons had released in her an extra burst of energy to 'make what she wanted' of the beloved young males around her – both her grandsons and her favourite. Though by all accounts Alexander Lanskoy was not particularly distinguished or gifted, he made the ideal companion for Catherine at this time, for he was eminently teachable – keen to learn and able to absorb information and what one might term 'cultivation' very quickly. He also had a large number of relatives who were delighted at his new-found wealth and status – for his position inevitably brought them great benefits too – and he seemed to love and respect the Empress as much as she loved him. He undoubtedly brought her much happiness and stability. He also seemed happy to accept Potemkin's place at the centre of Catherine's life and as a kind of father-figure in relation to himself.

Towards the end of 1779 and beginning of 1780 Catherine was preoccupied with the plans for the tour of inspection she had decided to undertake in May and June. Her intention was to see how her Guberniya Reform of 1775 was working in practice, to view for herself the new territories acquired by the Russian Empire as a result of the 1772 partition of Poland, and to meet Joseph II, the Holy Roman Emperor jointly ruling with his mother Maria Theresa. As she explained to Grimm, she had only one regret:

> It is true that Monsieur Alexandre will not be pleased to see me go, but what can I do? When he leaves my apartments under his own steam, he does so quite happily; but if I leave him, he cries loudly; he writes me letters from his room; if he is ill, he sends for me, and when I arrive he really livens up, whatever is the matter with him. He is a very unusual infant; he is a composite of instincts: those who do not observe him do not believe he has either spirit or imagination, but I maintain that he will be a very particular composite of instinct and knowledge; he already knows more things than other children of four or five. In addition analogies strike him in particular, and again it is I who has to explain them to him, and as I always speak simple reason to him and I have never deceived him about anything, he believes that he does not really know something until he knows it from me.

In addition to working on legislation and preparing for her journey, Catherine was compiling an 'ABC' of maxims for children. In this, she was influenced by Grimm's companion, Madame d'Epinay, the author of *Conversations d'Emilie*, a work in which she prescribed the moral upbringing of her granddaughter, using a question-and-answer technique which Catherine adapted:

> It begins by telling him straight that he is an infant born naked, like the hand which knows nothing, that all infants are born thus, that in birth all men are the same, but that by study they become infinitely different from one another, and thus we proceed from one thing to another, from maxim to maxim, like a string of pearls. I have only two goals in view: one is to open the mind to the impression of things, the other to elevate the soul while forming the heart.

Once published, Catherine's 'ABC' had some success; she reported to Grimm on 25 June 1781 that 20,000 copies of it had been sold in Petersburg in the preceding fortnight.

The news that Catherine and the Emperor Joseph II were planning to meet was causing some anxiety in Europe, particularly at the Prussian Court, in case such a meeting presaged a change in Russian foreign policy. An alliance between the Courts of Petersburg and Vienna would diminish Prussian influence in Russia, and Frederick the Great was determined not to let that happen. It was Sir James Harris's belief that Frederick made an attempt during the early spring of 1780 to suborn Prince Potemkin, insinuating that in return for the Prince's support he would guarantee to bring about a reconciliation between Potemkin and Grand Duke Paul, 'as to insure [Potemkin], in case of the Empress's demise, safety for his person, honours, and property; the danger of being deprived of which frequently haunts him, and there are moments when he is plunged in the profoundest melancholy'. But the Prince was as committed as the Empress to exploring closer links with Joseph, believing that this was the route to Russia's further expansion in the south and important in the event of future conflict with the Turks. And although Potemkin undoubtedly was anxious about his eventual fate under the sovereignty of Catherine's son, who might well have scores to settle, he did not think the answer was to entrust his fate to the King of Prussia. At the end of April he set off to take charge of the reception of the Russian Empress and the Holy Roman Emperor at Mogilyov, a port on the Dnieper which had become part of the Russian Empire in 1772 and was now the centre of the Mogilyov *guberniya*. Before her own departure Catherine arranged for the English painter Richard Brompton (who had moved from England to Russia at the Empress's invitation after she had settled all his debts) to attempt a portrait of Alexander, no easy task as the two-year-old had no inclination to sit still. His grandmother was amused at the child's response when she asked him how he held himself when he was being painted; 'I don't know,' he replied, 'I can't see myself.'

On 9 May the Empress departed from Tsarskoye Selo with a substantial suite – which included her young favourite Alexander (or, as she affectionately called him, Sasha or Sashenka) Lanskoy, but not the pro-Prussian Nikita Panin. The inspections of the newly reformed *guberniyas* and vice-regencies were meticulously planned, the eminent officials who had been selected as governors and vice-regents taking care to ensure that Catherine was given the best possible impression of their

administration, but there were nevertheless many genuinely good results
to be seen. Throughout her journey she wrote regularly to her son and
daughter-in-law, and they to her. Although this correspondence often
consisted of formulaic exchanges concerning health and mutual expressions of regard, the Empress's letters also contained much interesting
detail – Catherine clearly expecting Paul and Maria Fyodorovna to be
amused at whatever amused her. No one reading the letters would
guess how difficult face-to-face relations could be among this family:

> My dear children, I will not talk to you at all about my departure
> as I don't like to dwell on sad things; the first three versts were very
> sad, but I will tell you only that I arrived here towards four o'clock
> in good health, and I tell you this because I know it will give you
> pleasure, I ask you to stay well, and to enjoy yourselves while awaiting
> my return; I kiss both you and your children, especially my Alexander.
> Goodbye, I love you very much.

From her next letter, written the day after her departure, it is clear that
Paul and Maria Fyodorovna had also hastened to write to the Empress
as soon as she had left:

> My dear children, Your letters filled with tenderness affected me very
> poignantly and renewed my regrets at having left you. Be assured
> that I love you with all my heart and that I am very appreciative of
> all your feelings for me. I had a very heavy heart for several days,
> but didn't utter a word about it for fear of increasing your sadness,
> I saw your tears and often had difficulty in holding back my own.
> I will hurry to be reunited with you as soon as I can. Goodbye my
> dear children; I kiss you as well as my children's children; may God
> bless you and keep you in perfect health.

On 10 May, at eight o'clock in the evening, Catherine arrived at Narva
(now in north-eastern Estonia). She reported to Paul and Maria
Fyodorovna on the following day that her secretary Alexander
Bezborodko had been hunting for the courier since three o'clock in
the morning, and commented that Narva must be as large as Paris since
people could get lost in it so easily. Throughout her journey Catherine
made a habit of sending back locally manufactured presents to members
of her family, and from Narva she sent some dress material for Maria
Fyodorovna and a box of toys for 'my friend Monsieur Alexandre'. By

the end of that day she was feeling rather tired – and irritated by the way the women of the town insisted on crowding round her and serving her at table. Of the doctor's wife she commented: 'I was terrified that she was going to rub my plates with rhubarb the way they rub them with garlic.' She also remarked that 'the local beauties are ugly enough to scare you, yellow as though they've been dyed and emaciated as old nags'. The day's letter to her son and daughter-in-law concluded: 'may the good Lord preserve you from having seven or eight of the women of Narva behind your chairs at dinner; they breathed such hot air on me that I didn't feel the cold – though it's as cold here as it is with you'. On 13 May, Catherine was at Gdov on the river Gdovka (in recognition of her visit, Gdov formally acquired the status of a town), which she did not find very interesting as it was so sparsely populated. Then at nine o'clock in the evening she arrived in the ancient town of Pskov, which she declared to be very like Novgorod. En route she dined with, as she related to Paul and Maria Fyodorovna, a

> princess who was salted like a ham, but literally salted and here is how this lead substance was discovered: when I took leave of her, she came to kiss my hand, and I put my mouth to her cheek and then when the Master of the Horse was leading me down the stairs I had this odd feeling while I was talking to him that my lips were saturated with salt. Laughing, I told him this, and he looked at me and saw a finger of white on my lips. After I had got into my carriage Mademoiselle Engelhardt spent several minutes wiping me, and with difficulty got this wretched ceruse [white lead] off my lips. If her husband makes a habit of kissing her, he must get very thirsty.

On Sunday 17 May Catherine was in Ostrov, granted town status in 1777 and situated on the Velikaya river about 34 miles south of Pskov, which she found to be a beautiful place set among hills, with cultivated land and villages all around. She reported to Paul and Maria Fyodorovna that since her encounter with the 'salted Princess' her ladies kept a glass of water to hand in order to remove all traces from her face whenever people were presented to her. After attending the liturgy at Ostrov, the Empress and her suite set off for Opochka, another 46 miles or so further south, where they would spend the night. On the following day the travellers arrived in Dolostsi, in White Russia (now Belarus). Catherine reported of the region to Paul and Maria

Fyodorovna:'everywhere round here everyone lives pell-mell, Orthodox, Catholic, Uniates, Jews etc. Russians, Polish, Finns, Germans, Courlanders, there are no two people dressed in the same costumes who speak the same language correctly or accurately, it is a mixture of people and languages as at the building of the tower of Babel'.

On 19 May Catherine arrived in Polotsk on the river Dvina. She told Paul and Maria Fyodorovna that there was a large number of Poles there – hardly surprising, given that the town had belonged to Poland before the partition of 1772 – and went on to say, exhibiting conventional anti-semitic prejudices:

> At the moment I am equidistant between Petersburg and Moscow. It has been hot all day, and now it is thundering quite a lot. On arrival I saw something I have never seen before – Jesuits, Dominicans etc. and Jews lined up on parade. The latter are horribly dirty. The others make an august masquerade. Farewell, right now I'm exhausted and my eyes are tired by the candlelight. I am very well as is all my suite; I kiss you and your children and love you with all my heart.

On 20 May Catherine had a tour of Polotsk, which included a visit to the Jesuit college and church, where she witnessed a procession of the Blessed Sacrament. She remarked of this meeting with her Jesuit subjects: 'They have a very beautiful church here; they said all possible sweet things to me in all possible languages, except the ones that I understand.' Three days later the Empress and her retinue were hosted by Semyon Zorich – who was by now settled into his role as a high-spending (and indebted) ex-favourite – at his estate in Shklov, on the river Dnieper. There were now just 25 miles left to travel to Mogilyov, the appointed meeting place with Joseph II, who was travelling under the pseudonym of 'Count Falkenstein'.

In the latter stages of the journey the two rulers engaged in a race to see who could get to Mogilyov first, Catherine explaining to Grimm, 'When [Monsieur de Falkenstein] learned that I had shortened my journey by four days in order to get there ahead of him, he started running night and day and got ahead of me by two days.' Catherine arrived at Mogilyov on Sunday 24 May and arranged with Potemkin to have 'Count Falkenstein' waiting at her residence to meet her after she had attended the liturgy. Despite her initial nervousness – for it was very important to her to make a good impression on this most powerful monarch – she took to the Emperor at once, writing to Paul and Maria Fyodorovna after their first encounter: 'He likes talking, he is learned, he wants to put everyone at their ease, one has no idea what he looks like if one hasn't seen him, his portraits don't look like him at all.' When Catherine was nervous, she perspired, an affliction exacerbated by the humid weather in Mogilyov: 'Oh, how hot it is here, oh how I sweated, everyone said that I coped marvellously well and that no one could tell I was embarrassed; I'm very pleased that Countess Chernysheva has had a nice tub of water placed near my bedroom, first thing tomorrow morning I'll get into it.'

Certain of the Emperor's habits gained immediate approval from the Empress. If anything, he was even more abstemious and orderly in his life than she: 'he eats only once in 24 hours, he goes to bed early and gets up early, he eats what he is given and drinks only water'. He must also have been very loquacious, as Catherine repeatedly commented: 'He likes talking and knows a lot of things.' At least he wasn't a 'pea soup'! He did have one idiosyncrasy, for which Catherine intended to cater when he came to visit her in Tsarskoye Selo, which he would be doing in a few weeks' time: the Emperor Joseph had a particular predilection for staying in inns and taverns, so Catherine arranged for one of the bathhouse pavilions at Tsarskoye Selo to be fitted out as an inn, complete with sign, and for her gardener John Bush to dress himself up as the innkeeper. To add a final touch, this ersatz establishment was to be called 'The Falkenstein Arms'. Whether Joseph was flattered, amused or fooled is not recorded. Meanwhile, in Mogilyov, in addition to talking ('He talks with a lot of soundness and what he knows he knows very well, he likes making conversation and it is no trouble to be with him after the first encounter which made me sweat'), the two monarchs attended church. Joseph attended the Orthodox liturgy twice, and Catherine accompanied him to a Roman Catholic Mass, which she declared to Paul and Maria Fyodorovna to have been performed with less 'decorum' than the Orthodox celebration. Her subsequent comments to Grimm, however, throw a rather different light on things: 'Monsieur de Falkenstein and I heard a Catholic mass sung by the Bishop of Mogilyov assisted by Jesuits, ex-Jesuits and a quantity of religious and non-religious orders, we laughed and joked there more than we listened, with him as the cicerone and me the gawper.' They also laid the foundation stone of a new Orthodox church which was to be built of stone and where there was to be an inscription commemorating their meeting. This would eventually become the cathedral of St Joseph, designed by Nikolai Lvov and built by the Scot Adam Menelaws. (The cathedral was destroyed during Soviet times; there is now a hotel on the site.)

Catherine and Joseph left Mogilyov on 30 May, travelling together in a six-seater carriage, to spend the night in Shklov from where they departed on the following day for Smolensk. Here, in this town which had belonged to Russia since 1654, Catherine felt more at home than she had done in her more recently acquired dominions: 'It is very different here from those godforsaken towns of White Russia. The surrounding views are charming, the town picturesque, the cathedral superb, Monsieur de Falkenstein finds it more beautiful than the one in Kiev. A number of stone buildings have been begun . . . I am pleased with this place.' Even the weather was better in Smolensk. She also told Paul and Maria Fyodorovna: 'Don't sweat, the conversation with Monsieur de Falkenstein will not cause you any trouble, he is very intelligent and you will find him very learned. He will be a lot less of a pain than the King of Sweden, believe me.' A ball was given for the nobility of Smolensk, during which Catherine and Joseph absented themselves for a few hours to go for a drive round the town and its outskirts. At eight o'clock on the morning of 4 June they parted company. Joseph, accompanied by Potemkin, was to visit Moscow, while Catherine began her return journey to Tsarskoye Selo, where the Emperor would rejoin her in time for the feast day of St John Baptist on 24 June.

The journey from Smolensk was uncomfortably hot and very dusty. Catherine's return route, on which she seems to have found little to interest her, went via the village of Prechistoye, Velikiye Luki on the Lovat river, Porhkov on the Shelon river, Mshaga and Novgorod. She arrived back at Tsarskoye Selo on 12 June, very satisfied with the trip, which had consolidated her belief in the immeasurable benefits which membership of the Russian Empire had brought to its subject peoples. A year later she was still enthusing about this to Grimm: 'I must tell you the favourite saying of the Livonians, which is that since they have been under Russian domination, there is more silver and silverware in the province than there used to be copper; and in White Russia it's the same: their lands are better cultivated and have gone up in value; he who before had no hut is building one; he who did have one is improving it etc.'

'Count Falkenstein' duly arrived at the 'Falkenstein Arms' in time for the Feast of St John Baptist, which was also the anniversary of the battle of Chesme. On that day he attended the consecration of Chesme church, midway between Tsarskoye Selo and Petersburg and dedicated to St John Baptist (the foundation stone had been laid by Gustavus III during his visit in 1777). Thus Catherine ensured that two foreign monarchs were visibly reminded of the great Russian naval victory. Built by Yuri Felten, this distinctive red-and-white-striped church was designed to recall the kiosks and pavilions of the Bosphorus. Joseph left Tsarskoye Selo to return to Vienna on 10 July, after having also made the acquaintance of the Grand Duke and Duchess and stayed for some days with Catherine at Peterhof. A fortnight later Catherine described some of her impressions of him to Grimm; they were overwhelmingly positive:

> If I were to begin singing his praises, I would never finish; he has the soundest, most profound, most learned brain that I know: by God, anyone who wanted to get ahead of him would have to get up very early. My illustrious ally had a solemn service said for the repose of Voltaire's soul; I who believe that his soul is already at peace will not imitate his example, because I don't like to imitate everything that is done and because one should not wrong the living through love for the dead . . .
>
> Monsieur de Falkenstein told me that he had heard a thousand good things about you; I said to him that I begged him to believe that what he had heard about you was accurate. Addio, signor; Païsiello's music is very much to his taste; of all the arts I think that music is the one he loves the most, and also the one of which he has the profoundest knowledge.

The Empress received two further visitors during the late summer and autumn, both of whom served to strengthen the good impression the Emperor Joseph had made on her and to increase her determination to formalise an alliance between the Courts of Petersburg and Vienna. The first to arrive was the 50-year-old Charles Joseph, Prince de Ligne, who had the reputation of being one of the wittiest men in Europe. The Emperor had deliberately sent him to Petersburg to act on his behalf, knowing that he was precisely the sort of man to amuse and charm the Empress. And indeed on 7 September she described the Prince de Ligne to Grimm as 'one of the pleasantest people and easiest to get on with that I have ever met'. In this letter she also assured Grimm of the safe arrival of Anton Raphael Mengs' picture *Perseus and Andromeda*, and expressed her thoughts on people's varying ability to appreciate art: '[Andromeda] has been here for a fortnight in my Hermitage, on display to the eyes of both those who know how to look and those who take a quarter of an hour to see all that there is to see in this place. Great lords know everything without having learnt anything, says the proverb; by God, there are also plenty of people who see everything without seeing anything or who see everything in a single moment.' She went on to say that it was now time to stop buying so many paintings: 'After the paintings bought from Mr Jenkins I will buy no more, and all my acquaintances are forbidden to send me catalogues or suggest purchases to me, for I have no more money.' It is sometimes hard to tell which of Catherine and Grimm was the driving force behind her acquisition of artworks, both tending to spur the other on while attempting at the same time to put on the brakes. In one letter, Catherine rebukes Grimm both for criticising her for wanting too much – 'I cannot forgive you for accusing me of gluttony in connection with the fine arts' – and for trying to make her carry on spending – 'Why do you want me to buy everyone's paintings?'

The other visitor who arrived at the Court of St Petersburg that summer did not find such a warm welcome as either Joseph II or the Prince de Ligne. Anxious to repair any breach in his influence occasioned by Russia's rapprochement with the Habsburgs, Frederick the Great sent his own representative in the person of his nephew and heir, the 36-year-old Prince Frederick William. Unfortunately for the King's scheme, both Catherine's resolve to form an alliance with Austria and her personal antipathy towards this 'heavy' Prussian, so different from the charming and witty de Ligne and the talkative Joseph, resulted in her being barely able to treat him with courtesy, let alone favour. Prince Frederick William had been welcomed to the Court on 26 August by both Potemkin and Panin, and officially received by the Empress the following day. Sir James Harris immediately reported what he had learnt of the encounter:

The interview between him and the Empress, which took place yesterday morning with great ceremony and etiquette was, I believe, very little satisfactory to either. He appeared to her heavy, reserved, and awkward; and her reception struck him as cool, formal, and unpromising. In the evening, little ground was gained; and the Empress, though at her Hermitage, where she is generally very talk-

A portrait of King Stanislas II Augustus of Poland by Marie Louise Elizabeth Vigée-Lebrun. As Stanislas Poniatowski, he was Catherine's lover when she was still a Grand Duchess; he was elected King of Poland, at her instigation, in 1764.

The most significant man in Catherine's life, Prince Grigory Potemkin, painted by Johann Baptist Edler von Lampi, in about 1790.

A drawing by Louis Carrogis Carmontelle of Baron Friedrich Melchior Grimm, Catherine's art dealer, correspondent and *souffre-douleur*.

A portrait by Vigée-Lebrun of Giovanni Païsiello, the composer who came closest to giving Catherine an appreciation of music.

Catherine's uniform dress from 1763, modelled after the uniform of the Preobrazhensky Guards. Catherine had proclaimed herself Colonel of the Preobrazhensky Guards on her accession, and wore this dress at the ceremonial occasions of the regiment.

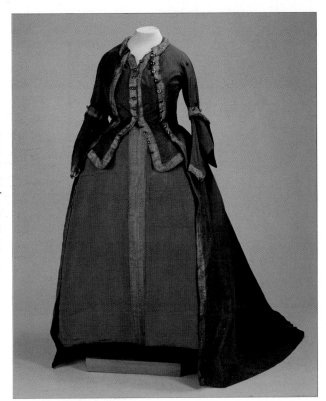

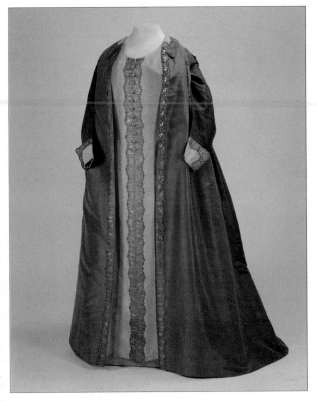

Another of Catherine's uniform dresses, modelled after that of the Life-Guards Cavalry regiment. This dress dates from 1773; it is noticeable how much the Empress's girth had expanded in ten years.

Grand Duke Paul, painted against a backdrop of the Neva with the spire of the Peter and Paul cathedral in the distance, by Alexander Roslin in 1777.

A portrait by the same artist and from the same year of Paul's second wife and mother of his many children, Maria Fyodorovna. A follower of exuberant fashion – in so far as her mother-in-law allowed – she also enjoyed gardens and garden design.

A portrait of Catherine's grandsons, Alexander and Constantine, by the English artist
Richard Brompton, whom the Empress rescued from penury.

Semyon Zorich, one of Catherine's *vremenshchiki*, or 'men of the moment', by an unknown artist. He survived as imperial favourite for just under a year.

Alexander Lanskoy, one of Catherine's longer-lasting young favourites, and her most beloved (also by an unknown artist).

Another young favourite, Alexander Dmitryev-Mamonov, painted by Mikhail Shibanov. The smitten Empress extolled his 'superb dark eyes, noble air and easy gait'.

Catherine wearing a 'kokoshnik',
a traditional Russian headdress, painted by
Virgilius Ericksen between 1769 and 1772.
(This is a copy from the 1830s.)

The Empress portrayed by Vladimir
Lukich Borovikovsky as she might appear
while walking in the grounds of Tsarskoye
Selo, accompanied by one of her favourite
greyhounds. The Rostral Column built
to commemorate the battle of Chesme is
visible in the background.

Catherine II in a travelling costume,
painted by Mikhail Shibanov in 1787.
This is how Catherine would have
looked during her great voyage to the
Crimea which took place that year.

The Empress as painted
by Anton Albertrandi.

An ageing Catherine,
painted by Alexander Roslin.

ative, took no further notice of him than decency or common attention required.

Not only did Catherine take little notice of the Prussian Prince, she went out of her way to indicate her lack of interest in him, refusing to put on an entertainment for him at Court, and suddenly breaking off a card game because she couldn't bear to sit next to him any longer. Quite apart from any political design in this behaviour, Catherine really did seem to have developed an antipathy for the unfortunate Prince, though she and Potemkin may also have been deliberately playing this up, in order to annoy and bewilder the pro-Prussian faction at Court, represented most strongly by Count Panin who, now that Catherine and Potemkin were taking over foreign affairs themselves, was rapidly losing his power and influence. After a few days the Empress told Count Panin that he was to send the Prince of Prussia on his way as soon as possible, because 'she felt if he stayed much longer she might say something rude to him'.

Catherine would have been well aware that such behaviour would be noted with fascination in all the Courts of Europe. She was sending a clear message not only to King Frederick that his days of influencing the Russian Court were over, but also to the Emperor Joseph that her allegiances had definitely shifted away from Berlin and towards Vienna. To underline the point, Catherine behaved very differently to Joseph's representatives, and was constantly singing the Emperor's praises both to his ambassador Count Cobenzl and to the Prince de Ligne. On 24 September there was a masquerade at Court, at which the Empress stayed from seven until ten. She used Sir James Harris as a buffer against the Prince of Prussia, instructing him to stay by her side in order to keep boring people at bay. Such an apparent mark of favour made the other foreign ministers very suspicious of Sir James, which doubly disgruntled the British ambassador as he felt he was making no progress at all in improving Anglo-Russian relations, the Empress's regard for him being purely personal.

The Prince de Ligne left towards the end of September, and on the 29th of that month Sir James reported: 'His Royal Highness has fixed his departure for Saturday next. He has presented Count Panin with his picture in a ring covered with a single diamond, and has given Major-General Potemkin a snuff-box, and a ring richly set in brilliants.' The Empress's presents for the Prince of Prussia were 'less profuse' than usual, consisting of 'four pieces of gold and silver brocade, forty pounds weight of rhubarb, and as much of tea', the whole reckoned to come to about 8,000 roubles in value. Prince Frederick William took his leave on 1 October. As soon as she had said goodbye to him, Catherine took to her bed with a cold she had already had for two days, though she was up again on the 2nd. On that day Sir James Harris summed up the results of the Prince's visit:

> There was not the smallest change in the Empress's behaviour to the last. She expressed a uniform disgust and ennui whenever her illustrious visitor was present, and in speaking of him, ever rated his talents and abilities at the lowest pitch. Notwithstanding the many powerful agents and friends he and his party have here, I am satisfied he has not succeeded in anything he has undertaken; that he has confirmed, not diminished, the high opinion the Empress entertains of Count Falkenstein, and that he has sunk the interests of his uncle still lower, instead of retrieving them. Prince Potemkin did not choose his niece should give him a supper.
>
> In short, he is gone away displeased and disgusted.

A month later Catherine was still grumbling about the Prince of Prussia:

> I swear to you that by making me endure such boredom he considerably worsened a rheumatic pain I had in my arm and which began to go away once he had left. When one has such a weighty nephew, one should never send him in the wake of characters such as those whose acquaintance we made at Mogilyov: just think, we [i.e. Catherine and Joseph] are now in correspondence and I have also received a letter as sweet as honey from Mamma [i.e. Empress Maria Theresa].

Any correspondence with Maria Theresa was short-lived, as she died on 18 November, leaving Joseph II as the sole ruler of the Habsburg dominions.★ Catherine sent three letters of condolence with a special envoy, and on 3 December Sir James Harris commented on the way

---

★ The Prince de Ligne relates that Sir James Harris asked for his opinion on what kind of Emperor Joseph would be, without the restraining hand of his mother, and that he had replied: '*Il b[ande] toujours, et ne d[écharge] jamais.*' ('He's always got a hard-on, and never comes.') (Ligne, *Mémoires,* p.362.)

the news had been received at the Russian Court: 'The extraordinary and universal sensation shewn here, on the news of the death of the Empress Queen, will better paint the sentiments and disposition of Her Imperial Majesty than anything I can say.' Negotiations to conclude an alliance between the two Empires now proceeded apace, Joseph proposing a defensive alliance and Catherine also hoping for Austrian assistance against the Turks in the event of another war (for, insisted the Empress, Turkey was repeatedly violating the terms of the Treaty of Kuchuk-Kainardji).

The British ambassador, still desperately trying to enlist active Russian support in the American War of Independence, had been working on Potemkin to get him to secure a private meeting with the Empress. On 7 December Potemkin told Sir James that Catherine had agreed to grant him an interview the following day:

> He told me to be unreserved, open and candid; 'for,' said he, 'she has excessive penetration, and if she perceives any inconsistency or prevarication she will suspect your sincerity; let her feel that you use no other weapons than those of truth and justice, and that you argue from these principles, and from the love of your country. Flatter as much as you can; *you cannot use too much unction*; but flatter her for what she *ought to be*, not for *what she is*.'

And so on 8 December Sir James was conducted by one of the Empress's valets through a back door into her private apartments. After the meeting he wrote up the conversation, which had of course been conducted in French. Sir James began by saying: 'I have come to represent to Your Imperial Majesty the critical situation in which our affairs find themselves. She knows our confidence in her; we dare to flatter ourselves that she will avert the storm, and that she will reassure us over our fears of having lost her friendship.' The Empress responded with: 'You know, Monsieur, my sentiments for your nation; they are as sincere as they are unchanging, but I have met with such a small return on your part, that I feel I should no longer count you among my friends.' Sir James then attempted to persuade her that her doubts about the British were a result of the machinations of England's enemies, particularly the French and – at the centre of her own Court – Count Panin. He took the daring step of telling her that her minister was in cahoots with the French ambassador, to which she responded rather crossly: 'Don't imagine that that signifies anything; I know

Monsieur Panin through and through; his intrigues have no effect on me any more; I'm not a child; nobody stops me doing what I want; I can see clearly.' Sir James pressed on, and told Catherine that Panin was entirely devoted to the King of Prussia, even that he served his interests before those of his own Empress. Later in the conversation, after Catherine had expressed her wish to act as intermediary in helping Britain make peace (which was not exactly the outcome Sir James desired), he said:

> The manner in which Your Imperial Majesty has just expressed herself touches me; she deserves and she has our entire confidence; we have never ceased to have it in her, but we are always afraid to entrust ourselves to her Minister, whom I have believed it my duty to represent to my Court as he is; and Your Imperial Majesty will allow me to observe that if I have to explain myself to him, he will betray me, or will give you only a very imperfect rendition of what I have said to him.

To this the Empress replied: 'Give him nothing except in writing; then he will not be able to change anything; if he is hiding the truth from me, I'll kick him out.' Part of Catherine's problem in her dealings with the English – even with as personable a representative of the race as Sir James – lay in their manner, and in the fact that they clearly did not perceive the Russian Empire to be as glorious as she herself considered it to be. And so she declared: 'Listen, my dear Harris, I am speaking very sincerely to you, and I expect you to make a very serious report to your Court; but if after all that I have just said to you, I find in it the same *indifference*, the same *stiffness*, what can I say, the same tone of *superiority* towards me, I will do nothing further to help.'

The advice Potemkin gave to Sir James after this interview, on how he should persuade his Court to respond, either demonstrates that Potemkin entirely shared the prejudices of his age about women, or that he was secretly laughing at the British ambassador and his hopes for support:

> 'For God's sake do not be ashamed to flatter her; it is the only road to her good-will, and she has so high an opinion of your nation, that a pleasant word from you will go further than a studied phrase from any other people. She asks for nothing but praise and compliment; give her that, and she in return will give you the whole force

of her Empire.' There, my Lord, are the Prince's own words, and they contain the *whole secret* of this Court.

In the first weeks of 1781 both Potemkin and Catherine were unwell, the former taking to his bed and Catherine suffering from colds and rheumatism (which had returned despite the absence of the 'heavy' Prussian Prince). She described her affliction to Grimm a couple of months later: 'But do you know that while you were stretched out on your bed and in Vienna all was in mourning, your very humble servant was horribly tormented by rheumatism in the left arm, which was only cured by Spanish fly which made the awful pain stop, and that even now the movements of this arm are still not perfectly free, especially during storms, which are very frequent this year.' The usual medicinal use of Spanish fly, or cantharides, was to produce vesication, or blistering. It is also a notorious, if dangerous and probably ineffective, aphrodisiac (it irritates the sexual organs), and it is possible that some of the scurrilous rumours which circulated about Catherine in her later years may have come from malicious misinformation about her use of this substance.

Rumours of a different sort had begun to circulate towards the end of 1780 about Grigory Orlov – to the effect that both he and his young wife were plagued by ill health and were travelling around Europe vainly seeking cures. Grimm told Catherine what he knew: 'I am very unhappy about all I hear of Prince Orlov. It is said that he has entrusted himself to an English doctor established in Brussels, a charlatan whom nobody knows. This man gives him remedies which would kill a horse. He uses them, always becomes worse, and continues . . . It is said that he is really very changed, and I am distressed about it.' Catherine was understandably alarmed. But the next news she received was that Grigory had visited Grimm and seemed rather better. His wife, however, was believed to be very ill (she was consumptive), though she looked well enough, and was pinning her hopes on some drugs that might enable her to have a child. Despite Grigory's experiences with quack remedies in Brussels, he had been fit enough to bait his old sparring partner, the priggish Princess Dashkova, who was there with her 16-year-old son, by telling the youth – who was shortly to go to St Petersburg – that he might have the necessary qualities to replace the imperial favourite. The Princess was horrified that Prince Orlov should allude so brazenly to the Empress's amours – about which she claimed to know nothing – and took him to task. He was of course unrepentant.

Five months later Grigory's wife died in Lausanne, and two of his brothers travelled there to bring the grieving widower back to Russia.

Count Panin also appeared unwell, although his taking to his bed may have had more to do with despair at recent developments in Russian foreign policy than with genuine illness. As for Potemkin, he continued to be ill into mid-February, which the British ambassador found most frustrating: 'My friend is ill in bed; his indisposition arises solely from his singular manner of living, and, till he changes this, he must not expect that sound health his robust constitution entitles him to. As his spirits and temper are always affected on these occasions, his illness naturally interrupts the progress of business, particularly as it prevents his going to the Empress, and as she does not now, as formerly, come to him.' Someone who now came increasingly to the fore in Sir James's reports, and of whom Catherine entertained an ever higher opinion, was her private secretary Alexander Bezborodko (who had originally been brought into her service at the same time as Peter Zavadovsky, on the recommendation of Field Marshal Rumyantsev). 'Count Alexis Orlov thinks highly of his parts and probity,' Sir James told Lord Viscount Stormont, 'and pronounces him to be a friend to England. Prince Potemkin very candidly informed me of the increase of his influence, and advised me to be attentive to him. These motives will sufficiently account for my lately having frequently applied to this gentleman, who, in everything which has passed between us, comes up perfectly to the character given of him.' In addition to having a prodigious memory, Bezborodko was very cultured, being a connoisseur of both literature and art, all of which qualities recommended him to Catherine. He was also very ugly, so there was no question of the Empress being physically attracted to him (although this did not prevent him indulging in a great number of sexual affairs himself).

Bezborodko worked closely with Catherine on the negotiations with Austria, which met with an unexpected hitch in late February. When a treaty was to be signed by two crowned heads, it was common practice to follow the 'alternative' protocol by which two identical copies of the treaty were drawn up; on one copy Monarch A would append his signature above that of Monarch B, while on the other copy Monarch B would sign above Monarch A. But Joseph, insisting on his supremacy as Holy Roman Emperor, refused to follow this procedure. Catherine was equally adamant that she was not going to be the junior partner, writing to Potemkin: 'If Cobenzl says to you, as he has often said, that there can be no alternative between the Emperor and the

Russian Empress, then please tell him to abandon such nonsense, which will bring the matter to an unavoidable halt, and that my principles have in fact been not to take anyone's place and not to concede my place to anyone.' There matters rested for several weeks.

Meanwhile Nikita Panin was resorting to desperate measures to regain his lost influence. Sir James Harris reported that he was spending his nights in forging letters 'calculated to hurt his enemies and serve his friends'. He would claim that these letters, which purported to have been written by the Austrian minister Count Cobenzl or by Sir James himself, had been intercepted at the post office, and as the rule was that once an intercepted dispatch had been copied and translated, the original was to be given back to the post office for sending on, no one could prove that the 'copies' were forgeries. Sir James also reported, however, that Catherine was aware of Panin's tricks: 'The Empress, indeed, seems to have entirely withdrawn her confidence from him, and though she still listens to his dark insinuations, because he has art enough to convey them in a way which speaks to her passions, yet she does almost the whole business of the Foreign Department through her Private Secretary.' More than a year later Sir James gave details to Lord Grantham of the kind of vilification he had had to endure from Count Panin: 'He accused me (and made the Grand-Duke actually believe it) of having attempted to set fire to the Russian fleet. He accused me of a design of poisoning the Grand Duke and Duchess and their children, by endeavouring to persuade them that some geraniums, and other equally inoffensive plants I had sent the Grand Duchess, were venomous.' On 23 April Sir James reported that Count Panin was soon to take his leave of the capital for some weeks to visit his estate in the Smolensk *guberniya*, a tactical withdrawal not unconnected with the intrigues he had been engaged in concerning the projected marriage of Grand Duchess Maria Fyodorovna's youngest sister, Elisabeth, who had unwittingly become a pawn in the Austro-Prussian struggle for influence at the Russian Court. Catherine had proposed that Elisabeth should be married to the nephew and heir of Joseph II, Archduke Franz, but Panin – with the full knowledge of Paul and Maria Fyodorovna – had been agitating for her to marry a Prussian prince instead. He had enlisted Frederick the Great's support, and a secret engagement had now been arranged between Elisabeth and the young Prince Henry of Prussia (the son of Ferdinand), who was only 10 years old at the time to Elisabeth's 14. Catherine had been kept in complete ignorance of this scheme to undermine her policy and wreck her plans for Elisabeth, but she was bound to find out before long, and the intriguers were understandably apprehensive. Sir James Harris expressed the opinion that the Empress's displeasure and surprise would

> certainly increase to a very great height when the whole intrigue is discovered; when she finds that Count Panin from the beginning has betrayed her; that it was he that urged the King of Prussia repeatedly to propose his own nephew; and that his own children and her own Minister have been acting in concert to oppose her. It would be easy for me to kindle this flame at once; but I am convinced it will blaze out more violently when the facts speak for themselves, and which no cunning or artifice can prevent their doing in a very short time. Count Panin is hastening his retreat, and the Grand Duke and Duchess pressing him to stay. Their apprehensions increase in proportion as the time for the return of the courier from Montbelliard [i.e. from the Grand Duchess's family] draws near, and they dread being left alone to resist the impending tempest.

Despite Panin's best efforts, and without his knowledge, Catherine and Joseph resolved their impasse by agreeing to a secret exchange of letters rather than the signing of an official treaty document. On 24 May 1781, a year after the two sovereigns had met, Catherine signed her letter to Joseph at Tsarskoye Selo. The agreement pledged a mutual defensive guarantee of Russia's current European possessions for eight years, and promised armed resistance in case of attack. Most importantly to Catherine and Potemkin, Austria was also committed to supporting Russia in her dealings with the Ottoman Empire. Very few people knew about this agreement to begin with, the general view being that the negotiations had fallen apart over the issue of the 'alternative' protocol. Sir James expressed his confusion on 8 June: 'I own, my Lord, I some-times think that on the score of this Treaty, there is some secret and mysterious transaction between the Empress and the Emperor, unknown to any one but themselves. Various circumstances confirm me in these suspicions, and I am endeavouring if possible to get at the truth, though it is very deeply concealed, and I do not know through what channel I may arrive at it.' Sir James also reported that Catherine had succeeded after all in getting her own way over young Elisabeth's marriage: 'I understand that the King of Prussia gave up his claim on the young princess of Wirtemburg in a manner very flattering to the Empress, and that she is perfectly satisfied with him.'

By 25 June Sir James knew what had transpired. His informant was Alexander Bezborodko's confidential secretary, and he believed that no one else apart from Bezborodko, Potemkin and the Empress herself knew about it. In the dispatch in which he reported this news, Sir James was at his most patronising:

> The two Imperial Sovereigns may be infinitely serviceable to us, but their good-will is to be purchased by very different attentions. The Emperor will listen to anything that may tend to the advancement and security of his empire; to propositions which might acquire him solid advantages and true glory: in a word, to the language of wisdom and sound policy. But the character of the great Lady near whom I have the honour of residing, is of a different cast. To please her, we must perpetually offer sacrifices to her vanity, avoid contradicting her opinions, affect to approve what she proposes, to admire her capacity, to respect her greatness, to place an equal confidence in her ability and in her inclination to assist us; and, by giving her credit for those eminent qualities she thinks she possesses, make her act as if she really possessed them.

Catherine would have been both infuriated and amused by such an assessment – especially as Sir James was uttering words put in his mouth by the devious Potemkin – and she would have drawn the ambassador's attention to the list of achievements of her reign which she was in the habit of enumerating on the anniversary of her accession. On 28 June of this year Alexander Bezborodko – her 'factotum', as she called him – presented her with an impressive list (which she duly sent on to Grimm). It specified 29 local government districts set up according to the new system, 144 new towns, 30 conventions and treaties, 78 military victories, 88 'memorable edicts concerning laws or foundations' and 123 'edicts for the relief of the people', making 492 achievements in all. And this was quite apart from anything artistic, architectural or musical.

Catherine's grandsons had not been neglected by her during this period. On the very day on which she had signed the letter to Joseph II, she had also written to Grimm, enclosing a sketch:

> This is how [Alexander] has been dressed since he was six months old: his whole outfit is sewn together, is put on in one go and is

fastened behind with four or five little hooks; around the costume there is a fringe, and in that he is perfectly well dressed; the King of Sweden and the Prince of Prussia asked for and received a copy of Monsieur Alexandre's costume. There is no tying to be done in any of it, and the child is hardly aware that he is being dressed; one stuffs his arms and feet into his costume at the same time, and it's done; this costume is a stroke of genius on my part, and I didn't want you not to know about it. I must also tell you that these two infants are growing and getting remarkably tall and that my method with them is succeeding marvellously. God knows what the elder one doesn't do: he spells, draws, writes, digs, fences, rides, makes twenty toys out of one, has an amazing imagination and asks questions endlessly. The other day he wanted to know why it is that there are men in the world, and what he himself has come to do in the world or on the earth; I don't know, there is a singular depth of thought germinating in this infant's head, and yet with all that he is very light-hearted; also I am very careful not to make him do anything: he does what he wants; one only prevents him hurting himself or others.

Alexander's younger brother Constantine had defied his grandmother's expectations by surviving babyhood, and she found him far more appealing now. 'As for [Alexander's] brother,' she told Grimm, 'his extreme liveliness does not yet allow him to concentrate on anything, but he has very intelligent eyes; moreover, he has the face of Bacchus, which makes a perfect contrast with the elder one, whom a sculptor could use as a model for Cupid.'

Having taken advice as to when children could safely be inoculated against smallpox, Catherine had decided that the right time would be the early autumn of 1781, when Alexander would be nearly four and Constantine nearly two and a half. Consequently she invited Baron Dimsdale to return to Petersburg to carry out the procedure. The 68-year-old Baron, accompanied by his new 48-year-old wife Elizabeth, arrived in August; the Baroness found much to admire:

St Petersburg is a much finer Place than I expected. On my entering it appeared very grand, as all the Steeples and Spires are covered with Tin and Brass, and some of them gilt, the Sun shining full upon them made a very gay appearance. The Palace is a prodigious fine Building, and a great many elegant Houses are dispersed about the

City. The Streets in general are very good, and particularly that which leads to the Admiralty, which I think was near two Miles in length; in general they are paved, but a few remain in the old state. The View upon the Banks of the River Neva exhibited the grandest lively Scenes I ever beheld.

John Howard, the prison reformer, was also visiting Petersburg at this time (he declined to be presented to the Empress, saying he was not there in order to see great people), and the Dimsdales encountered him one day beside the Neva. The Baroness recalled that he turned to her and said 'that it put him in mind of a Story he had heard of a Person who was so delighted with a fine Prospect that he said this and Heaven is too much'. Howard and the Dimsdales were also taken together by Ivan Betskoy to visit the Smolny Institute; Mr Howard seemed to approve of everything he was shown, except for the fact that the girls' hair was powdered which he considered unhygienic. The guests were entertained to a fine snack in the Institute's dairy: 'A Table was spread with Cheese and Cream, brown Bread, and the finest Butter I had tasted since I left England; we all partook of this delicious repast and were very merry.' The Baroness was altogether very impressed: 'This noble Establishment afforded me much pleasure, and the Sight of the great Order and regularity, and good management every thing was conducted with, and the happy Countenance of all the Children, impressed such an agreeable Idea on my Memory, that I think I shall never forget it.'

On 16 August the Dimsdales removed from Petersburg to Tsarskoye Selo, where the inoculation was to take place. They were accommodated on the first floor of the Catherine Palace. Once the Baroness got over her surprise that class distinctions were not observed as rigidly in the little British community at Tsarskoye Selo as in England, she seems to have enjoyed herself very much in the company of, among others, the Empress's Scottish physician, Dr John Rogerson:

Mr Bush from England with whom I was acquainted before he came to Russia paid me a Visit the morning after my arrival and very civilly invited me to dine with him as he knew the Baron was engaged to dine with the Empress, which distressed me a little as he was the Empress's Gardener, but it was soon explained by Dr Rogerson's coming in and saying to me I hear you and I dine together at Mr Bush's. I met some English ladies of my acquaintance from St Petersburg, and as we were sitting down to dinner, a Running-Footman in green and silver came and said if not inconvenient, Sir James Harris and the Imperial minister [Count Cobenzl] were coming to dinner: they soon arrived after the Messenger, and I spent a very agreeable day, and had a good English Dinner. Mrs Bush and her four Daughters are very agreeable good sort of People.

After being presented privately to the Empress, Baroness Dimsdale described her as 'a very fine looking Woman, not so tall as I am and lustier, very fine expressive blue eyes, and a sweet sensible look'. She also recorded her impressions of Paul and Maria Fyodorovna, to whom she was presented later in the day, and of the two little boys: 'The Duke is a little Man not handsome, said some civil things to me, and the Dutchess was very gracious, she is taller than I am, and a very healthy fresh coloured looking Woman, rather handsome, and aged about twenty two Years. The two young Princes are beautiful Children and extremely sensible and clever.' A number of supervisors and servants accompanied the children whenever they went out to play: 'They walked out in the Garden every morning if the Weather was fine, the Baron and I went with them and found it very agreeable, for the two Women that have the care of them Mrs Guslar and Mrs Nichols are Sisters and English Women and very civil and obliging. Of Footmen and under Women that belong to the Nursery, there are about twelve who attend when the Princes are in the Garden.' There is also in the Baroness's recollections a hint that Alexander and Constantine, for all the Empress's efforts to make what she wanted of them, were already chips off the old Romanov block, obsessed like their father and grandfather before them with military uniforms and parades: '[the Empress] is excessively fond of them and cannot refuse them any thing they ask for, but nothing pleases them like Soldiers and exercising . . . As to Prince Alexander it is said he knows every Uniform in the Empress's Service as much as the Officers in a manner that is very astonishing.'

Baroness Dimsdale's picture of daily life at Tsarskoye Selo included a description of how the Empress spent her time and what she wore:

The Empress is an early riser and very often in the Garden a little after six, she walks in leather Shoes, and several Dogs were with her, her Walk is usually over before nine, then while she is dressing, Prayers are read in her Apartment, she has two hairdressers, and always wore a large white Bonnet except on particular Days, and then her head was drest very low with two side Curls, and a piece of Gauze pinned on the top of it in the Shape of a Cap. All the Summer she lies on a leather Mattrass, and her Nightcap is an handkerchief, as the Russian Women are very partial to the use of handkerchiefs, and this is the old Russian Head-dress.

Good food was in plentiful supply at Tsarskoye Selo, the Baroness recording a typical dinner menu:

Soup, Fish, Boiled Chicken and Cauliflower,
Roast Leg of Mutton or Beef with Potatoes over it,
A small Dish with a ForeQuarter of Lamb roasted
Duck, Fowl, and two Snipes (all in one Dish)
Fine piece of Hamburgh Beef,
Cutlets and Sausages,
Hash Duck and stewed Mushrooms
Cray Fish. Apple Puffs
Seven dishes in the Desert. Oranges, Apples, Pears,
Cherries, Macaroons, Biscuits, Stewed Pippens, and Parmesan
    Cheese.

Catherine herself ate little, restricting herself to modest portions of no more than three or four dishes, her favourite being boiled beef with pickled cucumbers. She drank only one glass of hock or Hungarian wine. Supper for the guests regularly consisted of at least seven hot dishes. The Baroness was particularly partial to sterlet (one of the smaller species of sturgeon and something of a Russian delicacy), especially when it was served cold in jelly. According to the Baroness, it was on the Baron's advice that the Empress herself did not eat supper and that as a result she suffered far less from the severe headaches which had plagued her when she was younger. Most of the fruit served at Tsarskoye Selo was grown in the hothouses, of which John Bush gave Baroness Dimsdale a tour:

There are a great number of Hot Houses for all kinds of Fruits, and I think the best Melons I ever eat of Mr Bush's raising, and plenty of Water Melons, Peaches and Nectarines very good: and what surprised me most a very great plenty of exceeding fine China Oranges: they were not the Growth of Russia, but brought from some other place. Mr Bush shewed me the foundations of a hot house which was building, of eight hundred Feet in Length.

Alexander and Constantine were inoculated on 27 August. Alexander was quite badly affected, the Baroness commenting that he 'felt much indisposed before the eruption'. Sometimes footmen would come running to the Dimsdales' apartment, causing them considerable anxiety, but it usually turned out that they had been dispatched to ask whether Alexander was allowed to eat an orange, or some such query.

Once the alliance had been agreed between Russia and the Holy Roman Empire, Catherine knew that she had to find a way of communicating it to her pro-Prussian son. If Paul were perhaps to be given a splendid welcome by the Emperor in Vienna, he would be more likely to view the alliance with favour, and might even be less inclined to hold Frederick the Great in higher esteem than any other monarch, or so reasoned his mother. The idea of the Grand Duke making such a journey was first broached, probably by Joseph, when the two monarchs met in 1780, though nothing of this had been communicated to Paul. Catherine knew that any such suggestion coming from her would be viewed with suspicion by her son, and so she and Potemkin embarked on a plot to manipulate him into thinking he had had the idea himself. As a go-between she used Prince Repnin, Nikita Panin's nephew and a man whom the Grand Duke trusted, and she promised him due reward if the scheme was a success. Prince Repnin responded whole-heartedly to the challenge and proceeded to inculcate in both Grand Duke and Duchess a strong desire to travel, by expatiating on the benefits to be gained and talking all the time about foreign countries. With impeccable timing, a letter arrived from Joseph II inviting them to visit and also promising that he would arrange for the Grand Duchess to see her family during the trip. Excited yet still apprehensive, Paul and Maria Fyodorovna asked Count Panin for his opinion. No indication had leaked out that the Empress was behind the plan, and so Panin did not oppose it. On the contrary, he attempted to take it over, intending that Berlin rather than Vienna should be the main destination, and further rapprochement with Prussia, rather than the Holy Roman Empire, the goal. In mid-June the Grand Duke and Duchess duly made their request to the Empress, who received it with 'a countenance of surprise and uneasiness'. According to Sir James Harris,

[she] told them they had embarrassed her greatly by putting her in a situation where, either by granting what they asked, she must deprive herself for so long a time of their society, or by declining it, check in them a thirst after knowledge and instruction she could not but approve. After a good deal of conversation, in which they urged their request strongly, she gradually gave into their wishes. It was settled they should travel, but on condition that the Empress should draw the plan of their journey and name their attendants.

The Grand Duke and Duchess were then presented by the Empress with their itinerary and a list of their attendants (such details had of course been drawn up well in advance). They asked that Paul's friend (and another of Panin's nephews) Prince Kurakin should be added to the list, and this was agreed. They had to expend rather more effort to get the Empress to agree to add Versailles to the itinerary, but had no success whatsoever in persuading her to allow them to visit Berlin. Neither could representations from Frederick himself, made through his ministers and other agents, get her to change her mind on this point. The Grand Duke and Duchess were to travel as the Count and Countess of the North (an incognito which annoyed the King of Sweden, as it sounded as though Russia were laying claim to the whole of the north).

Count Panin now realised that he had been outmanoeuvred and he determined to use all his influence with the Grand Duke and Duchess to abort the trip. Sir James described the state of complete indecision in which Paul and Maria Fyodorovna found themselves, and the effect it had on their relations with the Empress:

As long as Count Panin remained here, the temper and disposition of their Imperial Highnesses suffered a perpetual revolution. Whenever a courier from Vienna brought them letters from the Emperor, they were quite Austrian, and delighted to a degree with their journey; when Count Panin had been with them, and had dealt out to them precepts from Potzdam, their sentiments changed, they scarce spoke to Count Cobenzel, and they seemed to be sorry they were to leave Petersburg. On Count Panin's going into the country, the scene changed; they became uniformly Austrian, talked to nobody but Count Cobenzel and his Lady; were full of the Emperor and of Vienna; and they never were on a footing of such cordiality with the Empress as during this period: they were even civil to Prince

Potemkin, and I came in for a very considerable share of their favour. This consistent and pleasing behaviour, which had really endeared them to the Empress, and which had been the cause of their passing two months with her on a footing of cordiality and affection before unknown to them, ended with Count Panin's return.

As Panin set to work to frustrate the grand ducal tour, the Empress counterattacked. On 2 September she issued an order that in future the Vice-Chancellor, Count Ivan Osterman, was to conduct all the business of the College of Foreign Affairs, including the signing of all acts and rescripts, and dealing with the foreign ministers and foreign correspondence. Osterman, despite being the son of a diplomat, had no interest or competence in the field of foreign affairs, and consequently the real power in this department would now reside in the hands of his deputy, Catherine's trusted and able secretary Alexander Bezborodko. Sir James Harris reported a few days later: 'This very singular and humiliating exclusion of Count Panin, was resolved on by the Empress about a week ago, but she kept her resolution secret till his arrival, making it, if possible, by this means, still more disgraceful for him. As it was quite unexpected here, and as most people supposed Count Panin too artful and too well informed a man to return to certain disgrace and shame, it has caused a very considerable sensation.'

Sir James spent the evening of 9 September with the Count, and reported the following day that Panin seemed to have recovered his spirits and was continuing his intriguing, stressing to the Grand Duke and Duchess that, by going to Vienna, they would be 'paying a visit to their most dangerous enemy'. His own disgrace only served to lend credence to this claim. He also worked on the Grand Duchess by representing to her the dangers attendant upon inoculation, so that she became worried about parting from her children while they were still convalescent. With the Grand Duke, whom he knew intimately, Panin used different tactics, as Sir James explained:

He had contrived to get at Prince Repnin's secret, and he discovered to the Grand-Duke that what he thought to be a *voluntary* act of his own, was a premeditated and deep-laid scheme of others; that it possibly concealed the most fatal intentions; that perhaps it was intended he should *never* return to Russia; perhaps his children would be taken from him; and though he asserted none of these facts, yet he endeavoured to give them credit, by suggestions and presumptive reasonings. He talked of the ambitious and unprincipled character of Prince Potemkin; of that of those who surrounded the Empress; and even she herself did not escape his animadversions. He then expatiated on what he called certain intelligence relative to the Emperor; averred that he never meant sincerely his nephew should marry the Grand-Duchess's sister; that when she was once at Vienna, he could dispose of her as he pleased; and said such things that, even in cypher and by messenger, my pen cannot write them.

Panin accomplished his task of scaremongering so well that on Monday 13 September the Grand Duke and Duchess suddenly announced that they would not leave until their sons completely recovered from their inoculations. The implication was that they would not go at all. For the next three days no one knew whether they were coming or going – including their suite of 60 attendants, the people in charge of managing the horses (about 240 of which were needed for each stage of the journey within the Russian Empire) and those who had been sent ahead to prepare the inns.

Sir James Harris claimed he was the catalyst for resolving the impasse – and maybe he did provide the final impetus Potemkin and Catherine needed for the Empress to insist that the journey go ahead, although he undoubtedly had an inflated view of his own role. (Years later, after Sir James had left Russia, Catherine referred to him as a 'muddler and intriguer' and commented: 'when he doesn't feel like making a muddle or intriguing, he gets jaundice'.) Sir James arrived at Tsarskoye Selo on the Wednesday, to find everyone in a flap. The ambassador spent some time with Potemkin, emphasising his belief that for the Empress to back down now and allow Paul and Maria Fyodorovna to abandon the trip would be tantamount to a total victory for Panin, and would damage Russian relations with Vienna and all the other Courts they were scheduled to visit. Potemkin then went to see the Empress, and in the space of an hour everything was settled.

Paul and Maria Fyodorovna finally left Tsarskoye Selo on the evening of Sunday 19 September. They were seen off by Prince Orlov, Prince Potemkin, Count Panin and most of the principal courtiers, while others watched from Baroness Dimsdale's windows inside the palace. The Duchess had been in tears all day at the prospect of leaving Alexander and Constantine. By the evening nearly everyone else was crying as well. Catherine had bade farewell to her son and daughter-in-law in her antechamber and had then gone to see her grandsons, annoyed that they should have been subjected to such emotional carryings-on.

Sir James, who had a man watching the scene for him, reported that on departure, Maria Fyodorovna's 'whole deportment and manner was of a person not about to undertake voluntarily an agreeable and instructive journey, but as one condemned to banishment. The Grand-Duke was nearly in the same state. On getting into the carriage, he drew up the blinds, and bid the coachman drive away as fast as possible.'

The following day, which happened also to be the Grand Duke's twenty-seventh birthday, Catherine dismissed Panin from his post as the senior member of the College of Foreign Affairs.

> The blow, though he ought to have expected it, came upon him unprepared; and, joined to what he had felt on taking leave of the Grand-Duke, produced such an effect, that about seven the same evening he was seized with a sudden attack of a violent fever, became immediately light-headed, and was so far lost as neither to know the persons he spoke to nor what he said. He continued in this state of delirium all night, and was not relieved till the faculty had exhausted the whole store of blisters, bleeding, etc. He then became entirely lethargic, and if nature had not thrown out erysipelas★ on his leg, it is probable he would have been carried off by apoplexy.

★ A contagious and infectious skin disease, once known as St Anthony's Fire.

# 16
# The Failures of Physicians
# (1781-84)

*It seems to me that as soon as someone falls into Rogerson's hands, he's as good as dead.*

Catherine II to Grigory Potemkin

About a mile outside Tsarskoye Selo the carriage bearing the Grand Duke and Duchess had to stop as Maria Fyodorovna had fainted. Her husband told her that if she did not pull herself together they would turn back, as he could no longer stand the emotional strain. This seems to have had the desired effect and Maria Fyodorovna calmed down. According to Baroness Dimsdale, the couple's sense of humour was restored by an Englishman: 'When she fainted the Dukes Coachman who was an Englishman, got off the Box, and dipped his hat in some water that was near, and offered it the Dutchess which very much entertained them. This Coachman is named Clark.'

A note Catherine wrote to the Grand Duke and Duchess in Russian (which language she seems to have reserved for the most personal communications to her son) a day or so later makes it clear that she had no intention of discussing the circumstances surrounding their departure: 'it would be inappropriate for me to touch upon your feelings by reminding you of the separation, when for your undertaking of such a protracted journey you are more than ever in need of health and courage of spirit'. She kept up the fiction that she would never have sanctioned the journey had she been able to predict the trouble it would cause: 'If I could have foreseen that [Maria Fyodorovna] would faint three times on leaving, and that she would be supported under her arms into the carriage, then simply the consideration of exposing her health to such severe trials would have stopped my consenting to this journey.' She also reported that the children, whom she had just been to see, were well on the road to recovery, and that Alexander's pustules were continuing to drop off.

On 25 September Catherine returned to Petersburg with her grandsons and the Dimsdales (who were provided with their own coach and eight horses). The Baroness wrote a description of the scenes of both departure and arrival:

There were ten Horses in the Empress's Coach (when she steps into her Carriage, there is always a Person in a very rich Dress, scarlet trimmed with Gold Lace, who sets a small stool covered with crimson Velvet trimmed with gold Fringe, for her to set Her Feet on, and the same at her getting out) fifteen Coaches attended in all, some with eight, and others with six Horses . . . A great number of Carriages, Horses, and Crouds [*sic*] of People stood before the Palace, and a little before we set off a hundred Cannons were fired. Trumpets and other Music played, altogether it was a very fine and Grand Sight. Our Coach was the fourth from the Empress's at going into St Petersburg and very great Crouds there were, the Windows were crouded with People who shewed the strongest expressions of Joy at the Sight of the Empress and the young Dukes who were in the Coach with her. In the Evening the City was illuminated and there were great Rejoicings.

The following day, a Sunday, a Te Deum was sung in celebration of the boys' recovery from their inoculations, and a ball was given in the evening. Baroness Dimsdale described Catherine's attire on this occasion as including 'a purple tissue Petticoat, and long white tissue Sleeves down to the wrist'. Catherine, as was her habit on such occasions, walked round to all the card tables to converse with people, desiring them not to stand as she approached. The Baroness also described the Empress's departure: 'Soon after ten it was whispered the Empress is going, and in an instant every body laid down their Cards – a Circle was made – I retain a strong remembrance of the majestic and pleasing manner with which she went out of the Room, and appeared to bow to every body.'

Two days later Catherine expostulated to Grimm over her disappointment and anger at the latest batch of paintings she had received, showing that she was by no means an indiscriminate collector and that the curators she now had working for her in Petersburg were at least as knowledgeable as her agents in foreign cities:

> One of the first things I did [on returning to Petersburg] was to go and see what Admiral Borisov had brought me from Italy, and to my great astonishment, apart from the Mengs and a few other things, all the rest, except for the Raphael loggias, are wretched daubs; I ordered Martinelli, the painter who looks after my gallery, to make a selection and send the daubs for auction in aid of the town's hospital. Oh my God! it is incredible how the divine [Reiffenstein] has let himself be fooled this time; also I beg you to tell him expressly not to buy anything more from Mr Jenkins; it is scandalous to pass off such poor things under the name of this or that painter; my people who work in the Hermitage were ashamed to allow anyone in there before me, and the consternation over these daubs was very great.

On 1 October Catherine reported to Paul and Maria Fyodorovna that the Dimsdales would soon be returning to England, and also that she had been very annoyed by the incompetence of the Narva post officials who had managed to leave two letters to her from the Grand Duke and Duchess at the bottom of a case for a fortnight. In addition she told them that she had a map of their projected route spread out on her table and that she marked every day where they had reached. The Empress became very restive whenever several days went by without a communication from them, as she expressed in her letter of 19 October:

> Here is the tenth letter which I have written to you, my dear children, without having had a syllable from you. The last which I received was from my dear son dated the 3rd of this month from Mogilyov. You can imagine how much this worries me, I do not know what to attribute this silence to; is it the roads? have the letters got lost? has the courier been eaten by wolves? – there are so many worries, that I live in expectation. Your children are very well and go for a drive around the town nearly every day. Yesterday Alexander made me a present of his portrait in silhouette and Constantine has promised me his.

Two days later Sir James Harris could report that Count Panin 'is out of immediate danger, but his faculties are not yet restored, and it will be many weeks before he will be able to leave his bed'.

In her letter of 11 November Catherine expressed curiosity about Paul and Maria Fyodorovna's recent meeting with the King of Poland, her erstwhile lover Stanislas Poniatowski:'I think that His Polish Majesty would have had a lot of difficulty in finding my physiognomy of 25 years ago in the portraits which you showed him. But the ability to converse this Prince used to have – so charming, amusing and knowledgeable – did you find he had it still or has it been lessened by royalty? It sounds to me as though there were traces of it in the way he proposed my health.' On the same day Catherine reported that her little grandsons had taken to going to court balls and dancing with as many ladies as they could, providing much entertainment for everyone. On 19 November she stressed the importance of using reading glasses – Maria Fyodorovna having remarked on arrival in Vienna that she thought the Emperor Joseph's eyes were looking red – and of rubbing one's eyes with a small piece of ice two or three times a day. At the beginning of December Alexander had a slight cough but, according to his grandmother, was cured by fresh air. He was learning to write to his parents by dictating what he wanted to say, having it written in pencil for him, and then tracing over it in ink. He was also beginning to do arithmetic ('we do not allow ourselves to be convinced that two plus two equals four, unless we have counted it for ourselves'). The Empress never mentioned her favourite in her letters to the Grand Duke and Duchess during their journey, making it sound as though her domestic circle consisted only of her grandsons and the dogs. In fact Sasha Lanskoy was with her constantly.

The winter of 1781–2 was extremely cold in St Petersburg, the temperature dropping to 28° Réaumur (35° Celsius) below zero on 20 December. Catherine related to Paul and Maria Fyodorovna how the children occupied themselves in such conditions:

Your children are as well as can be, they go out in sleighs every day when there's up to seven degrees of cold, and in a carriage up to ten degrees, any lower than that and we stay inside, and when it gets to twenty we stay in our rooms, always alert, agile and nimble. Alexander hops around the room on one leg like a bird and, believe it or not, he can put together whole words, after spelling out all the syllables; he does more: he is beginning to pin the geographical map of Russia on to a table, divided into guberniyas; he can also count to a thousand, beginning with two times two; if he goes on like this, on your return you will find him infinitely more knowledgeable than when you left him. Your children kiss your hands for the presents you send them, they are appreciative of what I said to them from you.

When more than 10 days went by without a letter from one or other of the travellers, Catherine would begin to accuse them of laziness and then have to retract her accusations when the delayed letters arrived. On 19 January she passed on a request, in Russian, from Alexander:

> Three days ago Alexander Pavlovich asked me to get him another brother; I suggested he pass on this request to you, dear children, but he specifically asked that I should write to you with the request that you bring him an extra brother. I asked him why he needed an extra brother, to which I received the reply that it was absolutely imperative he should have another brother for the important reason that when he was being a coachman, he had only one passenger, and he needed there to be two. Seeing the justice of his demand, I communicate to you, with my backing, the request of my beloved friend.

Paul and Maria Fyodorovna next visited Italy, and the early-to-bed Catherine asked them how they coped with being in Venice where the opera didn't start until 10 o'clock in the evening: 'did they start it for you at a better hour?' she asked, 'or have you taken to staying up all night?' She congratulated Grand Duke Paul on having been kissed by the Pope, and reported that when her son and daughter-in-law returned, they would see a good part of the Raphael loggias as well as several new statues – casts of ones they had seen in Rome. She remarked ruefully that it was a pity one couldn't also buy the climate of another country.

In March Sir James Harris was convinced that Lanskoy was about to be replaced in the Empress's affections:

> I may now venture to assure your Lordship with certainty, that there will, in a very short time, be a new favourite. He is the same I mentioned some posts back, and he is chosen by Prince Potemkin among his attendants. The only remaining difficulty is to get rid,

*decently*, of the present possessor, who has conducted, and still conducts himself, with such perfect complaisance and circumspection, that it is impossible to lay any charge at his door. He is neither jealous, inconstant nor overbearing; and, even in these moments, when he cannot be ignorant of his approaching fall, he preserves the same placid unexceptionable temper. This, however, will only tend to postpone, not to prevent, the public installation of his successor. The resolution is irrevocably taken, and my friend [i.e. Potemkin] is too much interested in this change to suffer it to be recalled. It will restore him to his plenitude of power, and, for the first month or six weeks, I see he will be in a manner omnipotent.

Sir James reported that all business was being neglected, as was usual at a time of turbulence in the Empress's private life, and that for the last fortnight Catherine had been 'visible to none but to those who compose her private society'. She had in fact been suffering from a cold accompanied by a sore throat. There was no change of favourite.

On 9 March the temperature in Petersburg was still 15° below zero and there was still much snow on the ground. Outside some court-yard entrances there were piles as tall as a man, and when Catherine went for a brief excursion to Tsarskoye Selo she found in some places that the snow was as high as the park walls. 'Your children are well,' she reported to Paul and Maria Fyodorovna. 'Alexander is very busy with his reading; I have made a little book for him with a dozen stories of good and naughty children, which have had an excellent effect; he reads and rereads them and models himself on them; he is polite, obedient and cheerful, as is Constantine; the latter copies his brother, and is a very pleasing character.' That spring Catherine's son by Grigory Orlov, Alexei Bobrinsky, graduated from the Cadet Corps school, and was sent on a tour of Russia which included visits to Moscow, Kazan, Astrakhan, Kherson and Kiev. He then went to Poland and Italy, before settling for several years in Paris.

Despite the anodyne nature of Catherine's correspondence with her son and daughter-in-law, she was actually both angry and anxious about a disturbance which had arisen in connection with a member of the Grand Duke's entourage, his friend Alexander Kurakin. A letter written to Kurakin by Pavel Bibikov, the son of the late general, had been intercepted. In it Bibikov had complained about the state of the Court and the Empire, alluded to other clandestine correspondents, and attacked Potemkin's influence. Worst of all, he had written that Russia could be saved only by the Grand Duke. As soon as she heard about it, the Empress ordered Bibikov's arrest and interrogation by the Secret Branch. But no evidence of a conspiracy could be found, and Potemkin advocated mercy. Pavel Bibikov was sentenced to lifelong banishment and exiled to Astrakhan, where he died two years later. Paul himself does not seem to have been involved. And although he complained frequently about his mother, her policies and his exclusion from all aspects of governance, in practical terms he was an unfailingly loyal subject. His concept of autocratic power, which one day he expected to inherit, could not have allowed him to be otherwise.

By 25 March the thaw had at last set in. Most of the snow disappeared from the town within the space of a week, though the ice on the Neva did not melt until 6 April and on the 10th there was still two feet of snow in the forested areas. Alexander and Constantine were asking eagerly when they would be going to Tsarskoye Selo. Sir James Harris was still anticipating Lanskoy's dismissal, taking as evidence the purchase of a house for him and the preparation of 'the usual magnificent leave-taking presents'. Meanwhile Catherine pursued her customary routine: 'We legislate,' she told Grimm, 'from six o'clock in the morning until nine; then comes the day's business until eleven when Messieurs Alexandre and Constantin arrive; the half-hour before and the hour after dinner is reserved for the said gentlemen when we do our abc, stories and memoirs; then two hours of perfect rest, and then an hour and a half for scribbling letters etc., after which the said gentlemen return to carry on their uproar until eight; then anyone who likes comes until ten.'

During this year she set up a Commission on National Education, to be chaired by Peter Zavadovsky, with the aim of establishing primary and secondary education in all districts and towns. She was also in the last stages of preparing a new Police Code, which included among its provisions assigning responsibility for the censorship of printed works to the chiefs of police. As had the Guberniya Reform, the Police Code made use of much of the material which had been generated by the Legislative Commission and its subcommittees. The police were exhorted in the Code (whose title meant literally 'Code of Good Order') to exercise common sense, goodwill, humanity, zeal for the common good, honesty and incorruptibility; specifically they were instructed not to accept bribes.

By Catherine's fifty-third birthday on 21 April, she and her grandsons (and Lanskoy) had been at Tsarskoye Selo for about a week. The children were getting very impatient as the snow, which was still covering almost half of the grounds, was preventing them running about in the garden. Instead they had to go out for daily carriage rides. Catherine boasted of Alexander and Constantine's progress to their parents: 'I flatter myself that you will be pleased with them when you see them again, their reason increases every day and they are as reasonable as they are lovable; we are unacquainted with crying, shouting and stubbornness and we are just as you would wish to see us.' Two days later she reported that the children were learning how to bow, and were being taught to dance a polonaise properly in time for the Feast of Sts Peter and Paul.

In her letter to Maria Fyodorovna of 5 May (by which time spring had finally arrived and the little boys were happily running around outside), Catherine described some of the latest additions to Tsarskoye Selo:

New statues have been cast; new pavilions which you cannot begin to imagine; a Chinese village; Chinese bridges; new alleyways, and apartments like a picture. You are free to praise and to criticise all that, but where I will ask you to exercise great restraint is in the extreme joy you will feel when you see your children again. Don't go frightening them for me with excessive transports of joy, may my dear daughter embrace them with moderation and, above all, may she not faint.

On 25 May the foundation stone of the new palace at Paul and Maria Fyodorovna's estate of Pavlovsk was laid. Charles Cameron, who was to begin work at the palace in the absence of its owners, John Bush and several others drove the three miles or so in a carriage from Tsarskoye Selo and were greeted by the Pavlovsk estate manager, Karl Kuchelbecker. There were already two smaller houses on the estate – the Grand Duke's residence Marienthal ('Maria's Valley') and the Grand Duchess's house Paulust ('Paul's Consolation') – both of which were surrounded by gardens on the English model and featuring the usual pavilions, such as a monk's hermitage, a charcoal burner's hut, a Chinese summerhouse, the statutory ruin and a mill. Many of these ideas had come not directly from England but via Maria Fyodorovna's home region of Würtemberg, where they were already popular. This rather piecemeal sort of garden design, in which a selection of pavilions was planted willy-nilly, without any overall schema or sense of a whole, was not really to Cameron's taste, but at Pavlovsk he had to cater to Maria Fyodorovna's enthusiasms (and she was a dedicated and knowledgeable gardener). In his planning of the landscape he also had to take into account Paul's passion for parades, marching and drill; from the start a significant amount of space at Pavlovsk was given over to military exercises.

Catherine was never so happy as when she was at Tsarskoye Selo, and on 1 June she compared her tranquillity there, sitting in the 'Grotto' pavilion by the side of the Great Pond and looking at the evening sun, with all the ceremonies the Grand Duke and Duchess were currently attending in Paris and Versailles. Though she was also aiming a sideswipe at the Court of France, Catherine, now she was in her fifties, really did prefer the informality of her life at Tsarskoye Selo – among friends, with children, with lover, usefully employed in reading and writing, in looking at pictures or poring over carved gems (Lanskoy's particular passion), in planning gardens and buildings and enjoying being in them, and in playing cards or billiards or just laughing and talking in the evenings – to the formal pomp and ceremony of major festivals and state occasions. She viewed the latter as a duty which she had to perform for the Empire – and a duty which she performed superlatively well – but her days of revelling in masquerades, fanfares and elaborate costume for their own sake were well and truly over. Physical comfort was becoming increasingly important to her, and during this year she introduced new regulations to simplify court dress: women were still to wear dresses of gold and silver brocade for major festivals, but for minor festivals and Sundays they were to adopt the *sarafan* or traditional loose Russian gown falling from the shoulders, with the traditional Russian headdress or *kokoshnik*.

Catherine told Grimm about some of the new rooms Cameron had built for her use in the Catherine Palace, all of which were designed as ideal living spaces in which by a subtle use of fine materials, space and light, symmetry and balance, an atmosphere of inner refreshment and spiritual peace was to be attained. Of course, in striving for this ideal, no expense was spared:

For example, I am writing to you in a study of solid silver, striped with red leaf; four pillars similarly striped support a mirror-glass which serves as a baldachin to a sofa of apple-green and silver material, the material coming from Moscow; the walls are made of mirrors, framed with silver pilasters, striped with the red leaf.

There is a balcony over the garden; the door makes a double mirror, so that it always looks open even when it's closed. This study is very rich, very striking, very cheerful, not at all over-loaded and very pleasant. I have another which is like a snuff-box, in white, blue and bronze; the white and blue is of glass and the design is arabesque.

Each room Cameron created was entirely original and different from every other room, in order that the visitor should be constantly enter-tained, surprised, impressed (of course), but also 'improved', the archi-tect being quite as committed to educating and refining people as was the Empress.

Catherine also made some rather disparaging remarks to Grimm over his encounter with the 'Count and Countess of the North' in Paris: 'I admit quite frankly that what you tell me about their success has surpassed my expectations; I thank you for the details you gave me and which have given me great pleasure ... It is quite true that the Countess told me that she thought you had got very fat; I expect you could have said the same about her.' In a letter to Potemkin, who had recently gone to Moscow on personal business, Catherine reveals how much she depended on him, needing his assistance and advice as relations between Russia and Turkey were becoming increasingly sensitive: 'You and I could have sorted all this out in half an hour, but now I don't know where to find you. I beg you in every way to hurry your arrival, as I fear nothing more than saying or doing the wrong thing.' Lanskoy was sustaining the role expected of him as the junior member of the triad, for Catherine added: 'I enclose a little note from someone who is extremely attached to you, and who longs for you cruelly.' (Potemkin, as requested, returned immediately.) On 29 June Catherine described Lanskoy's character to Grimm, beginning with a comment Grigory Orlov had made about him to one of his friends; her tone here is markedly similar to that which she habitually used when writing of her grandsons:

'Oh,' he said, 'you'll see what a man she'll make of him! he gobbles up everything.' He began by gobbling up the poets and the poems in one winter; several historians in another; novels bore us, but we gulp down the taste of Algarotti and friends. Without having been a student, we will have limitless knowledge, and we only enjoy ourselves in the company of all those who are of the highest quality and the most learned; in addition to that, we build and we plant, we are beneficent, cheerful, honest and very sweet.

On the evening of 5 August, Catherine and the children departed for Petersburg for the long-awaited unveiling of Falconet's equestrian statue of Peter the Great (the centenary of whose enthronement was celebrated that year), which took place two days later. As the statue which came to be such a potent symbol of Peter's city at last saw the light of day on its great plinth facing the Neva, and with its simple yet eloquent inscription 'To Peter I from Catherine II', the Empress was moved almost to tears, as she told Grimm some months later:

> When Peter the First was seen in the open, he looked as agile as great; one would have said he was fairly pleased with his creation; for a long time I could not look at him; I felt a welling-up of emotion, and when I looked around I saw that everyone had tears in their eyes . . . he was too far away to speak to me, but he seemed to me to have an air of contentment which gave me one too and which encouraged me to try to do better in the future, if I can.

Catherine was rather more prosaic in what she wrote to Paul and Maria Fyodorovna, telling them that the statue was 'very fine'. After the unveiling, she returned to Tsarskoye Selo, where she stayed until 11 September. Alexander and Constantine also spent some time at Pavlovsk, from where they sent flowers to their grandmother. Later that month the little boys visited the imperial porcelain factory, where they were allowed to buy some playthings for themselves. Alexander impressed everyone, as Catherine reported to Grimm, by his questions, his curiosity and his courtesy.

On 22 September 1782, the twentieth anniversary of her coronation, Catherine founded the order of St Vladimir, named after the Grand Prince of Kiev (to give him his official Orthodox title, Holy Equal of the Apostles Grand Prince Vladimir, in Holy Baptism Basil, the Enlightener of the Russian Land), who had been converted to Christianity in 988. This new order had symbolic resonance for Catherine and Potemkin's so-called 'Greek Project' – their dream of recreating Byzantium as part of the Russian Empire with Constantine as the ruler – as Potemkin had, with Catherine's permission, named the new Russian port by the Black Sea Kherson, in memory of the ancient Chersonessos which Prince Vladimir had conquered after his baptism.

On 1 October one of Maria Fyodorovna's brothers, Prince Frederick of Würtemberg, arrived in Petersburg a few days ahead of his wife (Princess Augusta of Brunswick, generally known as Zelmira), and was received by Catherine, who invited him to join her at dinner (he had come to serve in her army). By 8 October the Princess had also arrived, and though she was not feeling very well, she took part in dancing at the Hermitage. Catherine reported to her son and daughter-in-law that day: 'The weather here is as bad as the roads, so I am staying in my cage, like a marmot.' On 14 October both the Prince and Princess were suffering from 'Neva tummy', the Prince still feeling ill three days later while the Princess had recovered, attending the play at the Hermitage on the 16th.

A great sadness entered Catherine's life around this time, with the rapid deterioration of Grigory Orlov's health. His reason was affected, and it hurt her very much to see this once resourceful, dynamic, handsome and intelligent man, who had been a part of her life for over 20 years, becoming confused and helpless. On 25 October she told Paul and Maria Fyodorovna of Grigory's illness and of his imminent arrival in Petersburg:

I am going to have a very sad object before my eyes in the person of Prince Orlov, who is arriving today. Count Alexei came on ahead to warn me that his brothers had been guarding him in view of the derangement, or rather the enfeeblement of his reason, which they had observed in him, but that he was escaped from them. Marshal Chernyshev told me the same thing so that, however much pain this unfortunate circumstance causes me, it must be regarded as true; I admit that it grieves me sorely.

By 1 November Catherine had seen her former lover: 'Prince Orlov has arrived and his reason is so weakened that he hardly knows what he says or does. Nevertheless I have hopes that he will recover; we have here someone who performs extraordinary cures and in whom it is difficult not to believe; although I have little faith in doctors, medicines and charlatans.' Sir James Harris reported on the obvious distress Grigory's condition was causing Catherine: 'it should appear that at no period of her life, her feelings were so strongly and painfully moved as by this melancholy event, which has befallen her earliest favourite, and a man who at all times has been the first object of her affections, if not of her passions'. Sir James went on to describe how she was treating Grigory in this misfortune:

> Her conduct has been one of the most boundless regard, carried even to weakness. She absolutely forbids any harsh methods to be employed, rejects all ideas of confinement or discipline, and hoping, against all precedent, to restore him by gentleness and indulgence, she suffers him not only to visit and be visited, but admits him at all hours and in all dresses, whether she is alone, in company, or engaged in the most important concerns, to her presence. His situation of mind, when he is there, his wild and incoherent discourse ever affect her to tears, and discompose her so entirely, that for the remainder of the day she can enjoy neither pleasure nor business.

Catherine's care and concern for Grigory, and the time she was prepared to devote to him, appear to have offended both Potemkin and Lanskoy, who took to their beds in high dudgeon.

As the time drew near for Paul and Maria Fyodorovna's return – they were expected to arrive any day in Riga – Sir James Harris commented on Catherine's recent changes in the sumptuary laws to simplify women's dress, banning trimmings and flounces and high head-dresses, and on the effect this would have on the Grand Duchess,

> who returns passionately fond of the French nation, their dress and manners, and who, besides having settled a correspondence to be carried on in her hand with Mad$^{lle}$ Bertin [the famous Parisian dress-maker], and other French agents of a like cast, has no less than 200 boxes arrived or arriving here, filled with gauzes, pompons, and other trash, from Paris, together with new *valets de chambre*, and various designs for preposterous headdresses. It is impossible the Empress could have wounded Her Imperial Highness in a more sensible part. I am certain when the news of it reaches her, which it will at Riga, that it will hurt her more feelingly than any event which might have affected the glory and welfare of the empire.

On 13 November Catherine told her son and daughter-in-law that so far her hopes that a cure might be found for Grigory had proved vain: 'Prince Orlov's illness continues; for two days he has been in bed and his reason in childhood; today there is going to be a consultation of doctors. You can judge from that whether there is any hope for the healing of his mind.' She gave further details on the following day to Grimm (as well as telling him of little Alexander's disappointment in discovering that Alexander the Great was dead, as he had wanted to meet him personally):

> In addition to work I have been experiencing mortal grief at the state of Prince Orlov: he went to the waters at Tsaritsyn [now Volgograd]; hardly had he begun to take them than he began to talk nonsense; after having taken them, he went back to Moscow. There he found the means of escaping the vigilance of his brothers; they only had time to get ahead of him by a few hours; he came here; I have seen him three times; he is quiet and calm, but weak, all his thoughts are disconnected, and he has conserved only his unwavering attachment to me. Imagine all I have had to suffer at seeing him in this state; he is currently in bed, and it is believed that his illness is the result of an apoplectic stroke, and in consequence there is hardly any hope of recovery.

General Bauer, a long-time friend of Grigory's, was also ill, and had sent Catherine a letter which had made her cry at the thought of losing such a faithful servant. The unfortunate Dr Rogerson then arrived at just the wrong moment, and caught the rough edge of the Empress's tongue:

> I told him that no doctor could or knew how to heal even an insect bite, and I tore the entire faculty to shreds as it does not know how to heal anyone, even though they make people stay in bed for three months. I did not calm down until he agreed that he and all his colleagues were ignoramuses with no idea of how to heal anyone; then the truth softened me; I said: enough, go away, and I started writing to the scapegoat to comfort myself.

Three days later Catherine reported to Grimm that there had recently been a death in her greyhound family, the deceased being the wife of the patriarch Sir Tom. The two dogs currently spending time in the Empress's room were Lady Tom and Theseus Tom, the latter being trained by Lanskoy; the training seems to have been only partially successful, as Theseus had a tendency to nip the legs of anyone who tried to share the hearth with him. He made an exception for

Alexander and Constantine, who were great favourites with all the dogs.

Paul and Maria Fyodorovna arrived back in Petersburg on 20 November, having been away for a year and two months. A first, short meeting between the Empress and her son and daughter-in-law took place entirely in private, and then the Grand Duke was decorated with the newly instituted Order of St Vladimir. The warmth which appeared to have subsisted between Catherine and her 'dear children' throughout their correspondence did not withstand the reality of their presence. She was aware – for of course everything had been reported to her – that Paul had been unwise enough to criticise aspects of her rule, both its style and policies, at some of the Courts he had visited. He and his wife had also returned heavily indebted, and Maria Fyodorovna with innumerable purchases from Paris which she now had to return. For the Grand Duke and Duchess it was a difficult homecoming. Paul's former governor and mentor was dismissed, disgraced and ill; Pavel Bibikov was in exile as a result of correspondence sent to the Grand Duke's friend Alexander Kurakin; little Alexander and Constantine, though pleased to see their parents, had got on perfectly well without them and were more than ever attached to their grandmother; and Potemkin's position was even more secure. After having been the centre of attention and treated as a most important personage everywhere he and his wife had stayed during their travels, Paul found himself back in his customary position of complete insignificance at his mother's Court. Worst of all, he had heard rumours that Catherine was intending to disinherit him in favour of Alexander. He and Maria Fyodorovna seem to have decided to keep a low profile, avoiding any boasting about their experiences in foreign parts and giving every appearance of dutiful obedience. According to Sir James Harris, however, this overtly discreet behaviour did not succeed in gaining the approval of the Empress, who clearly much preferred her son and daughter-in-law when they were not there: 'She now calls them reserved, sulky, and solitary, that they are spoilt by foreign connexions, and cannot return to the habits of their country. In short, having in her own mind previously resolved to be displeased, it is not in their power to please her.' Catherine was also preoccupied with foreign affairs, in particular with ending the ambiguous position of the Crimea which, under the Treaty of Kuchuk-Kainardji, had been granted 'independence' under Russian protection. Turkey had never really accepted this – and neither had Potemkin, who urged the

Empress to annex the Crimea to the Russian Empire. On 14 December 1782 Potemkin received 'most secret' instructions from Catherine authorising the annexation to take place when the time was right. The other European powers, considered Catherine and Potemkin, were unlikely actively to challenge this latest expansion of Russian territory. Britain and France were preoccupied with finalising their peace treaty over the War of American Independence, and Joseph II had pledged to support Russia.

The new year, 1783, did not start well, as Catherine reported to Grimm: 'Prince Orlov is going from bad to worse, and he is already under the guardianship of his brothers; General Bauer is also not recovering as he should, and I am overwhelmed with work and the illness of people I love and esteem. One should just not get ill; listen, those who have ears to hear: do you hear?' General Bauer died on 11 February: 'I was very afflicted by the death of General Bauer. I curse all doctors, surgeons and the whole faculty; they are all as thick as two short planks. They have killed off another person who was close to me for thirty-three years; I would never get to the end of it if I were to tell you all the wrongs they have done to me in the past year. Monsieur Tom however is well – but then he steers clear of doctors.' Towards the end of February Catherine herself was obliged to spend a week in bed with a fever – but so acute were her distrust and anger towards the medical profession at this time that she refused to allow any 'Aesculapius'★ to cross her threshold. She was finding some consolation in writing a history of Russia for the use of Alexander and Constantine (and for other children once it was published). As always she worked quickly, completing the second part, which dealt with the period from AD 862 to halfway through the twelfth century in the space of about three months. There were to be five parts in all. On 9 March the Empress thanked Grimm for some pots of rouge he had sent her, but said the colour was so dark that it had made her look like a Fury, so she wouldn't be using it again.

On 31 March 1783 Sir James Harris reported to Lord Grantham: 'Count Panin was seized at five o'clock this morning with a violent stroke of apoplexy, and, though every remedy was immediately applied, he expired between ten and eleven.' The Grand Duke and Duchess were present at his deathbed, though Paul had seen little of his former governor during the last months of his life. Twelve days later Grigory

★ The Greek god of medicine.

Orlov died in Moscow, at the age of 49. Catherine received the news on her arrival at Tsarskoye Selo on 19 April, two days before her fifty-fourth birthday. The next day she wrote to Grimm:

> Although I was very prepared for this sad event, I admit to you that I feel the most acute affliction over it: in him I lose a friend and the man to whom I have the greatest obligations in the world and who rendered me the most essential services. It is no use saying to me, or me saying to myself, all the things one usually says on such an occasion; all I do is burst into tears, and I have been suffering terribly since the moment I received this fatal news; work alone distracts me, and as I have none of my papers here yet, I write to you to comfort myself. General Lanskoy is doing his utmost to help me bear my grief, but that makes me cry all the more.

She also commented on how taken aback Orlov and Panin would be to find themselves arriving together in the next world, after a lifetime's hostility. Panin, in Catherine's opinion, did not come out well in comparison with Orlov: 'Count Panin was naturally lazy, and he had the art of passing off this laziness as deliberate prudence; his disposition was neither so good nor so frank as that of Prince Orlov, but he was more worldly and knew better how to hide his defects and vices, of which he had plenty.' She had also never really forgiven Panin for his role in ending Grigory's reign as favourite, and manipulating her into a relationship with Alexander Vassilchikov. Catherine's physical reaction to her grief over Grigory's death manifested itself a few days later, in the shape of a swollen cheek, a very high temperature and delirium. On 1 May she felt so ill that she had a blood-letting and was still very weak two days later, having had nothing to eat for three days.

Potemkin was now in Kherson, supervising preparations for the annexation of the Crimea, which he intended to be bloodless (though regiments were of course positioned in readiness). The idea was to make it appear to be the will of the Crimean people. In the orders and undated manifesto which Catherine had sent to him earlier in the spring, the annexation was justified on political and economic grounds. It was declared that the Tatars had shown themselves unfit for freedom on account of their 'ignorance and savagery', and it was necessary for the Russians to forestall intervention by the Turks and to recoup the money they had already spent on Crimean affairs. On 11 May Potemkin wrote to Catherine to tell her that he had found everything in Kherson to be in great disarray but he was sorting it all out with his customary energy. He also expressed concern at not having heard from her for some time.

Catherine must have felt that illness and death were stalking her friends that year. She had been cross to hear during the spring that Diderot was ill, and on 1 June (while Alexander and Constantine were wading in a stream with their fishing nets) she wrote to Grimm to commiserate on the recent death of his companion Madame d'Epinay: 'I will not discuss your loss with you, as one must never nourish sad thoughts or resurrect them; but be assured that I shared your grief just as I am persuaded that you shared mine.'

Arrangements had been underway for several weeks for Catherine to have a meeting with King Gustavus III of Sweden in early June, in the town of Fredrickshamn (now known in Finnish as Hamina) on the Gulf of Finland. But on 7 June she reported to Grimm: 'There is my trip to Fredericksham curtailed or postponed, because the hero of the Swedes, through awkwardness and because he is not a good horseman, has fallen off his horse and broken his left arm between shoulder and elbow; he sent his gentleman of the bedchamber to me with this delightful piece of news.' The accident had happened during a troop inspection when the King's horse had been startled by a cannon shot.

Catherine was missing Potemkin, as well as wanting the Crimean matter to be settled soon. 'Not only do I often think of you,' she wrote to Potemkin, 'but I also regret and often grieve over the fact that you are there and not here, for without you I feel as though I'm missing a limb. I beg you in every way: do not delay the occupation of the Crimea. I'm now fearful of the plague for you and for everyone. For God's sake, get on and order all possible precautions . . . I believe that you have many anxieties, but I know that you and I can cope with anxieties.' The Empress was dreading a recurrence of the plague outbreak which had followed in the wake of the last Russo-Turkish War; she wrote again to Potemkin: 'Be so good as to let me know whether the plague continues, whether it is abating or has been stopped. This frightens me. I fear its stealing into Russia again as a result of some blunder along the frontier.'

The meeting with Gustavus was rescheduled for mid-June, when Catherine and a small entourage ('small' still comprised 51 carriages drawn by 296 horses) set off from Tsarskoye Selo. The party included Princess Dashkova (Catherine had decided it was time to make use of this lady's considerable talents, despite her difficult character, and had appointed her the first director of the newly founded Russian Academy in December 1782), Alexander Lanskoy, Ivan Chernyshev, Count Stroganov, Lev Naryshkin, Alexander Bezborodko and two chamberlains. They stopped for dinner in St Petersburg and then crossed the river in a longboat to the Vyborg side, where they found coaches waiting for them. After a hot and dusty journey, lasting two days, the Empress and her suite arrived in Fredrickshamn on the evening of 17 June. On the following day they were joined by the King of Sweden. Travelling under the name of 'the Count of Haga', Gustavus had his arm in a sling and was in some pain, but was otherwise well; Catherine showed him portraits of her grandsons, as they were on a snuff-box which she had with her (the Empress, like everyone else at Court, took snuff regularly). Though the two monarchs held no substantive discussions over the course of the next few days, Catherine did inform Gustavus of her intention to annex the Crimea and that war with Turkey might be a possible consequence of this action. The King had been warned in advance not to upset Catherine by mentioning the deaths of Grigory Orlov and General Bauer, and he complied with this request, only alluding to them after Catherine had done so herself.

In her letters to Paul and Maria Fyodorovna, Catherine told them how dreadful the weather was at Fredrickshamn; she was feeling stifled both by the noise of the wind and by being unable to open her windows. She was not enjoying herself in this 'most wretched country' and longed to be back at Tsarskoye Selo. 'In future,' she wrote, 'I will send anyone who speaks ill of the surroundings of Petersburg here for a few days.' Fortunately the trip lasted only a week.

The Russian annexation of the Crimea was completed in July, Potemkin personally administering the oath of submission on the 10th of that month. The news of this, however, took as usual a long time to arrive, and by the 15th Catherine was getting very fractious, writing to Potemkin:

> You can imagine how anxious I must be at not having had a word from you in more than five weeks. In addition, false rumours are being spread here, and I have nothing with which to refute them. I expected the Crimea would be occupied by the middle of May at the latest, and here it is half-way through July, and I know no more about it than the Pope of Rome. This leads inevitably to all sorts of talk, which is not at all to my liking. I beg you in every

way: inform me more frequently so I'm kept up to date with developments; the natural activity of my mind and head invents a thousand ideas which often torment me.

Catherine finally received the news she had been waiting for on 19 July, but her pleasure was spoilt by Alexander Lanskoy falling off his horse – an English animal that had already kicked him once before – and seriously injuring himself. Catherine told Grimm about this a few weeks later, when she also alluded to Lanskoy's passion for 'antique stones' – that is, for engraved gems and carved stones:

> When General Lanskoy heard that you had let go a collection of antique stones without buying them, he almost fainted, and was nearly suffocated by it; he learnt this news a few days after a dreadful fall he had from a horse and which put him in bed for several days, but from which he is completely recovered, although his chest was bruised and he was spitting blood, but thanks to his excellent constitution, he doesn't seem to feel it any more.

During the period of Lanskoy's convalescence, on 29 July, Catherine became a grandmother for the third time. This time the child was a girl, christened Alexandra, which must have somewhat disappointed Alexander in his hopes for another playmate and left Catherine less than enthralled, as she admitted to Grimm:

> My swarm has been augmented in the last few days by a young lady who in honour of Monsieur her elder brother has been named Alexandrine; to tell the truth, I greatly prefer boys to girls. Mine are perfectly well, running, jumping, skilful, agile, resolute, rowing in skiffs and steering them marvellously along the canals where there is a foot of water, and God knows everything they do: they read, write, draw, dance, all of their own volition; I recently took them with me to Peterhof, where we stayed at Monplaisir, where in truth I saw them climbing everywhere they could reach; they also went in and out through the windows as often as through the doors.

Catherine demonstrated even less enthusiasm for her new granddaughter in her letter of 27 September: 'The young lady Alexandra Pavlovna is a very ugly being, especially in comparison with her brothers.'

She reported on the same day that the five-year-old Alexander had been going through a phase of irrational fears and dislikes – including an aversion to the famous castrato Luigi Marchesi, whom he found 'unpleasant and his grimaces horrible'. As Marchesi was famed as much for his belligerence as his voice, Alexander's dislike may not have been as irrational as his grandmother supposed, but in any event the child decided to overcome his fears himself by examining closely the things which frightened him. This seemed to solve the problem – though how closely he examined the castrato is not recorded.

On 12 October 1783 there was another death which distressed the Empress, that of Field Marshal Prince Golitsyn, the former Governor-General of St Petersburg who had worked closely with Catherine for many years. She commented in a letter to Potemkin four days later: 'As for me, it's been a black year: this week Field Marshal Prince Alexander Mikhailovich Golitsyn died, and it seems to me that as soon as someone falls into Rogerson's hands, he's as good as dead.' At the end of 1783 Catherine also sustained the loss of her favourite composer, Giovanni Païsiello – not this time through death but through resignation, as he was finding it difficult to work with a change of management in the department responsible for court spectacles.

One practical consequence of Grigory Orlov's death was that Catherine decided to make a gift of his estate of Gatchina – comprising the village of Gatchina, the palace with all its furnishings, decorations and outbuildings, and 20 other villages, and situated about 26 miles to the south of St Petersburg on the main road to Moscow – to her son. This had the effect of removing him from her immediate environs for much of the time, as over the ensuing years the Grand Duke virtually established his own small kingdom at Gatchina, dominated by military exercises performed by his own regiment (which he formed largely of drop-outs from the regular army) in Prussian-style uniforms. Though in many ways Paul became absorbed in his own world at Gatchina, his resentment at being sidelined was by now considerable. A note he wrote to his friend Baron Sacken, the Russian ambassador to Denmark, at the beginning of 1784 was exceedingly bitter: 'I am infinitely obliged to you, my dear friend, for your compliments on the new year. I wish you a good one in return. Otherwise I do not articulate my wishes at all for fear of spoiling whatever they may be, my influence often being such that it suffices for me to mention an idea or a person to get the project aborted.'

While the Agate Pavilion above the new baths at Tsarskoye Selo was still in the process of completion, Charles Cameron submitted plans and a model of a long two-storey promenade gallery. He proposed that the gallery should be joined to the palace and the Agate Pavilion by a covered walkway, so that Catherine would have direct access to it from her own rooms. In fine weather she would be able to walk in the colonnade along the outer edges of the gallery, while when the weather was bad she could use the central part which would be enclosed by glass. The whole gallery was designed both to strike the viewer with its beauty and elegance from right over the other side of the Great Pond, and to provide a place from which the Empress could view the entire vista of her park and gardens. Cameron had been having some difficulty in finding Russian craftsmen able and willing to work to his specifications, and he now obtained permission from the Empress to import some from Scotland. Accordingly a notice advertising for them appeared in the *Edinburgh Evening Courant* on 21 January [N.S.].

The incorporation of the Crimea into the Russian Empire was formally ratified on 2 February, and Catherine appointed Potemkin Governor-General of the new district of Tauride (as the Crimea was now to be known, in another allusion to the 'Greek project', the region having been called Tauric Chersonese by the ancient Greeks) as well as president of the College of War, with the rank of field marshal.

Early in the year Catherine made another significant appointment. General-in-Chief Nikolai Saltykov became governor of her grandsons, and the Empress provided him with a set of instructions concerning their upbringing. These were by and large an amplification of the notes she had written around the time of Alexander's birth, and covered the areas of clothing, food, fresh air, washing and bathing, bed and sleep, childish amusements and high-spiritedness, illness and medicine, tears, desires, obedience, good and bad examples, the principal virtues to be instilled in children, courage, languages, and how their supervisors should relate to the children. The emphasis throughout is on fresh air, simplicity, order and a gently imposed discipline. Many of Catherine's instructions sound extraordinarily modern and enlightened. The children's clothing should, as she had always specified, be as simple, non-restrictive and light as possible. 'Food and drink should be simple, and simply prepared, without spicy potions or the sort of roots that heat the blood, and without too much salt.' If the children got peckish between meals, they were to be given a piece of bread, though it seems that here the Empress may not always have abided by her own precepts, at least when the children were younger, Baroness Dimsdale having noted in October 1781:

A few days before we left St Petersburg Prince Alexander and Constantine's physicians begged of the Baron that he would mention to the Empress (for they said they dare not) how improperly they were managed in regard to their manner of living as the Empress frequently had them with her in a morning and gave them a great deal of fruit, and likewise when they dined with her they eat of many different things. In consequence of this the Baron wrote her a letter mentioning how improper it was, and recommended in future how they ought to live to keep them in good health, and gave it himself.

They were not allowed to drink wine, except on doctor's orders. In summer in place of breakfast and between dinner and supper they could be given 'cherries, strawberries, currants, apples and ripe pears'. They were not to drink cold water if they had got overheated, and before drinking anything in such a case they should eat a piece of bread first.

Their rooms – which were not to be heated above 13° or 14° Réaumur (16° or 17° Celsius) – were to be aired at least twice a day, and they were to spend as much time as possible outside (but they were not to lie on damp grass after getting hot). They were to take Russian baths – sweating and going into cold water – every four to five weeks, in both summer and winter, as this had been demonstrated, asserted Catherine, to be good for the health. It was very important that they should learn to swim. They should also frequently have their feet washed in cold water; Catherine believed that this would help them to avoid colds as well as corns. They were not to sleep on soft mattresses, but on straw ones, to which they were already accustomed, and they should be 'early to bed and early to rise' – seven to eight hours' sleep should be enough. They should be woken up gently, so as not to startle them, by their names being called softly.

The little Grand Dukes' high-spiritedness must not be repressed, but channelled into play and exercise. Their supervisors should not join in the children's games, unless specifically invited by the children themselves. They should be allowed to play at whatever they wanted, provided there was nothing harmful in the games they chose or invented. Catherine understood the importance of play: 'Children's games are not just games, but the most diligent exercise of children.' Idleness, on the other hand, should never be allowed; if the children were not playing or studying, then they should be engaged in conversation suitable for their years. They were to learn to speak foreign languages, but Russian was never to be neglected; it was important for them to write and speak their own language well. There should be no force involved in teaching them; children, believed Catherine, are naturally curious and will want to learn of their own volition.

The Empress emphasised her instruction that the children, who were fortunate to be naturally healthy, were to be given medicine as rarely as possible. She was at great pains to explain this directive:

> Children's frequent little fits of the shivers, such as from the heat or from pain in a limb, are to do with growth or some such natural development, and they will go away without a physician, without medicine, without doctors and doctoring; indeed the use of medicine in such circumstances takes away the strength necessary for the production of that natural action; and as in the absence of real illness the use of medical prescriptions is unnecessary, so in the case of genuine illness, and when other means of healing have not worked, then it may be useful to ask for a doctor's advice.

For someone who was herself prone to tears, Catherine seemed very unsympathetic towards them:

> Small children usually cry for one of two reasons: first, from stubbornness, secondly, from sensitivity and the desire to complain. One can distinguish between these two sorts of tears by the child's voice, expression and appearance; but neither sort of tears should be allowed, all crying should be forbidden.
> When they cry from sensitivity, such as when they are ill, then one must try to give them relief but not take too much notice in their presence of their pain, tears and illness; one must tell them that crying will make them feel worse, and so therefore they must suppress their tears and stop crying; and it is better to put up with the illness and overcome it by being brave and patient. Try to get them to think about something else, or else turn their tears into jokes.

If they fell over while playing, no one was to make a fuss or run to pick them up − they were to be left to get up again for themselves.

Only if they really needed help should it be given, and then without unnecessary hurry or panic. They were to be told to be more careful in future, but that this is the way people grow up.

The boys were to be brought up to be unquestioningly obedient to the Empress and her imperial power; Catherine said that the idea of disobeying her should seem as impossible to them as changing the weather. But corporal punishment was absolutely prohibited (as it was in all the imperial educational establishments). Habits of obedience were to be formed through the exercise of reason and disapproval of bad behaviour. Their supervisors were never to leave them alone with the servants, and were themselves to treat the children more or less as they would treat adults. The boys were not permitted to issue commands to their instructors and carers; instead they were to ask properly for what they wanted and say thank you once they got it. No adults were to swear or use other unacceptable language in front of the children, neither were they to display anger. No conversations liable to encourage vice were to be tolerated within earshot of the children. Their guiding principle was to be: 'Do not do to others what you would not want done to you.'

On 28 March Catherine reported to Grimm that Alexander and Constantine were learning carpentry, under the direction of a German joiner, Herr Mayer. In addition a 30-year-old Swiss man, Frédéric César de La Harpe, became Alexander's tutor. La Harpe had earlier proved his worth to Catherine by helping to 'rescue' Sasha Lanskoy's younger brother, who had run off to Paris in pursuit of an unsuitable woman. In the same letter Catherine extolled Sasha's virtues; she said he rather resembled Alexander in his enthusiasms and desire to touch everything and that he was currently enjoying himself with an apothecary's set which some English person had given him and with which he was concocting and examining drugs.

Charles Cameron's advertisement in the *Edinburgh Evening Courant* had borne fruit, and on 3 May [N.S.] a party of about 70 workmen with their wives and children set sail from Leith. They included four master masons, three master plasterers, two master bricklayers, fifteen plasterers and five smiths. By the middle of June they had settled in Sofiya, a model town still under construction, established in 1779 and designed by Cameron, on the south side of the park at Tsarskoye Selo. This town, no less than the work Cameron did in the Catherine Palace and adjoining buildings, was intended to create perfection, designed to be an ideal living space for its inhabitants and to provide a pleasant and uplifting view from the grounds of the imperial palace. The town was even blessed with street lighting, very rare for the times – but the lamps were to be lit only when Catherine was in residence. The hours of work for the newly imported labourers were set out in an imperial decree: the normal working day was to end at six o'clock in the evening in spring and summer, though it could be extended to nine o'clock if necessary; there was to be a break for dinner at two o'clock and special arrangements were to be made for Sundays and feast-days.

Yet another significant death for Catherine had occurred during the winter. She had not been able to bring herself to tell Grimm about it until 19 May: 'Sir Tom Anderson, deceased this winter, has been placed with his inscription behind the granite pyramid [a construction of Cameron's at Tsarskoye Selo]; well, I have not yet had the heart to go and see it and I have not announced his death until today; he lived for sixteen years.'

The Portuguese singer Luísa Todi, who had been invited to Petersburg by Catherine, arrived with her husband and children on 27 May, and was received officially two days later. On the 30th she gave her first concert at Tsarskoye Selo, appearing in a performance of *Armida e Rinaldo* by Giuseppe Sarti, who had succeeded Païsiello as court composer. Catherine was so delighted by her performance that she gave her two diamond bracelets.

The series of illnesses and deaths which had so distressed Catherine and depleted her energy over the past 18 months culminated in June 1784, when the 55-year-old Empress suffered a catastrophe for which all her usual prescriptions of 'not thinking about it and carrying on' proved completely inadequate. Several months later, on 14 September, she gave her *souffre-douleur* an account of what had happened, this being the first time she had been able to write about the event, which began with Sasha Lanskoy getting a sore throat on the afternoon of Wednesday 19 June:

On that day he came to me the moment his throat began to hurt him, and he told me that he was about to have a severe illness from which he would not recover; I tried to banish this idea from his head, and he did seem to me to forget his illness: he went to his apartments at half-past four; at six I went for a walk in the garden; he came and walked round the pond with me. Back in my rooms he complained again, but he begged me to make up a party of reversis★

★ A card game for four players in which the main object was to avoid taking tricks containing penalty cards.

as usual; it was brief, because I could see that he was suffering. When everyone had left, I advised him to go to his apartments and to bed; he did so and sent for a very good surgeon we have at Tsarskoye Selo; the latter found his pulse to be intermittent, and the following day at seven o'clock in the morning he let me know that he would like to confer with some of his colleagues; I sent Kelchen and sent off a courier to Petersburg to summon Weikard [a German physician who could be relied upon to tell the truth]. The latter arrived toward mid-day; when I knew he had arrived, I went to see the invalid, who seemed to me to have a high fever . . . I called Kelchen; he, though more politic than [Weikard], did not hide how apprehensive he was either. The invalid, while waiting, had formed a very strong resolution not to take any drugs at all: he let himself be bled, put his feet in water, drank a lot of water and other drinks, but did not take the slightest thing; he slept a lot during Thursday, and all his features became extremely swollen, and the end of his nose went white. On Friday his friend Dr Sobolevsky arrived; he made him drink cold water and gave him cooked figs to eat; he didn't want to see either Weikard or the others until the evening, when the fever redoubled causing much anxiety; on Saturday he seemed a little better, but towards mid-day he began to vomit, and he vomited all day, after which came hiccoughs, and the purple rash appeared. Nevertheless on Saturday evening Weikard told me that if it didn't go to his brain, he could pull through. He was very hot; on Sunday he was moved to a more airy room. He walked there himself; I went to see him at three o'clock; he was feeling very ill in the evening, and he told me all the arrangements he had made. He was not wandering; but after an hour delirium set in; he knew everyone by name and patronymic; but he was wandering and was angry with everyone for not bringing his horses to harness to his bed. This anger made us hope that he would vomit bile, but he did not: throughout Monday he grew weaker by the moment. I left his room at eleven o'clock in the evening, I couldn't take any more.

Sasha died on Tuesday 25 June. On Monday Dr Rogerson had administered James's powders,★ but they had had no more effect than anything else. From the symptoms Catherine describes, the illness was most probably diphtheria.

★ 'Dr. James's Powders for Fevers, the Small-Pox, Measles, Colds, etc.'

For the first time in her life, Catherine was incapacitated by grief. A week after Sasha's death, she managed to write a paragraph to Grimm:

When I began this letter [on 7 June, when she had told Grimm how moved she had been by the singing of La Todi], I was happy and joyful, and my days passed so rapidly that I did not know where they went. It is no longer like that: I am plunged into the most acute grief, and my happiness is no more: I have thought I might die myself from the irreparable loss I have just suffered, a week ago, of my best friend. I had hoped that he would be the support of my old age: he applied himself, he profited, he had acquired all my tastes; this was a young man whom I had brought up, who was grateful, gentle and honest, who shared my sorrows when I had them and who rejoiced at my joys; in a word, I have the misfortune to tell you, while sobbing, that General Lanskoy is no more; a malignant fever accompanied by quinsy [inflamed tonsils] carried him off to the grave in five days, and my room, which I used to like so much, has become an empty cavern, in which I can barely drag myself around like a shade: I have nevertheless been out of bed since yesterday, but I am so weak and so grievously affected that at the moment I cannot see a human face without sobs robbing me of speech; I cannot sleep or eat; reading bores me, and writing is beyond my strength; I do not know what will become of me, but what I do know is that never in my life have I been so unhappy since my best and most lovable friend abandoned me thus. I opened my drawer; I found this letter which I had begun, I have traced these lines, but I can do no more.

Alexander Bezborodko sent an urgent message to the only person considered capable of bringing Catherine back to life. Prince Potemkin was then in Kremenchuk in central Ukraine, the capital of New Russia. On receipt of Bezborodko's summons he left immediately and arrived at Tsarskoye Selo on 10 July, having covered 760 miles in seven days Fyodor Orlov also arrived, and the two men provided some comfort for the Empress. As Catherine explained to Grimm, 'Until that moment I had been unable to bear a human face; those two went about it in a good way: they began to howl with me, and then I felt at my ease with them, but there was a long way to go . . .' Catherine kept asking about Sasha's body and was unwilling to allow it to be buried. The burial finally took place on 27 July, at Sofiya; the Empress did not attend, and on the same day she was bled.

Her depression lasted throughout the summer. She made no attempt to hide it – indeed, could not have done so - even from her son and daughter-in-law, to whom she wrote on 2 August: 'I have just received your letters, my dear children; I am replying straightaway. The news which you give me of your health and that of your daughter is very agreeable to me; mine is in precisely the same state as when you left. The news from here is more sterile than that which you give me, I do not even know if the harvest has been done. Farewell, keep well.' Even Alexander and Constantine seem to have been unable to afford Catherine any consolation during this period, and there was no question of her finding an instant replacement for Sasha Lanskoy. She nevertheless continued to carry out the most urgent business of the Empire, giving the necessary orders when required.

A spate of salacious and unkind rumours attended her beloved Sasha's death. Princess Dashkova was not alone in claiming that the young man's stomach had burst – 'literally burst' (and maybe some such thing had indeed happened in the long hot weeks between his death and burial) – while others claimed that Potemkin had poisoned him. It was also whispered that he had expired in the act of making love to Catherine, or that his death was the result of an overdose of aphrodisiacs (perhaps the apothecary's set had inspired this last rumour).

Towards the end of August, as Catherine subsequently told Grimm, 'at last some intervals came, at first calmer hours, and then days'. With the advent of autumn, it became necessary to light the stoves at Tsarskoye Selo and the one in Catherine's room started smoking. Without any warning, she made a sudden decision to return to Petersburg. On 8 September she attended the liturgy for the Feast of the Nativity of the Virgin in the chapel of the Winter Palace: 'in consequence also for the first time I saw everyone, and everyone saw me, but in truth it was such a great effort that on returning to my room I felt so exhausted that anyone else would have fainted, something which has never happened to me in my life'.

Several other deaths had occurred during the weeks of Catherine's seclusion, including that of senator and state secretary Adam Olsufyev on 27 June, Count Zakhar Chernyshev on 31 August, and Denis Diderot on 30 July [N.S.]. Catherine instructed Grimm to arrange for the latter's widow to receive a pension of 200 livres a year, initially to be paid five years in advance. She was still feeling too weak on 9 September to address all of Grimm's other outstanding queries. What she had managed to do during her prostration was more reading of ancient Russian history and work on comparison of languages, from which she hoped to demonstrate that the ancient Slavs had been responsible for naming most 'rivers, mountains, valleys and circles and countries of France, Spain, Scotland and other places'. Her depression was by no means over, and she could not bear reminders of Lanskoy – such as the engraved gems and stones he had loved so much – as is clear from what she wrote to Grimm, who had himself offered to come to St Petersburg if it would help her: 'I am very obliged to you for the suggestion you make of coming here; but I advise you to do nothing about it, for either you would see me die, or I would see you die, and that would only upset the one who remained. As for purchases, talk no more to me of them, and particularly of a certain sort. It has been a very long time since I bought them for myself.' She wrote again to Grimm on 26 September:

As regards carved stones, tell those who offer them to you that I never bought them for myself, because I don't understand them, and that I will not buy any more. If you want to know my true state, I will tell you that for three months from yesterday I have been incon-solable over the irreparable loss I have sustained, that the only thing which is better is that I have become reaccustomed to human faces, that otherwise my heart bleeds as it did at the first moment, that I do my duty and try to do it well, but that my grief is extreme, such as I have never felt in my life, and it is now three months that I have been in this cruel situation, suffering like the damned.

# 17

# Convalescence and Recovery
# (1784–86)

*I cannot complain that I lack people whose affection and care have been just right for distracting me and getting me to relax.*

Catherine II to Friedrich Melchior Grimm

W hen Catherine returned to St Petersburg in September 1784, she did not immediately go back to her normal apartments in the Winter Palace – she found too much there to remind her of Sasha Lanskoy – but instead moved into her Hermitage and in one small room, of under 20 square metres, sequestered herself with her books and manuscripts on Russian history and vocabulary. In shutting herself away like this, she was repeating the behaviour of her previous period of depression after Paul's birth in 1754. Potemkin stayed with her for the whole of that autumn and into the winter, constantly cajoling her and trying to bring her back to life – 'Oh, how he tormented me,' she wrote to Grimm, 'how I scolded him, how angry I got with him, but he did not stop.' By the New Year Potemkin had succeeded sufficiently for him to feel it was now safe to leave his Empress and partner for a few months, and in January he returned to the south of Russia.

On 16 February Catherine finally moved back to her apartments in the Winter Palace, where she resumed her correspondence with Grimm: 'I have nothing to tell you except how I have been during these six months in which I have not written to you; you know me well enough to judge; my health has stood up to it; I did not write to you, because in truth I had nothing cheering to say.' She mentioned that her grandsons were growing and that her latest granddaughter (born in December) was beautiful, which was why she had named her Elena (or Helen). She added: 'as you see, I am not dead, despite what the gazettes have said; neither do I have any trace of illness, but until now I have been an inanimate being, vegetating and spiritless'. On the positive side, Catherine had realised that she had some very good friends, chief among them Potemkin, but also others of her courtiers and officials – such as her lady-in-waiting Countess Anna Protasova, the Naryshkins and the Engelhardts (Potemkin's nieces) – who genuinely cared for her and had exerted themselves to restore her interest in life.

As Catherine had begun to emerge from the depths of depression, she had as usual found the act of writing – or 'scribbling' – therapeutic, and during the winter she had embarked on a new genre, that of playwriting. Plays were written to be performed, and the writing and staging of short theatrical pieces now became as staple a part of the entertainment of Catherine's immediate circle as were billiards and card games. Later that year she recommended the activity to Grimm: 'Why don't you write plays? it would keep you amused. I read mine to two or three people, and then I put them in my portfolio; it is as full of plays as of rulings.' Some of the dramatic works she wrote were also shown to a wider audience, though with her anonymity preserved (at least officially). On 3 April she told Grimm that her play *Le Trompeur* ('The Deceiver') had had a great success in Moscow, and she had also been amused by the seven-year-old Alexander donning a wig and acting out a scene from *Le Trompeur*, playing all three roles himself. Catherine's plays, like everything else she wrote, had a strong didactic element and she hoped to 'improve' her audience by poking gentle fun at various human foibles.

The Empress's interest in antique stones had also begun to return. Part of her mourning process was represented by the attention she was giving to her cabinet where these tiny objects – so beloved of Lanskoy – were contained, looking at it and adding to it every day (by now it had 125 full drawers) but showing the contents to very few people. Recently three members of the British community, including the new ambassador Mr Alleyne Fitzherbert (Sir James Harris had obtained his recall, partly because the Petersburg climate made him ill every winter), had been invited to a viewing and had been most impressed. On 30 April Catherine asked Grimm to find out the price of a collection belonging to the former French ambassador, Breteuil, which she had turned down the previous year. She also gave him a graphic description of how many stones she already possessed:

> My little collection of engraved stones is such that yesterday four people had difficulty carrying two baskets filled with drawers containing about half the collection; and, so you should be in no doubt, I ought to tell you that these baskets are the ones used for transporting wood into our rooms in the winter and that the drawers were greatly overflowing the baskets; by that you can tell how very greedy we've become on this subject.

To display her ever-increasing collection to best effect, Catherine commissioned a series of cabinets from the most renowned furniture-maker of the day, David Roentgen, cabinet-maker to Marie Antoinette.

In addition to writing plays and poring over her gems, Catherine had resumed normal work, one result of which was the publication on 21 April 1785, her fifty-sixth birthday, of twin charters to the nobility and the towns. The Nobles' Charter codified the privileges pertaining to the noble estate while, in addition to dividing citizens into six categories, the Urban Charter gave all citizens certain rights (such as not being deprived of property or reputation without the possibility of redress through the courts). On the day after the charters' publication, Catherine told Grimm that her spirits were gradually improving – though she could not be sure that she might not suffer a relapse: 'As for me, I can tell you that I have been better for the last two months – but one should not talk about ropes in the house of someone who's hanged himself.' Three days later she gave more details of her recovery and alluded to another way in which she was getting back to normal (or at least to what was normal for her):

> My inner self has regained its calm and serenity because we have, with the help of our friends, made an effort with ourselves; we have begun with a comedy which is said to be charming and is therefore proof of a little return of verve and gaiety; monosyllables have been banished, and I cannot complain that I lack people around me whose affection and care have been just right for distracting me and getting me to relax, but it took some time for me to notice this and even more to get used to it; in short, in a word, as in a hundred, I have a friend [un ami] who is very capable and worthy, and friends who do not abandon me.

The new 'ami' – a word which can mean friend or lover – was a 31-year-old officer called Alexander Yermolov, a tall blond man with almond-shaped eyes, who had been presented to the Empress by Potemkin (and had then had to bide his time until he was 'noticed').

Finally Catherine's recovery was marked by a return of enthusiasm for her grandsons – particularly, as ever, for Alexander:

> Messieurs Alexandre and Constantin are now in the hands of General Saltykov, who follows my principles and instructions in all matters, as do those who surround them. In truth these boys are ravishingly handsome, tall, strong, robust, sensible and obedient; it is a pleasure merely to see them. I am convinced that one will always be perfectly content with Alexander, who has a very equable disposition combined with a charm which is astonishing for his age; his face is open, smiling and prepossessing; his will is always good: he wants to succeed and he does succeed in everything beyond his age; he is learning to ride a horse, he reads, he writes in three languages; he draws – and he isn't forced to do anything; what he writes is either history or geography or selected sentences or something cheerful; he has an excellent heart.

Music was the one area in which Catherine did not think any effort should be spent in educating her grandsons, telling Grimm: 'Messieurs Alexandre and Constantin will not be learning music; they can scrape or play if they like, but they won't have lessons.' (She must in the end have been open to persuasion on this point, for Alexander did in fact have violin lessons from Henri Dietz, and became quite an accomplished player.)

On 24 May the Empress set off on a tour of inspection, the object of which was to view the canal system, inaugurated by Peter the Great and improved under herself (and part of what is now known as the Volga-Baltic Waterway), along which goods were transported into Petersburg. Her suite consisted of 16 people, including Potemkin, Count Ivan Chernyshev, the Grand Chamberlain Ivan Shuvalov, the Master of the Horse Lev Naryshkin, Alexander Yermolov, and the foreign ministers Count Cobenzl, the Comte de Ségur and Alleyne Fitzherbert (whom Catherine referred to as her 'pocket ministers' and part of whose unwritten contract was to repay her hospitality by praising her achievements to their respective Courts of Vienna, Versailles and St James). Before setting off, the party spent some time at Tsarskoye Selo, Ségur having left an account of what the daily routine was like there for a guest:

> Catherine worked nearly all morning, and each of us was free then to write, to read, to walk or to do in fact whatever one felt like. Dinner, few in dishes and in guests, was good, simple, without pomp; the time after dinner was employed in playing and in talking; in the evening the Empress retired early, and we would then get together, Cobenzl, Fitz-Herbert and I, either in one of our apartments, or in that of Prince Potemkin.

Ségur also described Catherine's appearance around this time:

> The majesty of her brow and the way she carried her head, as well as her proud glance and the dignity of her bearing, made her look taller than she really was. She had an aquiline nose, a charming mouth, blue eyes and black eyebrows, a very gentle look when she wanted, and an attractive smile.
>
> In order to disguise the corpulence of advancing years, which efface all the graces, she wore a full gown with wide sleeves, very like the ancient Muscovite dress. The whiteness and brilliance of her complexion were the attractions she kept the longest.

On the journey to inspect the canals, Catherine shared her carriage with Alexander Yermolov, her friend and lady-in-waiting Countess Protasova, and Countess Rostopchin; in addition Prince Potemkin and Count Cobenzl took turn and turn about, on alternate days, with the Comte de Ségur and Mr Fitzherbert. Sometimes, too, Lev Naryshkin joined them. On 28 May they arrived in Vyshniy Volochek, the location of the great locks designed and built in the days of Peter the Great; under Catherine they were being improved, wood being replaced by stone, and further sources of water being directed into the canals. In addition two further canals were being built, which would eventually join the Caspian to the Black Sea, and the Black Sea to the Baltic via the Dnieper.

As far as possible, the Empress adhered to her normal daily routine while travelling, as Ségur recounted:

> We would leave in the morning at eight o'clock; towards two o'clock we would stop for a dinner in a town or village, where everything

had been prepared in advance, so that the Empress would find herself as well served and almost as commodiously accommodated there as at Petersburg. We always dined with her. Our journey would stop at eight o'clock in the evening, and the Empress would employ the evening in her usual way with the entertainments of card-games and conversation. Every morning, after an hour of work and before leaving, Catherine would receive the homage of the magistrates, nobles and merchants of the place where she was staying; she gave her hand to everyone to kiss, and embraced all the women; this obliged her to have a sort of second toilet: for, as all the women in these provinces, even the bourgeoisie and the peasants, used powder and paint, the Empress's face at the end of these audiences would be covered in red and white.

On arrival at each place during the journey Catherine would first of all go to the church to make her devotions, knowing that this was indispensable in maintaining the affection and respect of the local populace.

The party left Vyshniy Volochek on 30 May, arriving the next day in Torzhok and the day after that in Tver. Catherine was enjoying the journey and feeling well, so much so that she was happy to accede to the request of Count Bruce, now the Governor-General of Moscow, to extend the itinerary to include a brief visit to the old capital, where she and her suite stayed for a few days. The Empress took the opportunity to inspect the various imperial palaces in the vicinity, including the Petrovsky palace, built by Matvei Kazakov between 1763 and 1768, and the very recently constructed palace at Tsaritsyno, where the architect was Vasily Bazhenov. During her return journey Catherine reported briefly to Paul and Maria Fyodorovna on her impressions of the various palaces: 'The Petrovsky palace is a very good pied-à-terre, the two others – that is, the new palaces of Moscow and Tsaritsyno – are not finished, the latter needs to be changed inside, or else it will be uninhabitable; otherwise Kolomenskoye is as I left it. The city of Moscow is improving, much is being built there and very well; the aqueduct is a great work in progress.' Catherine had in fact exploded in fury when she had visited Tsaritsyno. The most likely explanation for this was that she had noticed various masonic symbols introduced into the building by Bazhenov, who was a close friend of a leading exponent and propagandist of freemasonry in Russia, Nikolai Novikov. The Empress had always been suspicious of freemasonry. This was, after all, a secret male society from which she was by definition excluded. It had trans-national allegiances, including to foreign monarchs such as Frederick the Great, and there was always the possibility of the masons seeking to introduce Grand Duke Paul into their brotherhood, raising the spectre of a conspiracy against her. In addition, both as head of the Orthodox Church in Russia and as an exponent of Enlightenment principles, Catherine had an aversion towards what she saw as the superstitious elements of freemasonry. Much of what had already been built at Tsaritsyno had now to be rebuilt at the Empress's command. In 1786 Bazhenov was dismissed from his work there and replaced by Matvei Kazakov.

For the latter part of the return journey the party travelled by water, in galleys supplied with their own orchestras which played the travellers to sleep, along the river Msta to Novgorod, through Lake Ilmen and along the Volkhov river into the Ladoga canal and thence into the Neva. Catherine was pleased with both the journey and her travelling companions. 'One must do justice to Monsieur de Ségur,' she told Grimm. 'No one could be more agreeable and witty than he; he seems to enjoy himself with us, and is as merry as a lark. He writes verses and songs for us, and we have given him some bad prose. Prince Potemkin has made us die of laughing throughout the whole voyage, and it seems that everyone is bending over backwards to contribute. We are enjoying the nicest weather and charming views.'

The party arrived back in Petersburg on 18 June and on the following day Catherine travelled to Peterhof, where she was joined by Alexander and Constantine. There she remained for the celebrations of her accession and the Feast of Sts Peter and Paul at the end of the month. The foreign ministers had returned to their respective houses in the town, but Catherine remarked: 'by God, they would have gone to the end of the world with me, if I'd asked them to'.

During July Catherine went on another short excursion with her 'pocket ministers' and Potemkin's niece, Countess Alexandra Branicka (and, of course, Yermolov), to visit her new palace at Pella, returning again by water along the Neva. She commented of this very jolly journey: 'Monsieur Kelchen assured us on the way that it was impossible to die from laughing; this must be true, as no one is dead, even though we laughed fit to burst from morning to night.' She was back at Tsarskoye Selo by 21 July. That summer Alexander and Constantine extended their activities to exterior decoration, helping to whiten the outside of the Catherine Palace 'under the direction of two Scottish stucco workers'. And, to Catherine's delight, the Breteuil collection of carved stones arrived in August. On the 19th she returned to Petersburg, without fanfare or announcement, this being the one aspect of the previous summer of which she retained positive recollections, as she explained to Grimm:

> I came back to town yesterday, just like last year, on the spur of the moment. I find that delightful: no one to lead me, no one to receive me; I pass by like a tomcat without anyone noticing, and once I've arrived, everyone repeats for the next twenty-four hours: she came on the spur of the moment, and the hollow dreamers and politicians all find subtle reasons for that, slender enough to pass through the eye of a needle, and meanwhile your very humble servant strolls around the Hermitage, looks at pictures, plays with her monkey, looks at her doves, her parrots, her blue, red and yellow birds from America, and lets everyone say what they like as they do in Moscow.

Catherine continued to enjoy a very ordered way of life. The only real difference between her routines at Tsarskoye Selo and St Petersburg was that in the former she took long walks through her gardens while in town she promenaded through her galleries. That late summer and autumn she would get up as usual at six o'clock, make herself strong black coffee (it had become a habit to prepare her coffee herself, as she preferred neither to disturb nor to be disturbed by servants during the first hours of her day), then go in her *déshabillé* to her little study in the Hermitage to which she had become attached during her mourning for Lanskoy, where she worked on her 'scribbling'. Then she would go for a walk to look at pictures, or gaze through the windows at the Neva at all the boats. At nine o'clock her 'factotum' Count Bezborodko (the Empress having procured him the title of Count of the Holy Roman Empire in October 1784) would arrive with the day's reports and queries, followed by other officials with their reports. After which the Empress would return to her apartments to dress for dinner, while her grandchildren talked and played around her. Dinner was taken in the Hermitage with the usual company of select courtiers. Afterwards there would be some private time (with Yermolov) in her apartments, and at three o'clock she would return, usually with her favourite, to the Hermitage and settle down to examine, arrange and rearrange the latest additions to the engraved stone collection. She might also have a game of billiards, feed nuts to a white squirrel which she had tamed herself, play with her monkey or go for another walk through her galleries. Between four and six she would return to her rooms in the palace to write letters or read, and at six she would go out into her antechamber to receive courtiers who wished to speak to her. At eight she would go upstairs into her private *entresol*, where her select friends would join her to play cards and chat. She would be in bed by eleven.

In August Catherine had told Grimm that the new building by Giacomo Quarenghi, added to Felten's Hermitage and running alongside the Winter Canal, constructed specifically to house the copies of the Raphael loggias, would soon be having its roof put on. And on 28 October she told him about some of the other buildings for which Quarenghi was responsible, including her new Hermitage Theatre, which was then under construction on the other side of the Winter Canal. It would be connected to the rest of the Hermitage by a bridge. 'This Quarenghi makes charming things for us: the whole town is already stuffed with his buildings; he is building the bank, the exchange, quantities of shops, boutiques and private houses, and his buildings are of the best. He is building me a theatre in the Hermitage, which will be finished in a fortnight and whose interior delights the eye; it can hold between two and three hundred people, but no more.' The Hermitage Theatre, in which semicircular banks of seats looked down on a stage flanked by pink marble columns and classical statues, was an imitation on a small scale of the theatre built in Vicenza a century earlier by Palladio, who had himself copied the design of an ancient Roman theatre. Once it was completed, Catherine found it ideal for staging her plays. On 11 March 1786 she told Grimm: 'We are working at the moment on our seventh piece for the theatre in a year.' What she failed to mention was the amount of work her poor secretaries had to undertake in copying out her plays. On several occasions her secretary Alexander Khrapovitsky (who kept a secret diary of his working life) reports having had to work all night. Bonus payments were usually made for this work, but the secretaries had no choice but to do it, and usually at top speed. On 22 April, the day after Catherine's fifty-seventh birthday, the opera *Fevei*, with the libretto by the Empress and the music by Dmitry Bortnyansky (who was more often a composer of church music) was performed in the Hermitage Theatre, on the eve of the Court leaving for Tsarskoye Selo.

Catherine's third granddaughter, Maria Pavlovna, had been born on 3 February 1786, the Empress writing of the newborn: 'she's no beauty, but she's jolly big'. Another member of the Empress's family, though an officially unacknowledged one, had been causing her some concern for several months. Alexei Bobrinsky, her son by Grigory Orlov, had been running up debts in Paris (despite receiving a generous yearly income). He had been getting mixed up with what his mother certainly thought to be undesirable company, and also exhibiting some of the paranoid symptoms of his half-brother, Paul. Catherine asked Grimm to write to Bobrinsky with details of the arrangements for receiving his income and to reassure him that he was free either to stay abroad or to return home. She hoped Grimm might be able to persuade the young man to go and see him, commenting: 'you will see that he is not lacking in intelligence, but that it is very difficult to gain his confidence'.

On 17 June Catherine made another brief trip to Pella, taking with her Potemkin, Yermolov, the Comte de Ségur, Grand Duke Paul, Alexander and Constantine. That afternoon her two lively grandsons were making it difficult for her to write to Grimm:

> I'm telling you the time at which I'm beginning this letter, because my hand is shaking with laughter. I came here this morning from Tsarskoye Selo with my two grandsons; there is only one room between theirs and mine; consequently they have established themselves in mine and are kicking up a dreadful racket; I have had to chase them away to have a moment's peace; what's more, they have gone out singing a march from an opera, each holding a dog by the paw in the guise of a princess.

Despite the happy domestic scene Catherine portrayed here, all was not well in her personal life. The inexperienced and inconsequential Yermolov had been foolish enough to imagine that he could oust Potemkin. For a while, certain disaffected courtiers and officials (including the president of the College of Commerce Alexander Vorontsov, and Peter Zavadovsky, who had always felt some animosity towards Potemkin) were drawn to support Yermolov, and for a moment it looked as though he might succeed. The Comte de Ségur was a fascinated onlooker (and one of Potemkin's partisans):

> All those who were discontented with the eminence of Prince Potemkin rallied to Monsieur Yermolov; and soon, from all sides,

Catherine was bombarded with denouncements against the Prince's administration; they even accused him of embezzlement.

The Empress took notice of them and became fairly bad-tempered about it. Instead of explaining his conduct and justifying himself, the proud and audacious Prince countered her with brusque denials, a cold demeanour, most of the time an almost scornful silence; at last, he not only ceased all regular attendance on his sovereign, but he went away, left Tsarskoye Selo and spent his days in Petersburg with the Master of the Horse, appearing to be occupied with nothing other than parties, pleasure and love.

Potemkin was prepared to sit it out, telling Ségur: 'Don't worry, a *child* isn't going to topple me, and I don't know who *dare*.' 'Be careful,' said Ségur, 'before your time and in other countries, several celebrated favourites have pronounced those proud words *they wouldn't dare*, and they have not been slow in repenting of them.' 'Your friendship touches me,' replied Potemkin, 'but I scorn my enemies too much to fear them.'

Potemkin's tactics worked. The Empress needed him both emotionally and politically, whereas Yermolov was dispensable. Her decision was made easier when the Prince introduced another protégé and distant relative of his. This was the 26-year-old Alexander Matveyevich Dmitriyev-Mamonov (often referred to simply as Mamonov), a handsome Guards officer, greatly superior to Yermolov in looks, intellect and education. Yermolov was given his marching orders on 15 July. The dismissal was delivered on the Empress's behalf by her state secretary (and ex-favourite) Zavadovsky; the pay-off included 130,000 roubles, 4,000 peasants, leave of five years and permission to travel. He left Court the following day. Three days later Alexander Dmitriyev-Mamonov was appointed aide-de-camp to the Empress. Now that everything was sorted out to his satisfaction, Potemkin returned to Tsarskoye Selo, and the grateful Mamonov presented his benefactor with a golden teapot inscribed 'more united by heart than blood'.

In August 1786 the Statute of National Schools was issued and the Education Commission became the Main Administration of Schools. The Statute provided for the establishment of a secondary school in each provincial capital and a primary school in each district town. Children were to be taught mainly in Russian; the schools would be for both sexes and open to all classes of children (though the children of serfs would have to obtain permission from their landowners to attend). Attendance was to be free, but it would not be compulsory.

Catherine's play-writing continued apace. On 8 September Zavadovsky was given *Rurik* to read through; described by its author as an 'Imitation of Shakespeare', this play consisted of scenes from the life of Rurik, the Scandinavian chief called upon to unite the rival tribes around Novgorod and thus viewed as the founder of Russia. On the same day Khrapovitsky was set to work copying out the first act of another of the Empress's historical plays, *Oleg*. During the middle of that month Catherine had a cold and a swollen cheek, and was obliged to dictate her letter to Grimm. She used the occasion to introduce her new favourite (and scribe) to her friend, referring, as she did frequently, to Mamonov as 'Mr Redcoat' – for he liked to dress in this colour to show off his handsome dark eyes and finely chiselled eyebrows:

> We have just read, my companion and I, that the medals of the Duc d'Orléans are being sold at auction. Monsieur the Imperial scape-goat will kindly involve himself in this sale and buy the medals cabinet en bloc, likewise that of the engraved stones . . . I dictated plenty of other things, but the Coat in question didn't want to write them; in time you will find out who this Mr Redcoat is, if you don't already know.

A few weeks later Catherine realised it had been unwise not to give Grimm an upper limit for the purchase of the Duc d'Orléans' collections, and wrote in some anxiety to say he should not go above 40,000 roubles for each collection.

Unusually for one of Catherine's favourites, in the early days of his tenure Alexander Mamonov made some attempt to establish a relationship with the Grand Duke and Duchess, but this did not meet with the Empress's approval. There was an incident when the Empress gave her daughter-in-law a pair of ear-rings which had originally been a gift to her from Mamonov. This act seems to have prompted Maria Fyodorovna to invite Mamonov to come and pay his respects to her, but when Mamonov asked the Empress if he might go, Catherine replied: 'You? To see the Grand Duchess? What for?' and sent a message to her daughter-in-law to tell her this was not to happen again. Maria Fyodorovna was reportedly very upset and cried so much that she fell ill. Later the Grand Duke sent Mamonov a magnificent diamond-studded snuff-box, but refused to receive the favourite when he went to thank him for the gift. After this, normal relations resumed, the Grand Duke trying to take as little notice of his mother's young lover as possible.

On 17 December Catherine gave Grimm a 'metaphysical, physical and moral description' of Alexander Mamonov (again using the same kind of language in which she might describe her grandsons, particularly in the use of 'we' and 'our'); she was clearly very smitten:

> This Redcoat envelops a being who combines a most excellent heart with a great store of honesty; he has wit enough for four, a fund of inexhaustible gaiety, much originality both in how he conceives of things and how he expresses them, an excellent education, having been extremely well instructed in all that can add brilliance to the mind. We hide like murder our liking for poetry; we love music passionately; we understand everything with a rare ease; God knows what we do not know by heart; we declaim, we chat, we have the tone of the best company, we are exceedingly polite; we write in both Russian and French in a way that is rare here, as much as regards the style as the hand; our outward appearance corresponds perfectly with our inner self; our features are very regular; we have two superb dark eyes with eyebrows traced as one hardly ever sees them; above average height, a noble air, an easy gait; in a word, we are as sound in our inner self, as we are dexterous, strong and brilliant on the outside.

In December trouble suddenly erupted in the Grand Duchess's family, in the person of her sister-in-law Zelmira who, on the evening of the 17th of that month ran into the Empress's apartments after attending a performance in the Hermitage Theatre, flung herself on to her knees before Catherine and begged asylum from her violent husband, Maria Fyodorovna's brother Prince Frederick of Würtemberg. That Frederick had been abusing his wife (and mother of his three children) seems to have been known to Catherine, as she expressed no surprise over this turn of events and offered immediate protection to Zelmira. She wrote to Prince Frederick, effectively telling him to leave the Court at once (her claims not to be 'any kind of judge' are rather disingenuous, considering the action she was taking):

> Dear cousin. I announce to Your Highness that the Princess is with me; for the time being my residence is serving her as refuge. My intention is to send her back to her parents. Your Highness may in the future address himself to them. I am not, nor will be, any kind of judge in this affair. But as I have grounds for supposing that Your

Highness will not wish after this to stay here much longer, I grant him for the time being by this letter leave of one year, and I advise him to profit from it as soon as possible, and I dispense him from having to take leave of me. If Your Highness judges it appropriate to take his leave of my service, he will let me know, so that I can send him his release.

The following day Catherine wrote to tell Potemkin what had happened: 'The drubbings of the Prince of Würtemberg have at last obliged his wife to withdraw to my apartments, because she was genuinely in danger of her life; I have seized this very favourable opportunity to send them both away from here, and in a few days we'll be quit of them. I have done what I had to do and I have done well, the wife will go to her parents and the husband can go where he likes.' The Empress next had to inform her son and daughter-in-law of what was happening, and to ensure that they did not try to interfere. Accordingly, she wrote to them too, advising silence on the whole affair:

My very dear children. The Princess of Würtemberg having withdrawn to my apartments, I could not refuse to afford her refuge and protection; my intention is to send her back to her parents, and to procure for her the least unhappy fate her condition can allow; on this point I beg you to be calm. For the time being, do not try to see her. I am not nor will I be the judge in this affair; it is of a nature which it is best to conceal under a veil of oblivion and of the most profound silence; that is the wisest and most prudent thing I can find to say on this subject, and it is that to which I will try to reduce it. I advise you to do the same and to impose it on anyone who does not wish to observe it. I have written a letter to the Prince of Würtemberg, a copy of which I enclose.

I know very well that everything on this page and the enclosed could raise plenty of questions and comments, but I will refuse to answer them because I also know that I am doing what I have to do and that's all there is to it.

As the Empress had no doubt anticipated, her daughter-in-law was thrown into a complete frenzy by these events, particularly by the aspersions they cast on her brother. She wrote to Catherine to tell her so: 'Madame! My agitation is too great to be able to express to you all that I feel. My brother has served Your Imperial Majesty with zeal and affection, consequently he neither could nor should have expected such severity, which covers him with public opprobrium, which throws me into despair and which will be a dagger blow for those who gave me birth.' Catherine's reply left little room for further discussion. At no point was she prepared to take the contemporary conventional view that a wife ought to endure her husband's treatment, whatever its nature: 'It is not I who cover the Prince of Würtemberg with opprobrium; on the contrary, it is I who try to bury abominations in oblivion and it is my duty to suppress any further ones.' Catherine's attitude was not, however, shared by Zelmira's father who proved unsympathetic to his daughter's desire for a divorce; consequently Catherine, instead of sending Zelmira back to her parents, arranged for her to stay at the castle of Lohde, an imperial estate to the west of Reval.

The ructions between the Empress and her son and daughter-in-law were by no means confined at this time to the question of Prince Frederick and his wife. For some months Catherine had been preparing for a major voyage to inspect her latest imperial acquisition, the Crimea. Potemkin had been wanting to arrange this trip ever since the annexation in 1783. It had been put off until the threat of plague in the south had lessened, but in March 1786 it was scheduled to commence the following January. Paul and Maria Fyodorovna seem to have hoped to be included in the Empress's suite, but were more or less reconciled to their exclusion. What they were completely unprepared for was the news that Catherine intended to take Alexander and Constantine. They only learnt of this indirectly, when orders were received by the boys' governor to put preparations in hand for their departure. The children's parents wrote at once to express their consternation. As usual when Maria Fyodorovna was involved, they overdid it:

It is with the most acute affliction that we address these lines to Your Imperial Majesty, having just learnt that she intends to be accompanied by our sons in the great journey she is to undertake. In the first moments of agitation and grief which we feel at this news, and too acutely moved to be able to express ourselves face to face, we have recourse to the pen to tell you, Madame, all that we feel on the subject. The idea of being separated from Your Imperial Majesty for six months was already overwhelming for us, but duty obliged us to respect your silence on this subject, Madame, and to keep this feeling of sadness to ourselves, but the news of the orders which you have just given for the preparations for the journey of our sons has brought our sorrow to a head, for the idea, Madame, of being separated from you and from them is too overwhelming for us. It is our experience which makes us speak of it, the memory of what we suffered during a similar absence making us unable to bear the idea of going through that again. Deign to read these lines with kindness and indulgence; see in them above all, Madame, the tenderness with which we address them to you, we appeal with them to your maternal heart, may it be our judge, and we will then no longer fear a refusal. We make bold to reveal to you, Madame, the picture of our grief, our fears, our anxieties about our children's journey; you will easily imagine our grief, Madame, remembering the state we were in at the moment of our departure for foreign lands. The moment was such, Madame, that the memory of the leave we then took from Your Imperial Majesty and from our children, who were then only in their first infancy, still causes us such acute emotion that we truly do not feel we have the strength to bear a similar parting. Our fears, Madame, concern the health of our children, whose tender age must raise questions as to whether they will stand the fatigues of a long journey, undertaken in the depths of winter, and the change of climate, all the more so as our sons have not yet passed through all the usual childhood illnesses; our anxieties are also based on the fact that this journey and the distractions which will be a natural consequence of it may impede the progress of their education. There, Madame, is the faithful and sincere exposé of how we feel, and Your Imperial Majesty is too just, too good, her heart is too tender not to have any regard for the prayers of a father and mother who, after the respect and affection they bear for you, know no sentiments stronger than that of the tenderness which binds us to our children.

It can have come as little surprise to the Grand Duke and Duchess that Catherine was not to be dissuaded from her plan. Her reply was entirely predictable:

My dearest children. A mother who sees her children afflicted can only advise them to moderate their affliction, not to nourish sombre and painful ideas or to abandon themselves to the sorrows of an excited imagination, and to have recourse to reasons which can soften such pains and calm such alarms. Your children are yours, they are mine, they are the state's. From their earliest childhood I have made it my duty and my pleasure to take the most tender care of them. You have told me both face to face and in writing that you considered the care I gave them to be a genuine good fortune for your children, and the best thing which could happen to them. I love them tenderly. This is what I thought: it will be a consolation for me, separated from you, to have them near me. Out of your five children, three will stay with you; will it be that I alone should be deprived in my old age for six months of the pleasure of having someone from my family with me? As for your sons' health, I am quite persuaded that both their body and soul will be strengthened by this journey; the climate from January to April does not differ between here and Kiev, apart from some weeks more of spring. Neither will the progress of their education suffer, for their tutors will be accompanying them. For the rest I am infinitely grateful for the sentiments of tenderness which you give me and I embrace you both with all my heart.

Paul and Maria Fyodorovna's next letter revealed what their real wish had been all along:

It is with the most ardent gratitude and feeling that we read the reply which Your Imperial Majesty gave us. If the idea of a separation causes us pain, it is in her power to soften it and to replace it with consoling and agreeable emotions; we belong to you, Madame, even more closely than do our children and it is a precious happiness for us. Take us with you, Madame, and we will be near to you and to our sons. As for our daughters, they have as yet no needs other than physical ones, and the presence of their father and mother is not yet immediately necessary to them; we can do without everything and make light of it, provided that we are not separated either from you, or from our sons. This is the outpouring of our hearts, which are entirely yours, these are the sentiments of those who are, my very dear mother, your children, Paul and Maria.

The Empress's response to this, written in Russian, was unequivocal: 'I must tell you frankly that your latest proposal is of a sort that would cause the greatest of upsets, not to mention the fact that your smallest children would be left without any supervision; they would be entirely abandoned.'

That would seem to be that, but in the event, the 'usual childhood illnesses' came to the Grand Duke and Duchess's rescue. Alexander and Constantine went down with chickenpox and, to the Empress's great annoyance, had to be left at home.

# 18

# The Great Crimean Voyage, and 'Proverbs' in Petersburg (1787–89)

*All this so strongly resembles the dreams of the thousand and one nights that one does not know if one is awake or dreaming.*

Catherine II to Friedrich Melchior Grimm

The imperial convoy, consisting of 14 enormous coaches mounted on runners and 124 sleighs, with an additional 40 in reserve, departed from Tsarskoye Selo on 7 January 1787. Countess Protasova, Alexander Mamonov, Count Cobenzl, Lev Naryshkin and Grand Chamberlain Ivan Shuvalov travelled with the Empress in her coach, which was like a house in itself, containing a bedroom, sitting room, office and library, and pulled by 30 horses. The Comte de Ségur travelled in the second coach, with Alleyne Fitzherbert and Count Ivan Chernyshev. (Again the 'pocket ministers' took turn and turn about, Ségur and Fitzherbert swapping places with Cobenzl and Naryshkin or Shuvalov on alternate days.) Potemkin had travelled ahead to the Crimea to make some final arrangements. The numerous servants involved in this great journey included footmen, laundresses, doctors, apothecaries, cooks of all varieties, silver polishers and any other specialists required for the normal functioning of the itinerant court. Five hundred and sixty horses were waiting at each staging post. The temperature at times being as low as 30° Celsius below zero, everyone in the imperial party was enveloped in huge bearskin coats worn over pelisses, and sable hats. The days were very short and when darkness fell, at about three o'clock in the afternoon, great bonfires were lit by the sides of the road to light the imperial way. As the convoy approached towns and villages, the inhabitants would brave the cold and snow to come out and line the road to greet their sovereign – who during the journey kept as far as possible to her usual timetable. As described by Ségur: 'she got up at six o'clock and worked with her ministers; then she had breakfast and received us. We left at nine o'clock, and stopped for dinner at two. Then we got back in our conveyances and travelled until seven o'clock.' Catherine also worked most evenings, from nine o'clock until eleven.

Throughout the journey Maria Fyodorovna kept the Empress informed of all the minute details of family life back in St Petersburg:

> My husband throws himself at your feet, Madame, and will have the honour to write to you on Friday; in order to procure this happiness for ourselves more often without incommoding Your Imperial Majesty with too many letters at once, we will alternate our letters; our children are well apart from Constantine who still has a rash but is otherwise very cheerful, as you will see, Madame, from Monsieur Saltykov's report; Maria's cough is better, but she hasn't any teeth yet [Maria Fyodorovna had thought that perhaps the baby's cough was a sign that she was teething]; Alexandra is studying with great zeal, and in particular is trying to learn to write the word 'Grandmother', as for the pretty Elena, as soon as she sees her sister's tutor she says 'goodbye' to him in very urgent tones; she is always gaiety itself.

In reply the Empress commented: 'I hope that Alexandra will be as zealous at remembering the promise she gave me to be good during my absence as she is at learning to write; her sister is still too small to understand that study can be useful.'

Alexander Mamonov had been feverish at the start of the journey, and by the time the convoy stopped at Smolensk on 14 January he was suffering from a high temperature and sore throat. For his sake, the Empress decided to stay there several days longer than she had originally intended. On this occasion Dr Rogerson seems to have been lucky with his 'cures'. Mamonov was put to rights – or at least not prevented from recovering naturally – with doses of James's powders and Spanish fly. Several people were also afflicted with sore eyes from travelling through the cold and snow, so they too benefited from the respite. There was nevertheless little opportunity for rest. The Empress considered it her duty to use her time in each stopping place to the best advantage, hosting balls as well as receiving local dignitaries and representatives of the various classes of merchants and citizens. Ségur commented: 'I was pleased to see the end of these three days, which the Empress was pleased to call rest-days, and which, being employed in audiences and representations without respite, seemed to me a great deal more tiring than travelling days.' When the imperial party did have time off in the evenings, they would often amuse themselves with charades or rhyming games, as well as with conversation. On one occasion Catherine asked her companions what they thought she might have become, had she been born a man and a private individual; Ségur reported the answers:

> Mr FitzHerbert replied that she would have been a wise legis-lator; Cobenzl that she would have been a great minister or ambas-sador; I assured her that she would have become a very famous general.
>
> 'Oh,' she responded, 'for once you are wrong; for I know my head and how hot it is; I would have risked everything to search for glory and, being no more than a second lieutenant, I would have got my head broken in the first campaign.'

The convoy left Smolensk on 19 January, travelling on to Mstislav and then to Krichev, an estate in the Mogilyov *guberniya* belonging to Prince Potemkin. On 22 January the Empress was in Novgorod Severskiy in the Ukraine, where she hosted another ball (and where a triumphal arch built for the occasion of her visit still stands). On the 25th she arrived at Chernigov, where she gave yet another ball, and on the 28th she was in Nezhin. On 29 January the convoy reached Kiev. This completed the first stage of the journey. Now they had to wait until the ice was melted sufficiently for the Dnieper to be navigable. An elegant and richly furnished palace had been built for the Empress, where she received the town's clergy, authorities, nobility and merchants as well as foreigners who had come to see her. Here as elsewhere her aim was to work and to find out how well the local administration was functioning (and to ensure that her own popularity was main-tained). Ségur describes how she went about this:

> Everywhere the Empress, far from limiting herself to banal phrases, carefully questioned the authorities, the bishops, the landowners, the

merchants, on their situation, their means, their wishes and their needs: this was how she made herself loved, and how she allowed the possibility of discovering the truth including the enormous abuses which so many people were interested in hiding from her.

'One learns more,' she said to me one day, 'talking to ignorant people about their own affairs, than in addressing oneself to the experts, who have nothing but theories, and who would be ashamed not to reply with ridiculous assertions on things about which they have no real knowledge. How I pity them, these poor experts! they never dare pronounce these three words: *I don't know*, which are so useful to the rest of us ignorant people, and which sometimes prevent us making dangerous decisions; for, if in doubt, it's better to do nothing than to do the wrong thing.'

While the party was at Kiev, Potemkin arrived, accompanied by Prince Charles de Nassau-Siegen (a soldier of fortune and heir to a tiny principality). The Prince de Ligne also arrived from Vienna. Part of the massive expenditure incurred by this journey (and propaganda exercise) – an expenditure recouped in part by the levying of a special tax – was represented by the hospitality provided for the foreign ministers, as Ségur explained:

> On arriving in a very beautiful mansion which had been assigned to me, I found it filled with provisions of every sort: the Empress had provided a *maître d'hôtel*, valets, chefs, officers, footmen, coachmen, carriages, postilions, beautiful silverware, superb linen, several porcelain services, exquisite wines; so that nothing was lacking to maintain the most splendid state. She had forbidden us to be allowed to pay for anything. And so, for the duration of this great voyage, we were permitted to have no other expenses than that of giving presents to the owners of the mansions where we were staying, and which should be proportionate to the rank and quality of our hosts.

This splendid lifestyle seems rather to have palled on Ségur, who had hoped that the voyage might afford more interest than the normal court routine; in short, he had hoped to be more of a 'tourist' than a courtier. His frustration reached the Empress's ears, and drew forth a justification of her working journey:

I let fall the cross words that it was really annoying to travel so far to see nothing but a Court, to hear nothing but Orthodox masses, and to attend nothing but balls. Catherine knew what I thought and said to me: 'I am told that you criticise me for traversing my Empire in order to do nothing but give audiences and feasts in all the towns; but here are my reasons: I travel not to see places but people; I know enough about the places through maps, descriptions and information which I could not absorb from a quick visit. What I need is to give people the means to approach me, to allow access to their complaints, and to make those who might abuse my authority fear that I will discover their mistakes, their negligence or their injustices. That is the profit which I claim to draw from my travels; even the announcement of them does good: my maxim is that *the master's eye fattens the horses.*

The balls, feasts and masquerades came to an end with the beginning of Lent on Monday 8 February, and a week later the Empress visited the Pechersky (or Cave) Monastery and bowed to all the relics. Of Kiev itself she commented to Grimm: 'This is a strange town: it's all fortresses and suburbs, but I have yet to find the actual town which, according to all one has heard, was in ancient times at least as great as Moscow.' Potemkin meanwhile had installed himself in the Pechersky Monastery, scorning the palaces and great houses where the rest of the imperial suite was lodged, and holding there what Ségur referred to as an 'Asiatic court', reclining on his divan in a pelisse, his feet in large slippers, and his hair undressed.

During the weeks the imperial party spent in Kiev, Alexander Mamonov seems to have kept himself happily amused with the 'pocket ministers', in whose number Catherine included de Ligne. The latter noted that there was never anything remotely improper in Catherine's public behaviour towards her favourite: 'There is not the slightest indecency, not even an obvious fondness in public and the Empress never permits herself, or anyone else, the slightest flippancy about morals or religion.' The Comte de Ségur had had to learn this prohibition the hard way, as he related himself:

One day, when I was sitting opposite her in her carriage, she indicated to me the desire to hear some snippets of light verse which I had composed.

The gentle familiarity which she permitted to the people who were travelling with her, the presence of her young favourite, the memory of those who had preceded him, her gaiety, her correspondence with the Prince de Ligne, Voltaire and Diderot, had made me think that she could not be shocked by the liberty of a love story, and so I recited one to her which was admittedly a little risqué but nevertheless decent enough in its expressions to have been well received in Paris by the Duc de Nivernais, the Prince de Beauvau, and by ladies whose virtue equalled their amiability.

To my great surprise, I suddenly saw my laughing travelling companion reassume the face of a majestic sovereign, interrupt me with a completely unrelated question, and so change the subject of conversation.

Several minutes later, to make her aware that I had learnt my lesson, I begged her to listen to another piece of verse of a very different nature, and to which she paid the kindest attention: as she wished her weaknesses to be respected, so she took care to cover them with a veil of decency and dignity.

Back in the capital Alexander and Constantine's chickenpox had been succeeded by a light attack of scarlet fever, with Elena also getting suspicious symptoms. The Grand Duke and Duchess were worried as their little girls had not yet been inoculated for smallpox, and their doctors had been advising them that scarlet fever was not infrequently followed by smallpox. Maria Fyodorovna therefore wrote to the Empress on 20 March, requesting her permission to have her two elder daughters inoculated as soon as possible, the court doctors recommending a Dr Halliday to perform the operation. Catherine fully approved the request, clearly pleased with her daughter-in-law on this occasion for her good sense. The inoculation was to take place at Tsarskoye Selo. In her enthusiasm for the gardens there, Maria Fyodorovna was in harmony with her mother-in-law, as she also was in her quirky sense of humour and enthusiasm when she was not being melodramatic or overemotional. Catherine must have been both pleased and amused by the Grand Duchess's letter and enclosure of 17 April: 'I found on the lawn a clump of fresh grass, I picked it at once and it occurred to me that this specimen of the first greenery of dear Tsarskoye Selo might perhaps give you pleasure, my dearest mother, or that at least you would laugh for a moment at the idea of it being sent on a journey of over six hundred miles; therefore I am enclosing it.' Catherine reciprocated by sending back a sample of grass from Kremenchuk. Maria Fyodorovna also reported on the progress of Cameron's new gallery, its roof supported by Ionic columns and ending in a portico from which two graceful staircases descended to merge into one halfway down: 'We went to visit the great staircase of the gallery and found it adorned by the statue of Hercules, which makes a superb effect there; this whole ensemble is magnificent and really imposing.'

The imperial party finally left Kiev on 22 April, boarding seven gold and scarlet galleys specially constructed for the voyage by the Englishman Samuel Bentham (the philosopher Jeremy Bentham's shipwright brother, who had come to work in Russia to improve his career prospects and to be able to experiment on new designs) under Potemkin's supervision. Each galley, decorated inside in gold and silk, was supplied with its own orchestra. In the Empress's galley, named the *Dnieper*, Catherine travelled with Alexander Mamonov and the Countess Protasova. Count Cobenzl and Mr Fitzherbert shared another, the Prince de Ligne and the Comte de Ségur a third. Each person had a bedroom and a study, the rooms furnished with a commodious divan, a taffeta-clad bed and a mahogany writing-desk. The other galleys were occupied by Potemkin and his nieces, the Grand Chamberlain, the Master of the Horse, and various other ministers and important officials. There was also a great dining barge, and the galleys even featured lavatories equipped with their own water supply, a luxury unheard-of in most houses. A flotilla of 80 boats carrying 3,000 troops, baggage and munitions followed the galleys. Not surprisingly, this amazing sight attracted plenty of spectators, as described by Ségur:

> An immense crowd of people greeted the Empress with noisy acclamations, as soon as they caught sight of the sailors of her majestic squadron beating the waters of the Borysthène★ with their painted and shining oars in rhythm, to the sound of cannon.
>
> Along the riverbanks a crowd of onlookers, constantly renewing itself, came from all corners of the Empire to admire the progress of our cortège, and to offer the produce of their diverse climates in tribute to their sovereign.

All the villages and houses they passed were decked with flowers and triumphal arches (which is what may have given rise to the myth that

★ The ancient name for the Dnieper.

Potemkin had built pretend villages and towns – 'Potemkin villages' – all along the route). The galleys progressed very slowly down the sinuous river with its many shallows, and made frequent stops; Ségur described the routine of life on board:

> Only our mornings were free. We spent them agreeably in reading, in conversation, in visits from one galley to another, in walks along the riverbanks.
>
> Every day at one o'clock we assembled [summoned by the firing of cannons] on the Empress's galley, where we dined with her. As was customary, her table never had more than ten covers. Once a week only she invited all the people who had the honour of accompanying her. Then dinner was served on a very large boat where sixty covers could easily be laid.

On 25 April, while the galleys were moored opposite the town of Kaniv, a meeting took place which excited much interest among Catherine's entourage – that between the Empress and her former lover Stanislas Poniatowski. Catherine described the event very briefly to Grimm: 'The King of Poland spent nine hours on board my galley yesterday; we dined together; it is nearly thirty years since I saw him last; you can judge whether we found one another changed.' Ségur went into rather more detail – and sentiment - in his memoirs:

> The fleet's and town's artillery announced the approach of the two monarchs. Catherine sent several of her high-ranking officers on an elegant launch to greet the King of Poland.
>
> On their arrival the King, thinking that in order to avoid all embarrassing etiquette he ought to preserve an *incognito* which was hardly compatible with such splendour, said to them: 'Messieurs, the King of Poland has asked me to introduce Count Poniatowski to you.'
>
> When he climbed aboard the Imperial galley, we pressed into a circle around him, curious to witness the first emotions and to hear the first words of these august personages, meeting in such different circumstances from those in which they used to see one another, when they were united by love, separated by jealousy, and pursued by hatred.
>
> But our expectations were almost wholly disappointed; for after an exchange of greetings, grave, majestic and cold, during which

Catherine presented her hand to Stanislas, they entered a study and remained closeted there for half an hour.

When the two monarchs emerged from their private interview, the courtiers and ministers tried to guess from their faces what they were thinking, but failed. Catherine seemed unusually constrained, while Ségur thought he detected a hint of sadness in the King's eyes. Everyone was then conveyed in launches to the festival barge for dinner. The Empress had the King on her right and Count Cobenzl on her left. Opposite them sat Potemkin, Fitzherbert and Ségur, who remarked: 'We talked and ate little, and looked at one another a lot; we listened to beautiful music, and we drank the health of the King, to the accompaniment of a grand salvo of artillery.' The Empress, according to her secretary Khrapovitsky, described the dinner rather more prosaically: 'Prince Potemkin didn't say a word; I was forced to talk non-stop; my tongue got dry.' Afterwards there was a little scene of gallantry between the former lovers: 'On leaving the table, the King took the Empress's gloves and fan from the hands of a page and presented them to her. He then looked for and couldn't find his hat; the Empress, who had noticed it, had it brought and gave it to him. "Ah, madame," said Stanislas to her on receiving it, "once upon a time you gave me a far finer one."' The Empress and King then returned with some of the others to the imperial galley, the King departing at eight o'clock. A great firework display took place as soon as the sun had set, turning the mountain of Kaniv into the representation of a volcano; the flotilla was also illuminated. The King had arranged a magnificent ball, which members of the Empress's suite attended, but she did not go herself.

The King had hoped that the Empress would stay moored at Kaniv for at least another day, and he had made arrangements accordingly. But either he had not communicated his desires to the imperial party, or Potemkin had decided to ignore them and not tell the Empress, who was in any event desirous of pressing on to meet the Emperor Joseph, again travelling under the name of Count Falkenstein. She wrote to Potemkin that evening: 'Alexander Matveyevich [Mamonov] has told me of our guest's desire that I should stay here for another day or two, but you know yourself that this is impossible because of my meeting with the Emperor. And so please make him aware, in a courteous fashion, that there is no possibility of a change being made to my itinerary. And moreover I dislike every change of plan, as you well know.' When the King persisted, requesting that the Empress stay at least until after dinner on the following day, she made her refusal even clearer: 'When I make a decision it is not usually an idle whim, as is often the case in Poland. And so I leave tomorrow as I said, and I wish him every conceivable happiness and benefit.'

On 28 April Catherine wrote to concur with the arrangements her son and daughter-in-law were making for the inoculation of their two elder daughters, with the further proviso that the girls should be housed not only well away from the Catherine Palace but also at a distance from the pavilions in the garden at Tsarskoye Selo in which they loved to play, and where she feared that the infection might linger on the chairs, tables and cushions (this being a common fear at the time). Maria Fyodorovna wrote on the same day with a detailed account of the effects thus far of the inoculation (which had actually take place on 22 April):

Our little ones are still very well and so far without fever, though the doctors expect them to become feverish tomorrow or the day after. On the third day the place where the incision was made reddened and by yesterday it had risen and two little blisters, containing the aqueous matter, have already formed on both of them: finally Halliday and the others assure us that the appearances are very propitious, that is their expression which I pass on to Your Imperial Majesty, and they are persuaded that everything will proceed in the best manner possible. Yesterday evening Halliday made them take a Dimsdale powder, and this morning a little purgative, which has already had its effect. The children are cheerful and happy; their colouring is so good that nobody seeing them would believe them on the eve of having a fever. Their nourishment consists of milk and fruit; the apartments are fresh and kept very cool; they are dressed in their linen costumes like those of Your Imperial Majesty. Everyone who attends on them is also dressed in linen, in short everything is being done as it was with my sons . . . Alexandra has several little spots under her eyes which are equivocal, and might perhaps become pocks.

Tsarskoye Selo was particularly delightful that spring, added Maria Fyodorovna, the weather warm and the air fresh, the smell of new grass permeating the palace.

Meanwhile Catherine was in Kremenchuk, staying in 'a large, beautiful and charming mansion' built by Potemkin near an oak forest.

Potemkin had also managed, with the help of his gardener William Gould, a protégé of Lancelot 'Capability' Brown, to create within a matter of days an 'English garden' for the Empress, complete with trees, shrubs, flowers, gravel walks, seats and fountains. Catherine left by water on 3 May, her travelling companions still proving very entertaining: 'If you knew everything that was said and done every day on my galley, you would die laughing. Everyone travelling with me is so accustomed to being with me, that they act as though they are at home.' At one point the Comte de Ségur tried to teach the Empress to write poetry. She tried versifying for four days but, as she admitted later to Grimm, 'one needs to give too much time to it, and I started too late'. Fitzherbert tried to console the Empress, who was somewhat dispirited by her lack of poetic success, by telling her that no one could excel at everything and advising her to be content with the rhyme she had written about one of her greyhounds:

> Here lies Duchess Anderson,
> Who bit Mr Rogerson.

As the flotilla left Kremenchuk, it had been joined by the most extraordinary boat of all. This was Samuel Bentham's new invention (which he was also piloting), his 'vermicular', a six-section barge, 252 feet in length and almost 17 feet across and needing 120 oarsmen to row it. It was designed to go round bends in the river, like a worm. Twenty-five miles before reaching Kaydaki, where Catherine was expecting to meet Joseph, some of the boats in the flotilla ran aground and it began to look as though the whole expedition might end in disaster. But now Bentham's invention came into its own; leaving the rest of the flotilla behind, Potemkin embarked on the vermicular and set off to locate the Emperor. He returned with the news that Joseph was already at Kaydaki, and in the event the Emperor and Empress met in a field. Catherine described to Grimm how this had come about:

> On the seventh of this month, while I was on my galley near Kaydaki, I learnt that Count Falkenstein was riding hell for leather towards me; I immediately disembarked in order to run ahead of him, and we both ran so fast that we met one another nose to nose in the middle of the fields; the first words he said to me were that this had fooled all the politicians as no one would see our meeting;

he was with his ambassador, and I was with the Prince de Ligne, Mr Redcoat and Countess Branicka.

The Emperor and Empress ('their united majesties', as Catherine called them) then travelled on together to Kaydaki, where they met with an unanticipated problem – the absence of any dinner, the Empress's chefs and provisions still being several miles down-river with her flotilla. Potemkin had been too busy rushing about making arrangements to have thought of food. A dinner had to be hastily improvised, with Potemkin as chef, the Prince of Nassau as kitchen boy and Count Branicki as pastry-cook; even Catherine and Joseph, neither of them renowned gourmets, had to admit they had tasted better.

On 9 May the two monarchs jointly laid the foundation stone of the new town of Ekaterinoslav (now Dnipropetrovsk in Ukraine). They then travelled on for another three days to reach Kherson, which they entered together. Catherine described the place to her son and daughter-in-law: 'The town of Kherson is very beautiful for an adolescent of six years old, the terrain is admirable, as everything grows here as one would wish; it is also no exaggeration to say that everything is being built and planted here in the best way possible.' On 15 May Catherine and Joseph launched three warships, the seventh, eighth and ninth to have been built at Kherson.

Although the Emperor Joseph could appreciate Potemkin's abilities and therefore understand, to some extent, his powerful position in the Russian Empire and his influence with the Empress, he was bewildered by Catherine's penchant for Alexander Mamonov. 'What I don't understand,' he told the Comte de Ségur, 'is how such a proud woman, and one so mindful of her glory, can show such a strange weakness for the caprices of her young aide de camp Mamonov, who is really no more than a spoilt child.' The Empress for her part entertained doubts about certain aspects of the Emperor's behaviour. Her secretary Khrapovitsky reported her as saying: 'I see and hear everything, but I do not run around all the time like the Emperor. He has read a great deal and knows a lot of information; but, being strict towards himself, he demands indefatigability and an impossible perfection from everyone; he does not know the Russian proverb: activity should be mixed with inactivity.' Though Joseph may have censured Catherine for her relationship with Mamonov, he himself was not beyond reproach on this trip. According to the Prince de Ligne, early one morning the Emperor (incognito of course) had attempted to seduce a young peasant girl. But he had been surprised by the girl's master, who had beaten the girl and insulted 'Count Falkenstein', threatening to complain to the governor of the province. The embarrassed Emperor, petrified that the Empress might get to hear of the incident, confided in de Ligne. The latter resolved the situation by 'taking liberties' with the girl himself – which he claimed cheered her up – and by turning the tables on her master, threatening to denounce him to the Empress for having beaten his serf. Another incident of 'men behaving badly' landed de Ligne and Ségur in trouble with the Empress. These two, 52 and 34 years old respectively, decided their voyage would be incomplete without seeing some Muslim women unveiled. They managed to conceal themselves behind some bushes in order to spy on three women sitting by the side of a stream without their veils. But the men were disappointed to see that these women were neither young nor beautiful. De Ligne uncharitably commented: 'Perhaps Mohammed was right in wanting them to be covered up.' He then made the mistake of recounting this story over dinner, despite Ségur's attempts to silence him by pinching him, and it drew down on them an imperial rebuke:

> 'Messieurs, this joke is in very bad taste and a very bad example. You are in the midst of a people conquered by my arms; I want their laws, their religion, their customs and their prejudices to be respected. If someone had recounted this adventure to me without naming its heroes, far from suspecting you, I would probably have imagined some of my pages to be the perpetrators, and I would have punished them severely.'
>
> We had no response to offer. The Prince de Ligne was as silent as I, and moreover rather embarrassed by his indiscreet talkativeness.

Their contrition satisfied the Empress, who subsequently allowed them to hide behind a screen and watch during an audience she gave to an (unveiled) Muslim princess.

On 19 May Catherine and Joseph travelled to Perekop and on the 20th they arrived in Bakhchisaray, previously the capital of the Crimean khanate; its Tatar name translates as 'the Garden Palace'. Catherine was impressed by the scenery, particularly by the high mountains, which the Emperor Joseph compared to the Alps:

> It was a superb spectacle: preceded, surrounded and followed [by Tatars on horseback] in an open carriage containing eight people,

we entered Bakhchisaray and went at once to the mansion of the khans; here we are lodged between the minarets and the mosques where they shout, pray, sing and spin round on one foot five times in twenty-four hours. We can hear all this from our windows and, as it is the feast of Constantine and Helen today, we will hear mass in the courtyard in a specially erected tent. Oh, what an amazing spectacle it is here!

The next day Catherine and Joseph reviewed the Russian Black Sea fleet at Inkerman, and the Empress drank the health of her 'best friend, the Emperor'. (This toast was, however, excised from the official report of the voyage.) Meanwhile Alexander and Constantine set off from Tsarskoye Selo to meet their grandmother on her return journey. From Inkerman the imperial party travelled to Sevastopol, where Catherine commented in her letter to Grimm: 'by God, all this so strongly resembles the dreams of the thousand and one nights that one does not know if one is awake or dreaming'. The next towns to be visited included Simferopol, Karasubazar (now Belogorsk) and Staryy Krym. 'This tour of the Crimea has been a charming excursion,' the Empress wrote to her daughter-in-law, 'and I am not in the least bit tired. Count Falkenstein will leave us at Berislav [a town on the Dnieper] to go back home.'

Having duly said farewell to the Emperor, Catherine commenced her return journey, arriving in Kremenchuk on 4 June. Four days later she awarded Potemkin the honorific addition to his surname of Tavrichesky ('of the Tauride' or 'of the Crimea'); the award was announced in the symbolic setting of Poltava, where 50,000 Russian troops re-enacted for the delight of the Empress and her suite the great battle of 1709 in which Peter the Great had defeated the Swedish King Charles XII. On 9 June the Empress arrived in Konstantinograd and on the 10th in Kharkov. Here Potemkin took leave of her and returned to Kremenchuk.

Travelling through Kursk, Oryol and Mtsensk, Catherine arrived in Tula on 20 June. She was by now very tired and did not attend the ball given by the nobility of the town. On the 23rd she encountered her beloved grandsons at Znamensky, and they travelled on together to her palace at Kolomenskoye, a few miles outside Moscow, arriving there that evening. Two days later she told Grimm that the boys were making a dreadful din in her room but that, after six months apart, it would be cruel to send them away. The Empress made her public entry into Moscow on 27 June, in time to celebrate the twenty-fifth anniversary of her accession, and where she stayed until 4 July. The return journey was accomplished without mishap; journeying through Tver, Torzhok, Vyshniy Volochek and Novgorod, Catherine arrived back at Tsarskoye Selo on the afternoon of 11 July. Two days later she wrote to Potemkin to thank him and to tell him how his praises were being sung:

> Two days ago we finished our six-thousand-verst* journey, having arrived here in perfect health, and since that very hour we have been exerting ourselves in telling of the charming condition of the places – of the guberniya and districts – entrusted to you, of your labours, successes, zeal, effort and care, and the order that you have established everywhere. And so, my friend, our almost incessant conversations are devoted, either directly or indirectly, to your name or your work.

Grand Duke Paul was one of those who chose not to believe his mother's reports of all she had seen in the Crimea, remarking to the Prince de Ligne, with whom he got on well, that 'people did nothing but trick the Empress . . . and that everything we had done and seen in the Crimea was pure invention'. De Ligne riposted that though there may have been some 'conjuring', there was also a great deal of reality and that Catherine had really examined everything for herself and seen behind any smokescreens. But Paul countered that such clear sight was impossible for a woman, and that that was the reason why 'these Russian rogues' wanted to be ruled only by women. De Ligne commented on this outburst: 'The Grand Duchess lowered her eyes and, for a quarter of an hour, all three of us were equally embarrassed by what he had let slip.'

After the dream-like experience of the Crimea, Catherine had to confront the fact that a large part of her Empire was undergoing food shortages as a result both of a poor harvest and of the negligence of certain governors. On 7 August there was labour unrest in Petersburg. A delegation of 400 peasant workers arrived at the Winter Palace (to which Catherine had returned only the day before) in the hope of delivering a petition to the Empress in person. Despite her much-vaunted desire to provide open access to her subjects during her Crimean tour, this was not the kind of access Catherine had in mind, and the

* Approximately 4,000 miles.

palace guards were deployed to drive the workers away – which they achieved by arresting 17 of their number and charging them with illegal assembly and conspiracy. The practical consequence for the Empress of this event was that her dinner had to be delayed until three o'clock. The workers' grievances, which centred on accusations of ill-treatment by the merchant-contractor who had hired thousands of labourers to work on the granite embankments along the Fontanka river and Catherine (now Griboyedov) canal, were not completely ignored, however. In the days which followed, those who had been arrested were released and an official enquiry began. On 1 October, the work on the Fontanka having been completed, the workers were congratulated and given passports; Khrapovitsky commented that this was intended to stop them coming to the palace again.

Also in August word arrived of the arrest by the Turks of the Russian minister in Constantinople, which was tantamount to a declaration of war. On the 21st of the month a naval action took place off Ochakov on the Black Sea. Ten days later Catherine convened her Council for its first meeting of that year to discuss the impending war. On 7 September a counterdeclaration of war was signed, and on the 12th it was read aloud in the churches, including the imperial chapel, at the end of the liturgy. Despite her outwardly confident attitude, Catherine was in tears for part of that day.

For relaxation during this period of stress, and to continue the amusements that had been enjoyed by those close to the Empress on her Crimean voyage, Catherine and her circle turned to the writing and performance of what they called 'proverbs' – light comedies, often of only one act, which illustrated a particular saying or proverb. Similar to charades, except written down in play form, this form of entertainment had been initiated at the urging of Count Cobenzl – who, despite being middle-aged and prodigiously ugly, took singing lessons and had a great desire to be on stage. Ségur, Cobenzl, de Ligne, Mamonov, Ivan Shuvalov, Count Stroganov, Catherine herself and even Princess Dashkova all tried their hand at the writing of these proverbs and other light dramatic pieces, and most of the plays put on at the Hermitage Theatre during the winter of 1787–8 were examples of these little domestic comedies. Paul and Maria Fyodorovna were never asked to contribute, but they did attend most of the performances. Catherine's offerings in the genre were all very short and featured stock characters, sometimes even bearing the same names from play to play.

Another means of relaxation continued to be afforded by the

collection of engraved stones, Alexander Mamonov becoming particularly obsessive in this regard, as Catherine reported to Grimm:

> I must warn you that Mr Redcoat is even madder than I where engraved stones and medals are concerned; I had great difficulty today, after two hours of examining them, in tearing him away from the medal cabinet where he was so completely surrounded by chests and caskets that one could no longer walk through the room, and then he ended by carrying off the key of the room so that no one could spoil the nice arrangement he had made there and which bars the entrance and access so effectively that I defy anyone to penetrate into it even without that precaution, which is very unnecessary in my opinion but which he thinks exceedingly prudent.

Later in the year Catherine told Grimm that Mamonov was now learning to engrave stones himself, and that his teacher was astonished at his progress. So far he had carved a plumed helmet, a flag and a caduceus. Maria Fyodorovna also took up this craft and proved rather adept at it. The Empress's collection increased enormously towards the end of November with the arrival of nearly 1,500 stones purchased from the Duc d'Orléans. Mamonov unpacked them all himself, checking them against the catalogue to make sure they were all there.

On 15 October Catherine received the news of the first victory of the Russo-Turkish War at Kinburn, and two days later prayers were sung in thanksgiving in both the Winter Palace and the church of Our Lady of Kazan.

Lack of regular communication about the progress of the war added to Catherine's stress, as she explained to Potemkin: 'I would be extremely content with you, my friend, if you could force yourself to write to me more often and to dispatch a courier every week without fail. Not only would this calm my spirit, it would preserve my health against needless worries and would avert more than a thousand inconveniences. At this very hour it's been exactly a month since I had my last line from you.' For a while it looked as though Potemkin might have an extra difficulty to contend with at the front, in the shape of Grand Duke Paul, who had announced his intention of setting out to join the army. Catherine warned Potemkin about this on 11 January 1788, commenting: 'that's a further nuisance which I would be delighted to spare you'. A reprieve came in the form of another pregnancy, Paul deciding to stay at home until Maria Fyodorovna had given birth.

A different sort of war was being waged at Court at this time, to the amusement of the Empress and most of her courtiers. This was the 'war of Naryshkin's pigs', and the protagonists were Lev Naryshkin and Princess Dashkova. The issue was that Naryshkin's pigs had taken to straying on to Dashkova's land and trampling on her flowerbeds. Catherine commented of the pair: 'Dashkova and L.A. Naryshkin are having such an argument that, when they sit together, they turn away from one another and make a double-headed eagle.'

On the day after her fifty-ninth birthday, Catherine was not feeling well, and neither did she go out into her antechamber on the next day, 23 April. She spent the evening in Alexander Mamonov's apartments, where a private performance was given of her proverb *Le Flatteur et les Flattés* ('The Flatterer and the Flattered'), which was based on Aesop's fable of the fox and the crow. She was still feeling ill on the 26th, when she described to Khrapovitsky the unbearable colic she had had in the night: 'Nothing helped, nothing hot or cold, but it went away when I turned over in bed the way that a magpie lies down: I haven't had this for a year – I last had it on the galleys and in Chernigov.'

In May Alexander Mamonov was promoted to the rank of lieutenant-general, and also received the title of Count of the Holy Roman Empire. Early in the same month the Grand Duke and Duchess moved from Pavlovsk to join the Empress at Tsarskoye Selo, in preparation for the Grand Duchess's confinement. Catherine's fourth granddaughter, her namesake Ekaterina Pavlovna, was born on 10 May. It was a difficult birth, and Catherine was credited – even by the Grand Duke – with having been instrumental in saving Maria Fyodorovna's life. Two hours after the birth the placenta had still not come out and, while everyone else was panicking, Catherine suggested the application of mugwort, which fixed the problem. Maria Fyodorovna was upset at having produced yet another girl, and it was to console her that Catherine had given her own name to the child.

The international situation became even more fraught in mid-1788, with multiplying rumours that Sweden was about to attack Russia. On 2 June news was received that the Swedish fleet had appeared off the coast of Reval. This turned out to be a false rumour, the ships on this occasion being merchant vessels. But the visibly annoyed Empress was motivated to have all her maps and atlases brought so that she could examine the borders between Russia and Sweden. At such moments she longed for Potemkin's presence. 'Were you here,' she wrote, 'I would discuss matters with you for five minutes and would then decide what to do.' Nature was not doing anything to improve her spirits: 'We are having the nastiest cold weather and for five days there's been such a storm that branches are being snapped off the trees.' She was cheered on 15 June, however, with the arrival of a courier who reported a victory over the Turks at Liman in the Bug-Dnieper estuary. It happened to be on the day of that victory that Catherine had articulated the 'Greek project', the ultimate aim of Russo-Turkish conflict as far as Catherine and Potemkin were concerned, in Khrapovitsky's presence: 'Let the Turks go where they like. The Greeks can become a Monarchy for Constantine Pavlovich; and how does that endanger Europe? for it is better to have a Christian Power as a neighbour, than barbarians; but even a barbarian power will not be frightening, once it is divided up into pieces.' (In 1786 Monsieur de Reynival, a French diplomat who was well aware of the existence of the Greek project, had commented in a secret memoir: 'A few more years of Catherine, and Europe will be transformed.')

Catherine now discovered from intercepted dispatches that King Gustavus of Sweden really did intend to go to war with her over territorial claims in the south of Finland and Karelia. She ordered that Admiral Greig's fleet was to be positioned near Reval in order to observe the movements of the Swedish fleet and to be ready to fight if the Swedes initiated any action. Anxiety over this new conflict kept her awake all night on 17 June, and in the morning she ordered the naval fortress of Kronstadt to be on full alert. She expressed to Grimm her unshakeable faith in the justice of her rule and the confidence this gave her in facing her foreign enemies: 'as I know that my subjects have nothing to complain of, that I do not resent their liberty, that I do not employ ruse, pretence or duplicity in my dealings with them, that I never allow myself to undertake an unjust war, I am not at all afraid that foreigners will succeed in turning my subjects away from a loyalty which is as intimately united to their well-being as to their essential and true interests'. She also decided that it was time for Alexander Mamonov to be admitted to meetings of her Council. On 22 June Swedish troops bombarded the border fortress of Nyslott, supposedly in retaliation for raids by 'Cossacks' – but it was the Russian opinion that these 'Cossacks' were actually Swedes in disguise.

Two days later Grand Duke Paul wrote to the Empress from Pavlovsk to ask her permission for him to join the troops assembling in Finland. On her return from the annual commemoration of the battle of Chesme she confirmed that she had already given him permission; 'for the rest,' she wrote, 'war has not yet been declared, neither have any hostilities commenced. Our first moves so far have been defensive.' Steps were taken to ensure that the Swedes would not be able to gain control of Lake Ladoga, which would cut off Petersburg's communication lines. On 29 June Catherine was woken at midnight to be told that the Swedish fleet had definitely now appeared off Reval, and on the last day of the month she signed a declaration of war.

On 1 July Catherine received the official ultimatum signed by Gustavus III. He demanded the return of all Swedish territory in Karelia and Finland which had been ceded to Russia in 1721 and 1743. He also insisted that Sweden should act as mediator in resolving the Russo-Turkish conflict and that Russia should return all her gains in the Crimea and former Ottoman territory. Everything he demanded was completely unacceptable to Catherine (who considered that her cousin had gone mad). On the following day Catherine's declaration of war was proclaimed in the chapel of the Summer Palace after the morning liturgy.

The first engagement took place off the island of Hogland on 6 July, and was a victory for the Russian fleet. The weather was now extremely hot, and this combined with her anxiety to make the Empress feel ill. On 9 July she complained of pressure on her chest, and on the 10th she wrote to Paul: 'The heat has made me ill, it has given me a sort of rheumatism between my shoulders which incommodes me greatly; they assure me that it is not serious and I readily believe it.' Four days later she relaxed for a while with an impromptu visit to the out-of-town dacha belonging to Alexander Naryshkin and his wife, where she and her entourage were treated to fresh fruit from the garden and a cannon salute when they left. On 20 July – when Catherine commented that she had been feeling weak for 13 days – the weather broke with a thunderstorm, which smashed some of the windows in the Winter Palace. Her indisposition persisted into August, with colic, fever, headache and backache – all her usual symptoms of anxiety and distress. Some days she worked in bed, keeping up with the intercepted diplomatic mail and the foreign gazettes. Her anxiety was increased by Potemkin's continued failure to send her regular updates about the war with Turkey. On 23 August Maria Fyodorovna wrote to tell the Empress that the Grand Duke had seen the enemy for the first time and 'smelt their gunpowder'. To be precise, he had been on an expedition to reconnoitre the Swedish fortifications, during which a Russian horse had been shot. (The Grand Duke returned to

Petersburg on 18 September, two days before his thirty-fourth birthday.)

Despite intermittent illness and continuous anxiety, Catherine had not been neglecting her writing of 'proverbs' and she handed a new one over to Khrapovitsky on 27 August, with instructions that it should be conveyed for rehearsal to the actors to be performed as a surprise for Alexander Mamonov on his name-day three days later. This proverb was called *Les Voyages de Monsieur Bontems* ('The Travels of Mr Goodtime') and its dénouement was the unmasking of a fibber. She attended the all-night vigil at the monastery of St Alexander Nevsky on the eve of the saint's day (this does not mean she was there all night, the vigil consisting of a long service in the evening combining Vespers and Matins), and then Mamonov proceeded to spoil the feast day itself by being in a sulk and pretending to be ill. The reason for his bad temper was that he had been hoping the Empress would award him the Order of St Alexander Nevsky, but had discovered that she was intending to give him a jewelled cane instead. As a consequence of his 'illness', the surprise she had been preparing for him had to be postponed. On 1 September Mamonov was sufficiently 'recovered' to give Khrapovitsky (who shared the same name-day) a snuff-box from the Empress. The latter had by now discovered the reason for Mamonov's disgruntlement, and instructed Khrapovitsky to bring the insignia of the order with him in his pocket to the performance of a comedy in the Hermitage. After the play she ordered them to be put in her boudoir. No more was said about it until 8 September, when Mamonov finally received his coveted star and ribbon.

On 11 September Catherine handed over another proverb – *Il n'y a point de mal sans bien* ('Every cloud has a silver lining') – with instructions that this too was to be learnt in secret and performed with the earlier one for Mamonov's birthday, 19 September. The surprise duly took place and was followed by supper; the actors were paid 200 roubles each. Mamonov had been hard at work himself on a three-act proverb called *L'Insouciant* ('The Happy-go-lucky One'). This was a lampoon directed against Lev Naryshkin; in the play he is called Monsieur Sans-Souci, suffers from continual indigestion through overeating, is constantly in debt and refuses to do any work. The play was performed in mid-October, the small audience in the Hermitage including Lev Naryshkin, who joined in the general merriment.

The Empress's anxieties had increased on 4 October, when news was received that Admiral Greig was dangerously ill. He had gone down with a fever accompanied by jaundice on 23 September, and had been incapable of giving orders – or even of recognising people – since the 28th. Dr Rogerson was sent out to him and his ship was ordered to be brought into port at Reval, so that the Admiral could rest. Hostilities between Russia and Sweden were in any event now drawing to a temporary close with the onset of winter. The Ladoga canal had started to freeze over by 11 October and all the ships were recalled into harbour at Kronstadt and Reval. Admiral Greig died on 15 October, at eight o'clock in the evening. He had rendered inestimable service to Catherine for many years and she was very upset by his death. She ordered that he should be buried with full honours at Reval, and commented: 'This is a great loss, it is a loss for the state.'

On 21 October Khrapovitsky was given Catherine's *La Rage aux Proverbes* ('Proverb Fever') to copy out. In this piece Catherine pokes fun at herself through her portrayal of the main character, Madame Tantine, who is addicted to proverbs and bullies all her acquaintances into watching hers and composing their own. Two days later she handed over yet another proverb for copying, this one a satire on the 'pig wars' between Naryshkin and Dashkova. This was timely, as at the end of the month the argument escalated, Dashkova having beaten Naryshkin's pigs; laughing about this, Catherine said that the matter must soon be sorted out in court, before it led to murder. Dashkova sent an explanation of the affair to Alexander Mamonov, using him as a conduit to the Empress; the latter commented: 'He loves pigs and she loves flowers, and that's all there is to it.'

On 15 December, after another spell of ill health, Catherine heard about Potemkin's conquest of the port of Ochakov. He had been laying siege to it for weeks and Catherine had been longing for this event. She wrote delightedly to Potemkin:

> Having seized you by the ears with both hands, I kiss you in thought, my true friend, Prince Grigory Alexandrovich, for the news delivered by Colonel Bauer on the taking of Ochakov. Everyone is full of rejoicing at this happy event . . .
>
> You have shut the mouths of everyone, my true friend, and this happy occasion provides you with another opportunity to show magnanimity to your blind and empty-headed critics . . . I anticipate with certainty that, once you have attended to your army's needs, I shall have the pleasure of seeing you here, as I have already written to you in my previous letters and now repeat.

Despite the extremely low temperature of between 25° and 28° below zero, Catherine attended the Te Deum of thanksgiving for the victory. She suffered for it later, with severe pain in her stomach, back and left side. A sore throat followed and she spent the next three days in bed. She kept herself amused by reading Tobias Smollett's *The Expedition of Humphry Clinker* in a German translation (and asked Khrapovitsky to find someone to translate it into Russian).

Potemkin arrived back in St Petersburg on 4 February 1789. His official reception at Court took place a week later, to the accompaniment of 200 Turkish standards from Ochakov being paraded past the Winter Palace to the sound of trumpets. What should have been a glorious day was spoilt for Catherine by Mamonov, with whom she quarrelled after dinner. He made her cry, and she spent the evening in bed. She cried throughout the next day too, and the only person allowed in to see her was Bezborodko. In the evening Potemkin acted as mediator, and peace was – temporarily – restored.

Before the next campaign against the Swedes opened in the spring, Paul wrote to his mother to ask for her orders. She replied on 11 April:

> Here, my dear son, is the opinion you asked for from me on the subject of the future campaign; it will be defensive, static warfare, even more boring than last year's; that is why I cannot in conscience counsel you otherwise than, that in lieu of arousing tears and bitter regrets, you should stay in the bosom of your dear and charming family to share the joy of the successes with which I dare to hope it will please the All-Powerful to bless the justice of our cause.

Four days later the presentation of awards for the capture of Ochakov took place. Potemkin received a diamond-studded field marshal's baton, a gold medal with a charter celebrating the victory, and a loan of 100,000 roubles with which to finish off the new palace he was having built in Petersburg, near the Smolny Institute and the Horse Guards' barracks.

Catherine was 60 on 21 April 1789. She had been crying since the previous evening and spent her birthday in bed. Alexander Mamonov was making her unhappy by his aloofness, which was inexplicable to her, she was anxious about both the wars being waged by Russia (Potemkin would soon be returning to the south, where the Turks were preparing to resume the campaign) and she was also worried at the news from Vienna, where the Emperor Joseph was seriously ill. She had always disliked her birthday, the adding of another year, and the fact that her young favourite appeared not to be interested in her any more can only have made this milestone more bitter. A week later she set off for Tsarskoye Selo, where she hoped to find some respite.

The showdown between Catherine and Mamonov took place on Monday 18 June, immediately after dinner. One of the disadvantages of choosing such young men as her favourites was that they were rarely able to bring any degree of maturity to the ending of the relationship. Unable to bring himself to admit that it was his own desire to quit, Mamonov began by trying to blame Catherine, accusing her of coldness, and of ignoring him at the dinner table. She countered by telling him that, on the contrary, he had been difficult and cold towards her since the previous autumn, while she had been as patient with him as possible. But she promised, with characteristic generosity, to try to come up with a solution.

Her plan was that Mamonov should be offered in marriage the young daughter of Count Bruce. She was only 13 at the time, but an extremely desirable match in terms of fortune and, according to Catherine, 'already well-formed'. (Whether the girl herself would have been delighted to marry the Empress's cast-off is open to question – but Catherine thought her father would be pleased, which was what counted after all.) But her proposal precipitated a very different reaction from the grateful one she was expecting from Mamonov. He replied, 'in a shaking hand', to confess that he had been in love with one of the Empress's own maids-of-honour, 27-year-old Princess Darya Shcherbatova, for more than a year, and that six months ago he had promised to marry her. 'I nearly collapsed from shock,' Catherine told Potemkin, 'and I had still not recovered when he entered my room, fell at my feet and confessed to me his entire intrigue, his assignations, his correspondence and his secret dealings with her.' She was reduced to tears and speechlessness, and spent the rest of the day closeted with her friend Anna Naryshkina. The latter had more than made up for the Empress's lack of words, having castigated Mamonov severely in Catherine's presence.

Naryshkina spent the whole of the next afternoon and evening with Catherine as well, and the talk among the secretaries was that a certain Captain Platon Zubov was set to become the new favourite – nominated and seconded, so to speak, by Naryshkina and General Nikolai Saltykov. On 20 June Catherine told Khrapovitsky that she had agreed to Mamonov and Shcherbatova's wedding and that she hoped they would be happy. She also expressed her bewilderment that the couple were closeted in their apartments, weeping, and that Mamonov, who used to be so interested in everything, now seemed bored and always complaining of chest pains. Mamonov was in fact torn between the conflicting desires of marrying Shcherbatova and retaining his position of influence at Court. Catherine admitted to Khrapovitsky that Prince Potemkin had tried to warn her about what was going on during the winter, saying, 'Matushka, spit on him,' but she had not heeded the warning. She then instructed her secretary to draw up a decree to the effect that Mamonov was to receive the estate which had been bought by the crown from Prince Repnin, as well as over 2,000 serfs and 100,000 roubles. When Mamonov was informed of Catherine's generosity towards him, he was tearful and could not find words to express his gratitude. During her appearance in the antechamber that evening, the Empress herself betrothed Count Mamonov to Princess Shcherbatova. They knelt to beg her forgiveness.

After dinner on 21 June, Platon Zubov was taken upstairs into the Empress's *entresol* by Anna Naryshkina, and he and Catherine spent the evening alone together until 11 o'clock. By the following day he had been accepted into her circle of intimates.

Alexander Mamonov was married on 1 July. At nine o'clock in the evening Catherine placed a diamond headdress on the bride and blessed her with an icon, after which the wedding took place in the chapel of the Catherine Palace before a very small congregation. Count Mamonov came to say farewell to the Empress after her evening walk at 10 o'clock. Catherine commented in a letter to Potemkin: 'After marrying Princess Shcherbatova on Sunday, Count Alexander Matveyevich Dmitriyev-Mamonov went away with his spouse on Monday to stay with his parents [in Moscow], and if I were to tell you everything that went on during these two weeks, you would say he had gone completely mad.' On the Tuesday Platon Zubov was promoted to the rank of colonel and aide-de-camp. That same day (14 July 1789 according to the Gregorian calendar), events in Paris presaged changes in the political landscape of Europe which would threaten Catherine's whole outlook and poison her view of herself as an 'enlightened' autocrat.

# 19
# The Beginning of the End
## (1789–91)

*I've lost all strength and don't know what the end will be.*

Grigory Potemkin to Catherine II

The news of the storming of the Bastille arrived at Tsarskoye Selo by courier on 27 July. Catherine never had as much as a sliver of sympathy for the revolutionaries and their associates, and was puzzled by an intercepted letter to Ségur from the Marquis de Lafayette. 'Can a minister of the Crown write like that?' she asked Khrapovitsky, who replied: 'They're friends, and they were together in America.' 'It is a curious letter,' the Empress said, 'he congratulates him on what he calls a happy revolution, which has brought about the incapacity of several ministers, the weight of taxes and the excited ambition of Parliaments: I would rather fear it, because it could have destroyed France.'

Catherine's acquisition of a new favourite helped to take her mind off worrying political events, her immediate concern being to gain Potemkin's approval. Consequently when she wrote to him on 6 July she enclosed a note from Zubov and emphasised his admirable qualities herself: 'I'm enclosing with this a letter of recommendation to you from a most innocent soul, who has the best possible disposition along with a kind heart and an agreeable turn of mind. I know that you love me and would not offend me in any way. And just think what a fatal condition for my health I might be in without this man. Farewell, my friend, caress us, so that we can be completely happy.'

Platon Zubov was 22 years old to Catherine's 60. He was very handsome, with dark colouring – on account of which she called him 'le Noiraud' or Blackie – and he was also very ambitious. He may have felt some affection for the Empress, but he certainly had boundless affection for himself and a determination to use an elderly woman's weakness to his own and his family's advantage. Yet he also seemed to know how to keep Catherine happy, for which Potemkin was cautiously grateful while regarding Zubov as an unknown quantity. The young man's sponsors, Naryshkina and Saltykov, were no friends of Potemkin's, but Catherine, in a letter of 14 July, was at pains to remind him: 'You speak the truth when you write that you are in such favour with me that under no circumstances could anyone inflict harm on you. Please keep this confidence in me; it is precious to me and I deserve it.' In the same letter she continued to praise Zubov (using the familiar habit of referring to her favourite, like a small child, as 'we'):

We have a kind heart and a most agreeable disposition, without malice and cunning, and a very determined desire to do good. We have four rules which we try to keep, namely: to be loyal, modest, devoted and extremely grateful, with that this Blackie has very lovely eyes and is well-read, in a word he pleases me and so far no sort of problem has slipped in between us; on the contrary this is the fourth week which is passing very agreeably.

Potemkin wrote that he was prepared to accept her new favourite, and he also wished to assure her that he had had no proof of Dmitriyev-Mamonov's intrigue with Princess Shcherbatova, although he had long suspected it:

My beloved matushka, how could I not sincerely love a man who pleases you? You can be sure that I will have a genuine friendship towards him for his devotion to you. Do not imagine, matushka, that I knew about this vile intrigue and was hiding it. I had no definite proof, although I was firmly convinced of it in myself: their various machinations seemed suspicious to me . . . But tell me, my benefactress, how did you manage not to notice? – he used to send her fruit from your table, and when he went upstairs he always exhibited the greatest lethargy, yet in the mornings he would be busily running about. And now I hear that they used to meet in the mornings, and that they had a house on Vasilyevsky Island for their rendez-vous.

As a sign of his support, Potemkin made Platon's elder brother Nikolai one of his orderly officers, along with his own nephews Alexander Samoilov, Vasily Engelhardt and N.P. Vysotsky. Catherine was also very taken with Platon's younger brother, the 19-year-old Valerian, and recommended him to Potemkin too. Catherine herself was feeling on excellent form: 'I'm well and cheerful and have revived like a fly in summer . . . Farewell, my friend. I love you like my soul, and I know you love me too.'

After receiving news of a successful engagement against the Turks at Fokshany, Catherine travelled back to Petersburg for prayers of thanksgiving. On 15 August, the day on which the French National Assembly passed the Declaration of the Rights of Man and of the Citizen, the diplomat Count Stackelberg brought news of a victory over the Swedish fleet after a 14-hour battle in which seven ships had been taken from the Swedes. The Russians lost two galleys and a gunboat. Though such news buoyed Catherine, as did the novelty of her relationship with Platon Zubov, she was still beset by stress-related ailments and fell ill with a 'windy colic' on the evening of 17 August, the day on which the official account of the Paris revolution appeared in the Petersburg gazettes. It took her ten days to make a complete recovery, which she attributed partly to camomile pillows which the Metropolitan of St Petersburg had recommended she place around her body.

That autumn saw a series of victories over the Turks, culminating in the capture of Bender, the news of which was brought by the young Valerian Zubov, now serving with Potemkin. He was rewarded by being promoted to the rank of colonel and made an aide-de-camp.

Catherine was now predicting that Louis XVI would meet the same fate as Charles I of England. 'How times have changed!' she lamented to Grimm:

Henri IV and Louis XIV called themselves the first noblemen of their kingdom and believed themselves invincible at the head of this nobility. In their time the bishops and preachers found no other texts in the Bible and other holy scriptures than those which affirmed royal authority; the splendour of Louis XIV's reign was admired in foreign countries until our day. I confess to you that I do not like cordon bleus inscribed as night watchmen, nor justice with no justice, nor barbarous executions by stringing people up. Neither can I believe that bootmakers and cobblers are greatly talented in government and legislation; try to get a single letter written by a thousand people, give it to them to chew over for a time, and you'll see what will happen.

On 1 December the workaholic Catherine complained to Khrapovitsky that she did not feel she was achieving very much. He protested that she was defending her country against two enemies, but she replied, 'That's the business of the generals.' When Khrapovitsky countered that the generals were only carrying out her orders, she said, 'No, but what else am I doing?' He tried to persuade her that she was busy with legislation and writing history, and eventually she conceded that perhaps she was getting on with the history. On 6 December she felt unwell again with colic, and stayed in her bedroom.

By the spring of 1790 Catherine was wishing that the war with Turkey could soon be over, but the dispatch which arrived from Potemkin on 13 March held out no hope as yet of peace. Prussia had recently formed a 'secret' alliance with the Ottoman Empire, and the Holy Roman Emperor Joseph had died on 9 February. Apart from Catherine's personal liking for Joseph, she was well aware that his successor – his brother Leopold, Grand Duke of Tuscany – would not be as supportive of the Russian cause. He did not share the late Emperor's territorial ambitions and had no sympathy for the Greek Project – and indeed in June an armistice was concluded between Austria and Turkey. Catherine also felt very sorry for Marie Antoinette at having lost her brother at such a difficult time: 'No one could sympathise more with the sufferings of the Queen than I; I love her as the dearly beloved sister of my best friend Joseph II, and I admire her courage.'

On 22 April, the day after her sixty-first birthday, Catherine set off at four o'clock in the afternoon for Tsarskoye Selo, where she found some respite from her cares. In the early 1790s Charles Cameron created what was called the Hanging Garden, on a terrace built on arches in front of the Agate Pavilion and joining Catherine's apartments to the colonnade. The Hanging Garden was then joined to the rest of the gardens by a gentle slope, or *pente douce*, decorated with bronze statues of antique subjects and enormous vases in an antique style. This may have been a discreet design for an ageing and corpulent Empress who could no longer manage stairs, but it was also created deliberately to represent a gradual ascent into an ideal world of antiquity.

But the war was not far away. On 23 May a dreadful cannonade could be heard all day from dawn onwards. (Catherine later related to Grimm that she and Platon Zubov stayed calm by translating a volume of Plutarch into Russian.) At the end of the month Catherine paid a visit to Kronstadt, travelling via Peterhof, where the cannon fire had been so loud that the windows rattled. The Empress was also rattled by the anonymous publication in May of a book entitled *Journey from Moscow to St Petersburg*. It was critical of the government of Russia, of serfdom, and of Catherine herself. Enquiries about the identity of the author revealed it to be one Alexander Radishchev, a 41-year-old nobleman who had been a member as a child and youth of the Imperial Corps of Pages. He had been selected (in 1766) by Catherine herself to pursue his studies at Leipzig University. As far as the Empress was concerned, he had repaid these favours with ingratitude. He was arrested on 30 June and an order was also made for all copies of his book to be confiscated. In fact only about 30 had been sold, and as soon as Radishchev had discovered he was in trouble he had destroyed the rest himself. On the same day Catherine attended thanksgiving prayers at the church of St Nicholas the Wonder Worker, the sailors' church, for a victory against the Swedes on the 22nd. This was followed six days later by a resounding defeat for the Russians at the second battle of Svenskund. The Prince de Nassau-Siegen, who had been in command, had made considerable errors of judgement and was in despair. Catherine did not accept his proffered resignation, saying that she accepted that everyone made mistakes and urging him to repair the damage as best he could.

The Empress sent the notes she had made on Radishchev's book to the head of the Secret Branch, Sheshkovsky, and told Khrapovitsky that she thought the author was a rebel and worse than Pugachev. On 24 July Radishchev received a death sentence – but, as was customary, this sentence was commuted. He was instead condemned to 10 years' exile in the remote fort of Ilimsk in Siberia, and was also stripped of noble status and of all his decorations and ranks.

The war with Sweden ended on 3 August, and a peace agreement was signed at Verela. Neither side had gained anything and the borders remained exactly as they were. The following day there was a celebration for another naval victory on the Black Sea, and a large corn which had been troubling Catherine throughout the summer and preventing her walking properly now fell off her foot, which also pleased her greatly. But the Empress was missing Potemkin. 'I have designated the eighth day of September for the celebration of the Swedish peace here,' she wrote to him, 'and I'll do my best to manage. But I often feel, my friend, that there are so many times I would like to talk to you, if only for a quarter of an hour.' She also told him that now her anxiety was lessened she was starting to put on weight again: 'ever since 1787 my dresses have continually had to be taken in, but during these past three weeks they've started to get tight, so that soon they'll have to be let out a size. I'm also becoming much more cheerful. The pleasing disposition and manners of [Platon Zubov]* does much towards this end.'

On 8 September Alexander Radishchev was dispatched in chains to Siberia. By imperial order the chains were very soon removed, and Radishchev was supplied with all his material wants by his friend and patron Count Alexander Vorontsov. It seems that Radishchev had never had any intention of being a revolutionary and was hardly a focus of dissent – though he did become something of a symbol for later generations of Russian intellectuals. He was allowed to remain in Moscow for several weeks, and arrived towards Christmas in Tobolsk, where he stayed until the summer, having been joined by members of his family and servants. He finally arrived in Ilimsk in December 1791. On the day that Radishchev left Petersburg, the capital officially celebrated the peace with Sweden; among those to receive awards on this occasion was Platon Zubov, who was given the Order of St Alexander Nevsky. The next day Catherine felt unwell and lay on her sofa all day. Though still tired on 10 September, she attended a ball, had supper and played cards with the Swedish ambassador, Count Stedingk. After the peace festivities she fell ill with a cough and cold which she found difficult to shake off. 'Forgive me, my friend,' she wrote to Potemkin on 30 September, 'for writing poorly and briefly: I'm not very well, I have a cough, and my chest and back hurt a lot. I spent two days in bed, thinking I would overcome all this by lying there in my sweat, but now I'm weak and it's uncomfortable to write. [Platon Zubov] looks after me and takes such care of me that I can't thank him enough.'

Catherine's grandchildren continued to be a source of pleasure and solace to her, and in September 1790 she sent two prints of them to Grimm, along with a lengthy description of the character of each child. Alexander remained her favourite, the one in whom she saw hope for the future. She told Grimm that he was 'a personage rare in beauty, kindness and understanding', that he was 'lively and calm, quick and

---

* Catherine refers to Zubov as 'your Cornet', Potemkin having appointed him to this honorary post to please the Empress.

reflective' – in short that he united 'a quantity of contradictions, which means that he is singularly loved by those who surround him; those of his age easily fall into line with his opinion, and follow him willingly'. She had only one fear for Alexander, and that was women; she was quite sure that he would be 'run after', but so far he did not realise how handsome he was and those in charge of his upbringing were careful not to let him become conceited. He could, boasted his grand-mother, speak four languages, knew much history and was never idle; he had a capacity for immersing himself in whatever activity was on offer, from study to blind man's buff. He was also beginning to demon-strate an enjoyment of the fine arts.

Constantine was a rather more difficult character. He did everything 'by fits and starts'; he could be brilliant, but he was unpredictable and had a vivacity 'bordering on exuberance'. He was in fact similar in certain respects to his father as a child – Paul having been unable to sit still and of unpredictable temper – and even to his grandfather, Peter III. Catherine nevertheless considered that he would 'make a name for himself', and she was particularly gratified with his command of Greek (which he had been taught in preparation for the Greek Project). He would say to his brother: 'What are those wretched French translations you're reading? – I'm reading the originals', and Catherine boasted that 'seeing Plutarch in my room, he said to me: "Such and such a passage is very badly translated; I'll do a better translation and bring it to you" and, as promised, he brought me several passages . . . which he had signed: "Translated by Constantine".' Constantine also resembled his forebears in his enthusiasm for all things military, especially the navy, and he drew inspiration from heroic deeds such as that of a Captain Sacken who, 'seeing himself surrounded by Turks, blew his ship up into the air'.

The Empress had less to say of her granddaughters, though these too she found interesting once they were beyond the baby stage. In this she was similar to her own mother, who had had little time for her daughter when she was very small. Alexandra, now seven years old, had blossomed in the last 18 months, and was already accomplished in languages, music and dancing. She had had to work very hard to divert any of Catherine's attention away from her brothers. 'It is I, if you please,' Catherine remarked, 'who am her dominant passion, and to please me and claim my attention for an instant, I think she would throw herself into the fire.' Elena, or Helen, was slim and graceful, with very regular features, but also, according to her grandmother, 'feather-brained'. 'Her gaiety makes her beloved of all her sisters,' commented Catherine, 'and that is all I can say about her'. Maria, who had seemed to be a particular favourite of the Empress's when she was a baby (Catherine had referred to her as '*ma chéretka*' – 'my dear little thing' – and Machoutka), had suffered badly from her smallpox inoculation in September 1789 and her features had coarsened as a result. 'She is like a dragon,' said her grandmother, 'she fears nothing; all her inclinations and games are mannish, I do not know what will become of her'. In fact she married the Grand Duke of Saxe-Weimar-Eisenach in 1804, had four children, and died in Weimar at the age of 73. Little Ekaterina was not yet old enough to be of any interest to her grandmother: 'The sixth is too small, being only two years old, for anything to be said about her; but she seems to be behind compared with what her brothers and sisters were like at her age; she is a large white child with pretty eyes, who sits in a corner, surrounded by toys, chattering all day long and not saying a single word worth listening to.'

The autumn of 1790 saw various entertainments in the Hermitage, including the staging of Catherine's play *The Beginning of Oleg's Rule*, set to music by Sarti and featuring historical texts interspersed with some of Lomonosov's odes, old Russian songs and a scene from Euripides. This was performed for members of the imperial family and their guests on 22 and 25 October. Then on Sunday 10 November there was a special entertainment arranged by Catherine as a surprise for her courtiers. Following a grand ball and supper in the Hermitage, the guests were instructed to go to stalls manned by French actors and actresses where they were given costumes to put on over their court clothes – male costume for the women, female for the men – and there was then a masquerade. The Empress was perhaps trying to recapture her youth, when she had delighted in the transvestite masquerades so beloved of Elizabeth. The year ended on a high note, with Valerian Zubov arriving on 29 December with a report of the storming of the fortress of Ismail earlier that month. Catherine ordered immediate prayers of thanksgiving, with the firing of cannons. Valerian also brought a recommendation of himself from Potemkin: 'Valerian Alexandrovich proved himself worthy of your favour, and I always sought to give him an opportunity to deserve it. Be gracious toward him and do not tear him away from service. He has great potential.'

Potemkin himself was now anxious to come to Petersburg to see Catherine in person (and to check out Platon Zubov for himself and test the lie of the land as far as his own influence was concerned): 'Beloved matushka, I directed Valerian Alexandrovich to ask that should it be your will to allow me to come, then I would gallop there for a short while. But I haven't had a reply to this, which constricts me greatly, and I need, very much need, to speak with you myself.' Meanwhile, Catherine was writing to Grimm, lamenting the state of France – and seeming to anticipate the advent of Napoleon Bonaparte: 'one never knows whether you are alive in the midst of the murders, carnage and disturbances of that den of brigands who have seized the government of France and who are trying to turn it into the Gaul of the time of Caesar. But Caesar overcame them! When will the new Caesar arrive? Oh, he will come, don't you doubt it. He will appear . . .'

Prince Potemkin arrived back in Petersburg towards the end of February. According to Catherine, he was 'more handsome, more lovable, wittier, more brilliant than ever, and in the happiest mood possible'. Other observers were less certain of the Prince's 'happy' mood. Khrapovitsky reckoned that Potemkin was annoyed that Alexander Mamonov had not waited for him to return before ending his relationship with Catherine 'in a stupid way'. Had he waited a while, Potemkin might have been able to influence the choice of his successor.

Potemkin and Catherine were soon also embroiled in a tense disagreement over foreign affairs. There was a threat that Prussia, aided by Britain and Poland, might be about to launch a war against Russia. Prussia and Britain issued a joint ultimatum, stipulating that Russia was not to make any more territorial gains from the Ottoman Empire. Potemkin was in favour of Catherine making pacific overtures to King Frederick William II (the 'heavy Prussian' she had so disliked when he visited Petersburg in 1780, and who had succeeded to the throne on the death of Frederick the Great in 1786), but she refused. She was also resistant to Potemkin's suggestion that she take some medicine for the 'spasms and strong stitch' accompanied by breathlessness which afflicted her in March; she preferred to let nature take its course. There was much reported door-slamming and tearful scenes between the two, followed by equally tearful reconciliations. The British politician Charles James Fox unexpectedly now came to Catherine's aid, making a decisive speech to the Westminster Parliament against the plan for a naval expedition against Russia. (Catherine was so delighted with Fox's intervention that she ordered a marble bust to be made of him by the sculptor Joseph Nollekens, a bronze copy of which she had placed in Cameron's gallery, between those of Demosthenes and Cicero.) On 5 April Prime Minister William Pitt withdrew the British ultimatum and dispatched a secret emissary to Petersburg to find a peaceful way out of the 'Ochakov Crisis'. Before a courier finally arrived with this news on 30 April, Catherine had secretly authorised Potemkin to ready all the forces for action.

April was very warm in Petersburg, Catherine telling Grimm: 'It is nineteen to twenty degrees in the shade, something unheard of and which I have never seen before in my life: everything is turning green, and the leaves are beginning to come out; all the windows are open and we are dying of heat.' Towards the end of the month, however, the weather changed completely and it snowed. But the weather could do nothing to spoil the magnificent entertainment which Potemkin put on at his Palace on Horse-Guards (built by the architect Ivan Starov and later named the Tauride Palace by the Empress) on 28 April. He had spared no expense in creating a scene of unrivalled splendour and enchantment. The celebration began with a cockaigne, held outside and scheduled to begin as the Empress arrived at the palace at seven; but the crowd, eager to tuck in after having spent most of the day waiting in the pouring rain, pre-empted the signal. By the time Catherine arrived, they had seized most of the food laid out for them and taken it back home. Potemkin, unworried by this, knelt to receive his Empress and led her into his palace and its enormous colonnaded great hall. Beyond lay an equally enormous winter garden. The lady-in-waiting Countess Golovine described how the great hall and winter garden were illuminated for the event: 'Two porticos shut off the centre, and between the two porticos was a winter garden, magnificently illuminated by concealed padellas. There were trees and flowers in profusion. The principal illumination, however, came from an inverted dome on the ceiling, from the middle of which was suspended the Empress's monogram in paste. This monogram, lit up by an invisible reflector, gave out a dazzling light.' Certain items Potemkin had acquired from the Duchess of Kingston also featured on this occasion, including a silver wine cooler which was used as a container for fish soup, and two large gilded organs which contributed to the musical entertainment. Once the Empress was seated, two quadrilles made up of 24 pairs of young people dressed in pink and azure blue and covered in jewels emerged from the garden; Alexander was in one quadrille, Constantine in the other. Catherine was captivated by the dancing and with everything else during that extraordinary night, as she told Grimm the following morning (and with only a slight headache after having had so little sleep):

One could not see anything more beautiful, or more varied, or more brilliant than everything these two quadrilles executed. This lasted about three quarters of an hour, after which the host led me, and all the company, to the theatre, where a comedy was played; after that we returned to the hall where the ball began, in the middle of which, instead of the contredanse, our young people decided to repeat the appearance of the two quadrilles, about which everyone was extremely enthusiastic for the second time. When that had finished, I went to have a rest in the superb apartments of this enchanted palace; towards midnight supper was announced; it was set out in the theatre; the two quadrilles had their supper on the stage, NB. all the men of these two quadrilles were dressed in Spanish costume, all the women in Greek; the other tables filled the amphitheatre, which made a superb effect. And then after supper there was vocal and instrumental music in an anteroom, after which I left at two o'clock in the morning.

Potemkin's splendid entertainment had put Catherine in such a buoyant mood that not even the news of rebellion in Warsaw – where a new constitution had recently been proclaimed – could dispel it: 'we are perfectly prepared for every eventuality, and by God, we will not bend before the devil himself'.

On 1 May Catherine departed for Tsarskoye Selo, informing Khrapovitsky that she intended to keep this a secret, and leaving the Hermitage as though she were just going for a drive. It could hardly have remained a secret for very long, but she did seem to enjoy playing this particular game with her courtiers, leaving them guessing at least for a few hours, and avoiding the elaborate ceremonial of an official departure. On the following day Catherine wrote to Grimm to tell him of the anger and disappointment caused her by one of her 'pocket ministers' and a man she had previously thought of as a friend, the Comte de Ségur:

But there is a man whom I cannot pardon for his mischief: that is Ségur; shame on him, he is as false as Judas, and I am not at all surprised that no one in France likes him; it is necessary to have an opinion in this world, and he who doesn't have one, makes himself scorned . . .

In front of some he passes himself off as a democrat, in front of others as an aristocrat, and he finished by being one of the first to run to the *hôtel de ville* to swear this fine oath . . . I am delighted that he is not coming back here; he has written me a very long letter, in which he demands that I reply to him, because, he says, you accord this honour to the Prince de Ligne and the Prince de Nassau. I would like to reply to him that Ligne has not leapt on Van der Noot's bandwagon* and has remained faithful to his legitimate master, and as for the other it is indispensable I write to him as he is directly employed by and under me. And so, in order not to say to him what he deserves, it is necessary that it should not be I but another who replies to him for me.

Catherine felt ill that day, although she still went for an hour's walk in the gardens. Her colic persisted throughout the next day as well. She told Grimm that she felt the whole idea of freedom had been discredited by the French revolutionaries, and that theirs was the kind of freedom which people would come to regret. (She had defined what she meant in her Great Instruction of 1767: 'A Man ought to form in his own Mind an exact and clear Idea of what Liberty is. *Liberty is the Right of doing whatsoever the Laws allow.'*)

On 14 May Pitt's emissary, William Fawkener, arrived in Petersburg and was presented to the Empress at Tsarskoye Selo a week later, on which occasion he dined with her and went for a walk in the grounds. When he left Russia two months later, he was presented with a snuff-box worth 6,500 roubles. Catherine was particularly enjoying Tsarskoye Selo that spring and summer, especially the colonnade of Cameron's gallery and the vestibule which led from her apartments to the flower-garden, where she sat on a green leather sofa surrounded by descendants of Sir Tom Anderson. She described the scene to Grimm: 'this sofa is in a vestibule half open on to the garden and where I am like a Crimean khan in his kiosk, or like a parrot in his cage. You have no idea what Tsarskoye Selo is like when the weather is fine and warm!' The colonnade also proved a useful vantage point from which the Empress could view events taking place in the garden. On 6 July a prisoner captured while fighting on the side of the Turks at Anapa on the coast of the Black Sea, the 23-year-old Sheikh Mansour, was paraded near the gallery for her to be able to see him. A figure of some mystery, Elisha Mansour was said to have been an Italian Jesuit priest who had

---

* Henri van der Noot was a Belgian lawyer and political activist who led the abortive Belgian revolt of 1789 against the regime of Joseph II.

converted to Islam. In spite of the defeat in 1791 and his subsequent imprisonment, he has become a figure of inspiration to present-day Chechen separatists, and Grozny's airport is named after him.

Potemkin returned to the south on 24 July, leaving Tsarskoye Selo at five o'clock in the morning. Five days later there was a decisive victory over the Ottoman fleet, and on 10 August Potemkin's courier brought word of a preliminary peace with the Turks, which had been signed on 31 July. Thanksgiving prayers were offered in St Petersburg and Tsarskoye Selo on 15 August, and Catherine returned to the town after dinner on the 20th.

On 24 August the news was received of the death from fever of one of Maria Fyodorovna's brothers, Prince Karl Alexander of Würtemberg-Stuttgart, who had been serving with Potemkin. Catherine went to Pavlovsk on the 26th to comfort her daughter-in-law, returning to spend the night at Tsarskoye Selo. What she did not yet know was that Potemkin was also very ill. This news was received at Court two days later. There now began a period of great anxiety, with the inevitable time lags – such that medical bulletins reporting on the Prince's fluctuating condition were invariably out of date by the time they arrived – only adding to Catherine's concern.

In September Catherine was horrified to hear from France of Louis XVI's acceptance of the new constitution and his swearing of an oath of loyalty to it. She wrote in fury to Grimm:

> Well, is it not the case that Sire Louis XVI flings you his signature to this extravagant constitution, and that he is eager to make oaths which he has no desire to keep and, what's more, that no one is asking of him? But then who are these people with no judgement who make him do these stupid things? These are really unworthy acts of cowardice: one would say they had neither faith nor law, nor probity. I am terribly angry; I stamped my foot on reading these . . . these . . . these . . . horrors.

Meanwhile another courier had arrived from Jassy on 1 September, with a letter from Potemkin: 'Thanks to God the danger has passed, and I'm better. I remain very weak. The critical day was brutal. I had lost all hope of ever seeing you again, beloved matushka, Your Most Gracious Majesty.' Catherine replied: 'Your letter of 24 August calmed my soul's worry over you, for I saw that you are better, though before that I had been extremely anxious. Nevertheless, I don't understand how you can move about from place to place while so extremely weak.' A further courier arrived on 16 September, with the news that Potemkin was feverish again. But once more he rallied, writing to Catherine: 'Thanks to God I'm beginning to get my strength back, although only bit by bit. However, a ringing in one ear torments me. There's never been a year like this one – everyone's ill. My house looks like an infirmary . . . Oh, God, I can't write any more my head's so weak.' The message that came with the next courier on 29 September appeared to suggest that he was getting better, as it dealt with details of the peace negotiations and the names of those who had been appointed to act as the Turkish plenipotentiaries, and yet on the 21st Potemkin had written: 'My paroxysms continue for a third day. I've lost all strength and don't know what the end will be.' On 3 October two couriers delivered reports of the Prince's dangerous decline, along with the news that he had received the last rites. On 26 September Potemkin had been too ill to write himself, asking his confidant Vasily Popov to do it for him. On the 27th he had managed to write a few words: 'Beloved matushka, my not seeing you makes it even harder for me to live.'

Potemkin died on the morning of 5 October 1791, at the age of 52, on the road about 40 miles from Jassy. His last letter to his beloved Empress was written the day before:

Your Most Gracious Majesty. I've no more strength to endure my torments. My only remaining salvation is to abandon this town, and I have ordered myself conveyed to Nikolaev. I don't know what's to become of me.
Your most loyal and most grateful subject.

## 20

# *Last Years*
# *(1791-96)*

*Be assured that I will be unchanging and that, preaching perseverance to others, it will not be I who varies.*

Catherine II to Friedrich Melchior Grimm

*C*atherine received the news of Potemkin's death on 12 October. She did not sleep that night, and wrote to Grimm at half past two in the morning:

Yesterday another terrible staggering blow hit me. Towards six o'clock in the afternoon a courier brought me the very sad news that my pupil, my friend and almost my idol, Prince Potemkin-Tavrichesky, has died after about a month's illness in Moldavia! You can have no idea of how afflicted I am: he joined to an excellent heart a rare understanding and an extraordinary breadth of spirit; his views were always great and magnanimous; he was very humane, full of knowledge, singularly lovable, and always with new ideas; never did a man have the gift of *bons mots* and knowing just what to say as he had; his military talents during this war must have been striking, for he did not miss a single blow on land or sea. No one in the world was less capable of being led than he; he also had a particular gift for knowing how to employ his people. In a word, he was a statesman in counsel and execution; he was attached to me with passion and zeal; he scolded and became angry when he thought one could do better; with age and experience he was correcting his faults; when he was here three months ago, I said to General Zubov that I had noticed this change and that he no longer had the faults one used to know in him, and has not what I noticed now turned out, unfortunately, to be prophetic? But his most rare quality was a courage of heart, mind and soul which distinguished him completely from the rest of humankind, and which meant that we understood one another perfectly and could let those who understood less prattle away to their hearts' content. I regard Prince Potemkin as a very great man, who did not fulfil half of what was within his grasp.

Catherine was in tears for several days. 'How can I replace Potemkin?' she lamented to Khrapovitsky. 'He was a real nobleman, a clever man, no one could buy him. – Everything will be wrong. Who could have thought that Chernyshev and the other old men would outlive him? Yes, and now everybody, like snails, will begin to thrust out their heads.'

Count Bezborodko now set out for Jassy, having volunteered to take over the peace negotiations. Khrapovitsky thought this an unwise move, believing that Platon Zubov would use Bezborodko's absence to increase his own influence. Catherine was well aware that Potemkin's death had left her bereft on the political, as well as the personal, level:

Prince Potemkin did me a cruel turn by dying! The whole burden falls on me: I would like to ask you to pray for me; for, in the end, things must go on. But just think how I have Prince Vyazemsky who has literally been repeating himself for the last two years; and Count Chernyshev in the navy who, having had an apoplectic stroke this spring, has gone off travelling again – and they all live, while the man who promised to live the longest dies on me!

Catherine needed to build up a new team of men around her just as she had done when she first became Empress. But both her skill at selection and the human resources available to her had declined. She did not fully realise the extent of that decline:

Oh, my God! it is really now that I am Madame Resourceful; again I am reduced to training up people for myself, and it is certainly the two Zubovs who are the most promising; but the elder of the two is in his 24th year, while the younger is hardly 20; nevertheless they are people of spirit and understanding, and the elder has infinite knowledge, and everything is admirably ordered in his head; he is really a good soul.

The 'good soul' was quick to take advantage of the Empress's weakness, seizing as much power as he could, while Catherine was hardly in a state to notice what was going on. Khrapovitsky was well aware of the situation, and from now on his diary entries are charged with dislike and distrust of Zubov.

There was no question even now of involving her son in affairs of state, the Empress having concluded years ago that Paul was completely unsuited to the task. In the years following Potemkin's death the gulf between mother and son grew ever wider. Whereas Paul had previously been a fairly regular attender of dinners with the Empress and at evening gatherings at the Hermitage, he now only came on very special occasions – when he really had no choice in the matter – preferring for the most part to stay at Pavlovsk or Gatchina, where he spent his time in exercises with his private army. Catherine regarded this military preoccupation as a harmless, if faintly ridiculous, hobby; she seems to have had no fear that Paul would ever turn his forces on her.

Throughout the first months of her bereavement, Catherine's mood was unpredictable. Some days she seemed to function perfectly normally, while on others she dissolved in tears and felt unable to cope. On her name-day, 24 November, for instance, she seemed well to begin with. She had her hair done and her cap put on, but suddenly decided she was feeling ill and could not bear to go out in public. She was crying and did not go either to church, or to dinner, or to the ball, saying she could not stand noise. She was feeling better a couple of days later, and was able to attend the St George's Day celebrations on 26 November. That month saw more deaths among her contemporaries, the eldest Orlov brother, Ivan, dying on the 16th and Count Yakob Bruce on the night of the 29th–30th. On 12 December, Alexander's fourteenth birthday, Catherine told Grimm:

I am well, and affairs of state are proceeding despite the terrible loss I have suffered and which I announced to you on the very night following the evening on which I received the fatal news; I am still profoundly afflicted by it. To replace him is impossible, because someone would have to be born as he was, and the end of this century announces no geniuses; but in hoping for one perhaps we will get some able people; time, tests and application are needed. As for me, be assured that I will be unchanging and that, preaching perseverance to others, it will not be I who varies.

On Christmas Day Catherine attended the liturgy and the evening vigil, but on 26, 27 and 28 December she did not go out into her antechamber, complaining of a cold and spending her time lying on a sofa in her bedroom. On the 29th she went into her study, intending to work on her Russian history, but instead she lay down again. Reminders of Potemkin could be particularly distressing for her, as well as occasions that she wished he could be there to share, so that she cried while her hair was being dressed on 6 January 1792, after the peace treaty with the Turks had been delivered that morning. A hundred and one cannon were fired during dinner, but the Empress refused with anger to drink the health of anyone. She shed tears again on 12 January, when Vasily Popov arrived with Potemkin's papers, which included her letters to him, all faithfully preserved and read and re-read. Some even bore the marks of their recipient's tears during his final illness. She locked the papers away in a special box and hid the key. Then, on 30 January, Potemkin's nephew General Alexander Samoilov brought the Turkish ratification of the peace. Catherine dismissed everyone else, and she and Samoilov wept together.

One of the men who had been on Potemkin's staff, Adrian Gribovsky, now became one of Catherine's (and Zubov's) secretaries. In later life, he wrote his recollections of the Court and included a description of Catherine's attire during her old age. Her preference was now very much for comfort and simplicity. For working in the morning and before dressing for dinner she wore a simple white satin dress and crêpe cap (which usually slipped down over one ear), changing later into a lilac-coloured outer dress over a white underskirt, with another white cap with ribbons. On festival days she dressed more formally in a Russian silk or brocade gown, with her stars – and sometimes the ribbons – of St Andrew, St George and St Vladimir, and put on her small crown for public entrances. She wore her hair low, with two curls behind her ears, her old hairdresser Kozlov arranging her hair in this old-fashioned style for her. She favoured shoes with very low heels, as did the Grand Duchesses and indeed all the women of Petersburg at that time. Four elderly spinsters assisted Catherine with her toilet, one handing her ice with which she wiped her face, another passing her her cap, and the other two fastening it on for her with pins. Then she would return with her ladies of the bedchamber into her bedroom, where Maria Perekusikhina would help her on with her dress.

Count Bezborodko arrived back in Petersburg on 10 March and three days later Catherine received the shocking news that her cousin and sometime enemy, Gustavus III of Sweden, had been shot by a member of his own nobility at a masked ball. It took him nearly two weeks to die of his wounds. In such an atmosphere of fear, with a revolution in France, unrest in Poland and an assassination in Sweden, it is not surprising that rumours of Catherine being a likely target for an assassination attempt were rife. On 8 April a report arrived about a Frenchman who had supposedly been sent via Königsberg with instructions to kill her. Catherine commented on this and similar rumours to Grimm a few days later: 'Listen, the Jacobins publish everywhere that they intend to kill me and that to this effect they have despatched three or four men, about which everyone keeps sending me the particulars. I think that if they really had this intention, they wouldn't spread the rumour of it so that I would hear about it.' She also thought Voltaire was being falsely blamed for what was going on: 'So at the end of the 18th century, it is apparently a meritorious act to assassinate people, and then they come and tell me that it is Voltaire who preached this; that is how they dare to calumniate people; I think Voltaire would prefer to stay where he's buried than to find himself in the company of Mirabeau★ at St Geneviève.'

Despite Catherine's dismissive comments and apparent sangfroid, extra security precautions were put in place; in particular all foreigners in the vicinity of Tsarskoye Selo and Sofiya were to be carefully scrutinised. Nervousness about possible conspiracies was also evident in Catherine's order, issued on 13 April, for the eminent freemason and private publisher Nikolai Novikov's Moscow residence and provincial estate to be searched for proof of the publication of an unauthorised book treating religious matters from the perspective of the Old Believers. A former general, Prince Prozorovsky, was charged with the investigation, as well as being given a more general brief to investigate the sources of Novikov's wealth. He reported to the Empress by the end of the month that, though the book they were looking for had not been found, many other prohibited texts and masonic works had been uncovered. Novikov was now being held under guard at his estate, from where a further report arrived on 2 May; Catherine ordered it to be

---

★ The Comte de Mirabeau had died shortly after being elected President of the National Assembly in January 1791.

shown to Zubov and then sent to Sheshkovsky. A week later Catherine praised the former to Grimm: 'This General Zubov is hard-working, full of integrity and good will, and with a most excellent turn of mind; he is a man who will get himself talked about: all I need to do is make of him another factotum.'

On 10 May an order was issued for Novikov to be dispatched to the Schlüsselburg fortress for further questioning. He was placed in the same cell in which the unfortunate Ivan VI had lived and died. Further investigations unearthed correspondence with the architect Vasily Bazhenov from which it appeared that the freemasons were plotting to entice Grand Duke Paul to join their number (though Paul denied any involvement with the craft). On 1 August Catherine signed a decree sentencing Novikov to 15 years in Schlüsselburg, even though no direct evidence had been found to justify such a lengthy sentence. It was not made public.

Meanwhile a further partition of Poland was being plotted by the monarchs and statesmen of Russia, Austria and Prussia. This took place later in 1793, Russia's annexation of Polish territory being proclaimed on 27 March that year. Earlier in 1792 those leaders of the Polish nobility who were not in favour of the new constitution had entered into a secret agreement with Catherine. As a result the Confederacy of Targowica was organised in May, and the Confederates, supported by Russian troops, began military operations against Poland. Catherine now needed to ensure that neither Austria nor Prussia would do anything to help the Poles. Treaties guaranteeing this were in place by the end of July. Catherine was angered by the failure of King Stanislas Augustus to stand firm against the constitution and by his attempt to act independently. 'If I did not have the proof in my hand,' she told Grimm, 'I would never have been able to believe that the King of Poland could have been as ungrateful and ill advised as I have found him these past four years. He must either be being led or have fallen into imbecility to allow himself to be swept along with steps so harmful and contrary to the well-being of Poland, to probity, to gratitude.'

There was a new addition to the imperial family on 11 July 1792, with the birth of yet another daughter to Paul and Maria Fyodorovna, this one christened Olga. It was a difficult birth, labour lasting for two days and two nights and Catherine sitting up with her daughter-in-law for most of that time. When Olga finally arrived, Catherine commented that the baby's shoulders were nearly as wide as her own. The Empress was less than delighted at the prospect of having to find husbands for so many granddaughters, and Khrapovitsky reported that when the cannons started firing to announce the birth, Catherine exclaimed: 'Do they have to make so much noise for a rotten girl!' The need for her grandchildren to make suitable marriages (which for her grandsons meant the production of offspring to continue the Romanov dynasty, and for her granddaughters the securing of Russian influence at foreign Courts) now became a preoccupation of Catherine's, beginning of course with her beloved Alexander.

In September Catherine added another palace to the list of those she stayed in regularly – Potemkin's great palace by the Horse Guards' barracks which she renamed the Tauride Palace in memory of him. She spent four days there on this first visit; not only did she like it because it reminded her of Potemkin, but she liked the fact that it was built mainly on one floor, and level with the garden. That month Prince Alexander Vyazemsky retired as Procurator-General; he had been of limited usefulness to Catherine for some months as his faculties had declined with age and his mind had started to wander. He died soon afterwards, and was succeeded in the post by Alexander Samoilov.

On 30 September, Potemkin's name-day, Catherine cried, but was able to appear as normal in her antechamber, where she recalled the Prince with feeling. She spent the anniversary of his death alone, but apparently calm.

Though the 14-year-old Alexander had as yet shown no interest in women, his grandmother was determined to set events in motion for him to marry at the earliest possible opportunity. On the evening of 31 October 1792 the Princesses of Baden-Durlach – Louise aged 13 and Frederica aged 11 – arrived in Petersburg. They were related to Grand Duke Paul's first wife, their mother being the late Grand Duchess Natalya's elder sister. Catherine commented to Grimm: 'You will realise that one does not marry so young here; but this is not for now, rather it is provision for the future; while waiting they will get used to us and will adapt themselves to our ways and customs. As for our man, he doesn't give it a thought; he remains innocent of heart, and it's a diabolical turn I'm playing him, for I'm leading him into temptation.' The Princesses were accommodated in Potemkin's old apartments in the Shepilov house. Later, Princess Louise herself recounted to her friend Countess Golovine the details of her arrival and first introductions in Petersburg:

[The Empress] was with Prince Zoubov, at that time simply M. Plato Zoubov, and the Countess Branicka, niece of Prince Potemkine. The

Empress told me she was charmed to make my acquaintance, and I conveyed to her the messages with which my mother had entrusted me . . .

The second day after our arrival was entirely spent in arranging my hair in the Court fashion and in dressing us in Russian clothes, for we were to be presented in the evening to the Grand Duke and Grand Duchess. For the first time in my life I wore paniers [hooped petticoats], with powdered hair. At six or seven in the evening we were taken to the residence of the Grand Duke, who received us very kindly, while the Grand Duchess overwhelmed me with caresses and spoke to me of my mother, of my family, and of how sorry I must have been to leave them. Her manner won my affection altogether, and it is not my fault if this attachment did not grow into a genuine filial affection.

We sat down, and the Grand Duke sent for the young Grand Dukes and Grand Duchesses. I can see them coming in now. I looked at the Grand Duke Alexander as much as good manners permitted, and thought him very good-looking, but not as handsome as he had been described to me. He did not come up to me, and gave me a very hostile glance. After leaving the Grand Duke and Duchess, we went to see the Empress, who was already seated at her game of boston in the Diamond Room. We were placed at a circular table, Countess Chouvalov, the maids of honour in attendance, and the gentlemen of the bedchamber in attendance being with my sister and me. The two young Grand Dukes arrived soon after us. The Grand Duke Alexander let the evening pass without speaking a word to me and without approaching me, even avoiding me with a look of dislike. But by degrees he grew more civilised with regard to me. Little games at the Hermitage in a very small company, evenings passed together at the round table in the Diamond Room, where we played at secretary or looked at prints, very gradually brought about a softening in his feelings towards me.

Catherine was immediately taken with Princess Louise, commenting to Khrapovitsky: 'One cannot see her without being charmed by her.' On 3 November there was a court reception for the deputies of the Polish Confederates, during which the young Princesses of Baden stood near the throne. John Parkinson, an Oxford don acting as companion to the young Edward Wilbraham-Bootle during his grand tour of Europe, managed to gain admittance to this ceremony through the good offices of Dr Rogerson, and he wrote up his observations:

> The Empress took her seat on a throne placed under a Canopy of red velvet; the Crown and Globe and Sceptre lay on a table by her side. There were six [deputies] in all but not more than two or three of them were in the Polish habit. They entered by a door opposite to the throne accompanied by the proper Officers, bowing very low to her Majesty all together, first at the door and afterwards two or three other times till they reached the middle of the room. One of them, Branicki, addressed the Empress in a Polish speech which he delivered in a very audible, manly tone of voice . . . Her Majesty sat with a very dignified and imperious air; supporting her right hand with her fan . . . Count Osterman replied in the Russian language on the part of the Empress, but in so low a tone that if his speech had been in English, I could not have understood him . . . Count Osterman not venturing to depend on his memory held a copy of his oration in his hat, to which he was continually turning his eyes . . . As soon as the reply was finished the Polish deputies, preceded by Branicki, advanced towards the throne bowing to present the public letter of thanks with which they were charged and to kiss the Empress's hand: after which they retired the same way they had come, walking backwards and repeatedly bowing. The Empress then withdrew, handed from the throne as she had been handed to it by the grand Ecuyer, Nariskin.

In the evening the Princesses attended a play at the Hermitage Theatre. So did Parkinson, who described the protocol of the event and some of the participants:

> The Grand Duke, the Grand Dutchess, and the young Princesses of Baden who arrived on Sunday Night, entered before the Empress and took their seats on one of the Benches. On their entering the company all stood up. The Grand Duke makes rather an insignificant appearance. The Grand Dutchess is a large woman and seemed to behave with great decorum and good humour . . . M. Zeuboff accompanied and sat near the Empress, but I did not get [a] sight of him, or of the two Grand Dukes till they were going out. The Company all stood when the Empress came in and continued standing

till she sat down. The Grand Duke then set the example of doing the same.

Grand Duke Paul approved of Princess Louise straightaway, but Alexander remained shy for some time – hardly surprisingly as all eyes were on him, wondering if and when he would fall for the girl. On 7 December, Catherine told Grimm that Alexander was beginning to be 'a little bit in love' with Louise. In short, he was doing what was required of him, and it is clear from the Princess's own account of what happened around this time that so was she:

> One evening, about six weeks after my arrival, when we were sitting at the round table in the Diamond Room and drawing with the rest of the company, the Grand Duke Alexander slipped in front of me a letter that he had just written, and in which he told me that, *authorised by his parents to tell me that he loved me, he asked me whether I could accept the expression of his affection and return it, and if he might hope that I could find my happiness in marrying him.*
>
> I replied in the affirmative in the same manner, on a scrap of paper, adding that *I was obeying the wish that my parents had expressed in sending me here.* After that we were regarded as betrothed, and I was given a Russian master and a teacher of religion.

Sunday 12 December was Alexander's fifteenth birthday, and John Parkinson noted that during the ball that evening the Empress was exceedingly cheerful.

The Empress's happiness was short-lived. At the end of January she received the news of the execution of Louis XVI, and immediately took to her bed. On 1 February six weeks' official mourning was proclaimed 'For the death of the King of France who has been cruelly murdered by his rebellious subjects.' A week later a decree was published announcing the severing of political ties with France and the banishing from Russia of all French people, of both sexes, unless they swore an oath as laid down by the decree, pledging allegiance to the crown. A similar period of mourning was proclaimed in late October, following the guillotining of Marie Antoinette.

On 8 March Catherine suffered an accident as she made her way to the baths unaccompanied, toppling about 15 steps down a staircase. Her valet Zakhar Zotov heard her fall and, with difficulty, picked her up. She was bruised and shocked, and given a blood-letting to help her recover – which she did reasonably well by the next day, although the knee on which she had fallen most heavily gave her trouble for the rest of her life, particularly in bad weather. She spent Holy Week that year in the Tauride Palace, along with her three elder granddaughters, walking in the garden in between attending services in the palace's chapel. Alexander and Constantine had stayed behind with their parents and the Princesses of Baden in the Winter Palace, somewhat to the disgruntlement of Constantine, who had remarked: 'That means my brother has been left near his belle, but what am I supposed to do there?'

Princess Louise of Baden was received into the Orthodox Church, in the chapel of the Winter Palace, on 9 May and was given the name Elizaveta Alexeyevna. The following day she and Alexander were officially betrothed, at which point she also became a Grand Duchess. Four days later Catherine told Grimm: 'Everyone said that it was two angels getting betrothed; one could not imagine a more beautiful sight than these 15- and 14-year-old fiancés; in addition they are quite in love with one another.'

During the months since the death of Potemkin, the influence and power of Platon Zubov had been rising inexorably. In January 1793 he, his brothers and his father were awarded the title of Count of the Holy Roman Empire, and on 23 July Platon received the portrait of the Empress to wear and the Order of St Andrew, his colleague Arkady Morkov also being awarded this latter distinction. Morkov, who was 46 years old in 1793, thin and somewhat disfigured by smallpox scars, had originally been under the protection of Count Bezborodko but was astute enough to switch his allegiance to Zubov. Known to be very avaricious, Morkov never entertained anyone at his house; he was unmarried but supported a French actress, by whom he had a daughter. Two days after the Orders of St Andrew were awarded, Platon Zubov was also made Governor-General of Ekaterinoslav and the Crimea, a post formerly held by Potemkin.

On the evening of 4 August Count Bezborodko returned from a few weeks' leave in Moscow, and on the following day he communicated to Khrapovitsky some of his dissatisfaction with the administration of Zubov and Morkov, commenting that even Prince Potemkin had not interfered in everything to the extent that they did. It was also considered in official circles that whereas the credit for both the peace with Turkey and the plan for the occupation of Poland should have gone primarily to Bezborodko, those who had been rewarded were, in the first place, Alexander Samoilov, and in the second, Zubov and Morkov. The ascendancy of Zubov had also led to even further estrangement between the Empress and her son, whom the favourite – with an unwise lack of consideration for the future – treated with a disdain unequalled by any of his predecessors. During a dinner one day at which the Grand Duke was present but saying little, Catherine asked him for his opinion on what was being discussed. He said he agreed with Monsieur Zubov, at which the insolent young man cried out, 'Why? – did I say something stupid?'

A fortnight of festivities to celebrate the peace with Turkey commenced on 2 September. On this occasion Alexander Khrapovitsky was promoted to Privy Counsellor and Senator, and thus his work in the imperial palaces came to an end. (This may have been partly a tactful way to move him to a position where he had less access to sensitive information, Catherine having realised that he was keeping a diary.) He said farewell as secretary to the Empress in her study, and was given a present of three carved gems. He was also thanked for his work by Paul and Maria Fyodorovna on 5 September, when a ball was given in honour of the new Grand Duchess Elizaveta's name-day. The peace festivities concluded with a great fireworks display. Two weeks later the wedding of Alexander and Elizaveta took place in the chapel of the Winter Palace. Countess Golovine recorded her recollections of the event:

A raised platform, on which the ceremony was to take place, had been erected where it might be seen by everyone; and when the two beautiful children – for they were little more – appeared in their places, general enthusiasm broke out. The Lord Chamberlain, M. de Chouvalov, and Prince Bezborodko held the crowns. When the ceremony was over, the Grand Duke [Alexander] and Grand Duchess [Elizaveta] came down from the platform holding hands, and the Grand Duke fell on one knee before the Empress to thank her. She raised him, took him in her arms and kissed him, sobbing, then turned to the Grand Duchess, who received the same demonstrations of affection. They then embraced the Grand Duke and Grand Duchess, their parents, who also thanked the Empress. The Grand Duke Paul was greatly overcome, which was noticed by everybody. At that time he loved his daughter-in-law as if she were his own child.

Following the wedding there was a dinner, then a ball in the evening in the great hall of Alexander's apartments. The new husband and wife were conducted to their bridal chamber by Catherine, Paul and Maria Fyodorovna. Though Alexander did not yet have the emotional maturity to respond to the adoration of his young wife – for she really had fallen in love with him – the marriage appeared at least on the surface to be a success, though it brought no great happiness to either party. On 6 December Catherine reported to Grimm about Alexander, his wife, and his brother:

> Our newly-weds are very occupied, from what one can tell, with one another, and this clown of a Constantine jumps around them; you have no idea what a strange chap he is: first of all, he is not handsome but is extremely lively, full of wit and repartee, is as feather-brained as a cockchafer, admits his faults with frankness, has an excellent heart and desires to do good. In my opinion he is a charming individual and definitely distinguished among his contemporaries; he certainly does everything by fits and starts; but the public prefer, without comparison, his brother. Despite that I predict a brilliant future for this original who has been an unpolished bear since his childhood and still is.

On 9 February 1794 Catherine noted that it was exactly 50 years since she had first arrived with her mother in Moscow, and she enumerated for Grimm the people who were left who could still remember that day:

> First of all there is Betskoy, blind, decrepit and wandering, who asks young people if they knew Peter I. There is Countess Matushkina, who at 78 years old was dancing at the weddings celebrated yesterday. There is the chief cup-bearer Naryshkin, who was a gentleman of the bedchamber at Court when I arrived, and his wife. There is his brother, the Master of the Horse: though he denies having been here as it makes him too old. There is Grand Chamberlain Shuvalov, who hardly leaves his house any more on account of his decrepitude. There is an old chambermaid of mine, who forgets herself. And that's just about all my contemporaries.

Despite the awareness that she was getting old, Catherine retained a child-like spirit and loved watching her grandchildren and their friends playing blind man's buff and other games. And the children enjoyed her company too; it was not until adolescence set in, bringing with it an awareness of the Empress's questionable private life, that problems arose.

A couple of years earlier Catherine had defended Voltaire from charges of encouraging assassinations, but she was now changing her mind. The destruction of the monarchy in France and the continuing Revolution which inspired in her 'a just horror for all that overturns order, tranquillity, and the splendour of a great kingdom and fills it with murder and mayhem' encouraged her to repudiate those she had for years thought of as her mentors. She now saw the seeds of revolution in the work she had once offered to have printed in Russia, the *Encyclopédie*: 'Do you still remember,' she wrote to Grimm,

> how the late King of Prussia claimed that Helvetius had confessed to him that the project of the *philosophes* was to overturn all thrones and that the *Encyclopédie* had been made with no other aim than the destruction of all kings and all religions? Do you also remember that you never wanted to be counted among the *philosophes*? Well, you are right never to have wanted to be included among the *illuminati*, the enlightened ones, or the *philosophes*, for their only objective is destruction, as experience has shown.

As the cannons were firing from the Peter and Paul Fortress to announce that the ice had broken up on the Neva, Catherine wrote to Grimm about her former idol: 'You tell me that one day you will avenge Voltaire of the imputation that he contributed to preparing the revolution and that you will indicate the real authors of it. I beg you, tell me their names, and tell me what you know about it.' If, in her darkest moments Catherine ever reflected on the support she had once given the *philosophes*, she must have felt, like Frankenstein, that she had helped to unleash a monster on the world. But the indications are that her memory was selective on this point, and that she felt betrayed rather than duped.

The ageing Empress's disillusion was only exacerbated by the outbreak of further trouble in Poland. A patriotic military leader who had also fought in the American War of Independence, Tadeusz Kosciuszko, launched a revolt in Krakow which quickly spread to Warsaw where, in April, rebels killed or captured more than 3,000 Russians. There were also instances of rebellion at Vilna in Lithuania and in Courland. On

20 April, the day before Catherine's sixty-fifth birthday, Platon Zubov reported on the situation to the council. Russian forces, with assistance from Prussia and Austria, were being launched against the rebels, who suffered a defeat at Chełm on 29 May. By mid-July Catherine was conferring with Prussia on a third – and final – partition of Poland, having learnt from interceptions of Prussian correspondence that Frederick William II would settle for equal shares with Austria. The rebellion was quashed decisively by Ukrainian forces under General Alexander Suvorov, who carried out the infamous 'massacre of Praga', a fortified suburb of Warsaw. This led to the surrender of Warsaw on 29 October. Suvorov arrested the revolutionary leaders, including the King, disarmed the Polish forces, and confiscated the royal regalia.

The thirty-first of December 1794 marked the termination of the employment of Grand Duke Alexander's tutor, Frédéric César de La Harpe. Catherine had for some time had her suspicions about La Harpe's liberal tendencies and possible sympathy with the revolutionaries, and in any event considered that the 17-year-old – and married – Alexander no longer required a tutor. Alexander himself was very distressed at the dismissal of La Harpe, whom he had come to regard as a close friend. The letter he wrote to his tutor on learning that he was to leave reveals how deeply unhappy the young man was, how he hated the Empress's Court and dreaded the future:

> You know well enough the interest which I take in you, and everything that concerns you; I have no need to repeat it to you here, you will therefore know my dear friend, what pain I must feel in thinking that I must soon be separated from you, especially staying alone in this Court which I abhor, destined for a condition the idea alone of which makes me shudder . . . The only hope which remains to me is to think that I might be able to see you again after several years, as you have said to me yourself; all the more so as it seems to me, from what you tell me in your letter, that your discharge is honourable. Goodbye my dear friend. Be sure that I am until my last sigh all yours, and that I will never forget all that I owe you and all that you have done for me.

Yet another imperial granddaughter, Anna, was born on 7 January 1795 and baptised a week later. According to her grandmother, she was another enormous baby. Then, on the day following Anna's baptism, her two-year-old sister Olga died, after an agonising illness during which she had been unable to stop eating. Though genuinely upset about the little girl's suffering, Catherine dealt with the tragedy in her habitual fashion by refusing to dwell on it. No doubt she encouraged the child's parents to do the same. Catherine was now turning her attention to arranging suitable matches for the next two grandchildren in line, Constantine and Alexandra. For the latter, Catherine was considering the heir of her late cousin, Gustavus III of Sweden. This had been an idea mooted by Potemkin in December 1789 soon after the end of the war with Sweden, when he had written to the Empress: 'do everything possible to attach Sweden to you; for this purpose why not promise to marry one of the Grand Duchesses to their Prince? Indeed, my benefactress, this would be good, very good indeed.' Catherine had discussed this possibility with Gustavus while he was still alive, and it seems that he approved the idea. His successor, the young Prince in question, was officially his son, though whether the notoriously homosexual Gustavus had really fathered him is open to question. The rumour was that the King had tricked his wife into having sexual relations with his equerry, Count Munck, and that Gustavus Adolphus was the result of this union. But for the purposes of a dynastic marriage this was an academic question; Gustavus IV Adolphus was now King of Sweden, though still in his minority and not yet crowned, the actual business of ruling being performed by his uncle and Regent, the Duke of Södermanland. Catherine liked the idea of Alexandra becoming Queen of Sweden but was in no immediate hurry to effect the match, both parties still being very young. As she wrote to Grimm: 'the young lady can wait patiently for the King to attain his majority, before her fate is decided, for she is only eleven years old and will console herself, if he escapes her, with the reflection that it will be his loss'. Constantine's situation was more urgent as, according to his grandmother, he was envious of his brother's married state and desirous of emulating it. Catherine initiated the search for his bride-to-be on 16 April, asking Grimm to investigate the daughters of the Duchess of Mecklenburg and in particular to find out the attitude of that house towards religion.

Poland was virtually dismembered in 1795, Russia annexing Courland and Semigalia on 15 April. King Stanislas Augustus abdicated later in the year. One result of this dismemberment was the influx of a number of Polish noblemen into Russia, including the two young Czartoryski brothers, who arrived in Petersburg on 1 May. They were very soon made aware of the influence wielded by the Empress's favourite, and were presented to him shortly after their arrival. Adam Czartoryski left a vivid description in his memoirs of Zubov's daily ritual of receiving petitioners; it is very unlikely that Catherine, occupied with her work and her altogether less pretentious morning routines, had any idea of the airs her favourite was giving himself:

> Every day, towards eleven o'clock, he had a *lever*, in the strict sense of the word. An immense crowd of petitioners and courtiers of every rank would hurry to be present at his toilet. The street outside would be full of six- and four-horse carriages, just as at the theatre. Sometimes, after a long wait, it would be announced to the crowd that the Count would not be appearing, and everyone would leave, saying: 'Until tomorrow!' – Otherwise the double doors would open, and everyone from generals-in-chief and knights to Circassians and long-bearded merchants would vie with one another to crowd forward. Among these petitioners one would meet at that time many Poles who had come to claim the restitution of their goods, or the redressing of some injustice . . .
>
> This solemnity was always carried out in the following manner: the double doors would open. Zubov would amble in wearing a dressing gown, with hardly anything underneath: he would incline his head slightly in acknowledgment of the petitioners and courtiers gathered in a respectful circle, and would commence his toilet. The valets would draw near to put on his toupet and powder it. During this time other petitioners would arrive; they would also be honoured with a slight inclination of the head when the Count noticed one of them; everyone was watching with attention in the hope of catching his eye. We were among those who were always received with a kindly smile. Everyone remained standing up, no one dared breathe a word. It was through a dumb-show and an eloquent silence that each one recommended his interests to the all-powerful favourite. No one, I repeat, opened his mouth, unless the Count himself addressed a word to someone, and this was never on the subject of the request. Often he didn't say a word, and I don't remember him ever offering a seat to anyone, except to Field Marshal [Nikolai] Saltykov, who was the first personage of the Court, and who, from what was said, had made the Zubovs' fortune; it was thanks to his intervention that Count Platon had succeeded Mamonov . . .

Usually, while the favourite was having his hair dressed, his secretary, Gribovsky, would bring him papers to sign. The petitioners used to whisper to one another what it was necessary to pay this man in order to succeed with his master . . . The operation of hair-dressing completed, a few signatures written, and the Count put on his uniform or coat and retired into his apartments. All this was done with a certain nonchalance which might have been taken for gravity and dignity; there was nothing natural about it, everything was regulated according to a system. The Count eclipsed, everyone ran to his carriage, more or less discontented with his audience.

According to Czartoryski, Bezborodko alone had the courage not to kow-tow to Zubov; he did not even go to visit him. 'Everyone admired his courage, no one emulated it.' Zubov remained close to his benefactor Count Saltykov, who would sometimes go from the Empress's apartments to those of Zubov after dinner, using the small connecting staircase. Saltykov was 59 years old in 1795, small and thin with a sharp nose. A very devout man who spent a long time each morning at his prayers, he wore a high, powdered and pomaded toupet, and had something the matter with his foot which meant that he limped. He had a number of other mannerisms, including that of constantly pulling up his breeches.

The Czartoryski brothers were presented to the Empress at Tsarskoye Selo, and again Adam recorded the experience in his memoirs (it must be remembered that for him Catherine was the destroyer of his beloved country, and he could not help but see her in this light):

The Empress was still in the chapel when all those who were to be presented to her went to the salon. We were presented first of all to Count Shuvalov, the Grand Chamberlain and former favourite of Elizabeth. We were placed in line by him near the door in the passage of the Empress. The Mass over, the cortège began to file past two by two; it consisted of the gentlemen of the bedchamber, the chamberlains and the important dignitaries; finally the Empress herself appeared, accompanied by the dukes, duchesses and ladies of the Court. We didn't have time to look at her, for we had to bend the knee to kiss her hand, while our names were announced. Then, with this whole crowd of ladies and important personages, we ranged ourselves in a circle, and the Empress began to go round it, addressing a few words to each person.

She was an aged woman by now, but still sprightly, small rather than tall, and very fat. Her gait, her bearing, in fact her whole person bore the stamp of dignity and elegance. She had no sudden movements, everything about her was grave and noble; but she was like a river that swept all before her. Her face, wrinkled but full of expression, witnessed to her hauteur and spirit of domination. On her lips reposed an eternal smile but, for whoever remembered her acts, this studied calm hid the most violent passions and an inexorable will.

The Czartoryskis were invited to join the Empress for dinner at her table placed in the colonnade, a signal honour. Subsequently the brothers would attend at Tsarskoye Selo on Sundays and feast days, and join in the evening entertainments which, during fine weather, would take place in the garden. The Empress would either go for a walk, attended by her courtiers, or sit on a bank with some of the other older people and watch her grandchildren and their friends playing on the lawn. Grand Duke Paul would not stay for these times of relaxation, returning to Pavlovsk after divine service or, at the latest, after dinner. It was the habit of various people, including the Czartoryskis, to end these evenings in Platon Zubov's apartments. Zubov himself had become infatuated with Alexander's wife, Elizaveta, and his trailing after her was a source of considerable embarrassment to her. At one stage he even trained a telescope on the windows of her apartment, until Countess Golovine pinned the curtains together. At least one foreigner, a Dutchman whose report ended up with the French foreign office, interpreted this apparent infatuation of Zubov's as a ploy of his to gain influence with Alexander and his wife, in the hope and expectation that Alexander, rather than Paul, would become Emperor after Catherine's death. If this was so, his ploy didn't work. Alexander understandably was none too pleased at the realisation that his grandmother's favourite had designs on his wife.

In addition to being overweight, the Empress now had phlebitis and sometimes had open sores on her constantly swollen legs. At the time, however, it was considered that these helped to cleanse the body of phlegm. Catherine treated herself by bathing her feet and legs in sea water, which she believed did her a lot of good. Another sign of old age was a rather hoarse voice, but she was fortunate in having retained all but one of her teeth. That summer her old friend and assistant in many educational projects, Ivan Betskoy, died at the age of 93. 'He had been in a second childhood for nearly the last seven years,' Catherine told Grimm, 'and sometimes descended into madness; ten years ago he went blind. When anyone went to visit him, he would say: if the Empress asks you what I'm doing, tell her I'm working with my secretaries. He tried above all to hide from me the loss of his sight, so that I would not remove any of his posts from him; in fact all his offices were filled, but he didn't know it.'

The search for a suitable bride for Constantine had led Catherine to the three young Princesses of Saxe-Coburg, who duly arrived in St Petersburg with their mother on 6 October 1795. Constantine, rarely given to reflection, plumped almost immediately for the youngest one. 'I've been so tired all these days by Constantine,' Catherine reported to Grimm, 'and everything concerning him, apart from the usual commotion, that I haven't had a moment to myself. The hereditary Princess of Saxe-Coburg is a very decent and worthy lady; her daughters are very pretty; it is a pity that our groom-to-be can have only one, as all three would be good to keep, but it looks as though our Paris will give the apple to the youngest: you'll see it will be Julie who carries it off.'

The decision was finalised by the afternoon of 14 October: 'Our business is sorted. Constantine is marrying Julie; they find one another equally charming; her mother and everyone else laugh and cry by turns over this interesting couple; the groom is 16 years old, and the bride 14. They are two little imps together.' Catherine told Grimm about the arrangements that were being made for Constantine's young fiancée: 'The Princesses of Saxe-C[oburg] will leave on Saturday; the youngest stays and will live with Grand Duchesses Alexandra and Elena, until her wedding, the date of which is not yet fixed.' She also remarked: 'The day after tomorrow there will be a grand masquerade: why don't you come?' Princess Julie was for the time being placed under the authority of the Grand Duchesses' governess, Madame-General Lieven, and given the same tutors as the Grand Duchesses, with whom she would spend most of her time. From the Countess Golovine's observations, the future did not promise a great deal of happiness for Princess Julie:

The Grand Duke Constantine came to breakfast with his betrothed at ten o'clock in the morning in the heart of winter. He used to bring a drum and a trumpet, and made her play marches on the harpsichord, which he accompanied on these two noisy instruments. This was the only proof of affection that he gave her. Sometimes he twisted her arm and bit her, but these were only the preliminaries to what awaited her after marriage.

Among the promotions announced on 1 January 1796 were those of the Czartoryski brothers, who were named gentlemen of the bedchamber. Another recipient of imperial favour was Field Marshal Suvorov who, in recognition of his Polish triumphs, was given by the Empress a diamond-encrusted snuff-box engraved with her portrait. The Field Marshal's liveliness was one of the most notable features of the ball to celebrate the new year, as he danced about 20 dances like a youth instead of the old man he was (he was the same age as Catherine herself). The Empress was also in markedly good spirits, several times calling Suvorov over to her to laugh and joke with him while she was playing cards – with Zubov, and the Austrian and British ambassadors (the latter at the time being Charles Whitworth).

Princess Julie converted to Orthodoxy on 2 February and was given the name Anna Fyodorovna. The betrothal of Constantine and Anna took place the following day, and was swiftly followed by the wedding on 15 February. After the ceremony, dinner was served in the new St George's Hall, designed by Quarenghi, to the accompaniment of vocal and instrumental music. Healths were drunk to the sound of trumpets, drums and cannons – 51 guns for the Empress and 31 for everyone else. In the evening a whole procession of carriages joined the newly-weds on the short journey to the Marble Palace (the palace originally built for Grigory Orlov and now belonging to the crown, which was being lent to Constantine).

In the Countess Golovine's description of Constantine, he sounds like the young man the Empress Catherine herself had married. If anything, he had a crueller streak:

His behaviour, when he thought himself master in his own house, was proof enough of how badly he required strict supervision. Shortly after his marriage he used, among other things, to amuse himself with gun practice, in the riding school of the Marble Palace, with rats, which were loaded alive into the cannons, as ammunition. So, when the Empress went back to the Winter Palace, she gave him apartments near the Hermitage.

Constantine's poor young wife was also in urgent need of someone to instruct her:

The Grand Duchess Anne, who was fourteen years old, had a very pretty face, but neither grace of movement nor education, and she had a romantic little head that was the more dangerous to her because she was totally lacking in knowledge and in principle. She had a kind heart and was naturally quick-witted, but, not possessing any virtues likely to safeguard her against temptations, she was surrounded by dangers on every side, while the atrocious behaviour of the Grand Duke Constantine contributed further to bewilder her ideas.

But Constantine did seem to be very popular with the people, who thought they saw in him a true descendant of Peter the Great. It was said that soon after his marriage he had taken his new wife on a tour of Petersburg in an open sleigh, with no servants or ceremony. The people had liked this, but the Empress had subsequently forbidden Constantine to be given horses without her permission. In the letter which Alexander wrote to his former tutor, La Harpe, during the wedding celebrations, there is confirmation of Constantine's erratic behaviour, as well as of Alexander's own desire to escape his fate:

Dear friend! how often I think of you, and of all that you said to me when we were together! but that has not been able to change the resolution I have formed to rid myself, in the future, of my burden. It is becoming to me, day by day, more unbearable through all that I see being done around me. It is incomprehensible what is going on: everyone pilfers, one meets hardly a single honest man; it is dreadful ... I find my regime suits me very well, I am very healthy, I am cheerful most of the time, despite my sorrows, very happy with my wife and sister-in-law. As for the husband of the latter he often causes me grief; he is hotter than ever, very self-willed, and his desires do not often coincide with reason. The military turns his head, and he is sometimes brutal with the soldiers of his regiment; for he has one which he has formed, and of which you saw the beginning.

On 25 March Platon Zubov was awarded the dignity of Prince of the Holy Roman Empire, while Arkady Morkov received the title of Count.

Now that both Alexander and Constantine were married, Catherine turned her attention seriously to the projected match between her granddaughter Alexandra and the young King of Sweden. The first obstacle to be overcome was that, to Catherine's great annoyance, an engagement had already been entered into between Gustavus Adolphus and the Princess of Mecklenburg-Schwerin. But it seemed the Swedes were willing to break this off at the prospect of a Russian match. Catherine made her position clear in a letter to her ambassador in Stockholm, General Budberg:

> As I have always declared that I will never consent to tie this knot unless it is the result of a personal knowledge and a mutual liking, I still insist on the necessity of the voyage which the King and the Regent will want to make to my Court to make this acquaintance. I hold all the more to this idea as without letting myself be blinded by my tenderness for my granddaughter, in giving her as Queen to Sweden, I am making the finest present which could be made to the King and to his Kingdom: but it is necessary that she should also find there her happiness, which is the object of all my prayers and of my most tender solicitude.

By the time the Court moved to Tsarskoye Selo that May, Catherine had at last noticed what her favourite was getting up to. She told Platon Zubov to cease his attentions to Alexander's wife, and this year 'there were no more walks, and glances, and sighs'.

Catherine informed Grimm that she was in good health and getting plenty of exercise. They were waiting for Maria Fyodorovna to give birth again, Constantine declaring that he had never seen such an enormous belly and there must be room for four in it. The long-awaited third son, Nikolai Pavlovich, arrived on 25 June, the cannons sounding at Tsarskoye Selo at five o'clock in the morning to announce the birth. Catherine, who had as usual stayed up all night with her daughter-in-law, wrote to tell Grimm about her new grandson that very day:

> Monsieur Scapegoat is notified that Maman gave birth at three o'clock this morning to an enormous boy, on whom one has bestowed the name Nicholas. He has a bass voice with which he cries in an astonishing manner; his length is one arshin less two vershoks [just over two feet], and his hands are nearly as big as mine; I have never seen such a chevalier in my life. Goodbye, keep well. If he continues as he has begun, his brothers will be midgets alongside this colossus.

On 5 July Catherine told Grimm of her new grandson's astonishing progress: 'For the last three days Sir Nicholas has already been eating broth, because he wants to eat all the time; I think that no eight-day-old child has ever eaten such a meal; it is unheard-of. All the maids' arms are dropping off; if this continues, I think he will be weaned at six weeks. He looks at everybody, and holds and moves his head like me.' Nikolai's baptism took place the following day, his brother Alexander acting as one of his godparents.

On 4 August Count Schwerin, the equerry of the King of Sweden, announced the imminent arrival of the 17-year-old King Gustavus IV Adolphus, who would be travelling (as his father had before him) as the Count of Haga. He would be accompanied by his uncle, the Regent, who would be travelling as the Count of Wasa. The Swedish delegation duly arrived in St Petersburg on the evening of 13 August and was received at the Hermitage two days later, Catherine initially meeting the young King and the Regent alone. They were travelling with a suite of 140 people, including servants; the Swedish courtiers numbered 23 and were staying with their ambassador, Stedingk. When Catherine recounted her first impressions to Grimm, she may have been looking through rose-tinted spectacles, as later on she described the King as 'a melancholy and embarrassed dreamer' on his arrival:

On 15th August, at six o'clock in the evening, the Counts arrived at the Hermitage, where in the space of a quarter of an hour they made the acquaintance of everybody. The Count of Haga attracted not only the approval, but even the affection of everyone straight-away; moreover this, note this, has never happened here to anyone except him. He is a very distinguished figure; he is majestic and gentle; a charming physiognomy on which are written intelligence and charm; he is a very worthy young man, and assuredly no other throne in Europe can currently boast anything like as much hope. He has a good heart and is extremely polite, and to this he joins a prudence and restraint beyond his age; in a word, I repeat, he is charming. On the 16th he spent the evening with me at the Tauride Palace where, just as on the first day, there was a ball and supper. The scandalmongers claim to have noticed the eyes visibly getting softer and that majesty was beginning to take on a glow of great contentment. As for the young lady, misfortune would have it that on the 14th in the evening she lost her dog, which made her cry during the evening and morning, so that Madame-General Lieven, her governess, was dying of fear that she would have red eyes. Yesterday the 17th, although the dog has not yet been found, she nevertheless seemed more cheerful, and after dinner the Count of Haga talked to her for a long time, and although they were both standing in the sun, which was quite strong, one couldn't help remarking that neither one nor the other seemed to notice it.

Countess Golovine described her own first view of the young King:

> We were presented to the King at the Hermitage. Their Majesties' entry into the drawing-room was most striking. They held each other by the hand, the dignity and noble appearance of the Empress not in the least throwing into the shade the fine bearing of the young King, whose black Swedish coat, and long hair, reaching to his shoulders, gave something chivalric to the nobility of his appearance. We were all very favourably impressed.

On the evening of the 18th there was another ball and supper, this time in Grand Duke Alexander's apartments. Catherine seemed quite oblivious to Alexander's unhappiness at this time, remarking to Grimm: 'One seems to enjoy oneself here, and on that there is only one voice.' A week later she wrote to her son:

> I was, my dear son, very annoyed that an indisposition prevented your coming to dine in town yesterday; I am sending my valet to find out the state of your health. And here is what I have to communicate to you; yesterday, coming out from dinner, I went into the garden and went to sit down on the bank beneath the trees opposite the staircase; there the young King came to sit next to me. The rest of the company was taking coffee on the lawn of the parterre. Seeing himself alone with me, he told me that he was seizing the moment to open his heart to me, and after some compliments and a little embarrassment, he articulated to me very clearly the inclination which he felt towards your eldest daughter and the desire he had of obtaining her as his wife provided that she did not feel repugnance towards him. I replied to him that my friendship for him made me listen to his speech with satisfaction, but that I had to represent to him that the unfortunate ties he had contracted did not permit

him to form others until those had been completely broken off, and that on my side I should not listen to him before that time. He told me that this was indeed his intention also, and that he begged me to have confidence in his words and to give him my consent, but to keep the thing secret until the whole had been definitively arranged. I am taking a few days to think about it. I know that neither you nor my dear daughter are at all opposed to the plan, but it is necessary that it be done properly; you see where things are, I thought it necessary to warn you of them so that as soon as you are feeling better, you will come to town, because it is easier to talk than to write and because the dénouement is approaching. Farewell, I embrace you both. In case, God forbid, you should not be in a state to come to town between now and the day after tomorrow, send me an open letter from both of you with your consent and blessing for your eldest daughter which I will give to her myself and she will know nothing about it until the right time.

Paul did come to town as requested, and was happy to give his consent to the match. Catherine passed on the consent to Gustavus Adolphus, with the provisos that the engagement with the Princess of Mecklenburg should be unequivocally broken off and that the Grand Duchess should remain in the religion 'in which she was born and brought up' – for although Protestant princesses had to convert to Orthodoxy when they entered the Russian imperial family, there could be no question of the reverse process taking place. Here the real problems began. The Regent and Swedish statesmen charged with drawing up the accompanying treaty between the two countries – in conjunction with Osterman, Zubov, Bezborodko and Morkov on the Russian side – had no trouble agreeing to this condition, but the young King turned out to be highly evangelical about his religion.

It nevertheless seemed that his scruples could be overcome, and on 30 August Catherine was still very pleased with the prospective fiancé, as is clear from her letter to Grimm:

Everyone large and small adores the young King: he is of great courtesy, talks very well, chats extremely prettily. He has a charming face; his features are fine and regular, his eyes large and lively; he has a majestic bearing; he is fairly tall, but slim and agile; he likes jumping and dancing and all bodily exercises, and he acquits himself in them with dexterity and skill. He would appear to be enjoying himself very much here; he wanted to stay for ten days, but he has been here for nearly three weeks, and the day of his departure is not yet fixed, although the season is very advanced . . . The public claim to notice that from day to day His Majesty dances more often with Mademoiselle Alexandra and that they constantly have something to say to one another. It is further claimed that His Majesty has said to his people: 'Arrange it all as soon as possible, for I feel I will become madly in love, and once my head is turned I will have no more common sense.' It also seems as if the young lady has no repugnance for the above-mentioned lord: she has lost a certain air of embarrassment which she had at the beginning, and seems very much at ease with her admirer. One must admit that they make a rare couple. No one is interfering with it, neither is anyone preventing it happening, and it looks as though everything will be sorted or at least arranged before the departure of His Majesty, who is in no hurry to leave, although his majority is to be declared on 1st November new style.

On 2 September a ball was given by the Viennese ambassador, Count Cobenzl. The poor 13-year-old Alexandra sounds very innocent, her grandmother reporting an incident which took place at the ball:

I do not know how it happened, whether through gaiety or otherwise, that our lover took it upon himself to press his intended's hand a little while dancing; there she was becoming as pale as death and going to say to her governess: 'Imagine, pray, what he did: he pressed my hand while we were dancing; I did not know what would happen.' The other asked her: 'So what did you do?' She replied: 'I was afraid I was going to fall over.'

At the same ball the King came to tell Catherine that he was prepared to compromise on the religious issue. She had meanwhile written something for him, explaining her own position and what she thought ought to be his. She took the document out of her pocket and told him that he was to read it carefully once back at his residence. The idea of personal belief getting in the way of an advantageous treaty was completely foreign and incomprehensible to her; in her view, God could only support monarchs who put the interests of their country first. She was certain that Gustavus Adolphus's behaviour was primarily a result of his inexperience, and told him so: 'Be so kind as to trust the experience of thirty years of ruling during which I have succeeded in most of my enterprises; it is this experience joined to the most sincere friendship which dares to give you true and straight-forward advice, with no other aim than to ensure you enjoy a happy future.' On the question of her granddaughter's religion, it was more to do with imperial status and precedence – as well as the views of the Russian people – than of individual belief that made any idea of her conversion impossible; Catherine had after all argued at the time of her own conversion that there was no material difference between Orthodoxy and Lutheranism. She spelt out the position to the King, telling him that 'It is not appropriate for a Princess of Russia to change her religion' and using in support of her argument the example of her own late husband; having an Orthodox mother did not deprive him of his right to the Swedish throne. Catherine concluded: 'I invite Your Majesty to think carefully about what I have written, praying to God who directs the hearts of Kings, to enlighten his own and to inspire in him a resolution consonant with the good of his people and his personal happiness.'

On the evening of 3 September there was a big firework display, during which the King thanked the Empress for what she had written and said the only thing that upset him was that she could think him capable of tormenting anyone, 'still less an object so dear to his heart as the Grand Duchess'. All looked set fair for the treaty and the marriage plans to be concluded.

On 8 September, during a ball at the Tauride Palace, Catherine proposed to the Regent that a betrothal ceremony should take place according to the Orthodox rite and with a Bishop giving the blessing. This was readily agreed to by everyone, including the King, and it was arranged for Thursday 11 September. The ceremony would take place in the Empress's apartments rather than in a church or palace chapel. The Swedes had asked that it should be private, for the marriage could not be announced publicly until the King had attained his majority. 'Private' was to include all the members of the imperial family and the usual array of clergy and courtiers.

On the appointed day, the Russian and Swedish plenipotentiaries assembled around 12 o'clock for the signing of the treaty. The Russians who were to sign – Count Nikolai Saltykov and Madame-General Lieven – were startled to discover that the separate article promising Alexandra the freedom to exercise her religion was not present with the rest of the deeds. The Swedish representatives explained that the King had taken it, and wished to discuss it with the Empress. A message was sent to Catherine telling her that this problem had arisen. It was by now four o'clock in the afternoon. Catherine realised that there was no time before the betrothal for a discussion. Afterwards it would be too late to do anything about it (which was presumably what the young King was reckoning on). Consequently she sent Count Morkov to the King and the Regent to tell them that the article must be signed along with the rest of the treaty before the betrothal, as previously agreed. Morkov returned two hours later, having made no progress. Catherine then attempted to break the deadlock by writing another short form of words, and saying that if the King signed it, she would be content for the time being. The words she wanted him to sign read:

> I formally promise to leave to Her Imperial Highness Grand Duchess Alexandra Pavlovna, my future Wife and Queen of Sweden, entire liberty of conscience and of the exercise of the religion in which She was born and brought up and I beg Your Imperial Majesty to regard this promise as the most obligatory and solemn act which I could pass.

Count Morkov returned later with the King's written response:

> Having already given my word of honour to Her Imperial Majesty that the Grand Duchess will never be embarrassed in her conscience as regards her religion and Her Majesty having appeared to me to be content with that, I am sure that She can have no doubt that I know well enough the sacred laws which this engagement imposes on me for every other piece of writing to be entirely superfluous.

Catherine found this altogether too vague to be satisfactory.

By now it was 10 o'clock in the evening. People had been assembled for four hours in the Empress's antechamber, waiting for the betrothal to take place. 'The ladies-in-waiting, the maids-of-honour, the whole Court, the ministers, the Senate, many generals, were gathered together and standing in rows in the reception room,' Adam Czartoryski recorded. 'Everyone had been waiting for several hours, it was getting late; whisperings were noticed among the persons most likely to be in the know, comings and goings of people who were hurrying into the Empress's inner apartments, and who came running out of them; there were moments of agitation.'

The Empress now summoned her son, and they agreed to tell the

King that she was feeling ill, and that everyone should be sent away. And so, remembered Czartoryski, 'we were informed that the ceremony would not be taking place; the Empress sent her apologies to the Archbishops for their having been made to come in their pontificals to no purpose, to the ladies in their great paniers and to everyone in their rich and fine dress, and they were told to go away, that the ceremony, on account of some difficulties over unexpected details, had been postponed'. Quite how the young Grand Duchess Alexandra was feeling can only be imagined.

Such an embarrassing and public fiasco was without precedent in Catherine's reign. She was furious – principally with the King who, although younger than her eldest grandson, was prepared to stand up to her, but also with her ministers who should have ensured that all aspects of the treaty were firmly in place. It was the kind of situation which could never have arisen had Potemkin – or Alexander Vyazemsky, before he became old and enfeebled – still been in charge. Bezborodko appears to have taken a back seat in the negotiations, allowing Morkov and Zubov to deal with it themselves, while Osterman had never been an effective operator.

The next day, which happened to be Grand Duchess Anna Fyodorovna's birthday, the King and the Regent requested a meeting with the Empress. Catherine described the ensuing conversation to her ambassador in Stockholm, General Budberg, a few days later:

> I admitted them into my inner apartment. I saw the Regent was in despair. As for the King, he was as stiff as a poker. He put my form of words back on the table, I proposed to him to make a change in it as had been suggested to him the evening before, but neither the Regent's arguments, nor mine, could bring him to agree. He kept repeating Pilate's words: what I have written, I have written, I never change what I have written. In addition he was impolite, as stubborn and obstinate as a log, and not prepared either to speak or to listen. The Regent often spoke to him in Swedish and represented to him the consequences of his obstinacy, but I could tell that he was replying with anger. Finally, after an hour, they went away, on very bad terms with one another, and the Regent sobbing.

Seeing that no progress was likely, Catherine ordered all negotiations to be brought to a halt. That evening's ball, given in honour of Anna

Fyodorovna's birthday, was a sad affair. Adam Czartoryski reported:

> The Empress appeared there with her eternal smile on her lips, but
> in her look one could detect a dark expression of sadness and fury;
> one could not help but admire the impassive steadfastness with
> which she received her guests . . . Grand Duke Paul was said to be
> very irritated, although I suspect that he took a certain pleasure in
> the heavy *faux pas* of the cabinet. Grand Duke Alexander was indig-
> nant at the insult done to his sister, but put the blame on Count
> Morkov. The Empress was very pleased to see her grandson share
> her indignation.

Countess Golovine also remembered the ball: 'The King of Sweden
appeared sad and embarrassed, but the Empress was perfectly composed
and talked to him with all the ease and dignity possible. The Grand
Duke Paul was furious, and cast withering glances at the King.'

The stalemate continued on 13 and 14 September, during which the
Empress retired from public view. It was reported that tremendous arguments were raging in the Swedish residence, which could be heard on
all three floors of the house. On the evening of the 14th Catherine
received a letter from the Regent in which he apologised for the fool-
ishness of his nephew. Catherine replied that she really did not know
what to say. Eventually, on 17 September, the treaty, including the article
on religion, was signed on the authority of the Regent, but with the
proviso that it would only be executed if the King ratified it in two
months, after he attained his majority. Catherine did not think this very
likely, but realised that the manoeuvre helped to save the Regent's face.
Writing up this whole story to send to her ambassador, Catherine
admitted that it had made her think a great deal less of the King, that
in fact it completely destroyed the good opinion she had previously
entertained of him. She concluded her report: 'It is said they are taking
their leave tomorrow. Thank God.'

When the King and Regent came to say goodbye to the Empress
in the Diamond Room, the Regent told her that the King wished to
speak to her in private and hurriedly left the room. Catherine described
to her ambassador what then transpired between the ageing Empress
and the adolescent King:

> The Regent having gone out, I invited the King to sit down with
> me on a sofa . . . He then began to deliver a speech to me which

I thought seemed prepared. He began by thanking me for the way in which he had been received, that he would keep the memory of it and gratitude for it all his life; that he was very angry at the fact that unforeseen obstacles had prevented his desire of being united still more intimately with me; that he had had letters sent to Sweden to seek the opinion of his consistory; that this in no way compromised his authority as I seemed to fear, because he was a minor; that he had acted according to his conscience and in consequence of the perfect knowledge he had of his nation of which he needed to keep the affection.

I let him say all that he wanted, I listened to him with a great deal of attention and a very serious expression in total silence. When he had finished and was silent, I said that it was with great satisfaction that I heard he was pleased with the reception which I had given him and that he would always remember it; that I also saw the obstacles which had arisen to our more intimate union as very annoying; that I had acted as well as he according to my conscience and my duty. When I had said that, he praised my granddaughter and asked me the state of her health; I told him that all four of them were indisposed with a chill. He returned to the regret that he felt that the question of religion had given rise to obstacles to his desires. As conversation had now taken the place of prepared speeches, I said to him conversationally: You should know what you have to do, and you are the master of doing what you please; but I cannot alter my opinion which is that you should never talk of religion, in doing that you do a very great wrong to yourself, for if ever my granddaughter could become weak enough to change hers, do you know what would be the result? She would lose all consideration in Russia, and from that it would follow that she would also lose all consideration in Sweden. He wanted to argue with me about her consideration in Sweden. I said to him: all right, but would good would it do you if she lost that which she has in Russia? That appeared to strike him and he was silent. This silence lasted a long time, after which having talked about the rain and the weather, I proposed to ask the Regent to come back. He ran to the door to call him. When he entered we took our leave, I had the suite come in and they went away. During the whole conversation that I had with the King, he never proffered a word about the treaty, nor whether he would ratify it or not. He said to me only that he had thought it would have been sufficient to have given his word; to that I replied that one could adopt a principle in words, but that the consequences and development of these principles from State to State were made in writing.

And there the matter rested. On 19 September Catherine reported to General Budberg on the extent of the young King's duplicity, for she had now found out that while apparently whispering sweet nothings to his intended, he had in fact been trying to convert her:

The Grand Duchess Mother thought she had noticed in the King a great liking for her daughter because he often talked to her in a low voice for quite a long time. Well, I have found out what these interviews were – and it turns out that, far from telling her of his affection, his speeches concerned religion. He was trying to convert her to his, in complete secrecy, getting her to promise not to talk about it to a living soul. He wanted, he said, to read the Bible with her and even explain the dogmas to her himself; she was to take communion with him on the day when he would have her crowned etc. She replied to him that she would not do anything without my advice. But the King is only seventeen years old and does not foresee, being occupied only with his theological ideas, the grave temporal consequences which could result both for Grand Duchess Alexandra and for himself from a change of religion of this Princess.

Catherine spelled out for Budberg what those consequences would be:

To begin with, the first effect of this unconsidered action would be that she would lose all her consideration in Russia; neither I, nor her father, nor her mother, nor her brothers, nor her sisters, would ever be able to see her again and she would never dare set foot in Russia, in consequence of which she would also lose all consideration in Sweden and would remain with a very considerable dowry at the mercy of a poor and greedy country which would not refrain from depriving her bit by bit, under the pretext of a necessity of State, of her money and other precious effects.

Catherine instructed her ambassador that he was now to do nothing further in this matter, not to say anything, or press for ratification of the treaty, but just watch and see what the King did or said next – and tell her everything that was said when the delegation returned from

Petersburg. The Swedes departed on 20 September, Grand Duke Paul's forty-second birthday. The fact that they chose this particular day to leave, not staying to celebrate, struck the public as especially odd and underlined the fact that all was not well. No official announcement had been made as to what had happened. And after all the fanfare accompanying the Swedish delegation's arrival at Court, rumours were now rife as to what had gone wrong. One rumour was that Gustavus Adolphus had been handsomely bribed by the King of Prussia not to marry a Russian Grand Duchess, while another was that everything was Morkov's fault and he had been thrown out of the Court.

Grand Duke Alexander was pleased to see the back of the Swedes – not only because of the insult done to his sister, but also because he disliked what he called (in a letter to La Harpe) 'another racket of celebrations, balls, various suppers of all sorts'. Despite her proud boasts during his childhood, Catherine had not succeeded in making of 'Monsieur Alexandre' what she wanted. Not only did he evince a dislike of the atmosphere and style of his grandmother's Court and a distaste for the whole idea of becoming Emperor in his turn, he had also in the last few years grown disconcertingly close to his father. Both he and Constantine took part enthusiastically in Paul's military exercises at Gatchina and Pavlovsk. Catherine had imagined that by this time Alexander would have been sufficiently imbued with the scorn felt for Grand Duke Paul by all at Court to be impervious to his influence. But this had not turned out to be the case. Alexander seems to have feared both his father and his grandmother, but he had more respect for the former. Caught between the two, his solution was to prevaricate. The question to which his grandmother urgently wanted an answer was whether he would be prepared to assume the imperial throne after her death, thus cutting Paul out of the succession. The idea was abhorrent to Alexander on more than one count, but he could not quite bring himself to say so. In the summer of 1796 Catherine had also tried to enlist Maria Fyodorovna's support in this endeavour, asking her to persuade Paul to sign an act of renunciation. She thought she might be able to capitalise on the unhappiness of the grand ducal marriage, for Paul had become infatuated with one of his wife's maids-of-honour. But the Grand Duchess remained unfailingly loyal – and Paul could never have been brought to sign such a document anyway. In October Catherine approached her grandson directly; he confided in his mother, and made no clear response. By the end of the month the question of the succession had still not been resolved.

On 20 October Catherine wrote to Grimm: 'I preach and will go on preaching common cause with all the kings against the destroyers of thrones and of society, despite all the adherents of the wretched opposing system, and we will see who comes out on top: reason, or the nonsense talked by the perfidious partisans of an execrable system, which in itself excludes and tramples underfoot all sentiments of religion, honour and glory.' These could be said to be her final words both to Grimm and to the world.

## 21

# *Death and Burial*

On Wednesday 5 November 1796 Catherine got up early as usual, dressed, drank her coffee and sat down to work. When her faithful personal maid Maria Perekusikhina asked her if she had slept well, she replied that she had not slept so well for a long time. Soon after, she went to her water closet.

Unusually, she had not emerged after half an hour and her attendants began to wonder what had happened to her. At first they thought that perhaps she had gone for a walk in the Hermitage, slipping out without their noticing, but when her valet Zakhar Zotov checked to see whether any of her pelisses or other warm coverings had been taken from her wardrobe, he found nothing missing and consternation grew. Zotov decided to investigate; cautiously he opened the door of the water closet and saw that the Empress had collapsed. Zotov raised her head, and found that her eyes were closed and her face was purple; her breathing was harsh and laboured. He called out for help and a number of servants came running. They could not manage between them to lift the Empress, because of her weight and because one leg was wedged against the door. They summoned more valets and, after much effort, managed to carry Catherine into her bedroom where they placed her on the floor, on a mattress of Morocco leather. Then the doctors were summoned.

The first to arrive, after 45 minutes, was Dr Rogerson. He immediately diagnosed a stroke and held out no hope of recovery. Nevertheless he bled the Empress, and applied plasters of Spanish fly to her feet.

Count Nikolai Zubov, Platon's elder brother, was dispatched to Gatchina to alert the Grand Duke, and a footman was sent to find

Alexander. On arrival at the Winter Palace, the latter was not admitted to see his grandmother for several hours, Count Saltykov apparently fearing that he might try to proclaim himself Tsar.

Grand Duke Paul was dining that day at the mill at Gatchina, about three miles away from his palace. He and his guests returned to discover Count Zubov, who gave him all the details of the Empress's illness. The Grand Duke ordered eight horses to be harnessed to his coach at once, and he left with his wife for Petersburg, Count Zubov riding ahead to arrange a change of horses at Sofiya. At four o'clock Alexander sent his own courier to Paul, who met him en route. Indeed Paul encountered a number of couriers as he journeyed, various people being anxious to be among the first to bring him the news and thus signal their loyalty to him.

At five o'clock Alexander finally obtained permission from Count Saltykov to enter the Empress's apartments with his wife Elizaveta. In the dimly lit bedroom they found Catherine still unconscious, lying on the mattress, protected by a screen. Her dear friend and first lady-in-waiting, Anna Protasova, was with her, along with Maria Perekusikhina; they were constantly having to wipe away the dark liquid seeping from her mouth.

Alexander and Elizaveta did not stay long, Alexander demonstrating his generosity of spirit by going to see how Platon Zubov was and Elizaveta opting for the company of Constantine's wife, Grand Duchess Anna. Platon, dishevelled and anxious, did not know what to do with himself. He seems to have entirely given up any pretence of being in charge and was alternately burning potentially compromising papers and checking if any of the remedies being applied to the Empress were having any effect. At one point there was a rumour that Catherine had opened her eyes, and hope was briefly rekindled.

Grand Duke Paul arrived at the Winter Palace just after half past eight in the evening and went immediately to his mother's apartments. He met with Alexander and Constantine, instructing his daughters-in-law to remain at home. He then installed himself in a small room beyond his mother's bedroom, so that everyone who came to see him to receive orders had to tramp through the bedroom, past the stricken Empress lying on the floor.

At dawn on 6 November Paul asked the doctors whether there was any hope left. When they said no, he summoned the bishop and priests and ordered the last rites to be administered. News of the Empress's mortal illness had spread throughout the town, and all those with admission to

Court started to converge on the Winter Palace, most of them genuinely upset. The morning was spent waiting for the Empress to die. A change in administration was already very apparent, Catherine's courtiers and officials sitting dejected and in silence, while men in uniform whom most people had never seen before – they had come from Gatchina – were running hither and thither, looking important and giving orders. Alexander and Constantine had already changed into the Prussian-style uniforms of their Gatchina battalions.

At one o'clock Paul and Maria Fyodorovna dined together at a table that had been erected in the corridor behind the bedroom. At three o'clock Vice-Chancellor Osterman was ordered to go to Count Morkov's office and remove all the files relating to foreign affairs. He wrapped the papers up in two enormous bundles fastened by sheets, and lugged them back through the palace himself. During the afternoon Paul also went through all Catherine's personal papers, in the company of Count Bezborodko; these are believed to have included a document drawn up by the Empress removing Paul from the succession, which he threw on to the fire. Bezborodko was instructed to prepare the manifesto announcing the Grand Duke's accession.

Paul also found among his mother's papers the note from Alexei Orlov which appeared to confess to the murder of Peter III. It only confirmed what he had long suspected, and at least exonerated his mother from direct involvement in the deed. But he now performed his first act of filial devotion and restitution by sending home from the Court Prince Fyodor Baryatinsky, now Chief Marshal but 34 years ago one of the principal actors in the drama at Ropsha.

The Empress's pulse now began to weaken. Three or four times the doctors thought the end was approaching, but her robust constitution meant that the agony was prolonged.

At nine o'clock in the evening Dr Rogerson entered the room where Grand Duke Paul and Maria Fyodorovna were waiting, and told them it would not be long now. On Paul's order, Catherine's four eldest grandchildren – Alexander, Constantine, Alexandra and Elena – entered the bedroom with him and Maria Fyodorovna, followed by Madame-General Lieven, Prince Zubov, and Counts Osterman, Bezborodko and Samoilov, and gathered around the dying Empress. The doctors and personal attendants were already there. Catherine died at a quarter to ten, having never regained consciousness.

Some minutes later Paul, his face wet with tears, bowed to the corpse and left the room. At once the women who had served the Empress began to weep and wail. For almost everyone else, their first thought now was of their own survival under a very different regime. Count Samoilov went out into the Knights Guard room and announced the death of the Empress Catherine and the accession of the Emperor Paul. At 11 o'clock the Grand Duchesses Elizaveta and Anna were sent for. Alexander met them and told them to kneel when they kissed the new Emperor's hand. They greeted Paul and were then instructed to go through the late Empress's bedroom and into an adjoining room, where they found Alexandra and Elena in tears. Meanwhile Maria Fyodorovna was supervising with great efficiency and aplomb the washing and dressing of the body and the arrangement of the room.

Catherine's body was dressed in a simple gown and laid on the bed. Prayers for the departed were then recited, in the presence of the imperial family. They kissed Catherine's hand, before going to the imperial chapel to swear the oath of allegiance to Paul, along with everyone else present in the palace. Each person repeated the oath after a priest, then kissed the cross and the Gospel book, signed their name and kissed the hands of the Emperor Paul and the Empress Maria Fyodorovna. This went on until about two o'clock in the morning.

Later that day an autopsy was performed on the body of the late Empress, confirming the cause of death as a cerebral stroke. After the Empress's body had been embalmed, the courtiers and ladies-in-waiting, maids-of-honour, high officials and knights were ordered to keep watch beside her day and night, in two-hour shifts. This vigil was to last throughout the first six weeks of mourning. Paul, Maria Fyodorovna and all the imperial family came twice a day to meditate by her body, and kiss the deceased's hand. Meanwhile, the tomb of Catherine's late husband had been opened, by the order of the new Emperor and in the presence of the Metropolitan of Petersburg. The coffin had been removed and placed in the church of the Annunciation at the Alexander Nevsky Monastery.

On 15 November a procession made its way from Catherine's bedroom, with torches, incense and the chanting of funeral psalms, through the Knights Guard room, its floor, ceiling and walls shrouded in black, and into the throne room. Behind the clergy came the imperial family and finally the body of Catherine II, dressed in silver silk brocade and wearing all her decorations, borne on a magnificent bier covered with the imperial mantle. At the conclusion of the religious ceremony the imperial family took it in turns to prostrate themselves before the body and kiss Catherine's hand. The family then withdrew, a priest came to stand before the throne and begin the reading of the Gospels, and six members of the Imperial Guard took up their positions around the bier.

That same day a ceremony mirroring that of the late Empress's solemn procession to the throne room was carried out at the Alexander Nevsky Monastery, as the coffin containing the remains of Peter III was carried in an equally solemn procession the short distance from the church of the Annunciation to the Cathedral of the Holy Trinity. Here the coffin was opened. Peter's body not having been embalmed, it was found to contain only his hat, gloves, boots – and dust. A requiem was sung for him in the cathedral five days later, a cortège of 42 carriages making its way there from the Winter Palace, and Paul venerated the dust of his father, commanding his family to do the same.

On 25 November the Empress Catherine's body was placed in a coffin, a gold crown on her head, and carried to the Great Gallery, where in happier times balls were held. Here the coffin was placed on an elevated structure beneath a black velvet canopy with a silver fringe. Six candles were positioned round the coffin. A priest once again read the Gospels continuously and members of the Imperial Guard stood on the steps. At the same time, at the Alexander Nevsky Monastery, the imperial crown – which had been brought from Moscow – was placed on Peter's coffin (now re-sealed), in an act of posthumous coronation.

On 3 December, a sunny day of intense cold, Peter's coffin was loaded on to a wheeled platform pulled by eight horses and brought in slow and solemn state from the Alexander Nevsky Monastery to the Winter Palace. The Emperor Paul walked behind the coffin, followed by all the high-ranking court officials. The Emperor ensured that those who had played a part in his father's downfall and death were also participants in his posthumous restoration. Prince Baryatinsky and Governor-General Passek were ordered to walk in the cortège and Count Alexei Orlov was given the dubious honour of carrying the imperial crown on a cushion. Count Orlov, who reputedly had sat in a corner and sobbed on being given this order, bore himself on the occasion with a calm and resolute dignity, firm of tread and face impassive. The procession, accompanied by cannon fire, stretched the length of the Nevsky Prospekt and took several hours to reach its destination.

On arrival at the Winter Palace, Peter's coffin was placed beside Catherine's. So it was lying alongside her former spouse, whom she had despised and overthrown, that the late Empress received the homage of her subjects, who were now permitted to file past the double catafalque. This was seen by many as an insult to Catherine's memory, an act of disrespect to a mother by her son, and it did nothing to endear the new Tsar to his people.

The coffins lay exposed together for two days. Then, after the funeral service on 5 December, they were carried to the Cathedral of Sts Peter and Paul, the traditional burial place of the Romanovs, the imperial family following on foot across the solid ice of the Neva. Inside the cathedral the two remained exposed to public view for a fortnight, before being buried next to one another beneath marble tombs on which Paul had inscribed their dates of birth and burial, but not their dates of death. He had thus done all he could to make it appear as though Peter III had reigned alongside Catherine II. He was by no means the last among the rulers of Russia to attempt to rewrite history.

# *Epilogue*

On 22 February 1788 Catherine told Grimm not to confer titles upon her: 'I beg you no longer to call me, nor to give me any more the sobriquet of Catherine the Great, because, primo, I do not like any sobriquet, secondo, my name is Catherine II, and tertio, I do not want anyone to say of me as of Louis XV, that they find me badly named; fourthly, in size I am neither great nor small.' She believed that only posterity could make a true judgement, although she did compose a cheerful epitaph for her own entertainment, modelling it on that of her greyhound Sir Tom Anderson, and writing it on the reverse of his:

> Here lies Catherine the Second, born in Stettin on 21st April (2nd May) 1729. She came to Russia in 1744 to marry Peter III. At the age of fourteen she formed the threefold project of pleasing her husband, Elizabeth and the nation. She neglected nothing to succeed in this. Eighteen years of boredom and solitude made her read plenty of books. Arrived on the throne of Russia, she desired its good and sought to procure for her subjects happiness, liberty and propriety. She forgave easily and hated no one; indulgent, easy to live with, naturally cheerful, with a republican soul and a good heart, she had friends: she found work easy, she liked good society and the arts.

Though the 'republican soul', if it ever existed, became invisible in the years following the French Revolution, this is certainly an accurate reflection of how she saw herself. Humorous and succinct, but by no means self-effacing, this summing-up demonstrates a self-confidence and ease

505

with herself which her son did not inherit. Paul I was Emperor for a mere five years, his reign ending by assassination on 11 March 1801. Throughout his reign he had made himself unpopular by his self-important posturings. He insisted, for instance, that everyone, no matter what the situation or the weather, should kneel as the Emperor passed – even if that necessitated getting out of a carriage and kneeling in the snow.

Among the plotters of Paul's murder was his mother's last favourite, Platon Zubov. Paul had always feared assassination, and his abrasive, neurotic and domineering temperament made him a likely target. He thought he had taken steps to protect himself by building the fortified and moated Mikhailovsky Castle – on the site, alongside the Fontanka, of the Summer Palace which he had had demolished. But the conspirators, his own courtiers and officials, were inside the castle, and so moats and thick walls were of no use.

Catherine's beloved 'Monsieur Alexandre' thus became Emperor at the age of 23. The ambivalence he had always felt about his imperial calling was only exacerbated by the manner in which he had assumed the throne. He never recovered from the guilt he felt at having been implicated in the plot to overthrow his father (though he had tried to insist that Paul should not be murdered). Tsar Alexander I nevertheless won an honoured place in Russian history as the vanquisher of Napoleon Bonaparte. Alexander's desire to break free from his imperial inheritance may have resurfaced at the end of his life. His sudden death in Taganrog in 1825 became the subject of a strange legend – that he had not died at all. The body in the coffin (which was never exposed to public view) was rumoured to be that of some other man, while the Tsar had taken to wandering Russia as a holy fool under the name of 'Fyodor Kuzmich'.

Alexander and Elizaveta produced no sons, their only children being two daughters who died in infancy. (Alexander did father a large number of illegitimate children by several mothers, Catherine's prediction that women would be his undoing turning out to be accurate. Maybe in this, with the genders reversed, he was not unlike his grandmother.) The succession would have passed to Constantine, had not this erratic and difficult man renounced his claim to the throne in 1822, following his morganatic marriage to a Catholic Polish woman, Joanna Grudzínska. Few things would have horrified his grandmother more. Constantine's first marriage had broken down as early as 1801, when Anna Fyodorovna left him and returned home permanently. He was divorced from her in March 1820, remarrying two months later.

Constantine, who had become the father of an illegitimate son by another woman in 1808, died of cholera in 1831.

The confusion regarding the succession in 1825 was a catalyst for the Decembrists' revolt. Some of the rebels demonstrated in Constantine's name (or thought that was what they were doing), demanding that he should be made Emperor and bring in a constitution (not that such a move would have been at all in keeping with Constantine's illiberal, militaristic nature). The actual successor was Nicholas I, born as an enormous baby in the last months of Catherine's life and another of the Romanov males interested only in military affairs. Coming to the throne in the wake of a revolt, he brought in repressive measures in an attempt to strengthen the autocracy.

As for Catherine's granddaughters, husbands were found for them all. Alexandra Pavlovna, the victim of the débâcle over the King of Sweden in 1796, married an Austrian Archduke three years later, but died shortly after giving birth to a stillborn daughter in 1801 at the age of 17. The beautiful Elena fared little better, being married a week earlier than her sister to a Grand Duke of Mecklenburg-Schwerin and dying in 1803 at the age of 18. She was survived by a son and daughter who grew into adulthood. Maria, who had been so 'mannish' as a little girl, was made of sterner stuff and prospered, as has been mentioned earlier. Ekaterina Pavlovna's first husband was a Holstein-Gottorp and Duke of Oldenburg; she had two sons by him, who were christened Alexander and Constantine. After the Duke's death in 1812, she married King William I of Würtemberg, by whom she had two daughters. She died in 1819 at the age of 30. Anna married the King of the Netherlands in 1816, had five children, four of whom survived into adulthood, and died in 1865 at the age of 70.

Maria Fyodorovna, who produced one more son – Mikhail – after Catherine's death, remained a redoubtable presence as Dowager Empress throughout Alexander's reign, and died in 1828 at the age of 69.

One of the first acts of Paul I's reign had been to eliminate any possibility of there being another woman like his mother. By passing a law of succession in April 1797, he re-established the right of male primogeniture and forbade any woman to assume the throne. The age of the great Russian Empresses had come to an end, and a harsher male world had taken its place.

Nicholas I was succeeded by his son, the liberal Alexander II, renowned for the act emancipating the serfs in 1861, and rewarded for his pains by eight assassination attempts, the last of which was successful. The

church of the Saviour on Spilt Blood, one of the most striking land-
marks of present-day St Petersburg, was erected on the site of Alexander's
murder. The pendulum swung back to repression with Alexander III,
and his son Nicholas II inherited a situation for which the old ways
of autocracy were inappropriate and doomed. For a few months after
the collapse of the Empire the Alexander Palace, built by Catherine at
Tsarskoye Selo for her beloved grandson, became a prison for her
descendants, until the Tsar and his family were taken to Tobolsk and
then Ekaterinburg where they were killed in July 1918. The revolution
'trampling underfoot all sentiments of religion, honour and glory' which
Catherine had taken such pains to resist had finally came to pass.

In 1647 one Adam Olearius, a courtier from Holstein, published an
account of his travels in Russia in the 1630s in which he included an
observation that the Russians tended to indulge in sodomy, even with
horses. It was this unsubstantiated calumny that occurred to the minds
of particularly malicious gossipmongers in the decades following
Catherine's death. As she was known to have had an appetite for sex,
to have acclimatised herself very successfully to Russian customs and
to have been an expert horsewoman, it didn't require too much of a
stretch of the imagination to suggest that Catherine liked having sex
with horses and, indeed, that she had died in the act.

No one knows who first uttered the infamous 'horse story' – and
it seems likely that it was spread by word of mouth before being
written down – but one can identify certain rumours and supposi-
tions which fed into it. Even before her death, lewd images of Catherine
had appeared in satirical prints in Britain and France, particularly
around the time of the 'Ochakov Crisis' of 1791, when Britain and
Prussia nearly went to war with Russia over Turkey. Her vehement
opposition to the French Revolution – as well as the fact that the
male-dominated power circles of Europe could never quite get used
to the idea of this husband-less woman constantly increasing the size
and influence of her Empire – made her a continuing target for those
who would seek to denigrate her achievements. It is clear from an
entry in John Parkinson's journal of 1792 that Catherine's sex life was
also a common subject for ribaldry among the male society of
Petersburg: 'A party was considering which of the Canals had cost
the most money; when one of them archly observed there was not
a doubt about the matter; Catherine's Canal (this is the name of one
of them) had unquestionably been the most expensive.' Rumours had

always surrounded the death of Catherine's adored young favourite Alexander Lanskoy, and no doubt it had not been forgotten that during his final delirium he kept asking to have horses harnessed to his bed. This report, conflated with the rumours that he had died of an overdose of aphrodisiacs – and while actually making love to Catherine – was a probable first step, along with Olearius's earlier 'report' and Catherine's fabled skill as a horsewoman in her youth, on the path to the full-blown horse story.

I was first told the legend of how Catherine the Great died – and told it as though it were true (though not, thankfully, by a history lecturer) – when I was an undergraduate at the School of Slavonic and East European Studies. This scurrilous piece of fabrication, which would be funny were it not tragic in having attached itself to Catherine's memory – that the Empress died when a specially constructed hoist enabling her to have sex with a horse broke and the stallion fell on top of her, crushing her to death – is unfortunately the kind of story which once heard is never forgotten. I hope that the portrait of Catherine which has emerged from these pages will go some way to quashing this piece of arrant nonsense for ever.

Of course Catherine was no Virgin Empress. By the end of her life she had no doubt, as she indicated to Potemkin when telling him about Platon Zubov, that she needed a young man to love and be loved by for the sake of her health. And it is clear that she could not function effectively as Empress whenever these emotional and physical needs were not being satisfied.

Catherine was also addicted to acquisitions. She selected a new favourite, or agreed to the selection recommended by her 'experts', much as she selected a new painting for her collection. She acquired young men because they were there, available and willing – for even if a young man might not have relished the prospect of a physical relationship with an ageing woman, he and his family could not help but be attracted by the rewards on offer in terms of status and wealth.

There is a passage in Catherine's memoirs, suppressed in the edition published by the Russian Academy of Sciences in 1907, which casts some light on her love affairs and how they came about. For Catherine the onset of each new love had a feeling of inevitability; she could not imagine being attracted and failing to respond:

To tempt and to be tempted are closely allied; and in spite of all the finest moral maxims buried in the mind, when emotion interferes, when feeling makes its appearance, one is already much further involved than one realizes, and I have still not learnt how to prevent its appearance. Perhaps escape is the only solution, but there are situations, circumstances, when escape is impossible, for how can one escape, be elusive, turn one's back, in the atmosphere of a Court? Such an act itself might give food for talk. And if you do not run away, nothing is more difficult, in my opinion, than to avoid something that fundamentally attracts you. Statements to the contrary could only be prudish and not inspired by a human heart. One cannot hold one's heart in one's hand, forcing it or releasing it, tightening or relaxing one's grasp at will.

Catherine believed that she had a calling to rule Russia and to expend all her energy in the service of the country which had initially adopted her and which she then made her own. She believed that she had fulfilled this mission, that her reign had brought great benefits to Russia, benefits which outweighed any consideration that she had come by the throne – and held on to it – dishonourably, even criminally. She was in many ways absolutely right. Her achievements, so many of them shared with trusted officials and military men – and particularly with Prince Grigory Potemkin – were enormous. Under Catherine, the Russian Empire flourished politically and culturally, and became in many ways a better place to live. She carried on the work begun by Peter the Great in making Russia a major player on the world stage, and she improved the lot of many of her subjects, making great progress in reforms of local government and the spread of education. She may have deluded herself about how effective some of her reforms were, and she did nothing to change the basic structure of a society based on the institution of serfdom, showing little interest in her vast peasant population beyond wanting them to be fed and housed, enabled to work efficiently and contribute to population growth. But there seems little point in denigrating her for being in tune with the age in which she lived. Catherine's ideals, manifested in her desire for an ordered society in which everyone fulfils his allotted role and is given the means to enable him to do so, are very much those of the eighteenth century, before the cataclysm of the age of revolutions.

Catherine was a humane woman and her humanity filtered down to her subordinates. To compare the atmosphere of her Court with both those of her predecessors and her immediate successors is of course to notice the succession of favourites and the excesses represented by the massive spending, but it is also to see the absence of fear, the civilising influence of this most civilised of women. Catherine's officials and courtiers were not, in general, summarily dismissed, or executed, or tortured, or sent to the army, or exiled. Of course there were exceptions, and conspirators – or those suspected of conspiracy – were shown little mercy. But the men who worked with Catherine could by and large express their opinions, even when they were in conflict with her own, without fear – provided she could see they were being honest with her and that their fundamental loyalty was not in question – in a way that no official of her son, for instance, would be able to do and in a way that was unheard of before her reign. Catherine was not capricious in her dealings with her subordinates, nor unfair. And many of her personal attendants adored her.

Ultimately the scales come down in Catherine's favour, and posterity, while taking into account her weaknesses and failures, her prejudices and her pride, justly calls her Great.

# Notes

*Abbreviation*

SIRIO: Sbornik Imperatorskogo Russkogo Istoricheskogo Obshchestva: (Collection of the Imperial Russian Historical Society), St Petersburg, 1867–1912

Epigraph: SIRIO 23, p.177.


*Foreword*

Miss M. Trouncer . . . on the subject: J. Saumarez Smith (ed.), *The Bookshop at 10 Curzon Street: Letters between Nancy Mitford and Heywood Hill 1952–73*, Frances Lincoln, London, 2004, p.34.
Actually, if there is interest . . . interests him: Ibid., p.104.


*Prologue*

If memoirs are not history . . . crumbled to dust: R. Aldington, Introduction to *The Private Life of the Marshal Duke of Richelieu*, Routledge, London, 1927, pp.2–3.


*Chapter 1: From Feudal Anthill to the Court of Russia*

princes of Brunswick-Luneberg . . . archaic feudal anthill: Klyuchevsky, *A Course in Russian History*, p.32.

the widow of a certain Herr von Hohendorf: Maroger, *Memoirs of Catherine the Great*, p.25.

[he] considered me to be an angel: Ibid.

did not bother much about me: Ibid.

merely tolerated: Ibid.

Titus, Marcus Aurelius, and all the great men of antiquity: Ibid., p.29.

For speculation as to whether Catherine was masturbating: See, for example, Alexander, *Catherine the Great*, p.21.

insufferably forward: Maroger, *Memoirs of Catherine the Great*, p.31.

Really, this Princess . . . what future faces ours?: Ibid., pp.35–6.

I was given many mixtures to take, but God alone knows what they were!: Ibid., p.28.

of the sort one finds in Hamburg: SIRIO 7, p.16.

A detachment of cuirassiers . . . and stable hands: Ibid., p.13.

It never occurred to me . . . nothing at all: Ibid., p.15.

A squadron from His Imperial Highness's regiment . . . around my sleigh: Ibid., pp.17–18.

thousands: Ibid., p.19.

The Prince gave me his hand . . . inner apartments: Ibid., pp.19–20.

The shock that the sleigh received . . . a few bruises: Ibid., pp.22–4.

As we left Petersburg . . . for several hours: Maroger, *Memoirs of Catherine the Great*, p.57.

One of the coachmen . . . crush anyone: SIRIO 7, p.24.

And so we set off . . . as tenderness: Ibid., pp.25–6.

the benefits which she has showered . . . to her Court: Ibid., p.26.

She was a large woman . . . very beautiful: Maroger, *Memoirs of Catherine the Great*, p.60.

I have found out subsequently . . . gone out: SIRIO 7, p.26.

I don't know how many others, altogether a very numerous court: Ibid., p.27.

That day . . . way under me: Ibid.

infinitely more feared than loved . . . of his friends: Maroger, *Memoirs of Catherine the Great*, p.58.

I do not think . . . at my ease: Ibid., p.65.

brutality of the people: SIRIO 7, p.3.

One day I asked this Lutheran priest . . . and ceremonies: Maroger, *Memoirs of Catherine the Great*, p.29.

the Crown of Russia: Ibid., p.70.

The Court walked ahead . . . move through them: SIRIO 7, pp.31–2.

I was already so overcome . . . in their eyes: Ibid., pp.32–3.

Her demeanour . . . what she is: Ibid., p.33.

real little monsters: Ibid., p.35.

This whole ceremony . . . precede it: Ibid., p.39.

During the exchange of rings . . . of an hour: Ibid.

After coming out . . . here saw it: Ibid., p.40.


## Chapter 2: Engagement and Wedding

70,000 roubles: SIRIO 7, p.44.

Catherine's letter to her father: Ibid., p.5.

balls, masquerades, fireworks, illuminations, operas and comedies: Maroger, *Memoirs of Catherine the Great*, p.73.

romp about until early in the morning: Ibid.

uproar . . . childish spirits: Ibid.

made sour remarks at our expense while we were enjoying ourselves: Ibid., p.74.

very fair . . . of a court: Mrs Ward, *Letters from a lady who resided some years in Russia*, p.73.

altho' this is the most absolute . . . and cabals: SIRIO 103, p.268.

I had made it a general rule . . . in her favour: Maroger, *Memoirs of Catherine the Great*, pp.80–1.

Everything combined to make me hope for a happy future: Ibid., p.77.

Every Tuesday . . . as men: Ibid., p.78.

I had been told . . . oneself agreeable: Ibid., p.80.

the most extravagant woman . . . to have them: Ibid.

To please . . . the nation: Ibid.

his mind . . . gentlemen-in-waiting: Ibid., p.82.

He had grown a great deal . . . to look at: Herzen, *Mémoires de l'Impératrice Catherine II*, pp.30–1.

about as discreet as a cannon ball: Maroger, *Memoirs of Catherine the Great*, p.88.

I tried to be . . . politeness all round: Ibid.

very stricken: Ibid., p.92.

On the whole . . . I succeeded: Ibid., p.93.

He made me stand at arms . . . and mine: Ibid.

the differences between the sexes: Ibid., p.96.

Her Imperial Majesty's cortége . . . 40 lackeys: SIRIO 7, p.50.

a real little castle: Ibid.

magnificent: Ibid., p.56.

Her Imperial Majesty . . . to bed: Ibid., p.57.

Everybody left me . . . in bed together: Maroger, *Memoirs of Catherine the Great*, p.99.

but as soon as they noticed . . . their prey: SIRIO 7, p.63.

thus finished the most lavish of festivities ever perhaps to have taken place in Europe: Ibid., p.67.

performing military exercises and changing their uniforms twenty times a day: Maroger, *Memoirs of Catherine the Great*, p.100.

I would have been ready . . . this earth: Ibid., p.101.

cried abundantly . . . goodbye: Ibid., p.103.


## Chapter 3: Early Married Life

romped with his gentlemen-in-waiting in the other room: Maroger, *Memoirs of Catherine the Great*, p.105.

One pretended . . . went there: Ibid.

The great duke . . . being recalled: SIRIO 103, pp.25–6.

insipid: Maroger, *Memoirs of Catherine the Great*, p.108.

like a Fury: Ibid., p.111.

uneducated, malicious, and full of self-interest: Ibid., p.113.

The person selected . . . jerk his limbs: From *Arkhivi Knyaza Vorontsova*, Vol. 2, quoted in Gertrude Aretz, *The Empress Catherine*, Godfrey & Stephens Ltd, London, 1947, p.37.

She had the reputation . . . emulate it: Maroger, *Memoirs of Catherine the Great*, p.115.

I have every reason . . . Mlle Tatishchev: Ibid., p.118.

They formed a suite . . . for emptying: Ibid., p.180.

I remember dressing . . . and domestics: Ibid., p.118.

We were all . . . torches: Ibid., p.119.

I suppose . . . no harm: Ibid., p.123.

[he] immediately placed . . . mount guard: Ibid.

where the five or six . . . till night: Ibid.

Science and art . . . could write: Ibid., p.119.

In short that winter . . . and dancing: Ibid., p.125.

I realised his position . . . interminably: Ibid., pp.128–9.

stories of highwaymen or novels: Ibid., p.129.

He did not know . . . his instrument: Ibid., p.131.

had not been a king: Ibid., p.130.

She procured . . . Mme Krause: Herzen, *Mémoires de l'Impératrice Catherine II*, p.82.

I was tall . . . now and then: Maroger, *Memoirs of Catherine the Great*, p.133.

Pretending a headache . . . so prodigiously: Ibid., p.135.

When Lent came . . . matters worse: Ibid.

fraught with stupidity . . . nobody etc: Ibid., pp.135–6.

the Grand Duke . . . than censure: Ibid., pp.140–1.

Mme Krause screamed: 'It's an earthquake!': Ibid., p.142.

We often rounded . . . the skiff: Ibid., p.146.

During the day . . . my commode: Ibid., pp.151–2.

was naturally inclined . . . the room: Ibid., p.152.

as the houses . . . seemed delicious: Ibid., p.153.

hung up by the arms backwards for a considerable time: SIRIO 110, p.284.

Nothing could have been . . . the other: Maroger, *Memoirs of Catherine the Great*, pp.153–4.

At that time . . . in the world: Ibid., p.154.

She got married, and no more was said about her. Ibid.

an attack of constipation which threatened to become very serious: Ibid., p.155.

noticeably looking down their noses: Ibid.

taken proper measures . . . altho' in cypher: SIRIO 110, pp.292–3.

My cheerful disposition . . . with them: Maroger, *Memoirs of Catherine the Great*, p.160.

returned to his corner with his dogs and his violin: Ibid., p.155.

I rode like mad . . . or cared: Ibid., p.161.

Catherine's remedy for cold sores: Ibid.

tears streamed from my eyes and nose as though water had been poured from a teapot: Ibid., p.170.

whose fault it was: Ibid., p.174.

Lord Hyndford's report to the Duke of Newcastle: SIRIO 110, p.331.

small and hunchbacked: Maroger, *Memoirs of Catherine the Great*, p.173.

never had a mistress who was not hunchbacked, lame, or one-eyed: Ibid., pp.173–4.

never go much further than languorous ogling: Ibid., p.174.

two or three rather violent punches on the side: Ibid., p.176.

I cried a lot . . . had happened: Ibid.

I passionately loved riding . . . it back: Ibid., p.183.

superb clothes, all embroidered or of an elaborate style: Ibid., p.189.

The only woman . . . replace her: Herzen, *Mémoires de l'Impératrice Catherine II*, pp.148–9.

One day . . . present the apple: Ibid., p.149.

Resolved though I was . . . delightful pastime: Maroger, *Memoirs of Catherine the Great*, p.196.

Catherine's letters to Zakhar Chernyshev: *Russkiy Arkhiv*, Vol. 3, 1881.

## Chapter 4: Catherine Grows Up

unfortunately I could not help . . . the Court: Maroger, *Memoirs of Catherine the Great*, p.200.

knew how to conceal his faults: Ibid.

start upon his favourite subject: Ibid., p.201.

agreeable: Ibid.

I had believed . . . impossible task: Ibid., p.202.

grey below, blue on top, with a black velvet collar, and no other ornament: Ibid., p.203.

[she] replied . . . about it yet: Ibid. This passage was omitted from the 1907 Russian edition of Catherine's collected works.

It took several days . . . agree to do: Ibid., p.205.

At last . . . in her debt: Ibid.

with violent haemorrhages: Ibid., p.206.

We were living . . . or for me: Ibid.

The mention of Bestuzhev's drops in *Les Misérables*: 'In the eyes of M. Gillenormand, Catherine the Second had made reparation for the crime of the partition of Poland by purchasing, for three thousand roubles, the secret of the elixir of gold, from Bestucheff. He grew animated on this subject: "The elixir of gold," he exclaimed, "the yellow dye of Bestucheff, General Lamotte's drops, in the eighteenth century, – this was the great remedy for the catastrophes of love, the panacea against Venus, at one louis the half-ounce phial. Louis XV sent two hundred phials of it to the Pope." He would have been greatly irritated and thrown off his balance, had any one told him that the elixir of gold is nothing but the perchloride of iron.' Victor Hugo, *Les Misérables, Vol.III Book Second – The Great Bourgeois*, Chapter IV. A Centenarian Aspirant.

She started . . . to the rule: Maroger, *Memoirs of Catherine the Great*, p.208. This passage was also omitted from the 1907 Russian edition.

for in their state . . . Grand Duke: Ibid., p.211.

exposed to the public for three days: Ibid.

womanly ignorance of military law: Ibid., p.212.

so that a small lunatic asylum gradually collected at Court: Ibid.

I set off straightaway . . . to hurry: Herzen, *Mémoires de l'Impératrice Catherine II*, pp.196–7.

filled with vermin: Maroger, *Memoirs of Catherine the Great*, p.214.

as she was afraid of the dead: Ibid., p.219.

a sort of convulsion . . . or anxiety: Ibid., p.222.

Peter's violin playing: Stählin, *Muzyka i balet v Rossii XVIII veka*, p.93.

but all my troubles followed me relentlessly: Maroger, *Memoirs of Catherine the Great*, p.223.

they were dismal . . . no comfort: Ibid., p.224.

a very hard time: Ibid.

As soon as . . . follow her: Ibid.

It was enough . . . drag myself there: Ibid., p.225.

He was kept . . . than good: Ibid., p.227.

a miserable little necklace . . . my maids: Ibid., p.228.

I buried myself . . . my grief: Ibid., p.229.

I found him beautiful . . . carried away: Ibid.

two immense volumes of Baronius translated into Russian: Ibid., p.230.

in church . . . come through it: Ibid.

Everyone surpassed . . . than the last: Ibid., pp.230–1.

I waited . . . prevented him: Ibid., p.231.


## Chapter 5: Sir Charles Hanbury-Williams and Stanislas Poniatowski

I had to cross . . . heat was suffocating: Maroger, *Memoirs of Catherine the Great*, p.234.

once he had got it, would rush away again as fast as he had come: Ibid., p.240.

I remember . . . great admiration: Ibid., p.238.

We took no notice . . . than another: Smith. D. (ed. & tr.), *Love & Conquest: Personal Correspondence of Catherine the Great & Prince Grigory Potemkin*, Northern Illinois University Press, DeKalb, 2004, p.9. Copyright 2003 by Northern Illinois University Press. Used by permission of the publisher.

I forgot that Siberia existed: Poniatowski, *Mémoires secrets et inédits*, p.7.

She was 25 years old . . . her disposition: Ibid., pp.7–8.

In those days . . . same way: Maroger, *Memoirs of Catherine the Great*, pp.241–2.

There was a lot . . . nervous disorder: Ibid., pp.244–5.

water in the lower part of her belly: Catherine II, *Correspondence of Catherine the Great when Grand-Duchess*, p.32.

to disordered minds the same thing can appear as black and white at the same time: Ibid., pp.42–3.

wear the crown: Ibid., p.39.

There is short shrift . . . of breath: Ibid., p.35.

I implore you . . . so much: Ibid., pp.35–6.

My fondest hopes . . . the witchcrafts: Ibid., p.49.

I am told . . . tenderest feelings: Ibid., p.62.

Afterwards . . . upper hand: Ibid., p.45.

I shall either perish or reign: Ibid.

You are born to command and reign, and old age alone will kill you: Ibid., p.50.

the forty thousand roubles are at your disposal and await your orders: Ibid., p.64.

how pleased he is . . . and affection: Ibid., p.65.

First, I shall get . . . you money: Ibid., p.74.

I must tell you . . . your possession: Ibid., p.91.

to weigh things . . . never change: Ibid., p.56.

I shall never . . . flatter you: Ibid., pp.74–5.

There must always . . . read them: Ibid., p.47.

For six years . . . love him: Ibid., p.57.

in the case of any difficulty: Ibid., p.59.

The extreme hatred . . . on my part: Ibid., p.60.

While your friends . . . very least: Ibid., p.66.

My heart . . . your esteem: Ibid., pp.79–80.

live a great deal with you as a faithful servant and a humble friend: Ibid., p.82.

I should like . . . the Empress: Ibid.

I would like to feel . . . foolishly convinced: Ibid., p.90.

new penchant for a Greek girl, who is in my service: Ibid., p.101.

conflicted with all . . . so cross: Ibid., p.108.

very reasonable about many things: Ibid., p.109.

Here is something . . . her breath: Ibid., p.110.

He can do what you ask, if he pleases: Ibid., p.120.

you will make me speak . . . to you: Ibid., p.124.

I do not know . . . like this: Ibid., p.128.

One word from you . . . equal yours: Ibid., p.136.

As soon as . . . promised defence: Ibid., p.148.

the fingers . . . eyes sightless: Ibid., p.180.

My surgeon . . . carry her off: Ibid., p.183.

Everyone will bow . . . a meal: Ibid., p.180.

she wrung my hand . . . next day: Ibid., p.198.

went to shoot blackcocks . . . is better: Ibid., p.215.

The Grand-Duke . . . of Russia: Ibid., p.230.

I promise you . . . the opportunity: Ibid., p.236.

The Empress . . . no other comfort: Ibid., pp.238–9.

The kindness . . . opportunity arises: Ibid., p.244.

I am too much afraid . . . beyond repair: Ibid., pp.249–50.

He certainly keeps us waiting for him; he is said to be at Riga: Ibid., p.251.

marvellously well: Ibid., p.258.

The wish is very near my heart, Monsieur, that your son should have a brother: Ibid., p.276.

I am marvellously well . . . wish me well: Ibid.

advising him . . . excellent head: Ibid., p.277.

On a site . . . for supper: Maroger, *Memoirs of Catherine the Great*, p.275.

other frippery: Ibid., p.276.

there was not a breath . . . her feast: Ibid.

I explained . . . to me: Ibid., p.266.

Heaven alone knows . . . as such: Ibid., p.280.

Go to hell. Do not talk to me any more about it: Ibid.

he arranged great celebrations . . . of satisfaction: Ibid., p.282.

the commode: Ibid., p.283.

He was relieved . . . a prisoner: Ibid., p.286.

with the iron in my soul: Ibid., p.288.

according to which . . . the Admiralty: Ibid., pp.289–90.

The Grand Duke . . . would do so: Ibid., p.295.

Waiting for this interview . . . spectacular measures: Ibid., p.299.

that I did not consider . . . of women: Ibid.

listened with particular . . . of the moment: Ibid., p.308.

[Peter's] behaviour . . . in my heart: Ibid., p.309.

The Grand Duke . . . to mine: Ibid.

I began . . . the Grand Duke: Ibid., p.313.

The good fortune . . . his wife: Poniatowski, *Mémoires secrets et inédits*, pp.15–17.

I cannot tell you I have done something I have not done: Ibid., p.17.

I am sure . . . out of here: Ibid., p.18.

It was a wretched little carriage . . . in vain: Ibid., pp.18–19.

You have it in your power to make several people happy: Ibid., p.19.

How foolish . . . happened then: Maroger, *Memoirs of Catherine the Great*, p.273.

He was so flattered . . . satisfied everybody!: Ibid.

All that's missing . . . our friend: Poniatowski, *Mémoires secrets et inédits*, p.20.

I arrived . . . as I liked: Maroger, *Memoirs of Catherine the Great*, p.274.


*Chapter 6: Empress of All the Russias*

On Paul's fears: Poroshin, *Semyona Poroshina zapiski*, pp.602–7.

It is impossible . . . the succession: Maroger, *Memoirs of Catherine the Great*, p.329.

we would have managed to form sufficient subjects of our own nation to teach in the house: SIRIO 7, p.82.

Power without the trust . . . its aim: Ibid., p.85.

It is against . . . prejudiced landowners: Ibid., p.84.

able doctors . . . for the State: Ibid., pp.86–7.

The majority . . . flourish more: Ibid., p.87.

it is important that the obligation be owed to you, not to your favourites etc: Ibid., p.88.

he who does not . . . of reigning: Ibid.

Catherine on the favour shown towards her: Ibid., p.98.

wore a wig . . . Louis XIV: Fitzlyon, *Memoirs of Princess Dashkova*, p.56.

At the moment of H.I.M.'s death . . . and immature!: Maroger, *Memoirs of Catherine the Great*, p.330.

The body . . . light-coloured dresses: Ibid., p.331.

For a description of Elizabeth's lying-in-state: Cronin, *Catherine, Empress of All the Russias*, p.131.

taken with great pomp . . . the Fortress: Maroger, *Memoirs of Catherine the Great*, p.338.

The Emperor . . . of much talk: Ibid.

The Emperor himself . . . the refectory: Stählin, *Muzyka i balet v Rossii XVIII veka*, p.123.

The nobles . . . now inherited: Maroger, *Memoirs of Catherine the Great*, p.337.

perish or reign: Catherine II *Correspondence of Catherine the Great* when Grand-Duchess, p.45.

she: Fitzlyon, *Memoirs of Princess Dashkova*, p.52.

The abandonment . . . in her favour: SIRIO 140, p.2

The Empress . . . the whole table: Fitzlyon, *Memoirs of Princess Dashkova*, p.60.

The Guards . . . were against it: Maroger, *Memoirs of Catherine the Great*, p.341.

On reports of Peter receiving communion: SIRIO 140, p.1.

Alexei Orlov came in . . . had arrived: Maroger, *Memoirs of Catherine the Great*, p.341.

a frenzy of joy: Ibid.

Last Friday morning . . . the Emperor: SIRIO 12, p.2.

The atmosphere in the city: Ibid.

From that moment . . . his attendants: Ibid., p.5.

the fatherland, the people and my son: SIRIO 7, p.101.

a petty officer called Potemkin displayed discernment, courage and action: Maroger, *Memoirs of Catherine the Great*, p.348.

Frederick the Great's comments to the Comte de Ségur: Ségur, *Mémoires, ou Souvenirs et Anecdotes,* Vol. 2, p.134.

respectable and comfortable rooms were being prepared: Maroger, *Memoirs of Catherine the Great*, p.345.

A chance guest . . . appeared there: Klyuchevsky, *A Course in Russian History*, p.26.

Several other little circumstances . . . his understanding: SIRIO 12, pp.9–10.

Soldiers drinking out of their hats: Fitzlyon, *Memoirs of Princess Dashkova*, p.82.

The Orlovs shone . . . were here: Maroger, *Memoirs of Catherine the Great*, pp.347–8.

Princess Dashkov . . . this great writer: Ibid., p.348.

At last . . . hand of God: Ibid., p.349.


## Chapter 7: Murder, Coronation and Conspiracy

complaints of extortion . . . miscarriages of justice: SIRIO 10, p.380.

I beg you most urgently . . . in four days: Maroger, *Memoirs of Catherine the Great*, p.341.

I beg Your Majesty . . . her reign: Ibid., pp.345–6.

We and the whole detachment . . . had happened: Ibid., p.350.

[Peter] proposes . . . lacking is freedom: SIRIO 140, p.20.

Your Majesty, our little mother . . . lost our soul: *Arkhiv Knyazya Vorontsova*, Vol. 21, p.430.

Catherine, crowned and free . . . save her: Ségur *Mémoires, ou Souvenirs et Anecdotes*, Vol. 2, p.134.

What a picture . . . a regicide: SIRIO 140, p.26.

the late Emperor . . . died yesterday: Ibid., p.21.

face was extraordinarily black . . . his hands: Ibid., p.25.

Finally people claim . . . indicate poisoning: Ibid.

The late Emperor . . . the funeral: SIRIO 12, p.28.

All minds here . . . increasing it: Maroger, *Memoirs of Catherine the Great*, p.341.

Fright had given him . . . quite withered: Ibid., p.345.

I received your letter . . . little love-letters: Ibid., p.349.

everything was carried out . . . as such: Ibid.

I feel very embarrassed . . . is true: Ibid.

Good-bye, the world is full of strange situations: Ibid.

the acidity which dominates in his stomach and digestive tract: SIRIO 7, p.144.

oils, syrups and dilutants: Ibid., p.146.

engendered a slowness in the body's juices, by further weakening the solid parts: Ibid.

extraordinary wisdom . . . way of life: Ibid.

correct the juices . . . solid parts: Ibid., p.147.

according to the rules . . . the face: Ibid., p.149.

I was asked . . . better than us: Khrapovitsky, *Pamyatnye zapiski*, p.217.

At one of these moments . . . no repercussions: SIRIO 140, p.85.

The Empress . . . knew not why: SIRIO 12, p.46.

I had the honour . . . extremely gracious: Ibid., p.47.

The Chancellor . . . in this country: Ibid., p.52.

I do not know . . . these days: SIRIO 140, p.86.

I have no time . . . her Court: Ibid., p.20.

This man who plays today . . . particular protection: SIRIO 22, pp.69–70.

The Chancellor . . . upon every thing: SIRIO 12, p.83.

If the Treaty of Commerce . . . presents here: Ibid., p.71.

It was a Russian tragedy . . . justice to it: Ibid., pp.77–8.

When we consider . . . a few weeks: Ibid., pp.78–9.

The Empress's passion . . . highly gullible: SIRIO 140, p.163.

Her Imperial Majesty . . . her favour: SIRIO 12, p.89.

The foreign Ministers . . . a determination: Ibid., p.90.

People of all ranks . . . this country: Ibid., p.107.

a great rogue and the reason behind the whole business: SIRIO 7, p.291.

[Princess Dashkova] has lost . . . pleasure of it: SIRIO 22, p.66.

In those early days . . . and incorruptible: Ibid., pp.67–8.

I have noticed myself . . . much credit: Ibid., pp.68–9.

Returning to the source . . . this Court: Ibid., pp.72–4.

if an opinion . . . the world: Ibid., p.75.


## Chapter 8: Catherine Sets to Work

For details of Catherine's cabinet secretaries and the times allotted to them,
  see Alexander, *Catherine the Great*, p.69.

I get up regularly . . . manuscript paper: SIRIO 1, pp.261–2.

Listen Perfilyevich . . . as you do: SIRIO 7, p.351.

I will avoid . . . put anything: SIRIO 1, p.278.

Great as the delay . . . excusable: SIRIO 12, pp.182–3.

Count Panin . . . you kings: SIRIO 23, p.584.

If I see . . . towards business: SIRIO 7, p.346.

I have been watching them . . . their capabilities: Ibid.

In one you will find . . . betray you: Ibid.

the lack of application to work of several of my predecessors: Ibid., p.347.

She came in . . . half an hour: SIRIO 12, p.135.

Hasn't he already . . . on the carriage: SIRIO 7, p.355.

Don't mock me . . . when he heard: Ibid., p.321.

Dear Nikita Ivanovich . . . only a chill: Ibid., pp.373–4.

When I am speaking . . . for some time: SIRIO 12, p.136.

so charmingly . . . hardly be heard: Stählin, *Muzyka i balet v Rossii XVIII veka*, p.160.

His Highness woke up . . . should be: Quoted in Peskov, *Paul 1^er^, Empereur de Russie*, p.42.

Today I had a sore finger . . . he's working!: Ibid., pp.42–3.

It is asserted . . . his abilities: SIRIO 12, pp.125–6.

On the part . . . assured countenance: SIRIO 22, p.262.

I have read . . . part in it: SIRIO 7, p.365.

is a clever man, and will not go further than he is ordered: Ibid.

a speedy end to this whole mad business: Ibid., p.367.

not precisely handsome: *The Complete Memoirs of Casanova*, Russia and Poland, Ch. 1.

Catherine's letter to Nepluyev and Vyazemsky: SIRIO 7, p.371.

The Earl of Buckingham's report to the Earl of Sandwich: SIRIO 12, pp.170–1.

You like the truth . . . exact translations: SIRIO 1, p.264.

Well, the goal was reached . . . don't you?: Ibid.

If I were not afraid . . . very profitable: SIRIO 1, pp.258–9.

when I enter a room . . . at their ease: Ibid., p.260.

The hetman . . . said to me: SIRIO 7, p.375.

One must certainly consider . . . judgment and reason: Archives des Affaires Etrangères, Quai d'Orsay, Paris, Mémoires et Documents: Russie 11, f.9.

He is honest . . . these methods: Ibid., f.17.

His sentiments . . . of any importance: Ibid., f.18.

This is a very subtle young man . . . with him: Ibid.

His Highness . . . hurts him greatly: Quoted in Peskov, *Paul 1^er^Empereur de Russie*, p.44.

His Highness has the bad habit . . . the habit: Ibid., p.43.

pranced about in his own way, jumping and running around the room: Ibid., p.50.

His Highness has a fault . . . obeyed immediately: Ibid., p.45.

notwithstanding the general ferocity . . . civilised nations: SIRIO 12, p.200.

according to every appearance . . . to maturity: Ibid.

there are many paradoxes here that would demand uncommon ingenuity to reconcile: Ibid., p.201.

an enormous undertaking: SIRIO 1, p.268.

put everything . . . individual utility: Ibid., p.269.

For the state of the Russian legal system at the beginning of Catherine's reign: Madariaga, *Catherine the Great*, p.25.

the laws . . . system or design: Anon, *Authentic Memoirs of the Life and Reign of Catherine II*, pp.74–5.

eternal armchair: SIRIO 1, p.273.

There is enough . . . am leading: Ibid.

His Highness complained . . . impossible task: Quoted in Peskov, *Paul 1^{er} Empereur de Russie*, p.46.

After the meal . . . more and more: Ibid., pp.50–1.

not young and not of the Catholic religion: SIRIO 10, p.47.

wit, prudence, accomplishments: Ibid.

When you have found . . . all Courts: Ibid., p.48.

Madame! It is now . . . force of arms: Ibid., p.95.

the light of the northern star is only an aurora borealis: Ibid., p.93.

You have fought . . . have conquered: Ibid.

Lady of uncommon beauty . . . and travel: SIRIO 12, p.256.

The ill effects . . . her empire: Ibid., p.257.

He, who makes a profession . . . I owe it: SIRIO 1, p.288.

no one would give a glass of water to a doctor: SIRIO 10, p.104.

I will admit . . . well with them: Ibid., p.105.

Catherine's acquisition of Falconet: SIRIO 1, p.289.

At present . . . destruction of mankind: SIRIO 12, p.291.

I pity the poor Queen of Denmark . . . want it: SIRIO 10, p.164.

I will be leaving . . . God willing: Ibid., pp.165–6.


*Chapter 9: Laws, Smallpox and War*

Catherine's instruction to Ivan Glebov: SIRIO 10, p.170.

false air of Ispahan: Ibid., p.180.

whole house: Ibid., p.201.

I arrived here yesterday . . . before Sunday: Ibid., p.189.

Catherine's letter to Mikhail Vorontov: Ibid., p.190.

wept throughout dinner: Ibid., p.191.

They will tell you how I was received here: Ibid.

everything is going extremely decorously: Ibid., p.203.

Here the people . . . suffers need: Ibid., p.207.

and what a difference of climate, people, customs, even ideas!: Ibid., p.204

the Orthodox . . . as I am: Ibid., pp.35–6.

Nothing now remains . . . these Instructions: Catherine II, *Documents of Catherine the Great*, p.293.

About the titles . . . my desire: SIRIO 10, p.237.

the most beautiful monument of the century: Catherine II *Documents of Catherine the Great*, p.114.

For more details on Falconet's equestrian statue, see Zinovieff & Hughes, *Companion Guide to St Petersburg*, pp.76–7.

Monsieur Falconet . . . words to you: SIRIO 13, pp.10–11.

Petersburg seems like paradise compared to Ispahan: SIRIO 10, p.279.

I cannot resist . . . later years: SIRIO 37, pp.139–40.

[Panin] is very soon . . . five years ago: SIRIO 12, p.328.

I am extremely sorry . . . comfort you: SIRIO 10, p.290.

Ivan Perfilyevich . . . his fiancée: Ibid., p.291.

provided the Grand Duke is safe, then I would not worry about that: Ibid.

not be without reproach from the public: Ibid.

I am very anxious . . . is bad: Ibid.

Seeing from your letter . . . difficult days: Ibid., p.293.

I must not neglect . . . for him: SIRIO 12, p.331.

The palaces . . . of a forest: Richardson, *Anecdotes of the Russian Empire*, pp.13–14.

All the space . . . assembled without: Ibid., p.16.

supported upon eight pillars . . . with garlands: Ibid.

covered with crimson velvet, fringed with gold: Ibid.

two pieces of marble in the form of bricks: Ibid., p.17.

This young Prince . . . St Alexander Nevsky: Ibid.

The Empress of Russia . . . and courteous: Ibid., pp.19–20.

Count Orloff . . . very good French: SIRIO 12, p.352.

good-will and a loud noise: Richardson, *Anecdotes of the Russian Empire*, p.22.

The room seemed so full . . . they adjourned. SIRIO 12, pp.358–9.

[Betskoy] was so obliging . . . near finished: Ibid., pp.370–1.

extraordinary penetration and soundness: SIRIO 2, p.301.

Dinner consisted . . . and preserves: Ibid., p.302.

although small was very tasty: Ibid.

a secret which everybody knows: SIRIO 12, p.363.

charmed with their gracious and engaging behaviour towards him: Ibid.

Through the agency . . . the Empress: SIRIO 2, pp.310–11.

It is with great pleasure . . . happily over: SIRIO 12, pp.390–1.

The eruption took place . . . to fear: SIRIO 37, pp.163–4.

Madame! Whatever anyone . . . doing so: SIRIO 10, p.305.

Orlov hunting in a snowstorm: Catherine II, *Documents of Catherine the Great*, p.21.

certain old ladies: SIRIO 2, p.313.

of fine physique . . . congenital disease: Ibid., p.314.

My object . . . for his sheep: SIRIO 10, p.305.

On each side . . . and ejaculations: Richardson, *Anecdotes*, pp.33–6.

Baron Dimdale's comments about the Empress and the Grand Duke: SIRIO 2, pp.320–1.

For details of the Brühl collection, see Norman, *The Hermitage*, pp.32–3.

You tell me . . . the price: SIRIO 17, p.77.

I don't understand it enough to see what you see: Ibid., p.81.

the marble figure . . . on the marble: Ibid., p.150.

ignorance, superstition . . . all things French: Madariaga, *Catherine the Great*, p.92.

The half of Russia . . . the matter: Richardson, *Anecdotes of the Russian Empire*, p.38.

Cold! desperately cold! . . . chrystalline mass: Ibid., p.51.

something I found . . . in bed: SIRIO 10, p.332.

are men . . . of parts: SIRIO 12, p.427.

great pretensions . . . discerning friends: Ibid.

The Empress . . . difficult to imagine: Ibid.

Count Orloff . . . in others: Ibid., p.429.

is of a different turn . . . her government: Ibid., p.428.

though very little younger . . . private parties: Ibid.

a very promising Prince . . . without him: Ibid., p.431.

he has too much to do: Ibid., p.430.

Courage . . . fifty thousand Turks: SIRIO 10, p.338.


*Chapter 10: The Heroic Orlov*

my soldiers . . . to a wedding: Catherine II, *Documents of Catherine the Great*, p.32.

I think it is my duty . . . maritime power: SIRIO 19, pp.42–3.

the support . . . survive at all: SIRIO 17, p.78.

There is an old song . . . are good: Ibid., p.81.

I hear only praise . . . please everybody!: Ibid., p.107.

I know that you . . . wrong way: Ibid., p.112.

Right now I adore . . . my plantomania: Catherine II, *Documents of Catherine the Great*, p.163.

My fleet . . . had perished there: Ibid., pp.74–6.

Catherine's fear that Prince Henry was bored: SIRIO 13, p.45.

He is under the middle size . . . his toupée: Richardson, *Anecdotes of the Russian Empire*, p.326.

A great part . . . beautiful parrot: Ibid., pp.327–8.

He chattered . . . little amused: Ibid., pp.328–9.

lit by more . . . masked revellers: SIRIO 13, p.54.

at different intervals . . . old-fashioned romances: Richardson, *Anecdotes of the Russian Empire*, pp.329–30.

Thus ended . . . very pleased: SIRIO 13, p.55.

For further details about the conditions giving rise to plague in Moscow: Alexander, *Bubonic Plague in Early Modern Russia*

I have never . . . while writing it: SIRIO 13, p.59.

This city . . . much diverted: Richardson, *Anecdotes of the Russian Empire*, p.323.

If this war continues . . . monument erected: Catherine II, *Documents of Catherine the Great*, p.129.

If you need . . . given them: SIRIO 13, p.66.

The worst that could happen . . . be paid: Ibid., p.65.

because Protestants . . . their belief: Ibid., p.66.

I think that . . . our reciprocal satisfaction: Ibid., pp.66–7.

excessive corpulence: Ibid., p.91.

[She] has been described . . . her again: Ibid., pp.91–2.

what pleasure is there in celebrating a day that makes one a year older?: Ibid., p.94.

Tell whoever said . . . of plague: Ibid.

Since yesterday . . . breaking point: Ibid., pp.99–100.

I do not have . . . from Holland: SIRIO 17, p.133.

post-haste . . . everything in Russia: Catherine II, *Documents of Catherine the Great*, p.95.

When this nation . . . be overcome: SIRIO 10, p.411.

The Grand Duke's illness . . . his illness: SIRIO 37, p.488.

The signs . . . about his condition: Ibid., pp.490–1.

who is occupied . . . the Empress: Ibid., p.494.

I received your letter . . . to you: SIRIO 13, p.138.

we were anxious . . . detest them heartily: Ibid., p.142.

This morning . . . avail himself of it: SIRIO 19, pp.232–3.

She is said . . . no small addition: Ibid., pp.234–5.

For details about the Moscow plague riots, see Alexander, *Bubonic Plague in Early Modern Russia*, p.186ff.

The Archbishop . . . be killed!: SIRIO 13, p.173.

they broke down . . . murdered him: Ibid., p.174.

She is much affected . . . conceal it: SIRIO 19, p.237.

There is no appearance . . . a neighbour: Richardson, *Anecdotes of the Russian Empire*, p.450.

In truth . . . we have become!: Catherine II, *Documents of Catherine the Great*, p.135.

The weakness . . . with his dogs: SIRIO 13, p.180.

I forgot to say . . . been dismissed: Ibid., p.181.

Thanks to the indefatigable care . . . their feet: Ibid., pp.185–6.

Catherine's letter to Orlov of 3 December: SIRIO 2, p.288.

I regret very much . . . as a gardener: SIRIO 13, p.238.

## Chapter 11: Confusion and Unrest

for as [Orlov] believes . . . much circumspection: SIRIO 37, p.229.

if he ever hurries: SIRIO 10, p.321.

Catherine's letter of 12 May to Madame Bielke: SIRIO 13, p.241.

without exaggeration, the most handsome man of his time: Ibid., p.258.

the detestable, hateful Peterhof . . . St Paul there: Ibid., p.259.

favourite domicile: Ibid., p.260.

We have never . . . good number: Ibid., pp.259–60.

Several young and debauched . . . the throne: SIRIO 72, p.164.

the most extravagant plan . . . the Empire: Ibid., p.165.

No precautions . . . she resides there: SIRIO 19, p.297.

He has, I am told . . . with her: Ibid., p.299.

this is not a man . . . in society: SIRIO 72, p.226.

I have now seen . . . good fortune: Ibid., p.254.

the most handsome man of his time: SIRIO 13, p.258.

Luck presenting . . . prepared it deliberately: SIRIO 72, p.227.

maintained such good order among his men: Ibid., p.226.

Catherine's bad temper: SIRIO 13, p.260.

to be seen everywhere the Empress of Russia passed: SIRIO 72, p.226.

The person who . . . internal government: Ibid., p.228.

[Vassilchikov] is attached to Count Panin, who protects and directs him: Ibid., p.260.

air of bourgeois cordiality . . . prevented it: Ibid., p.256.

dejected, pensive and discontented: Ibid., p.255.

the violence and impetuosity . . . some alarm: SIRIO 19, p.315.

One fears . . . take their sides: SIRIO 72, p.255.

the best mood . . . and pleasure: Ibid.

There is no doubt . . . himself alone: Ibid., p.256.

sent provisions . . . in the past: Ibid., p.258.

not as a private individual, but as an equal: Ibid., p.263.

It is said . . . the town: Ibid., p.264.

It was expected . . . their advancement: SIRIO 19, p.330.

Count Orlov persists . . . must do: SIRIO 72, pp.264–5.

Count Panin . . . will not happen: Ibid., p.265.

The successor . . . to the report: SIRIO 19, pp.327–8.

The intention . . . to Mr Panin: Ibid., p.328.

The intrigues . . . sagacity to pierce: Ibid., p.329.

Catherine's letter to Ivan Orlov: SIRIO 13, pp.270–2.

The affair . . . degree of despair: SIRIO 72, p.266.

a sort of bravado: Ibid., p.268

she is sometimes affected by it to the extent of tears: SIRIO 72, p.270

In short . . . can understand anything: Ibid., p.271.

repeated and pressing request: Ibid., p.273.

[Orlov] has gained . . . beyond that: Ibid., p.275.

abandoning herself to it with all the vivacity of a young person: Ibid., p.304.

Very unexpectedly . . . never been absent: Ibid., pp.306–7.

Count Orlov is still . . . all this: Ibid., pp.307–8.

Unless the Empress . . . very late: Ibid., pp.308–9.

Count Orlov's first act . . . obtaining it: Ibid., pp.310–11.

to conciliate the nation: Ibid., p.315.

a stupid thing . . . cock-a-doodle-doo: SIRIO 13, pp.299–300.

Count Orlov's most recent stay . . . has elapsed: SIRIO 72, p.348.

It even seems . . . at the moment: Ibid., p.356.

anticipate their desires and study what would give them pleasure: SIRIO 13, p.329.

In order to avoid . . . Countess Bruce and I: Ibid., pp.346–7.

We are now waiting . . . is smitten: Ibid., p.348.

I only had . . . found it enough: SIRIO 13, p.353.

Catherine's 'Brief maxims' for Natalya Alexeyevna: SIRIO 13, pp.332–6.

I find his conversation . . . to think: Catherine II, *Documents of Catherine the Great*, p.189.

When I entered . . . our business: SIRIO 2, p.327.

At last, Madame . . . seven years: SIRIO 17, p.205.

A very gracious . . . he pleases: SIRIO 19, p.379.

Every thing relative . . . at present: SIRIO 19, pp.381–2.

Lieutenant-General and chevalier . . . well-disposed: SIRIO 13, p.373.

*Chapter 12: Passion and Pretenders*

one of the best heads of Europe: Smith, *Love & Conquest*, p.25.
Catherine's 'Sincere Confession': Maroger, *Memoirs of Catherine the Great*, p.356.
extremely restless people . . . the world: SIRIO 13, p.383.
It is very probable . . . and reason: Ibid., pp.383–4.
these very rare hangings . . . every day: Ibid., p.388.
Please tell . . . needed to know: Ibid., p.396.
As soon as . . . sleepless night: Potemkin, *Ot vakhmistra do feldmarshala*, p.33.
my doubt . . . Your Imperial Majesty: Smith, *Love & Conquest*, p.18.
He loves you . . . heed it: Potemkin, *Ot vakhmistra do feldmarshala*, p.33.
In order for me . . . more sensible: Ibid., pp.33–4.
Catherine's letter to Potemkin of 1 March: Smith, *Love & Conquest*, p.21.
A new scene . . . even consternation: SIRIO 19, pp.405–6.
His figure is gigantic . . . aspires to: Ibid., pp.406–7.
Fear not . . . unspeakably sad: Potemkin, *Ot vakhmistra do feldmarshala*, p.37.
I see them very often and our conversations never end: Catherine II, *Documents of Catherine the Great*, p.192.
It is a most extraordinary . . . useless pretensions: Ibid., pp.194–5.
I had long and frequent . . . our conversations: Ségur *Mémoires, ou Souvenirs et Anecdotes*, Vol. 3, pp.37–8.
How awful it is . . . I love you: Lopatin, *Ekaterina II i G.A. Potemkin*, p.19.
I think that the fever . . . to say: Ibid., p.21.
golden girl: SIRIO 13, p.388.
The day before yesterday . . . unheard-of manner: Ibid., pp.398–9.
getting old is a very disagreeable thing: Ibid., p.406.
I hate this day . . . delightful thing?": SIRIO 23, p.1.
We ask that in future . . . affectionate one: Lopatin, *Ekaterina II i G.A. Potemkin*, p.25.
on forays: Smith, *Love & Conquest*, p.36.
Something more . . . is now gone: SIRIO 19, p.416.
My dear soul . . . little sir: Potemkin, *Ot vakhmistra do feldmarshala*, p.39.
Giaour, Muscovite, Cossack . . . in you: Ibid.
My little dove . . . C[ossack]: Ibid., pp.39–40.
I really don't like . . . of smallpox: SIRIO 23, p.3.
Mr Thomas . . . philoso-comical conversations: Ibid.
who makes me laugh fit to burst: Ibid.
one of the greatest . . . iron century: Ibid., p.4.
This morning we received . . . to her: SIRIO 6, pp.74–5.
You will see . . . the empire: Smith, *Love & Conquest*, p.41.

I will willingly . . . has laws: Catherine II, *Documents of Catherine the Great*, pp.202–3.

Catherine's letter to Madame Bielke about Pugachev's execution: SIRIO 27, p.32.

Everything is done . . . in Europe: SIRIO 23, p.12.

I do not judge it . . . decide otherwise: SIRIO 42, p.356.

On the way . . . to be blind: SIRIO 27, p.27.

It is like drinking . . . true idea: SIRIO 23, pp.15–16.

If you ever see him . . . prodigious amount: SIRIO 27, p.36.

Farewell, madame . . . least bit tired: Ibid., p.37.

In the month . . . Countess of Bamberg: SIRIO 19, p.460.

Prince Golitsyn's first report on the female pretender: SIRIO 1, pp.170–1.

'Elizabeth's' deposition: Ibid., pp.172–82.

great advantages for your Empire: Ibid., p.184.

Send to say . . . her right mind: Ibid., pp.184–5.

she had never . . . eyes out: Ibid., p.187.

Catherine's explanation of her illness: SIRIO 23, p.41.

Description of Khodynskoye Field: Ibid., pp.20–1.

all those damn temples of divinities: Ibid., p.21.

to the great astonishment . . . in the world: Ibid., p.33.

## Chapter 13: New Lovers and a New Daughter-in-Law

bonds of Holy Matrimony: Smith, *Love & Conquest*, p.77.

My darling . . . meeting with you: Quoted in Alexander, *Catherine the Great*, p.350.

a stroke of the palsy: SIRIO 19, p.513.

a very warm altercation: Ibid.

Catherine's letter to Potemkin about her presence at Natalya's labour: Smith, *Love & Conquest*, p.80.

On 10 April . . . in the evening: SIRIO 23, pp.44–5.

in inexpressible distraction: SIRIO 19, p.515.

You cannot imagine . . . nothing will: SIRIO 23, p.45.

First thing tomorrow . . . is underway: SIRIO 27, pp.78–9.

I was very upset . . . any more: Ibid., p.81.

There were moments . . . their bearings: SIRIO 23, p.46.

Having seen the ship . . . and distraction: Ibid., p.49.

If my peace is dear to you, do me a favour and stop grumbling: Lopatin, *Ekaterina II i G.A. Potemkin*, p.99.

could not marry . . . the Empress: SIRIO 9, p.2.

I ask you . . . it currently is: Ibid., pp.5–6.

I don't know . . . greater than myself: SIRIO 23, p.50.

Several couriers . . . for the occasion: Harris, *Diaries & Correspondence of James Harris*, Vol. 1, p.146.

I believe that you love me . . . my heart: Lopatin, *Ekaterina II i G.A. Potemkin*, p.101.

You scolded me . . . her service: Ibid., p.102.

Catherine's letter telling Potemkin she would not dismiss Zavadovsky: Smith, *Love & Conquest*, p.85.

She already tears up . . . put together: SIRIO 23, p.47.

you know that . . . can't be dead: Ibid., p.48.

Petrusa dear, all will pass, except my passion for you: Quoted in Alexander, *Catherine the Great*, p.342.

Notwithstanding . . . the winter palace: SIRIO 19, p.520.

best refuge from the despair of an impotent ambition: Ibid.

The commotion . . . lace and embroidery: Harris, *Diaries & Correspondence of James Harris*, Vol. 1, p.147.

not one of them . . . and goodness: Ibid., p.150.

The Grand Duke's conduct . . . his adviser: Ibid., p.152.

On Sunday last . . . happy event: SIRIO 19, p.521.

Prince Potemkin arrived . . . had lost: Ibid.

You ask me about . . . is hurry: SIRIO 23, pp.53–4.

Her person . . . on this occasion: Harris, *Diaries & Correspondence of James Harris*, Vol. 1, p.151.

I admit to you . . . that's me content: SIRIO 27, pp.117–18.

I will be staying here . . . the comparison: SIRIO 23, p.56.

I want you to say . . . the negative: Ibid., p.697.

My advice is . . . kind deeds: Quoted in Alexander, *Catherine the Great*, p.344.

What a funny creature you have acquainted me with: Smith, *Love & Conquest*, p.94.

Païsiello's opera . . . much by it: SIRIO 23, p.63.

At ten o'clock . . . come of that: Ibid., pp.64–5.

Just imagine . . . beneath my windows: Ibid., p.67.

Today I woke up . . . their wits' end: Ibid., p.69.

the product of my eleven to twelve years of labour: SIRIO 17, p.245.

an object which [Your Imperial Majesty] has not yet seen: Ibid., p.247.

## Chapter 14: Grandsons and Other Acquisitions

Do you know Monsieur Alexandre? . . . Monsieur Alexandre: SIRIO 23, pp.71–2.

Children should not be dressed . . . the chest: SIRIO 27, p.140–1.

Do you know . . . scorn and indignation?: SIRIO 23, p.74.

Grigory Orlov laying claim to rabbit fur stockings: Ibid.

Prepared even as I was . . . a stranger: Harris, *Diaries & Correspondence of James Harris*, Vol. 1, p.161.

great good nature, great vanity, and excessive indolence: Ibid., p.164.

The present favourite . . . at Moscow: Ibid., p.173.

cut off the ears: Ibid.

capricious, headstrong, and very young: Ibid.

essence of prattle . . . often decided: SIRIO 23, p.96.

So go on! . . . he does: Ibid., p.83.

The Sèvres service . . . for me: Ibid., p.84.

It is a pleasure . . . ever crying: SIRIO 27, p.150.

the small aisle which adjoins the entrance door on the Gatchina side: SIRIO 23, p.86.

The Empress is gracious . . . the subject: Harris, *Diaries & Correspondence of James Harris*, Vol. 1, p.229.

the opposite party . . . and uneasiness: Ibid., p.191.

My head feels . . . I'm unhinged?: SIRIO 23, p.87.

that ardour for business she was used to be famous for: Harris, *Diaries & Correspondence of James Harris*, Vol. 1, p.187.

Persian candidate: Ibid., p.173.

A few days ago . . . this anecdote: Ibid., pp.198–9.

Your Lordship . . . of the empire: Ibid., pp.200–1.

Catherine's description of Rimsky-Korsakov: Smith, *Love & Conquest*, p.99.

Alas! I can only describe . . . feel like crying: SIRIO 23, p.93.

thanks to you . . . merry and well: Smith, *Love & Conquest*, p.99.

Rimsky-Korsakov's instruction that Catherine kiss Potemkin on the lips: Ibid., p.100.

The Grand Duke . . . do more: Harris, *Diaries of Correspondence of James Harris*, Vol. 1, p.228.

Do you know . . . very angry indeed: SIRIO 23, p.96.

I have not yet received . . . from Archangelsk: Ibid., p.97.

I'll die . . . in the world: Ibid., pp.101–2.

concealed by the most masterly hypocrisy: Harris, *Diaries & Correspondence of James Harris*, Vol. 1, p.210.

Many thanks . . . talk to you: Smith, *Love & Conquest*, p.101.

I don't write well enough for that: SIRIO 23, p.110.

you know my aversion . . . one laugh: Ibid., p.104.

I want them . . . ignorance etc: Ibid., pp.104–5.

Infatuation, infatuation! . . . thousand leagues away: Ibid., p.107.

very good-natured . . . Countess Bruce: Harris, *Diaries & Correspondence of James Harris,* Vol. 1, p.224.

It all depends . . . harmonious sounds: SIRIO 23, p.111.

You will excuse me . . . the race: Ibid., p.112.

But farewell . . . writing to you: Ibid., p.123.

Catherine's letter to Grimm of early January 1779: Ibid., pp.123–4.

die laughing: Ibid., p.127.

I think that . . . our ships: Ibid., pp.124–5.

but so far I've refrained from proving it to them: Ibid., p.125.

always cheerful: Ibid., p.130.

The Grand Duchess . . . Mother Nature's variations: Ibid., p.131.

Ma si il signor . . . what I need: Ibid., p.135.

The little rascal . . . on my left: Ibid., p.136.

One of the Thomases . . . from writing: Ibid., p.139.

But do you realise . . . and sounds: Ibid., p.143.

I am not putting . . . very amazed: Ibid., pp.144–5.

I legislate . . . hardly ever happens: Ibid., pp.148–9.

which says that . . . of that: Ibid., p.149.

The more I see it . . . is Païsiello's!: Ibid., p.152.

On Monday, 22 July . . . the ball-room: Harris, *Diaries & Correspondence of James Harris,* Vol. 1, pp.250–3.

Catherine's letter to Grimm of 23 August: SIRIO 23, p.156.

At present . . . gallery above: Ibid., pp.157–8.

But here comes Monsieur Alexandre . . . with him: Ibid., p.158.

At the entrance . . . formed for them: Coxe, *Travels into Poland, Russia, Sweden & Denmark,* Vol. 2, pp.280–3.

The great-duke . . . an inner apartment: Ibid., pp.283–4.

In the course of the evening . . . ball concluded: Ibid., p.285.

There is a drawing room . . . been presented: Ibid., pp.285–7.

The court-dress . . . scarcely a distinction: Ibid., pp.287–8.

This child loves me . . . anything yet: SIRIO 23, p.160.

it is impossible . . . than before: Ibid., p.330.

*Chapter 15: The Empress and the Emperor*

It is true . . . from me: SIRIO 23, pp.173–4.

It begins by telling him . . . the heart: Ibid., p.176.

as to insure . . . profoundest melancholy: Harris, *Diaries & Correspondence of James Harris,* Vol. 1, p.296.

I don't know, I can't see myself: SIRIO 23, p.176.

My dear children . . . very much: SIRIO 9, p.39–40.

My dear children, Your letters . . . perfect health: Ibid., p.40.

my friend Monsieur Alexandre: Ibid., p.42.

I was terrified . . . with garlic: Ibid., p.43.

the local beauties . . . old nags: Ibid.

may the good Lord preserve you . . . with you: Ibid.

princess who was salted . . . very thirsty: Ibid., p.44.

everywhere round here . . . tower of Babel: Ibid., p.48.

At the moment . . . all my heart: Ibid., p.49.

They have a very beautiful . . . I understand: SIRIO 23, p.182.

When [Monsieur de Falkenstein] . . . two days: Ibid., p.180.

He likes talking . . . at all: SIRIO 9, pp.52–3.

Oh, how hot . . . get into it: Ibid., p.53.

he eats only once . . . only water: Ibid.

He likes talking and knows a lot of things: Ibid., p.54.

He talks with a lot of soundness . . . made me sweat: Ibid., p.55.

Monsieur de Falkenstein . . . the gawper: SIRIO 23, p.181.

It is very different here . . . this place: SIRIO 9, p.58.

Don't sweat . . . believe me: Ibid., pp.58–9.

I must tell you . . . improving it etc: SIRIO 23, p.207.

If I were to begin . . . profoundest knowledge: Ibid., pp.183–4.

one of the pleasantest people and easiest to get on with that I have ever met: Ibid., p.185.

[Andromeda] has been here . . . single moment: Ibid., pp.185–6.

After the paintings . . . more money: Ibid., p.188.

I cannot forgive you for accusing me of gluttony in connection with the fine arts: Ibid., p.179.

Why do you want me to buy everyone's paintings?: Ibid., p.180.

The interview . . . attention required: Harris, *Diaries & Correspondence of James Harris,* Vol. 1, p.331.

she felt if he stayed much longer she might say something rude to him: Ibid., p.333.

His Royal Highness . . . in brilliants: Ibid., p.335.

less profuse . . . as much of tea: Ibid.

There was not the smallest change . . . disgusted: Ibid., pp.336–7.

I swear to you . . . from Mamma: SIRIO 23, p.192.

The extraordinary . . . I can say: Harris, *Diaries & Correspondence of James Harris*, Vol. 1, p.347.

He told me . . . what she is: Ibid., pp.350–1.

I have come . . . her friendship: Ibid., p.351.

You know, Monsieur . . . my friends: Ibid.

Don't imagine . . . can see clearly: Ibid., p.354.

The manner in which . . . to him: Ibid., p.356.

Give him nothing . . . kick him out: Ibid.

Listen, my dear Harris . . . to help: Ibid., p.358.

For God's sake . . . this Court: Ibid., p.362.

But do you know . . . frequent this year: SIRIO 23, p.197.

I am very unhappy . . . about it: SIRIO 33, p.87.

My friend is ill . . . to him: Harris, *Diaries & Correspondence of James Harris*, Vol. 1, p.389.

Count Alexis Orlov . . . of him: Ibid., p.392.

If Cobenzl says . . . to anyone: Smith, *Love & Conquest*, p.113.

calculated to hurt his enemies and serve his friends: Harris, *Diaries & Correspondence of James Harris*, Vol. 1, p.407.

The Empress, indeed . . . Private Secretary: Ibid., pp.407–8.

He accused me . . . were venomous: Ibid., p.537.

certainly increase . . . impending tempest: Ibid., pp.418–19.

I own, my Lord . . . arrive at it: Ibid., p.424.

I understand that . . . satisfied with him: Ibid.

The two Imperial Sovereigns . . . possessed them: Ibid., p.428.

Catherine's list of achievements: SIRIO 23, p.216.

This is how [Alexander] . . . or others: Ibid., p.205.

As for [Alexander's] brother . . . for Cupid: Ibid., p.214.

St Petersburg . . . I ever beheld: Cross, *An English Lady at the Court of Catherine the Great*, p.40.

that it put him in mind . . . too much: Ibid.

A Table was spread . . . very merry: Ibid., p.48.

This noble Establishment . . . forget it: Ibid., p.49.

Mr Bush from England . . . of People: Ibid., p.51.

a very fine looking Woman . . . sensible look: Ibid.

The Duke . . . sensible and clever: Ibid., p.52.

They walked out . . . the Garden: Ibid.

[the Empress] is excessively fond . . . very astonishing: Ibid.

The Empress is an early riser . . . Russian Head-dress: Ibid., p.56.

Soup, Fish . . . Parmesan Cheese: Ibid., pp.68–9.

There are a great number . . . in Length: Ibid., p.71.

felt much indisposed before the eruption: Ibid., p.63.

a countenance of surprise and uneasiness: Harris, *Diaries & Correspondence of James Harris,* Vol. 1, p.463.

[she] told them . . . their attendants: Ibid.

As long as Count Panin . . . Count Panin's return: Ibid., pp.463–4.

This very singular . . . considerable sensation: Harris, *Diaries & Correspondence of James Harris,* Vol. 1, p.450.

paying a visit to their most dangerous enemy: Ibid., p.451.

He had contrived . . . write them: Ibid., pp.466–7.

muddler and intriguer . . . gets jaundice: SIRIO 23, p.431.

whole deportment . . . as possible: Harris, *Diaries & Correspondence of James Harris,* Vol. 1, p.454.

The blow . . . by apoplexy: Ibid., p.470.


## Chapter 16: The Failures of Physicians

When she fainted . . . named Clark: Cross, *An English Lady at the Court of Catherine the Great,* p.65.

it would be inappropriate . . . of spirit: SIRIO 9, pp.64–5.

If I could have foreseen . . . this journey: Ibid., p.65.

There were ten Horses . . . great Rejoicings: Cross, *An English Lady at the Court of Catherine the Great,* p.72.

a purple tissue Petticoat . . . to the wrist: Ibid.

Soon after ten . . . every body: Ibid., p.73.

One of the first things . . . very great: SIRIO 23, p.221.

Here is the tenth letter . . . me his: SIRIO 9, pp.73–4.

is out of immediate danger . . . his bed: Harris, *Diaries & Correspondence of James Harris,* Vol. 1, p.470.

I think that His Polish Majesty . . . my health: SIRIO 9, pp.86–7.

we do not allow . . . for ourselves: SIRIO 23, p.222.

Your children are as well . . . from you: SIRIO 9, pp.109–10.

Three days ago . . . beloved friend: Ibid., p.113.

did they start . . . all night?: Ibid., p.118.

I may now venture . . . manner omnipotent: Harris, *Diaries & Correspondence of James Harris,* Vol. 1, p.491.

visible to none but to those who compose her private society: Ibid., p.492.

Your children are well . . . pleasing character: SIRIO 9, p.127.

the usual magnificent leave-taking presents: Harris, *Diaries & Correspondence of James Harris*, Vol. 1, p.496.

We legislate . . . comes until ten: SIRIO 23, p.231.

The Police Code: see Alexander, *Catherine the Great*, pp.192–3.

I flatter myself . . . to see us: SIRIO 9, p.140.

New statues . . . may she not faint: Ibid., pp.149–50.

For example . . . design is arabesque: SIRIO 23, p.239.

I admit quite frankly . . . about her: Ibid., pp.241–2.

You and I . . . wrong thing: Lopatin, *Ekaterina II i G.A. Potemkin*, p.150.

I enclose a little note . . . you cruelly: Ibid.

'Oh,' he said . . . very sweet: SIRIO 23, pp.244–5.

When Peter the First . . . if I can: Ibid., p.265.

very fine: SIRIO 9, p.174.

The weather here . . . a marmot: Ibid., p.185.

I am going . . . me sorely: Ibid., p.188.

Prince Orlov has arrived . . . and charlatans: Ibid., p.189.

it should appear . . . her passions: Harris, *Diaries & Correspondence of James Harris*, Vol. 2, p.11.

Her conduct . . . pleasure nor business: Ibid., pp.11–12.

who returns passionately fond . . . the empire: Ibid., p.9.

Prince Orlov's illness . . . his mind: SIRIO 9, p.191.

In addition to work . . . of recovery: SIRIO 23, p.252.

I told him . . . to comfort myself: Ibid., p.253.

She now calls them . . . please her: Harris, *Diaries & Correspondence of James Harris*, Vol. 2, pp.18–19.

Prince Orlov is going . . . do you hear?: SIRIO 23, p.267.

I was very afflicted . . . of doctors: Ibid., p.268.

Count Panin was seized . . . and eleven: Harris, *Diaries & Correspondence of James Harris*, Vol. 2, p.41.

Although I was very prepared . . . the more: SIRIO 23, pp.274–5.

Count Panin was naturally lazy . . . had plenty: Ibid., p.275.

I will not discuss . . . shared mine: Ibid., p.279.

There is my trip . . . of news: Ibid., p.280.

Not only do I . . . with anxieties: Lopatin, *Ekaterina II i G.A. Potemkin*, p.171.

Be so good . . . the frontier: Smith, *Love & Conquest*, p.140.

most wretched country: SIRIO 15, p.6.

In future . . . a few days: Ibid.

You can imagine . . . torment me: Lopatin, *Ekaterina II i G.A. Potemkin*, p.176.

When General Lanskoy . . . any more: SIRIO 23, p.282.

My swarm . . . through the doors: Ibid., pp.281–2.

The young lady . . . her brothers: Ibid., p.288.

unpleasant and his grimaces horrible: Ibid.

As for me . . . good as dead: Lopatin, *Ekaterina II i G.A. Potemkin*, p.186.

I am infinitely obliged . . . project aborted: SIRIO 20, p.444.

Catherine's instructions regarding her grandsons' upbringing: SIRIO 27, pp.303–23.

Food and drink . . . much salt: Ibid., p.303.

A few days before we left . . . it himself: Cross, *An English Lady at the Court of Catherine the Great*, p.84.

cherries, strawberries, currants, apples and ripe pears: SIRIO 27, p.304.

Children's games . . . of children: Ibid., p.305.

Children's frequent little fits . . . doctor's advice: Ibid., p.306.

Small children usually cry . . . into jokes: Ibid., p.308.

Sir Tom Anderson . . . sixteen years: SIRIO 23, p.314.

On that day . . . any more: Ibid., pp.319–20.

When I began this letter . . . no more: Ibid., pp.316–17.

Until that moment . . . to go: Ibid., p.317.

I have just received . . . keep well: SIRIO 15, p.17.

literally burst: Fitzlyon, *Memoirs of Princess Dashkova*, p.226.

at last some intervals . . . then days: SIRIO 23, p.318.

in consequence also . . . my life: Ibid.

rivers, mountains, valleys . . . other places: Ibid.

I am very obliged . . . for myself: Ibid.

As regards carved stones . . . the damned: Ibid., p.322.


## Chapter 17: Convalescence and Recovery

Oh, how he tormented me . . . not stop: SIRIO 23, p.326.

I have nothing . . . to say: Ibid., p.325.

as you see . . . and spiritless: Ibid., p.326.

Why don't you write plays? . . . of rulings: Ibid., p.361.

My little collection . . . this subject: Ibid., p.341.

As for me . . . hanged himself: Ibid., p.335.

My inner self . . . abandon me: Ibid., p.336.

Messieurs Alexandre and Constantin . . . excellent heart: Ibid., pp.336–7.

Messieurs Alexandre and Constantin will not . . . have lessons: Ibid., p.334.

Catherine worked . . . of Prince Potemkin: Ségur, *Mémoires, ou Souvenirs et Anecdotes,* Vol. 2, p.317.

The majesty of her brow . . . the longest: Ibid., p.195.

We would leave . . . and white: Ibid., pp.319–20.

The Petrovsky palace . . . work in progress: SIRIO 15, p.23.

One must do justice . . . charming views: SIRIO 23, p.342.

by God, they would . . . them to: Ibid.

Monsieur Kelchen . . . morning to night: Ibid., p.347.

under the direction of two Scottish stucco workers: Ibid., p.358.

I came back . . . in Moscow: Ibid., p.360.

This Quarenghi . . . but no more: Ibid., p.365.

We are working . . . in a year: Ibid., p.375.

she's no beauty, but she's jolly big: Ibid., p.374.

you will see . . . his confidence: Ibid., p.376.

I'm telling you . . . a princess: Ibid., p.377.

All those who were discontented . . . and love: Ségur, *Mémoires, ou Souvenirs et Anecdotes,* Vol. 2, p.398.

Conversation between Potemkin and Ségur: Ibid., p.399.

more united by heart than blood: Khrapovitsky, *Pamyatnye zapiski,* p.12.

We have just read . . . already know: SIRIO 23, p.385.

You? To see the Grand Duchess? What for?: 'Zapiski Mihkaila Garnovskogo' in *Russkaya Starina,* Vol. 15, No.1, p.17.

This Redcoat envelops . . . on the outside: SIRIO 23, pp.387–8.

Dear cousin . . . his release: SIRIO 15, pp.26–7.

The drubbings . . . where he likes: Smith, *Love & Conquest,* p.175 (translated from French).

My very dear children . . . is to it: SIRIO 15, pp.25–6.

Madame! My agitation . . . me birth: Ibid., p.27.

It is not I who cover . . . further ones: Ibid., p.28.

It is with the most acute . . . our children: Ibid., pp.37–9.

My dearest children. A mother . . . my heart: Ibid., pp.39–40.

It is with the most ardent gratitude . . . and Maria: Ibid., pp.40–1.

I must tell you . . . entirely abandoned: Ibid., p.41.


*Chapter 18: The Great Crimean Voyage, and 'Proverbs' in Petersburg*

she got up at six . . . seven o'clock: Ségur, *Mémoires, ou Souvenirs et Anecdotes,* Vol. 3, p.11.

My husband throws himself . . . gaiety itself: SIRIO 15, pp.43–4.

I hope that Alexandra . . . be useful: Ibid., pp.44–5.

I was pleased . . . travelling days: Ségur, *Mémoires, ou Souvenirs et Anecdotes*, Vol. 3, pp.29–30.

Mr FitzHerbert replied . . . first campaign: Ibid., p.102.

Everywhere the Empress . . . wrong thing: Ibid., pp.33–4.

On arriving . . . of our hosts: Ibid., pp.49–50.

I let fall the cross words . . . the horses: Ibid., pp.48–9.

This is a strange town . . . as Moscow: SIRIO 23, p.394.

Asiatic court: Ségur, *Mémoires, ou Souvenirs et Anecdotes*, Vol. 3, p.65.

There is not the slightest indecency . . . or religion: Ligne, *Mémoires*, p.117.

One day, when I was sitting . . . and dignity: Ségur, *Mémoires, ou Souvenirs et Anecdotes*, Vol. 3, p.18.

Catherine's letter of 1 April about the inoculation of her granddaughters: SIRIO 15, p.73.

I found on the lawn . . . enclosing it: Ibid., p.94.

We went to visit . . . really imposing: Ibid., p.101.

An immense crowd . . . their sovereign: Ségur, *Mémoires, ou Souvenirs et Anecdotes*, Vol. 3, pp.95–6.

Only our mornings . . . be laid: Ibid., p.97.

The King of Poland . . . one another changed: SIRIO 23, p.408.

The fleet's and town's artillery . . . half an hour: Ségur, *Mémoires, ou Souvenirs et Anecdotes*, Vol. 3, pp.106–7.

We talked and ate . . . of artillery: Ibid., p.108.

Prince Potemkin . . . tongue got dry: Khrapovitsky, *Pamyatnye zapiski*, p.28.

On leaving the table . . . finer one: Ségur, *Mémoires, ou Souvenirs et Anecdotes*, Vol. 3, p.108.

Alexander Matveyevich . . . you well know: Lopatin, *Ekaterina II i G.A. Potemkin*, p.215.

When I make . . . and benefit: Ibid.

Our little ones . . . become pocks: SIRIO 15, pp.103–4.

a large, beautiful and charming mansion: SIRIO 23, p.408.

If you knew . . . at home: Ibid., p.409.

one needs to give too much time to it, and I started too late: Ibid., p.423.

Here lies Duchess Anderson, Who bit Mr Rogerson: Ségur, *Mémoires, ou Souvenirs et Anecdotes*, Vol. 3, p.63.

On the seventh . . . Countess Branicka: SIRIO 23, p.410.

The town of Kherson . . . way possible: SIRIO 15, p.105.

What I don't understand . . . spoilt child: Ségur, *Mémoires, ou Souvenirs et Anecdotes*, Vol. 3, p.183.

I see and hear everything . . . with inactivity: Khrapovitsky, *Pamyatnye zapiski*, pp.29–30.

Perhaps Mohammed was right in wanting them to be covered up: Ségur, *Mémoires, ou Souvenirs et Anecdotes*, Vol. 3, p.163.

Messieurs, this joke . . . indiscreet talkativeness: Ibid., p.164.

It was a superb spectacle . . . is here!: SIRIO 23, p.411.

best friend, the Emperor: Khrapovitsky, *Pamyatnye zapiski*, p.30.

by God, all this so strongly . . . or dreaming: SIRIO 23, p.411.

This tour of the Crimea . . . back home: SIRIO 15, p.118.

Two days ago . . . your work: Lopatin, *Ekaterina II i G.A. Potemkin*, p.218.

people did nothing . . . pure invention: Ligne, *Mémoires*, p.120.

these Russian rogues . . . let slip: Ibid.

I must warn you . . . exceedingly prudent: SIRIO 23, p.419.

I would be extremely content . . . from you: Smith, *Love & Conquest*, p.217.

that's a further nuisance which I would be delighted to spare you: Lopatin, *Ekaterina II i G.A. Potemkin*, p.262.

Dashkova and L.A. Naryshkin . . . double-headed eagle: Khrapovitsky, *Pamyatnye zapiski*, p.44.

Nothing helped . . . and in Chernigov: Ibid., pp.58–9.

Were you here . . . to do: Smith, *Love & Conquest*, p.245.

We are having . . . the trees: Lopatin, *Ekaterina II i G.A. Potemkin*, p.291.

Let the Turks . . . into pieces: Khrapovitsky, *Pamyatnye zapiski*, p.66.

A few more years . . . be transformed: Archives des Affaires Etrangères, Mémoires et Documents: Russie 16, f.238.

as I know that my subjects . . . true interests: SIRIO 23, p.452.

for the rest . . . been defensive: SIRIO 15, p.136.

The heat . . . readily believe it: Ibid., pp.139–40.

smelt their gunpowder: Khrapovitsky, *Pamyatnye zapiski*, p.97.

This is a great loss, it is a loss for the state: Ibid., p.122.

He loves pigs . . . to it: Ibid., p.128.

Having seized you . . . now repeat: Lopatin, *Ekaterina II i G.A. Potemkin*, pp.329–30.

Here, my dear son . . . our cause: SIRIO 15, p.156.

already well-formed: Khrapovitsky, *Pamyatnye zapiski*, p.196.

in a shaking hand: Ibid.

I nearly collapsed . . . with her: Smith, *Love & Conquest*, p.291.

Matushka, spit on him: Khrapovitsky, *Pamyatnye zapiski*, p.195.

After marrying . . . gone completely mad: Lopatin, *Ekaterina II i G.A. Potemkin*, p.358.

## Chapter 19: The Beginning of the End

Can a minister . . . destroyed France: Khrapovitsky, *Pamyatnye zapiski*, p.201.

I'm enclosing with this . . . completely happy: Lopatin, *Ekaterina II i G.A. Potemkin*, p.358.

You speak the truth . . . deserve it: Ibid., p.360.

We have a kind heart . . . very agreeably: Ibid.

My beloved matushka . . . their rendez-vous: Ibid., pp.362–3.

I'm well and cheerful . . . love me too: Ibid., p.364.

windy colic: SIRIO 15, p.160.

How times have changed! . . . will happen: SIRIO 23, p.479.

Catherine's conversation of 1 December with Khrapovitsky: Khrapovitsky, *Pamyatnye zapiski*, p.213.

No one could sympathise more . . . her courage: SIRIO 23, p.490.

I have designated . . . an hour: Smith, *Love & Conquest*, p.358.

ever since 1787 . . . this end: Lopatin, *Ekaterina II i G.A. Potemkin*, p.430.

Forgive me, my friend . . . him enough: Ibid., p.436.

Catherine's description of her grandchildren: SIRIO 23, pp.497–9.

Valerian Alexandrovich . . . has great potential: Lopatin, *Ekaterina II i G.A. Potemkin*, p.444.

Beloved matushka . . . with you myself: Ibid., p.448.

one never knows . . . will appear: SIRIO 23, p.503.

more handsome . . . happiest mood possible: Ibid., p.504.

in a stupid way: Khrapovitsky, *Pamyatnye zapiski*, p.240.

It is nineteen . . . of heat: SIRIO 23, p.505.

Two porticos . . . a dazzling light: Golovine, *Memoirs: A Lady at the Court of Catherine II*, p.28.

One could not . . . the morning: SIRIO 23, p.519.

we are perfectly prepared . . . devil himself: Ibid.

But there is a man . . . for me: Ibid., pp.522–3.

A Man ought . . . Laws allow: Catherine II, *Documents of Catherine the Great*, p.219.

this sofa . . . fine and warm!: SIRIO 23, p.547.

Well, is it not the case . . . horrors: Ibid., p.560.

Thanks to God . . . Gracious Majesty: Smith, *Love & Conquest*, p.385.

Your letter of 24 August . . . extremely weak: Ibid., p.386.

Thanks to God I'm beginning . . . so weak: Ibid., p.388.

My paroxysms continue . . . will be: Ibid.

Beloved matushka, my not seeing you makes it even harder for me to live: Ibid., p.389.

Your Most Gracious Majesty . . . grateful subject: Ibid., p.390.

*Chapter 20: Last Years*

Yesterday another terrible . . . his grasp: SIRIO 23, p.561.

How can I replace . . . their heads: Khrapovitsky, *Pamyatnye zapiski*, p.252.

Prince Potemkin . . . dies on me!: SIRIO 23, pp.561–2.

Oh, my God! . . . good soul: Ibid., p.562.

I am well . . . who varies: Ibid., p.564.

Listen, the Jacobins . . . about it: Ibid., p.565.

So at the end . . . St Geneviève: Ibid.

This General Zubov . . . another factotum: Ibid., p.566.

If I did not have . . . to gratitude: Ibid., p.567.

Do they have to make so much noise for a rotten girl!: Khrapovitsky, *Pamyatnye zapiski*, p.270.

You will realise . . . into temptation: SIRIO 23, p.577.

[The Empress] was with . . . towards me: Golovine, *Memoirs*, pp.32–3.

One cannot see her without being charmed by her: Khrapovitsky, *Pamyatnye zapiski*, p.277.

The Empress took her seat . . . Nariskin: Parkinson, *A Tour of Russia*, pp.33–4

The Grand Duke . . . the same: Ibid., pp.35–6

a little bit in love: SIRIO 23, p.579.

One evening . . . teacher of religion: Golovine, *Memoirs*, pp.33–4.

For the death . . . rebellious subjects: Parkinson, *A Tour of Russia*, p.86.

That means my brother . . . do there?: SIRIO 23, p.582.

Everyone said . . . with one another: Ibid., p.583.

Why? – did I say something stupid?: Peskov, *Paul 1$^{er}$, Empereur de Russie*, p.106.

A raised platform . . . own child: Golovine, *Memoirs*, p.47.

Our newly-weds . . . still is: SIRIO 23, p.588.

First of all . . . my contemporaries: Ibid., p.592.

a just horror . . . and mayhem: SIRIO 42, p.188.

Do you still remember . . . has shown: SIRIO 23, p.593.

You tell me . . . about it: Ibid., p.599.

You know well enough . . . for me: SIRIO 5, pp.16–17.

do everything possible . . . good indeed: Lopatin, *Ekaterina II i G.A. Potemkin*, p.442.

the young lady . . . his loss: SIRIO 23, p.629.

Every day . . . with his audience: Prince Adam Czartoryski, *Mémoires*, Vol. 1, pp.56–9.

Everyone admired his courage, no one emulated it: Ibid., p.60.

The Empress was still . . . inexorable will: Ibid., pp.68–9.

He had been in a second childhood . . . know it: SIRIO 23, pp.644–5.

I've been so tired . . . carries it off: Ibid., p.658.

Our business is sorted . . . imps together: Ibid., p.660.

The Princesses . . . not yet fixed: Ibid.

The day after tomorrow . . . you come?: Ibid.

The Grand Duke Constantine . . . after marriage: Golovine, *Memoirs*, p.98.

His behaviour . . . near the Hermitage: Ibid.

The Grand Duchess Anne . . . her ideas: Ibid.

Dear friend! . . . saw the beginning: SIRIO 5, p.23.

As I have always declared . . . tender solicitude: SIRIO 9, p.245.

there were no more walks, and glances, and sighs: Golovine, *Memoirs*, p.101.

Monsieur Scapegoat . . . alongside this colossus: SIRIO 23, p.679.

For the last three days . . . like me: Ibid., p.681.

a melancholy and embarrassed dreamer: Ibid., p.692.

On 15 August . . . notice it: Ibid., pp.690–1.

We were presented . . . favourably impressed: Golovine, *Memoirs*, pp.108–9.

One seems to enjoy . . . one voice: SIRIO 23, p.691.

I was, my dear son . . . right time: SIRIO 42, pp.266–7.

in which she was born and brought up: SIRIO 9, p.301.

Everyone large and small . . . new style: SIRIO 23, pp.691–2.

I do not know . . . fall over: Ibid., p.692.

Be so kind . . . happy future: SIRIO 9, p.313.

It is not appropriate for a Princess of Russia to change her religion: Ibid.

I invite Your Majesty . . . personal happiness: Ibid., pp.314–15.

still less an object so dear to his heart as the Grand Duchess: Ibid., p.302.

I formally promise . . . could pass: Ibid., p.315.

Having already given . . . entirely superfluous: Ibid., pp.315–16.

The ladies-in-waiting . . . moments of agitation: Czartoryski, *Mémoires*, p.120.

we were informed . . . been postponed: Ibid.

I admitted them . . . the Regent sobbing: SIRIO 9, pp.305–6.

The Empress appeared . . . her indignation: Czartoryski, *Mémoires*, pp.120–2.

The King of Sweden . . . the King: Golovine, *Memoirs*, p.119.

It is said they are taking their leave tomorrow. Thank God: SIRIO 9, p.309.

The Regent having gone out . . . in writing: Ibid., pp.321–3.

The Grand Duchess Mother . . . this Princess: Ibid., pp.317–18.

To begin with . . . precious effects: Ibid., p.318.

another racket of celebrations, balls, various suppers of all sorts: SIRIO 5, p.26.

I preach and will go on . . . and glory: SIRIO 23, p.695.

*Epilogue*

I beg you . . . nor small: SIRIO 23, p.438.
Here lies Catherine the Second . . . the arts: Ibid., p.77.
trampling underfoot all sentiments of religion, honour and glory: Ibid., p.695.
A party was considering . . . most expensive: Parkinson, *A Tour of Russia*, p.49.
To tempt . . . grasp at will: Maroger, *Memoirs of Catherine the Great*, pp.300–1.

# Recommendations for Further Reading

## Memoirs, diaries and letters

Anon., *Authentic Memoirs of the Life and Reign of Catherine II, Empress of All the Russias. Collected from authentic mss, translations, etc of the King of Sweden, Right Hon. Lord Mountmorres, Lord Malmesbury, M. de Volney, and other indisputable authorities*, B. Crosby, London, 1797

Anon., *Memoirs of Prince Potemkin; comprehending numerous original anecdotes of the Russian Court, translated from the German*, Henry Colburn, London, 1813

Anspach, Margravine of (Lady Craven), *Memoirs*, Vol. 1, Henry Colburn, London, 1826

Bolotov, A.T., *Pamyatnik pretekshikh vremyon*, Yantarnyi skaz, Kaliningrad, 2004 (first published 1875)

Carrère d'Encausse, H. (ed.), *L'Impératrice et l'Abbé: Un duel littéraire inédit entre Catherine II et l'Abbé Chappe d'Auteroche*, Fayard, Paris, 2003

Casanova, J., *The Complete Memoirs of Casanova*, Globusz Publishing, New York/Boston, 2004

Catherine II, *Correspondence of Catherine the Great when Grand-Duchess, with Sir Charles Hanbury-Williams and Letters from Count Poniatowski*, ed. & tr. The Earl of Ilchester & Mrs Langford-Brooke, Thornton Butterworth Ltd, London, 1928

Catherine II, *Documents of Catherine the Great. The Correspondence with Voltaire and the Instruction of 1767 in the English text of 1768*, ed. W.F. Reddaway, Cambridge University Press, Cambridge, 1931

Catherine II, *Les Lettres de Catherine II au Prince de Ligne*, G. Van Oest, Brussels & Paris, 1924

Catherine II, *Mémoires de l'Impératrice Catherine II*, ed. A. Herzen, Trübner & Co., London, 1859

Catherine II, *Memoirs of the Empress Catherine II, Written by Herself*, tr. Hilde Hoogenboom & Markus I. Cruse, Random House, New York, 2005

Catherine II, *The Memoirs of Catherine the Great*, ed. D. Maroger, tr. Moura Budberg, Hamish Hamilton, London, 1955

Coxe, W., *Travels into Poland, Russia, Sweden & Denmark*, Vols. 1 & 2, T. Cadell, London, 1792

Cresson, W.P., *Francis Dana: A Puritan Diplomat at the Court of Catherine the Great*, The Dial Press, New York, 1930

Cross, A.G. (ed.), *An English Lady at the Court of Catherine the Great: The Journal of Baroness Elizabeth Dimsdale, 1781*, Crest Publications, Cambridge, 1989

Czartoryski, Prince A., *Mémoires*, Vol. 1, Plon, Paris, 1887

Diderot, D., *Mémoires pour Catherine II*, ed. Paul Vernière, Garnier Frères, Paris, 1966

Fitzlyon, K. (tr. & ed.), *The Memoirs of Princess Dashkova*, Duke University Press, Durham/London, 1995

Golovine, Countess, *Memoirs: A Lady at the Court of Catherine II*, tr. G.M. Fox-Davies, David Nutt, London, 1910

Gribovsky, A.M., *Vospominaniya i dnevniki*, University Press, Moscow, 1899

Harris, J., *Diaries & Correspondence of James Harris, First Earl of Malmesbury*, ed. Third Earl of Malmesbury, Vols. 1 & 2, Richard Bentley, London, 1844

Khrapovitsky, A.V., *Pamyatnye zapiski*, Moscow, 1862

Ligne, Prince de, *Lettres et Pensées*, Tallandier, 1989

Ligne, Prince de, *Mémoires*, Mercure de France, Paris, 2004

Lopatin, V.S. (ed.), *Ekaterina II i G.A. Potemkin: Lichnaya perepiska 1769–1791*, Nauka, Moscow, 1997

Masson, C.F.P., *Secret Memoirs of the Court of St Petersburg*, tr. from French, H.S. Nichols & Co., London, 1895

Oberkirch, Baroness d', *Memoirs of the Baroness d'Oberkirch*, ed. Count de Montbrison, London, 1852

Parkinson, J. (ed. William Collier), *A Tour of Russia, Siberia and the Crimea 1792–1794*, Frank Cass & Co., London, 1971

Poroshin, S., *Semyona Poroshina zapiski*, ed. M.I. Semyevsky, St Petersburg, 1881

Poniatowski, S.A., *Mémoires secrets et inédits*, Wolfgang Gerhard, Leipzig, 1862

Potemkin, G.A., *Ot vakhmistra do feldmarshala: Vospominaniya, dnevniki, pis'ma*, ed. Z.E. Zhuravlyeva, Pushkin Foundation, St Petersburg, 2002

Richardson, W., *Anecdotes of the Russian Empire*, Strahan & Cadell, London, 1784

Ségur, Comte de, *Mémoires, ou Souvenirs et Anecdotes*, Vols. 2 & 3, Alexis Eymery, Paris, 1827

Smith, D. (ed. & tr.), *Love & Conquest: Personal Correspondence of Catherine the Great & Prince Grigory Potemkin*, Northern Illinois University Press, DeKalb, 2004

Ward, Mrs., *Letters from a lady who resided some years in Russia to her friend in England, with historical notes*, J. Dodsley, London, 1775

## Monographs on Catherine (there are many more, but these are among the best)

Alexander, J.T., *Catherine the Great: Life and Legend*, Oxford University Press, New York/Oxford, 1989

Bilbasov, V.A., *Istoriya Ekateriny Vtoroi*, Vols. 1 & 2, Berlin, 1900

Carrère d'Encausse, H., *Catherine II: Un âge d'or pour la Russie*, Fayard, Paris, 2002

Cronin, V., *Catherine, Empress of All the Russias*, Collins Harvill, London, 1989

Dixon, S., *Catherine the Great*, Longman, London, 2001

Gooch, G.P., *Catherine the Great, & Other Studies*, Longmans, London, 1954

Lyubavsky, M.K., *Istoriya Tsarstvovaniya Ekateriny II*, Lan', St Petersburg, 2001

Madariaga, Isabel de, *Catherine the Great: A Short History*, Yale Nota Bene, New Haven & London, 2002

Madariaga, Isabel de, *Russia in the Age of Catherine the Great*, Phoenix Press, London, 2002

Safonov, M., *Zaveshchaniye Ekateriny II: Roman-issledovaniye*, LITA, St Petersburg, 2002

## Monographs on other characters

Bain, R.N., *Peter III, Emperor of Russia: The Story of a Crisis and a Crime*, Constable & Co., London, 1902

Bain, R.N., *The Daughter of Peter the Great*, Constable & Co., London, 1899

Leonard, C.S., *Reform & Regicide: the reign of Peter III of Russia*, Indiana University Press, Bloomington, Ind., 1993

McGrew, R.E., *Paul I of Russia 1754–1801*, Clarendon Press, Oxford, 1992

Mylnikov, A., *Pyotr III: Povestvovaniye v dokumentakh i versiyakh*, Molodaya Gvardiya, Moscow, 2002

Peskov, A., *Paul I^er, Empereur de Russie, ou le 7 novembre*, tr. Elena Balzamo, Fayard, Paris, 1996

Sebag Montefiore, S., *Prince of Princes: The Life of Potemkin*, Phoenix Press, London, 2001

Zamoyski, A., *The Last King of Poland*, Jonathan Cape, London, 1992

## *Art, architecture, costume, gardens, music and theatre*

Alekseyeva, M.A., *Mikhailo Makhayev: master vidovogo risunka XVIII veka*, Zhurnal Neva, St Petersburg, 2003

Althaus, F. & Sutcliffe, M., *Petersburg Perspectives*, Fontanka with Booth-Clibborn Editions, London, 2003

Berman, E. & Kurbatova, E., *Russkii Kostyum 1750–1830*, Vsyerossiiskoye Teatral'noye Obshchestvo, Moscow, 1960

Bradbury, M., *To The Hermitage*, Picador, London, 2001

Catherine II et al., *Théâtre de l'Hermitage*, 2 vols., F. Buisson, Paris, 1798

Cross, A., *By the Banks of the Neva: Chapters from the Lives and Careers of the British in Eighteenth-Century Russia*, Cambridge University Press, Cambridge, 1997

Figes, O., *Natasha's Dance: A Cultural History of Russia*, Allen Lane, London, 2002

Forbes, I. & Underhill, W. (eds.), *Catherine the Great – Treasures of Imperial Russia from the State Hermitage Museum*, Booth-Clibborn Editions, London, 1990

Norman, G., *The Hermitage: The Biography of a Great Museum*, Jonathan Cape, London, 1997

Ribeiro, A., *Dress in Eighteenth-century Europe 1713–1789*, Yale University Press, New Haven & London, 2002

Shvidkovsky, D., *The Empress & the Architect: British Architecture and Gardens at the Court of Catherine the Great*, Yale University Press, New Haven & London, 1996

Stählin, J. von, *Muzyka i balet v Rossii XVIII veka* (tr. from German B.I. Zagursky), Triton, Leningrad, 1935

Zinovieff, K. & Hughes, J., *The Companion Guide to St Petersburg*, Companion Guides, 2003

## Other background material

Alexander, J.T., *Bubonic Plague in Early Modern Russia: Public Health & Urban Disaster*, Johns Hopkins University Press, Baltimore/London, 1980

Cracraft, J., *The Revolution of Peter the Great*, Harvard University Press, Cambridge, Mass./London, 2003

Dukes, P., *The Making of Russian Absolutism, 1631–1801*, Longman, London, 1990

Freeze, G.L. (ed.), *From Supplication to Revolution: A Documentary Social History of Imperial Russia*, Oxford University Press, Oxford/New York, 1988

Hosking, G., *Russia: People and Empire 1552–1917*, HarperCollins, London, 1997

Kaun, A.S. & Kornilov, A.H., *Modern Russian History: Being a Detailed History of Russia from the Age of Catherine the Great to the Revolution of 1917*, Vol. 1, A.A. Knopf, New York, 1916

Klyuchevsky, I.V., *A Course in Russian History: The Time of Catherine the Great*, tr. Marshall S. Shatz, M.E. Sharpe, Armonk, NY, 1997

Molé-Gentilhomme & Saint-Germain Leduc, *Catherine II ou la Russie au XVIIIᵉ siècle: Scènes historiques*, Victor Lecou, Paris, 1854

Petinova, E.F., *Vo dni Yekateriny*, Knizhnyi Mir, St Petersburg, 2002

Pushkin, A.S., *History of the Pugachev rebellion*, tr. Paul Debreczeny, Vol. 14 of *The Complete Works of Alexander Pushkin*, Milner, Downham Market, 2000

Pushkin, A.S., *The Captain's Daughter*, Vol. 7 of *The Complete Works of Alexander Pushkin*, Milner, Downham Market, 1999

Radishchev, A.N., *A Journey from St Petersburg to Moscow*, tr. Leo Weiner, ed. Roderick Page Thaler, Harvard University Press, Cambridge, Mass., 1958

Wolff, L., *Inventing Eastern Europe: The Map of Civilization on the Mind of the Enlightenment*, Stanford University Press, Stanford, CA, 1994

# Acknowledgements

$\mathcal{I}$ would like to thank Fr Alexander Diaghilev of the church of the Epiphany, Gutuyev Island, St Petersburg and of Zagubie for always being ready to answer my queries on Russian Orthodoxy; Dr Brian Dix for sharing his knowledge of the gardens at Tsarskoye Selo with me; Dr Martin Dudley for being my first and constructively critical reader; Dr Louise Foxcroft for her helpful comments on the concoctions prescribed for Paul I's childhood illnesses; Gerlinde Friedsam for translating passages from German; Dr Lesley Hall of the Wellcome Library for the History and Understanding of Medicine and Professor Aileen Ribeiro of the Courtauld Institute for answering my queries on a specific aspect of women's dress; Melania Johnson for her help on obscure Russian words; Marc de Mauny, Andrei Reshetin and the Catherine the Great Orchestra of St Petersburg for so vividly bringing the music of Catherine's Court to life; and Bishop Seraphim Sigrist for also answering questions on the Orthodox Church. I also wish to record my thanks to my editor Paul Sidey, his assistant Tiffany Stansfield, and to my agent Clare Alexander.

I am grateful to the Direction des Archives of the Ministère des Affaires Etrangères, Quai d'Orsay, Paris for permission to quote from unpublished memoirs and documents, to Duke University Press for permission to quote from *The Memoirs of Princess Dashkova*, to Professor A.G. Cross and Mr Michael Dimsdale for permission to quote from *An English Lady at the Court of Catherine the Great: The Journal of Baroness Elizabeth Dimsdale, 1781* and to the Northern Illinois University Press for permission to quote from *Love & Conquest: Personal Correspondence of Catherine the Great & Prince Grigory Potemkin*, edited and translated by Douglas Smith. Every effort has been made to trace the copyright holder of Dominique Maroger's edition of *The Memoirs of Catherine the Great*, but so far to no avail.

# Index